GARNISH
Decorations on savoury dishes

GLAZE
Tool: pastry brush or spoon.
Meaning: to give a shine

GRILL
Tool: grill pan or flame-proof dish – grill.
Meaning: to cook under the heat of a grill

 **W9-BUK-257**

KNEAD
Meaning: to handle firmly

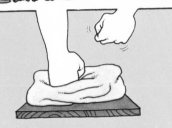

KNOCK BACK
Meaning: to knead dough that has 'proved' until it has returned to its original size

PAR-BOIL
Tool: pan – top of cooker.
Meaning: partially cook by boiling

PARE
Tool: sharp knife.
Meaning: to remove skin or rind

POACH
Tool: pan or dish – top of cooker or oven.
Meaning: to cook slowly in liquid

PROVE
Tool: basin or polythene bag.
Meaning: allow dough to rise

PUREE
Tool: sieve or liquidiser.
Meaning: to create a smooth, thick mixture

ROAST
Tool: tin – oven or rotisserie.
Meaning: to cook meat, poultry or vegetables in extra fat, or fat of meat, in the oven or over a rotisserie spit

ROUX
Tool: pan.
Meaning: mixture of fat and flour in a sauce

RUB-IN
Meaning: a way of incorporating fat and flour

SEASON
Meaning: 1 to add salt and pepper.
2 to prepare an omelette pan

SIEVE
Tool: sieve or strainer.
Meaning: to remove any lumps

SIMMER
Tool: pan or dish – top of cooker or oven.
Meaning: to cook below boiling point, 180-190°F. There should be an occasional bubble

SPONGE
Meaning: a type of light cake or the first stages in yeast cookery

STEAM
Tool: pan or steamer – top of cooker.
Meaning: to cook in steam

STEW
Tool: a covered pan or dish - top of cooker or oven. Meaning: to cook in liquid in a covered container

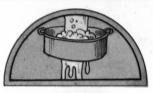

STRAIN
Tool: sieve, strainer, muslin or collander. Meaning: to remove solid food from the liquid

TOSS
Tool: palette knife, spoon.
Meaning: turning a pancake. Tossing food in fat, often called 'to sauté'.

WHIP
Tool: egg whisk or fork.
Meaning: to beat briskly i.e. to thicken cream or egg whites

WHISK
(See whip)

WORK
Tools: omelette pan, knife.
Meaning: technical term for moving eggs when making an omelette

PERFECT COOKING

PERFECT

Marguerite

COOKING

Patten

OCTOPUS BOOKS

Acknowledgements

The publishers would like to acknowledge the help of the following in providing photographs:
American Rice Council: Beef risotto Milanaise page 31, Risotto page 126, Shisk-kebabs page 130, Chinese vegetable soup page 186, Rice pudding page 224. **Argentine Beef Bureau:** Argentine beef soup page 114, Locro de trigo page 122. **British Egg Information Service:** Pastel de Tortillas page 85. **Cadbury Schweppes Food Advisory Service, Bournville, Birmingham:** Gooseberry sparkle page 9, Chocolate soufflé page 14, Dauphine potatoes page 189. **California Prune Advisory Bureau:** Ragoût of feef and prunes page 31, Yoghourt California Menu Maker 12. **Chiltonian Ltd:** Composite photograph page 203. **Danish Agricultural Producers:** Glazed forehock of bacon page 33, Danish open sandwiches pages 104–105, Cheese and bacon boats page 190. **Dutch Dairy Bureau:** Cheese soufflé page 90, Dutch vegetable flan page 187, Leeks mornay page 191. **Eden Vale Ltd:** Composite photograph page 1, Cottage cheese dip page 62, Cottage cheese and ham savoury page 107, Cottage cheese salads page 111, Lasagna al forno page 128, Paprikascsirke page 131, Yoghourt whip page 232, Composite photograph page 234. **Fruit Producers' Council:** Jellied fruit snow page 9, Pear and almond gâteau page 20, Chicken peach salad page 110, Prawn and rice salad page 112, Apple cream sponge page 235. **John West Foods Ltd:** Store cupboard omelette page 85, Salmon chowder page 117. **Kellog Co. of Great Britain Ltd:** Grape meringue flan page 237. **Herring Industry Board:** Preparing herrings page 162. Normandy herrings page 169. **National Dairy Council:** Prawn quiche page 94, Haddock and mushroom scallops page 168, Pineapple and strawberry ring page 225, Veal fricassée page 228, Creamed kidneys page 228, Stuffed plaice in cream page 229, Cream flan page 236. Peach and cherry trifle Menu Maker 4, Ganana and lemon cream Menu Maker 8, Orange coffee cream Menu Maker 24. **New Zealand Lamb Information Bureau:** Composite photograph page 21, Crown roast of lamb page 23, Roast lamb with apricot nut stuffing page 24. **Pasta Foods Ltd:** Mexican frankfurters page 106. Composite photograph page 205. **RHM Foods Ltd:** Christmas pudding page 3, Fruit flan page 5, Peach gâteau page 19, Ham en croûte page 33, Butterfly cake page 50, Economical Dundee cake page 52, Popovers page 56, Scotch pancake page 57, Cheese aigrettes page 74, Shrove Tuesday pancakes page 89, Old English chicken pie page 92, Pizza page 95, Green salad page 108, Leek and potato soup page 119, Marmalade page 150, Outlaw cabbage page 184, Tomatoes and mushrooms vinaigrette page 195, Mexican macaroni page 197, Stuffed peppers page 199, Eskimo risotto page 209, Chunky port supreme page 222. **Stork Cookery Service:** Composite photograph page 51. **Tabasco Sauce:** Roast pork with prune and apple stuffing page 24, Corned beef plate tart page 93, Creamed turkey duchesse page 180. **Tate & Lyle Ltd:** Brandy snaps page 49, Biscuits page 69, Composite photograph page 70, Cornflake flan Menu Maker 32. **Walls Ice Cream:** Composite photograph page 16, Ice cream gâteau page 225. **T. Wall & Son (Meat & Handy Foods) Ltd:** Sausage twists and sausage cheese savouries page 210. **White Fish Authority:** Sole Sevilla page 164, Goujons of fish page 167, Fish in a jacket page 170.

First published 1972 by
Octopus Books Limited
59 Grosvenor Street, London W 1

© Octopus Books Limited 1972

ISBN 0 7064 0072 0

Reprinted 1976, 1977

Printed in Czechoslovakia by Polygrafia, Prague

50338

Contents

Introduction

Most women, and some men, need to cook for themselves or their families, and interesting cooking and good food make a great contribution to the enjoyment of living and to good health. The majority of people have a fairly clear idea of how to cook basic dishes, but, judging by my post bag and by talking to people they are sometimes very disappointed by the result. This may just be 'bad luck' due to over or under-cooking, but it may be they have not realised the important techniques behind making each basic dish. For example, one is always told not to let a sauce or custard, containing fresh eggs boil . . . *why*? . . . *how do we stop this*? These are some of the things you will find covered in all basic recipes in Perfect Cooking.

However elaborate a dish may seem, you can be absolutely certain it is based on something fairly simple, straightforward and well-known. I have taken these basic dishes as my Blue Prints. Even if you do not wish to make the Blue Print Recipe, read it because in that recipe is the clue and the advice for success with all dishes *based upon* it.

Over the years I have demonstrated to some hundreds of thousands of people in Britain and across the other side of the world. I know the enjoyment many of you have in cooking meals and how you seek new ideas to provide variety for your family and friends. Some people though tell me they do not like cooking, even though they have to do this regularly and this is quite understandable for there is no reason why we all should enjoy the same skills. Even if cooking is *not* your favourite occupation I hope you will find help in these pages. I feel that in giving all the information for perfection, in making the dishes as interesting and quick as possible I am ensuring you have success and that your friends will enjoy the results and maybe in 'basking in their praise' you will come to like cooking more than in the past. Time, money and energy are important to all of us and this is why these points have been considered, not only in the special menus, but in the recipes throughout these pages.

I hope you enjoy our guide to Perfect Cooking. I have enjoyed writing it and would like to thank all the people who have helped to prepare this.

Many Australian readers will like to use a cup measure and you will find this given in the recipes. C =Australian (8 fluid ounce) cup.

Marguerite Patten.

one
PUDDINGS & DESSERTS

Few forms of cooking are more interesting and rewarding than producing a delicious pudding or dessert, often with the minimum of effort, for some of the most interesting recipes are the simplest. The dessert 'rounds off' the meal and helps to turn it into something exciting and memorable.

Many people feel that the old traditional puddings are no longer as popular as they were. I think this may be true to some extent, for iced desserts have now become so popular and are simple to make with modern refrigerators or home freezers. I still find though that the majority of people also delight in a truly feather-light steamed sponge or suet pudding topped with fruit or syrup, and there is a varied selection on pages 2 and 3 with the points for successful results.

The sauces to accompany puddings are important, be original in your choice of ingredients and combination of flavourings, for example a coffee sauce is splendid with a chocolate pudding.

Fruit flans are always a delight to look at, as well as to eat. However, often a perfect fruit flan is spoiled because the cook is too impatient to put the ingredients together, the method on page 5 shows the right way to do this.

A baked or steamed custard may seem very homely fare but it is the basis of so many interesting and indeed quite exotic desserts. I have lost count of the number of people who ask me why custards curdle or why the pastry rises and the custard sinks in a tart. You will find the answers on page 11 in the BLUE PRINT and the recipe for a Custard Tart. On most pages I have given you a BLUE PRINT RECIPE, for if you know how to make the simple basic dish, upon which so many other recipes are based, you have unlimited scope for imaginative and varied puddings.

Have you ever made your own ice cream or water ices? They are ridiculously simple, but how delicious. If you own a home freezer then make these in larger quantities so they are always available. With the development in freezing and excellent canning, practically every fruit can now be obtained in some form for most of the year, so fruit desserts should never be monotonous. A variety of these are on pages 7 and 8. For those of you who are watching your weight and counting calories the water ice recipes are very helpful in adding interest to a slimming diet. In fact on several pages you will find a special recipe, or adaptation of a recipe, that will enable you to eat a pudding and not 'upset' your diet.

The gâteaux on pages 19 and 20 may look ambitious but they are relatively easy to make and can be stored until ready to fill, or frozen complete with fillings.

Light Puddings

The puddings on this page are light in texture. They are all based on a type of sponge mixture.

Blue Print Recipe

Vanilla Sponge Pudding

4 oz. ($\frac{1}{2}$C) butter or margarine · 4 oz. ($\frac{1}{2}$C) sugar · 2 eggs · 6 oz. (1$\frac{1}{2}$C) self-raising flour (or plain flour and 1$\frac{1}{2}$ level teaspoons baking powder) · few drops vanilla essence · 3 tablespoons milk.

To make Cream together the butter or margarine and sugar until soft and light. Whisk the eggs well and beat gradually into the butter mixture. Sieve the flour or flour and baking powder, mix the vanilla essence and milk. Fold the flour and milk alternately into the creamed mixture. Grease a 1$\frac{1}{2}$–2-pint (5C) basin, put in the mixture and cover with greased greaseproof paper or foil.

To cook Put into a steamer over boiling water or stand on an upturned patty tin (so the basin will not crack) in a pan half filled with boiling water. Cook for 1$\frac{1}{4}$–1$\frac{1}{2}$ hours, filling up with boiling water as necessary.

To serve Turn out on to a heated dish and serve with jam or hot marmalade or the fruit sauce on this page. *All recipes based on this dish serve 4–6.*

When making light sponge puddings:
● **AVOID** *Too slow cooking at the start, this can cause a heavy pudding.*
● **TO RECTIFY** *This is almost impossible if the pudding is really heavy; you can only camouflage it by serving with a super sauce.*

For Family Occasions

Lemon Pudding

Follow the Blue Print recipe but cream the finely grated rind of 1 lemon with the butter and sugar. Mix with lemon juice and milk to give 3 tablespoons. Cook as Blue Print. Serve with fruit sauce.

Fruit Sauce

Put the juice of 1 orange and 1 lemon into a saucepan, add 2 oz. ($\frac{1}{4}$C) sugar, 4 good tablespoons ($\frac{1}{2}$C) orange or lemon marmalade and 2 teaspoons cornflour or arrowroot blended with 4 tablespoons water. Stir well over a gentle heat until clear and slightly thickened.

Chocolate Pudding

Omit vanilla from Blue Print recipe and substitute 2 tablespoons chocolate powder in place of the same amount of flour. Cook as Blue Print. Serve with Rich Chocolate or Coffee Sauce below.

Coffee Sauce

Blend 1 tablespoon cornflour with $\frac{1}{4}$ pint ($\frac{2}{3}$C) *strong* coffee. Put into a saucepan with 2–3 tablespoons sugar, small knob butter and $\frac{1}{4}$ pint ($\frac{2}{3}$C) milk. Stir over a gentle heat until thickened.

For Special Occasions

Fudge Pudding

Follow the Blue Print recipe but add 1 extra oz. butter and sugar and use *brown* sugar in place of white and 1 tablespoon golden syrup. Reduce the amount of milk to 2 tablespoons. Coat the inside of the basin with a generous layer of butter and brown sugar. Cook as Blue Print. Serve with Rich Chocolate Sauce.

Rich Chocolate Sauce

Melt 4–6 oz. plain chocolate with $\frac{1}{4}$ pint ($\frac{2}{3}$C) thin cream in a basin over hot water or top of a double saucepan. Flavour with a little vanilla essence or brandy. For family occasions use milk in place of cream.

Nut and Pineapple Upside Down Cake

Follow the proportions for the Blue Print recipe but use 1 extra oz. butter and sugar. Melt 2 oz. ($\frac{1}{4}$C) butter in a 7–8-inch cake tin or oven-proof dish, top with 2 oz. ($\frac{1}{4}$C) brown sugar. Arrange a design of pineapple rings, pecan or halved walnuts and Maraschino cherries on the butter and sugar. Top with the sponge mixture. Bake in the centre of a very moderate oven, 325–350°F, Gas Mark 3–4, for about 1 hour. Turn out, serve hot or cold with cream.

Storing and Freezing Prepare—*store up to 12 hours in a refrigerator or wrap and freeze. Thaw, cook as recipe.* Cook—*store in a refrigerator from 1–2 days or wrap and freeze. Thaw and reheat.*

To use any left over *The upside down pudding is eaten cold as a cake. The other puddings should be re-steamed for 30 minutes.*

Nut and pineapple upside down cake

1. Roll out suet crust thinly to form a round large enough to fill the basin. Cut out $\frac{1}{4}$ of the round, put on one side for the lid.
2. Lower the $\frac{3}{4}$ into the greased basin, seal the joins together.
3. Trim the top of the pastry. Add these pieces to the $\frac{1}{4}$ reserved.
4. Fill the pastry with fruit. Roll out remaining crust into a neat round. Damp top edges of pastry with water. Seal firmly.
5. Cover with greased foil or greaseproof paper, with a 'pleat' in to allow for the pudding rising during cooking.

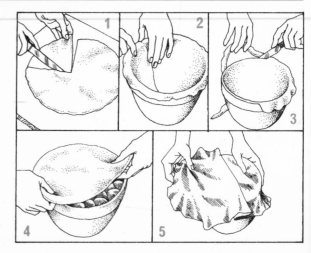

or Family Occasions

ruit Pudding

oll out the suet crust pastry, made as Blue
rint 1, line a 2-pint (5–6C) basin as Sketches
–3. Fill with halved stoned plums or peeled
nd sliced apples or mixed berry fruits. Add
ugar to taste and about 2 tablespoons water.
lavour apples with grated lemon rind or
pice and a few sultanas or mix with black-
erries. Cover the fruit with a 'lid' of pastry
nd foil or greaseproof paper as Sketches
–5. Cook as directions in Blue Print on page
, for about 2 hours. Turn out, sprinkle with
ugar and serve hot with cream or custard
auce.

offee Sultana Pudding

Make the suet pudding as Blue Print 2, but
dd 4 oz. (½C) sultanas to the flour. Grease
he basin, to be used for cooking the pudding,
enerously with butter, sprinkle with brown
ugar and put 2 tablespoons golden syrup at
he bottom. Add the suet pudding mixture,
over, as Sketch 5, and cook as the Blue
rint recipe.

or Special Occasions

raditional Christmas or
ich Fruit Pudding

ollow Blue Print 2, but use brown sugar,
eggs and ¼ pint ale or beer to mix; omit
he milk. Sieve 1 teaspoon mixed spice, ½
easpoon powdered cinnamon and ½ teaspoon
rated nutmeg with the flour. ADD 12 oz.
1½C) seedless raisins, 4 oz. (½C) sultanas,
oz. (½C) currants, 4 oz. (½C) chopped candied
eel, 2–4 oz. (¼–½C) chopped, blanched
lmonds, 4 oz. (⅔C) grated cooking apple,
rated rind· and juice of 1 lemon and 2
ablespoons brandy or sherry.
Mix very thoroughly and divide between 2
r 3 greased basins. Cover as Sketch 5, and

steam over boiling water, for a minimum of 5
hours. Remove the wet covers and put on dry
foil or greaseproof paper. Store in a cool, dry
place and cook for a further 2–3 hours on
Christmas Day. If more convenient cook for
the same length of time in a slow oven.
Stand the basin in a larger container half-
filled with cold water. Cover both the basin
and the container with foil to prevent the
water evaporating. Serve with Brandy Butter
or Hard sauce. *Serves 8–10.*

Brandy Butter or Hard Sauce

Cream 2 oz. (¼C) unsalted butter with 4 oz.
(¾C) sieved icing sugar. Gradually blend in
2 tablespoons brandy. Pile or pipe into a dish,
decorate with blanched almonds and glacé
cherries; chill thoroughly. *Serves 4–5.*

Golden Apricot Pudding

Make and cook as Christmas Pudding but use
chopped apricots in place of raisins and
currants and white wine in place of beer.

Steamed suet pudding

Suet Crust and Suet Puddings

Puddings made with suet crust pastry
are almost more adaptable than any
others, the pastry may be filled with
some kind of fresh fruit during every
month of the year. Suet puddings range
from the simple Blue Print to a rich
traditional Christmas recipe.

Blue Print Recipes

1. Suet Crust Pastry

8 oz. (2C) flour* · pinch salt · 4 oz.
(⅔C loosely packed) chopped or
shredded suet · water to mix.
*either self-raising to give a thicker
crust, or plain flour for a thin crust.

To make Sieve the flour and salt
together. Add the suet and enough
water to give a soft rolling consistency.
To cook As the Blue Print on page 2
for about 2 hours.

2. Suet Pudding

4 oz. (1C) self-raising flour (or plain
flour and 1 level teaspoon baking
powder) · 4 oz. (1C) soft fine breadcrumbs · 4 oz. (⅔C) suet (see above) ·
4 oz. (½C) sugar · 1 or 2 eggs · milk
to mix.

To make Sieve the flour or flour and
baking powder. Add the breadcrumbs,
suet and sugar together with the beaten
egg or eggs and enough milk to make a
sticky consistency.
To cook Put into a well greased 2-
pint (5–6C) basin. Cover well as Sketch
5. Steam as directions in Blue Print on
page 2 for about 2 hours.
To serve Turned out, with a sauce of
hot jam, marmalade, golden syrup or
fruit purée.
*All recipes based on these Blue Prints
serve 4–6 except where stated differently.*

● **AVOID** *Too slow cooking (except
for Christmas puddings) and too dry a
mixture. Always fill up the pan with
boiling water.*
● **TO RECTIFY** *See page 2.*
Storing and Freezing *The plain
puddings may be kept and frozen as
those on page 2, but rich puddings
mature better at room temperature.*
To use any left over *Re-steam, or
cut Christmas pudding into neat slices,
fry in a little butter, serve as fritters,
sprinkled with sugar.*

Fruit Pies and Tarts

It is strange how confusing these two terms can be. In the past one could assume that when a British cook talked about 'making a pie' she would mean fruit (or some other food) would be put into a deep dish and topped with pastry, whereas a tart was a base of pastry with a topping of fruit or other food.

Nowadays these two words are used less rigidly as you will see from the recipes such as the Lemon Meringue Pie on page 12. A flan is similar to a tart but has a more perfect, and often deeper, shape.

The Blue Print recipe is for sweet short crust, although similar to short crust, the small quantity of sugar helps to give an added crispness to the pastry.

Blue Print Recipes

Sweet Short Crust Pastry

6 oz. (1½C) flour, preferably plain · pinch salt · 3 oz. (⅜C) butter, margarine or fat · ½–1 tablespoon caster sugar · cold water to mix.

To make Sieve the flour and salt into a mixing bowl. Rub the butter, margarine or fat into the flour with your fingertips, as Sketch 1, until like fine breadcrumbs. Add the sugar, then *gradually* stir just over 1½ tablespoons water (or enough to bind the mixture) into the dough. Blend with a palette knife, gather together into a ball with the tips of your fingers but do not over-handle, see Sketch 2. Roll out the dough, use and cook as the recipes.

● **AVOID** *Over-handling the pastry: Using too much water, for this produces a dough that is over-sticky and difficult to handle, and a pastry that, when baked, is tough rather than crisp and short.*

● **TO RECTIFY** *If the pastry is damp and sticky, flour the pastry board and rolling pin generously, but this is not an ideal remedy as you alter the basic proportions.*

● **SHORT CUT** *Use frozen or packet short crust pastry. Mix sugar to packet mix before adding liquid, or sprinkle on frozen pastry as you roll it out.*

Fruit Pie

Use Blue Print recipe PLUS 1–1¼ lb. prepared fruit, a little water and sugar to taste. Make the pastry as the Blue Print. Prepare the fruit. Put into the pie dish; choose one which is small enough for the fruit to come to the top or use a pie support. Add about 4 tablespoons water with firm fruit or 1–2 tablespoons water with very ripe or soft fruit with sugar to taste. Roll out the pastry until sufficiently large to cover the pie and give an extra band round the edge of the dish. Moisten the rim of the pie dish with water, cut a long strip of pastry, and put on to the rim. Lift the rest of the pastry on to the top of the pie using the rolling pin for support, see Sketches 1 and 2 opposite. Press the edges lightly, cut away the surplus, and decorate as shown in the picture and Sketch 3. Fruit pies are left plain on top. Stand the pie dish on a baking tray,

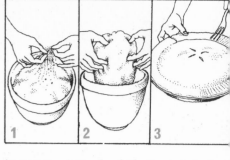

in case any juice should boil out. Bake in, or just above, the centre of a hot oven, 425°F, Gas Mark 6–7, for 15–20 minutes to set the pastry then lower the heat to very moderate to moderate, 350–375°F, Gas Mark 4–5, for a further 20–25 minutes to make sure the fruit is cooked. *Serves 4–5.*

Fruit Tarts

Use the Blue Print or the fleur pastry opposite. Roll out the pastry and line small or medium-sized individual tins. Prick the pastry with a fork and bake 'blind', see opposite, until golden brown. Cool, then either fill with fruit and glaze as for a fruit flan opposite, or put a layer of whipped cream in the bottom of the case and top with fresh fruit, such as raspberries, strawberries or blackberries.

Storing and Freezing *Fruit Flans, opposite, and tarts are better eaten fresh. They can be frozen, but the filling tends to soften the pastry as they defrost. Pies keep well when frozen; thaw before reheating.*

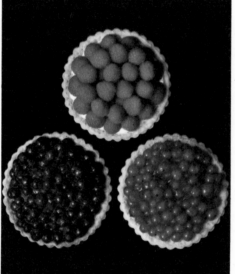

Fruit tarts
Simple fruit pie

Cherry flan

There are various types of pastry you can use for the flan case but fleur pastry, often called flan or biscuit crust, combines best with the fruit and glaze.

Blue Print Recipe

Fleur Pastry

Sufficient for one 8-inch flan ring: 3 oz. ($\frac{3}{8}$C) butter or best quality margarine · 2 oz. ($\frac{1}{4}$C) caster sugar · 1 egg yolk · 6 oz. ($1\frac{1}{2}$C) flour, preferably plain · little cold water.

To make Cream the butter or margarine and sugar until soft and light. Beat in the egg yolk, add the sieved flour and blend with a palette knife. Gradually stir in enough water to bind. Roll out to a circle about 10 inches in diameter.

If using a sandwich tin grease lightly. If using a flan ring stand on an upturned baking tray or sheet.

Putting the rolling pin under the pastry to support it, lower into the tin or flan ring, see Sketch 1. Slip the rolling pin away as you do so, Sketch 2. Press the pastry into the case with your fingers.

Either cut away any surplus pastry with a sharp knife, or else take the rolling pin backwards and forwards over the pastry, as Sketch 3.

To cook To keep the flan case a perfect shape it should be weighted to prevent the pastry base rising and the sides losing their shape, this is called 'baking blind'. The two best methods to use are either to prick the base of the flan case, then put in a double thickness of foil and press firmly against the pastry. Or grease a round of greaseproof paper lightly and place greased side downwards into the flan case. Fill with dried haricot beans or crusts of bread, see Sketch 4.

Bake in the centre of a moderate to moderately hot oven, 375–400°F, Gas Mark 5–6, for 15–20 minutes, or until the pastry is just set. Remove the foil, or paper and beans or bread, then continue baking for a further 5–10 minutes until golden brown. Lift away the flan ring and if the pastry is a little pale return to the oven for a few minutes. Cool slightly, put on to a wire cooling tray. When cold fill and glaze.

To Fill the Flan

You will need about 1 lb. of fruit. If using *cooked fruit*, poach carefully (as page 7). Lift from the syrup and put in a sieve over a bowl. Retain the syrup. *Canned fruit* should be drained in the same way. *Frozen fruit* should be *almost* defrosted, then drained as above. It spoils the appearance and taste of *ripe cherries, raspberries and strawberries* if they are poached in syrup. Make a syrup from sugar and water (see page 7). Put the fruit into the syrup while it is still warm. Leave for 2–3 minutes, lift out and strain as above. Put the drained fruit into the flan case carefully.

To Make the Glaze

If the flan case is fairly shallow use $\frac{1}{4}$ pint ($\frac{2}{3}$C) syrup, but if it is fairly deep, use $\frac{1}{2}$ pint ($1\frac{1}{3}$C). Blend the syrup with 1 or 2 teaspoons arrowroot or cornflour. Put into the saucepan, stir well and cook until thickened. Add a few drops of colouring if necessary, or about 2 tablespoons red currant jelly or sieved raspberry jam for extra flavour. When thickened and clear, cool but do not allow to set. Brush or spread over the fruit, see Sketch 5. *Serves 6.*

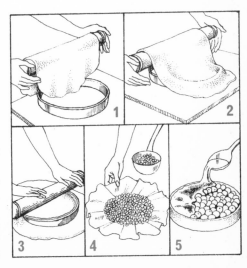

Charlottes and Crumbles

Contrasting textures in food add interest to many dishes and both Fruit Charlottes and Crumbles are excellent examples of combining ultra crisp toppings and soft fruit. They are quick and easy to make and ideal for family or special occasions.

Blue Print Recipes

1. Fruit Charlotte or Brown Betty

1–1¼ lb. prepared fruit · little water · sugar to taste. For the charlotte mixture: 4–5 large slices bread · 3 oz. (⅜C) butter or margarine · 2 oz. (¼C) sugar (preferably brown).

To make If using firm fruit, such as apples, plums, etc., cook in a covered saucepan with a *little* water and sugar to taste until softened. Berry fruit (such as raspberries, loganberries, etc.) may also be cooked first, but if you prefer these to remain firm then do not heat.

There are two ways of making a charlotte. The first is to remove the crusts and then cut the bread into neat fingers; the second method is to make fairly coarse crumbs from the bread. Heat the butter or margarine in a large frying pan and fry the bread in this until just golden coloured. Put one third of the bread slices or crumbs into a pie or oven-proof dish, sprinkle with some of the sugar. Add half the fruit purée. If using uncooked soft fruit sprinkle with sugar. Put a second layer of bread and a sprinkling of sugar, then the rest of the fruit purée or fruit and sugar. Top with an even layer of bread and sugar.
To cook Bake for about 35–40 minutes in the centre of a moderate oven 350–375°F, Gas Mark 4–5.
To serve In the dish or invert this on to a hot serving plate and decorate with cooked or raw fruit.
To vary See below under Crumble.

2. Fruit Crumble

1–1¼ lb. prepared fruit · little water · sugar to taste. For the crumble: 4 oz. (1C) flour* · 2 oz. (¼C) butter or margarine · 2–3 oz. (¼–⅓C) sugar.
*can be plain or self-raising.

To make Put the fruit into a pie or oven-proof dish. If cooking soft berry fruit use no water or about 1 tablespoon if very firm; with harder fruit use 3–4 table-spoons. Add sugar to sweeten. Cook gently in the oven for 10–15 minutes. If you prefer berry fruit to be firm, do *not* cook this before adding the crumble top-ping. Sieve the flour, rub in the butter or margarine, add the sugar. Sprinkle over the top of the fruit.
To cook Bake in the centre of a moderate oven 350–375°F, Gas Mark 4–5, for 25–30 minutes until crisp and golden brown.
To serve In the baking dish, with cream or custard sauce. It is nicer served hot rather than cold. *All recipes based on these Blue Prints serve 4–5.*
To vary Sieve ½–1 teaspoon ground ginger, cinnamon or other spice with the flour, or add the grated rind of 1 or 2 oranges or lemons. Use the same flavour-ings in the charlotte and either mix with the crumbs and sugar or sprinkle over the fingers of bread, after frying.

● **AVOID** *Too much fat in a crumble mixture, this prevents it becoming crisp: Too much liquid when cooking the fruit, this will spoil both the appearance and texture of the topping.*
● **TO RECTIFY** *If you find the fruit is too soft strain away surplus moisture before adding the topping.*
● **SHORT CUT** *Use canned fruit or canned fruit pie filling.*

Apricot fruit crumble (above right)
Cornflake Brown Betty (left)

Cornflake Brown Betty
Use Blue Print 1, but substitute 4–5 oz (3–3¾C) cornflakes for the breadcrumbs Toss the cornflakes lightly in the hot butte or margarine then mix with the sugar. Bak as Blue Print 1.

Coconut Crumble
Ingredients as Blue Print 2 PLUS 2 oz. desi ccated coconut.
Make the crumble, then add the coconut Bake as Blue Print 2.

For Special Occasions

Choose the 'luxury' fruits for either the Frui Charlotte or Crumble.

Apple Raisin Brown Betty
Use Blue Print 1 PLUS 4 oz. (½C) seedless o stoned raisins, 1 good tablespoon brandy o lemon juice and 2 tablespoons blanched chopped almonds.
Follow the Blue Print, but mix the raisin and brandy or lemon juice with the cooked fruit (in this case apples) and blend the chopped almonds with the breadcrumbs before tossing in the hot butter or margarine. Bake as Blue Print 1 and serve with Hard Sauce (see page 3).

Chocolate Chip Crumble
Ingredients as Blue Print 2 PLUS 3 oz. plain chocolate.
Prepare the crumble as the Blue Print, add the coarsely grated or chopped chocolate with the sugar. Bake as Blue Print 2, but take care not to over-cook, to avoid scorching.

Storing and Freezing *Both Char-lottes and Crumbles may be made over-night, stored in a cool place and cooked as the recipe. They may be frozen, wrapped and stored for 2–3 months. Thaw out before cooking or re-heating.*

One of the simplest and most enjoyable desserts is fresh fruit. Serve it plain or with cream or ice cream, or give additional flavour with a liqueur, wine or other fruit juice (see page 8). Other fruits are better cooked and it is important that they retain colour, texture and flavour by careful cooking. In either case it is important that the fruit is well prepared and given interesting flavours.

To Prepare and Flavour Fruit

Wash in cold, not hot water and use immediately after washing.

Apples and Pears Peel thinly unless retaining peel on eating apples. Core and slice. Both these fruit discolour easily, so sprinkle with lemon juice or keep in cold water until ready to use or cook. Flavour with spices, dried fruit, lemon rind and/or juice or cook with sliced quince.

Apricots and Plums Halve or use whole. Flavour with lemon juice.

Bananas If using raw sprinkle with lemon juice to prevent discoloration.

Blackcurrants Remove from stalks singly, or as redcurrants.

Cherries Choose cooking or black cherries when possible. Flavour with almond essence or Maraschino.

Gooseberries Top and tail, i.e. remove stalk and flower ends with kitchen scissors. Flavour with finely grated orange rind, 1–2 leaves of Ivy geranium and/or a little white wine.

Grapes Split carefully, remove pips, skin if wished, use raw.

Oranges and Citrus Fruits Cut away peel with the pith. Do this over a basin to retain the juice, Sketch 1. Cut the segments of fruit between the skin and discard any pips, Sketch 2. When all the fruit has been removed squeeze pith and skin remaining to extract any juice.

Raspberries Prepare and flavour as directions for strawberries.

Redcurrants Pull the fruit very carefully from the stalk with the prongs of a fork. A delicious dessert can be made by flavouring redcurrants with vanilla sugar and leaving for 1 hour; stir once or twice. This is particularly good as a topping on sliced fresh peaches.

Rhubarb Cut into neat lengths. Flavour with orange rind, sultanas and/or spices.

Strawberries Remove stalks i.e. 'hull' them. Flavour with wine but other additions are unnecessary.

Blue Print Recipe

Compôte of Fruit

Water (see method) · sugar (see method) · approximately 1 lb. prepared fruit.

To make Allow between ¼–½ pint (⅔–1⅓C) water and 2–4 oz. (¼–½C) sugar to cook very firm fruit, such as hard plums, or half the quantity of water for soft fruit, such as blackcurrants.

To cook Put the water and sugar into a large pan, stir until the sugar has dissolved. Put in the prepared fruit, lower the heat, cover the pan to prevent the liquid evaporating and simmer gently until tender. This varies a great deal, firm fruit takes 10–20 minutes, soft fruit about 5 minutes.

Another way of cooking soft fruit is to put this, and sugar to taste, in the top of a double saucepan and cook over hot water until tender. This is particularly suitable for forced rhubarb, blackcurrants and raspberries.

If preferred the fruit may be cooked in a covered casserole in a very moderate oven, 325°F, Gas Mark 2–3. It is best to make the sugar and water syrup in a pan, put this into a warm casserole and *then* add the fruit. In this way you retain more colour.

To serve Hot or cold with cream, custard or ice cream. *Serves 4–6.*

● **AVOID** *Putting the sugar, water and fruit in the pan at the same time if you wish to keep the fruit in good shape: Too rapid cooking softens the outside of the fruit before the centre is tender.*

● **TO RECTIFY** *If you find the fruit is cooking too rapidly remove the pan from the heat, cover with a tightly fitting lid, and let the fruit continue cooking in the steam retained in the pan.*

● **SHORT CUT** *By cutting fruit in smaller pieces you shorten the cooking time but run the risk of it becoming over-soft and looking less attractive.*

● **TO SLIMMERS** *Make as much use of fruit desserts as possible, particularly the citrus fruits. Use sugar substitute instead of sugar for sweetening fruit salad.*

To Cook Dried Fruit

Cover 8 oz. (1C) dried fruit with ½ pint (1⅓C) cold water and soak overnight. If preferred give additional flavour by soaking in cider or white wine, or add lemon juice to apples, pears and apricots, weak tea to prunes and weak coffee to figs. Tenderized fruit does not need soaking. Add sugar to taste and simmer until tender. The time varies, some tenderized fruit will need only ½–¾ hour. Others are better given longer.

Fresh fruit salad

There is infinite variety in a fresh fruit salad depending on the time of the year. Try to have a good blending of colour and texture, i.e. add firm apple and pear slices to balance the softness of oranges and bananas. The easiest way to prepare a fruit salad is, as the picture on this page, to blend canned and fresh fruit. Choose canned pineapple or peaches with fresh oranges, apples, grapes and pears. The syrup from the can provides the liquid. If preferred sweeten with fresh orange juice, or make a sugar and water syrup as the Blue Print and flavour with pieces of orange rind or a liqueur. A fruit salad is suitable for family or special occasions.

More Fruit Desserts

Fruit is so adaptable that it can be used in a great variety of ways and pages 4–7 cover some of these.

One of the best simple fruit desserts is a Baked Apple, and since this can be varied in innumerable ways I have made it one of my Blue Prints on this page.

Blue Print Recipes

1. Baked Apples

4 medium-sized to large cooking apples · approximately 1 tablespoon brown or white sugar.

To make Core the apple, do this either with an apple corer or a pointed knife. In order to prevent the skin 'bursting' during cooking either slit this round the centre or cut as in the picture. Put the apples into an oven-proof dish, fill the centres with sugar.
To cook Bake for approximately 1 hour in the centre of a moderate oven, 350–375°F, Gas Mark 4–5, or allow 15 minutes longer in a very moderate oven, 325°F, Gas Mark 2–3.
To serve The skin may be left on the apples unless planning either of the last two variations below. Serve with custard sauce, cream or ice cream. *All recipes based on this dish serve 4.*

2. Fruit in Rum

2 oz. ($\frac{1}{4}$C) butter · 2 oz. ($\frac{1}{4}$C) brown sugar · 2–3 tablespoons orange juice · 2–3 tablespoons rum · fruit (see method).
To make and cook Heat the butter and sugar in a frying pan stirring until the sugar has dissolved. Add the orange juice and rum, stir to make a syrup. Put 4 halved bananas or skinned peaches, or 8 apricots into the syrup and simmer gently for 10 minutes.
To serve Hot with cream. *All recipes based on this dish serve 4.*
Storing and Freezing *Most of the dishes on pages 7 and 8 may be kept a day or two in a refrigerator, but do not freeze well.*

● **AVOID** *Cooking the apples too quickly, this gives an ultra-soft outside before the fruit is cooked through to the centre.*
● **TO RECTIFY** *If you find the fruit cooking too quickly lower the heat or move the dish to a cooler part of the oven.*

Baked apple with orange filling

For Family Occasions

Orange Filling

As Blue Print 1 MINUS the sugar. Blend 2–3 tablespoons of orange marmalade with the finely grated rind of 1–2 oranges and approximately 2 tablespoons orange juice.
Put into apples before cooking. While the apples are cooking, cut neat pieces of fresh orange (as page 7). Remove the apples from the oven a few minutes before serving, spoon the orange segments on top, return to the oven to heat, or omit orange pieces and decorate with strips of rind as in the picture.

Ginger-Apricot Filling

As Blue Print 1 MINUS sugar. Blend 2–3 tablespoons of apricot jam with 1–2 tablespoons chopped preserved ginger.
Put into apples and cook as the Blue Print. Serve with cream which may be flavoured with a little syrup from the preserved ginger.

Coconut-Fudge Filling

As Blue Print 1 (choose brown sugar), PLUS 1 oz. butter and 2–3 tablespoons desiccated coconut.
Prepare the apples as the Blue Print but mix the sugar with the butter and coconut. Put into the centre of the apples and cook as the Blue Print.

For Special Occasions

Macaroon Apples

As Blue Print 1 PLUS 2 tablespoons ground almonds, 2 eggs, almond essence, 2 oz. ($\frac{1}{4}$C) caster sugar and 1 tablespoon chopped blanched almonds.

Prepare the apples as the Blue Print. Blend the ground almonds with the sugar in the Blue Print, egg yolks and a few drops of almond essence. Put into the centre of the apples and cook as the Blue Print. Remove the apple skins. Whisk the egg whites until very stiff, gradually whisk in the caster sugar. Spread over the apples. Top with the almonds then return to the oven for a few minutes. Serve at once.

Coconut Apples

Follow the recipe for the Coconut-Fudge filling. When the apples are cooked remove from oven, take off the skins and coat with desiccated coconut.

Baked Oranges

4 large or 8 medium-sized oranges; 1 oz. butter; 2 oz. ($\frac{1}{4}$C) brown sugar, 1–2 tablespoons sherry or rum; 4 glacé cherries.
Cut the peel and pith from the oranges. Cut into thick slices then put together again as Sketch 3, page 7, with cocktail sticks. Put into an oven-proof dish. Spread the softened butter on the top of the oranges, sprinkle with the sugar and add the sherry or rum. Bake for 30 minutes as Blue Print 1. Decorate with the cherries, serve hot.

Luxury Touches with Fresh Fruit

Prepare the fruit, put into a dish with wine, liqueur or fruit juice, see below, and leave for about 1 hour. Do not add sugar as everyone differs in the amount of sweetening they like. Some combinations you might like to try are strawberries in white wine; sliced ripe peaches in a mixture of white wine and crème de menthe; sliced fresh pineapple sprinkled with kirsch or apricot brandy; sliced bananas in orange juice and Curaçao.

Gelatine, obtainable both in sheet and powder form, can be used to set clear liquids such as fruit juices, fruit purées, milk and/or cream mixtures. However, it is not always used as successfully as it might be, so Blue Print 1 covers the correct way to dissolve and incorporate it into other foods. Commercial jellies are favourites with all the family and make interesting dishes with the minimum expenditure of time and trouble.

Blue Print Recipe

1. To use Gelatine

The instructions on the packet will give exact quantities. Generally one uses 1 envelope, which is ½ oz. or 1 tablespoon to 1 pint (2⅔C) clear liquid or half this quantity for thickened liquids (see page 15), or the equivalent in sheet gelatine.

To dissolve Put the gelatine into a basin, add 2–3 tablespoons *cold* liquid from the 1 pint (2⅔C). Stand the basin in, or over, a pan of hot water, leave until the gelatine has dissolved. There is no need to stir *as the gelatine softens*, do this just before blending with the other ingredients. Heat the remainder of the liquid, pour over the gelatine, stir until well blended.

To set Rinse a mould or basin in cold water, leave damp. Pour in the jelly, when set invert on to a *damp* serving dish. This means you can slide the jelly easily into the centre of the dish. *All recipes based on this serve 4.*

Blue Print Recipe

2. Fruit Filled Jelly

1 packet jelly · water and fruit juice or syrup from a can · canned, cooked or fresh fruit.

Read the instructions on the packet for the exact amount of water or liquid required; this varies slightly according to different makes. If using canned or cooked fruit strain off the syrup, dilute with water to make up to the quantity given on the packet *less* about 1 tablespoon. This is because the fruit is moist and will dilute the strength of the jelly. If using fresh fruit such as bananas or berries you can use the full quantity of water because these are firm. If you wish to use a little fresh orange or lemon juice then this counts as part of the total amount.

Dissolve the jelly according to the instructions. Pour a little into the rinsed mould (see Blue Print 1). Allow this to become nearly set and arrange the first layer of fruit on top. It is easier to do this if you dip the fruit in liquid jelly. When set pour over a little more jelly and continue filling the mould like this to give an interesting design. Allow to set and turn out as Blue Print 1.

● **AVOID** *Adding gelatine to hot liquids, soften first (see Blue Print 1).*
● **TO RECTIFY** *If gelatine does not dissolve well, due to putting it into hot liquid without softening, allow to stand until cool, stir well and reheat gently.*
● **SHORT CUT** *To speed the setting of jellies use some crushed ice instead of the same quantity of water.*
● **TO SLIMMERS** *Many jelly recipes are suitable for low calorie desserts. Use sugar substitute instead of sugar.*

Jellied fruit snow

Fresh Orange Jelly
2–3 large oranges; 1 small lemon; water; 2–3 oz. (¼–⅜C) sugar; 1 tablespoon gelatine.
Pare the rind from the oranges and lemon, put into a saucepan with about ½ pint (1⅓C) water. Simmer for 10 minutes, strain, add sugar while hot. Squeeze the juice from the fruit and measure. The juice *plus* fruit liquid should give 1 pint (2⅔C). Soften the gelatine in a little cold liquid as Blue Print 1. Heat the rest of the liquid, pour over the gelatine mixture. Stir until dissolved, then follow Blue Print 1 for setting and turning out the jelly.

Fresh Lemon Jelly
Recipe as above but use 2 large or 3 medium-sized lemons.
You will note I added a lemon to the orange jelly above. You may like to omit this but it does *not* conflict with the orange flavour, and it seems to give a more refreshing jelly.

Jellied Fruit Snow
½ pint (1⅓C) thick sweetened fruit purée*; 1 teaspoon powdered gelatine; 2 tablespoons water or fresh fruit juice; ¼ pint (⅔C) thick cream; 3 egg whites.
*in the picture apple purée was used and tinted with a little green colouring.
Warm the purée gently, soften the gelatine in the water or fruit juice as Blue Print 1. Mix with the purée, stir until dissolved. Allow to cool, fold in half the lightly whipped cream and 2 stiffly beaten egg whites. Spoon into 4–6 serving glasses and allow to set lightly (this will never be sufficiently stiff to turn out). Whip the remainder of the cream and the third egg white in separate basins, fold together and pile on top of the dessert. Decorate with lemon slices if wished. *Serves 4–6.*

Gooseberry Sparkle
Method as Blue Print 2. Choose canned gooseberries and a lime jelly. Decorate with whipped cream, chopped glacé cherries and chopped crystallised ginger.

Gooseberry sparkle

Egg Custards

Eggs or egg yolks have the ability to thicken liquids (generally milk), to make either a pouring sauce, or quite a firm pudding. The higher the proportion of eggs used, the more solid the result, 2 eggs or egg yolks and 1 pint (2⅔C) milk produces a lightly set custard or a custard sauce, however, 4 eggs or 2 whole eggs and 2 egg yolks, or 5 egg yolks and 1 pint (2⅔C) liquid will give a custard sufficiently firm to turn out of the dish such as the Caramel Custard on the opposite page.

Blue Print Recipe

Baked Egg Custard

1 pint (2⅔C) milk · 2 eggs · 1 oz. sugar · nutmeg.

To make Heat the milk but do not let it boil; it should be about blood temperature. Beat the eggs and sugar together, then add the hot milk, stirring all the time.

To cook Strain into a greased pie dish, grate a little nutmeg on top. Stand the dish in a 'bain-marie', i.e. another dish containing cold water, and bake in the coolest part of a slow oven, 275–300°F, Gas Mark 1–2, for approximately 45 minutes to 1 hour until the mixture is set.

To serve In the pie dish. It is not sufficiently firm to turn out. This can be a pudding by itself or it can be served with cooked fruit. *All recipes based on this dish serve 4–5.*

● **AVOID** *Over-heating, which causes the mixture to curdle (separate). You can see when this has happened by the 'watery' liquid in the dish: Pastry rising and custard sinking in a custard tart. The recipe gives the best way of preventing this, i.e. to bake the pastry 'blind' first and then to pour in the hot custard mixture.*

● **TO RECTIFY** *Whisk sharply, this is quite often effective in a sauce. If unsuccessful emulsify in a liquidiser. This gives a thinner mixture. If time permits whisk in an extra egg or egg yolk, cook again to thicken. The only other alternative is to spoon the pudding carefully from the dish, leaving the 'watery' liquid behind.*

● **SHORT CUT** *Make a sauce with custard powder or cornflour, when thickened add an egg or egg yolk. Simmer gently for 2–3 minutes only.*

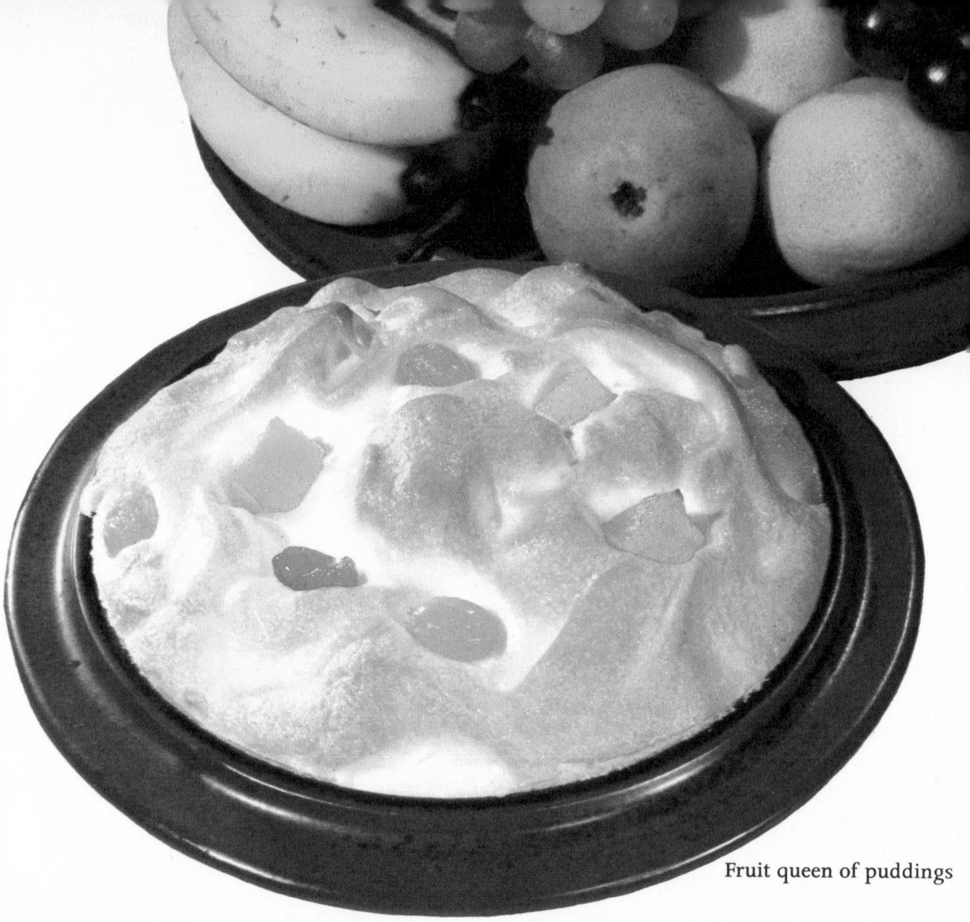

Fruit queen of puddings

For Family Occasions

Custard Sauce

Ingredients as Blue Print. Strain the custard into the top of a double saucepan, or basin balanced on a pan, over *hot* but not boiling water. Cook gently, stirring well, until the custard coats the back of a wooden spoon. If serving cold cover with damp greaseproof paper to prevent a skin forming.

Custard Tart

Sweet short crust pastry made with 6 oz. (1½C) flour, etc. (page 4). Half ingredients as Blue Print (i.e. ½ pint (1⅓C) milk, etc., but use 2 eggs for a firmer filling).

Line a 7–8 inch flan case or a sandwich tin with the pastry. Bake 'blind' (see page 5) in the centre of a hot oven, 425–450°F, Gas Mark 6–7, for 10 minutes to set the pastry and prevent it rising. Prepare the custard as the Blue Print, strain the hot custard into the hot pastry case, top with grated nutmeg. Lower the heat to very moderate, 325–350°F, Gas Mark 3–4, cook for a further 35–40 minutes until the custard is set. Serve hot or cold.

Small custard tarts are made in the same way. Set the pastry cases for 5 minutes, fill with custard, cook for 20–25 minutes.

Bread and Butter Pudding

Ingredients as Blue Print PLUS 4 large slices bread and butter, 2–4 oz. (¼–½C) dried fruit and 1 extra tablespoon sugar.

Cut the bread and butter into triangles. Put into a pie dish with the fruit. Strain over custard and top with the sugar and grated nutmeg, if wished. Bake as Blue Print.

For Special Occasions

Snow Eggs or Floating Islands

Ingredients as Blue Print PLUS 2 oz. (¼C) caster sugar and a few drops vanilla essence or a vanilla pod.

Pour the milk into a shallow pan or deep frying pan. Separate the eggs. Whisk the egg whites stiffly, cover the egg yolks to prevent them from drying. Gradually whisk the caster sugar into the egg whites. Heat the milk to about 190°F, i.e. until simmering. Drop spoonfuls of the meringue mixture on top of the hot milk, poach for 2 minutes. Turn with a perforated spoon, or fish slice, and poach for the same time on the second side. Lift the meringues from the milk, drain on a large sieve. Meanwhile strain the milk on to the beaten egg yolks and sugar. Add the vanilla essence or pod. Cook as custard sauce on this page. If using a vanilla pod remove this. Pour into a shallow dish, cool, top with meringue balls.

Fruit Queen of Puddings

2 tablespoons jam; 2 oz. (½C) soft breadcrumbs; 2 eggs; ¾ pint (2C) milk; 3 oz. (⅜C) caster sugar; 3 tablespoons fresh or canned fruit.

Spread half the jam in an oven-proof dish. Add the crumbs. Separate the egg yolks and make the custard as Blue Print using the yolks, milk and 1 oz. sugar. Pour over the crumbs and bake as the Blue Print, until firm. Spread with the jam and most of the fruit. Whip egg whites until very stiff, fold in remaining sugar. Pile on to the custard and top with the remaining fruit. Bake for 15 minutes in a moderate oven, 375°F, Gas Mark 4–5. Serve hot.

More Egg Custards

As caramel combines well with egg custards, a caramel sauce is the Blue Print on this page.

Blue Print Recipe

Caramel Sauce

3 tablespoons granulated or caster sugar (or equivalent in loaf sugar) · 3 tablespoons water.

To make Put the sugar and water into a strong saucepan.
To cook Stir over a low heat until the sugar has dissolved. If the sugar and water splash against the sides of the saucepan brush with a pastry brush dipped in cold water. This helps to prevent the mixture crystallising. Allow the sugar and water syrup to boil steadily until golden brown, then use in individual recipes.

● **AVOID** *Leaving the sugar and water* until *the sugar has dissolved, stir all the time. When the sugar has dissolved do not stir, or you will hinder the syrup reaching the right temperature and it could crystallise and never become brown: Too dark a coloured caramel, this tastes unpleasantly bitter: Adding milk to the very hot caramel, this could cause curdling.*
● **TO RECTIFY** *Add a little more water if mixture crystallises. Stir until a clear syrup, proceed as usual: If the caramel is going too dark, immediately add 2 tablespoons cold water or put pan into cold water to lower the temperature.*
● **SHORT CUT** *Use 3 tablespoons golden syrup instead of 3 tablespoons sugar. Do not add water. Brown the syrup for a very few minutes.*

Storing and Freezing *All the recipes on these two pages keep for 2–3 days in a refrigerator. Only the Crème Brûlée can be frozen because it contains a high percentage of cream.*

For Family Occasions

Caramel Custard or Crème Renversée
Caramel as Blue Print PLUS 1–2 tablespoons water, custard made with 4 eggs, 1 tablespoon sugar and 1 pint (2⅔C) milk.
Make the caramel as the Blue Print. When golden brown add the extra water and heat. Coat a 7–8-inch, oval or round oven-proof dish with the caramel. Make the custard as the Blue Print opposite. Strain into the dish. Bake as Blue Print but allow 1½–2 hours until firm. Cool for about 10 minutes, invert on to a serving dish. *Serves 4–6.*

For Special Occasions

Crème Brûlée
Caramel as Blue Print PLUS ½ pint (1⅓C) milk, 4 eggs, 1 tablespoon sugar, ½ pint (1⅓C) thick cream. *For the topping:* 2 tablespoons blanched almonds, 2 tablespoons sieved icing sugar.
Make the caramel as the Blue Print. Leave in the saucepan, cool slightly. Add the milk, heat gently until blended with the caramel. Beat the eggs with the sugar and cream, add the caramel and milk. Strain into an oven-proof or soufflé dish. This can either be a deep dish, as in the Caramel Custard above, or you can cook it in a shallow dish, as in the photograph, in which case you may like to use a little extra topping. Bake as Blue Print on the opposite page, allowing 1½–2 hours until firm. Top with almonds and sugar and brown for a few minutes under the grill. *Serves 4–6.*

Coconut Meringue
Ingredients as Blue Print opposite PLUS 3 tablespoons desiccated coconut, 2 tablespoons glacé cherries, 2 tablespoons apricot jam and 2 tablespoons caster sugar.
Separate the egg yolks and whites. Make the custard as the Blue Print opposite with the egg yolks only. Pour on to 2 tablespoons coconut. Leave for 30 minutes. Add most of the chopped glacé cherries. Pour into a pie dish and bake as Blue Print. Spread with the jam. Whip the egg whites until very stiff, fold in the caster sugar. Pile this on the custard. Top with the rest of the coconut and glacé cherries. Return to the oven for 20–25 minutes. Serve hot with cream.

Chestnut Meringue
Substitute sliced marrons glacés for the coconut in the above recipe.

To use any left over *Eat cold, or emulsify the plain or caramel custard in a liquidiser. They make a delicious sauce to serve with fruit. Any left over egg whites can be used for meringues (see page 12).*

Crème brûlée (above left)
Caramel custard or crème renversée (below)

Meringues

A meringue topping on a dessert, as the Lemon and Lime Meringue Pies illustrated, gives a look of luxury as well as a pleasant taste. Meringues are also one of the best 'stand-by's' in a tin. Small meringues may be sandwiched together with cream or ice cream, or a large meringue case may be turned into a party gâteau (see page 20).

Blue Print Recipe

Meringue

2 egg whites · 4 oz. ($\frac{1}{2}$C) caster sugar (or use half caster and half sieved icing sugar).

To make First check that the bowl is free from grease and that the egg whites are not too cold. If you have brought them out of the refrigerator allow to stand an hour before whisking.

Separate the egg yolks from the whites, cover the yolks with a little cold water to prevent hardening, store in a cool place until they may be used. Check no yolk has gone into the whites. If there is a particle remove with the half egg shell as a scoop, or the corner of a damp, clean tea towel or damp kitchen paper.

Whisk the egg whites until very stiff. If they seem slow in whisking, after taking the precautions above, then it may be the kitchen is too hot, so move to an open window.

To test The egg whites are sufficiently stiff when they stand up in peaks and you can turn the bowl upside down without the mixture moving.

There are several ways of incorporating the sugar. The best way is *gradually* to beat in *half* the sugar, then fold in the remainder gently and slowly. A softer meringue is given if you *gradually* fold in *all* the sugar and a very firm meringue (only successful if you have a mixer) is obtained if you *gradually* beat in *all* the sugar.

To cook As individual recipes.

● **AVOID** *Adding the sugar until the egg whites are* really *stiff (see the Blue Print): Adding the sugar too rapidly: Baking the meringue mixture too quickly, unless serving hot.*

● **TO RECTIFY** *If egg whites are not becoming stiff consult the Blue Print: If sugar is added too rapidly you will have a softer meringue, which can be used for a dessert but is not good for small meringues or a gâteau.*

Lemon Meringue Pie

Fleur pastry (page 5); 2 lemons; water; 2$\frac{1}{2}$ tablespoons cornflour; 4–8 oz. ($\frac{1}{2}$–1C) caster sugar (see method); $\frac{1}{2}$–1 oz. butter; 2 eggs.

Make the flan case and bake 'blind' (as page 5). Grate the top rind (zest) from the lemons, squeeze out juice, measure and add water to give $\frac{1}{2}$ pint (1$\frac{1}{3}$C). Blend the cornflour with the lemon juice and water, put into a pan with the grated rind, 2–4 oz. ($\frac{1}{4}$–$\frac{1}{2}$C) sugar (depending on whether you like a sharp or sweet flavour) and the butter. Stir over a gentle heat until thickened. Remove from the heat, separate the eggs, add the beaten yolks. Cook *gently* for several minutes.

Taste, add even more sugar if wished. Spoon into the pastry case. Whisk the egg whites until very stiff, add 2 or 4 oz. ($\frac{1}{4}$ or $\frac{1}{2}$C) sugar as the method in the Blue Print. Spoon over the lemon mixture, so meringue touches the pastry rim.

To serve freshly cooked Use the smaller quantity of sugar if desired. Brown for 20 minutes in the centre of a very moderate oven, 325–350°F, Gas Mark 3–4, or 5–8 minutes in a hot oven.

To serve cold Use full proportions of sugar as Blue Print, bake for at least 1 hour in the centre of a very slow to slow oven, 225–250°F, Gas Mark $\frac{1}{2}$–1.

Lime Meringue Pie

Use bottled or fresh lime juice in place of lemon juice. Allow 4–5 tablespoons bottled juice and add grated lemon rind if fresh limes are not available. If liked decorate with a twist of lime.

Graham Crust Pie

Instead of the pastry case make the flan of biscuit crumbs. Crush 8 oz. plain graham or cream crackers or similar biscuits. Cream 4 oz. ($\frac{1}{2}$C) butter and 2 oz. ($\frac{1}{4}$C) caster sugar. Add the crumbs, form into an 8-inch flan shape, do not bake. Fill with the lemon or lime mixture, proceed as above.

Lemon meringue pie (above left)
Lime meringue pie (below)

Removing the pancake from the frying pan

For Family Occasions

Fruit Fritters

Ingredients as Blue Print PLUS 1 tablespoon flour; pan deep fat or oil for frying or 3–4 oz. (½C) fat for shallow frying; 4 good-sized cooking apples or bananas, 8 pineapple rings (drain canned pineapple well) or 12 plums; caster sugar to coat.

Prepare the batter as the Blue Print in a large basin (this makes it easier to coat the fruit). Put the flour on a large plate. Heat deep fat or oil—*test if correct temperature*—a cube of bread should turn golden in 30 seconds. Lower the heat so the fat does not over-heat. Peel and core apples, cut into ½-inch rings. Halve large bananas. Coat the fruit first with flour (this makes sure the batter adheres well) and then in the batter. Lift out with a fork, hold over the basin to allow surplus to drop into the basin. Drop into the hot fat, cook steadily for 4–5 minutes, until golden brown. Lift out, drain on absorbent paper, coat in sugar and serve hot. *If frying in shallow fat* heat this *as you* coat the fruit. Turn the fritters after 2–3 minutes and brown other side. *Serves 4.*

Lemon Pancakes

Ingredients as Blue Print (or economical variation) PLUS ¼ pint (⅔C) milk or milk and water, oil or fat for frying, 1–2 tablespoons caster sugar, 1 or 2 lemons.

Make the batter as the Blue Print, adding the extra liquid. Put 1–2 teaspoons oil or a small knob of fat into a frying pan, heat thoroughly. Pour or spoon enough batter into the pan to give a *paper thin* layer. Cook quickly for 1–2 minutes until brown on the under side, turn

or toss, cook on the second side. Remove from the pan, see picture, put on to sugared paper, roll and keep hot on a plate over a pan of boiling water. Continue until all the batter is used. Serve with sugar and sliced lemon. *Serves 4.*

Syrup Waffles

Ingredients as Blue Print PLUS 1 teaspoon baking powder (if using plain flour), 1½ tablespoons melted butter or oil *and* butter, and butter, golden or maple syrup for serving.

Make the batter as the Blue Print, sieving the baking powder and flour and adding the extra butter or oil and butter. Heat the waffle iron, oil if necessary. Spoon enough batter on to the iron to give a good coating. Close the lid, cook until the steaming ceases. Lift the lid, remove the waffle and serve hot topped with butter and syrup. *Serves 4.*

For Special Occasions

Almond Cream Fritters

Stone large plums, ripe apricots or small peaches. Fill with cream cheese and chopped blanched almonds. Omit 1 tablespoon milk from the Blue Print and add 1 tablespoon brandy instead. Coat, fry and serve as Fruit Fritters.

Chocolate Ice Cream Pancakes

Make the pancakes as directed. Keep hot until ready to serve. Fill with ice cream, top with hot chocolate sauce (see page 16) and serve at once.

Apple fritters

Making Batters

The batter for pancakes, fritters and waffles is basically the same, it is just the consistency that varies. A batter for pancakes has a higher percentage of liquid to give a wafer thin result. When coating fruit with batter (for fritters), or for making waffles, it needs to be thicker.

Blue Print Recipe

Fritter Batter

4 oz. (1C) flour, preferably plain · pinch salt · 2 eggs · ¼ pint (⅔C) milk or milk and water · 1–2 teaspoons melted butter or olive oil.

To make Sieve the flour and salt. Gradually beat in the eggs and liquid giving a smooth thick batter. Add the butter or oil just before cooking.

To vary *For a lighter texture:* separate the eggs. Add the yolks to the flour, then the milk and oil. Fold the stiffly beaten egg whites into the mixture *just before coating* the fruit.

Economical batter: use 1 egg only.

● **AVOID** *Cooking too slowly, this makes a heavy mixture inclined to stick to the pan or waffle iron.*

● **TO RECTIFY** *If the first pancake or waffle cooks too slowly heat the pan, or iron, to a higher temperature before adding more mixture. The method of testing fat is given in the recipe for Fruit Fritters.*

● **SHORT CUT** *Emulsify ingredients in a liquidiser. Put milk and eggs in first then add flour, etc.*

Storing and Freezing *Batters may be stored for several days in a refrigerator. Wrap cooked pancakes and waffles in aluminium foil, store for several days in a refrigerator or 10–12 weeks in a home freezer. Reheat as required.*

Hot Soufflés

A hot sweet soufflé is one of the most delicious puddings. It is so light in texture that it is a perfect choice after an elaborate main dish. The secrets of success are to make a smooth sauce and to incorporate the egg whites carefully, folding them gently but thoroughly into the mixture with a metal spoon or palette knife. If you choose a large-sized saucepan, in which to prepare the mixture, it gives room to do this well.

Soufflés are economical as well as interesting; and can be varied in so many ways. If you like a firm-textured dessert use the smaller quantity of liquid. For a more delicate and moist texture use the larger amount.

Blue Print Recipe
Vanilla Soufflé

1 level tablespoon cornflour · $\frac{1}{4}$ pint—12 tablespoons ($\frac{2}{3}$–1C) milk · vanilla pod or vanilla essence · 2 oz. ($\frac{1}{4}$C) sugar · $\frac{1}{2}$ oz. butter · 4 eggs (see To vary) · little icing sugar.

To make Butter a 6–7-inch soufflé dish or prepare as the Blue Print opposite (this is not essential for a hot soufflé, unless using a very small soufflé dish). Put the cornflour into a basin and blend with 3 tablespoons cold milk. Heat the remainder of the milk, in a large saucepan, with the vanilla pod or essence. Pour over the cornflour, stirring well, then return to the pan. Remove the vanilla pod. Bring to the boil, add the sugar and butter, stir well and cook steadily until a thickened smooth mixture. Remove from the heat. Separate the eggs and gradually beat in the egg yolks. Whisk the egg whites stiffly and fold into the mixture, see photograph. Spoon into the greased soufflé dish, smooth flat on top.

To cook Bake in the centre of a moderate oven, 350–375°F, Gas Mark 4–5, for approximately 25 minutes, until well risen. Have the icing sugar ready.

To serve Take the dish from the oven, shake the icing sugar through a sieve as quickly as possible, remove the paper (if you have used this) and serve at once. To give a pleasant caramellised top to the soufflé pull the oven shelf out gently and carefully about 6 minutes before the end of the cooking time. Dredge the soufflé with the icing sugar and push the shelf back into the oven. *All recipes based on this dish serve 4–5.*

To vary You make a lighter soufflé if you use 3 egg yolks and 4 egg whites. If you care to omit the yolks completely and use just the egg whites, the soufflé has less flavour but sinks far less rapidly.

● **AVOID** *Too slow cooking: Keeping the cooked dish waiting—this means that you should time the cooking carefully, so the soufflé can be served as soon as it is cooked.*
● **TO RECTIFY** *A 'fallen' soufflé (and it will fall if kept waiting) never rises again. The flavour is still very pleasant though, providing the mixture is still hot.*
● **SHORT CUT** *Cook in individual dishes for 10–12 minutes only.*

Chocolate Soufflé

Although one can make a chocolate soufflé as the Blue Print, adding 2 oz. melted plain chocolate or $\frac{1}{2}$ oz. sieved cocoa to the sauce *before* the egg yolks, the following variation gives a light and very moist soufflé.

Melt 3 oz. plain chocolate in $\frac{1}{2}$ pint ($1\frac{1}{3}$C) milk. Heat 3 oz. ($\frac{3}{8}$C) butter in a large pan. Stir in 1 oz. cornflour or 2 oz. ($\frac{1}{2}$C) flour and cook for several minutes. Gradually blend in chocolate liquid. Bring to boil and cook until thickened. Beat in 2 oz. ($\frac{1}{4}$C) sugar and 4 egg yolks. Fold in the 4 whisked egg whites. Proceed as Blue Print but bake for 40 minutes. Dust with sieved icing sugar if wished, and serve with cream.

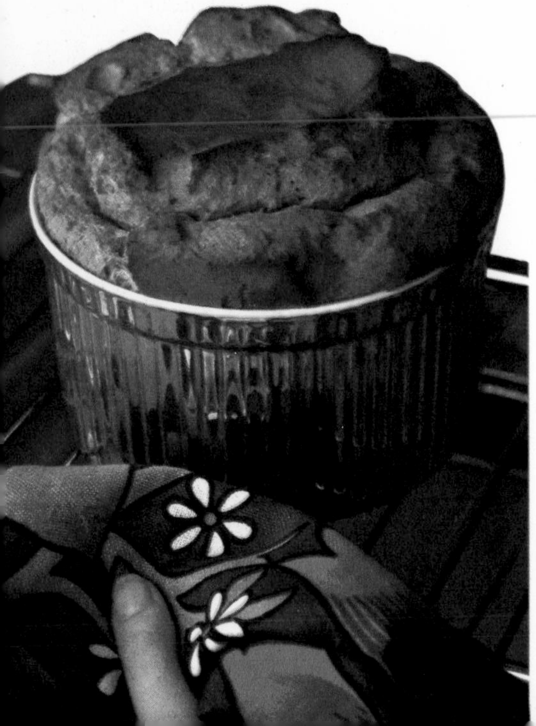

Coffee Soufflé

Recipe as Blue Print, but use either *all* strong coffee instead of milk, or half coffee and half milk. Make and cook the soufflé as the Blue Print.

Liqueur Souffle

Follow the Blue Print recipe but reduce the amount of milk by 2–3 tablespoons and use

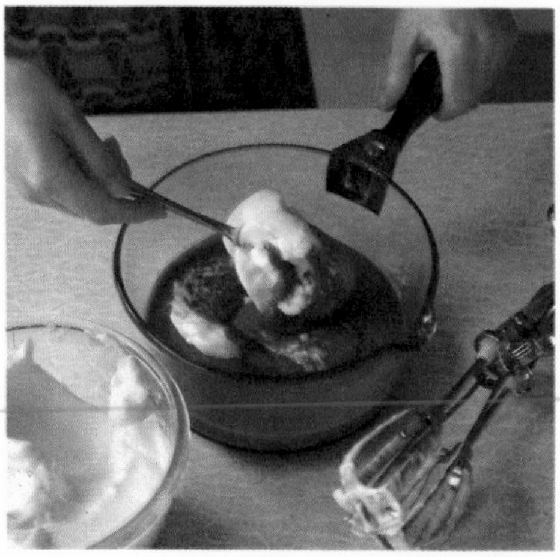

2–3 tablespoons liqueur instead. Some of the most suitable are Apricot Brandy, Cherry Brandy, Curaçao, Crême de Menthe, Tia Maria (which can be used with milk, as in the Blue Print, or with coffee). Bake as Blue Print.

Fruit Soufflé

There are several ways of incorporating fruit flavours into hot soufflés.

If using citrus fruits, i.e. orange, tangerine, lemon or lime. Follow the Blue Print recipe but use fruit juice (or fruit juice PLUS fruit liqueurs such as Curaçao or Apricot Brandy) instead of milk PLUS 2–3 teaspoons very finely grated fruit rind.

With most other fruits, particularly apricots, blackcurrants and gooseberries, use the Blue Print recipe but substitute thin smooth fruit purée for milk.

Cooked or canned cherries and canned pineapple make excellent soufflés. Follow the Blue Print recipe but use $\frac{1}{4}$ pint ($\frac{2}{3}$C) of the syrup instead of the milk, reduce the amount of sugar if wished. When the sauce has been prepared add 3–4 tablespoons well drained diced fruit *before* the egg yolks and whites. Bake as Blue Print.

Folding in the egg whites (left)
Chocolate soufflé (far left)

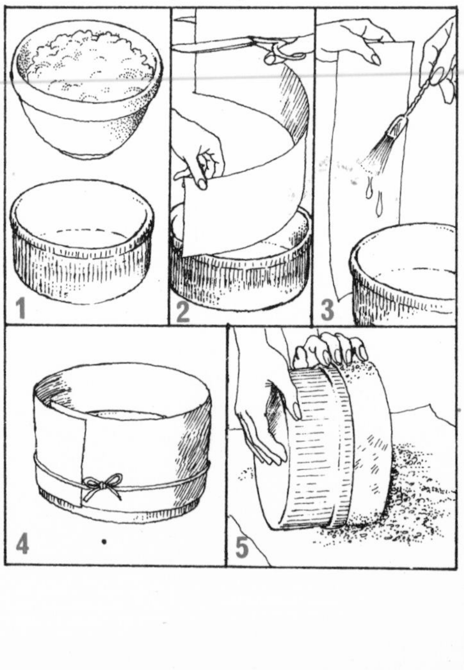

Put together beaten eggs, thick cream, flavouring (this can be fruit, rich chocolate or coffee) and bind them with gelatine and you have the ingredients to produce one of the most elegant of desserts—a cold soufflé. Naturally any soufflé is a fairly expensive dish, which is why I have included a simple 'family' adaptation: Orange Soufflé.

Blue Print Recipe

Five Stages to a Perfect Soufflé

Stage 1 Separate the egg yolks from the whites, put the yolks, sugar, flavouring and liquid (where used) into a basin over a pan of very hot water. Whisk until thick and creamy.

Stage 2 Soften the gelatine in some cold liquid. Add to the mixture above, stir over the heat until the gelatine has dissolved. Cool and allow to stiffen slightly.

Stage 3 Whip the cream lightly, fold into the jellied mixture.

Stage 4 Whisk the egg whites until stiff, but not too dry, fold into the mixture. Spoon into the prepared soufflé dish.

Stage 5 Allow to set and remove the paper slowly and carefully. Decorate the top and sides with whipped cream, finely chopped nuts, ratafia biscuits or mimosa balls.

Preparing the Soufflé Dish

It is traditional that a cold soufflé should look as if it has 'risen' in the dish, as the hot soufflé opposite. In order to achieve this result choose a soufflé dish with a smaller capacity than the amount of mixture produced, see Sketch 1. A 6-inch dish is ideal for all the recipes on this page.

Cut a band of greaseproof paper three times the depth of the dish, see Sketch 2.

Fold the paper to give a double thickness and brush the part that will stand above the

dish with a very light coating of melted butter, see Sketch 3.

Tie or pin the band of paper *very securely* round the outside of the soufflé dish, see Sketch 4.

● **AVOID** *Over-whipping the cream, this makes it difficult to incorporate: Beating the egg whites until too stiff: Adding the cream and egg whites too early; wait until the jellied mixture is lightly set.*

● **TO RECTIFY** *If the cream or egg whites have been beaten too stiffly then soften with a few drops of water. Fold this in gently and carefully.*

● **SHORT CUT** *Use the mixer to whisk the egg whites, do not over-whip: Make a smooth fruit purée in the liquidiser.*

Storing and Freezing *Keep in a cool place immediately before serving. The cold soufflé, with the high percentage of cream may be frozen, but tends to lose some of its light texture. The hot soufflé cannot be stored or frozen.*

To Use Any Leftover *Put spoonfuls of the soufflé into glasses and top with a whirl of whipped cream.*

Lemon Soufflé

Finely grated rind of 2 lemons; 4 tablespoons lemon juice; 3 eggs; 4–6 oz. ($\frac{1}{2}$–$\frac{3}{4}$C) caster sugar; $\frac{3}{4}$ tablespoon powdered gelatine; 4 tablespoons water; $\frac{1}{2}$ pint (1$\frac{1}{3}$C) thick cream. *To decorate*: small ratafia biscuits.

Put the lemon rind, juice, egg yolks and sugar into a basin. Whisk as Stage 1 in Blue Print. Soften the gelatine in the cold water, add to the egg yolk mixture and continue as Blue Print. Press some finely crushed ratafia biscuits on to the sides, see Sketch 5, and decorate the top with ratafias. *Serves 5–6.*

Fruit Soufflé

If using dessert fruit, such as raspberries and strawberries, sieve the raw fruit and measure. If using firm fruit, such as apricots, blackcurrants and gooseberries, cook in the minimum of water until soft, sieve and measure. If sugar has been used in cooking the fruit omit a little in the recipe below.

$\frac{1}{4}$ pint ($\frac{2}{3}$C) thick fruit purée; 3 eggs; 4 oz. ($\frac{1}{2}$C) caster sugar; $\frac{1}{2}$ tablespoon powdered gelatine; 2 tablespoons water; $\frac{1}{2}$ pint (1$\frac{1}{3}$C) thick cream. *To decorate*: nuts and cream.

Put the fruit purée, egg yolks and sugar into a basin. Whisk as Stage 1 in Blue Print. Soften gelatine in the cold water, add to egg yolk mixture and continue as Blue Print. Chop a few nuts very finely, press against the sides of the soufflé, see Sketch 5. Decorate the top of the soufflé with cream.

Chocolate Soufflé

4 oz. plain chocolate; 2 tablespoons milk; 3 eggs; 3 oz. ($\frac{3}{8}$C) caster sugar; $\frac{1}{2}$ tablespoon

powdered gelatine; 2 tablespoons water; $\frac{1}{2}$ pint (1$\frac{1}{3}$C) thick cream. *To decorate*: grated chocolate and cream.

Break the chocolate into pieces, put into a basin with the milk, egg yolks and sugar. Whisk as Stage 1 in Blue Print. Soften the gelatine in the cold water, add to the egg yolk mixture, continue as Blue Print. Decorate with coarsely grated chocolate and whipped cream. *Serves 5–6.*

Orange Soufflé

Dissolve an orange flavoured jelly in $\frac{3}{4}$ pint (2C) very hot water. Add grated rind of 1 orange and 2 tablespoons orange juice. Cool slightly. Whisk 1 egg yolk and pour on the warm orange jelly. Allow to cool and stiffen slightly then fold in 2 tablespoons cream or evaporated milk (lightly whipped) and 1 beaten egg white. Put into a 5-inch soufflé dish. Decorate with cream. *Serves 4–5.*

Lemon soufflé

15

Although one can buy excellent cream ices the home-made variety enables you to add any flavouring you wish. It also provides a nutritious dessert for the family. The Blue Print is for a fairly rich ice, creamy yellow in colour. You will also find variations under the Blue Print.

If you have a home freezer, it is a good idea to make up a larger amount than that given in the Blue Print. Several different flavours, i.e. coffee, chocolate and fruit, can of course be made from the basic mixture.

Blue Print Recipe

Basic Cream Ice

2 large eggs · 2 oz. ($\frac{1}{4}$–$\frac{3}{8}$C) sugar (preferably icing sugar) · $\frac{1}{4}$ pint ($\frac{2}{3}$C) thick cream · $\frac{1}{4}$ pint ($\frac{2}{3}$C) thin cream · flavouring.

To make Whisk the eggs and sugar until thick and creamy. Whip the thick cream until it *just begins* to hold its shape then gradually whisk in the thin cream. Add flavouring required. Fold into the egg mixture.

To freeze Spoon into the freezing tray or other utensil and freeze until firm. This mixture does not need beating during freezing.

If using an electric mixer whisk the eggs and sugar, pour the thick cream on to the beaten eggs and sugar, continue whisking until thick again, then gradually whisk in the thin cream and flavouring.

Cream Ices

To serve Spoon or scoop into serving dishes. *All recipes based on this dish serve 4 or 6 with other ingredients, such as fruit.*

To vary *For a whiter ice cream* use the egg whites only. Whip these until very stiff and fold into the whipped cream.

For a more economical ice cream use the egg yolks to make a custard sauce (see page 10) with $\frac{1}{2}$ pint (1$\frac{1}{3}$C) milk and sugar. Cool, fold in the whipped cream, flavouring and finally the stiffly whisked egg whites.

Use $\frac{1}{2}$ pint (1$\frac{1}{3}$C) evaporated milk in place of the thick and thin cream. To whip evaporated milk boil the tin of milk in water for 15 minutes, cool then whisk until thick.

Flavourings for ice cream
Add $\frac{1}{2}$–1 teaspoon vanilla or other essence. Add 1 tablespoon liqueur (remember this is very sweet and adjust sugar accordingly). Add $\frac{1}{2}$–1 tablespoon sweetened coffee essence.
Add $\frac{1}{2}$–1 oz. sieved cocoa.
Add $\frac{1}{4}$–$\frac{1}{2}$ pint ($\frac{2}{3}$–1$\frac{1}{3}$C) thick fruit purée. The most suitable fruits are raw sieved strawberries, raspberries and bananas, or cooked, sieved apricots (shown in the picture), blackcurrants, gooseberries and damsons.

● **AVOID** *Too slow freezing: A recipe too low in fat content encourages the formation of ice splinters in the mixture as it freezes: Too solid a mixture.*

● **TO RECTIFY** *Modern refrigerators and home freezers are sufficiently cold to freeze ice cream without adjustment. The older refrigerators freeze more slowly and should be turned to the coldest position at least half an hour before freezing the mixture and returned to normal setting when the ice cream is firm: Use a high percentage of cream or evaporated milk in the recipe to provide the fat content: Do not over-beat the cream. You have a lighter consistency by using half thick and half thin cream and by aerating the eggs or egg whites.*

● **SHORT CUT** *Use commercial ice cream in some of the ice cream desserts.*

Apricot ice cream

For Special Occasions

Poires Hélène

For the chocolate sauce: 4 oz. plain chocolate; $\frac{1}{2}$ oz. butter; 2–3 tablespoons water. 4 small pears or large pear halves; ice cream as Blue Print or 4 portions bought ice cream.
Melt the chocolate in a basin over *hot* water with the butter and water. Stir. Peel and core pears (do this at the last minute to prevent discoloration). Put scoops of ice cream into individual dishes with the pears and pour over the sauce. *Serves 4.*

Harlequin Flan

Fill a sponge or pastry flan with lightly whipped cream. Top with chopped glacé cherries, crystallised ginger, angelica and chocolate ice cream. *Serves 6–8.*

Storing and Freezing *Freeze as instructed on this page. Store in the freezing compartment of a refrigerator for several days or in a home freezer. If a little hard stand at room temperature for a short time before serving.*

Harlequin flan and a simple ice cream coûpe

Water ices are some of the most refreshing desserts, giving the flavour of fresh fruit in an interesting way.

Sorbets or water ices, were originally served in the middle of the dinner to freshen the palate before proceeding to the next course. Although at some elaborate dinners, this practice is still occasionally continued, it is more normal to serve them now as a dessert.

Blue Print Recipes

1. Orange Water Ice

3 large oranges · 1 small lemon · ¾ pint (2C) water · minimum 4 oz. (½C) sugar · 2 teaspoons powdered gelatine · 1 egg white.

To make Pare the rind thinly from the oranges and lemon (do not use the white pith, which would give a bitter flavour to the ice). Put into a saucepan with the water and sugar, simmer for 8 minutes. Squeeze the juice from the oranges and lemon. Soften the gelatine in 2 tablespoons cold orange juice, add to the liquid in the pan, stir until dissolved, strain and add to the remainder of the fruit juice. Taste, add a little extra sugar if required, but do not make the mixture too sweet. Cool, then freeze.

To freeze Pour into freezing trays or a deeper utensil. Freeze on the normal setting in the refrigerator or home freezer. Leave

Water Ices

until lightly frosted. Remove and blend with the stiffly beaten egg white. If wishing to serve as the picture on this page, pile the mixture into the orange cases (you will need 6 cases altogether) and support in individual dishes or cups. If preferred, spoon the mixture back into the freezing trays or original utensil. They also look most attractive served in a ring mould with fresh or canned fruit in the centre or in a jelly mould.

To serve In orange cases or sundae glasses. *All recipes based on this serve 6.*

2. Apple Water Ice

1 lb. cooking apples · 1 lemon · ½ pint (1⅓C) water · 4 oz. (½C) sugar · 2 teaspoons powdered gelatine · colouring · 1 egg white.

To make Wash and chop the apples, do not remove peel or cores, as these give flavour. Put into a saucepan with the thinly pared lemon rind, water and sugar. Simmer until the apples are very soft. Sieve the mixture, return to the pan to keep warm. Soften the gelatine in the cold lemon juice, add to the warm apple mixture, stir until dissolved. Taste, add extra sugar is desired, or if the apples are rather sweet add a little more lemon juice. Tint a delicate shade of

green or pink. Cool, then freeze.

To freeze As Blue Print 1. When lightly frosted, remove and blend with the stiffly beaten egg white. Return to the freezing compartment or freezer and continue freezing.

To serve In glasses, or pile into canned peach halves and decorate with mint leaves. The combination of the sharp apple mixture and the sweet peach is delicious. *All recipes based on this serve 6, or 8 when served with other ingredients, such as peaches.*

To vary Use other fruit in place of apples. Plums, damsons, rhubarb, gooseberries, etc., should be cooked. Raspberries, strawberries and other soft fruits should be used raw then blended with the syrup, made by heating the water, sugar and lemon rind. Two fruits can also be blended together, e.g. apples and raspberries; rhubarb and orange juice.

● **AVOID** *The formation of ice splinters, the mixture should be smooth when frozen: Too hard a texture.*

● **TO RECTIFY** *Use a little gelatine in the mixture, this prevents splinters of ice forming: Add an egg white to the mixture to give additional aeration. Never serve the water ice when too solid, allow time at room temperature for it to soften.*

● **SHORT CUT** *Use canned fruit juice or a smooth canned fruit purée. The canned fruits sold for baby foods are an excellent basis for water ices.*

● **TO SLIMMERS** *Sweeten with sugar substitute and you have a low calorie dessert.*

For Family Occasions

Lemon Water Ice

3 large or 4 smaller lemons; ¾ pint (2C) water; 5–6 oz. (¾C) sugar; 2 teaspoons powdered gelatine; 1 egg white.
Method as Blue Print 1.

To vary Use pineapple, grapefruit and other juices as Blue Print 1.

For Special Occasions

Orange Curaçao Sorbet

Ingredients as Blue Print 1 PLUS 1–2 tablespoons Curaçao and 2 *additional* egg whites. Make the orange water ice mixture as Blue Print 1, but use only 2 oz. (¼C) of the sugar when simmering the orange and lemon rinds. Add the Curaçao just before freezing for the first time. Freeze until lightly frosted. Whisk 3 egg whites until very stiff. Gradually beat in the remaining 2 oz. (¼C) sugar. Fold the meringue mixture into the orange ice and freeze again. Serve in glasses or freeze and serve in orange cases, as described in Blue Print 1.

Orange water ice

Melon Water Ice

Ingredients as Blue Print 2, but substitute the flesh from a ripe honeydew or water melon for apples and reduce the amount of water to ¼ pint (⅓C).

Make the syrup with the water, sugar and lemon rind, add the gelatine, softened in the lemon juice and stir until dissolved. Cool. Halve the melon, discard the seeds and sieve the pulp. Blend with the lemon syrup, continue as Blue Print. Serve in glasses or the melon case. Decorate with cherries or other fruit. The mixture can be tinted if wished and given additional flavour by adding a little dry sherry or white wine.

Cream and Cold Desserts

So many desserts are improved by topping or decorating with cream, or incorporating cream among the ingredients, but often the piping or dessert itself can be less than perfect because the cream has been over-whipped.

Blue Print Recipe

To Whip Fresh Cream

Put thick cream into a basin. Use an electric or hand whisk or a fork to whip the cream. The latter is slow, but safer if the cream is very rich. Whip slowly and steadily until the cream *begins* to stand in peaks. This consistency is ideal when adding cream to desserts. If using the cream for piping the cream should be stiffer and stand in peaks.

To make a lighter cream
1. Whip as Blue Print and then fold in an equal quantity of thin cream. Whip again until it stiffens. This will be rarely firm enough to use for piping.
2. To each $\frac{1}{4}$ pint ($\frac{2}{3}$C) thick cream add one egg white. Whip the cream and egg white in separate basins and fold together *just before* serving. You can pipe this, although it tends to be much softer than thick cream alone.

● **AVOID** *Over-whipping cream because if you do it will separate, giving you a solid butter-like substance and watery liquid.*
● **TO RECTIFY** *If the cream begins to separate add a little milk or water and fold gently into the mixture.*
● **SHORT CUT** *Use an electric mixer for whisking but choose a very low speed and watch the cream as it thickens to avoid over-beating.*

For Special Occasions

Banana Cream Syllabub
3 ripe firm bananas; 2 tablespoons lemon juice; 2 tablespoons white wine; 2 tablespoons caster sugar; $\frac{1}{2}$ pint ($1\frac{1}{3}$C) thick cream.
Peel the bananas and mash with the lemon juice, wine and sugar. Whip the cream as the Blue Print. Fold into the banana mixture. Spoon into serving dishes and chill before serving. *Serves 4–6.*

Creamy Apple Crunch

This recipe, somewhat similar in texture to a Charlotte (page 6) uses soured cream to give additional interest to the apple mixture.
4 oz. ($\frac{1}{2}$C) caster sugar; $\frac{1}{4}$ pint ($\frac{2}{3}$C) water; 4 or 5 medium-sized cooking apples; 10 fl. oz. ($1\frac{1}{4}$C) soured cream; $2\frac{1}{2}$ tablespoons soft brown sugar; 4–6 gingernut biscuits; 2 tablespoons chopped blanched almonds.
Make a syrup with the caster sugar and water in a large pan. Peel, core and slice the apples and poach in the syrup until just tender, but unbroken. Lift the apple segments into a basin, blend with the soured cream and 2 tablespoons brown sugar. Spoon into a heat proof dish. Crush the biscuits with a rolling pin; do this between 2 sheets of greaseproof paper or put the biscuits into a large bag. Blend with the almonds and remaining brown sugar. Sprinkle over the fruit and brown for 2–3 minutes only under a hot grill. Serve cold. (Illustrated on page 1.) *Serves 4–6.*

Apple Surprise Pie
One of the old fashioned farmhouse traditions, when making a fruit pie, was to cover the fruit with thick cream before baking. This has been done in the pie shown on page 1. Apples or plums are the most suitable fruit for this purpose.

Either put the prepared fruit into the pie dish with sugar and water as page 4, or, to give a firmer fruit layer, poach the fruit for about 10 minutes with the sugar and water in a saucepan. Lift out the fruit only, (serve the liquid with the pie if wished,) and put this into the pie dish. Whichever method is used, top the fruit with $\frac{1}{4}$–$\frac{1}{2}$ pint ($\frac{2}{3}$–$1\frac{1}{3}$C) whipped cream, then with the pastry. Bake as the fruit pie on page 4.

Storing and Freezing *Dairy cream, and any desserts using cream, must be used when fresh unless stored in a home freezer.*

Banana cream syllabub

Special Gâteaux

On this and the following page you will find a selection of gâteaux. They are all simple to make, and are based on the Blue Prints in this section.

Fruit Cream Bande
This and the following recipe, are based on puff pastry. The excellent frozen pastry enables you to make a seemingly elaborate dessert very easily.
12–13 oz. packet frozen puff pastry or puff pastry made with 6 oz. ($1\frac{1}{2}$C) flour etc.; 2 tablespoons custard powder or cornflour; $\frac{1}{2}$ pint ($1\frac{1}{3}$C) milk; 2 tablespoons sugar; $\frac{1}{4}$ pint ($\frac{2}{3}$C) thick cream; 6–8 dessert plums; 1 red skinned dessert apple; 1 dessert pear; 3–4 tablespoons apricot jam.
Roll out about $\frac{2}{3}$ of the pastry into a rectangle about 11 inches × 8 inches. Put on to a baking sheet or tray. Roll out the rest of the pastry into a long strip, cut 2 pieces 11 inches × $\frac{1}{2}$–$\frac{3}{4}$ inch wide and 2 pieces $6\frac{1}{2}$ inches × $\frac{1}{2}$–$\frac{3}{4}$ inch wide. Damp the edges of the pastry rectangle and press the bands into position. The pastry case should look like a 'picture frame'. Bake just above the centre of a very hot oven, 450–475°F, Gas Mark 8, for about 5 minutes, then lower the heat to moderately hot, 400°F, Gas Mark 5–6 for further 15 minutes or until the pastry is golden brown. Allow to cool. Blend the custard powder or cornflour with the milk. Put into a saucepan with the sugar, cook gently, stirring all the time until thickened. Allow to cool, stirring from time to time to prevent a skin forming. Blend with the whipped cream, spread over the pastry. Halve the plums, remove the stones, slice the apple and peeled pear. Arrange on the cream layer and top with the warmed and sieved jam at once to keep the fruit a good colour. (Illustrated on page 1.) *Serves 5–6.*

Blackberry Milles Feuilles
12–13 oz. packet frozen puff pastry or puff pastry made with 6 oz. ($1\frac{1}{2}$C) flour, etc.; 1 lb. blackberries; sugar to taste; $\frac{1}{4}$ pint ($\frac{2}{3}$C) thick cream; $\frac{1}{4}$ pint ($\frac{2}{3}$C) thin cream.

Roll out the pastry very thinly, cut into 3 equal-sized rounds and 1 ring to fit over the top, as shown in the picture. Put on to a baking sheet or tray and bake as the recipe above, allowing about 12–15 minutes only. Allow to cool. Mash about half the blackberries with sugar. Whip the thick cream, add the thin cream and whip again. Spread the first layer of pastry with mashed fruit and cream, put on the second layer of pastry, spread with cream, add third layer, spread with cream and top with the pastry circle. Fill the centre with the whole fruit. *Serves 5–6.*

Peach Gâteau

Half the ingredients as Blue Print on page 2 (2 oz. (¼C) butter or margarine, etc.); 6 canned peach halves and some of the syrup; 3–4 tablespoons sherry; 4–5 tablespoons raspberry jam; ¼ pint (⅔C) thick cream; little angelica.

Butterscotch fruit gâteau (above left); Peach gâteau (right); Blackberry milles feuilles (below)

Make the mixture as the Blue Print on page 2. Grease and flour a 7-inch sandwich tin, put in the mixture, bake for about 15–18 minutes above the centre of a moderate oven, 350–375°F, Gas Mark 4–5. Allow to cool. Lift the peach halves from the syrup, blend about 3 tablespoons syrup and the sherry. Put the cake on or in a dish, spoon the syrup and sherry over this. Arrange the peach halves on top. Warm and sieve the jam and glaze the fruit with this. When glaze is quite cool, whip the cream and pipe, as in the picture. Decorate with angelica. *Serves 6.*

To vary Instead of using angelica decorate with ratafia biscuits. To make about 24, whisk 1 egg white lightly, add 3 oz. (¾C) ground almonds, 2 oz. (¼C) caster sugar and a few drops almond essence. Roll mixture into tiny balls, put on a greased tin and bake for 6–8 minutes in the centre of a very moderate oven, 325–350°F, Gas Mark 3–4.

Butterscotch Fruit Gâteau

Ingredients as Blue Print on page 2 but substitute brown sugar for white sugar in the recipe. Make the mixture and bake in two

7–8-inch sandwich tins as for Peach Gâteau above. When cold, sandwich the ckaes together with approximately ¼ pint (⅔C) whipped cream and chopped canned and fresh fruit. Top with a selection of fruit as in the picture. Heat 3–4 tablespoons apricot jam and spoon over the fruit, to give a generous layer of glaze. *Serves 6–8.*

Pear and Almond Gâteau

Ingredients as Blue Print on page 2; 4 oz. (nearly 1C) blanched almonds; 4 ripe dessert pears; ½ pint thick cream; little sugar; 6 tablespoons apricot jam; grapes to decorate.
Make the mixture as the Blue Print on page 2. Grease and flour two 7-inch sandwich tins and divide the mixture between these. Bake for about 15–18 minutes above the centre of a moderate oven, 350–375°F, Gas Mark 4–5. Allow to cool. Meanwhile flake the almonds and brown on a baking tray in the oven. If you like the 'bite' of burnt almonds leave half of the nuts until very dark brown. Peel, core and slice 1 pear. Whip the cream and sweeten to taste. Sandwich the cakes together with a little jam, cream, the sliced pear and about ¼ of the nuts. Spread the outside of the cake with half the remaining jam and all the remaining cream. Press the nuts firmly against the cream, as shown in the picture. Warm the last of the jam. Peel, halve and core the 3 pears, put on top of the cake and arrange the grapes round the pears. Brush the jam over the fruit. *Serves 6–8.*

Pavlova

4 egg whites; 8 oz. (1C) caster sugar, or use half caster and half sieved icing sugar; ½ pint (1⅓C) thick cream; fresh or canned fruit; sugar or vanilla sugar (see below).
Follow the Blue Print for making the meringue (page 12). Brush 1 or 2 baking trays with a very little olive oil or melted butter or cut out 3 or 4 rounds of greaseproof paper, put on the trays, then brush with oil or butter. Spread or pipe the meringue mixture to give 3 or 4 rounds. 'Dry out' in the coolest part of a very slow oven, 225–250°F, Gas Mark 0–½, for about 2 hours until crisp. Lift off the tins with a warm palette knife, store in an airtight tin until ready to use. Whip the cream and prepare the fruit. Sandwich the layers of meringue with the cream and fruit sweetened with ordinary or vanilla sugar. *Serves 6–8.*
To prepare vanilla sugar: Cut a vanilla pod in half and stand in a jar of caster or icing sugar, leave for some days before using the sugar then fill up the jar.

Fresh Blackberry Cheesecake

1 lb. blackberries; 6 tablespoons water; 6 oz. (¾C) caster sugar; 2 eggs; 1 tablespoon powdered gelatine; 12 oz. (1½C) cottage cheese; ½ pint (1⅓C) thick cream; 4 oz. (1C) digestive biscuit crumbs; 1 tablespoon brown sugar; 2 oz. (¼C) butter.
Put a few blackberries on one side for decoration. Cook the remainder of the blackberries with 4 tablespoons water and ⅓ of the sugar. Sieve the fruit or put into a liquidizer,

More Gâteaux

allow the pulp to cool. Separate the egg yolks and whites and whisk the yolks and the rest of the caster sugar until thick. Soften the gelatine in the remaining cold water, then stand over a pan of hot water until dissolved. Add to the eggs and sugar with the fruit purée and sieved cottage cheese. Finally add ¾ of the lightly whipped cream and the stiffly

whisked egg whites. Line an 8-inch cake tin (with a loose base) with damp greaseproof paper. Spoon in the cheesecake mixture, smooth flat. Blend the biscuit crumbs, brown sugar and melted butter, sprinkle over the top of the cheesecake and allow to set. Invert on to the serving plate and decorate with the last of the cream and blackberries. (Illustrated on page 1.) *Serves 6–8.*

Yoghourt Greengage Flan

Fleur pastry (page 5); 15 fl. oz. (2C) natural yoghourt; 3 egg yolks; 2 tablespoons sugar; 1 lb. greengages.
Make the pastry and line an 8-inch flan ring, as directions on page 5. Blend yoghourt, egg yolks, sugar. Pour half into the pastry case and bake in the centre of a moderately hot oven, 400°F, Gas Mark 5–6 for 20 minutes. Arrange greengages on top and spoon remainder of the filling round the fruit. Return to the oven and cook for a further 20 minutes. Serve hot or cold. (Illustrated on page 1.) *Serves 6.*

Pear and almond gâteau
Pavlova (above right)

two

MEAT COOKERY

Meat is one of the most popular and important protein foods in most countries of the world. It is also one of the most expensive and, in order to make the best use of meat, it is worthwhile learning about the various cuts, and to recognise them in the butcher's shop or supermarket, so you may choose the best kind of meat for each and every purpose.

When one is busy the quick cooking cuts of meat for frying and grilling are an obvious choice. Because these are prime cuts they are appreciably more expensive than meat for stewing. The Blue Prints on pages 25 and 26 give information on the best way to grill and fry meats to make them as tender and appetising as possible. One of the secrets of success when frying and grilling meat is to seal the outside of the meat quickly, so the meat remains moist, which is why the Blue Prints stress the importance of this. I hope they will also give some new suggestions of the meats that may be fried and grilled. For example, the obvious choice when one wants a Wiener Schnitzel is veal, but fillets of pork are cheaper and really have more flavour than veal.

Nothing is more imposing than a really good joint of roasted meat; again this demands high quality, but if you make use of the slow roasting method on page 23 you can use the slightly cheaper cuts of meat. Stuffing and interesting accompaniments not only add flavour and help to keep the meat moist, but enable one to serve more portions from a joint, and many fruits, vegetables and herbs can be used in stuffings and sauces.

Every country has its own traditional way of cooking meat and in countries where the quality of meat is not perhaps as good as one would wish, the cooks have become experts in slow cooking to ten-

derise meat in casseroles, stews and curries. There is a wide range of such recipes from pages 28–32. Be adventurous in the vegetables and fruit you add to meats in stews and casseroles. Acid fruit is like wine, it gives flavour and helps to tenderise meat.

Britain has a reputation for excellent meat puddings and pies and the well-known and new recipes on pages 34 and 35 give the kind of meat dishes you will enjoy throughout the year. I have also included meat patties and cold meat dishes, such as galantines and meat pies, that are admirable for out-of-doors eating.

Never feel that offal, or the specialist meats, are less interesting or nutritious than other cuts. The very wide variety of textures and flavours provided by these meats (liver, sweetbreads, tripe, kidneys) make them appetising and adaptable.

When one is making a fairly complicated meat dish, or buying a large quantity of meat, it is a good idea to freeze part of the dish or some of the meat to use on future occasions. On most pages in this part you will find information on home freezing of the meat or the completed dish.

There is nothing to beat the flavour of a succulent roasted joint; when you buy prime cuts there is no point in 'dressing-up' the meat, except to serve it with appropriate sauces and stuffings.

In most homes today the accepted method of roasting is in a meat tin in the oven; purists argue that this is *not* roasting, it *is* baking and that the only correct method is to cook the meat on a turning spit over open heat. If you have a rotisserie attachment on your cooker use this, for you do obtain more even browning over the *whole* joint than in a tin. If the rotisserie is under the grill then the cooking times are the same as given for fast roasting. If in the oven you can select which method you prefer—fast or slow cooking.

For top quality meat you may choose the heat at which you cook this. Personally I prefer fast roasting, for I believe the meat retains more flavour although it may shrink a little more in cooking. If the meat has been chilled, frozen or is of slightly cheaper quality then the slower cooking is better for you achieve a more tender joint.

The table that follows the Blue Print assumes the meat is fresh *not* frozen.

● AVOID *Trying to roast cuts of meat recommended for stewing: Using more fat than necessary, for this only hardens the outside:*

Roasting Meat

Over-cooking, this destroys flavour and texture and dries the joint.
● TO RECTIFY *Look at the joint during cooking, if you have been too generous with the fat pour away any excess: Dried meat is spoiled meat, so you must camouflage it with sauce or gravy.*
● TO SLIMMERS *A sensible way to cook meat, avoid the fatty outside, stuffings and thickened sauces or gravy.*

Blue Print Recipe

Roasting Meat

To prepare Buy meat to give a *minimum* of 8–12 oz. per person (including the weight of the bone). *Allow frozen meat to defrost.* Wash and dry the meat. Make any stuffing required, see this page and page 24. Put the meat into the roasting tin, in foil, or on the spit. Spread any fat recommended over the top of the meat. The amount of fat suggested

under the meats must be increased by about 2 oz. ($\frac{1}{4}$C) if roasting potatoes round the joint.
To cook
1. IN AN OPEN ROASTING TIN Allow the times given under each meat. You can 'baste' with a little fat during cooking if wished. This means spooning some of the hot fat over the meat. The advantage of this is that it keeps the meat moist and encourages it to crisp, but it is not essential.
2. IN FOIL You need to wrap the meat and any fat in the foil and to time as under each meat, but you must allow about 20 minutes extra cooking time or set the oven 25°F or 1 Mark higher on the gas cooker. If you wish the meat to crisp and brown, open the foil for the last 20–30 minutes. There is no need to 'baste' during cooking.
3. IN A COVERED ROASTING TIN Try and use one large enough to give some space above and around the meat. This means the fat splashes the lid, drops back on to the meat and so is self-basting; it will brown well. If required, to be crisp, the lid should be removed for the last 20–30 minutes. Allow higher temperature or extra time as for foil.
4. SPIT ROASTING Time as for slow or fast roasting, but melt the fat and brush over the whole joint. 'Baste' if wished during cooking.
To serve As the suggestions on this page, and seasonal vegetables or cold with salad.

Choice and Timing for Roast Meat

Fast roasting: Set the oven to hot, this varies slightly with cookers, start at 425–450°F, Gas Mark 6–7. After 15–20 minutes lower to moderately hot, 375–400°F, Gas Mark 5–6.
Slow roasting: Set the oven at very moderate to moderate, approximately 350°F, Gas Mark 3–4. Keep at this setting.
Very small joints: accepted timing for meat has been based on larger-sized joints than

many of us buy today. For a really small joint (about 2 lb.) allow an extra 10–15 minutes on the *total* cooking time.

BEEF

Cuts: *Fast or slow roasting:* Châteaubriand, sirloin, rib.
Slow roasting: topside, aitch-bone, fresh brisket.
It is a sin to over-cook prime beef, but cheaper cuts are better medium-cooked.
Fat required and timing: Use minimum of fat 1–2 oz. Sirloin needs no fat.
Fast roasting: Underdone (rare)—15 minutes per lb., 15 minutes over.
Medium to well done—20 minutes per lb. and 20 minutes over.
Slow roasting: Underdone (rare)—25 minutes per lb., 25 minutes over.
Medium to well done—35 minutes per lb. and 35 minutes over.
Serve with: Yorkshire pudding, horseradish sauce, thin gravy.
To give interest: Insert tiny strips of peeled onion into meat at regular intervals.

LAMB

Cuts: *All joints suitable for fast or slow roasting:* leg, shoulder, loin, saddle, best end of neck, breast.

Fat required and timing: Use minimum of fat 1–2 oz.
Fast roasting: Medium-cooked—20 minutes per lb., 20 minutes over. Reduce time slightly if preferred slightly 'pink'.
Slow roasting: 35 minutes per lb., 35 minutes over.
Serve with: Mint sauce, thin gravy.
To give interest: Put 1–2 sprigs fresh rosemary over lamb before roasting, or cut 1–2 cloves garlic into thin 'slivers' and insert into joint before roasting.

MUTTON

Cuts: As lamb, but better slow roasted.
Fat required and timing: Mutton needs no fat. Timing as lamb.
Serve with: Onion sauce or red currant jelly.
To give interest: As lamb.

PORK

Cuts: Use open roasting tin for a crisper crackling.
I suggest fast roasting for pork but joints are suitable for fast or slow roasting: leg, fillet, bladebone, spare-rib, loin.
Fat required and timing: Use a little melted fat, lard or oil, brushed over the meat fat. Sprinkle a little salt over joint if wished. Score fat to encourage crispness.

Roast rib of beef

Blue Print Recipe

Good Gravy

Gravy can 'make or mar' a roasted joint. It should incorporate the delicious flavours from the roasting tin.

To make If you have stock from meat bones then use this as the basis of the gravy, but if no meat stock is available then use vegetable stock, obtained after straining the vegetables. This contains valuable mineral salts, so it is nutritious as well as being a source of flavour. Allow about $\frac{1}{2}$–$\frac{3}{4}$ pint ($1\frac{1}{3}$–2C) gravy for 4 people; the amount depends upon personal taste.

When the meat is cooked pour away all the fat from the roasting tin except for about 1 tablespoon. The fat poured out can be used for dripping. If convenient make the gravy in the meat tin, if not pour the fat and any 'residue' of tiny pieces of meat, etc. into a pan.
For a thin gravy Blend 1 level tablespoon flour into the fat.

To cook Heat for a few minutes or until the 'roux' turns golden brown. This is quite a risky business as it can burn, so you may like to add a little gravy browning (and flavouring) instead and just use the flour as a

Roasting Meat

thickening. Gradually work in about $\frac{1}{2}$ pint stock, bring to the boil and cook until slightly thickened. Strain and use.
For a thick gravy Proceed as above but use nearly 2 level tablespoons flour to the 1 tablespoon fat.

Buy loin of lamb or 2 best end of neck joints, or loin of pork. Chine the meat, or ask the butcher to do this, and trim the bones. Tie into a circle (Crown).

Put into the roasting tin, protect the bones with foil and put the stuffing in the middle. Calculate weight of joint *and* stuffing, roast as this page.

If serving underdone beef the juices that flow from the meat may be served instead of gravy.

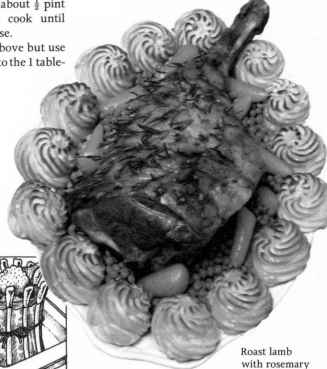

Roast lamb
with rosemary

Fast roasting: 25 minutes per lb., 25 minutes over.
Slow roasting: 35 minutes per lb., 35 minutes over. Pork must be well cooked.
Serve with: Apple sauce, sage and onion or other stuffing, thick gravy.
To give interest: Put 1–2 leaves fresh sage on joint before roasting. Add whole cored, not peeled, dessert apples to the roasting tin, cook about 30–40 minutes. Pour over fresh orange juice during cooking.

VEAL

Cuts: *All joints suitable for fast or slow roasting:* leg, fillet, loin, best end of neck, breast.
Fat required and timing: Use plenty of fat, about 4 oz. ($\frac{1}{2}$C) and keep basting during cooking or wrap in foil to keep joint moist.
Fast roasting: 25 minutes per lb., 25 minutes over.
Slow roasting: 35–40 minutes per lb., 35–40 minutes over. Veal must be well cooked.
Serve with: Veal stuffing, roasted sausages, bacon rolls, thick gravy.
To give interest: Roll joint in a little seasoning to which is added finely grated lemon rind. Baste with a little fresh lemon juice during cooking.

Crown roast of lamb

Well chosen accompaniments provide extra flavour, counteract undue richness, as with pork, give a moist texture to drier meat, such as veal, and turn a *good* roasted joint into a memorable dish. Make a 'pocket' in the meat and put in the stuffing, or spread on boned meat, roll and tie firmly, then roast. *Always calculate the total weight of meat plus stuffing for cooking time.* If preferred put the stuffing into a separate dish and bake in the oven for 40–50 minutes.

● **AVOID** *Too dry stuffings.*
● **SHORT CUTS** *Use the liquidiser to make crumbs, or buy packet stuffing or bottled or canned sauces.*

TO SERVE WITH BEEF

Horseradish sauce: Whip $\frac{1}{4}$ pint ($\frac{2}{3}$C) thick cream, gradually whisk in $\frac{1}{4}$ pint ($\frac{2}{3}$C) thin cream and 2–3 teaspoons lemon juice or vinegar. Add 3–4 tablespoons grated fresh horseradish, seasoning and 3–4 teaspoons sugar. *Serves 5–6.*
New look: Blend 2–3 tablespoons shelled chopped walnuts with the sauce.

TO SERVE WITH LAMB

Apricot nut stuffing: Drain a medium-sized can of apricots, chop the fruit and blend with 3 oz. (1C) soft breadcrumbs, 2–3 tablespoons chopped peanuts or walnuts, 2 oz. ($\frac{1}{4}$C) softened margarine and the grated rind and juice of 1 orange and 1 lemon. Season well and bind with some of the juice from the can and 1 egg. *Serves 5–6.*
Pineapple nut stuffing: Use canned pineapple instead of apricots.
Mint sauce: Chop enough mint leaves to give about 5 tablespoons, add 2–3 tablespoons sugar and 3–4 tablespoons vinegar. *Serves 4–5.*
Onion sauce: Peel, chop and cook 2 large onions in about $\frac{1}{2}$ pint (1$\frac{1}{3}$C) well seasoned water. Strain the liquid and make a sauce

Accompaniments to Roast Meat

with 1$\frac{1}{2}$ oz. butter, 1$\frac{1}{2}$ oz. flour, $\frac{1}{2}$ pint (1$\frac{1}{3}$C) milk and $\frac{1}{4}$ pint ($\frac{2}{3}$C) onion stock. When thickened add the onions and season well. *Serves 5–6.*

TO SERVE WITH PORK

Apple sauce: Simmer peeled, sliced apples in a very little water until soft, sieve, beat or emulsify in the liquidiser until smooth, sweeten to taste.
New look: Add ground cinnamon, a little dried fruit or orange segments to the sauce, or serve an orange sauce (see page 36).
Sage and onion stuffing: Peel, chop and cook 2–3 large onions for 10 minutes in $\frac{1}{4}$ pint ($\frac{2}{3}$C) water. Season well, strain, then blend with 3 oz. (1C) soft breadcrumbs, 1–2 teaspoons chopped fresh sage or $\frac{1}{2}$ teaspoon dried sage and 2 oz. ($\frac{1}{4}$C) shredded suet. Bind with onion stock and/or an egg. *Serves 5–6.*
Prune and apple stuffing: Soak 8 oz. (1C) prunes overnight, drain, stone and chop. Mix with 2 oz. ($\frac{3}{4}$C) soft breadcrumbs, 2 peeled diced raw apples, grated rind and juice of 1 orange, seasoning, 1 teaspoon ground cinnamon, 1–2 tablespoons chopped parsley and 1 egg blended with $\frac{1}{2}$ teaspoon Tabasco sauce. Tabasco sauce is very hot, so reduce to $\frac{1}{4}$ teaspoon if wished. *Serves 7–8.*

TO SERVE WITH VEAL

Veal (parsley and thyme) stuffing: Blend 4 oz. (1$\frac{1}{3}$C) soft breadcrumbs, 1–2 tablespoons chopped parsley, 2 oz. ($\frac{1}{4}$C) shredded suet, 1–2 teaspoons chopped fresh thyme or good pinch dried thyme, grated rind and juice of 1 lemon and 1 egg. *Serves 5–6.*

Roast Potatoes

These are the favourite accompaniment with most roast joints. Peel the potatoes. If you like them to be 'floury' inside, then par-boil in salted water for about 10 minutes only and strain, otherwise use them uncooked. Roll the potatoes in the hot fat in the roasting tin (round the joint) or heat 2–3 oz. ($\frac{1}{4}$–$\frac{3}{8}$C) fat, lard or clarified dripping in a separate tin. Cook for approximately 45 minutes (for small to medium-sized potatoes) at the temperature given for fast roasting. Slow roasting is not suitable for potatoes.

A Perfect Yorkshire Pudding

Although this is the 'classic' accompaniment to roast beef, many people enjoy it with other roast joints. Sieve 4 oz. (1C) flour (preferably plain) with a good pinch salt, add 1 egg then gradually beat in $\frac{1}{2}$ pint (1$\frac{1}{3}$C) milk or milk and water.

There are two ways of producing the perfect Yorkshire pudding. The old traditional way is to lift the meat from the roasting tin and pour away all the fat, *except* about 1 tablespoon. Pour the batter into the tin and cook with the meat on a trivet, or on the shelf above. Alternatively to give a very well-risen pudding, put about $\frac{1}{2}$–1 oz. fat in a tin. Heat, then pour in the batter. Cook in the hottest part of the oven until well risen and brown.

You cannot cook a Yorkshire pudding slowly, so it is only possible if you have chosen fast roasting of the meat. Even then it is best to raise the oven temperature, it must be hot to very hot, 450–475°F, Gas Mark 7–8. Pour in the batter, cook for 10 minutes at this temperature, then lower the heat again to moderately hot. Complete the cooking, total time about 35 minutes, lift out and serve.

Roast pork with prune and apple stuffing (left)

Roast lamb with apricot nut stuffing (below)

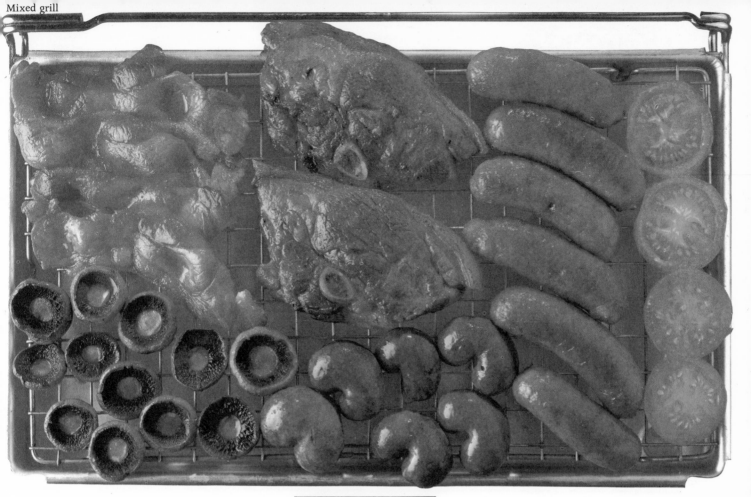

Grilling is undoubtedly one of the best methods of cooking prime quality meats, for they retain the maximum flavour and are more easily digested than when fried.

Blue Print Recipe

Grilling Meat

Switch or turn on the grill, so it is very hot before cooking commences, except for gammon.

To prepare To grill tomatoes and mushrooms put into the grill pan, top with a little melted butter or margarine or fat, season. Grill for a few minutes, then put the meat on the grid of the pan and cook with the meat; or see Mixed Grill.

Choose The same cuts of meat and time the cooking as for frying on the next page. Season the meat if wished. Brush with a little melted fat (the amount needed is about half that for shallow frying).

To cook Grill quickly for 2–3 minutes, or until the outside is sealed. Turn the meat with two knives or tongs, do not pierce with the prongs of a fork as this allows the meat juices to escape. Cook quickly for 2–3 minutes on the second side. Lower the heat slightly and/or move the grill pan further away from the heat and continue cooking until meat is tender. A Châteaubriand (very thick steak) can be grilled easily as you can move the grill pan away from the heat after sealing the outside.

To serve With grilled tomatoes, mushrooms or maître d'hôtel butter and watercress.

● **AVOID** *Grilling too slowly or putting the food under a cold grill (with the exception of gammon, where the grill is only heated when the gammon is put under to prevent the fat 'curling'): Allowing the food to dry, baste well with melted fat. Serve grilled food as soon as it is ready.*

● **TO RECTIFY** *If the grill is too cool, remove the pan, heat the grill until red and glowing, then replace the pan: If the grilled meat is dry top with a sauce or maître d'hôtel butter.*

● **TO SLIMMERS** *An ideal cooking method.*

Mexicali Lamb

1 tablespoon oil; $\frac{1}{2}$–1 tablespoon vinegar; 1 tablespoon tomato purée; 1 tablespoon made mustard; seasoning; good pinch garlic salt; 4 large or 8 small lamb chops; 4 tomatoes.
Blend the oil, vinegar, purée, mustard and seasonings. Halve the tomatoes, brush meat and tomatoes with oil mixture and grill as Blue Print. Serve with chipped potatoes and mushrooms. *Serves 4.*

Mixed Grill

4 lamb chops (in the picture are chump chops); 4–8 sausages; 4 tomatoes; about 12 mushrooms; seasoning; little fat, margarine or butter; 4 rashers bacon. *To garnish:* watercress.
Put the chops and sausages on the rack of the grill pan. Halve the tomatoes, wash and dry the mushrooms (there is no need to skin good quality mushrooms, simply cut the base of the stalks). Season lightly. Put the vegetables on to the rack, as in the picture, or into the grill pan, see Blue Print. Brush the food with melted fat, margarine or butter, cook as the Blue Print until meat is nearly tender (by this time the vegetables can be removed and kept hot if there is not much space on the grid of the grill pan). Add the bacon, cook for a further 2–3 minutes. Arrange on a hot dish with watercress. *Serves 4.*

For Special Occasions: Add halved lamb's kidneys, fingers of lamb's or calf's liver, steak and fried eggs. Serve with maître d'hôtel butter.

Maître d'Hôtel (Parsley) Butter

2 oz. ($\frac{1}{4}$C) butter; little grated lemon rind (optional); 1 tablespoon chopped parsley; 1–2 teaspoons lemon juice; seasoning.
Cream all the ingredients together, chill. Form or cut into pats. Put on the meat just before serving. *Serves 4.*

Storing and Freezing *Keep uncooked chops and steaks for 2–3 days only in the refrigerator, but store good stocks in the home freezer. Separate with squares of waxed or grease-proof paper, peel-off as required, grill or fry as pages 26 and 27 from the frozen state.*
To use any left over *Grilled or fried meats are not good cold or reheated.*

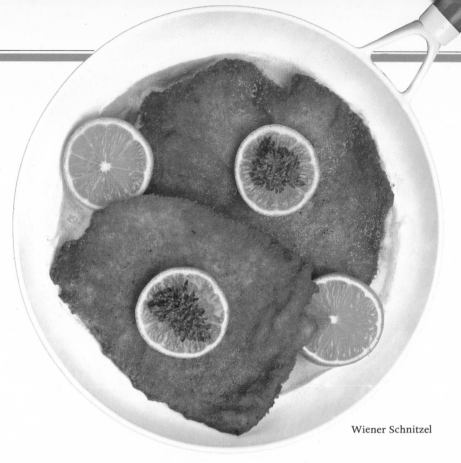
Wiener Schnitzel

Frying Meat

Frying is a method of cooking that can be used for tender pieces of meat, as outlined in the table below, and some 'made-up' meat dishes, such as croquettes, rissoles and Hamburgers. Shallow frying is generally chosen for cuts of meat, also Hamburgers, but shallow *or* deep frying can be used for coated meats, such as rissoles.

Modern 'non-stick' pans enable you to fry meat with little, if any, fat, but the amount of fat given in the Blue Print pre-supposes that an ordinary pan is being used.

Blue Print Recipe

Shallow Frying of Meat

Choose a good-sized *solid* frying pan, too light a pan is inclined to over-cook the outside of the meat before it is cooked through to the centre. The amount of butter or fat suggested is enough for 3–4 portions, but this must vary according to the amount of natural fat on the meat. If frying in butter, add a few drops of olive oil, this lessens the possibility of the butter burning and discolouring.

To prepare Season the meat if wished. Coat as individual recipes. Tie fillet steaks into a round to make into tournedos if following a recipe that requires these (the butcher will do this for you). If frying mushrooms and tomatoes as an accompaniment prepare these and either fry in a separate pan or fry *before* the meat if the meat is to be very *under-done*, then keep the vegetables hot, while cooking the meat. If the meat is to be *well cooked*, then this may be fried first, lifted on to a hot dish and kept hot while the mushrooms and tomatoes are fried.

To cook Heat the butter, or butter and oil, or other fat in the pan. Add the meat and cook quickly on one side, turn with tongs or two knives (do not pierce with the prongs of a fork as this allows the meat juices to escape). Fry quickly on the second side, lower the heat and continue cooking as the timing below.

To serve Garnish with fried mushrooms and tomatoes or with watercress, parsley, lettuce or as the individual recipes.

● **AVOID** *Frying too slowly, this gives a greasy outside to the meat, which makes it less easy to digest: Keeping fried food (particularly meat) waiting before serving.*
● **TO RECTIFY** *If the meat does not begin cooking the moment it is put into the hot fat or hot pan, raise the temperature immediately.*
● **SHORT CUTS** *Have the meat cut thinly (as minute steaks) or choose very small slices of veal or pork fillet.*

● **TO SLIMMERS** *If you cannot use a 'non-stick' pan avoid frying, particularly if following a fat-free slimming diet.*

Wiener Schnitzel (or Escallops of Veal or Pork)

Choose 4 fillets veal or pork. As Blue Print PLUS seasoning, 1 tablespoon flour, 1 egg, 3–4 tablespoons fine soft breadcrumbs, 1 lemon and a little chopped parsley.
The meat must be very thin, so flatten with a rolling pin if necessary. Coat the slices of meat in seasoned flour, then beaten egg and breadcrumbs. Cook as the Blue Print, but allow a total cooking time of about 10 minutes only. Garnish with slices of lemon and chopped parsley. If the lemon and parsley are put on the meat *in* the pan (as in the picture) and warmed for 1–2 minutes, the maximum flavour can be extracted.

For a more elaborate garnish top the lemon slices with chopped hard-boiled egg, capers and anchovy fillets. *Serves 4.*

Veal Parisienne

As above, but coat the fillets of veal in seasoned flour, beaten egg and packet sage and onion stuffing or veal (thyme and parsley) stuffing instead of crumbs. Cook as Wiener Schnitzel.

Choice and Timing for Fried Meat

BEEF

Cuts: Entrecôte, fillet, minute (very thin slices), rump, point, porterhouse, sirloin, T-bone. (Châteaubriand is very thick for frying.)
Fat required: 2–3 oz. ($\frac{1}{4}$–$\frac{3}{8}$C) fat.
Timing: *Steaks about $\frac{1}{2}$–$\frac{3}{4}$-inch thick.*
Under-done (rare): 2–3 minutes on either side.
Medium: 2–3 minutes on either side, then 5–6 minutes on lower heat.
Well done: 2–3 minutes on either side, then 8–10 minutes on lower heat.
Minute Steaks: 1–2 minutes only on either side.

LAMB

Cuts: Chops or cutlets from loin or best end of neck, chump chops, fillet from leg.
Fat required: 1 oz. fat for chops, but a little more for very lean cutlets or fillet.
Timing: *For medium-sized chops about $\frac{3}{4}$-inch thick:* About 3 minutes on either side, then 6–8 minutes on a lower heat.

PORK

Cuts: Chops or cutlets from loin, or spare rib or chump chop or fillet (see individual recipes).
Fat required: 2–3 oz. ($\frac{1}{4}$–$\frac{3}{8}$C) fat for fillet, but grease the pan lightly for other cuts. Remove the rind from chops and snip the fat at $\frac{1}{2}$-inch intervals to encourage this to crisp.
Timing: *For medium-sized chops about $\frac{3}{4}$-inch thick:* 4–5 minutes on either side, then 8–10 minutes on lower heat.
For fillet: 3 minutes on either side, then about 4 minutes on lower heat. Never under-cook pork.

VEAL

Cuts: Chops or cutlets from loin, or fillet (see individual recipes).
Fat required: 4 oz. ($\frac{1}{2}$C) fat.
Timing: As pork.

Deep Fat Frying of Meat

Prepare the meat as the individual recipes. Heat the pan of deep fat or oil, never have this more than half filled. Heat steadily. To test if it is the correct temperature, put a cube of day-old bread into the hot fat or oil; this should turn golden brown in just over $\frac{1}{2}$ minute (no quicker). Lower the basket into the pan of fat, this makes sure it is well coated and that food will not stick to it. Raise the basket from the fat, put in the food, lower gently into the fat and fry as individual recipes. Lift out and drain on absorbent paper.

● **AVOID** *Serving without draining.*

Steak au Poivre (Peppered steak)

Choose 4 fillet or rump steaks.
Version 1 : As Blue Print PLUS $\frac{1}{2}$–1 tablespoon crushed peppercorns.
Version 2: As Blue Print, using butter for frying, PLUS $\frac{1}{2}$–1 tablespoon crushed peppercorns, 5–6 tablespoons thick cream and 1–2 tablespoons brandy.
Season the steaks with salt and press half the peppercorns into one side, then turn and repeat on the second side. Cook as the Blue Print. For the more luxurious version, prepare as above and fry as the Blue Print then add the cream and heat gently, with the meat, for 1–2 minutes. Add the brandy and ignite if wished. If preferred the cooked meat may be lifted on to a hot dish before adding first the cream and then the brandy to the pan. *Serves 4.*

Rissoles

12 oz. cooked meat (lean beef, corned beef, lean lamb or veal, or use a mixture of meats); 1 oz. butter or margarine; 1 oz. flour, $\frac{1}{4}$ pint ($\frac{2}{3}$C) brown stock or milk (see method); 2 oz. ($\frac{3}{4}$C) soft breadcrumbs; seasoning; pinch mixed herbs. *To coat:* 1 tablespoon flour; 1 egg; 2–3 tablespoons crisp breadcrumbs. *To fry:* 2 oz. fat or deep fat.
Mince the meat, or chop very finely. Heat the butter or margarine in a fairly large pan, stir in the flour and cook over a low heat for several minutes, stirring carefully. Gradually add the liquid—stock naturally gives a more 'meaty' flavour; milk a creamy one. Bring to the boil and cook until thickened. Add the crumbs, minced meat, seasoning and herbs. Allow the mixture to cool then form into 8 round flat cakes. Coat in flour, then beaten egg, then in crumbs. For shallow frying heat the fat in a large pan and fry the cakes until golden brown on either side and heated through to the centre. For deep frying follow the Blue Print on this page, allow about 5 minutes only and do not turn. Drain on absorbent paper and serve with the brown or tomato sauce given below.

Sauces for Fried Meats

Brown sauce Chop a medium-sized onion and fry in $1\frac{1}{2}$ oz. fat until soft. Stir in 1 oz. flour and cook gently for a few minutes. Gradually add $\frac{1}{2}$ pint ($1\frac{1}{3}$C) brown stock, bring to the boil, cook until thickened and season well. Sieve or emulsify in the liquidiser if wished.

Tomato sauce Use the recipe for brown sauce but substitute 4–5 large chopped tomatoes and 4–5 tablespoons water for the brown stock.

Hamburgers

Hamburgers can be varied in many ways, but this is the basic recipe.
1 lb. minced beef (choose rump, sirloin or other prime steak for tenderness, chuck steak for economy); seasoning; 1 egg yolk (optional); pinch mixed herbs; 2–3 teaspoons oil (optional); 1 large onion (optional); 1 tablespoon seasoned flour (optional); 1–2 oz. fat for frying.
Mix the beef, seasoning, egg yolk and herbs together. If wished omit the egg yolk. If the meat is very lean add the oil. Form into 4 round flat cakes. If wishing to top the Hamburgers with onion, peel and cut into rings, then coat in seasoned flour. Fry in the fat and keep hot, then add the meat cakes and cook on both sides as the Blue Print opposite. Lower the heat and continue cooking for 2–6 minutes according to personal taste and type of meat used (chuck steak naturally takes longer). Serve with vegetables or on toasted halved Hamburger rolls.

Plus Cheese

Ingredients as above, PLUS 4 slices Cheddar or processed cheese.
Cook the onion rings and Hamburgers. Put the Hamburgers on top of halved toasted rolls, cover with the cheese and brown under the grill. Top with the onion rings. If preferred omit the fresh onion and top with rings of tomato and several small pickled onions.

Hamburger Indienne

Ingredients as above, but add 1–2 teaspoons curry powder with the seasoning, together with a little finely grated onion; OMIT onion rings.
Cook as the basic Hamburger. Top with rings of fried pineapple and a little chutney.

Nutty Hamburger

Ingredients as above, PLUS 2–3 tablespoons salted peanuts.
Cook as the basic Hamburger, top with peanuts before serving. A few chopped nuts can be added to the Hamburger mixture if liked.

Pimento Hamburger

Ingredients as above, PLUS sliced rings red and/or green pepper.
Cook as the basic Hamburger and top with the rings of fried pepper.

From the top:
Basic hamburger, Hamburger Indienne,
Hamburger plus cheese, Nutty hamburger,
Pimento hamburger

Boiling Meat

Never despise a joint of 'boiled meat' for some of the most appetising dishes are prepared by this method. The word 'boiling' is really incorrect, for the liquid in the pan should simmer gently, *not* boil rapidly.

Normally one chooses fairly economical joints for this purpose and it is ideal for salted meats, such as brisket, silverside and tongue although there is no reason why all joints cannot be cooked by this method if wished.

Allow minimum 8–12 oz. fresh meat with bone; less without bone. Salted meats shrink during cooking so allow minimum 8 oz. without bone.

Blue Print Recipe

Boiling Meat

Choose a large pan so that the liquid surrounds the meat. If the meat fits too tightly into the pan, the outside tends to be dry and the meat does not cook as well as it should. Make sure the lid fits well so the liquid does not evaporate too quickly.

To prepare Wash and dry then tie the meat into a neat shape if necessary and prepare any vegetables. If using salted meat then soak for about 12 hours before cooking.

To cook Put the meat with any vegetables into the saucepan. Add seasoning if required. Salted meat should have only a few peppercorns or pepper, no salt. Add herbs, other ingredients as the particular recipe and liquid, generally water. Bring to the boil, remove any grey scum that may float to the top and cover the pan tightly. Lower the heat and allow the liquid to simmer steadily for the time given in the table below.

To serve Hot or cold, according to the individual recipes. If serving hot then serve some of the unthickened liquid with the meat and vegetables.

● **AVOID** *Cooking too quickly, for this means the outside of the meat becomes over-cooked before the centre is tender: Cooking salted meats before soaking.*

● **TO RECTIFY** *Reduce the heat when the liquid in the pan boils too quickly: If you should start to cook salted meats without soaking, pour away the original cooking liquid and fill up with fresh cold water. Add plenty of vegetables to help absorb the salt.*

● **TO SLIMMERS** *A splendid way of cooking meat as no thickening is used in the liquid.*

Choice and Timing for Boiled Meat

BEEF

Cuts: Fresh or salted brisket, silverside or ox-tongue or for a very economical joint choose shin, but this is mainly used for stock. For special occasions choose rump or other prime joints, see Pot-au-feu.

Timing: 30 minutes per lb. and 30 minutes over (slightly less for prime joints).

Add: Vegetables or accompaniments such as dumplings (see recipes) or serve cold.

LAMB OR MUTTON

Cuts: Scrag or middle neck, breast, tongues or head, shank can be used but is mainly for soups. Leg could be used for special occasions.

Timing: 25 minutes per lb. and 25 minutes over for a joint. Allow 1½ hours for scrag or middle neck.

Add: Vegetables or accompaniments such as caper sauce (see recipes).

PORK

Cuts: Loin, spare rib or head, belly or trotters.

Timing: 30 minutes per lb. and 30 minutes over.

Add: Vegetables to give flavour as the meat cooks, generally served cold.

VEAL

Cuts: Boned and rolled breast, head or tongue.

Timing: 30 minutes per lb. and 30 minutes over.

Add: Mixed vegetables, and serve with parsley or brain sauce.

BACON OR HAM

See page 33.

For Family Occasions

Boiled Silverside or Brisket

Choose salted meat as it has a better flavour and colour when boiled than fresh meat. Prepare and cook as the Blue Print, adding a selection of root vegetables. Prepare dumplings and add these to the stock about 25 minutes before serving the joint. Lift the meat on to a dish, arrange the dumplings and vegetables round and serve with stock. This is excellent cold with salads.

Dumplings

4 oz. (1C) self-raising flour (or plain flour and 1 teaspoon baking powder); pinch salt, pepper and dry mustard; 2 oz. (⅓C) shredded suet; water to mix.

Sieve the flour and seasonings, add the suet and bind with water to a slightly sticky dough. Roll into 8–12 small balls with lightly floured hands. Drop into the liquid in the pan and cook for 20–25 minutes. Make sure the liquid boils when the dumplings are first put into the pan, then reduce to simmering again after about 8 minutes.

Note: Whilst dumplings are usually made with suet, other fats such as margarine or cooking fat can be used and Australian readers may prefer to use this.

Boiled Tongue

Although ox-tongue is cooked more often than others, the smaller lambs' tongues or calf's tongue are excellent for smaller families. Try to buy the tongues salted as this gives a better colour to the meat. Prepare and cook as the Blue Print, adding herbs, a few strips lemon rind and vegetables to flavour if wished. When the tongue or tongues are tender allow to cool sufficiently to handle. Meanwhile boil the liquid in the pan rapidly so you have just enough to cover the meat;

Boiled salt beef and tongue

this is about ¾ pint (2C) with a large ox-tongue. Remove the skin, bones and gristle from the tongue and press the meat into a round tin or pan (it needs to be a tight fit to give a good shape). Soften 2 teaspoons powdered gelatine in 2 tablespoons cold water, add to the hot liquid in the pan. Stir until the gelatine has dissolved, pour over the tongue, allow to cool, then cover with foil and a light weight and leave until firm. Turn out and serve with salad.

Boiled Lamb or Mutton

Remember the bone content of scrag or middle neck is high so buy a generous amount of meat. Put the meat into a pan with a selection of vegetables and cook as the Blue Print. Arrange on a dish and serve with the caper sauce below.

Caper Sauce

1½ oz. butter or margarine; 1½ oz. flour; ½ pint (1⅓C) milk; ¼ pint (⅔C) stock from cooking the lamb; seasoning; 2–3 teaspoons capers and a little vinegar from the jar.
Heat the butter or margarine in a pan, stir in the flour and cook the 'roux' for several minutes. Gradually add the liquid, bring to the boil and cook until thickened. Add the seasoning, capers and vinegar. Keep hot but do not boil. *Serves 4–6.*

For Special Occasions

Pot-au-Feu

Approximately 3–3½ lb. joint boned sirloin or rump steak; small piece salted bacon or uncooked ham; 1 small veal knuckle or 2 pig's trotters; about 1½ lb. mixed root vegetables (carrots, turnips, celeriac, small piece parsnip); seasoning; *bouquet garni*; 6–8 small onions; 1 lb. garlic sausage; mayonnaise; tomato sauce; French mustard.
Put the meats, half the sliced vegetables, seasoning and *bouquet garni* into a pan and cook as the Blue Print for about 1½ hours. Add the rest of the sliced vegetables, the onions and sliced sausage and cook for a further 1–1½ hours.
Slice the meats, arrange on a dish with the cooked vegetables round. Strain the liquid, serve in a sauce boat. Dishes of mayonnaise, tomato sauce and French mustard are generally served as well.

Storing and Freezing *Uncooked non-salted meat may be kept for several days in a refrigerator or some weeks in a home freezer. Salted meat, cooked or uncooked, keeps well in a refrigerator for some days but uncooked does not store as well in a home freezer as unsalted meat. Cooked unsalted meat freezes reasonably well but cooked salted meat, when frozen, should be used within 5–6 weeks.*
To use any left over *See above. Boiled meats may be turned into rissoles, meat pies, etc.*

Killarney hot-pot

Most meats can be served in a stew or casserole. The great advantage of these methods of cooking is that they 'tenderise' the cheaper cuts of meat and with imaginative use of spices, herbs, fruits and vegetables, provide both interesting and economical dishes.

Blue Print Recipe

Irish Hot-Pot

8–12 oz. belly of pork · 12 oz. leanest possible meat from a hand of pork or 4 chump chops · 1 lb. onions · 2–3 large carrots · seasoning · 1–2 teaspoons chopped fresh sage or about ¼ teaspoon dried sage · 1½ lb. potatoes · ¼ pint (⅔C) stock or water · 1 oz. margarine.

To make Cut the belly and hand of pork into neat pieces. If using chump chops leave on the bone, or remove the meat and dice if more convenient (this means the meat takes up less space in a small casserole). Peel and cut the onions and carrots into rings. Season the meat and mix with the sage. Peel and slice the potatoes thinly, keep in water until ready to use, so they do not discolour. Put about one third of the potatoes into the casserole, season well. Add half the onions and carrots, half the meat, then another layer of potatoes (save plenty for the topping). Season each layer of vegetables. Next add the last of the meat, onions and carrots and cover with the stock or water. Arrange the last of the potato slices over the vegetables, in a neat overlapping design. Put the margarine in small pieces on the potatoes.

To cook Leave the hot-pot uncovered for about 15 minutes if possible, so the margarine melts and gives a good coating on the potatoes (this stops the lid 'sticking'). Put on the lid after 15 minutes, but remove again for the last 20 minutes to encourage the potatoes to brown and crisp. Cook for about 2 hours in the centre of a slow to very moderate oven, 300–325°F, Gas Mark 2–3.
To serve With cooked red cabbage or pickled red cabbage and apple sauce or sliced cooked beetroot. *All recipes based on this dish serve 4–5.*

● **AVOID** *Using too much stock or water, the vegetables keep the mixture moist. If you use too much liquid the potatoes on top will not crisp.*
● **SHORT CUT** *Use canned meat and canned potatoes, bake for about 45 minutes only in a moderately hot oven to crisp the potatoes.*

For Family Occasions

Welsh Hot-Pot

Method as Blue Print but choose about 1½–2 lb. middle or scrag end of neck of mutton and substitute sliced leeks for onions.
Bake and serve as the Blue Print.

Lancashire Hot-Pot

Method as Blue Print, but MINUS the carrots and sage and use 1½–2 lb. scrag or middle end of neck of lamb in place of pork. 1 or 2 thinly sliced lambs' kidneys may be mixed with the meat.
Bake and serve as the Blue Print.

For Special Occasions

Killarney Hot-Pot

Method as Blue Print but use 8 oz. belly of pork or fairly fat ham and 1 lb. lean fresh brisket or best quality chuck steak. Substitute ¼ pint (⅔C) brown ale for stock or water. Bake and serve as the Blue Print.

Family Stews

Although the Blue Print recipe and variations on this page give details for simmering the stew in a covered saucepan you can transfer the ingredients into a casserole, cover this tightly, and cook the food in a slow to very moderate oven, 300–325°F, Gas Mark 2–3.

The cooking time will be the same, but you can *reduce* the liquid in each recipe by 25 per cent for there is *less* evaporation in a covered casserole in the oven than in a covered saucepan on top of the cooker.

Blue Print Recipe

Beef and Vegetable Stew

1¼ lb. chuck beef · 1 oz. flour · seasoning · 8 small or medium-sized onions · 8 small carrots · 2–3 sticks celery · 4 oz. (1C) small mushrooms · 2 oz. (¼C) fat or dripping · 1 pint (2⅔C) brown stock · bouquet garni · To garnish : chopped parsley.

To make Cut the beef into neat cubes. Blend the flour and seasoning. Roll the meat in the seasoned flour. Peel the onions and carrots but leave whole. Cut the celery into neat pieces. Wash the mushrooms, do not peel.

To cook Heat the fat in a large pan. Toss the onions and meat in this for a few minutes, turning round until the meat is well coated with the fat. This initial cooking in fat helps to 'seal in' the flavour of the meat. Stir in the liquid gradually. Bring the liquid to the boil, stir well until a smooth slightly thickened sauce. Add the rest of the vegetables, herbs and season to taste. Cover with a well-fitting lid. Simmer for 2¼–2½ hours.

To serve In a hot dish or casserole. Remove the *bouquet garni* and garnish with chopped parsley. *All recipes based on this dish serve 4–5.*

● **AVOID** *Cooking the stew too quickly (unless using a pressure cooker). The long slow cooking tenderises the meat and produces a good blending of flavours.*
● **SHORT CUT** *Use ready prepared· sauce as the speedy alternative to stock and flavourings.*
● **TO SLIMMERS** *Omit the flour, to give a non-thickened liquid and reduce the quantity of fat.*

Creamed Veal Stew

Method as Blue Print but use veal in place of beef and half stock and half milk instead of all stock.

Spring-time Lamb Stew

Method as Blue Print but use 2 lb. middle neck of lamb in place of beef. Add peas instead of celery and top with freshly chopped mint.

Beef Goulash

1¼ lb. chuck or flank beef; 2–3 onions; 2 oz. (¼C) butter or dripping; ½ pint (1⅓C) stock; 2–3 teaspoons paprika; 1 lb. skinned chopped tomatoes; seasoning; 1 lb. potatoes. *To garnish :* natural yoghourt (optional); chopped parsley.

Dice the meat, peel and slice the onions and toss the meat and onions in the hot butter or dripping. Blend the stock and paprika (sweet red pepper), add to the pan with the tomatoes and seasoning. Simmer gently for 1¾ hours then add the potatoes and continue cooking for a further ½–¾ hour. Spoon carefully into a dish, top with yoghourt if wished, and parsley. *Serves 4–5.*

To vary Use all veal or half veal and half beef. Omit the potatoes and serve with cooked noodles if wished. Add diced red pepper with the tomatoes.

Somerset-Style Pork

5 or 6 loin or chump pork chops (or thick slices pork); 2–3 onions; ½ pint (1⅓C) cider; pinch fresh or dried sage; 2–3 dessert apples; seasoning; little olive oil.
Fry the chops in a large pan for about 5–8 minutes until lightly browned. Lift out of the pan. Peel and chop the onions and toss in any fat left in the pan until tender but not brown. Add the cider, sage, peeled and chopped apples and seasoning. Spoon into a large shallow casserole. Arrange the chops on top. Try to keep the skin above the cider so it crisps, as in the picture, and brush this with oil. Do not cover the dish. Cook for 40–45 minutes in the centre of a moderate oven, 350–375°F, Gas Mark 4–5. *Serves 5–6.*

Normandy Pork

As above, but use white wine and 1 tablespoon Calvados (optional) instead of cider.

Normandy pork (above)

Beef and vegetable stew (left)

New Look Stews and Casseroles

A stew or casserole is ideal when you entertain, for it can be left to 'look after itself'. A little extra cooking time does not spoil the dish.

For Special Occasions

Fluffy Topped Bobotee

1–2 medium-sized aubergines; 1–2 large onions; 3–4 large tomatoes; 2–2½ tablespoons oil; 2 lb. meat from leg of lamb; 1 teaspoon curry powder; seasoning; ½ pint (1⅓C) *brown* stock; *bouquet garni*; 2–3 tablespoons chopped blanched almonds. *For the topping:* 6 tablespoons very smooth mashed potato; 2 tablespoons thin cream; 3 eggs; 1–2 tablespoons finely grated Parmesan cheese; seasoning.

Dice the aubergines, the peeled onions and tomatoes and toss in the oil. Dice or mince the lamb and mix with the vegetables. Add the curry powder, seasoning and stock. Simmer for about 15 minutes, stirring well to mix the meat with the vegetables. Transfer to an oven-proof dish, add the *bouquet garni* and nuts. Cover the dish and cook in the centre of a very moderate oven, 325–350°F, Gas Mark 3–4, for 45 minutes. Remove the *bouquet garni*. Mix the potato, cream, egg yolks, cheese and seasoning. Fold in the stiffly whisked egg whites. Spread over the meat and cook for a further 20 minutes. (Illustrated on page 21.) *Serves 5–6.*

Ragoût of Beef and Prunes

1 pint (2⅔C) brown stock; about 18 prunes; 1¼ lb. chuck steak; seasoning; 1 oz. flour; 2 oz. (¼C) fat or dripping; 1 tablespoon tomato purée; 2 bay leaves; 4–5 tomatoes.

Heat the stock, pour over the prunes and soak for about 12 hours (unless using tenderised prunes which need 1 hour only). Dice the meat, roll in the seasoned flour and cook in the hot fat for a few minutes. Strain the stock from the prunes, add to the meat, bring to the boil and cook until thickened. Add the tomato purée, about 6 finely chopped prunes and the bay leaves. Cover the pan and simmer for 1¾ hours. Add the rest of the prunes and cook for a further 15 minutes. Skin the tomatoes if wished, add to the ragoût and cook for 15 minutes. *Serves 4–5.*

Beef Risotto Milanaise

2 tablespoons oil; 2 onions; 1–2 cloves garlic; 1 lb. minced beef; 1 medium-sized can tomatoes; 4 carrots; 1 tablespoon tomato purée; seasoning; 1 bay leaf; 8 oz. (1C) long grain rice; 1 pint (2⅔C) water. *To garnish:* parsley.

Heat the oil in a pan. Peel and cut the onions into thin rings and slice the garlic. Toss the onions and garlic in the oil until the onions are transparent. Put a few rings on one side for garnish. Add the beef to the pan, stir well to break up any lumps. Add the tomatoes and liquid from the can, the roughly chopped carrots, tomato purée, seasoning and bay leaf. Cook gently in a covered pan for 45 minutes, stirring once or twice. Put the rice and cold water into a saucepan with ½–1 teaspoon salt. Bring the water to the boil, stir briskly then cover the pan. Lower the heat and cook for approximately 15 minutes until the rice is tender and the liquid absorbed. Fork the rice on to a hot dish. Spoon the beef mixture in the centre and garnish with onion rings and a sprig of parsley. *Serves 4–5.*

Lamb Ratatouille

2 onions; 1–2 cloves garlic; 1½ lb. tomatoes; 1–2 green peppers; 1–2 aubergines (optional); 4 courgettes; 8 lamb cutlets or 2 lb. lamb from leg or shoulder; 2 tablespoons oil; 1–2 tablespoons chopped parsley; seasoning to taste.

Peel and chop the onions, crush the garlic, skin and chop the tomatoes, dice the peppers (discard core and seeds). Slice the aubergines and courgettes thinly. Fry the cutlets or cubed lamb in a pan for a few minutes on all sides. Lift out, then add the oil. Toss the onion and garlic in the oil for a few minutes then add the rest of the vegetables and the parsley. Season very well. Cover the pan and simmer for 25 minutes. Add the meat and blend with the vegetable mixture so it absorbs the flavour. Cover the pan again. Cook gently for a further 25–30 minutes. (Illustrated on page 21.) *Serves 8 for a light meal or 4–5 for a main meal.*

Storing and Freezing *Cooked stews and casseroles keep well for 2–3 days in the refrigerator and always seem to taste better when reheated. If cooking to freeze do not thicken, or use cornflour in place of flour.*

Ragoût of beef and prunes (above)

Beef risotto Milanaise (below)

The spicy flavour of a good curry surely provides one of the most interesting meals. Do not imagine a good curry *must* be very hot, there are many versions of this dish and the Blue Print is for a moderately hot curry sauce only.

Blue Print Recipe
Beef Curry

2 medium-sized onions · 1–2 cloves garlic · 2 oz. ($\frac{1}{4}$C) fat, butter or ghee * · 1 small sweet apple · $\frac{1}{2}$–1 tablespoon curry powder · 1–2 teaspoons curry paste · 1 tablespoon flour · $\frac{3}{4}$ pint (2C) brown stock · 1–2 tablespoons desiccated coconut or grated fresh coconut · 1–2 tablespoons sultanas · 1–2 tablespoons chutney · 1–1$\frac{1}{4}$ lb. uncooked beef (see method) · 1 teaspoon sugar · 1 teaspoon lemon juice or vinegar · seasoning. To accompany: 6–8 oz. (1C) long grain rice · saffron powder (optional) · chutney · sliced peppers and tomatoes · Poppadums · Bombay duck · nuts · raisins · grated coconut · sliced banana · rings of raw onion or spring onions.
*ghee is clarified butter.

To make   Chop the peeled onions and crush the cloves of garlic. Toss in the hot fat. Peel and slice the apple, add to the onion mixture with the curry powder, paste and flour. Fry gently for several minutes, stirring well to prevent the mixture burning. Gradually blend in the stock and bring to the boil and cook until slightly thickened. Put the coconut, sultanas and chutney into the sauce, then add the diced meat. For special occasions, choose diced topside, rump or fresh brisket; for economy choose diced chuck or flank steak.

To cook   Simmer for about 1 hour in a tightly covered pan then add the sugar, lemon juice or vinegar and seasoning. Taste the sauce and add more sweetening or seasoning as desired. Cover the pan again and continue cooking for a further 1$\frac{1}{2}$–2 hours.

To cook the rice put this with about 2$\frac{1}{2}$ times the amount of cold water (i.e. to 8 oz. rice use 20 fl. oz.—1 pint water; to 1 cup use 2$\frac{1}{2}$ cups water). Add seasoning and a pinch saffron powder if desired. Bring to the boil, stir briskly, cover the pan tightly and allow to simmer for approximately 15 minutes or until the rice has absorbed the water and is tender.

To serve   Arrange the curry in a border of saffron or plain rice or serve the rice in a separate dish. Arrange all the accompaniments in dishes so everyone may help themselves. The Poppadums should be fried in a very little fat until crisp. The Bombay duck (which is a dried fish) should be sprinkled over each portion of curry. *All recipes based on this dish serve 4–6.*

● **AVOID**   *Cooking too quickly, one needs prolonged cooking for a true blending of flavours.*

● **TO RECTIFY**   *Give yourself plenty of time to cook the sauce. If using cooked meat then allow the sauce to simmer for an hour or so before adding the meat. This prevents overcooking the meat.*

● **SHORT CUT**   *Use a canned mulligatawny soup as a ready-made sauce or buy canned curry sauce and add your own flavourings.*

● **TO SLIMMERS**   *Do not thicken the sauce and have very small portions of cooked rice, chutney and the fattening accompaniments.*

For Family Occasions

To vary

Very hot curry   As Blue Print PLUS 2–3 sliced red chilli peppers, pinch cayenne pepper, little ground ginger or sliced stem ginger.
Mild curry   As Blue Print but OMIT the curry paste and use only half the amount of curry powder.
Sweet curry   As Blue Print PLUS 1–2 grated carrots and 1 medium-sized can pineapple, guavas or mangoes. Add the carrots and most of the fruit to the onion and apple mixture, and use about $\frac{1}{2}$ pint (1$\frac{1}{3}$C) only of stock and $\frac{1}{4}$ pint ($\frac{2}{3}$C) syrup from the can instead of the remainder of the stock. Garnish the curry with the remaining pieces of fruit just before serving.

Bhoona Goast

This is a very dry curry, and can be made as the Blue Print, but reduce the amount of stock to a few tablespoons only. Cook gently until the meat is tender, stirring from time to time to stop the mixture from burning. Choose diced lean mutton instead of beef and omit the apple.

For Special Occasions

Aubergine Curry

Ingredients as Blue Print, but use only 8 oz. meat, PLUS 4 thinly sliced aubergines (egg plants) and 1 or 2 lemons. The aubergines should be sprinkled with salt and left standing for about 15 minutes before adding to the curry sauce. Cook and serve as Blue Print, but garnish with thick wedges of lemon.

Lamb and Courgette Curry

Method as Blue Print but use diced lamb (from leg or shoulder) in place of beef. Cook as Blue Print. Add 3–4 thinly sliced unpeeled courgettes about 30 minutes before the end of the cooking period. Serve as Blue Print. (Illustrated on page 21.)

Storing and Freezing   *Store cooked curry in the refrigerator for one or two days and reheat. Curry may be frozen but it can destroy some of the flavour.*

Sweet curry

Bacon and ham provide a wide selection of dishes for various meals, ranging from a simple breakfast dish of bacon and egg to the more elaborate Ham en Croûte and Glazed Bacon or Ham here.

Blue Print Recipe

Glazed Bacon or Ham

Choose gammon or a joint of ham for special occasions; oyster cut for medium quality; forehock or collar for family economy. Soak the bacon or ham overnight in cold water to cover, unless you have chosen 'green' or sweet-cure. This does not need soaking. Put the bacon or ham into a large pan, cover with cold water, or with cider, ginger beer or ginger ale. Add vegetables if wished. Bring the liquid to the boil, lower the heat and simmer very gently for $\frac{2}{3}$ of the total cooking time (see below). Allow the bacon or ham to cool sufficiently to remove the skin. Score (cut) the fat at regular intervals, this allows the glaze to penetrate the fat and gives more flavour to the joint. Lift into the roasting tin. Spread the glaze, as the recipes below, over the joint of bacon or ham and roast in the centre of a moderately hot oven, 400°F, Gas Mark 5–6, for the remainder of the cooking time.

Timing Prime gammon or ham. A wide joint that is not very thick cooks more quickly, so allow 20 minutes per lb. and 20 minutes over, while a thicker joint needs 25 minutes per lb. and 25 minutes over. More economical joints need 30–35 minutes per lb. and 30–35 minutes over. Therefore a 4 lb. piece of gammon would take either 4×20 plus 20 minutes or 4×25 plus 25 minutes, i.e. either a total of 1 hour and 40 minutes or 2 hours and 5 minutes.

To serve Hot with vegetables, cold with salad. Some of the stock may be used for a clear sauce or for parsley sauce.

Roasting Bacon or Ham

If preferred the bacon or ham can be roasted for all the cooking time. Soak as above and either fast roast (see page 23) for 20–25 minutes per lb. and 20–25 minutes over or slow roast for 35–40 minutes per lb. and 35–40 minutes over. Forehock and collar should be slow roasted, gammon, ham or oyster cut can be slow or fast roasted.

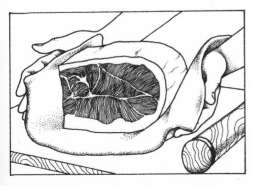

Glazed forehock of bacon

Glazes for Bacon or Ham
These are sufficient to coat the fat on a joint weighing about 4 lb. which will serve about 8.

Honey Ginger Glaze
Blend 4 tablespoons thick honey, 2 teaspoons ground ginger and 2 tablespoons finely chopped preserved ginger together. Spread over the fat and roast as the Blue Print.

Pineapple Glaze
Blend 3 tablespoons brown sugar, 3 tablespoons syrup from canned pineapple and 1 teaspoon made mustard together.
Spread over the fat and roast as the Blue Print. Put the pineapple rings from the can round the joint and cook for about 10 minutes before serving.

Sugar and Spice Glaze
Blend 3 tablespoons brown sugar, 2–3 tablespoons soft breadcrumbs (optional), 1–2 teaspoons mixed spice and 1 tablespoon golden syrup together.
Moisten to a spreading consistency with a very little stock from boiling the joint. Spread over the fat. Roast as the Blue Print, then serve hot with mixed vegetables as shown in the picture.

Ham en Croûte
Joint middle gammon or ham about $3\frac{1}{2}$–4 lb.; 1 lb. (4C) flour, preferably plain; pinch salt; 8 oz. (1C) fat; water to mix. *To glaze:* 1 egg.
Soak the gammon or ham for 12 hours in cold water unless 'green' or sweet-cure. If very salt soak for 24 hours. Lift out of the water, dry thoroughly and cut away the skin. Sieve the flour and salt, rub in the fat until the mixture is like fine breadcrumbs. Mix with cold water to a rolling consistency. Roll out to about $\frac{1}{4}$-inch in thickness and cut off $\frac{2}{3}$ of the pastry. Place the gammon or ham on this, bring up the pastry to encase the sides of the meat, see Sketch 1. Roll out the remaining pastry for the 'lid' and place over the meat. Cut away any surplus pastry, brush the edges with beaten egg and pinch together very firmly. Lift on to a baking tray. Brush with beaten egg. Cut a slit in the top to allow the steam to escape and make small 'leaves' of pastry. Press on top of the croûte and brush with beaten egg. Bake in the centre of a moderate oven, 350–375°F, Gas Mark 4–5, for 30 minutes, then reduce the heat to very moderate, 325–350°F, Gas Mark 3–4, for the remainder of the time. Allow 25 minutes per lb. and 25 minutes over, so a 4-lb. joint will take 2 hours 5 minutes. Serve hot or cold, cut into thin slices. *Serves 8–10.*

Ham and Pâté en Croûte
Ingredients as Ham en Croûte PLUS about 3–4 oz. pâté and 8 oz. mushrooms. Roll out $\frac{2}{3}$ of the pastry as Ham en Croûte. Spread with most of the pâté and finely chopped mushrooms. Wrap round the gammon. Spread the top of the gammon with pâté and mushrooms, cover with the pastry lid and proceed as Ham en Croûte.

Ham and Corn Scallops
1 oz. butter or margarine; 1 oz. flour; $\frac{1}{4}$ pint ($\frac{2}{3}$C) milk; seasoning; $\frac{1}{2}$–1 teaspoon made mustard; 8 oz. cooked ham; small can corn; 2 packets potato crisps.
Make a thick sauce with the butter or margarine, flour and milk. Add the seasoning and mustard. Add the diced ham and corn (plus any liquid from the can). Put into 4 scallop or individual dishes. Crush the potato crisps and sprinkle over the ham mixture. Heat for 15–20 minutes in the centre of a very moderate oven, 325–350°F, Gas Mark 3–4. *Serves 4.*

Ham en croûte

Meat Puddings

Most men (and a percentage of women) would choose a home-made steak and kidney pudding as one of the (if not *the*) ideal cold weather meat dishes. If correctly made, with a coating of not-too-thick, feather-light suet crust pastry, and a richly flavoured steak and kidney filling it is satisfying, without being 'stodgy'. The points below apply to all meat puddings.

Blue Print Recipe
Steak and Kidney Pudding

For the filling: 1½ lb. stewing steak (chuck is a good choice) · 8–12 oz. ox kidney or 6 lambs' kidneys · seasoning · 2–2½ tablespoons flour · 1 or 2 onions (optional) · water or stock · For the pastry: 10 oz. (2½C) flour* · pinch salt · 5 oz. (nearly 1C) shredded suet · water.
*this can be self-raising (or plain flour with 2½ level teaspoons baking powder) to give a thicker crust, or plain flour for a thin crust that does not rise.

To make   Either cut the steak into neat cubes, as shown in the picture, or narrow strips. Dice the kidney, remove any gristle and skin. Either mix *with* the meat or put a small piece of kidney on each strip

Steak and kidney pudding

of steak and roll firmly. Mix the seasoning and flour on a plate or in a bag, turn or toss the meat and kidney in this until evenly coated. Chop the onions finely, if adding these, and blend with the meat. Put the liquid on one side to add later. Sieve the flour and salt together, add the suet and mix to a soft rolling consistency with cold water. Roll out and use about ¾ to line a 3-pint (8C) basin; trim the edges, put trimmings with the ¼ reserved. Put in the meat filling, add just enough water or stock to come halfway up the meat mixture. Damp the edges of the pastry. Roll out the remaining dough to form the 'lid', put on top of the meat filling, press the edges firmly. Alternatively follow instructions for lining the basin on page 2. Cover with greased greaseproof paper and foil; make a 'pleat' in the centre to allow the pudding to rise.

To cook   Either put into a steamer over a pan of boiling water, or lower into a saucepan of boiling water, to stand on an upturned saucer or patty tin. Steam or boil for 4–5 hours so the meat is tender. Fill-up the pan with *boiling* water during cooking.

To serve   In the basin. If this is attractive, as in the picture, there is no need to cover this. If using a less pleasing basin wrap a white or coloured table napkin round this. Top with a sprig of parsley. Either make a gravy to serve with the pudding, or when you cut out the first portion add a little good hot beef stock to the filling and use this as the gravy. *Serves 6–7.*

For Family Occasions

A smaller sized pudding for 4 people is made with about 1 lb. steak and 8 oz. (2C) flour, etc.

Steak and Vegetable Pudding
Ingredients as Blue Print MINUS the kidney and PLUS 2–3 sliced carrots, 2–3 sticks diced celery and a few mushrooms. Cook as the Blue Print.

Minced Steak Pudding
Ingredients as Blue Print but mince the steak, kidney and onions. Blend with 1–2 tablespoons rolled oats or oatmeal and 1–2 tablespoons tomato purée as well as the flour and liquid in the Blue Print. Steam for 2½–3 hours.

Mutton Pudding
Method as Blue Print, but use about 2½–3 lb. middle neck of mutton or lamb. Bone this and use instead of steak and kidney. Flavour with 1–2 teaspoons chopped parsley, little chopped mint, 12 mushrooms and 12 tiny onions *instead of* sliced onions.

For Special Occasions

Flemish Pudding
Ingredients as Blue Print (choose prime quality chuck steak) PLUS 2–3 rashers diced lean bacon and a few mushrooms. Use beer or red wine instead of water or stock in the pudding and flavour with 1 teaspoon chopped mixed herbs. Cook as the Blue Print.

Steak and Pheasant Pudding
Method as Blue Print, but omit the kidney and use the meat from a small boned pheasant instead.
Cook as the Blue Print. Serve with redcurrant jelly.

● **AVOID** *Making the suet crust pastry too dry, it needs to be a soft rolling consistency: Adding too much liquid to the filling, it boils out and spoils the appearance of the dish.*
● **SHORT CUTS** *Use ready shredded packet suet; or pastry and canned meat filling and cook for a much shorter time (about 2 hours); or cook in a pressure cooker (following the maker's instructions).*

Storing and Freezing   *The cooked pudding can be stored for 2–3 days in a refrigerator and reheated. It can be frozen with great success. Cook for 2–2½ hours (to set the pastry), cool, freeze then wrap or remove from the basin and wrap.*
Allow to thaw out if using a breakable basin before completing the cooking for 2–2½ hours.
To use any leftover   *Cover and re-steam.*

Forfar Bridie

For Family Occasions

Thrifty Pasties
Ingredients as Blue Print, but use chuck steak instead of rump.
Put the chuck steak through a coarse mincer. Make as Blue Print, bake for 15 minutes in a hot oven, lower the heat to very moderate and cook for 40–45 minutes.

Steak and Kidney Pasties
Ingredients as Cornish Pasties PLUS 2–3 lambs' kidneys and MINUS the swede.
Skin and dice kidneys and mix with the meat. Make and bake as the Blue Print.

Forfar Bridies
Pastry ingredients as the Blue Print, using 6 oz. (¾C) fat only to 1 lb. (4C) flour.
Cut 1¼–1½ lb. good quality stewing steak into thin strips about 1-inch in length and ½-inch wide, spread with a little butter or press shredded suet on to each strip and season well. Dice about 3 large onions and mix with the meat strips, do not add stock or water. Roll out the pastry, cut into 4 large ovals or rectangles instead of rounds. Divide the filling between these. Damp pastry edges, fold one half over, seal edges and flute or crimp. Bake as the Blue Print in a hot oven for 15 minutes, then lower the heat to very moderate for just over an hour.

For Special Occasions

Gammon Pasties
Ingredients as Blue Print but substitute about 1¼ lb. lean gammon for the steak. Dice this finely and mix with the diced potatoes, onions and 1 dessert apple in place of the swede. Season well and flavour with a very little powdered sage. Blend with 1 tablespoon only white wine or stock. Make and bake as the Blue Print.

Burgundy Pasties
Ingredients as Blue Print but substitute fillet steak and Burgundy wine for stock. Omit swede and use extra onion and a crushed clove garlic. Make and bake as Blue Print.

Storing and Freezing *Uncooked pasties store for 1–2 hours only in the refrigerator as the filling makes the pastry 'soggy'. The uncooked potato and meat filling does not freeze well. Cooked pasties freeze excellently.*
To use any left over *Do not keep long. Re-heat before serving.*

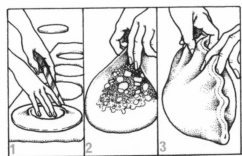

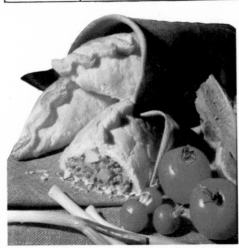

Cornish pasties

On this page are two of the best known meat pasties, together with variations.

Blue Print Recipe
Cornish Pasties

For the pastry: 1 lb. (4C) flour, preferably plain · pinch salt · 6–8 oz. (¾–1C) fat (see method) · water to mix. For the filling: 1 lb. rump steak · 2 medium-sized potatoes · 2 medium-sized onions · 1 small or ½ medium-sized swede (optional) · 2 tablespoons stock or water · seasoning. To glaze: 1 egg (optional).

To make Sieve the flour and salt and rub in the fat. Choose the smaller amount if carrying the pasties on a picnic for this ensures that the pastry is not too 'short' and fragile. Bind to a rolling consistency with the water. Cut the meat, peeled potatoes, onions and swede into neat small pieces. If omitting the swede, add a little more potato and onion to give the same amount of filling. Mix with the stock or water and seasoning. Roll out the pastry, cut round 4 teaplates, see Sketch 1. Put the filling in the centre of each round. Damp the edges of the pastry with water, bring up to form a pasty shape, see Sketch 2. Flute the edges with your fingers, as Sketch 3. Lift on to a baking tray. If wishing to give the pastry a good shine blend a beaten egg with about 2 teaspoons water and brush the pasties with this glaze.
To cook Bake for approximately 15–20 minutes in the centre of a hot oven, 425–450°F, Gas Mark 6–7, or until the pastry is golden then lower the heat to moderate, 350–375°F, Gas Mark 4–5, and cook for a further 20 minutes, or to very moderate, 325–350°F, Gas Mark 3–4 for 25–30 minutes.
To serve Hot with vegetables and a brown sauce (see page 27) or cold with salad or as part of a packed meal. *All recipes based on this serve 4.*

● **AVOID** *Making the filling too moist, add only half the stock and if you find it looks fairly liquid then omit the rest. Do not dice the potatoes, etc. too early for they discolour and become over-moist.*
● **TO RECTIFY** *If the mixture is too soft sprinkle with a little flour. with a little flour.*
● **SHORT CUT** *Use canned steak, warm slightly then strain away surplus moisture and serve this as part of the sauce if you intend having the pasties hot.*

Offal is often called specialist or variety meats and the latter name is very appropriate, for there are many kinds of meat grouped under this heading and they can be cooked in an unlimited number of ways. The most popular offal are:

LIVER

Liver is an excellent source of iron as well as protein, but can be spoiled by over-cooking. Choose calf's liver for the best quality, lambs' or pig's liver for tender, but less delicately flavoured liver. The simplest way to cook tender liver is to slice it fairly thinly, coat lightly in seasoned flour and fry for about 6–7 minutes in butter, dripping or bacon fat until tender. Serve with fried or grilled bacon. Ox-liver needs longer, slower cooking, as in the Ragoût Sicilienne below.

Liver Ragoût Sicilienne

$1\frac{1}{4}$ lb. ox-liver; 1 oz. flour; seasoning; 3 medium-sized onions; 1–2 cloves garlic; 2 oz. ($\frac{1}{4}$C) dripping or fat; $\frac{1}{2}$ pint ($1\frac{1}{3}$C) stock; $\frac{1}{2}$ pint ($1\frac{1}{3}$C) cider or inexpensive red wine; a generous tablespoon red currant jelly; $\frac{1}{2}$ teaspoon grated lemon rind; 2–3 tablespoons green olives.
Cut the liver into narrow strips. Mix the flour with seasoning, coat the liver in this. Cut the peeled onions into rings and crush the cloves of garlic. Heat the dripping or fat in a pan, toss the liver in this, lift out and fry the onion rings and garlic for a few minutes. Gradually blend in the stock and cider or wine, bring to the boil and cook until slightly thickened. Add the jelly and lemon rind. Replace the strips of liver, put a lid on the pan and simmer very slowly for about 2 hours. Add the olives just before serving. Serve with creamed potatoes, boiled rice or noodles. (Illustrated on page 38.) *Serves 4–5.*

Kidney Ragoût Sicilienne

Use sliced ox-kidney in place of liver.

Liver Kebabs with Orange Sauce

For the sauce: 2 oranges; $\frac{1}{2}$ pint ($1\frac{1}{3}$C) brown stock; 1 oz. cornflour; 1 oz. butter; seasoning; $\frac{1}{2}$–1 teaspoon sugar. *For the kebabs:* 1 lb. calf's liver (cut in one piece about 1-inch thick); seasoning; pinch mixed dried herbs; about 12 mushrooms; 12 small cocktail onions; 4 rashers bacon; 2 oz. ($\frac{1}{4}$C) melted butter. *To serve:* boiled rice.
Pare the rind very thinly from the oranges and simmer this in half the stock for about 5 minutes. Strain, return to the pan. Blend the cornflour with the rest of the stock, add to the liquid in the pan with the juice of the oranges, the butter, seasoning and sugar. Bring to the boil, cook gently and stir until smooth and thickened. Meanwhile cut the liver into cubes, roll in seasoning and herbs, put on to 4 metal skewers with the mushrooms, onions and halved bacon rashers, in neat rolls. Brush with the melted butter and cook under a hot grill for about 8 minutes. Turn several times during cooking, so the

food cooks evenly. Serve on a bed of boiled rice with the orange sauce. *Serves 4.*
Note Extra orange segments can be added to the sauce, if liked.

Kidney Kebabs

Use 8–12 skinned whole or halved lambs' kidneys in place of the calf's liver.

KIDNEY

Kidney adds flavour to many dishes such as the steak and kidney pudding on page 34 and the less expensive, but less tender ox-kidney can be used for this purpose. Lambs' kidneys can be grilled or fried and form an important part of a mixed grill. They make a delicious dish for Special Occasions when cooked in red wine, as in the recipe below. Smaller quantities can be used as a filling for pancakes and omelettes or to serve on toast as a light snack.

Kidneys Bordelaise

About 20 lambs' kidneys; $1\frac{1}{2}$ oz. flour; seasoning; good pinch grated nutmeg; 2 medium-sized onions; 2 rashers bacon; 2–3 oz. ($\frac{1}{4}$–$\frac{3}{8}$C) good dripping or butter; 1 tablespoon chopped parsley; $\frac{1}{2}$ pint ($1\frac{1}{3}$C) brown stock; $\frac{1}{4}$ pint ($\frac{2}{3}$C) red wine. *To serve:* about $1\frac{1}{2}$ lb. creamed potatoes. *To garnish:* parsley. Skin the kidneys, halve for quicker cooking if wished. Mix the flour, seasoning and nutmeg and coat the kidneys in the flour mixture. Peel and cut the onions into thin rings, cut the bacon into narrow strips. Heat the dripping or butter in a pan, fry the onion rings and bacon gently for a few minutes, then add the kidneys and cook gently for 5 minutes, stirring well. Add the parsley, mix thoroughly, then gradually blend in the stock and wine. Bring the sauce to the boil, stir and

cook until thickened. Cover the pan and simmer for about 15 minutes. Meanwhile pipe the creamed potatoes on to a heat-proof serving dish, brown under the grill. Spoon the kidney mixture into the centre of the potatoes and garnish with parsley. Sliced pigs' kidneys may be used instead. *Serves 5–6.*

Kidneys Marengo

Recipe as above, but omit the potatoes. Top the kidney mixture with 5–6 fried or poached eggs and garnish with fried croûtons of bread.

Boiled Calf's Head

Follow the directions for cooking Brawn on page 40, but remove the meat from the head and put back into the stock to keep hot (keep the brains separate). Make the brain sauce below, arrange the meat and any vegetables on a dish and serve the sauce separately. *Serves about 6 according to the size of the head.*

Brain Sauce

$1\frac{1}{2}$ oz. butter or margarine; $1\frac{1}{2}$ oz. flour; $\frac{1}{2}$ pint ($1\frac{1}{3}$C) stock from cooking the head; $\frac{1}{4}$ pint ($\frac{2}{3}$C) milk; the brains from the head; seasoning.

Heat the butter or margarine in a pan, stir in the flour and cook the 'roux' for several minutes. Gradually add the liquid, bring to the boil and cook until thickened. Add the chopped brains and season to taste.
If preferred, parsley sauce can be served instead of brain sauce. Add 1–2 tablespoons chopped parsley to the sauce in place of the brains.

Kidney kebabs with orange sauce (above)
Kidneys Bordelaise, Ox-tail hotch-potch with mustard dumplings,
Fricasée of sweetbreads and Tripe—French style (right)

Both tripe and sweetbreads are very easily digested. Before using in individual recipes they need 'blanching'. This simple process ensures that the meat is a good colour.

Blue Print Recipe

To Blanch Tripe and Sweetbreads

To blanch First cut the tripe into neat pieces. Wash the tripe or sweetbreads in cold water. Put into a saucepan. Cover with cold water. Bring the water to the boil then strain the meat and discard the liquid.

To cook As individual recipes.

Storing and Freezing *Offal is highly perishable so use within 48 hours if stored in a refrigerator. All offal freezes well when raw but should be used within 6–8 weeks. Cooked ox-tail and kidneys freeze excellently, but I find most other cooked dishes, except liver pâté, tend to lose flavour.*
To use any left over *Cooked liver may be minced, blended with butter and garlic for a quick pâté.*
Reheat kidneys, ox-tail, but use quickly.

OX-TAIL

Ox-tail is a meat with a full, rich flavour. It has an excessive amount of natural fat so take care that dishes made with ox-tail are not too greasy. The easiest way to avoid this is to cook the dish, allow it to cool, remove the excess fat, then reheat.

Ox-Tail Hotch-Potch with Mustard Dumplings

1 good-sized ox-tail; 3 onions; 3–4 large carrots; 2 pints water or beef stock; grated rind 1 lemon; *bouquet garni*; seasoning; 1½ oz. cornflour. *For the dumplings*: 4 oz. (1C) self-raising flour (or plain flour and 1 teaspoon baking powder); 1 teaspoon dry mustard; seasoning; 2 oz. (⅓C) shredded suet; water to mix.

Ask the butcher to joint the tail. Put this into a strong pan and fry steadily until golden brown. Lift out of the pan and toss the peeled sliced onions and half the sliced carrots in the fat remaining for about 5 minutes. Replace the joints of ox-tail. Cover with the water or stock, lemon rind, *bouquet garni* and seasoning. Simmer for about 1½ hours. Add

the rest of the sliced carrots and simmer for a further 1 hour. Let the mixture become quite cold, remove the surplus fat. Reheat and add the cornflour blended with a little cold water. Stir well until a thickened sauce. Sieve the flour or flour and baking powder with the mustard and seasoning. Add the suet and enough water to make a fairly soft mixture. Roll into 8 balls with floured hands. Drop into the boiling mixture and cook steadily for 20 minutes. Spoon into a serving dish. (Illustrated on page 37.) *Serves 4–6.*
For Special Occasions Use a little red wine in the sauce and add a few olives and cooked or canned haricot beans.

Fricasée of Sweetbreads

1½ lb. sweetbreads; ½ pint (1⅓C) white stock; 1 onion; *bouquet garni*; 1 lemon; seasoning; 1 oz. butter; 1 oz. flour; ½ pint (1⅓C) milk; 2 tablespoons thick or thin cream. *To garnish*: 3–4 slices bread; 2 oz. (¼C) dripping or butter.
Blanch the sweetbreads as in the Blue Print. Put into a saucepan with the stock, whole peeled onion, *bouquet garni*, thinly pared lemon rind and a little lemon juice. Season well and simmer gently for about 30–35 minutes when the sweetbreads should be tender. Strain the stock (keep this), allow the sweetbreads to cool sufficiently to handle. Remove any pieces of skin. Make a white sauce with the butter, flour and milk, allow to thicken. Stir about ¼ pint (⅔C) of the stock into the sauce. Put in the sweetbreads and heat thoroughly, add extra seasoning if necessary, and the cream. Meanwhile remove the crusts from the bread and cut the slices into triangles. Fry in hot dripping or butter until crisp and golden brown. Arrange

round the edge of a dish and spoon fricasée into the middle. (Illustrated on page 37.) *Serves 5–6.*
To vary Add well drained fried button mushrooms to the fricasée. If liked add a generous amount of chopped parsley or parsley with sage and thyme to the sauce.

Tripe—French Style

1½–2 lb. tripe; 2–3 onions; 2–3 carrots; 2–4 oz. mushrooms; 1 clove garlic (optional); 1½–2 tablespoons oil; 1 tablespoon flour; ½ pint (1⅓C) stock; seasoning; 4 tablespoons thick or thin cream; 1–2 tablespoons brandy or sherry.
Blanch the tripe as in the Blue Print. Peel and slice the vegetables and garlic. Toss in the hot oil for a few minutes. Stir in the flour and cook for 2–3 minutes then add the stock. Bring to the boil, add the tripe and seasoning. Cover the pan tightly and simmer for 40 minutes, or until tender. Blend the cream and brandy or sherry. Add to the tripe and heat *without* boiling for 5–6 minutes. Serve with crusty French bread. (Illustrated on page 37.) *Serves 4–6.*

For Special Occasions

Tripe Parmesan

Tripe is very inexpensive but it can be very interesting. Cook the tripe with onions and carrots to flavour as the recipe above until *just* tender, but not too soft. Lift out of the liquid, drain and coat in beaten egg and grated Parmesan cheese mixed with soft breadcrumbs. Fry until crisp and golden brown. Serve with thick wedges of lemon. *Serves 4–6.*

Liver ragoût Sicilienne

38

Cold Meat Dishes

Although many of the dishes covered in the previous pages are equally good served hot or cold, the meat loaves and other interesting ideas on this, and the following page, are specially planned for eating cold.

Blue Print Recipe

Ham and Beef Loaf

1 lb. lean cooked ham · 1 lb. chuck steak · 1 medium-sized onion · 8 oz. pork sausagemeat · 2 tablespoons tomato purée · 2 eggs · 1 large slice bread, about 1-inch thick · ¼ pint (⅔C) stock · seasoning. To garnish: 1 or 2 hard boiled eggs · small piece cucumber · 2 tomatoes · parsley.

To make Put the ham, steak and onion through a fine mincer. Blend with the sausagemeat. Add the tomato purée and beaten eggs and blend thoroughly. Meanwhile cut the crusts from the bread, put the crumb into a basin and add the warm stock. Allow to stand for 15 minutes, beat until smooth. Blend with the meat mixture and season very well. Grease a 3-lb. loaf tin and put in the mixture. Cover with greased foil and stand in a 'bain-marie' of cold water.
To cook Bake for 1½ hours in the centre of a very moderate oven, 325–350°F, Gas Mark 3–4. Allow to cool in the tin.
To serve Turn out and garnish with sliced egg, cucumber, tomato and chopped parsley. *All recipes based on this dish serve 8–10.*
  If using half quantities bake for 1 hour only.

● **AVOID** *Over-cooking meat loaves as the meat continues to cook as it cools: Making the mixture too dry. A good meat loaf or mould should have a moist texture.*
● **TO RECTIFY** *Stand the tin or cooking container in a 'bain-marie' to keep the mixture moist and prevent it over-cooking.*
● **SHORT CUTS** *Meat loaves may be cooked in a pressure cooker. Allow about ⅓ of the usual cooking time at 15 lb. pressure.*
● **TO SLIMMERS** *Choose the recipes that contain the minimum of bread and fat.*

Ham and chicken mould

For Family Occasions

Fruity Meat Loaf

Ingredients as Blue Print PLUS 3–4 tablespoons well drained chopped pineapple and 1 tablespoon sweet chutney.
Make and cook as the Blue Print. Garnish with rings of pineapple and tomato slices.

Cheese Meat Loaf

Method as Blue Print but use only 8 oz. beef and 8 oz. diced Gruyère cheese (instead of all beef). Cook as the Blue Print.

Crisp Coated Meat Loaf

Use the Blue Print or any of the other recipes, but coat the baking tin with a generous layer of butter or fat and crisp breadcrumbs, crushed cornflakes or potato crisps. Cover the top of the meat with melted butter or oil and a layer of crumbs, cornflakes or crisps. Bake as the Blue Print but without the 'bain-marie'.

For Special Occasions

Liver Cream Loaf

Method as Blue Print but choose 1 lb. calf's liver instead of 1 lb. beef and ¼ pint (⅔C) thin cream instead of stock. Mix the ingredients together and add several chopped anchovy fillets. Cook as the Blue Print.

Stuffed Meat Roll

Ingredients as Blue Print PLUS 3 or 4 hard boiled eggs and 2–3 tablespoons canned or home-made liver pâté.

Prepare the ingredients as the Blue Print. Put half the meat mixture into the tin. Shell and halve the eggs. Put the yolks into a basin and blend with the pâté. Press this pâté into the white cases. Press the cases together to form whole eggs again. Lay these in the centre of the tin, cover with the rest of the mixture and cook as the Blue Print.

Glazed Veal Loaf

Method and ingredients as Blue Print but substitute fillet of veal for beef PLUS 2 teaspoons aspic jelly powder, 1 teaspoon powdered gelatine, ½ pint (1⅓C) white stock or water and ¼ pint (⅔C) *thick* mayonnaise. *To garnish:* small pieces of gherkin, cooked carrot and cucumber.
Make and cook the meat loaf as the Blue Print. Allow to cool then turn out of the tin. Soften the aspic jelly powder and gelatine in 2 tablespoons cold stock or water. Heat the remainder of the stock or water. Add the gelatine mixture, stir until dissolved. Allow to cool and stiffen slightly, then blend with the mayonnaise. Stand the meat loaf on a wire cooling tray with a large plate underneath to catch any 'drips'. Brush the mixture over the loaf until evenly coated. Dip the pieces of gherkin, carrot and sliced cucumber into the mixture on the plate and press them on to the loaf to form an attractive design. Leave for 1–2 hours in a cool place before serving.

Storing and Freezing *All the dishes on this page keep for 2–3 days in a refrigerator and freeze well with the exception of the Glazed Veal Loaf. The mayonnaise coating prevents successful freezing.*
To use any left over *Slice and use as a sandwich filling.*

More Cold Meat Dishes

All the dishes on this page have one thing in common, the meat is set in a jelly. This jelly is made from aspic, or other flavouring and gelatine, or from the natural setting qualities of the meat itself, as in the Brawn.

Blue Print Recipe

Ham and Chicken Mould

2 envelopes aspic jelly powder (enough to set 2 pints (5½C) liquid) · 2 pints (5½C) white stock or water · 2–3 hard boiled eggs · about 1–1¼ lb. cooked chicken · about 1–1¼ lb. cooked ham (make a total of 2¼ lb. meat in all) · few cooked peas · large can asparagus tips.

To make Dissolve the aspic in the stock or water according to the directions on the packet. Allow to cool. Pour a little into the bottom of a lightly oiled or rinsed 4-pint mould or basin and leave this to set. Shell the eggs, slice, then arrange in a neat design on the jelly. Spoon a very little aspic over the egg slices and put into the refrigerator or stand over a basin of ice. When the jelly is firm put a layer of neatly diced meat and peas into the mould, cover with liquid jelly. Leave once again to set. Continue like this, using the *very well drained* asparagus for the final layer. Cover with the last of the jelly and leave until the mould is firmly set.
To serve Dip the mould for a few seconds in warm water. Invert on to the serving dish and serve with salad. (Illustrated on page 39.)
Serves about 8.
   Naturally a smaller mould may be made with half the above quantity.

Storing and Freezing *These jellied moulds keep for several days in a refrigerator but tend to stiffen slightly. In a home freezer they keep well for 2–3 weeks but after this they dry out slightly.*
To use any left over *Part of a mould looks rather unsightly so slice neatly before serving.*

For Family Occasions

Lemon-Flavoured Lamb's Brawn

1 lamb's head; 1 or 2 extra lamb's tongues; 1 lemon; 1–2 bay leaves; 1–2 onions; *bouquet garni*; 2 pig's trotters; seasoning.
Wash the lamb's head in plenty of cold water. Put the head, the tongues, thin strips of lemon rind, bay leaves, whole onions, the *bouquet garni* (mixed fresh herbs tied in a neat bunch or in muslin), the trotters and seasoning into a large pan. Cover with cold water. Bring slowly to the boil and remove any grey scum from the top of the liquid. Cover the pan and simmer slowly for about 2 hours, or until the meat on the head, tongues and trotters is tender. If preferred cook for about 45 minutes at 15 lb. pressure in a pressure cooker, allow the pressure to drop at room temperature. Lift the head, tongues and trotters from the liquid and when cool enough to handle cut all the meat from the bones and arrange in a 3-pint basin or plain mould. Squeeze the lemon juice into the liquid in the pan and boil rapidly until you have about ¾ pint (2C). Strain over the meat in the basin or mould and allow to set. Turn out and serve as the Blue Print. *Serves 8–12 according to the size of the head.*

Calf's or Pig's Head Brawn

As instructions for Lamb's Head Brawn. Omit the extra tongues and pig's trotters and instead use 1 lb. diced shin of beef or chuck steak and a small piece diced lean ham or bacon, if wished. Simmer for about 2½–3 hours then follow instructions above.

For Special Occasions

Ham and Tongue Mousse

1½ lb. cooked ham and tongue (adjust the proportions to personal taste); 2 teaspoons powdered gelatine or enough to set ½ pint (1⅓C); ¼ pint (⅔C) white stock; ¼ pint (⅔C) thick cream; 2 tablespoons dry sherry; seasoning.
Mince the ham and tongue finely and blend together. Soften the gelatine in a little of the cold stock, then dissolve in very hot stock as the aspic jelly in the Blue Print. Blend the meats with this and allow to cool. Whip the cream lightly, add the sherry and whip again, fold into the meat mixture then season. Put into an oiled or rinsed 2-pint basin or mould and allow to set. Turn out as instructions in the Blue Print. *Serves 4–5 as a main course or 8–10 as an hors d'oeuvre.*
To vary Use all ham or all tongue.
For family occasions, substitute corned beef for ham and tongue. Omit the sherry and add extra stock.

Lemon-flavoured lamb's brawn

three
HOME BAKING

There is a great sense of achievement in producing a perfect cake, home-made bread or a selection of biscuits. The secrets of perfection can be summed up as follows:

1. To use (and follow) a well balanced recipe, by this I mean a recipe that gives the right proportions of fat, sugar, etc. For example, if you have too much fat in proportion to flour the cake will be heavy and greasy, the biscuits will spread in cooking and will not crisp. Too little fat, on the other hand, will make most cakes dry and unappetising unless eaten when very fresh. If you 'cut down' too much on the sugar in a recipe the cake will not only be lacking in flavour, but much heavier, for sugar lightens sponges and cakes. One must have a good proportion of eggs in relation to the fat and flour used, otherwise the mixture will not 'bind together'.

2. To select the best method of blending the ingredients together for that particular type of cake and to follow the recommended method of handling the ingredients, i.e. 'folding gently' when advised

to do this. Rubbing-in is an ideal method for family type cakes, for it is quick and easy, but the cakes are generally less light and smooth in texture than those produced by creaming the fat and sugar or by whisking eggs and sugar. The whisking method on the other hand gives such an ultra-light texture that it is quite unsuitable for fruit cakes. There is more about these methods in the various Blue Prints.

3. To bake the cake, loaf or biscuits correctly. It is essential to appreciate that individual ovens vary a great deal and that suggested temperatures in recipes can be based on the 'average' oven only.

Always consult your own manufacturer's instruction card or book the first time you bake a particular type of cake.

Baking too quickly will set the outside of a cake in too short a period, make it over-brown and prevent the heat penetrating to the centre, so you may well have an over-cooked cake or loaf on the outside and a nearly 'raw' mixture in the centre.

Baking too slowly can prevent a cake or loaf from rising properly and gives a heavy texture.

4. Take care when turning cakes out of the tins. Many a perfect cake is spoiled by a little part 'breaking-away' as it is turned out; this could probably be avoided. Allow all cakes to stand for 2–3 minutes in the tin before turning out, this allows the mixture to contract slightly. Certain cakes and biscuits should be cooled completely before being handled and this information is given in the recipes.

Perhaps you have never made your own bread, please try it once in a while as the Blue Print on page 58 gives very detailed instructions.

I have chosen some of the cakes and buns made by rubbing the fat into the flour as 'family' cakes, for these are quickly made and most of them are reasonably economical.

● **AVOID** *Making the mixture too soft, for since the fat is rubbed into the flour, it often looks deceptively stiff. Sketch 2 shows the consistency for small cakes, Sketch 4 the slow dropping consistency ideal for most large cakes: Using too much fat for this type of mixture, unless in a specific recipe: Baking too slowly.*
● **TO RECTIFY** *If you feel you have made the mixture for small cakes too soft either work in extra flour (which will slightly spoil the proportions and flavour) or put the mixture into patty tins or paper cases so it does not spread too badly.*
● **SHORT CUT** *There are many cake mixes on the market which will enable you to follow most of the recipes on these pages.*

Blue Print Recipe

Vanilla Buns

8 oz. (2C) self-raising flour (or plain flour with 2 teaspoons baking powder) · 4 oz. (½C) fat (choose margarine, butter or cooking fat) · 4–6 oz. (½–¾C) caster sugar · ¼ teaspoon vanilla essence · 2 eggs* · little milk. To decorate: few lumps sugar. *If wished use 1 egg only.

To make Sieve the flour or flour and baking powder into a mixing bowl. Add the fat then rub this into the flour with the tips of your fingers until like fine breadcrumbs. Lift the mixture as Sketch 1 to incorporate air. Add the sugar. Beat the vanilla essence with the eggs and stir into the fat mixture, blend well. Add a very little milk, if necessary, to make a sticky mixture.
To cook Grease and flour 2 flat baking trays or sheets. Lift out teaspoons of the mixture and put on the trays. Shape into rounds with the help of a second teaspoon, see Sketch 3. Leave room for the cakes to spread in cooking. Crush the lumps of sugar lightly and sprinkle over the cakes. Bake for 12–15 minutes above the centre of a moderately hot to hot oven, 400–425°F, Gas Mark 5–6.
To serve With coffee or tea. *All recipes based on this make 12–14 buns.*

Rich Vanilla Buns

Ingredients as Blue Print but use nearly 6 oz. (nearly ¾C) fat, 2 eggs and no milk. These are very brittle when cooked so cool for a few minutes before removing from the trays.

Jam Buns

Ingredients as Blue Print MINUS crushed sugar topping and PLUS a little jam and caster sugar.
Prepare the buns as the Blue Print, put the mixture on to the trays. Make an indentation in each bun with a floured finger. Put in some jam and bring the mixture up round the jam. Sprinkle with a little caster sugar. Bake as the Blue Print.

Rock Buns

Ingredients as Blue Print MINUS vanilla essence and sugar topping and PLUS 4–6 oz. (½–¾C) dried fruit.
Add the fruit with the sugar. Bake as the Blue Print. (Illustrated on page 41).

Orange Buns

Ingredients as Blue Print MINUS vanilla essence and sugar topping and PLUS grated rind of 2 oranges and a little chopped candied orange peel. Add the orange rind and peel with the sugar. Bake as the Blue Print, allow to cool and then dust with sieved icing sugar or decorate as the recipe below.

Orange Jamaican Buns

Orange buns above; 6–8 oz. (1¼C) icing sugar; little orange juice; 2–3 tablespoons candied orange peel; 2–3 tablespoons chopped plain chocolate or chocolate 'dots'.
Allow the orange buns to cool. Blend the icing sugar with enough orange juice to give a stiff spreading consistency. Spread in the centre of each bun and top with the candied peel and chocolate.

From the top: Orange Jamaican buns, Orange buns, Rock buns, Vanilla buns and Jam buns

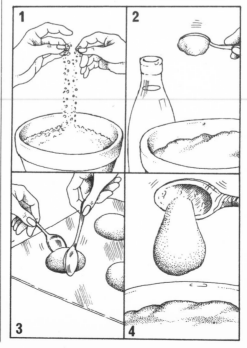

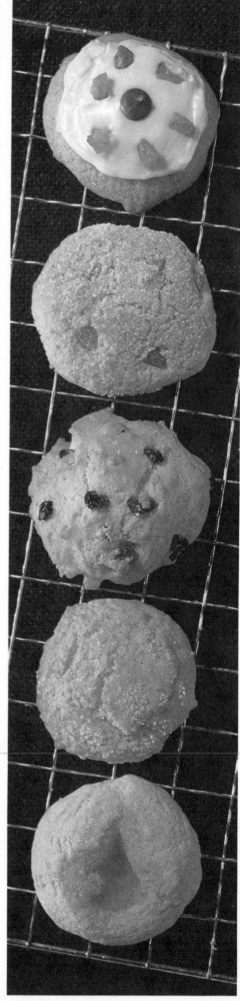

Orange Raisin Cake

Ingredients as Blue Print using all raisins, MINUS the spice and PLUS the grated rind of 2 oranges, which should be added with the sugar.

Bake as the Blue Print or bake in a loaf tin as illustrated for barely 1 hour.

To vary Top the cake with warmed marmalade and cover with a thick layer of coconut.

Coat the top of the cake with orange flavoured icing (see Orange Jamaican Buns opposite). Sprinkle a neat band of coconut round the top edge of the cake and decorate with glacé cherries.

Cherry Coconut Cake

6 oz. (1½C) self-raising flour (or plain flour and 2 *level* teaspoons baking powder); 4 oz. (½C) fat (see Blue Print opposite); 6 oz. (¾C) caster sugar; 2 oz. (generous ¾C) desiccated coconut; 3 oz. (⅜C) glacé cherries; 2 eggs.
Sieve the flour or flour and baking powder. Rub in the fat as the Blue Print opposite. Add the sugar and coconut. Halve the cherries, add ⅔ to the cake mixture then bind with the beaten eggs. Grease and flour an 8-inch cake tin or baking dish as shown in the picture. Put in the mixture and press the remaining halved cherries on top. Bake in the centre of a moderate oven, 350–375°F, Gas Mark 4–5, for approximately 1 hour. Test by pressing firmly on top.

Although this is delicious cold with tea or coffee it is equally good served hot as a dessert.

Oslo Apple Cake

For the apple layer: 3 large cooking apples; 1 oz. (¼C) sugar; 1 teaspoon finely grated lemon rind; 1 tablespoon lemon juice.
For the cake layer: 8 oz. (2C) self-raising flour (or plain flour and 2 *level* teaspoons baking powder); 4 oz. (½C) fat (see Blue Print opposite); 4 oz. (½C) caster sugar; 1 small egg.
Peel, core and slice the apples and cook with the sugar, lemon rind and juice. If necessary add a little water but keep a very firm mixture. When soft, strain to remove any surplus moisture and cool thoroughly. Sieve the flour or flour and baking powder. Rub in the fat. Add half the sugar and the egg. Knead together well then add the rest of the sugar. Roll or press out ⅔ of the dough to make an 8-inch round. Put into a well greased 8-inch cake or deep sandwich tin (preferably with a loose base). Top with the apple mixture. Roll out the remaining dough, cut into strips and make a lattice design over the top of the apples. Bake in the centre of a moderate oven, 350–375°F, Gas Mark 4–5, for about 40 minutes. Either eat hot with coffee or tea or allow to cool, but serve when fresh – delicious with fresh cream.

Empress Cake

Ingredients for the cake layer as Oslo Apple Cake but MINUS the apple layer and PLUS 3 oz. (⅜C) caster sugar, 3 oz. (¾C) finely chopped blanched almonds, ½ egg white and little water.
Prepare the base of the cake as recipe above. Mix the sugar, almonds, egg white and water together. Spread over the base, top with the lattice and bake as the Oslo Apple Cake.

To vary Blend 1 small boiled, sieved potato and a few drops almond essence with the ingredients for the almond layer above. This gives a soft moist texture which is very pleasant.

Storing and Freezing *Keep in an airtight tin for a very limited period. The uncooked cake dough may be stored overnight before baking. The cakes on these two pages freeze well, particularly the Empress Cake and Oslo Apple Cake and these may be heated gently from the frozen state. The other cakes are better thawed out slowly.*
To use any left over *Use these cakes as quickly as you can as they 'dry-out' easily.*

Granny's spice cake

You will often find that large cakes made by the rubbing-in method have a tendency to crack slightly on top as the cake on this page. This is not a fault in rather 'short' crumbly cakes that have a pleasantly crisp textured crust. All spoon measures throughout this book are level, but where I insert the word it is of particular importance.

Blue Print Recipe

Granny's Spice Cake

12 oz. (3C) self-raising flour (or plain flour and 3 *level* teaspoons baking powder) · 1–2 teaspoons allspice · 6–8 oz. (¾–1C) fat (see Blue Print opposite) · 6–8 oz. (¾–1C) caster or light brown sugar · 6–8 oz. (about 1C) mixed dried fruit · 2 eggs · milk to mix.

To make Sieve the flour or flour and baking powder and spice together. Rub in the fat as described in the Blue Print opposite, add the sugar, fruit, the beaten eggs and enough milk to make a sticky consistency, see Sketch 4. Put into a greased and floured 7–8-inch round cake tin, smooth flat on top.
To cook Bake in the centre of a moderate oven, 350–375°F, Gas Mark 4–5, for approximately 1 hour for an 8-inch tin, 1¼ hours for a 7-inch tin. Reduce the heat to very moderate, 325–350°F, Gas Mark 3–4, after 45 minutes. Test by pressing quite hard on top, and the cake is cooked when quite firm to the touch.
To serve When fresh, this type of cake is delicious with cheese.
To vary Omit the spice or use ground ginger or cinnamon.
Use all one kind of fruit such as currants or sultanas.

Cherry coconut cake and Orange raisin cake

The biscuits and cookies on this and the next page are based on several methods of mixing the ingredients and reference will be made to relevant Blue Prints. The points listed below, however, apply to all biscuits and biscuit-type cookies.

● **AVOID** *Making any biscuit dough too soft and sticky by adding excess liquid. You cannot over-handle most biscuit doughs, the more you knead the better the texture and if the dough seems too dry, knead very well before adding extra liquid. You will probably find that handling produces the right texture: Baking too quickly, most biscuit doughs need steady baking.*

● **TO RECTIFY** *If you have made a somewhat soft biscuit dough, chill for several hours and then try to handle it: If the biscuits seem to be baking too rapidly, lower the oven temperature immediately.*

● **SHORT CUTS** *Use the quick creaming fats which save time in blending: See the short cuts suggested in the sketches.*

Blue Print Recipe
Orange Biscuits

These are made by the rubbing-in method.
8 oz. (2C) flour, preferably plain · 5 oz. ($\frac{5}{8}$C) margarine or butter · 4–6 oz. ($\frac{1}{2}$–$\frac{3}{4}$C) caster sugar · very finely grated rind of 1 or 2 oranges.
To make Put the flour into a mixing bowl. Rub in the margarine or butter as the Blue

Print on page 42. Add half the sugar and orange rind. Knead firmly and work in the rest of the sugar. This dough should need *no* liquid but if necessary add a *few* drops orange juice.

Put the dough on to a very lightly floured pastry board. Roll out very firmly until about $\frac{1}{8}$-inch in thickness. Cut into rounds about 2–2$\frac{1}{2}$-inches in diameter or follow the directions in Sketches 1 and 2. Put on to un-greased baking trays. These biscuits should not spread (with self-raising flour they may spread a little). Prick lightly with a fork.
To cook Put as near the centre of the oven as possible and bake for about 10–12 minutes in a very moderate oven, 325–350°F, Gas Mark 3–4. Cool on the baking trays.
To serve With tea or coffee or as an accompaniment to ice cream. *Makes 14–18.*

Orange Laurel Rings

Ingredients as Blue Print PLUS angelica and a little sieved jam or marmalade (optional).
Prepare the dough as the Blue Print but cut into rings instead of rounds. Bake as the Blue Print. Decorate with pieces of angelica. These can be brushed first with a little jam

or marmalade to make sure they stick on t the biscuit. *Makes 18–20.*

Orange Cream Cookies

Ingredients as Blue Print PLUS 2 oz. ($\frac{1}{4}$C butter, 4 oz. (nearly 1C) sieved icing suga and finely grated rind of 1 orange.
Make the dough as the Blue Print. Roll ou and cut an equal number of rounds and ring (the size to fit on top). Bake as the Blue Prin allow to cool. Do not decorate until the da you intend to serve these as the butter icin can soften the biscuits. Cream the butte nearly all the icing sugar and grated orang rind together. Spread the rounds with a thi layer of the butter icing. Place the rings o top, dust with the remaining icing sugar Use the remaining butter cream to pip rosettes to fill the centre 'hole'. *Makes 8–9*

Sugar Rings

Ingredients as Blue Print but MINUS grate orange rind and PLUS 1 egg white, 2 oz. ($\frac{1}{4}$C caster sugar and few drops vanilla essence Make the dough as the Blue Print but cu into rings. Bake as the Blue Print for abou 8–9 minutes until well set and nearly cooked Remove from the oven. Whisk the egg whit until it begins to hold its shape. It must no be as stiff as a meringue. Fold in nearly all th sugar and the vanilla essence and sprea over the nearly cooked biscuits. Dredge wit the remaining sugar. Return to the oven but lower the heat to very cool, 250–275°F Gas Mark $\frac{1}{2}$–1, and leave for about 4 minutes until the topping is very crisp bu still white. *Makes 18–20.*

Left to right: Orange laurel rings, Cherry ginger cookies, Chocolate shortbreads, Sugar rings, Zebra biscuits and Orange cream cookies

Zebra Biscuits

Ingredients as Blue Print MINUS the currants and PLUS ¾–1 teaspoon instant coffee, little water and 2–3 oz. plain chocolate.
Method as Blue Print. Blend the coffee with the egg yolk, mix well then beat into the creamed fat and sugar. Add the flour and a few drops of water, if necessary. Roll out and bake as the Blue Print; but there is no need to grease the baking trays. Allow to cool. Do not ice until the day you intend to serve the biscuits.
Melt the chocolate in a basin over hot, but not boiling, water. Put into a greaseproof bag with a small hole at the base or use a fine writing pipe. Pipe lines of chocolate across the biscuits. *Makes 20–24.*

Traffic Light Biscuits

Ingredients as Blue Print MINUS the currants and PLUS a little raspberry jam or some glacé cherries, lemon curd or marmalade and greengage jam.
Make the biscuit dough as the Blue Print, roll out and cut into neat fingers. Make small holes in half the fingers with a very tiny cutter (or use a thimble). Bake as the Blue Print. When cooked and cold, sandwich with

a little jam. Put either red jam or half a cherry in one 'hole', curd or marmalade in the next space and the greengage jam in the third. Jam does not soften biscuits like a soft icing so these may be decorated and stored. *Makes 10–12.*

Bourbon Biscuits 1.

Ingredients as Blue Print MINUS the currants and 1 level tablespoon flour and PLUS 2 level tablespoons cocoa, a little caster sugar, 2 oz. (¼C) butter and 4 oz. (nearly 1C) sieved icing sugar.
Sieve the flour and half the cocoa together then make the biscuit dough as the Blue Print. Roll out and cut into fingers. Prick neatly and dust with a very little caster sugar. Bake as the Blue Print and shake a little more sugar over the biscuits while still warm. Allow to cool. Cream the butter, sieved icing sugar and sieved cocoa together. Flavour with a few drops vanilla essence if wished. Sandwich the biscuits with this mixture. As the filling is stiff the biscuits store for a few days without softening. *Makes 14–16.*

Chocolate Shortbreads

Ingredients as Blue Print MINUS the currants and PLUS 1½ oz. fat and 2–3 oz. chocolate and use self-raising flour (or plain flour with 1 teaspoon baking powder).

More Biscuits

The biscuits on this page are based on the creaming method; they are all easy to make and not too extravagant. Remember you can put biscuits on to ungreased baking trays and sheets, unless the recipe contains syrup or treacle, oatmeal, dried fruit or glacé fruit or nuts (including ground almonds), chocolate or cheese. In these cases it is wiser to grease the trays lightly.

Blue Print Recipe

Currant Crisps

These are made by the creaming method.
4 oz. (½C) butter, margarine or cooking fat · 4 oz. (½C) caster sugar · 1 egg yolk · 4 oz. (generous ½C) currants · 8 oz. (2C) flour, preferably plain

To make   Cream the butter, margarine or cooking fat and sugar until soft and light. Add the egg yolk and beat again. Stir in the currants and flour. Knead well, then roll out until about ⅛–¼-inch thick. If using quick creaming margarine or cooking fat put all the ingredients listed in the above recipe into a bowl. Beat for about 2 minutes then knead well, roll out and cut into shapes. Put on to lightly greased baking trays.
To cook   Bake for 10–12 minutes in, or near, the centre of a very moderate oven, 325–350°F, Gas Mark 3–4. Cool on the baking trays.
To serve   With tea or coffee. *Makes 20–24.*
To vary   Add a little mixed spice to the flour. Use mixed fruit or chopped glacé cherries.

Currant crisps

Method of mixing dough as Blue Print using the larger quantity of fat, but roll the mixture into about 15–16 balls. Put on the baking trays allowing room to spread. Bake as the Blue Print but allow about 15 minutes. Leave to cool. Melt the chocolate in a basin over hot, but not boiling water. Spread the chocolate over the biscuits placed on a wire rack and allow the chocolate to flow evenly and make thin lines on the biscuits.
To vary   Make as above, but roll out and cut into small squares.

Storing and Freezing   *All these biscuits (unless coated with soft icing) store well in airtight tins away from cakes, pastry or bread. There is no point in freezing them.*
To use any left over   *Put back into the tin. If they become soft, crisp for a short time in the oven.*

Bourbon biscuits

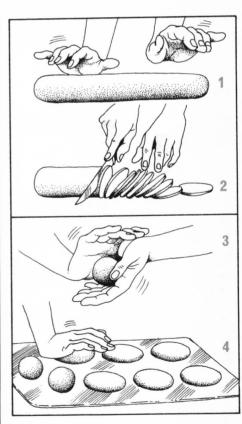

1. Make the biscuit dough into a long 'sausage-shape'. Chill if slightly sticky.

2. Cut into thin slices with a sharp knife—this is quicker and easier than cutting

with a pastry cutter.

3. Roll into small balls.

4. Put on baking tray. Flatten with a palette knife or the palm of your hand.

45

Viennese orange shortbreads

These piped Viennese shortbreads, delicately flavoured with orange, are delicious for a special occasion. They are prepared as the creaming method on the previous page. In order that they may hold their shape do not exceed the recommended amounts of butter and icing sugar. If you do not wish to pipe the mixture then roll in balls as the Cherry Ginger Cookies on this page.

Viennese Orange Shortbreads
Grated rind 1 large orange; 4 oz. (1C) plain flour; 4 oz. (1C) cornflour; 6 oz. (¾C) butter; 4 oz. (nearly 1C) sieved icing sugar. *For the filling and coating of icing sugar:* grated rind 1 large orange; 3 oz. (⅜C) butter; 6 oz. (nearly 1¼C) sieved icing sugar.
Put the grated orange rind into the mixing bowl. Make certain you have taken just the top orange 'zest', not the bitter white pith that lies under the skin. Sieve the flour and cornflour into a small basin. Add the butter

For Special Occasions

and icing sugar to the orange rind and cream very well, by hand or mixer, until very soft and light. This is most important if you wish to pipe the mixture. Gradually beat in the flour and cornflour. Put the mixture into a cloth piping bag with a ½-inch rose nozzle and pipe out about 14–16 large neat rose shapes on an ungreased baking tray. Bake in the centre of a very moderate to moderate oven, 325–350°F, Gas Mark 3–4, for about 15–20 minutes. Look at the shortbreads as

they cook, for they must crisp without becoming too brown. Allow to cool on the baking tray. Cream the finely grated orange rind, butter and nearly all the icing sugar together. Sandwich the biscuits together with the butter icing and dust with the remaining icing sugar. *Makes 7–8 complete shortbreads.*

Cherry Ginger Cookies
Use the recipe above for the biscuit dough, but not the filling. Omit the orange rind and sieve 1 teaspoon powdered ginger with the flour and cornflour. Roll into about 14–16 balls, flatten into rounds and bake as the recipe above. When cold and ready to serve, top with icing made by blending 8 oz. (nearly 2C) icing sugar with enough water to make a spreading consistency. Spoon the icing into the centre of each cookie and top with a glacé cherry (Illustrated on page 44). *Makes 14–16.*

Macaroons and Meringues

These are delicious to serve not only with tea or coffee, but also as a dessert. They can be varied in many ways to give interest to meals and are suitable for both Family and Special Occasions.
Macaroons may be topped with ice cream for a special occasion and meringues can be filled with cream, cream and fruit or ice cream.

Blue Print Recipe

Coconut Macaroons

2 egg whites · 5–6 oz. ($\frac{5}{8}$–$\frac{3}{4}$C) caster sugar · approximately 6 oz. (nearly 2C) desiccated coconut · rice flour or corn-flour (optional, see method) · rice paper (see method). To decorate: glacé cherries.

To make Put the egg whites into a mixing bowl and whisk lightly; do not over-whip, the whites should just be 'frothy' not stiff. Add the sugar (the amount given above is on the generous side and if wished you can use as little as 4 oz. ($\frac{1}{2}$C)). Stir in the coconut steadily, as since egg whites vary in size you may need a little less than the amount given. The mixture should just roll into balls. If you wish a firmer texture then use a little less coconut and add 1–2 teaspoons rice flour or cornflour. When blended roll into about 10–12 balls. Either put on rice paper on baking trays or sheets, or grease these lightly and put on the balls. Allow room for the mixture to flatten out during cooking. Press half a glacé cherry on top of each biscuit.

To cook Bake in the centre of a very moderate to moderate oven, 350–375°F, Gas Mark 4–5, for about 18–20 minutes. If you like a slightly sticky macaroon then put a dish of water in the oven while cooking.

To serve Remove from the baking trays or sheets when nearly cold, cut or tear round the rice paper and serve with tea or coffee or top with a scoop of ice cream. I like to put the ice cream on about 5 minutes early so it softens the macaroon slightly. *All recipes based on this make 10–12.*

● **AVOID** *Cooking macaroons too slowly otherwise they become too hard: Cooking meringues too quickly or they brown on the outside before becoming crisp.*

● **TO RECTIFY** *As you cannot rectify mistakes check the baking carefully.*

Storing and Freezing *Macaroons become dry after 1 or 2 days if stored in a tin. Meringues keep well for weeks. Macaroons can be wrapped and frozen and they store for some weeks without losing their soft texture inside. Meringues contain such a high percentage of sugar that they never become frozen.*

To use any left over *Macaroons can be crumbled and added to trifles. Meringues can be put back into the tin, unless they are filled with cream, etc., when they will soften very quickly. You can therefore freeze left over filled meringues.*

Put the egg whites into a bowl, free from any specks of dust or particles of egg yolk. Whisk until very stiff. Gradually whisk in half the sugar and fold in the remainder (alternative ways of adding the sugar are given on page 12). Brush the baking trays with a very little oil or butter, or brush greaseproof paper on the trays with oil. Either spoon or pipe the meringues on to the trays as Sketches 1 and 2. Bake in the coolest part of a very slow oven, 225–250°F, Gas Mark 0–$\frac{1}{2}$, for about 2 hours until crisp, but still white. Lift from the tin with a warm, but dry, palette knife. Store in an airtight tin until ready to fill.

Coconut macaroons

The meringues may either be filled with whipped cream or with butter icing, see recipe opposite for orange butter icing. You can flavour with vanilla instead of orange or other essences or a little sieved cocoa (as in the picture) or instant coffee. They are delicious if filled with fruit or ice cream. To incorporate more filling press the base of each meringue gently so you break this slightly and make a 'hollow', then sandwich two together with the filling. A 'nest' shape also enables you to use a generous amont of cream and other filling.

To tint meringues add a few drops of colouring essence to the egg whites before they are quite stiff.
To flavour meringues add a few drops essence to the egg whites before they are quite stiff. If you wish to add cocoa or instant coffee powder, blend either of these with the sugar.

Almond Macaroons
Flavour with almond essence, use ground almonds in place of coconut. Top with blanched almonds.

Oatmeal Macaroons
Use all rolled oats or half rolled oats and half coconut or ground almonds. Top with almonds or glacé cherries.

Crumb Macaroons
Use all crisp fine breadcrumbs or half crumbs and half coconut or ground almonds. Flavour breadcrumbs version well with essence, i.e. almond, rum or vanilla.

Meringues
The Blue Print on page 12 gives details about making the meringue mixture but some of the most important points are repeated below.
2 egg whites; 4 oz. ($\frac{1}{2}$C) caster sugar (or use half caster and half sieved icing sugar).

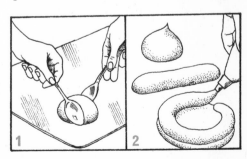

1. Take a spoonful of meringue mixture. Hold over the baking tray and form into a neat shape with a second spoon.

2. Put the mixture into a piping bag with a $\frac{1}{4}$-inch pipe. Pipe into rounds, fingers or nest shapes.

This method of blending ingredients is often used for cakes containing a high percentage of syrup, treacle or honey. The cakes are generally moist in texture, such as a gingerbread.

Blue Print Recipe

Golden Ginger Loaf

Melting Method for Mixing Cakes

10 oz. (2½C) plain flour · 1 level teaspoon bicarbonate of soda · ½ teaspoon ground ginger · 6 oz. (⅜C) clear honey · 4 oz. (½C) fat · 6 oz. (¾C) sugar · 2 tablespoons syrup from jar preserved ginger · 1½ tablespoons milk · 2 eggs · To decorate: 1 tablespoon honey · few leaves angelica · 2–3 tablespoons preserved ginger (cut in neat pieces).

To make Sieve the dry ingredients into the mixing bowl. To weigh the honey, put an empty saucepan on the scales, note the weight, then add 6 oz. honey. If the measuring cup is floured the honey (syrup or treacle) pours out easily into the saucepan. Add the fat and sugar. Heat gently until the fat melts, pour over the flour and beat well. Warm the syrup and milk in the pan, add to the flour mixture with the eggs and beat until smooth. Line a 2½–3-lb. loaf tin with greased greaseproof paper. Pour in the mixture.

To cook Bake in the centre of a slow to very moderate oven, 300–325°F, Gas Mark 2–3, for 1–1¼ hours until *just firm* to the touch, do not over-cook. Remove from the oven, cool in the tin for about 15 minutes. Remove from the tin, take off the paper, then brush the top with the honey and press the pieces of angelica and ginger into position.

To serve As a cake with coffee or tea, or spread with butter as a tea-bread. This is also delicious sliced and topped with apple purée.

To vary To make a darker, stronger flavoured loaf use golden syrup or black treacle, or a mixture of these, in place of honey. The amount of ground ginger may be increased to 2 teaspoons as the Blue Print has a very mild flavour.

● **AVOID** *Having the mixture too dry, most recipes produce a very soft texture before baking which gives a pleasantly moist cake: Baking too quickly, otherwise you will burn or over-cook the outside before the cake is set: Turning the cake out of the tin when freshly baked, or it could break due to the weight of the syrup, honey or treacle.*

● **TO RECTIFY** *If the cake should appear dry, store for a week with an apple in the cake tin and this should produce the right texture.*

Iced Ginger Loaf

Make the variation of the Blue Print with all black treacle and 2 teaspoons ground ginger. When the loaf is cooked and cold, top with icing made by blending 6–8 oz. (1¼C) icing sugar with enough warm water to give a flowing consistency. Pour on top of the loaf and allow to 'trickle' down the sides. Leave until nearly set then top with pieces of preserved or crystallised ginger. (Illustrated on page 41).

Golden ginger loaf

The true gingerbread was served, as the name suggests, as a rich tea-bread. It is excellent with cheese or topped with fruit, especially apple sauce, and ice cream as a dessert. A rich gingerbread matures and improves in texture and taste if kept for at least a week before cutting.

More Cakes and Biscuits by the Melting Method

Gas Mark 3–4. It is advisable to put in one tray at a time so you do not have too many biscuits ready to roll at once. Remove from the oven, cool for 2–3 minutes, roll round the greased handle of a wooden spoon. Hold until biscuit begins to harden, remove care-

Almond sultana gingerbread

Brandy snaps

Make the gingerbread as the recipe above then add the sultanas and chopped almonds. Put the mixture into the prepared tin, top with the flaked almonds and bake as the Old Fashioned Gingerbread.

Brandy Snaps

These classic biscuits are ideal to store in a 100% airtight tin and to fill with whipped cream as a dessert, or to serve with ice cream instead of wafers. They are also a perfect choice for tea or coffee.

2 oz. ($\frac{1}{4}$C) butter or cooking fat; 2 oz. ($\frac{1}{4}$C) caster sugar; 2 oz. ($\frac{1}{8}$C) golden syrup; 2 oz. ($\frac{1}{2}$C) plain flour; $\frac{1}{4}$–$\frac{1}{2}$ teaspoon ground ginger; 1 teaspoon brandy or lemon juice (optional). If not using the brandy or lemon juice I always take away about 1 teaspoon of flour so the mixture is not too thick.

Melt the butter or fat with the sugar and golden syrup in a pan. Sieve the flour and ginger, stir into the syrup mixture and blend well, adding the brandy or lemon juice. Grease 2–3 baking trays or sheets. Put teaspoons of the mixture on these, allowing room for them to spread out into rounds of 3–4 inches. Bake for approximately 8–10 minutes near the centre of a very moderate to moderate oven, 325–350°F,

fully, cool on a wire cooling tray. Continue until all the biscuits are rolled. If some have hardened on the trays, warm for 1–2 minutes in the oven. *Makes 14–16.*

Yorkshire Parkin

Ingredients as the Old Fashioned Gingerbread PLUS 4 oz. ($\frac{2}{3}$C) coarse oatmeal and $\frac{1}{4}$ pint ($\frac{2}{3}$C) milk instead of 4 tablespoons, but MINUS half the bicarbonate of soda as this does not rise as well as a true Gingerbread.

Prepare as the Old Fashioned Gingerbread mixing the oatmeal with the flour. Bake as the Old Fashioned Gingerbread in an 8-inch tin. This is delicious covered with warmed golden syrup, after baking, then topped with a thick layer of chopped nuts and chopped preserved ginger and finally dusted with sieved icing sugar.

Storing and Freezing *The gingerbreads keep well in tins for several weeks, but can be wrapped and frozen if wished. Do not freeze the brandy snaps.*

To use any left over *If the gingerbread has become stale, steam gently until soft and serve hot with fruit or syrup sauce.*

Old Fashioned Gingerbread

8 oz. (2C) plain flour; $\frac{3}{4}$ teaspoon bicarbonate of soda; $\frac{1}{2}$–1 teaspoon ground cinnamon; 1$\frac{1}{2}$–2 teaspoons ground ginger; 4 oz. ($\frac{1}{2}$C) butter or cooking fat; 4 oz. (nearly $\frac{3}{4}$C) moist brown sugar; 5 oz. (just over $\frac{1}{4}$C) black treacle; 2 eggs; 4 tablespoons milk.

Sieve the dry ingredients. Put the butter or fat, sugar and treacle into a pan and melt carefully. Add to the dry ingredients, beat well, then add the eggs and milk. Beat again. Put into a 7–8-inch square tin, lined with well-greased greaseproof paper and bake in the centre of a slow to very moderate oven, 300–325°F, Gas Mark 2–3, for about 1$\frac{1}{4}$ hours. A 7-inch square cake takes rather longer than an 8-inch cake because of the greater depth of the mixture. Cut into squares to serve. (Illustrated on page 41).

Almond Sultana Gingerbread

Ingredients as the Old Fashioned Gingerbread PLUS 4–5 oz. (generous $\frac{1}{2}$C) sultanas and 2 tablespoons finely chopped blanched almonds and 2–3 tablespoons flaked blanched almonds.

The Creaming Method for Making Cakes

This method is used for making the largest selection of cakes, from a light Victoria sandwich to a Christmas cake.

Blue Print Recipe

Victoria Sandwich or Butter Sponge

4 oz. (½C) margarine, butter or cooking fat · 4 oz. (½C) caster sugar · 2 large eggs · 4 oz. (1C) self-raising flour (with plain flour use 1 teaspoon baking powder).

To make Cream the margarine, butter or fat with the sugar until soft and light in colour, use a wooden spoon for this. If using the mixer warm the bowl *but not the fat* to ease mixing. Gradually beat in the eggs, then fold in the sieved flour or flour and baking powder with a metal spoon. Divide the mixture between two 6–7-inch greased and floured sandwich tins.

To cook Bake above the centre of a moderate oven, 350–375°F, Gas Mark 4–5, for 15–20 minutes until just firm to the touch. Cool for 2–3 minutes in the tins, turn out carefully.

To serve Fill with jam or jam and whipped cream and top with sieved icing sugar or caster sugar and serve with coffee, or for tea, or fill with fruit and cream.

● **AVOID** *Melting the fat, for the secret of success is to incorporate as much air as possible into the mixture by beating well: Adding the eggs too quickly, for this could curdle the mixture: Over-beating the flour, as this spoils the texture.*

● **TO RECTIFY** *If the fat has been melted, allow to cool and solidify again before trying to cream the mixture: If the eggs have been added too quickly and the mixture shows signs of curdling, blend in a little sieved flour.*

● **SHORT CUTS** *Use the quick creaming margarines and fats and put all the ingredients into the basin and beat for about 2 minutes. As less air has been beaten into the mixture it is advisable to sieve an extra level teaspoon baking powder with each 4 oz. (1C) flour. This means however that the cakes tend to dry out more easily.*

Orange Layer Cake

Ingredients as Blue Print PLUS 2 tablespoons orange juice and an extra 1 oz. flour. Use 2 small eggs. *For the filling:* 4 oz. (½C) butter or margarine; 8 oz. (1¾C) sieved icing sugar; grated rind 1 orange; little orange juice. *For the icing:* 6 oz. (1¼C) icing sugar; little orange juice; pink colouring; few crystallised orange slices; little pieces of angelica.

Make the sponge as the Blue Print, but mix the orange juice with the beaten eggs and bake in 7-inch tins. When the cakes are cool, split to give 4 layers. Cream the butter or margarine and icing sugar, add the orange rind and enough juice to make the consistency of a thick whipped cream. Sandwich the cakes together with most of this, top with the icing made by blending the sugar with enough orange juice to give a soft spreading consistency and 2 or 3 drops of colouring. When firm, pipe rosettes of the remaining butter icing and decorate with portions of crystallised orange slices and little pieces of angelica.

Walnut Layer Cake

Method of mixing cake as Blue Print, but use 6 oz. (¾C) margarine or cooking fat; 6 oz. (¾C) caster sugar; 3 large eggs; 6 oz. (1½C) self-raising flour (or plain flour and 1½ teaspoons baking powder).

Make the cake as the Blue Print, but bake in two 7–8-inch sandwich tins for about 20–25 minutes. Make vanilla butter icing with 8 oz. (1C) butter, etc. (see page 54). Use two-thirds of this to sandwich the cake and coat the sides, then roll the sides in chopped walnuts. Spread the rest of the butter icing on top of the cake and mark neatly with a skewer,

Butterfly cake

then decorate with glacé cherries. (Illustrated on page 41.)

Butterfly Cakes

The basis of these cakes is a small plain sponge cake, which can be made exactly as the Blue Print but as you wish the little cakes to rise into peaks it is better to use only 3 oz. (⅜C) margarine to give a firmer texture. The sugar can be reduced to 3 oz. (⅜C) if wished or left as the Blue Print. Put the mixture into about 12–15 well greased and floured patty tins or into paper cake cases. Bake for about 10–12 minutes towards the top of a moderately hot to hot oven, 400–425°F, Gas Mark 5–6. When cold cut off the tops, pipe or spread a little butter icing (see page 54) or whipped cream on top of the cakes. Halve the slices removed, press into the icing or cream to form 'wings'. Dust with sieved icing sugar if wished. *Makes 12–15.*

Orange layer cake

Honey and Lemon Cake

For the cake: 6 oz. (¾C) quick creaming margarine or fat; 5–6 oz. (⅝–¾C) caster sugar; 3 large eggs; 1 tablespoon clear honey; 6 oz. (1½C) self-raising flour and 1 level teaspoon baking powder (with plain flour use 2½ level teaspoons baking powder); few drops almond essence. *For the icing:* 4 oz. (½C) quick creaming margarine; 8 oz. (nearly 2C) sieved icing sugar; generous tablespoon lemon juice. *To decorate:* few blanched almonds; angelica; violet petals or mimosa balls.

Put the margarine, sugar, eggs and honey into the mixing bowl. Sieve the flour and baking powder into the bowl, add the essence. Beat until smooth. Grease and flour, or line two 7–8-inch sandwich tins with greased greaseproof paper. Divide the mixture between the two tins, bake just above the centre of a very moderate to moderate oven 325–350°F. Gas Mark 3–4 for approximately 30–35 minutes until firm. Turn out and allow to cool.

Note: Choose a lower temperature than for Victoria Sandwich because of the honey content.

Beat the ingredients for the icing together and use half to sandwich the cakes together. Spread the remaining icing on top of the cake. Decorate as in the photograph, forming flower petals with the almonds, leaves and stalks with the angelica and flower centres with pieces of violet petals or mimosa balls.

To vary Omit the almond essence from the cake and add the finely grated rind of 2 lemons or 2 oranges.
Omit a little icing sugar and add 1–2 teaspoons honey in the icing.
Use orange juice to flavour the icing instead of lemon juice.

The quantities of icing given in the recipe are fairly modest. For a thicker layer use proportions suggested on page 54.

Mocha Torte

For the cake: 3 oz. (⅜C) quick creaming margarine or fat; 3 oz. (½C) soft brown sugar; 3 large eggs; 2 tablespoons sweetened coffee essence; 3 oz. (¾C) self-raising flour and 1 level teaspoon baking powder (with plain flour use 1¾ level teaspoons baking powder); 3 oz. digestive biscuits. *For the icing:* 4 oz. (½C) quick creaming margarine; 12 oz. (nearly 3C) sieved icing sugar; 3 oz. (¾C) sieved cocoa; 5 tablespoons hot water. *To decorate:* few digestive biscuits.

Put the margarine or fat, sugar, eggs and coffee essence into the mixing bowl. Sieve the flour and baking powder into the bowl, add the coarsly crushed biscuits, beat together until smooth. Line the bottoms of three 7-inch sandwich tins with greaseproof paper, grease and flour the tins. Divide the mixture between the tins, bake in, or near, the centre of a very moderate oven, 325°F, Gas Mark 3 for about 20–25 minutes until firm. Cool for 5 minutes, turn out carefully, allow to cool.

To make the icing beat all the ingredients together. Sandwich the cakes together with about ⅓ of the mixture. Spread another ⅓ round the sides of the cake and roll in finely crushed digestive biscuit crumbs. Spread the top of the cake with most of the remaining icing. Pipe a design, as shown in the picture, with a star pipe and decorate with the biscuit crumbs.

Primrose Cakes

For the cakes: 6 oz. (¾C) quick creaming margarine or fat; 6 oz. (¾C) caster sugar;

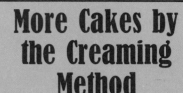

More Cakes by the Creaming Method

The cakes shown in the picture on this page were made with soft table margarine and by the speedy one stage method described on page 50 and in the Blue Print. To compensate for the very short creaming period extra baking powder is added. In both the Mocha Torte and Lemon and Honey cake the extra amount is slightly less than the usual 1 teaspoon to each 4 oz. (1C) flour, this is to ensure that the cake rises with an *even flat* surface for perfect icing.

Blue Print Recipe

One Stage Mixes

Choose quick creaming margarine or fat.
Choose a large mixing bowl for easy beating.
Put in *all* the ingredients (or ingredients as specified in the recipe).
If creaming by hand use a wooden spoon, beat gently for about ½ minute so the flour etc. does not 'fly' out of the bowl, when blended increase the beating action. If using an electric mixer switch to the lowest speed until the ingredients are blended, then use medium speed.

3 large eggs; 6 oz. (1½C) self-raising flour and 1½ level teaspoons baking powder (with plain flour use 3 level teaspoons baking powder). *For the icing:* 3 oz. (⅜C) quick creaming margarine; 8 oz. (nearly 2C) sieved icing sugar; 1 tablespoon milk. *To decorate:* 2 oz. (¾C) desiccated coconut; few drops green colouring; 18 mimosa balls or silver balls.

Mix the ingredients for the cake together, then put into an oblong tin approximately 11 × 7-inches lined with greased greaseproof paper and bake as the Honey and Lemon cake, on this page, for about 25 minutes until firm. Turn out and cool then cut into 18 rounds with a 2-inch cutter (any pieces left may be used in a trifle). Beat the ingredients for the icing together. Colour the coconut by blending the green colouring into this. Allow to dry for an hour before using. Coat the sides of the cakes in some of the icing, then in the coconut.

Pipe a design on top of the cakes with the rest of the icing, as shown in the picture, and decorate with the mimosa balls. *Makes 18.*

Honey and lemon cake, Mocha torte and Primrose cakes

Fruit Cakes by the Creaming Method

The essential points for cakes made by the creaming method are described on page 50, so the Blue Print on this page simply adds information on preparing dried fruit and nuts.

Blue Print

Preparing Fruit and Nuts

When you wash dried fruit, use hot water if the fruit seems very dry, for this will make it 'plump'. Use cold water though if the fruit is pleasantly moist. Spread out on flat trays and leave in the air for 48 hours to dry. Chop candied peel, remove excess sugar (this could be used for stewing fruit, but is too 'solid' for cakes). Halve glacé cherries and mix with the flour, this prevents the cherries sinking to the bottom of the cake, but see the special remarks under cherry cake. Blanch almonds, dry well and chop. Use chopped angelica, for a change.

● **AVOID** *Using damp fruit.*
● **TO RECTIFY** *If you have washed the fruit and cannot allow the recommended time for it to dry, rub dry in a cloth and reduce the amount of liquid in the recipe. This is not ideal however, it is far better to allow the correct drying time.*
● **SHORT CUT** *Use pre-packed cleaned fruit and ready-chopped peel.*

Dundee Cake

6 oz. ($\frac{3}{4}$C) margarine or butter; 6 oz. ($\frac{3}{4}$C) caster sugar; 3 large eggs, 8 oz. (2C) flour*; 1 lb. (2C—well filled) mixed dried fruit; 2 oz. ($\frac{1}{4}$C) glacé cherries; 2 oz. ($\frac{1}{4}$C) chopped candied peel; little milk. *To decorate:* 1–2 oz. ($\frac{1}{5}$–$\frac{2}{5}$C) blanched almonds.
*Either half self-raising and half plain flour or all plain flour with 1$\frac{1}{2}$ level teaspoons baking powder.
Cream the margarine or butter and sugar together and add the eggs, as the Blue Print on page 50. Fold in the sieved flours or flour and baking powder gently, then the fruit, cherries and peel and just enough milk to make a soft consistency. Put into a 7–8-inch greased and floured, or lined and greased tin and cover with the almonds. Brush these with a little egg white (there is enough left in the egg shells after making the cake). Bake for 2–2$\frac{1}{4}$ hours in the centre of a very moderate oven, 325°F, Gas Mark 3, reducing the heat to slow after about 1–1$\frac{1}{2}$ hours. Cool slightly, turn out carefully.

To vary
Economical Dundee cake Use only 5 oz. ($\frac{5}{8}$C) fat and sugar, 2 eggs and all self-raising flour, or plain flour with 2 teaspoons baking powder. Mix with milk to give a soft dropping consistency. The amount of dried fruit can be reduced to 12 oz. (generous 1$\frac{1}{2}$C). Reduce the baking time to about 1$\frac{3}{4}$ hours. This cake tends to rise in a pleasant round instead of being flat.
Spiced Dundee cake Sieve 1–2 teaspoons mixed spice with the flour.

Almond Cake

Ingredients as the Dundee cake but add 2 oz. ($\frac{1}{2}$C) ground almonds to the flour.

Put the mixture into the tin, but do not cover with blanched almonds. Bake as the Dundee cake. Brush with a little egg white or apricot jam when the cake is cooked, cover with a thick layer of blanched and flaked almonds and brown for a few minutes under the grill.

Cherry Cake

6 oz. ($\frac{3}{4}$C) margarine or butter; 6 oz. ($\frac{3}{4}$C) caster sugar; 3 large eggs; 8 oz. (2C) plain flour; 6 oz. ($\frac{3}{4}$C) glacé cherries.
Cream the margarine or butter and sugar, add the eggs and then fold in the flour. Use no more moisture. The cherries may be rinsed in cold water, then dried on kitchen paper. This makes sure they will not drop to the bottom of the cake, but personally I find in this particular cake that if I halve them and blend them with the flour they 'stay put'. Obviously the cake does not rise a great deal as it has all plain flour. If you want a lighter type of cake use half self-raising and half plain flour or all plain flour with 1 teaspoon baking powder. Bake for about 2 hours in a slow to very moderate oven, 300–325°F, Gas Mark 2–3 until firm to the touch.
To vary Use 6 oz. (1$\frac{1}{2}$C) flour and 2 oz. ($\frac{1}{2}$C) ground almonds.

Storing and Freezing cakes made by the creamed method *Rich fruit cakes keep well in tins. All other cakes freeze well.*
To use any left over *Plain cakes can be used in puddings (instead of breadcrumbs) or for trifles. Stale fruit cakes can be sliced, fried in hot butter as fritters and served as a pudding.*

Economical Dundee cake (above)
Almond cake (below)

Whisking Method of Making Cakes

The sponges made by this method are often considered the only 'true' sponges. This is also the method for the classic French Genoese pastry (see page 139).

Blue Print Recipe

Sponge Sandwich

3 large eggs · 3–4 oz. ($\frac{3}{8}$–$\frac{1}{2}$C) caster sugar · 3 oz. ($\frac{3}{4}$C) flour*.
*So much air has been beaten into the eggs and sugar that raising agent is really unnecessary, but you can use self-raising flour if wished.

To make   Put the eggs and sugar (the larger quantity produces a lighter sponge) into a basin and whisk hard until a thick mixture. You should see the mark of the whisk. Sieve the flour very well, then fold into the whisked eggs with a metal spoon or palette knife. The mixture should flow readily, so if it seems a little stiff add up to a tablespoon hot water or flavouring (see below). Divide between two 7–8-inch well-greased and floured sandwich tins or tins lined with greased greaseproof paper. If preferred coat the tins with fat then with an equal amount of caster sugar and flour.

To cook   Bake above the centre of a moderately hot oven, 400°F, Gas Mark 5–6, for approximately 15 minutes. If preferred bake in one prepared cake tin for 30–35 minutes in the centre of a very moderate to moderate oven, 325–350°F, Gas Mark 3–4. Cool for 2–3 minutes before turning out of the tins or tin. When cold sandwich the sponges with jam or jam and cream, or split the one cake if wished and fill.

To serve   With tea or coffee or as a dessert, particularly suitable when filled with cream and fruit.

● **AVOID** *Overhandling the flour when blending the ingredients. It must be folded carefully into the eggs and sugar.*

● **TO RECTIFY** *There is no remedy for a sponge where the flour has been over-beaten. You are sure to have a rather heavy 'tight' texture, instead of a light one.*

● **SHORT CUT** *Make use of the packet sponges which do produce very acceptable results.*

Orange Sponge

Ingredients as Blue Print PLUS finely grated rind of 1–2 oranges and 1 tablespoon hot orange juice. *To fill and decorate:* orange marmalade or orange curd; $\frac{1}{2}$ pint ($1\frac{1}{3}$C) thick cream; little sugar; Curaçao (optional); crystallised orange slices.

Make the sponge as the Blue Print, but add the orange rind to the eggs and sugar, and fold the hot orange juice in after the flour. Bake as the Blue Print. When cold, fill with marmalade or orange curd and a little whipped cream. Sweeten the remainder of the cream and flavour with a few drops of Curaçao if liked. Pipe round the edge of the sponge as shown in the picture. Decorate with the orange slices.

Lemon Sponge

As the Orange Sponge, but use lemon rind and juice, fill with lemon curd and cream and decorate with fresh lemon slices. If wishing to flavour the cream use an apricot brandy.

Chocolate Sponge

Ingredients as Blue Print MINUS 1 tablespoon flour and PLUS 1 tablespoon cocoa sieved with the flour. Fill with chocolate butter icing or cream.

Coffee Sponge

Ingredients as Blue Print but use 1 tablespoon very strong hot coffee instead of the hot water in the Blue Print.

Sponge Flan

Use the same method of making as the Blue Print, but use only 1 egg etc., for a 6–7-inch flan tin or 2 eggs etc., for an 8–9-inch flan tin. Bake as the sandwich in the Blue Print, allowing about 10–12 minutes. Turn out, allow to cool, then fill with fruit and glaze as a fruit flan made with pastry (see page 5).

Storing and Freezing   *The sponge should be cooked as soon as possible after mixing. The cooked sponge tends to dry if kept more than 1 or 2 days, but freezes well.*
To use any left over   *Any stale sponge is excellent for making trifles.*

Orange and lemon sponges

The recipes on this page can turn a simple Victoria sandwich (page 50) or light sponge (page 53) into a special gâteau. The Royal icing opposite is ideal for rich fruit cakes.

● **AVOID** *Using too heavy or stiff an icing on these delicate cakes, for they would break the sponge and make it difficult to cut.*
● **TO RECTIFY** *While one cannot change a firm icing, such as Royal icing, it is possible to make other icings softer in texture so they do not break the cake.*
● **SHORT CUT** *Do not bother to sieve the icing sugar for simple glacé or water icings (unless in very hard lumps), if mixed with the liquid and allowed to stand for a while the icing will be quite smooth. The icing sugar must be sieved for other icings though.*

Choice for Fillings and Toppings

Use whipped cream, flavoured with a little vanilla and sweetened, as either a filling or topping.
Another excellent filling for light cakes (as well as pastries) is the Vanilla Cream, below. This is rarely used as a topping.
Butter icing is not only ideal to pipe on light cakes, but is excellent for fillings too.
American frosting, below, is equally good as a filling and topping for sponges as for fruit cakes.
Glacé or water icing is one of the best toppings for light cakes, but is rarely chosen for a filling.

Blue Print Recipes

1. Water or Glacé Icing

In this simple icing, the icing sugar is blended with liquid (often just water) and colouring and flavouring, if desired. The consistency varies slightly, the icing shown in the picture on page 41 was sufficiently soft to 'trickle' down the sides, but generally it should be slightly stiffer.

To 8 oz. (1¾C) icing sugar use about ¾–1 tablespoon liquid for a firm mixture, or 1½–2 tablespoons for a very soft consistency. Blend the icing sugar with cold liquid or

Coating the sides of the cake.

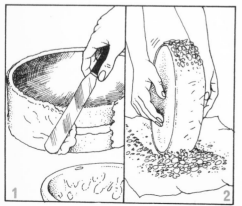

Icings & Fillings

Mocha hazel-nut gâteau

heat the liquid and sugar in a pan over a gentle heat for a better gloss.
Flavourings can be given by using orange, or other fruit juice, or coffee instead of water or adding a little cocoa, chocolate or essences.
The quantity given above would coat the top of an 8-inch cake.

2. Butter Icing

This is made by creaming butter, margarine or fat with *sieved* icing sugar and flavouring. To 4 oz. (½C) butter or other fat allow 4 oz. (nearly 1C) icing sugar and flavouring for a soft butter icing, or up to 8 oz. (1¾C) icing sugar for a firmer texture.
Flavouring is given by adding very finely grated fruit rind (with a very little juice if wished), or instant coffee powder, or strong coffee or coffee essence, or chocolate or cocoa. Always add liquids gradually to prevent curdling.
The quantity above is enough to give a good layer of filling *or* topping for an 8-inch cake. If making butter icing for coating and filling you may like to be less generous with the amounts. The Mocha Gâteau pictured on this page uses coffee butter icing for filling and topping.

Mocha Hazel-nut Gâteau

6 oz. (¾C) butter or margarine; 6 oz. (¾C) caster sugar; 3 large eggs; 5 oz. (1¼C) self-raising flour (with plain flour use 1¼ teaspoons baking powder); ½ oz. cocoa; 1½ oz. very finely chopped hazel-nuts; 1 tablespoon strong coffee. *For the filling:* 10–12 oz. (1¼–1½C) butter or margarine; 1–1¼ lb. (3½–4½C) sieved icing sugar; 1–1½ tablespoons coffee essence or very strong coffee; 3–4 table-spoons chopped hazel-nuts; whole hazel-nuts to decorate.

Cream the butter or margarine and sugar, gradually add the beaten eggs, then fold in the sieved flour or flour and baking powder and cocoa. Add the chopped hazel-nuts and coffee. (For details of the creaming method see page 50.) Divide between two 8–8½-inch greased and floured sandwich tins and bake for 20–25 minutes above the centre of a moderate oven, 350–375°F, Gas Mark 4–5, until firm to the touch. Turn out carefully. Allow to cool. Make the butter icing as Blue Print 2 (the variation in amounts depends on the thickness and firmness preferred). Use about ¼ of the mixture to sandwich the cakes together and another ¼ to coat the sides, see Sketch 1. Roll the cake in the chopped nuts, see Sketch 2, then cover the cake with some of the remaining icing sugar and pipe rosettes on top with the last of the icing. Decorate with whole hazel-nuts.

Vanilla Cream

¾ oz. flour; ½ oz. cornflour; ½ pint (1⅓C) milk; vanilla pod or ½–1 teaspoon vanilla essence; 2 oz. (¼C) caster sugar; 1 oz. butter; 1 whole egg or 2 egg yolks; 1 tablespoon thick cream or milk.
Blend the flour and cornflour with the cold milk, put into a saucepan with the vanilla pod or essence and cook gently, stirring well, until thickened. Add the sugar and butter as the mixture begins to stiffen. Remove the pan from the heat, take out the vanilla pod (rinse in cold water and dry). Blend the egg or yolks with the cream or milk, add to the mixture in the pan and cook gently for several minutes without boiling. Stir from time to time as the mixture cools to prevent a skin forming. If wished, blend in ¼ pint (⅔C) lightly whipped cream when the filling is cold. This is also known as Confectioners' Custard or Crème Patissière.
The quantity above fills about 12 good-sized pastries or would provide 2 thick or 3 thinner layers in a layer cake.

American Frosting

In this icing it is essential to heat to the correct temperature. If you have a sugar thermometer then use that, otherwise have a basin of cold water for testing.
Stir 8 oz. (1C) granulated sugar and 4 tablespoons water over a low heat until the sugar has dissolved. Add a pinch cream of tartar, then boil steadily until the mixture reaches 238–240°F. Choose the lower temperature for a smooth coating icing and the higher temperature when you wish the icing to stand in peaks, or if the weather is very damp. To test without the thermometer drop a little of the icing into cold water; when ready it should form a soft ball. Beat the syrup in the pan until slightly cloudy, then pour on to 1 stiffly beaten egg white and beat well. Pile the icing over the top of the cake, either smooth flat or sweep up in peaks. The quantity above is enough to give a good topping on a 6–7-inch cake.

Blue Print Recipes

1. Marzipan

Although there are many variations of this recipe (you can increase the amount of sugar and decrease the quantity of ground almonds), the recipe I prefer is to blend 8 oz. (2C) ground almonds with 4 oz. (½C) caster sugar, 4 oz. (nearly 1C) sieved icing sugar, a few drops almond essence and 2 egg yolks or 1 large whole egg to bind. You can use a little less egg and some sherry. The marzipan is then rolled out on a sugared board and put on to the cake as shown in the sketches. The secret is *not* to over handle the marzipan; if you do the natural oils from the almonds 'seep through' the icing and spoil the colour. If you handle the marzipan lightly you may ice the cake at once; if you feel it has been kneaded and rolled rather firmly then allow it to 'dry out' for 48 hours before putting on the icing.

The quantity above is sufficient to coat the top and sides of a 7½–8-inch round cake (about 2½-inches in depth).

The easiest way to calculate the amount of marzipan required is to take the *total* weight of the cake, then allow *half* this weight in marzipan.

Marzipan trimmings left from coating the cake may be coloured and used to decorate the top of the cake.

Icings & Fillings

2. Royal Icing

This is the icing used on the wedding cake pictured on this page. It is essential to sieve the icing sugar. Do not over-beat, particularly in a mixer, for if you do you have large 'air bubbles' which spoil the smoothness of

Traditional three-tiered wedding cake

the icing. Beat only until the mixture stands in soft peaks (for coating) and firm peaks (for piping).

Blend 1 lb. (good 3½C) sieved icing sugar with 2 lightly beaten egg whites and ½–1 tablespoon lemon juice. To give a less hard icing add up to 1 teaspoon glycerine or use only 1 egg white and a little water to blend. If using water do not try and pipe the icing. The quantity above is sufficient to give one coating only on a 7–7½-inch round cake—with none left for piping.

The cake shown on this page would need Royal icing made with 5 lb. icing sugar, etc. This would allow for two coats of icing and the piping as shown.

Storing and Freezing *Icings harden with storage, and this makes them difficult to spread or pipe. Always cover bowls of icing with damp paper and keep surplus marzipan in a polythene bag or foil. Butter icings freeze well and many people find it an excellent idea to store small containers of different flavoured butter icings. Cakes coated with glacé icing and American frosting can be frozen, but Royal icing keeps well without freezing.*

To use any left over *Any icing left can be used at a later date, if well covered, see above. Frosting tends to lose its fluffy texture if handled again so it is better to use all of this after making.*

1. Roll out the marzipan. Cut a round the size of the top of the cake and a band the depth and circumference of the cake.

2. Brush the sides of the cake with sieved apricot jam or egg white.

3. Roll the cake along the strip of marzipan.

4. Brush the top of the cake and put on the round of marzipan.

5. Roll the top of the cake lightly. Roll the sides of the cake with a jam jar.

6. Brush the marzipan with egg white to form a 'seal'.

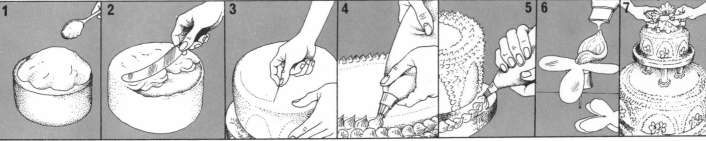

1. To coat the cake with icing, put the total amount for the first coating i.e. about ⅓ on the cake.

2. Spread out until evenly coated with a palette knife or icing spatula.

3. Let the first coat dry before putting on the second coat and when this is dry 'prick out' the design with a fine needle.

4. Pipe the design with a fine rose or star pipe.

5. When dry pipe the borders, you could use the same pipe. Hold the bag at an angle as shown in the sketch.

6. To make flowers, put a piece of waxed paper on an icing nail. Pipe out the petals.

7. Place the flowers in position and stand the top tier on the pillars. Complete the cake with a spray of real flowers and ribbon on top.

Scones and Muffins

There are few things more delicious than a feather-light, freshly baked scone, topped with plenty of butter.

Blue Print Recipe

Plain Scones

8 oz. (2C) flour* · good pich salt · 1 oz. margarine or cooking fat · milk to mix.**

*Either use self-raising flour or plain flour with 3–4 level teaspoons baking powder or plain flour with ½ teaspoon bicarbonate of soda and 1 teaspoon cream of tartar. The amounts of baking powder added to plain flour are more than the raising agent in self-raising flour, so you *can* add 1–2 teaspoons baking powder to self-raising flour for a lighter scone. Remember that the greater amount of baking powder gives a very well risen scone, but I find it crisps less, so you can choose the type you wish.
**If you have buttermilk or sour milk, use plain flour and only the cream of tartar.

To make Sieve the flour or flour and raising agent with the salt. Rub in the margarine or fat, then blend with milk to a soft rolling consistency. The dough will make your fingers slightly sticky as you handle it. Turn out of the bowl on to a lightly floured pastry board and roll out to about ½–¾-inch in thickness. Cut into triangles or rounds, or make one round as the picture on page 41. Lift the small scones or round on to an ungreased baking tray or sheet. Mark the round into 8 sections.

To cook Bake small scones towards the top of a hot to very hot oven, 450–475°F, Gas Mark 7–8, for about 10–12 minutes until firm to the touch. The scone round should be baked in the centre of the oven for about 20 minutes. Reduce the heat to moderately hot after 10–12 minutes.

To serve When fresh, with butter or whipped cream and jam. *All recipes based on this make 8–12 scones.*

To vary

Sweet Scones Add 1–2 oz. (⅛–¼C) sugar. This not only gives flavour, but helps crisp the scones.

Fruit Scones Add sugar as above, plus 2–3 tablespoons dried fruit.

Flavoured Scones Add a little spice, grated lemon rind, etc. to the flour to flavour the mixture.

Cream Scones Mix with 1 egg and thin cream instead of milk.

Cheese Scones Add a generous amount of seasoning to the flour and 3–4 tablespoons finely grated cheese.

● **AVOID** *Making the mixture, or any tea-breads based on a scone dough, too dry; the mixture should be slightly sticky (see Blue Print): Baking too slowly.*

● **TO RECTIFY** *If the mixture is too dry be sure to add a little extra liquid: See baking instructions in Blue Print.*

● **SHORT CUT** *The scone round shown on page 41 is very speedy to prepare, although it takes longer to cook than small scones.*

Popovers

Fruit Loaf

Ingredients as the Blue Print PLUS 1 teaspoon mixed spice, 2 oz. (¼C) sugar, 1 tablespoon golden syrup and about 4 oz. (½C) dried fruit.

Method as Blue Print, the spice should be sieved with the flour and the sugar, golden syrup and fruit added after rubbing-in the fat. Add enough milk to make a slightly stickier dough than for the scones. Put into a well greased and floured 1½-lb. loaf tin and bake in the centre of a moderate oven, 350–375°F, Gas Mark 4–5, for approximately 40 minutes. Lower the heat to very moderate after about 25 minutes. Use while fresh, spread with butter.

Popovers

Although these do not resemble a scone, they are delicious served hot with butter or butter and jam or syrup or topped with savoury ingredients.

Ingredients as Blue Print opposite, PLUS 1 extra egg, and use ⅜ pint (1C) milk in place of ¼ pint (⅔C), and 2 teaspoons oil or melted butter.

Make the batter as the Blue Print opposite. Add the oil just before cooking. Grease really deep patty tins, custard cups or proper Popover tins and heat them for a few minutes in a hot oven, 425–450°F, Gas Mark 6–7. Half fill with the batter and bake in a hot oven for about 20 minutes, then lower the heat to very moderate and cook for a further 15–20 minutes until really crisp and brown. Serve hot immediately. *Makes 8–12.*

Bran and Nut Muffins

3 oz.—poor weight (1C) bran; 1 large egg; ⅜ pint (1C) milk; 4 oz. (1C) plain flour with 2 teaspoons baking powder (or use self-raising flour with 1 teaspoon baking powder); pinch salt; 2 oz. (¼C) sugar; 1 oz. melted butter; 2–3 tablespoons chopped pecans or walnuts. Make a batter with the bran, egg and milk. Allow to stand for 15 minutes. Beat in the sieved flour, baking powder and salt, then add the rest of the ingredients. Grease deep patty tins or muffin tins. Bake in the centre of a moderate to moderately hot oven, 375–400°F, Gas Mark 5–6, for about 20 minutes until firm. Serve hot or cold with butter. *Makes about 12–16.*

Storing and Freezing *The batter for the Scotch pancakes and the uncooked scones on this page may be stored in a refrigerator overnight before baking. All the scones freeze well when cooked. The popovers and muffins do not freeze quite as well.*

To use any left over *Left over scones, as on this page, can be freshened if you dip them in a little milk then heat in the oven for a few minutes. Otherwise split and toast. The Scotch pancakes on the opposite page should be eaten when fresh.*

There are many kinds of scones and all of them are delicious to serve with tea or coffee, or to take on picnics or packed meals.

The Blue Print is for one of the oldest types of scone, i.e. a Scotch Pancake or Drop or Dropped scone (often called a Flapjack or Griddle pancake).

Blue Print Recipe

Scotch Pancakes

4 oz. (1C) flour* · pinch salt · 1 egg · $\frac{1}{4}$ pint ($\frac{2}{3}$C) milk or milk and water · very little fat.

*Use either self-raising flour or plain flour with 1 level teaspoon baking powder or plain flour with $\frac{1}{4}$ level teaspoon bicarbonate of soda and $\frac{1}{2}$ level teaspoon cream of tartar.

To make Sieve the flour or flour and raising agent well with the salt. Add the egg and beat, then gradually whisk in the milk until a smooth batter.

To cook The old-fashioned griddle (sometimes called a girdle or bakestone) has become difficult to find, but modern versions are being made. The alternatives are to use a solid hotplate on an electric cooker (again becoming less plentiful with modern type cookers) or a frying pan. If the frying pan is heavy then use in the normal way, but if light-weight the scones are inclined to burn and I find the best thing is to turn the frying pan upside-down and cook the scones on the base. Grease the griddle or substitute and warm. Test by dropping a teaspoon of the batter mixture on to the warm plate and the batter should set almost at once and begin to bubble within 1 minute. If this does not happen then heat a little longer before cooking the scones.

Drop from the tablespoon on to the griddle and cook for 1–2 minutes until the top surface is covered with bubbles (as shown in the picture). Put a palette knife under the scone and turn carefully and cook for the same time on the second side. To test if cooked, press gently with the edge of the knife and if no batter 'oozes out' then the scones are cooked. Lift on to a clean teacloth on a wire cooling tray and wrap in the cloth until ready to serve.

To serve Either cold with butter or warm topped with butter and jam, or cooked, well

drained, fruit or syrup, as a quick and easy dessert. They are also excellent if served with cooked sausages and beans as a supper snack. *All recipes based on this make 10–12.*

To vary Add 1 tablespoon cooled, melted butter or other fat to the batter just before cooking.

● **AVOID** *Making the batter too wet, otherwise the mixture spreads too much: Cooking too slowly.*
● **TO RECTIFY** *Add a little more flour if you have been generous with the liquid: Test heat of griddle, or pan, as described above.*

Buttermilk Pancakes

Ingredients as Blue Print using plain flour and bicarbonate of soda but MINUS the cream of tartar and using buttermilk or sour milk in place of milk or milk and water. Make and cook as the Blue Print.

Oatmeal Griddle Pancakes

Method as Blue Print but use half flour and half quick-cooking rolled oats. Allow the batter to stand for several hours before cooking as the Blue Print. A tablespoon sugar can be added if wished.

Scotch pancakes

Cooking with yeast is most rewarding, for it produces delicious buns and bread with the minimum of expenditure. Many people feel it takes a very long time to prepare, but for most of the time the yeast mixture is rising or 'proving' and you have nothing to do but leave it until it is ready.

Cooking with Yeast

and some dried fruit. Fold as puff pastry (page 60) then repeat this once or twice more adding the lard, sugar and fruit. Form into required loaf shape and score the top. Bake as the Blue Print, but allow a little longer cooking time. (Illustrated on page 41.)

Blue Print Recipe

White Bread

3 lb. strong PLAIN white flour*· 3–7 teaspoons salt**· 1 oz. fresh yeast · 1 teaspoon sugar · approximately 1½ pints (4C) tepid water.

*It is possible to buy strong flour now and this is worth using, since it gives a better texture to bread.

**The first time you make bread use the smaller quantity of salt until you are sure how much you like. Remember refined table salt is less strong than cooking salt.

To make Sieve the flour and salt into a warm bowl. Cream the yeast with the sugar, add *most of the liquid*. Make a well in the centre of the bowl of flour, pour in the yeast liquid and sprinkle flour on top. Cover the bowl with a clean cloth and leave for about 20 minutes, until the surface is covered with bubbles. Mix the liquid with the flour, if too dry then add sufficient tepid liquid to give an elastic dough. Turn out of the bowl on to a floured board and knead until smooth (see below for method of testing this). Either put back into the bowl and cover with a cloth or put into a large greased polythene bag. Leave to rise until almost double the original size. Turn on to the board again and knead. Form into the shaped loaves you like, for the tin loaf illustrated grease, flour and warm the tins. Form the dough into an oblong shape, fold into three to fit the tin and lower into the tin. The dough should come just over half-way up the tins. If you brush the loaves

with a little melted fat or oil it produces an excellent crust. Covers the tins with a cloth or polythene, allow to rise for 20 minutes.
To cook Bake for about 20–25 minutes in the centre of a hot oven, 425–450°F, Gas Mark 6–7, after this lower the heat to very moderate and complete cooking. A 1 lb. tin loaf takes a total of about 35–40 minutes.
To test Turn the loaves out of the tins; knock firmly on the base, the bread should sound hollow. If it does not, return to the oven for a little longer. *Makes 3 loaves.*
To vary
Richer bread Use half milk and half water and rub 1–2 oz. fat into the flour.
Milk loaf Use all milk for mixing, plus an egg if wished and rub 2 oz. butter or margarine into the flour.
Brown bread Use half white and half wholemeal flour.
Wholemeal bread Use all wholemeal flour but this absorbs more liquid.

● **AVOID** *Putting the yeast mixture in too warm a position, room temperature is generally ideal: Over-kneading the dough.*
● **TO RECTIFY** *If you have put the dough in too hot a place you have 'killed' the yeast too early and the dough will not rise. Test to see if you have kneaded sufficiently, then stop. The way to test is to press with a lightly floured finger; if the impression comes out the dough is ready for the next stage.*
● **SHORT CUT** *One can buy risen, partially cooked bread doughs.*
● **TO USE DRIED YEAST** *Allow half the quantity of fresh yeast (½ oz. dried yeast = 1 oz. fresh yeast). Mix the sugar with the tepid liquid. Sprinkle the yeast on top, wait for about 10 minutes, stir well then proceed as fresh yeast.*

Lardy Bread
Ingredients as the Blue Print using 1 lb. flour, etc. PLUS a little lard, sugar and dried fruit. Roll the risen dough out to an oblong shape. Spread with a very thin layer of softened lard, about 1 oz., the same amount of sugar

Bun Dough
Most small buns are made as the Blue Print, but to each 1 lb. flour rub in about 2 oz. (¼C) fat, add about 2 oz. (¼C) sugar and mix with an egg and enough tepid liquid to bind.

Soft Topped Baps
Ingredients as the Blue Print PLUS a little milk and flour for topping.
Make the dough as the Blue Print; be quite sure it is a soft consistency. Allow it to 'prove' in bulk as the Blue Print but form into small rounds instead of a loaf. Put on to warmed, lightly greased baking trays. Press these slightly with your hand to flatten, brush with milk and sprinkle with flour. Allow to 'prove' for about 15 minutes. Bake for about 12 minutes towards the top of a hot oven.

Fruit Loaf
Ingredients and method as Blue Print but add 2–4 oz. (¼–½C—good measure) dried fruit to the flour.

Fruit Malt Loaf
Ingredients and method as Blue Print PLUS 1–2 tablespoons powdered malt and 2–4 oz. (¼–½C—good measure) added to the flour. (Illustrated on page 41.)
Storing and Freezing *This is a somewhat complex subject so consult your freezer book, but you can store the unproven dough overnight in the refrigerator where it will begin to rise slowly or you can freeze both unbaked and baked yeast breads.*
To use any left over *Stale bread can be freshened by heating in the oven or by dipping quickly in a little liquid if very stale and heating in the oven.*

The mixture for doughnuts may be either the bread or bun dough opposite or the baking powder version below.

Blue Print

Perfect Doughnuts

To make Choose the dough you prefer. For round doughnuts roll in balls (remember those made with yeast dough rise to about twice the original size). Make a depression with the tip of your finger or the handle of a spoon and fill with jam, then re-roll the ball to cover the jam. For ring doughnuts roll out and cut into rings. Allow yeast doughnuts to 'prove' as instructions opposite.
To cook In deep fat or oil. Heat oil or fat until it reaches 370–375°F; a cube of bread should turn golden in 30 seconds. Slide the doughnuts into the hot oil or fat, put in as many as you can but allow space between to turn them over. Cook quickly until they

Making Doughnuts

rise to the surface and begin to colour underneath, turn carefully and continue to cook until golden brown all over. Lift out carefully with a perforated spoon or fish slice. Drain over the pan for a few seconds then on absorbent paper. Roll in sugar, spread on a plate, or drop into a bag of sugar and shake vigorously until coated.
To serve When fresh with coffee, tea or instead of a dessert.

● **AVOID** *Making the dough too dry.*
● **TO RECTIFY** *Blend with enough liquid to give a soft pliable dough.*
Storing and Freezing *See opposite.*
To use any left over *If fried for 1 minute only, until very hot, you freshen a rather stale doughnut but of course the sugar coating spoils the oil or fat so it is wiser to warm through in the oven.*

Baking Powder Doughnuts

8 oz. (2C) self-raising flour (or plain flour and 2 teaspoons baking powder); good pinch salt; 1 oz. melted butter or oil; 1 egg; 1–2 oz. ($\frac{1}{8}$–$\frac{1}{4}$C) sugar; approximately 6–7 tablespoons milk or better still use milk and water. *To fill:* jam (see Blue Print). *To cook:* oil or fat (see Blue Print). *To coat:* sugar (see Blue Print). Sieve the dry ingredients together. Add the butter or oil, the egg and sugar and mix, then gradually add enough milk to make a soft rolling or handling dough. If slightly sticky, cover and stand for about 10 minutes. Prepare and cook as Blue Print. *Makes about 8.*

Pastries

There are many delicious ways in which to use pastry for tea or coffee time.

Blue Print Recipe

Cream Horns

8 oz. frozen puff pastry or pastry made with 4 oz. (1C) plain flour · pinch salt · squeeze lemon juice · water to mix · 4 oz. (½C) butter · To glaze: egg white · little caster sugar · To fill: jam and ¼–½ pint (⅔–1⅓C) thick cream.

To make If using frozen pastry allow to thaw. If making the pastry, sieve the flour and salt, add lemon juice and enough water to make an elastic dough. Roll out to an oblong shape, place the piece of butter, which should have been softened slightly, in the centre of the dough. Fold the dough, bringing up the bottom third, then bringing down the top third so the butter is completely covered. Turn the pastry at right angles, seal the open ends and depress the pastry at regular intervals. Roll out, fold and repeat the process above. You need a total of 7 foldings and 7 rollings for puff pastry, putting it away in a cool place in between these, so it is not too sticky. When the pastry has been made, or thawed, roll out until very thin, see Sketch 1. Cut the pastry into strips, 1-inch in width. Brush 12 cream horn tins with a *little* melted butter or oil. Starting from the bottom of each cream horn tin, wind the pastry round this, allowing each round to overlap the previous one. Take care not to pull the pastry, see Sketch 2. Neaten the tops, place on to a baking tray or sheet. Brush the pastry with lightly whisked egg white, sprinkle with sugar.

To cook Bake above the centre of a hot to very hot oven, 450–475°F, Gas Mark 7–8, for 8–10 minutes. Check after 5 minutes that the pastry is not becoming too brown. If it is, lower the heat slightly. Remove from the oven, cool for a few minutes, gently pull out the tins. When quite cold, fill with jam and then spoon in whipped cream.

To serve With tea or coffee or as dessert. *All recipes based on this make 10–12.*

● **AVOID** *Filling too many pastries with cream, for they will soften easily and you cannot reheat the pastry when once filled or coated with cream: Pulling the pastry out of shape (see Blue Print).*

● **TO RECTIFY** *If you have stretched the pastry there is little you can do except to chill the shapes before cooking and hope that will assist.*

● **SHORT CUTS** *Use the frozen or packet pastry mixtures.*

60

Raspberry Cream Horns

Ingredients as Blue Print MINUS the caster sugar and jam and PLUS 8–10 oz. fresh raspberries and sieved icing sugar. Use ½ pint (1⅓C) cream.

Prepare the cream horns as the Blue Print, brush with egg white but omit the dusting of caster sugar. Bake as Blue Print. Crush half the raspberries, add a little sugar, blend with half the whipped cream. When the horns are cold fill with this mixture. Spoon slightly sweetened whipped cream on top, decorate with raspberries and sieved icing sugar.

Chocolate and Rum Horns

Ingredients as Blue Print MINUS the jam and PLUS little sieved icing sugar, 1–2 tablespoons rum and 2–3 oz. plain chocolate. Make and bake the horns as Blue Print. Whip the cream, add sugar and the rum to taste. Chop the chocolate into pieces, blend with the cream. Fill the horns.

Eccles Cakes

Ingredients for puff pastry as the Blue Print PLUS 4 oz. (½C) currants, 2 oz. (¼C) chopped candied peel, ½ teaspoon mixed spice, 1–2 tablespoons brown sugar, 1 oz. butter or margarine.

Roll out the pastry to a thin layer and cut into large rounds, about 3½–4-inches in diameter. Mix all the ingredients together,

softening the butter so it binds the fruit. Divide the mixture between the pastry rounds, putting it in the centre. Brush the edges of the pastry with water. Gather up the dough to form into ball shapes, see Sketch 3. Turn over and roll gently to make into a flattish round again, as Sketch 4. Cut 2 or 3 slits on top, brush with the egg white and dust with sugar, as the Blue Print. Bake as Blue Print but in the centre of the oven, allowing about 12–15 minutes cooking time. *Makes about 12–15.*

Banbury Cakes

These are made like Eccles Cakes but about 2–3 tablespoons fine biscuit or cake crumbs are added to the mixture which is moistened with orange juice or brandy or rum for a more luxurious filling. The pastry is formed into ovals rather than rounds.

Storing and Freezing *Uncooked puff pastry stores well in the cabinet of the refrigerator for several days or for several months in the home freezer. Any cooked pastry that is left may be frozen, but if filled with cream the pastry will soften very quickly as it is defrosted.*

To use any left over *Any left over uncooked pastry may be stored or frozen as above. In fact all the recipes on this page can be made with the trimmings of puff, flaky or rough puff pastry.*

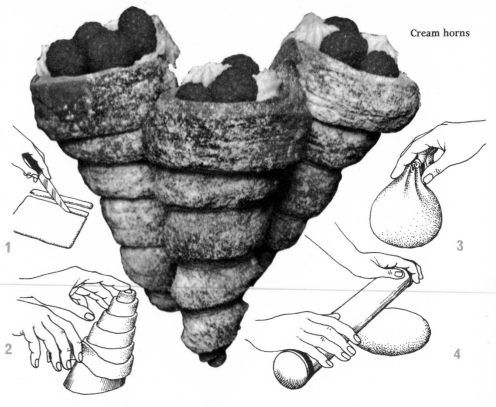

Cream horns

four

ENTERTAINING FOR ALL OCCASIONS

In this part you will find suggestions for most types of entertaining, from simple coffee and biscuits to a special dinner party or buffet, suitable for celebrating a wedding, birthday or other occasion.

Never let entertaining be a worry and tiresome 'chore'. Obviously it entails extra planning and effort, but the results should be so pleasant they compensate for this.

The golden rules of entertaining may be summed-up as follows:

1. Plan ahead if possible, but do not make the mistake of thinking informal 'on the hop' entertaining will be less successful.
2. When you plan the meal or dishes remember about last-minute touches. Avoid these as far as possible if you have no one who can help you in the kitchen—plan the kinds of dishes that *look* and *taste* delicious, but will not spoil if your guests should be a little late or talk longer than expected with a pre-meal drink.
3. If uncertain about your guests' tastes avoid very definite flavours—imagine having to eat avocado pears, followed by curry, if you hate both of these! You can of course offer a choice of menu, but that

does entail extra work.
4. Often it is a problem to keep a variety of dishes hot without drying. The hints given below pre-suppose you have no hot-plate and have just a gas or electric cooker.

To Keep Food Hot and Looking Fresh

Transfer soups and sauces to a basin over a pan of hot water or stand the basin in a dish of water in the oven with the heat turned low. This prevents any possibility of the sauce burning or becoming too thick. If you cover the sauce with a round of very damp greaseproof paper it prevents a skin forming, while it is kept

waiting.

Put the vegetables into very hot dishes, remember to toss or top with melted butter or margarine, so they do not dry, then cover with foil. Keep hot in the oven with the heat turned very low, or over hot water, see above.

If serving roasted meats or poultry put on the serving dish in a very low oven and cover with foil, unless the outside should be crisp (e.g. pork), then leave uncovered.

Salads should be covered with damp kitchen paper or foil, so they do not dry. Keep in the refrigerator until serving.

Pastry-topped pies keep well with the oven turned very low. If you are afraid of the pastry becoming too brown, lay a piece of greaseproof paper or foil *lightly* on top.

Often the easiest way to plan a meal is to have two courses that are served cold, so saving many problems in keeping the food at just the right temperature, without drying or over-cooking. I would never plan over-ambitious dishes that cause you a great deal of worry. Comparatively simple dishes, well made and served elegantly will be just as impressive.

Drinks and a Dip

The modern fashion of having trays of savoury mixtures to use as dips is a very practical one. The mixtures may be prepared beforehand and stored or frozen, brought out and the tray with all the interesting 'bits and pieces' arranged just beforehand.

Blue Print

Choosing Dips

The flavour of the dip or dips is of course the most important consideration. If you plan a limited selection then have those that most people will enjoy. Base them on a cream or cottage cheese with rather 'gentle' flavours, i.e. tomato, onion and shell fish. If, however, you plan several dips then one of these can be really unusual such as avocado pear, curry-flavoured or devilled dip. Check the consistency just before your guests arrive, for some mixtures stiffen as they stand. The dip should be like a thick whipped cream, this means it is easy to 'pick up' on the biscuits, crisps and vegetables and yet not so soft that it drips.

Have a colourful and well chosen selection of foods to put into the dip: small very crisp savoury or plain biscuits; potato crisps; pieces of celery; strips of tiny raw carrots; sprigs of cauliflower; thick fingers or slices of cucumber (delicious used with fish dips); chicory; melon balls; radish roses.

● **AVOID** *Having pieces of food in the dip that could fall off the biscuit: Having too stiff or soft a consistency.*
● **TO RECTIFY** *Chop small pieces of food into such small particles that they blend with the rest of the mixture: If the dip seems too stiff then blend in a little soured cream or mayonnaise; if too soft then stiffen with a little grated or cream cheese.*

Blue Print Recipe

Cottage Cheese Dip

1 lb. cottage cheese · ¼ pint (⅔C) soured cream or thin cream and 1 tablespoon lemon juice · 2–3 tablespoons mayonnaise or salad dressing · flavouring (see below) · seasoning. To garnish: paprika or chopped chives.
To make   Mix all the ingredients together seasoning to taste.
The cottage cheese can be sieved if wished.
To serve   Put into a bowl, top with paprika or chives. Stand on a large dish or tray and arrange a variety of ingredients round, as shown in the pictures on this page. *Serves 4–6.*

To Flavour Cottage Cheese Dip

There are excellent commercial dip flavourings on the market which can be blended with the Blue Print. As they consist of dehydrated ingredients mix some time before required and allow to stand so the dried ingredients may soften.
Crabmeat dip   Open a small can crabmeat or use a small dressed crab. Flake the meat and mix with the Blue Print, add a little extra lemon juice and 2–3 tablespoons finely shredded fresh cucumber.
Curried dip   Blend curry powder, curry paste and a little chutney with the Blue Print. Add a few seedless raisins and grated fresh or desiccated coconut. Leave to stand for a while before serving.
Devilled dip   Blend 2–3 teaspoons made English or French mustard with the ingredients in the Blue Print together with 2–3 tablespoons chopped pickled onions and chopped gherkins and 1–2 teaspoons Worcestershire sauce. To make it hotter, add a few drops chilli sauce.
Herb dip   Blend chopped chives, parsley and crushed garlic with the Blue Print.

Drinks that blend well with Dips

Sherry, dry or medium, but not sweet.
Campari or Martinis.
Red wines, especially with the stronger flavoured dips, see page 68 for a choice of red wines. Those listed blend with the recipes on these pages equally as well as with cheese. *White wine or a rosé* to serve with the more delicately flavoured dips or in hot weather. Suggested wines page 68. Also serve beer or lager, cider, soft drinks, and try the White Burgundy Cup for a summer drink or the Mulled Lager for a cold weather drink.

White Burgundy Cup

2 large oranges; 2 lemons; ½ pint (1⅓C) water; 1 tablespoon clear honey; 2 oz. (¼C) sugar; 2 bottles white Burgundy; 2 wineglasses brandy; crushed ice. *To decorate:* orange and apple slices.
Cut the zest from the oranges and lemons, do not use the bitter white pith. Simmer for 5 minutes with the water, honey and sugar. Strain into the serving bowl. Add the juice from the oranges and lemons, wine, brandy and the crushed ice. Decorate with slices of fruit. *Gives 15–18 glasses.*

Mulled Lager

Heat 3 pints lager with a cinnamon stick, 3–4 cloves, pinch ground ginger and 1 tablespoon sugar. Add 1–2 wineglasses brandy and pour into a well heated bowl. *Gives 8–10 glasses.*

Cottage cheese dips
(above and below)

More Dips

Some well-known sauces make excellent dips and are particularly interesting with hot savouries, as shown in the picture.

● **AVOID** *Making the sauce too thin, see the comments about the consistency of dips opposite.*
● **TO RECTIFY** *If the sauce is too thin, add a few tablespoons of very fine breadcrumbs, mix well with the mixture and allow to stand. Instead of crumbs you can add sieved cottage cheese or cream cheese.*
● **SHORT CUT** *Use ready prepared sauces.*

Storing and Freezing *All the dips on this page and the page opposite keep in a refrigerator for 1–2 days, but do not freeze as they contain mayonnaise. Cover well with foil to prevent top surface looking dry.*

To use any left over *The meat balls are excellent as an alternative to sausages in a 'Toad in the Hole' or can be served with a gravy or sauce. The dips can be used for tart or sandwich fillings.*

Scampi with Tartare Sauce

Coat about 24 fresh or defrosted frozen scampi in a little seasoned flour then in beaten egg and breadcrumbs. Fry in hot oil or fat for several minutes. Drain on absorbent paper and serve with tartare sauce below.
Tartare Sauce Buy or make a *thick* mayonnaise. To ½ pint (1⅓C) sauce, add 2 tablespoons chopped gherkins, 1–2 tablespoons chopped parsley and about 1 tablespoon capers. *Serves 5–6.*

Goujons of Fish

Cut skinned fillets of sole, plaice, whiting or fresh haddock into small strips. Coat and fry as scampi and serve with tartare sauce.

Tomato Shrimp Dip

2–3 tablespoons cottage cheese (sieved if wished); ½ pint (1⅓C) thick mayonnaise; 1–2 tablespoons tomato ketchup* or concentrated tomato purée*; 2–3 drops chilli sauce; 2–3 teaspoons lemon juice; very little finely grated lemon rind; ½–1 teaspoon anchovy essence; about 8 oz. shelled shrimps or chopped prawns.

*the former gives a somewhat bland dip, the latter a more 'biting one'.
Mix all the ingredients together. *Serves 8–10.*

Savoury Cheese Dip

This is an excellent alternative to tartare sauce. Blend ¼ pint (⅔C) mayonnaise, juice of ½–1 lemon, 4 oz. (1C) finely grated Cheddar cheese and ¼ pint (⅔C) thick cream, lightly whipped. Add seasoning and gherkins, parsley and capers as tartare sauce. *Serves 5–6.*

Other sauces that make good dips are *thick* tomato sauce, *thick* curry sauce and *thick* Madeira sauce.

Miniature Meat Balls

1 lb. cooked meat (either one kind or a mixture of meats or meat and poultry); 2 oz. (¼C) butter, dripping or margarine; 2 oz. (½C) flour; ½ pint (1⅓C) stock or use half stock and half milk; 3 oz. (1½C) soft fine breadcrumbs or use cheese biscuit crumbs; seasoning; 2–3 teaspoons chopped fresh herbs; 1 egg. *To coat:* 2 eggs; about 3 oz. (¾C) crisp breadcrumbs. *To fry:* deep fat or oil.
Pound the meat until smooth, this makes it easier to form into balls that do not break when lifted with a cocktail stick. Make a thick sauce of the butter or other fat, flour and liquid. Add the meat, crumbs, seasoning, herbs and egg. Allow the mixture to cool, form into tiny balls. Coat with beaten eggs then crumbs and fry for just a few minutes. Drain on absorbent paper. These can be crisped in the hot fat, then reheated in the oven for a short time, or they are very good cold. *Makes about 40.*

Chickens' Livers and Bacon

Cut chickens' livers into tiny pieces, wrap in pieces of bacon and spear with cocktail sticks. Cook for about 10–15 minutes in a moderately hot oven. If you wish to keep these hot, cover the dish with foil when the bacon has crisped, and turn the oven to a very low heat.

Salmon Dip

As Blue Print opposite, but use flaked canned salmon in place of cottage cheese. Flavour with a little chilli sauce, chopped gherkins and capers. *Serves 6–8.*

Scampi with tartare sauce, Goujons of fish, Tomato shrimp dip and Miniature meat balls

Avocado Dip (Guacamole)

As Blue Print opposite, but use 2 mashed avocado pears in place of cottage cheese, flavour with chopped onion and chopped fresh tomatoes. *Serves 4–6.*

Creamed Chicken Liver Dip

As Blue Print opposite, but use 1 lb. chickens' livers, cooked in 2 oz. (¼C) butter in place of cottage cheese. Sieve, blend with ingredients as Blue Print, flavour with mustard and cream. *Serves 6–8.*

Blue Cheese Dip

As Blue Print opposite, but use half mashed Danish Blue cheese and half cottage cheese. *Serves 6–8.*

Quantities to Allow

Dips

This depends upon the variety served, and the serving quantity is given after each recipe. If you allow about 4–5 good tablespoons per person, plus about 8–12 'pieces' to put into the dip that should be sufficient.

Drinks

Sherry—12–15 glasses per bottle, and one assumes people will have 2 or 3 glasses.
Wines—6–8 glasses per bottle, and one assumes people will have 2–3 glasses.
Spirits—a bottle gives 16 'doubles' or 32 'singles', plus soda, tonics etc. and one assumes you will serve 2–3 glasses per person.
Beer and Cider—about 1 pint minimum.

It is difficult to state accurately the amount to order, for it depends upon the duration of the party.

Grapefruit cocktails

If it is possible I would arrange an evening meal, rather than a tea time celebration for older children. It is not only more simple and less 'time consuming' to prepare, but it implies you realise the children have become more sophisticated in their tastes.

Blue Print

Concentrate on savoury dishes with one or two rather 'super' desserts. Choose spaghetti with a meat or tomato sauce as a 'starter', melon, Grapefruit Cocktails or soup.

Follow this with lots of Hamburgers (see page 27) and fried potatoes and salads or with fried chicken with jacket potatoes. The picture illustrates a very delicious form of fried chicken, Chicken Maryland.

Follow this with a choice of one or two fairly simple but pleasant-looking desserts, e.g. ice cream with various fruits, an Alaska, rather similar (although not as luxurious) to that shown on page 74. A fruit-filled gâteau or a fruit flan would be other wise choices.

Have a tray of cheese and biscuits, fruit, coffee, soft drinks and cider or an interesting Ginger-ale Punch or Cup.

Quantities to Allow

If serving spaghetti as a 'starter', then allow about $1-1\frac{1}{2}$ oz. uncooked spaghetti per person, i.e. 1 lb. serves about 10 people and you need about 2 pints ($5\frac{1}{3}$C) sauce for the same number.

A medium-sized melon gives 6 portions.

For Grapefruit Cocktails, 2 fresh grapefruit (or a medium-sized can), a small can of mandarin oranges and a medium-sized can cherries (or equivalent in cooked or fresh cherries) will serve 6–8.

Allow about $\frac{1}{3}$ pint (1C) soup per person. Hungry children will eat 2–3 Hamburgers (unless very large) or 1 large portion or 2 smaller portions of fried chicken.

Cater for 2 scoops or large spoonfuls of ice cream per person plus the fruit, etc.

Allow about 3 glasses of soft drinks, Ginger-ale Punch or Cup or cider (remember you can buy non-alcoholic cider) and 2 cups coffee. Also have milk, for many children enjoy ice cold milk.

Grapefruit Cocktails

Use canned grapefruit or halve fresh grapefruit and remove the segments. Blend with well drained, canned mandarin oranges and canned, cooked or fresh cherries, sweeten if wished. Frost the rims of the glasses, see Sketches 1–4, and spoon the cocktails into these.

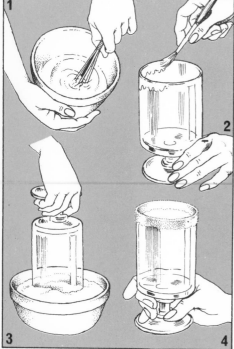

1 Whisk an egg white lightly.

2 Brush on to the rims of the glasses.

3 Turn the glasses upside-down over caster sugar.

4 The finished glass.

Ice cream sundae

Ginger-ale Punch or Cup

2 pints (5⅓C) canned pineapple juice; 3 pints (8C) ginger-ale or ginger-beer. *If serving hot:* 2–3 tablespoons preserved or crystallised ginger; little powdered ginger; few glacé cherries. *If serving cold:* ice cubes; frozen or fresh strawberries; slices of cucumber.

Blend the pineapple juice and ginger-ale or beer. *If serving hot:* put into a saucepan, heat then pour into a heated bowl and top with the sliced ginger, a sprinkling of powdered ginger and the cherries. *If serving cold:* crush the ice cubes, add the pineapple and ginger-ale or beer, then top with strawberries and sliced cucumber. *Makes about 16–20 small glasses.*

Chicken Maryland

Allow 1 large portion or 2 smaller portions of frying chicken per child. Remember they must be young chickens and if they have been frozen, allow to thaw out before coating and frying. Wash and dry the portions well. To each 4–6 portions you will need about 1 oz. seasoned flour, 1 egg and 2–3 tablespoons fine soft or browned breadcrumbs. Coat the portions with the flour, then the egg, beaten with a few drops of water, then in the crumbs. Fry quickly in deep or shallow fat until crisp and golden brown, then lower the heat and fry for about 8–10 minutes. It may be easier though to fry the chicken until just brown, then to put it on to flat baking trays in the oven and continue cooking above the centre of a moderate oven, 350–375°F, Gas Mark 4–5, for about 30–35 minutes. Drain well on absorbent paper before serving. Garnish with parsley. Bake jacket potatoes for 1–1¼ hours in a moderate oven. Serve with butter.

Fried Bananas

Allow 1 small or half large banana per person. Coat in a little seasoned flour, allow 1 oz. flour to each 6 bananas. Fry the bananas for a few minutes only in shallow fat or oil. Drain (see Note below Corn Fritters).

Corn Fritters

4 oz. (1C) flour (with plain flour use 2 teaspoons baking powder, a level teaspoon baking powder can be added to self-raising flour); good pinch salt; 1 egg; ¼ pint (⅔C) milk or milk and water; can (about 1 lb.) sweetcorn. *To fry:* fat or oil.

Make the batter with the sieved flour or flour and baking powder, salt, egg and milk or milk and water. Open the can of corn, drain this, but put about 2 tablespoons of the liquid into the batter, then add the corn. Mix well, then put spoonfuls into shallow fat or oil and fry until golden brown on the underside, turn and brown on the second side, then lower the heat and continue cooking for a further 4–5 minutes. Drain on absorbent paper. *Makes 8 large or 12 small fritters.*

Note Both the bananas and the fritters may be fried beforehand, put on kitchen or other absorbent paper and kept hot in the oven for a short time.

The fried chicken does not *need* a sauce, but can be served with a good brown gravy or a tomato sauce.

Storing and Freezing *The ready-coated chicken may be stored for 24 hours in the refrigerator or the fried chicken may be frozen and just heated for the party. The fritters also freeze well.*

To use any left over *The chicken is excellent cold, but the bananas and fritters need eating when fresh. The Grapefruit Cocktails will keep for 1–2 days in the refrigerator.*

Cocktail Parties

This is an ideal way to entertain a large number of people, either at mid-day or early in the evening. The drinks can be as varied as you wish—either a selection of cocktails or those suggested on page 62.

The food can be simple or original and hot or cold. A good selection of cocktail savouries should look gay and colourful. The tray pictured opposite shows a well planned selection of canapés. You may also like to incorporate some dips from pages 62 and 63.

● **AVOID** *Making any savouries too large, they should be 'bite-sized' so your guests need not hold plates for the food: Greasy fried canapés.*
● **TO RECTIFY** *Use special cocktail patty tins for tartlet cases, and tiny cutters for the base of other savouries.*
● **SHORT CUT** *Make use of the wide range of ready-to-serve foods—cocktail onions, gherkins, olives, crisps, nuts and biscuit-type savouries.*

Blue Print Recipe

Cheese Pastry

This pastry is not only used for cheese straws and other cheese biscuits, but it can be used for tiny tartlet cases instead of short crust pastry.

8 oz. (2C) flour, preferably plain · good pinch salt · shake pepper · shake cayenne pepper · pinch dry mustard · 4 oz. ($\frac{1}{2}$C) butter, margarine or cooking fat · 3 oz. (1C) grated Parmesan cheese · 2 egg yolks · water to mix.

To make Sieve the dry ingredients together. Rub the butter, margarine or cooking fat into the flour. Add the cheese, then the egg yolks and sufficient water to make a rolling consistency. Roll out and use as the individual recipes. You can make a batch of pastry and use it for several recipes.

To cook As individual recipes.

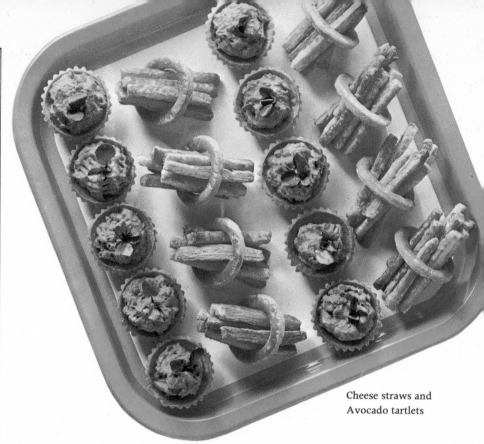

Cheese straws and
Avocado tartlets

Cheese Straws

Ingredients as Blue Print PLUS 1–2 egg whites. Roll out the pastry until about $\frac{1}{3}$-inch in thickness. Cut into fingers about $\frac{1}{3}$-inch in width and 3–4-inches in length. Lift on to well greased baking trays. Brush with egg white. Also cut out some rings of the pastry. Bake for 8–10 minutes towards the top of a hot oven, 425–450°F, Gas Mark 6–7. Allow to cool on the tin, then lift off carefully and store in an airtight tin until ready to serve. Put some of the straws into the pastry rings. *Makes about 60 straws and 8–10 rings.*

Savoury Twists

Ingredients as Blue Print PLUS little yeast extract and 1–2 egg whites. Make the cheese pastry as the Blue Print. Roll out to just under $\frac{1}{4}$-inch in thickness. Cut the dough into two equal-sized rectangles. Spread one piece of dough with yeast extract, top with the second piece of dough. Cut into narrow fingers, as Cheese Straws. Twist gently, put on to greased baking trays, brush with egg white and bake as Cheese Straws. (Illustrated opposite.) *Makes about 60.*

Avocado Tartlets

Ingredients as Blue Print PLUS 1–2 egg whites. *For the filling:* 2 large ripe avocado pears; 2 tablespoons lemon juice; 2 tablespoons thick mayonnaise; 2–3 tablespoons whipped cream or soft cream cheese; seasoning. *To garnish:* watercress.
Make the pastry as the Blue Print. Roll out thinly and cut into rounds to line about 36 tiny cocktail tartlet tins. Prick the base of the tarts with a fork, brush with egg white to give a shine and bake as the Cheese Straws. Allow to cool. Do *not* fill until just before serving. To make the filling, halve the pears, remove the pulp, mash with the lemon juice

and mayonnaise, then blend with the cream or cream cheese. Season well. Spoon into the tartlet cases and top with watercress leaves. These small tartlet cases may be cooked earlier and stored until ready to fill. You can make a smaller amount of the avocado mixture, fill some of the tartlet cases with this, then fill the rest with scrambled eggs and chopped prawns, flaked cooked or canned salmon and mayonnaise or chopped ham blended with cream cheese and mayonnaise.

Cheese Savouries

These cheese savouries are suitable for serving at cocktail parties or as a savoury for a buffet or dinner party. Make the pastry as the Blue Print with 1 lb. (4C) flour etc.
Divide the pastry into three parts. One third makes the Quiche opposite. Roll out the second third and line boat-shaped tins. Bake 'blind' for about 10 minutes in a hot oven, 425–450°F, Gas Mark 6–7, cool then fill with 3–4 scrambled eggs, blended with a little mayonnaise and chopped shrimps or prawns. Top with whole prawns or shrimps. Roll out the last third and cut into 12–14 rounds. Mince about 8–10 oz. ham, blend with 1–2 teaspoons curry powder, 1–2 tablespoons sweet chutney, $\frac{1}{2}$–1 tablespoon desiccated coconut, 1–2 tablespoons sultanas and a little chopped parsley. Put into the centre of the rounds. Brush the edges with water, fold (as shown in the picture) and seal the edges. Cut small slits on top and brush with beaten egg. Bake for 15 minutes in the centre of a moderately hot oven, 375–400°F, Gas Mark 5–6. The total amount of pastry makes about 36–48 savouries for dinner or about double if cocktail size.

Asparagus Rolls

About 12 small *thin* slices *fresh* brown bread;

butter; soft cream cheese or mayonnaise; 12 cooked or canned asparagus heads.

Cut the crusts from the bread, roll each slice with a rolling pin; this makes it easier to roll up. Spread with butter, then cheese or mayonnaise. Lay the asparagus diagonally on the prepared bread and roll, so the asparagus tips just show. *Makes 12.*

Base for Assorted Canapés

The base for these can be rounds of toast, short crust pastry, well drained fried bread or crisp cheese biscuits, or use the Cheese Pastry Blue Print opposite. Roll out the dough, cut into rounds or triangles and bake as the Cheese Straws opposite, allowing about 10 minutes. Store in airtight tins until ready to serve.

Cheese Whirls

Blend Demi-sel cheese, or a cream cheese spread, with enough butter, mayonnaise or soured cream to make a piping consistency. Put into a piping bag with a rose pipe and form rosettes on to a biscuit, pastry or bread base. Sprinkle with paprika.

Devilled Sardine Canapés

Drain canned sardines well. Bone, mash and blend with a little cayenne pepper, a few drops chilli and Worcestershire sauces and tomato purée or ketchup. Spread on a biscuit, pastry or bread base and top with sprigs of parsley.

Anchovy and Egg Canapés

Hard boil 2 eggs, remove the yolks and mash or sieve with 2 oz. ($\frac{1}{4}$C) butter, anchovy essence and pepper to season. Pipe on to a biscuit, pastry or bread base and top with sliced olives. *Makes about 18–20.*

Grape and Cheese Bites

Cut neat pieces of rather under-ripe Danish Blue or other cheeses, top with black grapes and put cocktail sticks through the fruit and cheese. Alternatively, use stoned black olives or pieces of pineapple or balls of melon in place of grapes.

Walnut Cheese Bites

Cut squares of Cheddar, or other firm cheese, top with a walnut half and secure with a cocktail stick at one end.

Pineapple and Cherry Savouries

Cut pieces of firm Cheshire or Cheddar cheese, top with pineapple pieces and glacé or Maraschino cherries and spear with cocktail sticks.

Caviare Canapés

Spread rounds of brown bread with butter and cover with rings of hard boiled egg. Top with caviare. If the caviare is blended with a very little thick cream and lemon juice it makes it firmer and easier to eat as a cocktail savoury.

Cocktail Quiche Lorraine

Line small cocktail-sized tartlet tins with short crust or cheese pastry (see Blue Print opposite). The quantity of cheese pastry in the Blue Print lines about 36 tartlet cases. If using short crust pastry you need 10 oz. ($2\frac{1}{2}$C) flour, etc. to line the same number of tins. Fry 4–6 rashers bacon lightly, then chop finely and divide between the tartlets. Beat 3 eggs with 3 oz. (1C) grated Parmesan cheese, add $\frac{3}{4}$ pint (2C) milk and seasoning. Spoon carefully into the uncooked pastry cases and bake for 7–8 minutes in the centre of a moderately hot to hot oven, 400–425°F, Gas Mark 5–6. Lower the heat to very moderate and set for a further 10–15 minutes. *Makes about 36.*

Prawn Balls

Chop about 12–16 large shelled prawns. Mix with a thick sauce made of 1 oz. butter, 1 oz. flour, $\frac{1}{4}$ pint ($\frac{2}{3}$C) milk, 2–3 tablespoons soft breadcrumbs and seasoning. Form into about 24–30 small balls. Coat in a little flour, then beaten egg and crumbs. Fry until crisp and golden brown. Serve hot or cold. Garnish with lemon slices and whole prawns. *Makes 24–30.*

Quantities to Allow

Suggested quantities of drinks are given on page 63.

Allow about 6–7 fairly substantial cocktail savouries per person plus nuts, olives, etc.

Storing and Freezing *Cheese pastry keeps well in an airtight tin, apart from biscuits and cake. It may soften slightly and need a few minutes crisping. It also freezes well. The Cocktail Quiches freeze excellently and any toppings or fillings that do not contain mayonnaise or hard boiled egg can be frozen.* **To use any left over** *This can be quite difficult as toppings soften the base.*

Mixed cocktail canapes

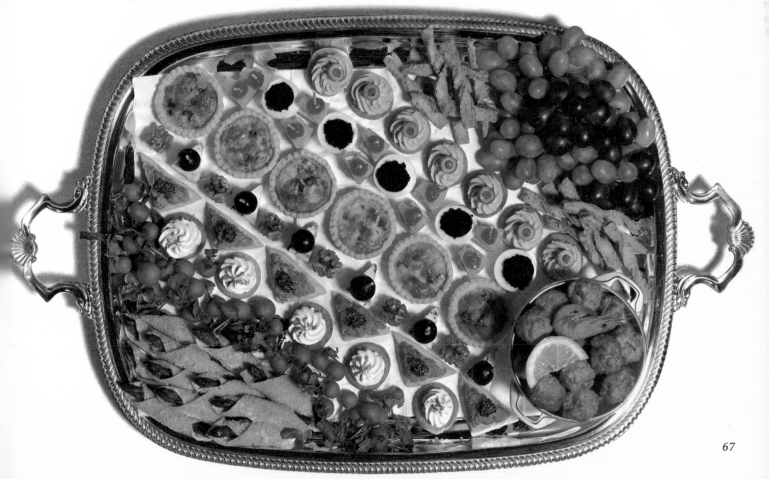

One of the easiest, and most enjoyable, of buffet-type parties is to serve a variety of cheeses with suitable wines. The Blue Print suggests some types of cheese to choose, but this, of course depends entirely upon personal choice and the selection available.

If you are expecting rather a large number of guests and have relatively little space in which to entertain them, you can dice the cheese beforehand, so it is easier to serve.

The cheese looks more inviting, in this case, if the cubes are placed on cocktail sticks and speared into red and/or green cabbages and grapefruit. Obviously cheese that crumbles easily, such as mature Danish Blue and Roquefort, cannot be served in this way, and should be arranged in bowls or on dishes with colourful garnishes. The usual arrangement though is to have several cheese boards on the table, each one containing a selection of cheese and garnished with bunches of grapes, orange segments, radishes, celery, etc., so your guests may then help themselves.

You may care to serve one hot dish. If the weather is cold, cups of an interesting soup would be appreciated; or a Quiche Lorraine, or Cheese Aigrettes (as page 74) or large dishes of hot sausages. If you feel 'just cheese' could be dull combine your cheese selection with dips such as those on pages 62 and 63, or various kinds of pâté.

Blue Print

It is wise to 'play for safety' by having some well known, also much liked, Cheddar cheese. If you have this then choose either Cheshire or Double Gloucester as a second firm cheese.
Have a full flavoured cheese, such as Danish Blue, Roquefort, Stilton, Gorgonzola.
Choose a 'creamy' type cheese with plenty of flavour such as a Brie or Camembert or Pont L'Eveque and a really creamy cheese such as Bel Paese, or a local cream cheese.
Many people today are calorie conscious

Wine and Cheese Party

so have bowls of low calorie cottage cheese. As this is very colourless you may like to mix it with chopped herbs or chopped fresh fruit. The above are the basic ideas, there is such a variety of cheeses from which to choose that your Cheese Party need never be dull.

Some extra cheeses I personally would include would be a Smoked Cheese, a Port du Salut, a very good Caerphilly and a Sage Derby (Derby cheese with the flavour of fresh sage), plus garlic-flavoured cream cheese. If your party includes children then the milder processed cheeses might well be popular.

The suggested wines are given below. If you wish to provide just a choice of one red, one white or rosé (and this is certainly easier for serving), then I would choose the wines that come at the beginning of the lists. On the other hand it is enjoyable for your guests to sample a variety of wines on such an occasion.

Red wines
Mouton-Rothchild or Mouton-Cadet, Médoc, St. Emilion, Nuits St. Georges, Gevrey-Chambertin, Volnay, or an Italian Valpolicello.

White Wines
Pouilly-Fuissé or better still if you like an interesting flavour, a Pouilly Fuissé Fumée, Puligny-Montrachet or some of the German Hocks—Liebfraumilch is one of the most popular. Try also a German Moselle, such as a Riesling or a Soave di Verona from Italy.

Rosé Wines
The best known Portuguese Mateus Rosé blends well with many cheeses, but less

hackneyed is the French Tavel rosé or Beaujolais rosé or a really dry Pradei rosé.

Remember many people might enjoy a beer or lager or cider with the cheese.

Serve white and rosé wines well chilled, red wines at room temperature.

Some of the best accompaniments to cheese will be crusty French bread or crisp rolls. Have crispbreads, various biscuits and fingers of a rich fruit cake (or tiny hot mince pies) to blend with the creamy cheese.

Include plenty of salads and fruit too. The fruits I would choose would be fingers of ripe melon, crisp apples, firm, but ripe, pears and cherries when in season.

Quantities to Allow
If you are serving cheese, with no dips or other savoury dishes then allow 6–8 oz. per person. Buy generously for the cheese will keep, see Storing and Freezing. If you are having other dishes then you can allow about 4 oz. per person.

Allow about 3 rolls or the equivalent in bread with several biscuits or crispbreads per person, also a finger of cake (have some over though as I find this very popular).

On an occasion like this people will doubtless use a lot of butter on the bread, so allow about 2 oz. per person.

If you allow $\frac{1}{2}$ bottle of wine per person that should be sufficient.

Remember coffee will also be appreciated so allow 2 cups of coffee per person.

Storing and Freezing *Keep the hard cheeses and cream cheese in the refrigerator (cover well). Cheeses such as Camembert and Danish Blue should be kept at room temperature. Bring cheeses out of the refrigerator an hour or so before serving. For freezing see below.*
To use any left over *Store carefully as above or wrap and freeze. There may be a slight loss of flavour due to freezing but this is better than wasting cheese.*

This may sound very informal, but it is quite a good idea to have friends for a coffee morning and a splendid way of raising funds for your favourite charity. If you are very busy and cannot spend time cooking for a dinner or supper party, then ask friends to join you for coffee after dinner and serve biscuits with the coffee. Make sure you have plenty of coffee ready together with supplies of hot milk, cold milk and/or cream and choose a good selection of biscuits.

Blue Print

Biscuits for Coffee

Have a well balanced selection of biscuits. The recipes on this page include biscuits flavoured with chocolate, ginger and oatmeal. Include some savoury recipes too, for many people prefer a cheese or other strongly flavoured biscuit (see Blue Print page 66). There is no 'last minute' rush when planning this type of entertainment, for all the biscuits can be made well beforehand and stored.

Quantities to Allow

Allow 3–4 biscuits per person. If serving white coffee for mid-morning you need to allow an average of $\frac{1}{2}$–$\frac{3}{4}$ pint ($1\frac{1}{3}$–2C) per person and a little less milk, or serve thin cream. This means everyone can be offered 2–3 good-sized cups.

For after-dinner coffee (if serving in small cups) about $\frac{1}{2}$ pint ($1\frac{1}{3}$C) coffee per person should be ample, plus hot or cold milk or cream.

Oatmeal Biscuits

8 oz. (2C) self-raising flour (or plain flour and 2 teaspoons baking powder); $\frac{1}{2}$–1 teaspoon salt; 8 oz. ($1\frac{1}{3}$C) medium oatmeal; 5 oz. ($\frac{5}{8}$C) margarine or cooking fat; 2 oz. ($\frac{1}{8}$C) golden syrup; approximately 4 tablespoons hot water.
Sieve the flour, or flour and baking powder, and salt together. Add the oatmeal and rub in the margarine or cooking fat. Dissolve the syrup in half the water, add to the mixture in the bowl and knead well. Gradually add the rest of the hot water, or as much as is re-

quired to form a firm rolling consistency. Roll out on a lightly floured board, until approximately $\frac{1}{4}$-inch in thickness. Cut into small rounds, or large rounds and mark into four triangles. Lift on to lightly greased baking trays or sheets and bake in the centre of a very moderate to moderate oven, 325–350°F, Gas Mark 3–4 for approximately 15 minutes. Cool on the tray then lift off carefully.

Serve with butter or cheese, or spread with marmalade or jam. These biscuits are not only excellent with coffee, but can be served at any time. *Makes 20–24.*

Chocolate Stars

$3\frac{1}{2}$ oz. (nearly 1C) plain flour; $\frac{1}{2}$ oz. cocoa; 3 oz. ($\frac{3}{8}$C) butter or margarine; 2 oz. ($\frac{1}{8}$C) golden syrup. *To fill:* 2 oz. ($\frac{1}{4}$C) butter; 4 oz. (nearly 1C) sieved icing sugar; 1 level tablespoon sieved cocoa. *To coat:* little icing sugar.
Sieve the flour and cocoa. Cream the butter or margarine and golden syrup until soft and light. Work in the cocoa mixture then put into a piping bag with a large rose pipe and form large stars on a greased baking tray or sheet. Bake in the centre of a very moderate oven, 325°F, Gas Mark 3, for approximately 15 minutes until firm. Cool on the tin. Cream the butter, icing sugar and cocoa. Sandwich the biscuits together with butter icing and dust with sieved icing sugar. *Makes 10–12.*

Bourbon Biscuits 2

6 oz. ($1\frac{1}{2}$C) plain flour; 2 oz. (generous $\frac{1}{4}$C) fine semolina; 1 oz. cocoa; 4 oz. ($\frac{1}{2}$C) margarine or butter; 2 oz. ($\frac{1}{8}$C) golden syrup; 1 egg yolk or about 1 tablespoon beaten egg; 3 oz. ($\frac{3}{8}$C) caster sugar. *To dust:* granulated sugar. *To fill:* 2 oz. ($\frac{1}{4}$C) butter; 4 oz. (nearly 1C) sieved icing sugar; 1 level tablespoon sieved cocoa.

Sieve the flour, semolina and cocoa. Cream the margarine or butter, syrup and egg, then work in the sugar and the cocoa mixture. Knead well, add a very little more egg if necessary to make a firm rolling consistency. Roll out to just over $\frac{1}{4}$-inch in thickness. Cut into fingers, lift on to greased baking trays, prick and dust with granulated sugar. Bake as chocolate stars above. Allow to cool. Cream the butter, icing sugar and cocoa. Sandwich the biscuits together with this mixture. *Makes 24–30.*

Australian Biscuits

$2\frac{1}{2}$ oz. (just over $\frac{1}{2}$C) plain flour; $3\frac{1}{2}$ oz. (nearly 1C) rolled oats; 2 oz. ($\frac{1}{4}$C) caster sugar; 4 oz. ($\frac{1}{2}$C) butter or margarine; 1 oz. golden syrup; $\frac{1}{2}$ level teaspoon bicarbonate of soda; 1 tablespoon hot water.
Mix the sieved flour and rolled oats. Cream the sugar and butter or margarine with the golden syrup, then add the bicarbonate of soda, dissolved in the hot water. Blend well, add the rolled oats and flour and mix well. Knead thoroughly. Roll into about 18 small balls with damp hands. Put on to well greased baking trays or sheets, allowing space to spread out. Bake in the centre of a very moderate to moderate oven, 325–350°F, Gas Mark 3–4 for about 15–18 minutes. *Makes 18.*

Storing and Freezing *All these biscuits keep perfectly for some weeks in airtight tins. The butter filling is very stiff, so it will not soften the biscuits for several days. However, it is a good idea to fill limited quantities only if you wish them to keep for a long time. Freezing is quite unnecessary.*
To use any left over *Crisp if necessary for a few minutes in the oven.*

Chocolate stars,
Bourbon biscuits
and Australian biscuits

Come to Tea

This is probably one of the most usual occasions for entertaining friends, particularly when they have children. It means planning a menu that will suit both the parents and the children. The picture on this page illustrates very well four types of cookies and biscuits that will be appreciated, i.e. Gingerbread Boys and Girls (especially for the younger guests), Florentines for adults (the recipes for these are on page 71), small Mexican Cookies with chocolate chips and light Syrup Ginger Buns that will please most people.

Blue Print Recipe

Most guests, young and old, enjoy something savoury as well as sweet things for tea, so serve a selection of small sandwiches, as the suggestions on this page.

Follow with bread and butter or scones (see pages 56 and 57) with butter and/or jam, or cream and jam.

Have a selection of small cakes or cakes and cookies and a large cake or gâteau (see pages 48–52, 71 and 79).

Quantities to Allow

For each person allow

3 or 4 small sandwiches. 1 scone (have a few extra) or 2 thin slices of bread and butter. 2–3 small cookies or cakes, and a slice of cake.

Allow 2–3 cups of tea and have plenty of milk, in case the children prefer this to tea. Also be prepared to serve soft drinks, lemon or orange squash. If your guests include hungry school-children then incorporate some of the suggestions on pages 64 and 65.

Some Savoury Sandwiches

Cut the bread and butter very thinly. Fill with one or more of the following: Lightly scrambled eggs, blended with a little mayonnaise and finely diced green pepper and/or cucumber (have some plain egg sandwiches for young children); cream cheese and shredded lettuce; lettuce and home-made pâté (see page 79); mashed sardines, flavoured with lemon juice and seasoning and blended with finely shredded lettuce.

Syrup Ginger Buns

4 oz. (½C) margarine or butter; 4 oz. (½C) caster sugar; 6 oz. (⅜C) golden syrup; 1 egg; 8 oz. (2C) plain flour; ½ level teaspoon mixed spice; 1 level teaspoon ground ginger; ½ level teaspoon bicarbonate of soda; ¼ pint (⅔C) water; 1–2 tablespoons finely chopped pre-

served ginger. *To decorate:* small pieces of preserved ginger.

Cream together the margarine or butter with the sugar and syrup, until soft and light. Gradually beat in the egg. Sieve the flour with the spice and ginger. Blend the bicarbonate of soda and the hot, but not boiling, water. Stir the flour and liquid alternately into the creamed mixture. Lastly add the finely chopped ginger. Put about 20 paper cases on to flat baking trays or support them in patty tins. Half fill with the mixture, top with the pieces of ginger and bake for 15–20 minutes just above the centre of a moderately hot oven, 400°F, Gas Mark 5–6. *Makes about 20.*

Mexican (Chocolate Chip) Cookies

4 oz. (½C) margarine or butter; 4 oz. (just over ½C) moist brown sugar; 3 oz. (nearly ¼C) golden syrup; 1 egg; 8 oz. (2C) plain flour; ½ level teaspoon bicarbonate of soda; 1 tablespoon hot water; ½ teaspoon vanilla essence; 4 oz. plain chocolate.

Cream together the margarine or butter, sugar and golden syrup. Add the egg and the sieved flour. Blend the bicarbonate of soda in the hot water and vanilla essence, add to the dough and knead very well. Chop the chocolate roughly, add to the mixture. Drop about 36 small piles of mixture on to several greased baking trays or sheets; allow about 4 inches in between for these to spread out. Bake in or near the centre of a very moderate to moderate oven, 325–350°F, Gas Mark 3–4, for about 20 minutes. Cool on the trays. *Makes 36.*

To vary Walnut or Pecan Chocolate Chip Cookies are made as above with the addition of 2–3 tablespoons chopped nuts.

Storing and Freezing *All sandwiches, with the exception of those filled with hard boiled egg (scrambled egg is not very good either), can be frozen. Sandwiches store well for about 24 hours if wrapped in foil or polythene and put in the refrigerator. Biscuits keep in airtight tins and the buns will keep for 24 hours.*

To use any left over *Return biscuits and cakes to their tins. Dip sandwiches in beaten egg and fry until crisp and brown.*

Syrup ginger buns,
Gingerbread boys and girls,
Mexican cookies
and Florentines

Specialities when you Entertain

The recipes on this page can be used for many occasions. The gingerbread figures are ideal for Christmas and children's parties, as well as family teas. The Florentines are sufficiently sophisticated to serve with after-dinner coffee (see page 69), for tea or instead of a dessert for lunch. Cheesecakes are possibly the most versatile of all desserts and the particular recipe on this page can be varied in many ways.

Gingerbread Boys and Girls

8 oz. (2C) plain flour; 1 level teaspoon baking powder; 1–2 level teaspoons ground ginger; $\frac{1}{2}$ level teaspoon bicarbonate of soda; 3 oz. ($\frac{3}{8}$C) margarine or butter; 3 oz. ($\frac{1}{2}$C) moist brown sugar; 3 oz. (nearly $\frac{1}{4}$C) golden syrup. *To decorate:* currants; glacé cherries; about 6 oz. (just over 1C) icing sugar.

Sieve the dry ingredients very well. Cream the margarine or butter, sugar and syrup until soft and light. Work in the dry ingredients and knead very thoroughly. Roll out the dough until about $\frac{1}{4}$-inch in thickness. Cut into the shapes of boys and girls. If you have no cutters, then mark out the shapes in stiff paper and cut round these, as Sketches 1–4. Lift on to lightly greased baking trays or sheets, and press currants into the dough for 'eyes' and pieces of cherry for 'mouths'. Bake in the centre of a hot oven, 425°F, Gas Mark 6–7, for about 10 minutes; check that the shapes are not scorching after about 6 minutes. Cool on the trays, then decorate. Blend the icing sugar with warm water to give a flowing consistency. Put into a piping bag with a fine hole at the base (or use a fine writing pipe). Draw the designs as shown in the picture. Allow to harden. *Makes 8–12.*

Florentines

3 oz. (nearly $\frac{1}{4}$C) golden syrup; 3 oz. ($\frac{3}{8}$C) butter; $1\frac{1}{2}$ oz. ($\frac{3}{8}$C) flour, preferably plain; 1 oz. sultanas; 2 oz. ($\frac{1}{4}$C) chopped glacé cherries; 3 oz. ($\frac{3}{4}$C) flaked almonds; 1 teaspoon lemon juice; 4 oz. plain chocolate.

Melt together the syrup and butter, do not boil. Stir in the sieved flour, then all the rest of the ingredients, except the chocolate. Allow the mixture to cool and stiffen slightly before cooking. Grease 2–3 baking trays or sheets and put on about 10 small piles of the mixture, allowing 4 inches for them to spread out. Bake in or near the centre of a moderate oven, 350–375°F, Gas Mark 4–5, for about 15 minutes until golden brown. Allow to cool before removing from the trays. Melt the chocolate in a basin over hot, but not boiling, water. Coat the under-side of the biscuits with the chocolate and mark lines with a fork or icing spatula. *Makes 10.*

If preferred, make half the size above for petits fours to serve with after-dinner coffee. Bake for about 10 minutes. You need to chop the nuts and cherries very small for this variation and to cut the sultanas in half. *Makes about 20.*

Rich cheesecake

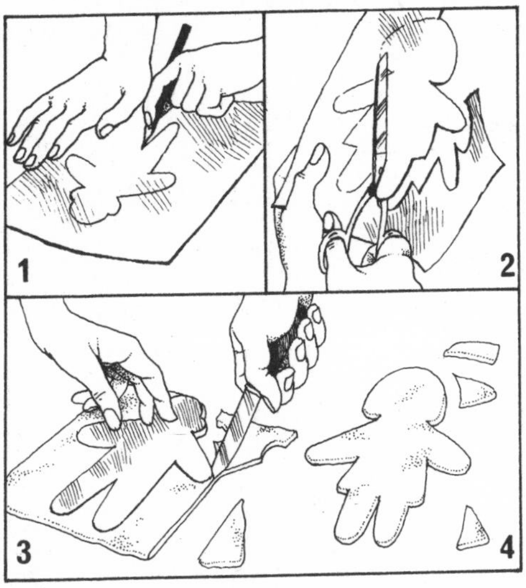

Rich Cheesecake

$7\frac{1}{2}$–8 oz. semi-sweet biscuits; 4 oz. ($\frac{1}{2}$C) butter; $1\frac{1}{2}$ lb. cream or cottage cheese; 6 oz. ($\frac{3}{4}$C) caster sugar; 2 eggs; flavouring (see below).

Crush the biscuits between two sheets of paper, put into a basin and blend with the melted butter. Line the base and sides of a 7–8-inch oven-proof serving dish (about 2–3-inches deep), or cake tin with a loose base, with the crumb mixture and allow to set for about 1 hour in a cool place. Cream the cheese with the sugar and eggs. If using cottage cheese (which gives a lighter texture than cream cheese) this may be sieved. Add flavouring; this can be the grated rind of 1–2 lemons plus about 1 tablespoon lemon juice or $\frac{1}{2}$–1 teaspoon vanilla essence, or little mixed spice, or you can put some firm fresh fruit, strawberries, diced pineapple or halved apricots over the crumb mixture. Spread the cheese mixture over the crumbs and bake in the centre of a slow oven, 300°F, Gas Mark 2, for 30–40 minutes until set. Turn off the heat, but keep the cheesecake in the oven until cold, this prevents it 'wrinkling'. It is a good idea to chill this overnight if possible before removing from the tin. If liked, decorate with fresh fruit as in the picture, or with cream. *Serves 8–10.*

Storing and Freezing *Florentines keep reasonably well in a tin apart from other biscuits for 2–3 days. Other biscuits can be stored in airtight tins, away from cakes, pastry and bread. The cheesecake keeps for 2–3 days in a refrigerator, but like all cheesecakes (except any very savoury ones containing mayonnaise), freezes splendidly. Omit fruit from cheesecake if wishing to freeze and allow plenty of time for it to thaw out at room temperature before serving.*

To use any left over *Use broken biscuits in a coating as in the cheesecake on this page, others can be crisped then returned to their tins. The cheesecake can be stored as above.*

A party for small children often means entertaining the mothers as well, so plan to prepare some adult food as well as cooking for the younger generation.

● **AVOID** *Serving all sweet dishes, most modern children enjoy, and often prefer, savoury dishes: Planning all 'childish' drinks, like squash and milk; many children like weak tea to drink: Cooking unusual foods, children are often very conservative and like familiar foods.*

Blue Print

Plan the food to be small in size—little sandwiches, cakes and biscuits. Have a selection of savoury foods. I find some of the most popular are small sausages. To make these, take a larger sausage and decide how many tiny sausages you want to make. Move the flesh in the skin to 'divide' the sausage, then twist firmly. Cut into portions at the twisted skin. Children also seem to enjoy crisps. I would suggest open sandwiches so that it is apparent just what they are. Small children are not generally given pastry, so I would avoid sausage rolls. Serve milk, milk shakes, tea and squashes.

Biscuits of various kinds are popular. The recipe on this page is a good one for cutting into shapes, but see also other biscuit recipes. The cakes should be simple and not too rich and creamy. If the party is to celebrate a birthday, then the birthday cake should have a simple sponge-like base or plainish fruit cake, not a rich fruit cake. Crisp little meringues, without cream, are generally popular.

Jellies should be fairly plain and I find small children prefer them not *too* firm. Ice cream will be a popular choice with most children. Choose a not-too-rich recipe, or buy the non-full cream type. Little children get rather excited about parties and it *is* important that the food served is not too rich.

Quantities to Allow
For each child allow:
3 or 4 small open sandwiches (halved bridge rolls or fingers of buttered bread).
2 or 3 tiny sausages plus a few crisps. 1 table-spoon dip (this is 'copying' an adult taste and some children may be a little suspicious of a 'new look' like this). 2 or 3 biscuits. 1 or 2 cakes.
2 cups, beakers or glasses of drink. About ⅛ pint (⅔C) jelly and 1–2 tablespoons ice cream

Open Sandwiches
Split bought or home-made bridge rolls spread with a very thin layer of butter or margarine, then put on the topping. The quantities given below are each enough to top 8 sandwiches (i.e. 4 bridge rolls), so if you choose about 4 different toppings you will cover 32 open sandwiches.

Savoury toppings
Scrambled egg Scramble 3 beaten eggs lightly in 1 oz. butter or margarine. You can add 1–2 teaspoons mayonnaise when the eggs are nearly ready (this stops them becoming too firm). Season lightly. Top with twists of tomato as illustrated, a curl of fried crisp bacon, a finger of cooked ham or a light sprinkling of grated cheese.
Cream cheese Do not choose too rich a cream cheese, you can blend a little milk with grated Cheddar cheese to make it soft for spreading. You need about 4 oz. cheese for a

not-too-thick topping on the rolls. Top with segments of mandarin oranges as illustrated (drain canned oranges well), or use segments of fresh tangerine or orange (remove the pips and skin), rings of apple (dipped in a little lemon juice) or dates or a very few peanuts.
Yeast extract   Spread the rolls with yeast extract and top with small lettuce leaves or rings of tomato, or use potted fish or meat.

Sweet toppings

Mashed banana   Mash 2 large or 3 small, really ripe bananas (choose those with brown marks on the skins). Add 1–2 teaspoons lemon juice, to prevent the banana discolouring and a sprinkling of sugar if wished. Top with dates as illustrated, rings of apple (dipped in a little lemon juice) or segments of well drained canned mandarin oranges.

Honey   Spread honey over the buttered rolls and top with fruit or a light sprinkling of desiccated coconut.

Peanut butter   Use peanut butter in place of dairy butter or margarine and top with fruit, or with a savoury ingredient if preferred.

Cheese and Carrot Dip

Grate 1 lb. Cheddar or other similar type cheese very finely. Blend with enough top of the milk to give a consistency like very thick cream, then add just enough mayonnaise to give a piquant taste. Add 2–3 finely grated carrots and blend well. Top with a little more grated carrot, as shown in the picture. Stand the bowl on a large dish and surround with small cooked, well drained, sausages on 'sticks' and potato crisps. *Serves 12–16.*

10-Minute Rolls

1 lb. (4C) self-raising flour (with plain flour use 4 teaspoons baking powder); 1 teaspoon salt; 1 oz. margarine or cooking fat; milk or milk and water to mix. *To glaze:* 1 egg (optional).
Sieve the flour and salt. Rub in the margarine or cooking fat, add the milk or milk and water and blend to a slightly sticky consistency, but one you can handle. Knead lightly and form into a long roll, then divide into about 32 portions. Handle with lightly floured fingers. Form each portion into a long shape, like a small bridge roll. Put on to ungreased baking trays. Glaze with beaten egg if wished, but if these are being served as open sandwiches the topping on the rolls will not show. Bake for 10 minutes towards the top of a hot to very hot oven, 450–475°F, Gas Mark 7–8. Eat when fresh. *Makes about 32.*

Iced Rabbit Biscuits

6 oz. (¾C) margarine, butter or cooking fat; 6 oz. (¾C) caster sugar; 12 oz. (3C) flour, preferably plain; little milk or egg to bind. *To decorate:* 8 oz. (nearly 2C) icing sugar; little water or orange juice; colouring; currants.

Cream the margarine, butter or cooking fat and sugar until soft and light. Add the sieved flour, knead well and add enough milk or egg to make a firm rolling consistency. Knead once more, roll out on a lightly floured board until ¼-inch in thickness. Cut into 'rabbit' shapes, either using a metal cutter, or cut round a cardboard shape. Save enough dough to cut oblong pieces, upon which the rabbits will stand when iced.

Put on to ungreased baking trays, bake for 12–15 minutes in the centre of a very moderate to moderate oven, 325–350°F, Gas Mark 3–4. Cool on the trays, store in airtight tins until ready to ice. Blend the icing sugar with water or orange juice to give a soft coating

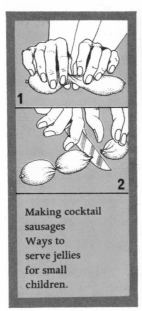

Making cocktail sausages
Ways to serve jellies for small children.

consistency. Colour three quarters with a few drops yellow or orange colouring and the remainder with 2 or 3 drops cochineal. Spread the orange icing over one side of the 'rabbits' and when nearly set press currants in position as 'eyes'. Coat the oblong pieces with pink icing, when nearly set stand the 'rabbits' on top. If you wish to ice both sides of the 'rabbits' then you need about 12–14 oz. (just over 3C) icing sugar. *Makes about 12–16.*
To vary   Do not ice the biscuits, and put the currants for the eyes into the dough before baking. You can stick the rabbits on to the bases with a little butter or glacé icing; leave to set.

Baby Meringues

Follow the method of making meringues on page 75. Use 2 egg whites and 4 oz. (½C) caster sugar for the plain white meringues and 2 egg whites and 4 oz. (½C) caster sugar mixed with 2 *level* tablespoons chocolate powder, for the chocolate ones. Pipe into rosette shapes on lightly oiled baking trays and dry out for about 1½ hours in the coolest part of a very slow oven, 250–275°F, Gas Mark 0–½. Lift off the trays, cool, then store in airtight tins. *Makes about 48.*

Milk Shakes

Blend special flavouring syrup (sold for milk shakes), rose hip syrup or blackcurrant syrup with cold milk. If this is done in the liquidiser you produce a very fluffy milk shake. A little ice can be added if wished, or the milk shakes could be topped with teaspoons of ice cream.

Birthday Cake

Make a Victoria sandwich by creaming 8 oz. (1C) margarine or butter with 8 oz. (1C) caster sugar. Add 4 beaten eggs and 8 oz. sieved self-raising flour or plain flour and 2 level teaspoons baking powder. Divide between two greased and floured 8–9-inch sandwich tins and bake for approximately 25–30 minutes above the centre of a moderate oven, 350–375°F, Gas Mark 4–5. Turn out carefully and cool. Prepare the icing with 8 oz. (1C) butter or margarine, 1 lb. (3½C) sieved icing sugar, the finely grated rind of 1 orange and about 2 tablespoons orange juice and a few drops yellow or pink colouring. Sandwich the cakes together with about ⅓ of the icing. Coat the sides with ⅓ and top with the remainder. Decorate with a chocolate figure, as the picture, candles and a ribbon band. *Serves about 16 small children.*

Ways to serve jellies

1. Whisk the jelly when set and put into ice cream cones.
2. Whisk a jelly and put on to saucers. Top with 'pear mice'.
3. Cut slices off oranges, remove pulp, squeeze out juice and use to make jellies, then put back into the cases and place 'lids' in position.

Storing and Freezing   *The sandwiches would freeze, and so will the rolls, see page 70. The biscuits keep well in an airtight tin until ready to ice and the cake can be frozen if wished.*

A Luxury Luncheon

Although the main course and the dessert may appear rather ambitious looking, they are both simple to prepare.

Blue Print

Cheese Aigrettes

Trout Nansen with Cucumber Salad, Asparagus and New Potatoes

Pacific Delight

Coffee

I have suggested hot Cheese Aigrettes for this menu, since the main course is cold and the dessert a combination of hot and cold ingredients. If you do not wish to fry these at the last minute then serve a hot soup, or a pâté, or hot globe artichokes with melted butter (in this case choose another vegetable, *not* asparagus).

The main course, Trout Nansen, is both delicious and sustaining, it could be made with grey mullet instead.

The dessert is a combination of fresh pineapple, ice cream and meringue. Choose a well chilled white wine or a rosé for this menu (see page 68).

Quantities: The menu is planned for 4 people, although the aigrettes and this rich dessert could serve 6 people easily, so all you need to do is allow extra fish and vegetables.

● **AVOID** *Over-cooking the fish, for it must look firm for this dish: Making the savoury jelly too stiff, it should be lightly set: Cooking the meringue too slowly.*

● **TO RECTIFY** *If the jelly has become a little stiff, whisk in a small quantity of white wine and pile the whisked jelly over the fish, instead of the smooth coating shown in the picture: Have the oven very hot before putting in the meringue.*

Cheese Aigrettes

1 oz. butter or margarine; 3 tablespoons water; 2 oz. ($\frac{1}{2}$C) flour, preferably plain; 2 large eggs; 1$\frac{1}{2}$ oz. ($\frac{1}{3}$C) grated Parmesan cheese; seasoning. *To fry:* deep oil. *To garnish* (optional): grated Parmesan, or Parmesan and Cheddar cheese or flaked almonds.

Put the butter or margarine with the water into a pan. Heat until the butter or margarine has melted, remove from the heat, stir in the flour. Return to the heat and cook gently for several minutes, until a firm ball. Again re-

move from the heat, gradually beat in the eggs until a smooth sticky mixture. Add the cheese (do not replace over the heat), season well. Heat the oil to 350°F (until a tiny piece of the mixture turns golden coloured within about a minute). Drop spoonfuls of the mixture into the hot oil, lower the heat and cook for about 7 minutes, turning during cooking. Drain well on absorbent paper and serve on a napkin as in the picture. Sprinkle with the garnish if wished. *Makes about 16–20.*

Note These can be fried, put on a flat tray in a low oven and kept hot for a *very limited time only.*

To vary An excellent alternative is to use shredded suet in place of the butter or margarine, as in the picture. As this is blended with flour you may need a little extra egg to give the right consistency.

Trout Nansen

4 large trout; *little* seasoning; $\frac{1}{2}$ pint (1$\frac{1}{3}$C) white wine or use half wine and half water; $\frac{1}{4}$ pint ($\frac{2}{3}$C) fish stock*; *bouquet garni*; enough aspic jelly powder to set $\frac{1}{2}$ pint (1$\frac{1}{3}$C); 2–3 tablespoons thick mayonnaise; little chopped parsley; 2–3 teaspoons chopped capers; 1 tablespoon chopped gherkins. *To garnish:* 2 lemons; shelled prawns or shrimps (amount as required); 2 skinned tomatoes; little cooked or canned asparagus; parsley.

*made by simmering the back bones for a short time or by simmering a small cod's head.

Slit the trout along the stomach and carefully remove the backbones (or ask the fishmonger to do this). If using frozen trout allow to defrost, then bone. Try to leave the heads on the fish as shown in the picture. Wash and dry the fish well, season *very* lightly. Put into a large pan with the wine or wine and water and fish stock. Add the *bouquet garni*, but no more seasoning. Simmer very gently until tender, i.e. about 8–10 minutes. Lift the fish out of the liquid and drain well.

Strain the liquid most carefully, measure and

if necessary add a little more wine or water to give just *over* $\frac{1}{2}$ pint (1$\frac{1}{3}$C). Soften the aspic jelly powder in a little of the liquid, heat the rest, then add the softened aspic jelly, stir until dissolved. Put on one side and leave until cool and beginning to stiffen. Meanwhile blend the mayonnaise, parsley, capers and gherkins and spread a little inside each fish. Put the fish on a serving dish with the sliced lemons (serrated as sketches) and the prawns or shrimps. Peel the tomatoes, slice and cut one or two slices into small pieces, put these on the lemon rings. Arrange the rest of the sliced tomatoes and asparagus on the dish, as shown in the picture. Spoon the cold and slightly stiffened jelly over the fish and garnish and leave until set. Top with parsley.

Cucumber Salad

Peel the cucumber if wished, and slice thinly. Top with a little seasoning, lemon juice or white wine vinegar and chopped parsley and chopped chives.

Pacific delight

Cheese aigrettes

Asparagus

Cut the ends from the asparagus, wash in cold water, tie in bundles and stand in boiling salted water. If you have no asparagus-boiler use the tallest pan possible (I find a deep pressure cooker, used as an ordinary saucepan, excellent). Put a lid on the pan, or cover with foil to retain the steam. Cook for about 20–25 minutes, until tender. Drain and serve with well seasoned melted butter.

Pacific Delight

1 ripe medium-sized pineapple; ice cream to serve 4 or 6. *For the meringue:* 4 egg whites; 4 oz. ($\frac{1}{2}$C) caster sugar.

Cut the top from the pineapple very carefully. Put on one side to be used for decoration. Cut the pineapple into 4 or 6 rings then remove the skin from each slice with a sharp knife or kitchen scissors. Take out the centre core with an apple corer, see Sketches 1 and 2. This can all be done well ahead. Make sure the ice cream is firm. Whisk the egg whites until very stiff. Gradually whisk in half the sugar then fold in the remainder. Put the first slice of pineapple on to an oven-proof serving dish. Fill the centre 'hole' with ice cream. Top with a second slice of fruit and ice cream, see Sketch 3, continue like this until the fruit is put together. Put the meringue mixture into a cloth piping bag with a $\frac{1}{4}$-inch rose and pipe over the fruit to look like the original shape of the pineapple. Put into a very hot oven, 475–500°F, Gas Mark 8–9, and leave for about 3 minutes only, until the meringue is tinged with golden brown. Remove from the oven. Put the leaves into position, on the top of the meringue shape, and serve at once, or this dessert will stand for about 25–30 minutes without the ice cream melting.

Note When fresh pineapple is not available, use rings of well drained canned pineapple, in which case use a little less sugar in the meringue.

There is another way to serve this dessert, and that is to peel the pineapple and cut it into slices downwards, removing the hard core. Put a block of ice cream on to the dish, press the slices against the ice cream so it looks like a whole pineapple again, then coat with meringue as the recipe above.

Storing and Freezing *The fish dish can be made the day beforehand and stored in the refrigerator. I do not find it very satisfactory to freeze this. The aigrettes and dessert must be made freshly.*

Trout Nansen

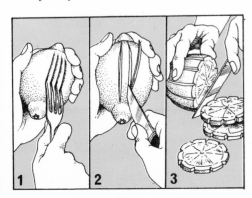

1 To serrate lemon peel, either drag the prongs of a fork down the skin.

2 Or cut thin strips.

3 Slice the lemon.

1 Cut the skin from each ring of pineapple.

2 Lay the rings on a board and cut out the centre core with an apple corer.

3 Assembling the pineapple with ice cream.

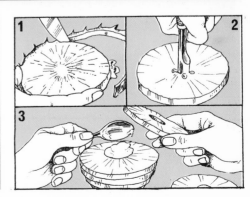

Celebration Dinner Menu

Here is a menu for a celebration dinner. The menu is planned for 6 people, but would serve 8 if desired.

Blue Print

Mixed hors d'oeuvre

Paella with Green Salad or Broccoli

Apricot Lemon Soufflé

Cheese

Coffee with Caramelled Grapes

A mixed hors d'oeuvre is an excellent start to a meal. It looks colourful, can be prepared beforehand and allows guests to select the items they prefer. Choose ingredients to give a variety of colour and texture. Blend the oil and vinegar dressing and use as required (I would choose olive oil and white wine vinegar for this particular hors d'oeuvre).

So many people have enjoyed Paella in Spain and would be delighted to have it again, so it is a clever choice. Paella also can be adapted to the ingredients available, see under the recipe. The ideal accompaniment to Paella is a good green salad, or choose a firm green vegetable like broccoli.

The cold Apricot Lemon Soufflé has a sharp refreshing taste which contrasts with the previous courses.

There is no need to have a wide range of cheeses after such a satisfying meal, those shown are Cheddar and Grape cheese (Tôme au Marc de Raisin).

Bunches of caramelled grapes are delicious with the coffee.

Suggested wines A dry sherry, dry white wine (page 68 gives suggestions) or a hock as shown in the picture. Try a claret with the Paella, the one selected for this menu is a Chateau d'Arche, or a Spanish Villa Zaco (a claret type).

Mixed Hors d'Oeuvre

Salami Cornets Twist 12 slices of salami into cones. Slice about 12 small white raw button mushrooms, toss in oil and vinegar, season well. Spoon into the cones, top with halved stuffed olives. Alternatively pipe rosettes of thick mayonnaise and top with olives.

Red Pepper and Cucumber Salad Blend 3–4 tablespoons diced cucumber with 3–4 tablespoons diced canned red pepper. Toss in well seasoned oil and vinegar.

Carrot Creamed Coleslaw Blend a little cream and lemon juice into mayonnaise. Toss 5–6 tablespoons shredded white cabbage and

the same amount of coarsely grated carrot with the dressing.

Tomato and Onion Salad Blend oil and vinegar with seasoning and a pinch sugar. Cut 1 large onion and about 4 medium-sized tomatoes into rings. Toss in the dressing.

Corn Potato Salad Blend 2–3 tablespoons mayonnaise with a little oil and vinegar to make a thinner dressing. Blend 3–4 tablespoons cooked or canned sweetcorn, 2–3 tablespoons cooked or canned peas and 5–6 tablespoons diced cooked or canned potatoes. Toss in the dressing.

Stuffed Egg Mayonnaise Hard boil 3–4 eggs, halve, remove the yolks. Mash the yolks and blend with 4–5 chopped anchovy fillets. Press back into the white cases. Put into the dish and top with mayonnaise flavoured with a little tomato ketchup and thin cream. Garnish with chopped parsley. Serve with crisp toast or French bread.

Paella

¼ teaspoon saffron powder or few strands saffron; 1½ pints (4C) chicken stock; 3–4 tablespoons olive oil; 2 onions; 1–2 cloves garlic; about 1½ pints (4C) mussels; seasoning; parsley; 1–1½ lb. diced raw young chicken; 7 oz. (1C) long grain rice; approximately 8 oz. shelled prawns; few cooked peas.

Blend the saffron powder, or infuse the strands in the stock for about 30 minutes,

then strain. Heat the oil in a large pan and fry the chopped onions and crushed garlic for a few minutes. Meanwhile put the washed mussels into another pan with just enough water to cover. (Discard any mussels that do not close when sharply tapped.) Add seasoning and a bunch of parsley. Heat until the mussels open. Allow to cool enough to handle, remove most of the mussels from *both* shells, but save a few on halved shells. Add the diced chicken and rice to the onions and garlic, toss in the oily mixture, then pour in the saffron flavoured stock. Simmer steadily in an uncovered pan, stirring from time to time, until the rice is almost tender

(about 25 minutes). Add the prawns, peas, mussels and seasoning and complete the cooking.

To vary Add pieces of salami or smoked sausage (Frankfurters would be excellent) towards the end of the cooking time. Use all fish and omit the chicken. Fry sliced skinned tomatoes with the onions.

Apricot Lemon Soufflé

1 large can halved apricots; 2 lemons; 1 oz. powdered gelatine—enough to set 2 pints (5⅓C); 5 eggs; 3 oz. (⅜C) caster sugar*; ¾ pint (2C) thick cream; chocolate vermicelli.
*little more if wished.

Drain the fruit from the syrup and put 8 halves on one side for decoration. Sieve (or emulsify) the rest of the fruit, then add the juice from the 2 lemons and enough syrup to give ¾ pint (2C). Soften the gelatine in a little of the cold apricot mixture. Heat the remainder, stir the softened gelatine into this and continue stirring until thoroughly dissolved. Beat the egg yolks with the sugar and then whisk in the warm apricot mixture. Allow this mixture to cool and begin to stiffen slightly then fold in ½ pint (1¼C) whipped cream and the stiffly beaten egg whites. Spoon into the prepared soufflé dish (see page 15) and leave to set. Remove the band of paper from the mixture and press chocolate vermicelli against the sides of the soufflé. Top with piped cream and apricots.

Caramelled Grapes

Put 6 oz. (¾C) caster or granulated sugar into a saucepan with 6 tablespoons water. Stir until the sugar has dissolved then boil steadily until a pale golden caramel. Dip small bunches of grapes into the caramel and allow to harden. Eat within a day.

Storing and Freezing *The hors d'oeuvre should be freshly made. The Paella also needs to be cooked just before the meal, although all the ingredients could be prepared earlier. The soufflé should not be stored more than 24 hours unless frozen. It does tend to lose its light texture if stored or frozen.*

Preparing the paella (above) The dinner party (righ

There are many different types of buffet party, so I have given a selection of menus. These menus are planned for 10–12 people.

Menu 1

Fried Scampi and Fried Chicken
with Various Sauces

Oranges in Rum Sauce

Cheese Savouries (page 66)

Party Punch

Coffee

Fried Scampi and Fried Chicken

These two fried foods may be served together, as in the picture, or can be served separately if wished. For a buffet party, cut the joints of chicken into smaller pieces, removing bones where possible. Coat the scampi and chicken in seasoned flour, then in batter. Allow about 4 scampi per person plus about 2–3 small pieces of chicken. For about 48 scampi and 36 pieces of chicken you will need : 3–4 oz. ($\frac{3}{4}$–1C) well seasoned flour and a batter made with 1 lb. (4C) flour, preferably plain, seasoning, 4 eggs, 1 pint ($2\frac{2}{3}$C) milk and nearly $\frac{1}{2}$ pint (about 1C) water. Coat the fish and the chicken in the batter. Fry scampi in deep fat for about 2–3 minutes, and chicken about 6–8 minutes. Drain and serve hot.

Sauces to Serve

Olive tartare sauce Mix 2–3 tablespoons chopped gherkins, 2–3 tablespoons capers, 2–3 tablespoons chopped parsley and 2–3 tablespoons sliced stuffed olives with $\frac{1}{2}$ pint ($1\frac{1}{3}$C) mayonnaise. Add a little lemon juice and extra seasoning.

Spiced pickled cucumber sauce Open a small jar of pickled cucumbers, chop or slice the cucumbers. Blend 1–2 teaspoons peppercorns, little mixed spice, 1–2 teaspoons made mustard with the liquid from the jar of cucumbers. Put the cucumbers into a dish, pour the spiced liquid over these.

Herbed chutney Take any sweet chutney, mango, tomato, etc., and blend with finely chopped parsley, chives and any other fresh herbs you like.

Capsicum sauce Blend 1–2 medium-sized chopped green and 1–2 chopped red peppers together (discard the core and seeds—use canned red peppers if the fresh are not available). Blend 2 tablespoons olive oil, 2–3 tablespoons white malt or wine vinegar, 1 teaspoon made mustard, 1 teaspoon sugar, 1–2 teaspoons peppercorns or a very good shake black pepper and salt. Pour over the capsicums and allow to stand for about 1 hour. 1–2 tablespoons sultanas or raisins may be added if wished.

Oranges in Rum Sauce

12 medium-sized oranges (buy seedless variety if possible); ½ pint (1⅓C) water; 8 oz. (1C) granulated sugar; 4–5 tablespoons rum.
Cut away the peel from the oranges, so you remove all the pith as well. Cut the orange part of some of the peel into very narrow strips, as shown in the picture. Soak in half the water for 1 hour, then simmer in this water in a covered pan for about 20 minutes. Stand in the liquid until ready to add this to the caramel. Put the sugar and the remainder of the water into a strong pan. Stir over a low heat until the sugar melts, then boil steadily, without stirring, until the mixture turns golden brown. Strain the liquid from the orange peel into the caramel, stir until blended over the heat, then add the rum.

Put the oranges into a dish, pour the syrup over slowly so it soaks into the fruit, top with the peel.

Party Punch

Blend 2 bottles of rosé wine with about 1 pint (2⅔C) soda water, and 2 glasses brandy. *If wishing to serve as a hot punch*: heat with 2–3 tablespoons sugar and the juice of 1–2 lemons. Top with lemon slices. *If wishing to serve cold*: I do not add sugar, or lemon juice but just pour the wine, soda and brandy mixture over a little crushed ice and decorate with slices of lemon and mint. *Gives about 12–16 glasses, size as shown in the picture.*

Menu 2

Avocado dip
(page 63)
Kedgeree
Shish-kebabs
Fresh fruit
Cider or beer or soft drinks
Coffee

Make the avocado dip and serve with the ingredients shown in the picture.

Kedgeree

Heat 4 oz. (½C) butter or margarine in a large pan. Add about 1 lb. cooked rice, 1½ lb. cooked flaked smoked haddock and ¼ pint (⅔C) thin cream. Heat gently, then add the chopped whites of 3–4 hard boiled eggs and seasoning. Top with chopped or sieved egg yolk.

Shish-Kebabs

Put cubes of tender lamb, rolled in seasoning and a little chopped fresh rosemary on to metal skewers, with rings of courgette or cucumber and/or rings of green pepper and/or slices of lemon. You can also add small mushrooms, tomatoes and tiny onions (parboil these first). Brush with oil or melted butter and grill until tender. Serve with various sauces, those shown on the opposite page would be excellent.

Menu 3

Chilled Chicken Cream Soup
Beef and Ham Pâté Loaf with
Sweet and Sour Onions (Menu 24)
and Various Salads
Sponge Finger Gâteau
Cheese Savouries
(page 66)
Chianti or a light wine
Coffee

This menu is illustrated on page 61.

Chilled Chicken Cream Soup

2 pints (5⅓C) chicken stock; 2–3 onions or leeks; 2–3 old potatoes; *bouquet garni*; seasoning; about 8 oz. cooked chicken breast; ½ pint (1⅓C) thin cream; chopped chives and chopped parsley.
Put the stock into a pan, add the onions or leeks, potatoes and *bouquet garni* with some seasoning, simmer for about 20 minutes. Add the chicken and continue cooking for a further 10 minutes. Remove the *bouquet garni*, then sieve, or emulsify the mixture in a liquidiser. Add the cream, more seasoning and a generous amount of chives and parsley. Serve very cold.

Menu 2

Beef and Ham Pâté Loaf

1½ lb. rump steak; 8–12 oz. calf's liver; 1 lb. cooked ham; 2 oz. (¼C) butter or margarine; 2 oz. (½C) flour; ¼ pint (⅔C) brown stock; ½ pint (1⅓C) milk; 4–5 tablespoons thick cream; 2–3 tablespoons dry sherry; 5 eggs; seasoning; 1–2 teaspoons chopped fresh herbs.
Mince the steak, liver and ham very finely. Make a fairly thick sauce with the butter or margarine, flour, stock and milk. Add the cream, sherry, 2 beaten eggs, plenty of seasoning and the herbs. Add all the meats

and blend well. Hard boil the 3 remaining eggs, shell. Put half the meat mixture into a large 3–4-pint (8–11C) buttered mould, arrange the eggs on this, cover with the rest of the meat mixture, then with well buttered foil or greaseproof paper. Stand in a tin of cold water and bake for 1½ hours in the centre of a very moderate oven, 325°F, Gas Mark 3. Cool in the tin, then turn out just before serving. Serve with salads and mayonnaise.

Sponge Finger Gâteau

About 30 sponge fingers; 1 pint (2⅔C) thick cream; sugar to taste; 1½–2 lb. fresh fruit.
Put ⅓ of the sponge fingers on a flat serving dish. Whip the cream, add sugar to taste. Spread some of the cream over the sponge fingers, top with some of the fruit. Add more sponge fingers, more cream and fruit, then a final layer of sponge fingers, cream and fruit. Allow to stand for 1–2 hours before serving.

Storing and Freezing *In the first menu you can store the ready-coated scampi and chicken overnight in the refrigerator. They could be frozen, if wished, on a flat dish ready to fry. (Do not freeze the scampi or chicken again if it has been frozen once.) The various sauces keep overnight, but do not freeze. The oranges do not freeze well but will keep about 48 hours if covered in a refrigerator.*

Only the shish-kebabs freeze well in the second menu. The dip will keep for 1–2 days but be very generous with lemon juice to prevent it darkening. Do not freeze or store the Kedgeree.
In the third menu the soup can be kept overnight or frozen for a limited time. The pâté loaf will store for 24 hours or can be frozen if you omit the hard boiled eggs. The dessert does not store or freeze if you wish the sponge fingers to keep firm. It makes an equally good dessert with softened fingers, so sprinkle them with sherry or wine then store overnight or freeze and wrap.

Hot Weather Menu

The luncheon or dinner menu on this page is a wise choice when you wish a meal for hot weather.

Blue Print

Seafood Scallops

**Cyprus Chicken Salad
in Orange Rice Ring**

Chestnut and Rum Swiss Gâteau

Cheese

Coffee

Suggested wines A really well chilled Chablis or other dry white wine would be perfect.

Quantities The menu is planned for 6–8 people.

Seafood Scallops

Pastry made with 8 or 10 oz. (2 or 2½C) flour, etc. *For the filling:* 2 oz. (¼C) butter or margarine; 2 oz. (½C) flour; ¾ pint (2C) milk; 1 small onion; *bouquet garni*; seasoning; 2–3 tablespoons thick cream; 2 egg yolks; small canned red pepper; 8–12 oz. cooked fish; 8 oz. shell fish (either all prawns or some prawns and some crabmeat); 1–2 tablespoons dry sherry. *To garnish:* 1 oz. butter; 1–2 rashers lean bacon; few mushrooms; parsley. Roll out the pastry and line 6 or 8 large patty tins or scallop shells. If the scallop shells are rather large you need the 10 oz. (2½C) flour etc. Bake 'blind' (see page 5) for about 15 minutes until crisp and golden brown above the centre of a hot oven, 425–450°F, Gas Mark 6–7. To make the filling, heat the butter, stir the flour into this, cook for several minutes. Gradually blend in the milk, add the onion and herbs, bring to the boil, cook until a thick sauce. Remove onion and herbs and whisk the sauce sharply. *Heat gently* again, add seasoning, the cream blended with the egg yolks, the chopped red pepper, flaked fish, shell fish and sherry. *If serving hot:* put the *hot* filling into the *hot* pastry cases, top with the garnish and serve. *If serving cold:* allow the pastry to cool, and also the filling. Put the cold filling into the cold pastry and top with the garnish.
To prepare the garnish: heat the butter, fry the bacon and the sliced mushrooms. Chop the bacon, spoon on to the fish with the mushrooms and top with the parsley.

Cyprus Chicken Salad in Orange Rice Ring

For the rice ring: 7 oz. (1C) long grain rice; 1 pint (2⅔C) very well clarified chicken stock;

¼ pint (⅔C) fresh orange juice; seasoning; 2–3 tablespoons olive oil; 1–1½ tablespoons white wine vinegar. *To garnish:* finely shredded peel 2–3 oranges. *For the chicken salad:* 5 lb. cooked chicken; ¼ pint (⅔C) mayonnaise; about 3–4 tablespoons white wine; 1 tablespoon olive oil; seasoning; 1 green pepper; 1–2 teaspoons freshly chopped herbs; about 8 oz. grapes; 2–4 tablespoons blanched shredded almonds.
Put the washed rice into a pan with the stock, orange juice and seasoning. Bring to the boil, lower the heat, cover the pan and simmer gently for about 15 minutes until the rice is just tender and the liquid evaporated. While the rice is cooking, blend the oil and vinegar and soak the shredded peel in this to soften. Drain the peel well, then blend enough oil and vinegar into the rice, with extra seasoning, to make it slightly moistened and full of flavour. Form into a ring on the serving dish, allow to cool, then top with the orange rind. To make the salad, cut the meat from the bones, save some of the very best pieces of breast for the top garnish. Blend the mayonnaise with the white wine and oil, season well. The dressing should have a slightly sharp flavour. Cut the green pepper into neat pieces, discarding the core and seeds. Blend the diced chicken, pepper and herbs into the dressing, pile into the centre of the rice ring. Garnish with the grapes and the browned almonds. Serve with lettuce.

Chestnut and Rum Swiss Gâteau

For the cake: 3 large eggs; 4 oz. (½C) caster sugar; 3 oz. (¾C) flour (plain or self-raising); 2 oz. (¼C) butter; little extra caster sugar. *For the filling:* small can unsweetened chestnut

purée; 1 egg yolk; 4 oz. (about ¾C) sieved icing sugar; 1–2 tablespoons rum. *For the coating:* 1 egg white; 10 oz. (good 2C) sieved icing sugar; little warm water; 2–3 oz. plain chocolate.
Whisk the eggs and sugar until thick. Sieve the flour, melt and cool the butter. Fold the flour, then the butter into the egg and sugar mixture. Pour into a Swiss roll tin lined with well greased greaseproof paper. Bake for approximately 12–15 minutes just above the centre of a moderate to moderately hot oven, 375–400°F, Gas Mark 5–6. Turn on to sugared paper, roll round the paper, allow to cool.
Blend the chestnut purée with the egg yolk, icing sugar and enough rum to give a soft creamy-like filling. Unroll the cold sponge, spread with the filling and re-roll. Whisk the egg white lightly, add the icing sugar and enough water to give an icing soft enough to flow. Smooth over the roll and 'swirl' slightly then leave to set. Melt the chocolate in a basin over hot, but not boiling water. Arrange several well washed and dried leaves on a flat dish, spread the melted chocolate over these, allow to set. Lift the chocolate off the leaves carefully, arrange on top of the cake.

Storing and Freezing *The pastry can be made beforehand and stored or frozen. The filling for the scallops is better made just a few hours beforehand. The chicken salad can be prepared a day beforehand, but does not freeze (although you can use frozen uncooked or cooked chicken). The gâteau keeps for about 24 hours or can be frozen, but do not freeze the chocolate leaves.*

Hot weather meal

EGG COOKERY, PIES AND FLANS

This part covers a wide variety of cookery skills and dishes. Pages 82–91 and page 100 deal with eggs in cooking. An egg is probably the most versatile ingredient in cooking. It forms the basis of main dishes that can be served at all meals of the day, it gives light cakes, puddings, soufflés, omelettes and it is the 'thickening agent' in many classic sauces. If you consider the price of an egg, it is still very inexpensive compared to other foods. Remember eggs are not only invaluable in cooking, they also have a very high food value.

One often hears the expression, (describing a not very talented cook), she (or he) 'cannot boil an egg'. You know boiling eggs cannot be said to be difficult, but they do need care in timing. You will therefore find the Blue Print on the next page deals with the right way to boil an egg so the white is light and not tough. The page also gives some new ways of serving boiled eggs.

The rest of the egg cookery section covers pancakes, soufflés and some very interesting egg dishes (such as the French classic, Piperade). If you have never made Hollandaise sauce, fearing it is too difficult, may I suggest you follow the Blue Print on page 100. It is a surprisingly simple sauce—and quite delicious. Here you will also find the Italian classic dessert Zabaione.

Page 92 commences the section on savoury pies and flans. These can be served hot or cold for main meals, quick family or party snacks. The fillings for flans can be 'cheesey', 'fishy', 'meaty' or full of colourful vegetables.

Some of the best known tarts and flans for tea have been popular for several centuries. The recipe on page 98 is for the *real* Maid of Honour, which has been known since Tudor times. There is a more modern recipe that I find very popular on the same page.

During the past years the Italian Pizza, which is a savoury yeast flan or tart, has grown in popularity. This can be a very inexpensive or quite luxurious dish, according to the topping selected. If you do not wish to make the yeast dough (which is very simple), then try the other variations on page 95.

Can you make perfect puff pastry? The Blue Print on page 98 gives the 'do's and don'ts' for success. Of course if you do not have the time to spare you can make all the recipes with the frozen puff pastry that is readily available.

Boiling an Egg

The flavour of an egg, when boiled, is very pronounced and therefore one should be ultra-fussy that the eggs are very fresh.

Blue Print Recipe

To Boil an Egg

Regular boiling of eggs can darken a pan slightly, so you may like to keep a small pan specially for this purpose. There are two ways in which you can boil an egg. Method 1 gives a lighter texture to the egg white and is therefore ideal for small children and invalids.

Method 1 Put the eggs carefully in enough *cold* water to cover. Bring the water to the boil *as quickly as possible*, and time the cooking from the moment the water is boiling. Since the egg cooks slightly *as the water heats*, the cooking time is shorter than that for Method 2.

Method 2 Lower the eggs into boiling water and time the cooking.

Timing	Method 1	Method 2
Lightly set egg	2½–3 min.	3½–4 min.
Firmly set egg	4 min.	5 min.
Hard boiled egg	8–9 min.	10 min.

● **AVOID** *Boiling any eggs that have even the finest cracks, for these could develop into larger cracks and some of the egg could be wasted: Over-cooking eggs when you wish them to be hard boiled; if over-cooked they develop a dark ring round the yolk and an unpleasantly strong flavour.*

● **TO RECTIFY** *Put a teaspoon vinegar in the water if you have to boil a slightly cracked egg, this helps the egg white to stop spreading out into the pan: Put hard boiled eggs into cold water as soon as they are set, then crack the shells. This cools the eggs quickly, so stops continued cooking and should prevent the dark line round the yolk (unless the egg has been cooked for too long a period).*

● **TO SLIMMERS** *A boiled egg is very low in calories, as there is no added fat or sauces, so is ideal for a 'slimmer's meal'.*

Storing and Freezing *Boiled eggs do not store well and they are one of the few things that do not freeze, they become like 'rubber'.*

For Family Occasions

Eggs Mornay

4 eggs; 1 oz. butter or margarine; 1 oz. flour; ½ pint (1⅓C) milk; seasoning; 4 oz. (1C) grated Cheddar cheese.

Boil the eggs, these can be firmly set or hard boiled, according to personal taste. Plunge into cold water to cool, crack the shells, then remove these. Heat the butter or margarine in a pan, stir in the flour and cook for several minutes. Gradually blend in the milk and bring to the boil, then cook until the sauce has thickened. Season well, stir in the grated cheese. Do not continue cooking after the cheese has melted. Arrange the whole or halved eggs in a dish, top with the cheese sauce and serve at once. *Serves 4 as an hors d'oeuvre or 2 as a main dish.*

Eggs Florentine

Ingredients as above (or use poached eggs if preferred). Put on a bed of cooked spinach, coat with the sauce as above.

Eggs au Gratin

These are the same as Eggs Mornay, but topped with a layer of fine breadcrumbs and grated cheese, so you have a crisp topping. If the sauce is hot the dish may just be browned under the grill. If the sauce and eggs have become cold, then heat and brown

in a moderately hot oven for about 15–20 minutes.

Scotch Eggs

4 eggs; little flour; seasoning; 12 oz.–1 lb. sausagemeat. *To coat:* 1 egg; 2–3 tablespoons crisp breadcrumbs. *To fry:* fat or oil.

Hard boil the eggs and cool, as the Blue Print. Coat each egg in a little seasoned flour, this makes the sausagemeat 'stick' round the egg better. Divide the sausagemeat into four portions, press out into neat squares on a floured board. Wrap round the eggs, then seal the ends and roll until neat shapes. Coat in beaten egg and crumbs.

These may be fried in deep fat or oil, in which case turn once to brown and fry for about 5–6 minutes. If using shallow fat or oil then turn several times and cook for about 10–12 minutes. Remember it is essential to ensure that the sausagemeat is thoroughly cooked. If preferred, bake for about 25 minutes in the centre of a moderate to moderately hot oven, 375–400°F, Gas Mark 5–6. Serve hot or cold. *Serves 4.*

For Special Occasions

STUFFED EGGS

These can be used for a main dish with salad or as an hors d'oeuvre.

Cold stuffed eggs

The quantities of filling are enough for 4 hard boiled eggs.

Hard boil, cool and shell the eggs as the Blue Print, remove the egg yolks, mash or sieve and continue as the suggestions below. In each case the yolks are put back into the white cases.

For Hot Stuffed Eggs

Creamed eggs Mix the yolks with 3 tablespoons thick cream and seasoning. Top with fine crumbs and melted butter, brown under the grill.

Cheese eggs Mix the yolks with 3 oz. ($\frac{3}{4}$C) grated Cheddar or Parmesan cheese and 1–2 tablespoons thick cream. Top with fine crumbs and brown under the grill.

Curried eggs (good cold as well as hot) Blend the yolks with 2 tablespoons mayonnaise, 2–3 teaspoons chutney and 1–2 teaspoons curry powder. Top with fine crumbs and brown under the grill.

For Cold Stuffed Eggs

Anchovy eggs Blend the yolks with a little mayonnaise and a few drops anchovy essence if wished. Top with rolled anchovy fillets. or with anchovy stuffed olives.

Corn eggs Blend the yolks with well drained canned corn, seasoning and a little mayonnaise (grated cheese can be added if wished). Top with strips of fresh or canned red pepper (capsicum).

Crabmeat eggs Blend the yolks with flaked crabmeat, use some of the dark as well as the light flesh. Moisten with a little cream or mayonnaise and lemon juice, season well. Top with paprika and piped rosettes of really thick mayonnaise if desired.

Seafood eggs Flavour the yolks with anchovy essence and a few drops soy sauce if wished. Add chopped prawns or other fish if wished, then top with shelled prawns.

Other fillings can be caviare, mashed sardines, diced ham and tongue or flaked salmon. Always use a moist filling or moisten with mayonnaise or a little thick cream. Season well.

Cover with foil or greaseproof paper so the eggs do not dry.

Scotch eggs

To Make an Omelette

A perfect omelette should be moist in texture, very light and served 'piping hot'. In order to achieve this, cook the mixture quickly so the eggs set in a short time; too slow cooking toughens them. Never keep omelettes waiting; they should be cooked *as required* then served immediately, this means all fillings and garnishes should be prepared before you start to cook the omelette. Omelettes are suitable for serving either as an hors d'oeuvre or as a main dish for any meal.

● **AVOID** *Putting too many eggs into the pan, this 'slows up' the cooking. A 5–6-inch omelette pan should be used for a 2–3 egg omelette: Using too large a pan for the number of eggs, for this means you have a wafer thin layer which becomes dry and slightly hard in cooking: Washing the pan after use, it is the main reason why omelettes stick.*

● **TO RECTIFY** *Make several small omelettes if you have only a small pan. This does mean the first omelettes are kept waiting, unless you can persuade your family to eat them as they are cooked, rather than serving them altogether. If you make a lot of omelettes it is worth while investing in two omelette pans, so you can cook two omelettes simultaneously: If the only pan you have is really too big for the number of eggs then* work on half the pan, *Sketches 4, 5 and 6 illustrate this: Treat an omelette pan with great respect, season it when new, see Sketch 1 and wipe out with soft paper or a soft cloth after use.*

Blue Print Recipe

To Make a Plain Omelette

2 or 3 eggs · seasoning · 1 tablespoon water · 1 oz. butter · filling or flavouring (see individual recipes) · garnish as recipes.

To make Beat the eggs, seasoning and water lightly. I use a fork only for a plain omelette like this, for I find over-beating gives a less moist result.

To cook Heat the butter in the omelette pan, make quite sure it is hot, but do not let it darken in colour, otherwise it spoils the look of the omelette. Pour the eggs into the hot butter then *wait* $\frac{1}{2}$–1 *minute* until the eggs have set in a thin film at the bottom. Hold the handle of the omelette pan quite firmly in one hand, then loosen the egg mixture from the sides of the pan with a knife and tilt the pan slightly (it should be kept over the heat all this time). This is known as 'working' the omelette and it allows the liquid egg from the top of the mixture to flow to the sides of the pan and cook quickly. Continue tilting the pan, loosening the sides and moving the mixture until it is as set *as you like*. People vary considerably in the way they like their omelettes cooked, some prefer them just set, others fairly liquid in the centre. Add any filling mentioned in the recipe.

To serve Fold or roll the omelette away from the handle of the pan, see Sketch 2. Hold the pan firmly by the handle, then tip the cooked omelette on to the very hot serving dish or plate, see Sketch 3. Garnish as the recipe and serve at once. *All recipes based on this serve 1 person as a main course or 2 people as an hors d'oeuvre unless stated otherwise.*

Storing and Freezing *Omelettes cannot be stored or frozen.*

1. To season a new omelette pan. Sprinkle a thick layer of salt over the base. Heat gently for some minutes, tip out the salt then rub in oil.

2. Folding or rolling the omelette.

3. Tipping the omelette on to the dish.

4. To make an omelette in a too large pan. Heat the butter as the Blue Print.

5. Pour in the eggs and before they have had time to set tilt the pan so they run back and cover half the pan only.

6. Continue cooking as Blue Print 'working' the omelette but using only half the pan.

SOME FLAVOURINGS AND FILLINGS FOR OMELETTES

Omelette aux Fines Herbes

Ingredients as Blue Print PLUS 1–2 teaspoons freshly chopped herbs or $\frac{1}{4}$–$\frac{1}{2}$ teaspoon dried herbs. Mix the herbs with the beaten eggs. Cook and serve as the Blue Print. Garnish with freshly chopped herbs.

Bacon Filled Omelette

Ingredients as Blue Print PLUS 2 rashers of bacon and 1 tomato. Chop and fry the bacon, keep hot. Cook the omelette as the Blue Print, add the bacon then fold or roll. Serve as the Blue Print, garnished with cooked or raw tomato slices.

Cheese Omelette

Ingredients as Blue Print PLUS 1–2 oz. ($\frac{1}{4}$–$\frac{1}{2}$C) grated cheese. Cook the omelette as the Blue Print but add the cheese just before it is completely set. Fold or roll and serve as the Blue Print. Garnish with a little more grated cheese and parsley.

Ham Omelette

Ingredients as Blue Print PLUS 2 oz. ($\frac{1}{4}$C) diced cooked ham. Mix the ham with the beaten eggs. Cook as the Blue Print.

Mushroom Omelette

Ingredients as Blue Print PLUS 1–2 oz. ($\frac{1}{4}$–$\frac{1}{2}$C) chopped fresh mushrooms and a little extra butter. Cook the mushrooms in some of the butter. Mix with the beaten eggs. Cook as the Blue Print. Garnish with more mushrooms or parsley.

Prawn Omelette

Ingredients as Blue Print PLUS 2 oz. ($\frac{1}{4}$C) chopped shelled prawns. Mix the prawns with the beaten eggs. Cook as the Blue Print. Garnish with a thick slice of lemon.

Pastel de Tortillas (Omelette Cake)

8 eggs; seasoning; 3 tablespoons water; about 2 oz. butter. *For the sauce:* 1$\frac{1}{2}$–2 lb. tomatoes; 2 oz. ($\frac{1}{4}$C) minced raw beef; 1 clove garlic; 1 onion; seasoning; good pinch dried or fresh basil. *Layer one:* about 4 oz. (1C) mixed cooked vegetables; little butter. *Layer two:* 4 oz. (1C) mushrooms; 1–2 oz. butter. *Layer three:* 4 oz. (about 1C) cooked shrimps or other shell fish; little butter.

This is an unusual variation of the Spanish omelette or Tortilla.

The omelettes are made just as the Blue Print, but do not cook these until all the fillings and sauce are ready. To make the sauce, chop the tomatoes, put into a pan and simmer until the juice flows, then add the beef, crushed garlic, chopped onion, seasoning and herbs. Simmer for about 30 minutes, sieve if wished, then reheat. The sauce must be fairly stiff, so allow any surplus liquid to evaporate in an uncovered pan.

Heat the vegetables in the minimum of butter (they must not be greasy). Slice or chop the mushrooms, simmer in the butter. Toss the shrimps or shell fish in butter.

Make four omelettes as the Blue Print. Put the first omelette on a hot dish, cover with the vegetable layer, then add the second omelette and the mushroom layer, the third omelette and the shell fish and the final omelette to cover. Top with some of the sauce and serve the rest separately. *Serves 4–5 as a main course, 8–10 as an hors d'oeuvre.*

Store Cupboard Omelette

Ingredients as Blue Print (using 3 eggs) PLUS can asparagus spears, can diced potatoes, little extra butter or use 1–2 tablespoons oil, 1–2 oz. ($\frac{1}{4}$C) diced Cheddar cheese and parsley.

Open the cans, cut the tips from the asparagus spears. Chop the stalks. Heat the tips and put on one side for garnish. Fry the drained diced potatoes in hot butter or oil until golden, drain. Mix the chopped asparagus stalks, fried potatoes and cheese. Make the omelette as the Blue Print but add the potato mixture while it is still fairly soft. Fold. Slide out of the pan (as you have a very generous filling) on to a hot dish. Garnish with hot asparagus tips and parsley. *Serves 2 as a main dish.*

Bacon filled omelette (opposite)
Pastel de Tortillas (Omelette Cake), below left
Store cupboard omelette (below)

Poached and Scrambled Eggs

All too often a poached or scrambled egg is spoiled by over-cooking. This produces a tough hard poached egg or a dry scrambled egg, or one that 'curdles' and becomes 'watery' due to too much heat.

Blue Print Recipes

1. Poached Eggs

METHOD 1. To Make Half fill a shallow pan or frying pan with water. Add a good pinch salt and bring to boiling point. Pour in 1–2 teaspoons vinegar if wished, this helps to prevent the white spreading in the water, but does give a faint vinegar taste to the eggs. Break the first egg into a cup or saucer, slide into the water. Continue like this, adding the number of eggs required.

To cook Lower the heat once the eggs have been added, so it bubbles very gently. Move the water round the eggs in a 'whirling' movement, this, like the vinegar, assists in keeping the eggs a good shape. Cook for 2–3 minutes only until set.

To serve Lift each egg out with a fish slice or perforated spoon, allow to drain over the water. Serve on hot buttered toast or as the suggestions below.

METHOD 2. To Make Put water into the base of an egg poacher. Add a small knob of butter or margarine to each small metal cup and allow to melt as the water boils. Break an egg into each cup, season lightly if wished.

To cook Until just set, be careful they do not become too firm.
To serve As above.

● **AVOID** *Boiling the water too rapidly, this produces a very badly shaped egg and one where the white breaks away.*
● **TO RECTIFY** *If this has started to happen, reduce the heat at once and gather the white together with a metal spoon or spatula.*
● **TO SLIMMERS** *Choose Method 1 for poaching the eggs.*

2. Scrambled Eggs

3 or 4 eggs · seasoning · 1–2 tablespoons milk or thin cream (see method) · 1 oz. margarine or butter.

To make Beat the eggs with seasoning and the milk or cream. It is not essential to add milk or cream, although this gives a lighter scrambled egg.
To cook Melt the margarine or butter in a saucepan. Add the eggs, make sure the heat is low then leave the eggs for about 1 minute. Stir gently with a wooden spoon until lightly set.
To serve Spoon on to hot buttered toast or fried bread or serve as the suggestions below. Scrambled eggs make a light meal served with piped creamed potatoes. *All recipes based on this serve 2–3.*

● **AVOID** *Leaving the eggs too long without stirring, for they then set too firmly.*
● **TO RECTIFY** *If the eggs have become rather firm, add either another raw, seasoned egg, or a little milk or cream and blend gently with the firm egg.*
● **TO SLIMMERS** *Omit the cream.*

For Special Occasions

Eggs Hollandaise

Make Hollandaise sauce as page 100. Poach 6 eggs as Blue Print 1, put on rounds of fried bread or buttered toast. Coat with the Hollandaise sauce. Top with paprika or sliced cooked mushrooms. *Serves 3 as a main dish or 6 as an hors d'oeuvre.*

Oeufs en Matelote

Poach the eggs as Blue Print 1, but use meat stock instead of salted water. Top with a thick, well seasoned onion purée and serve on rounds of toast. Garnish with anchovy fillets. The mixture of meat and fish in this particular recipe is most interesting and a very pleasant combination.

Piperade

1–2 oz. butter or use half butter and half olive oil; 1 green pepper; 1 red pepper (optional—or use half a green and half a red pepper); 1–2 onions: 1–2 tomatoes; 1 clove garlic; 6 eggs; seasoning.
Heat the butter, or butter and oil in a pan. Add the prepared peppers, either diced or cut into thin rings, (discard the seeds and core), the peeled sliced or chopped onions and tomatoes and the crushed clove of garlic. Cook gently until tender, then add the beaten seasoned eggs and scramble as Blue Print 2; *do not add milk or cream.* Serve with crusty French bread or with crisp toast. *Serves 2–3 as a main dish or 6 as a light hors d'oeuvre.*

Eggs with Asparagus

Heat the tips of canned or cooked asparagus in butter or margarine, then add the eggs, beaten with cream or milk, and scramble as Blue Print 2.
To vary Add diced ham or cooked chicken or prawns in place of asparagus.

Storing and Freezing *You can store the cooked, scrambled eggs for sandwich fillings and they can be frozen although they do become slightly tough. Poached eggs are quite unsuitable for freezing, they can however be stored then chopped to add to sauces etc. in place of hard boiled eggs. Naturally they must be poached until firm for this purpose.*

Piperade

Scrambled eggs

Fried bacon and eggs

Fried Eggs Hussarde

4 small slices bread; 2 oz. ($\frac{1}{4}$C) fat; 2 slices cooked ham; 1–2 tomatoes; seasoning; 4 eggs. Cut the bread into neat rounds. Heat most of the fat, fry the bread until crisp and golden brown on both sides. Lift out of the pan on to a hot oven-proof dish. Top with chopped ham, thickly sliced tomatoes and seasoning. Put into the oven to soften the tomatoes while frying the eggs. Heat the remainder of the fat in the pan. Fry the eggs as Blue Print 1, put on top of the tomato slices and serve at once. *Serves 2 as a main dish, 4 as a snack.*

Savoury Snow Eggs

4 thick slices Gruyère or Cheddar cheese; little made mustard; 4 slices cooked ham; 4 eggs; seasoning. *To garnish:* paprika; chopped parsley.

Put the cheese into a shallow oven-proof dish. Spread with the mustard and top with the ham. Put into a moderate to moderately hot oven, 375–400°F, Gas Mark 5–6 for about 10 minutes. Meanwhile, separate the egg yolks and whites. Beat the yolks with seasoning, pour over the ham and cheese. Bake for 5 minutes. Whisk the egg whites until very stiff, add seasoning and pile over the egg yolk mixture. Return to the oven, lower the heat to very moderate and leave for about 10–15 minutes. Garnish with paprika and chopped parsley. *Serves 4.*

Fried Eggs Turque

4–6 chickens' livers; 2 oz. ($\frac{1}{4}$C) butter; $\frac{1}{2}$ tablespoon chopped parsley; 4 large tomatoes; seasoning; 4 eggs; French bread.

Slice the chickens' livers and fry in half the hot butter until tender. Add the chopped parsley and arrange in the centre of a hot dish. While the livers are cooking, heat the skinned chopped tomatoes with seasoning until a thick purée. Spoon over the livers. Fry the eggs in the remaining hot butter as Blue Print 1 and arrange round the tomato and liver mixture. Serve with hot French bread. *Serves 4.*

Storing and Freezing *None of these dishes store or freeze.*

Perfectly fried eggs with grilled or fried bacon are one of the best and quickest dishes to serve at breakfast time, or any other meal of the day. The soft yolk of the egg gives moistness to grilled meat or fish. I enjoy hot fried eggs on thick slices of cold boiled bacon or ham or as a topping on Welsh Rarebit (instead of poached eggs).

Baked eggs are equally good for a light main dish, or an hors d'oeuvre. They can be varied in many ways. As the baked eggs are generally served in the cooking container it is worth while investing in interesting oven-proof dishes if you serve them frequently.

Blue Print Recipes

1. Fried Eggs

To cook If you have fried bacon or sausages there may be enough fat left in the pan; if insufficient then heat a small knob of fat, check it is not too hot. Break the first egg into a cup or saucer or directly into the hot fat. Tilt the pan for a few seconds to encourage the white to set in a neat shape. Add the second egg, tilt the pan, then continue like this. If very fussy about the shape, you can put an old round metal pastry cutter into the pan and heat this as you heat the fat, then break the egg into it. When set, lift away the cutter and use for each egg.

Lift the eggs from the pan with a fish slice so they are drained of any surplus fat.

Some people like the yolk covered with a layer of white, in which case spoon the fat over the yolk as its sets.

To serve As soon as possible after cooking.

● **AVOID** *Over-cooking, fried eggs cook very quickly: Too hot fat, if you dislike a crisp skin at the bottom of the eggs: Too cool fat, as this allows the white to spread over the pan which gives a bad shape to the*

egg and makes it difficult to 'dish-up'. Too cool fat also produces a greasy egg.
● **TO RECTIFY** *Check cooking progress carefully and 'dish-up' as soon as the eggs are set. Remember they continue cooking if kept warm for any length of time.*
● **TO SLIMMERS** *Choose a 'non-stick' pan so you need the minimum of fat.*

2. Baked Eggs

$\frac{1}{2}$–1 oz. butter or margarine · 2 eggs seasoning.

To make Put half the butter or margarine into one or two containers (use one container for a main dish, two for hors d'oeuvre).
To cook Heat the butter or margarine for a few minutes in a moderate to moderately hot oven, 375–400°F, Gas Mark 5–6. Break the eggs over the hot butter or margarine, add a little seasoning, then the rest of the fat in one or two small knobs. Bake for just over 10 minutes towards the top of the oven.
To serve With a teaspoon, while still very hot. *All recipes based on this serve 2 as an hors d'oeuvre or 1 as a main meal.*

To vary This is a very basic way of baking the eggs, you can:
Put grated, cottage or cream cheese into the dish or dishes, with the butter or margarine. Heat this for a few minutes, then add the egg or eggs, seasoning, more grated (not cream or cottage) cheese and butter or margarine. Cook as Blue Print 2.
Put a layer of thin or thick cream over the hot butter or margarine, then add the egg or eggs, seasoning, another layer of cream and the remaining butter or margarine. Cook as Blue Print 2.
Add chopped ham, chicken, prawns or asparagus tips to the butter or margarine, heat, then add the egg or eggs, seasoning and the rest of the butter or margarine. Cook as Blue Print 2.
All these variations make excellent light dishes.

● **AVOID** *Cooking the eggs too slowly, they become 'leathery'.*
● **TO RECTIFY** *Check on the cooking after about 6–7 minutes, the egg whites should be setting, if they are still very transparent raise the oven temperature.*
● **TO SLIMMERS** *Use as little butter as possible and choose low calorie flavourings.*

Do not imagine that pancakes 'belong' just to Shrove Tuesday. It is an old and cherished tradition to make pancakes, served with sugar and lemon, for this special day, but they are excellent as a savoury or pudding throughout the year.

Blue Print Recipe

To Make Pancakes

For the batter: 4 oz. (1C) flour, preferably plain · pinch salt · 1 egg · ½ pint (1⅓C) milk or milk and water. **For frying:** oil or fat (see method).

To make   Sieve the flour and salt, add the egg and a little milk or milk and water. Beat or whisk thoroughly to give a smooth thick batter. Gradually whisk in the rest of the liquid.

To cook   For each pancake you cook, put about 2 teaspoons oil or a knob of fat the size of an unshelled almond into the pan. If using a 'non-stick' pan then brush with oil or melted fat before cooking each pancake. This is essential if you want really crisp pancakes. Heat the oil or fat until a *faint* blue haze is seen coming from the pan. Pour or spoon in a little batter, then move the pan so the batter flows over the bottom, it should give a paper thin layer, see Sketches 1 and 2. Cook fairly quickly until set on the bottom. This takes about 1½–2 minutes. To test if ready to toss or turn, shake the pan and the pancake should move easily if cooked on the under surface. Toss or turn carefully as directions given with the sketches. Cook for about the same time on the second side.

To serve   Lift or slide the pancake out of the pan. Keep hot (see below), while cooking the rest of the pancakes. *This batter should give enough pancakes for 4 people, but you may*

1. Spoon or pour a little thin batter from a jug.

2. Immediately turn and tilt the pan to allow the batter to coat the bottom of the pan in a paper thin layer.

3. To turn the pancake, slip a palette knife under the pancake and turn carefully.

4. To toss a pancake, hold the pan in a relaxed fashion pointing slightly downwards.

5. Flick the wrist very briskly upwards so the pancake lifts from the pan, turns and drops back again.

be able to serve a greater number if using a substantial filling, as in the Savoury Pancake Boat and Orange Pancake Gâteau opposite.

To keep pancakes hot   Either put a large plate over a pan of boiling water and place each cooked pancake on this or keep hot on an uncovered dish in a cool oven.

● **AVOID** *Making the batter too thick: Insufficient heating of the oil or fat before cooking each pancake: Pouring too much mixture into the pan: Trying to turn or toss before the pancake is properly set (this is the main reason why pancakes break): Washing the pan after use.*

● **TO RECTIFY** *Follow the proportions in the Blue Print. This gives a very thin batter. Always whisk the batter just before cooking, as it tends to separate slightly as it stands; so that the batter at the bottom of the basin is slightly thicker than at the top: Check the heat of the oil or fat very carefully: Learn the 'knack' of pouring a little batter into the pan, see the sketches: Shake the pancake well before trying to toss or turn; if it does not move easily it is* not *ready: Wipe the used pan with soft paper immediately after use. If using a 'non-stick' pan follow the maker's directions.*

● **SHORT CUTS** *There are commercial pancake mixes, or blend the ingredients in the liquidiser. Emulsify the liquid and egg first, then add the flour and salt. In this way you prevent the flour sticking round the sides of the goblet.*

Storing and Freezing   *The uncooked batter may be stored for several days in a refrigerator and can be frozen for a few weeks. Wrap cooked unfilled pancakes in aluminium foil (separate each pancake with squares of greaseproof or waxed paper). Store for several days in a refrigerator or 10–12 weeks in a freezer. Most filled pancakes can be frozen.*

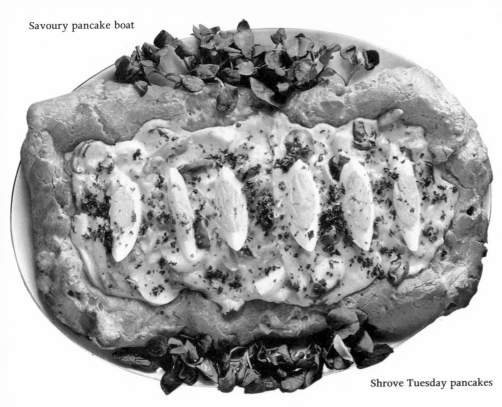

Savoury pancake boat

Red Currant Pancakes

Ingredients as Blue Print opposite PLUS red currant jelly and caster sugar.
Make the pancakes as the Blue Print. Fill with hot red currant jelly and top with sugar. *Serves 4–6.*
To vary Use hot jam or fruit purée instead of jelly.

Crisp Coated Pancakes

Ingredients as Blue Print opposite PLUS jam, jelly or fruit purée, oil or fat for deep frying and sugar.
Put a little of the pancake batter on one side, make and cook the pancakes with the remainder of the batter as Blue Print. Keep warm. Spread with a little jam, jelly or fruit purée, then fold in the sides of the pancakes and roll firmly. Dip each rolled pancake in the reserved batter and fry in hot deep oil or fat until very crisp and golden brown. Put on to a hot dish, top with sugar and hot jam, jelly or fruit. *Serves 4–6.*
To vary Dip in batter, then in fine soft breadcrumbs or chopped nuts before frying.

Shrove Tuesday pancakes

The pancake batter, covered by the Blue Print opposite, enables you to make a variety of savoury and sweet dishes.

Savoury Pancake Boat

Ingredients as Blue Print opposite MINUS fat for frying and PLUS 1 oz. fat; 3–4 hard boiled eggs; 3 oz. ($\frac{3}{8}$C) butter or margarine; 2 oz. ($\frac{1}{2}$C) flour; $\frac{1}{2}$ pint (1$\frac{1}{3}$C) chicken stock; $\frac{1}{4}$ pint ($\frac{2}{3}$C) milk; seasoning; about 4–6 oz. (1C) diced cooked chicken; 2–3 tablespoons thin cream; 2–4 oz. ($\frac{1}{2}$–1C) button mushrooms; chopped parsley. To garnish: sprigs of watercress.
Make the batter as the Blue Print opposite. Heat the fat in a shallow tin, pour in the batter and bake for approximately 25–30 minutes towards the top of a hot to very hot oven, 450–475°F, Gas Mark 7–8. Reduce the heat after about 15 minutes to moderate. Meanwhile slice the eggs, make a sauce with 2 oz. ($\frac{1}{4}$C) of the butter or margarine, the flour, chicken stock and milk. When thickened and smooth, add the seasoning, chicken and cream; do not allow to boil. Heat the remainder of the butter or margarine, fry the whole or sliced mushrooms. Add most of the sliced eggs and mushrooms to the chicken mixture. Lift the batter from the tin on to a hot serving dish, spoon the sauce mixture over this. Top with the remainder of the eggs, mushrooms and chopped parsley. Garnish with watercress. *Serves about 6.*

Orange Pancake Gâteau

Ingredients as Blue Print opposite PLUS 2 cans mandarin oranges, fresh orange juice (optional—see method), 2 tablespoons honey, 2 tablespoons sieved apricot jam, 3 teaspoons

arrowroot or cornflour and 1 glacé, fresh or canned cherry.
Cook the pancakes as the Blue Print opposite and keep hot. Strain the syrup from the cans of oranges, measure and allow $\frac{3}{4}$ pint (2C). If insufficient add a little fresh orange juice. Put most of the fruit syrup into a saucepan with the honey and jam, heat gently until the jam has melted. Blend the arrowroot or cornflour with the remainder of the syrup, add to the mixture in the pan, stir until thickened and clear. Put the first pancake on to a hot dish, top with some mandarin oranges and sauce. Continue like this, ending with a pancake. Arrange a few orange segments and the cherry on top and coat with a little sauce. Serve cut into slices, like a cake. *Serves 6–8.*

Shrove Tuesday Pancakes

Make the pancakes as the Blue Print opposite, serve in the traditional way with sugar and lemon slices. *Serves 4–6.*

A New Look to Pancakes

1 Flavour the batter with $\frac{1}{2}$ teaspoon ginger, cinnamon, allspice or grated lemon rind.
2 Fill the cooked pancakes, fold the ends in and roll. This prevents the filling coming out. Dip in a stiffly beaten egg white blended with 1 teaspoon cornflour and fry in deep fat or oil. If the filling is savoury, roll in grated cheese after frying. If the filling is sweet, roll in chopped nuts or desiccated coconut.
3 Use pancakes instead of omelettes in the recipe for Pastel de Tortillas (page 85).

A savoury soufflé is ideal for a light meal or can be served at the end of a formal dinner. For serving as a savoury at the end of a meal, the best flavours to choose are cheese, ham or smoked haddock.

The Blue Print gives a fairly firm textured soufflé. If you are having this with vegetables, as a main course, I would increase the amount of liquid by up to an extra ¼ pint (⅔C). This means that you have a very soft texture in the centre which serves as a sauce with any vegetables.

Blue Print Recipe

Cheese Soufflé

1 oz. butter or margarine · 1 oz. flour · ¼ pint (⅔C) milk (see introduction above) · seasoning · 4 eggs · approximately 3 oz. (¾C) grated cheese*.

*You can vary the cheese—Dutch Gouda gives a pleasant mild, creamy texture, a Cheddar or Gruyère a fairly definite taste and Parmesan a very strong taste and a drier texture.

To make Heat the butter or margarine in a large saucepan, stir in the flour then gradually blend in the milk. Cook until a thick sauce (if using the higher percentage of

Savoury Soufflés

liquid it will be a coating consistency). Season well. Remove from the heat and add the egg yolks, then the cheese and finally fold in the stiffly beaten egg whites. Put into a greased soufflé dish.

To cook Bake in the centre of a moderate to moderately hot oven, 375–400°F, Gas Mark 5–6, for approximately 30 minutes. If using the larger quantity of liquid use the lower temperature so the mixture does not over-brown before it is cooked.

To serve As quickly as possible. *All recipes based on this serve 4 for a main dish or 6 as a savoury.*

● **AVOID** *Handling the mixture too much when putting in the egg whites, for this destroys the fluffy texture.*
● **TO RECTIFY** *You can tell if you are overhandling the mixture because you lose the very light appearance. If by chance you have been too rough, the best remedy is to incorporate an extra whisked egg white.*
● **SHORT CUT** *Instead of making the sauce, use ¼–½ pint (⅔–1⅓C) condensed soup,*

either mushroom, chicken or asparagus, to blend with the other flavouring.
● **TO SLIMMERS** *This is a relatively low calorie, high protein dish.*
Storing and Freezing *You cannot freeze or store a hot soufflé.*

Spinach Soufflé

Ingredients as Blue Print but substitute spinach purée for the milk. Cheese may be added if wished. Make and bake as the Blue Print.

Fish Soufflé

Ingredients as Blue Print but use flaked cooked fish (white fish, salmon or shell fish) in place of cheese and flavour the sauce with a few drops of anchovy essence. Make and bake as the Blue Print.

Smoked Haddock and Cheese Soufflé

This is a very pleasant combination.
Follow the Blue Print recipe but use only 2 oz. (½C) grated Parmesan cheese and 2–3 oz. cooked flaked smoked haddock. Substitute fish stock (or liquid from cooking the fish) for milk if possible.

Cream Soufflé

Follow the Blue Print recipe using the smaller quantity of milk and add 3–4 tablespoons thick cream to the sauce with the egg yolks.

A soufflé omelette is made by separating the egg yolks and the whites, then whisking the whites until very stiff and folding them into the egg yolks. In this way you produce a thick, ultra-light type of omelette.

A soufflé omelette makes an excellent basis for a hot dessert. Although you can add sweet fillings to the plain omelette on page 84, they blend better with the lighter texture of the soufflé type.

The savoury fillings given on pages 84 and 85 may be incorporated into this type of omelette, although I prefer more moist fillings as indicated by the suggestions on this page.

The points under AVOID and TO RECTIFY on page 84 also apply to this type of omelette.

Blue Print Recipe

To Make a Soufflé Omelette

2 or 3 eggs · seasoning or 1 teaspoon sugar for a sweet omelette · 1 tablespoon water · 1 oz. butter · filling or flavouring (see individual recipes).

To make Separate the yolks from the whites. Beat the yolks with seasoning or sugar, and water. Whisk the egg whites until very stiff, fold into the yolks.

Making a Soufflé Omelette

To cook Heat the butter in the pan (see page 84). Switch on or light the grill. Pour the fluffy egg mixture into the hot butter. Allow to set and 'work' as the Blue Print on page 84. You will find this more difficult as the mixture is less liquid. When the omelette is about half-cooked, put the pan under the grill (with the heat to medium) and complete the cooking.

To serve Add any filling required. This thicker omelette is more difficult to fold (you cannot roll it) so make a shallow 'cut' across the centre, then fold, see Sketches 2 and 3 (page 84). Slide or tip on to the hot serving dish or plate. *All recipes based on this serve 1 as a main dish or 2 as a light hors d'oeuvre or dessert.*

SWEET FILLINGS
Nut Omelette

Follow the Blue Print and blend 1–2 tablespoons chopped blanched almonds, hazel, pecan or walnuts with the egg yolks. Fill with hot sweetened apricot purée or jam.

Fruit Omelette

Use thin cream instead of the water in the Blue Print. Fill with hot fruit purée or sliced uncooked sweetened fresh fruit. The fruit can be flavoured with brandy or liqueur.

Jam Omelette

Make the omelette as the Blue Print and fill with hot jam (or jelly). A delicious omelette is made by adding finely grated orange or lemon rind to the egg yolks then filling with hot marmalade.

SAVOURY FILLINGS WITH SAUCES

Thick cheese, curry, mushroom, or tomato sauces all make excellent fillings.

Vegetable Filling

Blend diced cooked vegetables with any of the sauces above or with a thick fresh tomato purée (made more piquant with the addition of a little canned concentrated tomato purée).

Fish and Meat Filling

Blend cooked ham, tongue, chicken, white fish or shellfish with the selected sauce and flavour with chopped fresh herbs.

Storing and Freezing *You cannot store or freeze a soufflé omelette, but it is a good idea to freeze different fillings in small containers.* **To use any left over** *I quite like a cold soufflé omelette cut in strips and served in place of hard boiled egg.*

Making Short Crust Pastry

Short crust is undoubtedly the most useful of all types of pastry. It is quick to make, relatively simple, keeps well and is equally good with sweet as with savoury ingredients.

Blue Print Recipe

Short Crust Pastry

8 oz. (2C) flour, preferably plain · pinch salt · 4 oz. ($\frac{1}{2}$C) fat* · cold water to mix.

*This can be cooking fat, margarine, butter, shortening or a mixture.

To make   Sieve the flour and salt. Cut the fat into convenient-sized pieces, drop into the bowl. Rub in with the tips of your fingers until the mixture looks like fine breadcrumbs. *Do not overhandle.* Lift the flour and fat as you rub them together so you incorporate as much air as possible and keep the mixture cool. *Gradually* add water to give enough moisture to bind the ingredients together. Use a palette knife to blend. Flour varies a great deal in the amount of liquid it absorbs, but you should require about 2 tablespoons water. When blended, form into a neat ball of dough with your fingers. Put on to a lightly floured pastry board, and roll out to a neat oblong or round about $\frac{1}{4}$-inch in thickness unless the recipe states to the contrary. Always roll in one direction and do not turn the rolling pin, instead lift and turn the pastry. This makes sure it is not stretched badly.

To cook   As the individual recipes, generally short crust pastry needs a hot oven to set the pastry, but you may need to reduce the heat after a time.

● **AVOID** *Making the pastry too wet, this produces a tough instead of a crisp, short result: Overhandling the dough: Baking too slowly.*

● **TO RECTIFY** *If you have made the pastry over-moist either chill thoroughly, this does allow it to 'dry out' slightly, or use a generous amount of flour on the pastry board; unfortunately the latter remedy spoils the basic proportions of the pastry.*

● **SHORT CUT** *Use ready-prepared frozen short crust pastry for the various dishes in this section.*

For Special Occasions

Old English Chicken Pie

Short crust pastry made with 8 oz. (2C) flour etc. as Blue Print. *For the filling:* small quantity of sage and onion stuffing or $\frac{1}{2}$ packet stuffing; 12 oz. (nearly 2C) diced raw chicken meat; 2 oz. ($\frac{1}{2}$C) flour; seasoning; 3 sausages (skinless if possible); 2 oz. ($\frac{1}{4}$C) butter or fat; $\frac{3}{4}$ pint (2C) chicken stock or water and 1 chicken stock cube; 2 hard boiled eggs. *To glaze:* 1 egg.

Make the pastry as the Blue Print and put on one side while preparing the filling. Form the stuffing into 6 small balls. Toss the chicken meat in half the flour, blended with a little seasoning. Halve the sausages. Toss the stuffing balls, coated chicken and sausages in the hot butter or fat until golden brown. Remove from the fat and put into a 2-pint (5–6C) pie dish. Stir the remaining flour into any fat remaining in the pan, then gradually add the stock or water and stock cube. Bring to the boil, cook until thickened. Add the coarsely chopped eggs. Pour the sauce over the chicken, stuffing balls and sausages. Cool slightly, then cover with the pastry as the sketches below. Make a slit in the centre of the pie to allow the steam to escape. (This encourages the pastry to crisp.) Decorate with pastry leaves made from the trimmings. Brush with the beaten egg and bake in the centre of a hot oven, 425–450°F, Gas Mark 6–7, for about 20–25 minutes until the pastry is golden brown. Reduce the heat to moderate and cook for a further 20–25 minutes. Serve hot. *Serves 6.*

To make tartlets
1. Cut the pastry into rounds (about 2-inches in diameter, but depending upon the size of the patty tins). Use a plain cutter for savoury tarts and a fluted cutter for sweet tarts.
2. Put the rounds into the patty tins, press down and continue as the individual recipes.

To make a pie
3. Put the filling into the pie dish. Cut a band of pastry to fit round the moistened edge of the pie dish. Brush the rim of pastry with a very little water.
4. Support the rest of the pastry over the rolling pin. Arrange on top of the pie (slip the rolling pin away).

5. Press the edges together, then cut away the surplus pastry.
6. Decorate the edges by fluting.

Old English chicken pie

Savoury Tarts and Pies

Corned Beef Plate Tart

Short crust pastry made with 8 oz. (2C) flour, etc. as Blue Print opposite. *For the filling:* 2 × 12 oz. cans corned beef; 2 medium-sized onions; 1 tablespoon oil; seasoning; 1 teaspoon Tabasco (pepper) sauce; 1 egg; 2–3 diced cooked or canned carrots; 4 oz. (about ½C) cooked or canned peas. *To glaze:* 1 egg. *To garnish:* parsley.

Make the pastry as the Blue Print opposite and put on one side. Flake the corned beef and put into a basin. Peel and chop the onions, toss in the hot oil until tender, blend with the corned beef, seasoning, Tabasco sauce, egg and vegetables. Roll out the pastry, use half to cover a 7–8-inch pie plate or tin. Cover with the filling and the rest of the pastry as sketches below and opposite. Decorate with leaves of pastry, made from the trimmings, and glaze with the beaten egg. Bake for 25–30 minutes in the centre of a moderately hot to hot oven, 400–425°F, Gas Mark 5–6, then lower the heat to moderate for a further 20–25 minutes. Serve hot or cold, garnished with parsley. *Serves 6.*

Note As you see, by comparing the cooking temperatures of this tart with the Old English Chicken Pie opposite, it is advisable to use a slightly lower oven temperature, and longer cooking time, when you have pastry above and below a substantial filling. This ensures that the bottom pastry sets and browns as well as the top pastry. If the filling is fairly dry in texture, as above, it is not essential to make a slit in the pastry 'lid'.

Chasseur Chicken Pie

Ingredients as Old English Pie opposite, but substitute 4–6 oz. mushrooms for the sage and onion balls and about 4 firm, halved skinned tomatoes for the hard boiled eggs.
Make as the Corned Beef Plate Tart with pastry above and below the filling. *Serves 6.*

Steak and Vegetable Pie

The pie shown on page 81 is made with steak and vegetables. Cook the steak as in the Steak and Kidney pie on page 97 for about 1 hour, then add about 12 oz. diced uncooked vegetables and continue cooking until the steak is almost tender, i.e. approximately 2–2¼ hours. Put into the pie dish and cover with flaky or short crust pastry. Cook as the instructions for that pastry. *Serves 6.*

Golden Crust Pie

Short crust pastry made with 6 oz. (1½C) flour etc. as Blue Print opposite. *For the filling:* 2 oz. (¼C) butter; 1 large onion; 2 large tomatoes; 8 oz. (1C) minced cooked meat or chicken; seasoning; 1 tablespoon chopped parsley; ½–1 teaspoon chopped thyme or pinch dried thyme; 2 eggs; 2 oz. (½C) grated Cheddar cheese.

Make the pastry as the Blue Print opposite. Roll out and line an 8-inch flan ring or tin. Bake 'blind' in the centre of a hot oven, 425–450°F, Gas Mark 6–7 until crisp and just golden in colour, this takes approximately 15–18 minutes. While the pastry is cooking, prepare the filling. Heat the butter in a frying pan and cook the peeled chopped onion and tomatoes until soft. Add the meat or chicken, seasoning and herbs and heat thoroughly. Add the beaten egg yolks then spoon the hot filling into the hot pastry case. Whisk the egg whites until very stiff, fold in the cheese and seasoning, pile this over the meat mixture. Lower the oven temperature to very moderate and cook for 10 minutes. Serve at once. *Serves 4–5.*

To vary Omit the meat or chicken and add the same quantity of cooked or canned haricot beans. Children love this variation.

Salmon Pie Florentine

Short crust pastry made with 6 oz. (1½C) flour etc. as Blue Print opposite. *For the filling:* 1 lb. fresh spinach or large packet frozen spinach; 2 oz. (¼C) butter; 2 tablespoons thick cream; seasoning; medium-sized can salmon; ¼ pint (⅔C) milk; 1 oz. flour. *To garnish:* 1 lemon.

Make the pastry as the Blue Print opposite. Roll out and line an 8-inch flan ring or tin. Bake 'blind' as the recipe above but allow a little longer until golden brown. Meanwhile cook the spinach, drain well, sieve or chop and blend with half the butter, the cream and seasoning. Open the can of salmon, strain this and blend the juice from the can with the milk. Make a thick sauce with the rest of the butter, flour and milk (plus salmon liquid). Add the flaked fish and seasoning. Put the creamy spinach at the bottom of the pastry, top with the salmon mixture. Garnish with lemon slices, serve at once. *Serves 4–5.*

To make a plate tart
7. Cover the baking tin or pie plate with pastry, neaten edges, add filling. Cover with pastry as described under the pie, Sketches 4–6.

Corned beef plate tart

To make a flan
8. Lower the pastry into the flan ring on an upturned baking sheet or tray, or put into a sandwich tin. Neaten edges by cutting or rolling. This is described in detail on page 5.

Savoury Cheese Flans

The best known of all the savoury flans is a Quiche Lorraine, i.e. an egg custard filling flavoured with cheese and crisp bacon. This is only one of the many interesting flans of the same type. A Quiche is an excellent hors d'oeuvre and ideal for buffet parties.

Blue Print Recipe

Making a Quiche

To make Prepare the pastry, roll out and line the flan ring (put this on an upturned baking tray, for easy removal) or use a sandwich tin or oven-proof serving dish. Prepare ingredients for the filling.

To cook Bake the pastry 'blind' (see page 5) in a moderately hot to hot oven, according to the type of pastry used, until just set and pale golden; do *not* over-cook. Remove the pastry from the oven and pour the *warm* filling into the *warm* pastry. Lower the heat to very moderate to moderate, as directed in the recipe and continue cooking until the filling is set. The *greater* the depth of filling, the *longer* the cooking time and the *lower* the oven setting.

To serve Hot or cold.

● **AVOID** *Having pastry that is not crisp: Allowing the custard filling to curdle.*

● **TO RECTIFY** *Although not all recipes bake the pastry case 'blind', I find this the perfect solution. You have crisp pastry, by baking in a hot oven, and a custard filling that is perfectly set but does not curdle, by cooking the filled flan at a lower temperature, see the Blue Print.*

● **SHORT CUTS** *Use frozen or ready-prepared pastry: Use the quick method of filling as in the Onion and Cheese Flan.*

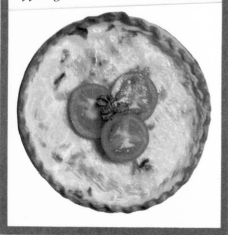

For Family Occasions

Prawn and Cheese Quiche

For the pastry: 6 oz. (1½C) flour, preferably plain; pinch salt; 3 oz. (⅜C) margarine, butter or cooking fat; water to mix. *For the filling:* 2 eggs; seasoning; ¼ pint (⅔C) milk; 4 oz. (1C) crumbled Lancashire cheese; 4 oz. (½C) shelled chopped prawns. *To garnish:* few whole prawns; parsley.

Sieve the flour and salt, rub in the fat then add sufficient water to make a firm rolling consistency. Roll out and line a *shallow* 8-inch flan ring, sandwich tin or oven-proof baking dish. Bake 'blind' for about 15 minutes in the centre of a hot oven, 425–450°F, Gas Mark 6–7, until just set. Meanwhile beat the eggs with seasoning, add the *warmed* milk, cheese and chopped prawns. Pour into the partially baked pastry case, return to the oven and continue baking in a moderate oven, 350–375°F, Gas Mark 4–5, for about 25–30 minutes until the filling is firm. Serve hot or cold garnished with whole prawns and parsley. *Serves 4–5.*

Note This filling is rather shallow, as shown in the picture. This means it will set fairly quickly and is a firm filling, so ideal to cut and serve for a buffet. For a less firm filling you can use *nearly* ½ pint (1⅓C) milk to the 2 eggs for an 8-inch, reasonably shallow, dish. Allow about 40–45 minutes to set the filling in a very moderate oven.

Quiche Lorraine

A simple Quiche Lorraine can be made in a very similar way to the Prawn and Cheese Quiche above. Use crisply fried bacon in place of the prawns. If preferred you can use grated Cheddar or Gruyère cheese in place of the crumbled Lancashire cheese.

For Special Occasions

Rich Quiche Lorraine

For the pastry: 8 oz. (2C) flour, preferably plain; good pinch salt; 4 oz. (½C) butter; 1–2 egg yolks and water to bind. *For the filling:* 4 large eggs; good pinch salt; shake pepper; pinch dry mustard; ¼ pint (⅔C) milk and ½ pint (1⅓C) thin cream or use all milk or all thin cream or partly milk and partly thick cream, but make the total amount ¾ pint (2C); 8 oz. (2C) grated Gruyère cheese; about 6 rashers lean bacon (chopped, fried until crisp and well drained). *To garnish:* parsley.

Make the pastry as the Prawn and Cheese Quiche, but binding with the egg yolks and water, then line a deep dish. I use a 2-pint (5–6C) pie dish or similar sized dish. Make sure you make the pastry sides fairly high. If you wish a more shallow Quiche then line a 9–10-inch tin instead. Bake 'blind' in a hot oven for about 15 minutes. Prepare the filling as the Prawn and Cheese Quiche, heating both the milk and the cream. Pour into the pastry case. Lower the heat and bake

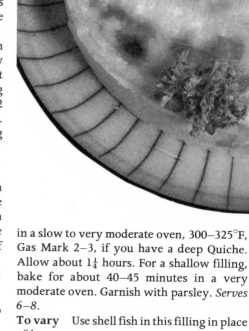

in a slow to very moderate oven, 300–325°F, Gas Mark 2–3, if you have a deep Quiche. Allow about 1¼ hours. For a shallow filling, bake for about 40–45 minutes in a very moderate oven. Garnish with parsley. *Serves 6–8.*

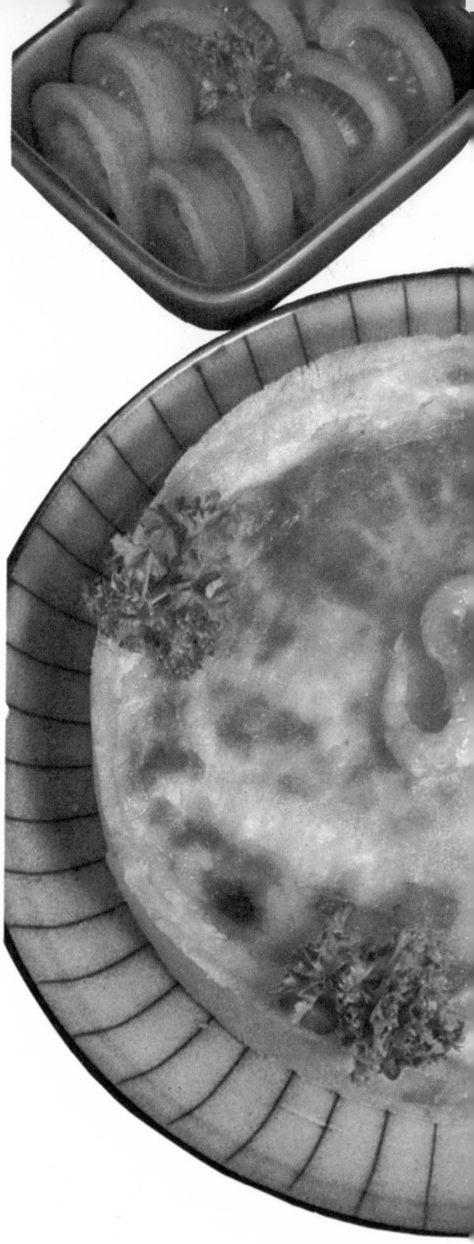

To vary Use shell fish in this filling in place of bacon.

Use cooked chopped ham, or cooked chicken in place of the bacon.

Use a mixture of cooked vegetables, sliced onions, mushrooms, potatoes, peas. Do not use tomatoes, for they might cause the filling to curdle.

Onion and Cheese Flan

For the pastry: 6 oz. (1½C) flour, preferably plain; good pinch salt; shake pepper; pinch dry mustard; pinch cayenne pepper; 3 oz. (⅜C) margarine or butter; 1 oz. (¼C) grated Parmesan cheese; 1 egg yolk and water to bind. *For the filling:* 2 large onions; little water; seasoning; 1 level tablespoon cornflour; ¼ pint (⅔C) milk; 2 eggs; 2 tablespoons cream; 4 oz. (1C) grated Cheddar or Gruyère cheese.

Sieve the flour and seasonings together. Rub in the fat, add the cheese, then bind with the egg yolk and water. Roll out and line an 8-inch tin or flan ring or dish. Bake 'blind' in a

Making a Pizza Pie

The famous Italian Pizza Pie has a yeast base but can be made with a baking powder dough. It is also possible to fill a short crust pastry flan with the savoury mixture.

Blue Print Recipe

Pizza Pie

For the base: 12 oz. (3C) plain flour · pinch salt · 1 tablespoon olive oil · scant ½ oz. fresh or ¼ oz. (1 teaspoon) dried yeast · scant ¼ pint (barely ⅔C) water · **For the topping:** 2 large onions · 1–2 cloves garlic · 1 tablespoon olive oil · 1½ lb. tomatoes · 1–2 tablespoons concentrated tomato purée · seasoning · ¼ teaspoon dried or 1 teaspoon fresh chopped oregano or marjoram · 4–6 oz. Cheddar, Mozzarella or Gruyère cheese · few anchovy fillets · few black olives · sprinkling grated Parmesan cheese.

To make Sieve the flour and salt into a mixing bowl. Make a well in the centre and add the oil. Cream the fresh yeast and add the tepid water, or sprinkle the dried yeast over the water. Pour the yeast liquid over the oil. Sprinkle flour over the yeast liquid. Cover the bowl with a cloth and leave in a warm place for about 15–20 minutes until the yeast liquid bubbles. Blend all the ingredients together and knead until smooth. Return to the bowl and cover. Leave in a warm place for about 1½ hours until the dough has doubled its bulk. Knead again. Roll out to a 9–10-inch round then put on to a warmed greased baking tray. While the yeast dough is rising (proving) for the first time, prepare the topping.

Peel and chop the onions and garlic. Toss in the hot oil, then add the skinned chopped tomatoes, the purée and seasoning. Simmer until the mixture is thick in an uncovered pan. Stir in the oregano (wild marjoram) or marjoram. Spread the tomato mixture over the yeast round. Top with the sliced or grated Cheddar, Mozzarella or Gruyère cheese, the anchovy fillets, olives and a sprinkling of Parmesan. Allow to 'prove' for about 20 minutes (although this stage is not essential).

To cook Bake in the centre of a hot oven 425–450°F, Gas Mark 6–7 for about 15–20 minutes. If the yeast mixture is not quite cooked, then put a piece of foil over the topping to protect it, lower the heat to very moderate and leave a little longer.

To serve Hot or cold. *All recipes based on this serve 5–6 or up to 8 as an hors d'oeuvre.*

Speedy Pizza

Ingredients as Blue Print, but OMIT the yeast. Use self-raising flour or plain flour and 3 teaspoons baking powder. Blend the oil and water (or you can use milk) with the sieved flour and salt. Knead lightly, roll into a round, add the topping and proceed as the Blue Print recipe.

Seafood Pizza

Ingredients as Blue Print PLUS about 4 oz. (1C) shelled prawns and use a whole can of anchovy fillets. Prepare as the Blue Print but add the prawns and most of the anchovy fillets to the *cooked* tomato mixture. Proceed as Blue Print.

Ingredients for base as Blue Print, but OMIT the tomatoes and tomato purée from the topping and use double the amount of onions and garlic, and a whole can of anchovy fillets. Cook the onion and garlic as the Blue Print, add the seasoning and herbs and spread over the dough. Continue as Blue Print.

Pizza Flan

Another way of serving the delicious pizza topping is as follows.

Make a really deep 8–9-inch flan with short crust pastry using 8 oz. (2C) flour etc. Bake 'blind' until crisp and just golden, *do not over-cook*. Prepare the filling as the Blue Print. Spoon the hot tomato filling into the hot flan, top with the cheese, anchovies and olives as Blue Print. Return to the oven for a few minutes to melt the cheese.

Crisp Topped Pizza Flan

Make and fill the flan as above. Bring out of the oven when the cheese has almost melted and top with a layer of soft breadcrumbs and grated Gruyère or Cheddar cheese. Either return to the oven to crisp the crumbs, or protect the pastry with foil and crisp under a moderate grill.

Storing and Freezing *The dough and filling should be stored separately in the refrigerator before baking. The 'unproven' dough keeps for 12 hours and rises very slowly in the refrigerator. Allow to stand at room temperature for about an hour before topping and baking. You can freeze the uncooked or cooked pizza. Allow to thaw out before cooking, but reheat from the frozen state if wished.*
To use any left over *Heat gently so you do not dry the topping.*

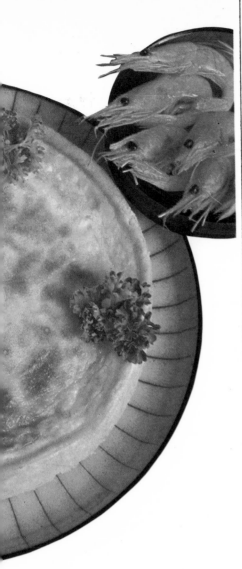

moderately hot oven 400°F, Gas Mark 5–6, until quite cooked. Meanwhile cook the neatly sliced onions in just enough water to cover. Season, cover the pan tightly, so the liquid does not evaporate. When the onions are cooked, blend the cornflour with the milk, add to the onions and liquid and cook steadily until thickened. Remove the pan from the heat. Blend the beaten eggs with the cream, stir into the onion mixture and cook *without boiling* for about 3 minutes. Add the cheese and heat until melted. *If serving the flan hot:* put the hot filling into the hot pastry and serve as soon as possible. *If serving the flan cold:* allow the filling and pastry to cool then put the filling into the flan case. *Serves 4–5.*

Storing and Freezing *The uncooked pastry may either be stored overnight or for 1–2 days in a refrigerator or for some weeks in a freezer. The cooked Quiche keeps 2–3 days in a refrigerator or for some time in a freezer. The higher the proportion of cream used in the filling, the better the flan will freeze. Allow to defrost at room temperature.*

Quiche Lorraine (left)
Prawn and cheese quiche (above)
Pizza (right)

Making Flaky Pastry

Flaky pastry has a light texture, should rise well, and is easier and quicker to make than puff pastry.

Blue Print Recipe

Flaky Pastry

8 oz. (2C) flour, preferably plain · pinch salt · 6 oz. ($\frac{3}{4}$C) butter or other fat* · water to mix (as cold as possible).
*A favourite combination is half margarine and half lard.

To make Sieve the flour and salt into a mixing bowl. Rub in one third of the fat. Add enough water to make an elastic dough. Roll out to an oblong on a lightly floured board. Divide the remaining fat in half, if hard soften by pressing with a knife, Sketch 1. Put over the top two thirds of the pastry in small pieces, Sketch 2. Bring up the bottom third of the pastry dough and fold like an envelope, Sketch 3. Bring down the top third, Sketch 4.

Turn the pastry at right angles, seal the ends of the pastry then depress this at regular intervals with a lightly floured rolling pin—this is called 'ribbing' the pastry, Sketch 5. Roll the dough out into an oblong shape again. *If you find it feels sticky and is difficult to roll* then put away in a cool place for about 30 minutes. Repeat the process covered above and by Sketches 1–5. Put away in a cool place for another 30 minutes, or longer if wished. Roll out to the required shape.
To cook As the individual recipe, but flaky pastry needs a hot to very hot oven to encourage the pastry to rise and to prevent it being greasy.
To serve Hot or cold.

● **AVOID** *Overhandling the pastry both when rubbing the small amount of fat into the flour and when folding: Pressing too firmly when you roll out the dough: Allowing the pastry to become warm and sticky.*
● **TO RECTIFY** *Rub the fat into the flour carefully as for short crust pastry, (see page 92): Lift the dough as gently as you can when folding: Use short sharp movements when rolling out the pastry: Put the pastry away in a cool place from time to time.*
● **SHORT CUT** *Although given a different name, i.e. rough puff pastry this has the same proportions of fat to flour as flaky pastry and so can be considered a good alternative. The number of rollings and foldings for rough puff pastry is greater than when making flaky pastry, but the method of incorporating the fat is much quicker.*

Chicken vol-au-vents

Rough Puff Pastry

Ingredients as the Blue Print.
Sieve the flour and salt into a basin. Drop in the fat, cut this into tiny pieces with 2 knives. Mix with water to an elastic dough. Roll out to an oblong as flaky pastry above, fold, as Sketches 3 and 4. Turn, seal the ends and 'rib' as Sketch 5. Continue as flaky pastry but allow a total of 5 rollings and 5 foldings. Use as flaky pastry.

For Special Occasions

Vol-au-Vent Cases

Choose flaky pastry as the Blue Print, rough puff pastry, as above, or puff pastry (see page 98).
Roll out the pastry until about $\frac{1}{2}$-inch in thickness for fairly shallow cases or up to 1-inch for deep ones. Cut into required shape, or shapes, i.e. either 1 large round or square or a number of smaller shapes. Take a smaller cutter and press into the pastry as Sketch 6; let this cutter mark the pastry about half-way through. Bake a large vol-au-vent case in the centre of a hot to very hot oven 450–475°F, Gas Mark 7–8 for about 25–30 minutes, reduce the heat to very moderate after about 15 minutes. Small cases take from about 10 minutes (for cocktail size) to 15–20 minutes for the size shown on this page. There should be no necessity to lower the heat. Remove the pastry case or cases from the oven. Lift out the pastry 'lid' very carefully. If you find there is a little uncooked mixture in the centre, return the cases to a very moderate oven until this is cooked.

If serving the vol-au-vent cases cold, then put the *cold* filling into the cold pastry. Place the lids in position, if wished. If serving hot, make quite sure both pastry and filling are very hot. Put together and serve at once.

Flaky or rough puff pastry made with 8 oz. (2C) flour etc. as the Blue Print will give 1 large vol-au-vent to serve about 6 people, 6–8 medium-sized cases or about 12–14 tiny ones. Puff pastry made with 8 oz. (2C) flour etc. produces rather more vol-au-vent cases.

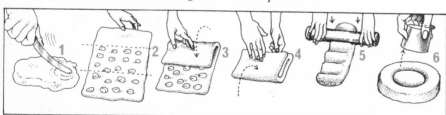

Using Flaky Pastry

Although an excellent steak and kidney pie can be made with short crust pastry I always feel the lighter texture of flaky pastry blends rather better with the meat filling.

For Family Occasions

Steak and Kidney Pie

For the filling: 1¼–1½ lb. stewing steak; about 8 oz. ox-kidney; nearly 1 oz. flour; seasoning; 1–2 oz. fat; ¾ pint (2C) stock or water and 1 beef stock cube. *For the flaky pastry:* 6 oz. (1½C) flour; pinch salt; 4½ oz. (just over ½C) butter or other fat (see Blue Print opposite); water to mix. *To glaze:* 1 egg plus 1 tablespoon water or a little milk. Cut the steak and kidney into neat pieces. Blend the flour and seasoning. Roll the meat in the seasoned flour then fry gently in the hot fat. Use the higher amount of fat if the meat is exceptionally lean. Blend the stock into the mixture gradually. Bring to the boil and cook until thickened. Cover the pan *very* tightly and allow the meat to cook over a low heat until almost tender, 2–2¼ hours. Make sure the liquid does not evaporate too much, add a little more stock if the gravy becomes too thick. Make the flaky pastry as the Blue Print opposite while the meat is cooking. Spoon the meat into a 2-pint pie dish, allow to cool, then cover with the pastry. Flake the edges with a knife to encourage the pastry to rise. Make a slit in the pastry so the steam escapes during baking and arrange pastry leaves, made from the trimmings, on top. Beat the egg (or use just the yolk) with the water. Brush over the pastry to give a shine when baked. Milk can be used in place of egg, but is not so effective. Stand the pie dish on a baking tray or baking sheet, this is a precaution in case any liquid boils out.* Bake in the centre of a hot to very hot oven 450–475°F, Gas Mark 7–8 for 15–20 minutes. Re-set the heat to moderate, 350–375°F, Gas Mark 4–5 and continue cooking for a further 30–35 minutes until the pastry is brown and firm and the meat very hot. *Serves 6.*

*If you like a generous amount of gravy then put a little into the pie with the meat and heat the rest to serve separately.

To vary   Add sliced onions or other vegetables to the steak and kidney.
Use a little red wine in the gravy in place of all stock.

Chicken Pie

Use joints of raw chicken and diced vegetables in place of steak and kidney or a mixture of raw chicken and diced bacon.

Fillings for Vol-au-Vents

Savoury   Blend diced cooked chicken, ham, cooked vegetables, flaked cooked fish or shell fish with a moderately thick sauce or with thick mayonnaise. The picture opposite shows chicken vol-au-vents.
Sweet   Fill with jam, lemon curd or well drained fruit.

Using Trimmings of Pastry—

Often there are trimmings of pastry left, which can be used for unusual savoury or sweet 'tit-bits' which can be served either as cocktail snacks or with tea or coffee.
The baking temperature will be as the particular pastry, which is covered in the Blue Print on the various pages.

Sardine Cigars   Mash sardines, season and flavour with lemon juice. Roll out narrow strips of pastry, put the fish mixture in the centre, fold as sausage rolls (page 98) and bake for about 12 minutes in a hot to very hot oven.
Jam fingers   Roll out the pastry to a square or rectangle, spread half with jam. Fold the plain pastry over the top, brush with a very little water and sprinkle lightly with caster sugar. Bake for about 15 minutes in the

Steak and kidney pie

centre of a hot to very hot oven. Cut into fingers while warm. Mincemeat, honey and chopped nuts, chocolate spread and banana mashed with lemon juice and a little sugar, all make interesting sweet fillings. Use grated cheese and chopped dates or raisins, yeast extract and chopped peanuts for savoury fillings.

Nut crisps   Roll out the pastry very thinly. Top with chopped nuts (fresh or salted peanuts, blanched almonds, walnuts, hazelnuts, brazils or pecans) and bake until crisp.

Storing and Freezing   *Uncooked flaky pastry keeps well for several days in a refrigerator. Wrap in foil or polythene to prevent the outside hardening. It freezes very well. Cooked flaky pastry keeps for several days but needs to be crisped for a short time in the oven. It freezes well, but naturally the success depends upon the filling. A steak and kidney pie is excellent.*
It is better to freeze the uncooked or cooked vol-au-vent cases without the filling and freeze the fillings separately. You cannot freeze fillings containing mayonnaise, and sauces are better if made with cornflour rather than flour.

97

Puff is the richest of all pastries, yet, in spite of the high percentage of fat, it should not be greasy. The two important factors when making and cooking puff pastry are:

1 The way you roll the dough. Do not 'cut-down' on the number of rollings, for this blends the fat into the flour and incorporates air at the same time. You should see the bubbles of air forming in the dough as you roll. Read the comments about using the rolling pin in the same direction on page 92 and on handling flaky pastry on page 96. These are even more important when making puff pastry.

2 The baking temperature. Do not be afraid of using a very hot oven to encourage the pastry to rise and to 'seal-in' the fat. Reduce the heat as directed in the recipes to prevent over-browning.

Blue Print Recipe

Puff Pastry

8 oz. (2C) plain flour · pinch salt · water to mix (as cold as possible) · 8 oz. (1C) butter.* *preferably unsalted. Other fats could be substituted. Soften slightly with a knife if very hard.

To make Sieve the flour and salt into a mixing bowl. Gradually add enough water to make an elastic dough. Roll out to an oblong shape on a lightly floured board. Place the butter in the centre of the pastry dough, Sketch 1. Fold the bottom part of the dough over the butter, Sketch 2; bring down the top part, Sketch 3. Turn, seal the ends and 'rib' the pastry as described under flaky pastry (page 96). Continue rolling and folding as flaky pastry but allow a total of 7 rollings and 7 foldings. Puff pastry must be kept cool, so put away between rollings.

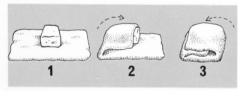

To cook As individual recipes, but puff pastry needs a very hot oven at the beginning of the cooking period. This enables it to rise well and prevents it being greasy. It is suggested sometimes that puff pastry is cooked on damp baking sheets but I have never found this necessary.

To serve Hot or cold. With sweet or savoury ingredients.

● **AVOID** *Overhandling the pastry—see the comments on page 96.*
● **TO RECTIFY** *See page 96.*
● **SHORT CUT** *Frozen puff pastry is one of the most successful convenience foods. Remember though that when a recipe says puff pastry made with 8 oz. (2C) flour etc., or 8 oz. puff pastry you need to buy 1 lb. frozen pastry.*

Puff Pastry

The following recipes all use puff pastry, several are equally successful with flaky or rough puff. An indication is given where the less rich pastries could be substituted.

Vanilla Slices (Mille Feuilles)

Puff pastry made with 8 oz. (2C) flour etc. as Blue Print. *For the filling:* ½ pint (1⅓C) thick cream; sugar to taste; few drops vanilla essence; jam or jelly; little sieved icing sugar (optional).

Roll the pastry out until wafer thin. Cut into about 15 or 18 fingers. Put on to baking trays or sheets, leave in a cool place for about 30 minutes; this makes sure they keep a good

shape. Bake just above the centre of a very hot oven, 475°F, Gas Mark 8–9. Bake for approximately 10 minutes at this high temperature until well risen and golden, then lower the heat to very moderate or switch the oven off for about 5 minutes. Allow to cool, then trim the edges with a very sharp knife. Whip the cream, add a little sugar and vanilla essence. Spread one third of the slices with the cream, top with another slice, then the jam or jelly and a final pastry slice. Dust with sieved icing sugar. (Illustrated opposite.) *Makes 5 or 6.*

Note Flaky or rough puff are not as good in this recipe as puff pastry.

To vary The three layers of pastry gives a tall and very impressive slice, but two layers of pastry are often used, in which case spread the bottom layer of pastry with jam and then with cream and top with the second layer of pastry.

Coat the top of the slices with glacé icing.

Fill the slices with Vanilla cream (page 54) instead of whipped cream.

Maids of Honour

Puff, flaky or rough puff pastry made with 6 oz. (1½C) flour etc. (see above and page 96). *For the filling:* little jam; 6 oz. (¾C) cottage

cheese; 2 oz. (nearly ⅓C) sultanas; ½ teaspoon almond essence; 2 tablespoons ground or finely chopped almonds; 2 eggs. *For the topping:* 4 oz. (nearly 1C) icing sugar; little water; few drops almond essence.

Roll out the pastry until wafer thin. Cut into 12–15 rounds, to fit into fairly deep patty tins about 3-inches in diameter. When gathering-up the 'pieces' lay these carefully one over the other, and re-roll to use for some of the rounds. Do not squeeze into a ball, as this spoils the pastry. Put a teaspoon of jam into each pastry case. Sieve the cheese, add the other ingredients for the filling and beat well until a smooth mixture. Spoon into the pastry cases and bake for 10 minutes in the centre of a hot to very hot oven, 450–475°F, Gas Mark 7–8. Lower the heat to moderate and cook for a further 15 minutes, or until both pastry and filling are set. Allow to cool. Blend the icing sugar with enough water to make a flowing consistency. Add a few drops of almond essence. Spoon a little into the centre of each tartlet and leave to set. *Makes 12–15.*

Traditional Maids of Honour

Blend 4 oz. (1C) ground or finely chopped blanched almonds with 2 oz. (¼C) caster sugar, the yolks of 2 small eggs and the white of 1 egg. Add 1 oz. plain flour or fine cake crumbs, then a teaspoon orange flower water or orange or lemon juice and a very little finely grated lemon rind. Use this filling in place of that given above. Do not ice.

Sausage Rolls

Puff, flaky or rough puff pastry made with 8 oz. (2C) flour etc.* (see above and page 96); 8–12 oz. sausagemeat. *To glaze:* 1 egg plus 1 tablespoon water.

*this gives a very thin layer of pastry only.

Roll out the pastry and cut into strips, these should be sufficiently wide to cover the sausagemeat. The pastry must be very thin if using the larger quantity of sausagemeat. Form the sausagemeat into long rolls. Lay on the pastry strips. Moisten the edges of the pastry and fold over the sausagemeat. Press the edges together and 'flake' these with the knife. Cut into the required lengths and make several slits on top if wished. Brush with the egg mixed with the water. Put on to baking sheets or trays and bake in the centre of a hot to very hot oven, 450–475°F, Gas Mark 7–8 for 10–15 minutes, then lower the heat to moderate and cook for another 5–10 minutes, depending upon the size of the sausage rolls. Serve hot or cold. *Makes 8 large, 12 medium-sized or about 18 tiny rolls.*

Storing and Freezing *See the comments on page 97 about uncooked pastry.*
Vanilla Slices freeze extremely well, but they should be served as soon as they have been defrosted at room temperature, otherwise the pastry becomes very soft.
Maids of Honour, Sausage Rolls etc., all freeze extremely well.

Maids of honour (above left) Vanilla slice (right)

Eggs in Sauces

An egg is an invaluable ingredient in many sauces. It adds flavour, food value and is either the sole thickening agent or helps the flour or cornflour to thicken the mixture. Although Zabaione (often known as Zabaglione) is really a complete dessert rather than just a sauce, I have given it on this page, for the principles of making this frothy egg mixture are the same as the Blue Print recipe.

● **AVOID** *Having the water under the mixture too hot; this is essential, otherwise the eggs could set or curdle, instead of being light and fluffy: Leaving the eggs without whisking, they could become hard around the sides of the cooking utensil.*

● **TO RECTIFY** *If the water begins to boil, remove from the heat and add a little cold water.*

● **SHORT CUT** *Soften the butter for the sauce, this means it is incorporated more readily.*

● **TO SLIMMERS** *Although no sauces can be 'slimming' the simple egg-thickened sauces are less fattening than those with a high percentage of flour.*

Hollandaise sauce with asparagus

Blue Print Recipe

Hollandaise Sauce

3 egg yolks · salt · pepper · cayenne pepper · 2 tablespoons lemon juice*· 3 oz. (⅜C) butter.
*Or use white wine vinegar.

To make Put the egg yolks, seasoning and lemon juice into a basin over a pan of hot water or into the top of a double saucepan. Make sure the basin or alternative utensil is sufficiently large to be able to whisk well; a very narrow container hampers movement.
To cook Beat with a hand or electric whisk until the mixture is light and fluffy. If using an electric whisk check that the egg mixture really is thickening well. To do this remove from the heat, if the eggs remain thick all is well. Sometimes one can whisk so vigorously that the mixture *appears* to thicken, then 'flops' as it has just been aerated, *not* cooked as it should be. When the eggs are thick, add a small piece of butter, whisk hard until well blended. Continue like this until all the butter is incorporated.
To serve Hot or cold over vegetables or with fish. This is an excellent sauce for cauliflower or broccoli. *All recipes based on this serve 6–7.*

Rich Hollandaise Sauce

Ingredients as Blue Print recipe PLUS extra 3 oz. (⅜C) butter. Method as the Blue Print but use the larger amount of butter.

Fluffy Mayonnaise

Ingredients as Blue Print PLUS ½ teaspoon *made* English or French mustard and ½–1 teaspoon sugar. Method as Blue Print. Add the mustard and sugar with the other seasoning. Allow the sauce to cool, then fold 2–3 tablespoons whipped cream into the egg mixture. Taste the sauce then add extra seasoning and lemon juice if required.

To give a more pronounced flavour, add the finely grated rind of 1 lemon to the egg yolks.

Tartare Sauce

Ingredients as Blue Print PLUS 1–2 teaspoons capers, 2–3 teaspoons chopped parsley and 2–3 teaspoons chopped gherkins (or use freshly chopped cucumber).
Make as the Blue Print recipe, then add the ingredients above. This is delicious with any fish.

Zabaione

3 egg yolks; 2–3 oz. (¼–⅜C) caster sugar; 3–4 tablespoons Marsala.
Put the egg yolks and sugar into the container, whisk as the Blue Print. When the mixture is thick, gradually whisk in the Marsala. Serve warm by itself as a dessert or over fruit. *Serves 2.*
To vary
Orange Zabaione Add the finely grated rind of 1–2 oranges to the egg yolks and flavour with 1 tablespoon Curaçao and 2 tablespoons orange juice in place of the Marsala.

Storing and Freezing *Although Hollandaise sauce can be stored for up to 24 hours it does lose some of its light texture. It can however be frozen very successfully, but use as soon as possible after defrosting. Zabaione is nicer served freshly made.*

six

SOUPS, SALADS AND SNACKS

At the beginning of this part of Perfect Cooking, you will find a selection of interesting sandwiches of all kinds. It is recorded that the word 'sandwich' was added to our language in memory of the 4th Earl of Sandwich (who lived in the 18th century) and who once spent 24 hours without a pause at the gaming tables, with no other food than beef between slices of bread.

The traditional British-type sandwich is still two slices of bread with a filling in the centre. This can be meat, fish, salads, etc., but whatever the filling, it is important that the bread is fresh, generously spread with butter or other fat and the filling kept moist, so the sandwich is never dry and 'hard to eat'.

The most colourful looking sandwiches in the world originated in Denmark, but you will be offered these delicious open sandwiches in other parts of Scandinavia too. They can be sufficiently sustaining to serve with a knife and fork for a light meal or small and elegant enough to eat with

your fingers at a cocktail party.

Toasted sandwiches provide the quick and easy snack for cold weather and there are few things more appetising than a freshly cooked bacon and egg or bacon and cheese toasted sandwich.

It is a mistake to think that salads are just for hot weather. With the wide variety of ingredients available from which to create good salads, they can be served throughout the year. Often one can serve a crisp green or mixed salad with a hot

dish as a change from cooked vegetables. You will find old favourite recipes and new ideas on pages 108–113.

I am a great lover of home-made soups. I find if I am very tired that a bowl of interesting hot soup is a wonderful light meal. The soup is easy to digest and gives one a feeling of warmth and well being. Because so many of us are 'calorie-conscious' these days I have also included some soups for slimmers. Many soups can provide a 'meal in a bowl'; others are more suitable for the start of a meal. Do not forget that soups are excellent in hot weather, when they can be served cold, iced or jellied.

Making soups today need not be a long and tiresome job. If you have a pressure cooker, use this for making stocks and soups and reduce the cooking time to a matter of minutes. If you possess a liquidiser (blender), then emulsify the soup in this to give a smooth texture. It takes almost no time at all to produce a smooth purée, and saves the tiresome 'chore' of sieving.

A plate of sandwiches can be prepared very quickly, but, if properly made, and if the fillings are chosen with a thought to food values, the sandwiches can be as nutritious as a cooked meal. If your family need to take sandwiches regularly to work, or school, make sure they have protein foods plus raw vegetables in the fillings to give the nutritional balance needed.

Blue Print

To Make Perfect Sandwiches

Make sure the bread is reasonably fresh.
Cut the bread with a really sharp knife (unless using ready-sliced bread).
Make sure the butter or margarine is sufficiently soft to spread without 'breaking' the bread, do not oil the fat though, otherwise it soaks into the bread and spoils the sandwiches. If you leave the fat at room temperature for a short time it should be soft; choose a flat-bladed knife for spreading the fat on the bread.
If the filling is very moist in texture, lay lettuce leaves on the bread before adding the filling, so preventing the filling making the bread and butter too soft.
Wrap sandwiches, or cover, as soon as they are made. This prevents them from becoming dry. Use kitchen paper, foil, greaseproof or polythene wrappings.
Cut the crusts off the bread for dainty-sized sandwiches, but if they are to take the place of a meal, then you can leave the crusts on the bread.

A NEW LOOK TO THE BREAD IN SANDWICHES

Make sandwiches with one slice of white and one slice of brown bread and arrange as the picture on this page.
Use very fresh bread, remove the crusts, spread with the filling and roll.
Make double-decker sandwiches, i.e. a slice of buttered bread, then filling, then a slice of bread, buttered on both sides, more filling and a final slice of buttered bread—just the thing for hungry children. You can either

Sandwiches of all Kinds

use the same filling or have two different fillings.
Ribbon sandwiches are made by preparing double-decker sandwiches as above, or even having four slices of bread—use white and brown breads alternately. Cut into narrow fingers.
Have a change of breads; wholemeal, malt and fruit breads of all kinds can be used in sandwiches with appropriate fillings, so can some of the interesting crispbreads available. Use firm fillings for crispbreads, so they remain firm and crisp.

SOME INTERESTING SANDWICH FILLINGS

Here are a few of my favourite sandwich fillings, but obviously it is very easy to plan an infinite variety.

With Cheese

Blend cream or cottage cheese with:
Chopped green pepper and mayonnaise.
Mashed banana.
Chopped well drained pineapple and/or pineapple and nuts. Or top the cream cheese with pineapple as in the French loaf.
Seedless raisins and nuts.
Chopped dessert apple.
Grated raw carrots and a little mayonnaise.
Little red currant or other jelly.
Blend grated Cheddar or other cheese with:
A little mayonnaise to soften.
Any of the fillings above.
Chopped or sliced cucumber.
Chopped or sliced tomato and watercress.
Chopped lean ham or other meats.
Flaked cooked fish or chopped shell fish.
Fish pâtés or pastes (spread the pâtés or pastes over the bread and butter, then add the cheese filling).
Shredded lettuce and chopped celery.

With Egg

The eggs may be soft boiled for a moist filling, hard boiled or scrambled. Hard boiled or scrambled eggs can be blended with mayonnaise for extra flavour. If you chop hard boiled eggs, instead of slicing, they are easier to eat in a sandwich.
Blend the cooked eggs with:
Chopped or sliced smoked salmon and/or a little caviare as in the French loaf.
Chopped ham, salami, other meat or chicken.
Flaked cooked fish or chopped shell fish.
Chopped stuffed olives and/or chopped gherkins or cucumber.
Chopped green pepper by itself or with chopped tomato and watercress as in the French loaf.

With Fish

Flaked white fish, mixed with chopped cucumber, shredded lettuce and mayonnaise.
Chopped shell fish mixed with plain or curry flavoured mayonnaise and lettuce as in the French loaf.
Mashed cooked cod's roe, blended with chopped crisply fried bacon.
Smoked cod's roe, mixed with a very little horseradish cream and lettuce. Use other smoked fish with the same ingredients.

With Meat

Mix chopped cooked ham with:
Well drained pineapple and lettuce.
Peanuts, and spread the bread with peanut butter.

Chequerboard and double-decker sandwiches

Finely chopped mustard pickle and watercress.
Top sliced ham with:
Very thick apple sauce or apple jelly, lettuce or watercress and some chopped dessert apple as in the French loaf.
Mix chopped cooked beef or tongue with:
Horseradish sauce and lettuce.
Cooked halved prunes and watercress.
Mix chopped cooked lamb with:
Lettuce and mint jelly.
Halved grapes, sweet chutney and lettuce.
Mix chopped cooked chicken with:
Mayonnaise, chopped pepper and lettuce.
Chopped almonds, shredded lettuce and mayonnaise.
Sliced cooked mushrooms, mayonnaise and cress.
Top sliced cooked chicken with:
Pâté and a little lemon juice.

Storing and Freezing *Wrap the sandwiches well and store in the refrigerator as far away from the freezing compartment as possible. Sandwiches freeze well, wrap and allow time for them to thaw out before serving. Avoid freezing sandwiches containing boiled eggs (scrambled eggs are reasonably good), mayonnaise, lettuce and other crisp salad ingredients.*
To use any left over *Wrap and store or freeze, or fry the sandwiches in hot butter.*

Toasted Sandwiches

These sandwiches are excellent for a hot snack, and allow you to blend hot toast with cold ingredients or with cooked food, whichever is available.

Blue Print

To Make Toasted Sandwiches

Do not be too conservative in your selection of bread, most breads toast well. Choose brown, white, wholemeal and fruit bread, as well as large soft topped rolls.
If the filling is to be hot, prepare this before

Toasted Club sandwich

toasting the bread, for the fresher the toast, the better the sandwich.
Put the hot sandwiches on a very hot plate, so they do not cool too quickly.

Cold Fillings
Raw mushrooms, sliced, mixed with cream cheese and shredded lettuce.
Flaked cooked or canned salmon or tuna, blended with cucumber and mayonnaise.
Scrambled egg, mixed with chopped anchovy fillets (this can also be served hot).

Mashed sardines, blended with a little lemon juice and finely chopped gherkins and pickled onions to taste.
Flaked crab mixed with a little mayonnaise, curry powder and capers (other shell fish can be substituted).

Hot Fillings: With Cheese
In order to heat the cheese, make the toast, put the cheese filling on one piece of buttered toast, heat under the grill for a minute then top with the second slice of toast. Choose a good cooking cheese; Cheddar, Gruyère, Emmenthal, Dutch Edam or Gouda.
Sliced cheese, topped with anchovy fillets.
Grated cheese, blended with little mustard, cream, and chopped pickled onions.
Grated cheese and pickled walnuts.
Sliced cheese, grilled until melted then topped with sliced banana and toast.

With Egg
Cook the egg, so it is just ready at the same time as the toast.
Scrambled egg, mixed with minced ham and chopped red pepper.
Scrambled egg, blended with asparagus tips.
Scrambled egg and fingers of cheese (shown in the middle layer of the sandwich on this page).
Fried eggs and crisply fried or grilled rashers of bacon.
Fried egg and fried tomatoes.
Fried egg and sliced fried or grilled sausages.
Fried egg and sliced fried mushrooms.

With Meat
Have bacon fried or grilled, other meats boiled, roasted or grilled.
Bacon and made mustard (shown in the top layer of the sandwich on this page).
Bacon and fried apple rings.
Bacon and fried bananas.
Bacon and hot pineapple rings.
Bacon and hot prunes.
Boiled salted beef and pickled onions.
Boiled salted beef, crisp lettuce and horseradish sauce.
Boiled tongue and cranberry sauce or red currant jelly.
Boiled ham, chopped and mixed with chopped hard boiled egg and cream cheese, heated for about 1 minute on the toast, then covered with more toast.
Diced chicken, blended with a thick white or cheese sauce, or curry sauce.

With Fish
Chopped smoked salmon or smoked trout, blended with very hot scrambled egg and watercress.
Flaked grilled herrings, mixed with mustard and chopped cucumber.
Flaked white fish, blended with fried mushrooms (shown in the bottom layer of the sandwich on this page); do not over-cook mushrooms.
Fried scampi (large prawns), blended with tartare sauce.
Fried fillets of fish, topped with tartare sauce.

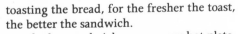

Open Sandwiches

While it is very quick and easy to place food on top of buttered bread, it takes time, practice and a real appreciation of colour and garnish to produce professional looking open sandwiches.

Blue Print

To Make Open Sandwiches

Choose a firm type of bread, this can be white, brown, rye or crispbread.

Cut it fairly thinly and spread generously with butter or margarine.

Select the toppings with an eye to colour as well as flavour and food value.

Learn to make your garnishes 'stand-up' as in the pictures (the sketches show how this is done).

Keep the sandwiches very fresh until ready to serve. Lay light weight polythene wrapping over the top of the sandwiches, heavy paper or foil can crush the toppings. If you wish to pack open sandwiches for picnics, choose toppings that do not spoil with covering. Lay a square of waxed or greaseproof paper over the top of each sandwich (instead of a second slice of bread and butter, as in an ordinary sandwich).

The following hints apply to all sandwiches:

● **AVOID** *Having too much filling or topping, so the sandwiches look untidy: Using 'tired' looking ingredients, all fillings and toppings must be fresh and retain their texture: Keeping sandwiches exposed to the air for too long before serving.*

● **TO RECTIFY** *Cover fillings before they are used: Cover the sandwiches and keep in a cool place.*

● **SHORT CUTS** *Buy ready-sliced bread: Cut loaves lengthways if you are slicing the bread, this gives a large strip of bread to be buttered and covered with filling and topping: Halve soft rolls or long French loaves, spread with butter and filling or topping and make a large sandwich, rather than a number of small individual sandwiches.*

● **TO SLIMMERS** *Use low calorie breads and crispbreads instead of ordinary breads and choose the less fattening fillings or toppings.*

SOME TOPPINGS FOR OPEN SANDWICHES

Because a number of varying ingredients are used in the true Danish open sandwich it is a little difficult to group them under a basic food. However, I *have* done this and have given the food used more plentifully than any other on the sandwich. The choice of bread is a personal one, most of the toppings are improved by being put on crisp lettuce.

With Cheese

Sliced Danish Danbo cheese (with or without caraway seeds) topped with fruit; this can be halved apricots, rings or segments of orange (fresh or mandarin oranges), prunes or nuts. Garnish with a glacé cherry, lettuce and parsley. Other cheeses can be used.

Sliced Danish Blue cheese, topped with grapes and slices of radish. This cheese is also excellent with mayonnaise and nuts; with twists of cucumber and tomato; crisply fried or grilled twists of bacon and/or Frankfurter sausages; ham rolls and potato salad. Other cheeses can be used.

Sliced Camembert with fresh or canned fruit and mayonnaise.

Sliced Danish Samsoe topped with sliced hard boiled egg, twists of tomato and mixed vegetable salad.

Sliced Danish Danbo cheese on sliced cucumber or lettuce and thick mayonnaise, topped with grated raw carrot.

With Eggs

Scrambled egg, topped with twists of smoked salmon and twists of lemon and tomato. Add a little horseradish sauce if wished. Other smoked fish can be used with the scrambled egg.

Scrambled egg, topped with fingers of thinly sliced Danish Havarti or Esrom cheese, sliced olives and radish roses.

Sliced hard boiled egg, mayonnaise and twists of crisp bacon.

Sliced hard boiled egg, pâté and potato salad.

With Fish

Small fried fillets of fish, with thick mayonnaise, mustard flavoured mayonnaise or tartare sauce and topped with twists of cucumber, lemon and tomato.

Shelled prawns, topped with thick mayonnaise, parsley and lemon and/or cucumber twists.

Bismarck or other herring. (There is a wide variety of flavourings given to herrings in Scandinavia, some sweet, some savoury, which you can buy in cans. These are splendid for open sandwiches.) Top with single rings of raw onion, parsley and slices of tomato. Also excellent topped with scrambled egg or served with slices of apple dipped in lemon juice or mayonnaise.

With Meat

Luncheon meat slices or rolls, topped with slices of cucumber and tomato and twists of lemon; or add potato salad or cottage cheese, cooked well-drained prunes and orange twists to the meat. Other meats blend well with these accompaniments.

Liver pâté, topped with crisply fried bacon, tomato and parsley; or add fried sliced mush-

rooms, bacon, gherkins and sliced tomato to the pâté.

Cooked ham, topped with fingers of cheese or scrambled egg, chopped chives, twists of cucumber and tomato. Thinly sliced smoked pork loin is an even more delicious topping for these open sandwiches. Ham or smoked pork blends well with prunes, potato salad and raw onion rings, or with prunes, potato salad and orange twists.

Slices of salami, laid flat, or rolled, then topped with scrambled egg and chopped gherkins or a gherkin fan, or just with raw onion rings. The rolls of salami (or cooked ham) can be filled with potato or mixed vegetable salad or soft cream cheese.

Steak Tartare: blend minced raw fillet steak, with seasoning, very finely chopped onions, gherkins and capers. Form into a neat round, put on buttered bread, topped with lettuce. Place an egg yolk in half an egg shell on top of the meat.

Serve hot or cold portions of fried chicken on buttered bread and lettuce. Garnish with crisply fried bacon or pâté, twists of cucumber and tomato and more lettuce or watercress.

Storing and Freezing *See comments under other sandwiches. It is less simple to store or freeze this particular type of sandwich.*

Two selections of Danish open sandwiches

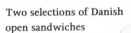

Some Garnishes for Open Sandwiches

Twists

1. Making lemon, orange, cucumber and tomato twists. Cut slices of fruit, tomato or cucumber; these should be fairly thin, but sufficiently thick to stand upright.

2. Make a cut at one side.

3. Twist so the garnish stands upright.

Gherkin fans

4. Slice a gherkin several times.

5. Open to form a fan.

Radish roses

4. Cut the radish from the base downwards.

7. Put into ice cold water to open out.

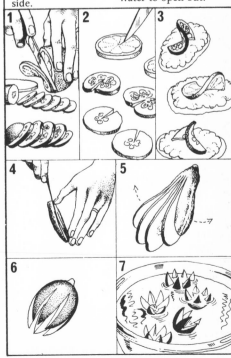

Mexican frankfurters

25 Quick Snacks

On this page you will find snacks that can be served for a light meal. Many of them are fried or grilled. Undoubtedly the frying pan is one of the most useful cooking utensils, for food that is fried cooks quickly. However, do not serve too much fried food, it can be fattening (for the fat used in frying adds calories to the other ingredients) and some people find it indigestible. The grill is perhaps less versatile than the frying pan, but provides a more easily digested form of cooking.

● **AVOID** *Too 'starchy snacks', those on this page are relatively low in bread and potatoes: Too much fat when frying, obviously if you have 'non-stick' pans you can reduce the amount of fat appreciably.*

● **SHORT CUTS** *As a snack is often chosen because you are short of time I have given very quick ideas on this page.*

● **TO SLIMMERS** *Reduce the bread or toast given in the recipes*

Storing and Freezing *The completed snacks should be eaten as soon as they are made, but some of the preparation could be done beforehand and the dish put in a cool place. Many of the ingredients in the snacks can be frozen, e.g. the cooked mushroom and tomato purée (1), the raw or cooked kidneys (2), sausages (12) (which may be cooked from the frozen state), the sliced bread (which can be fried or toasted from the frozen state) etc.*

Mainly Fried

Fried bread may be served instead of toast, or the bread may be omitted in recipes where it is given.

1. Savoury Eggs Fry thinly sliced mushrooms and tomatoes until a thick purée, season well, put on toast and top with fried eggs.

2. Bacon and Kidneys Fry rashers of bacon and sliced lambs' kidneys, put on toast and top with fried, poached or scrambled eggs.

3. Cheesey Hamburgers Fry frozen Hamburgers and tomatoes, serve on toast and top with grated cheese.

4. Autumn Bacon Fry rashers of bacon and thick apple rings. Add fairly thick slices of Cheddar cheese to the pan and heat for 1 minute only until the cheese starts to melt.

5. Fried Cheese Dreams Make sandwiches of bread and butter and sliced cheese and chutney, or cheese and ham or cheese and sliced chicken. Dip the sandwiches in a little beaten egg (dilute each egg with about 2 tablespoons milk). Fry steadily in hot fat until crisp and golden brown on both sides.

6. Corn Paella Cut 3 or 4 rashers of bacon into strips, fry until nearly crisp. Add 2 oz. ($\frac{1}{4}$C) butter, allow to melt, then add several diced cooked or canned potatoes, a medium-sized can drained sweet corn and a few sliced olives or chopped parsley. Beat 4 eggs, add 2 oz. ($\frac{2}{3}$C) grated cheese. Pour over the hot mixture and allow to set. Serve at once.

Mainly in a Saucepan

7. Kidney Scramble Chop 2–3 lambs' kidneys very finely, cook gently in a little margarine or butter. Add about 2 skinned, sliced tomatoes and cook until a purée. Beat 4 eggs, season well, add to the kidney and

tomato mixture and scramble lightly. Serve with or on toast.

8. Mushroom Fondue Heat a medium-sized can mushroom soup, add a little diced cooked ham, small can sweet corn and 2–3 oz. ($\frac{2}{3}$–1C) grated Cheddar cheese. Serve as a quick Fondue, with squares of toast or bread.

9. Tomato Prawns Heat a can of tomato soup, add shelled prawns and heat for 2–3 minutes. Turn into a heat-proof dish, cover with crisp breadcrumbs and brown under the grill (use home-made tomato purée instead of soup if wished).

10. Beans Mornay Heat a can of baked beans. Serve on toast, top with thick slices of cheese and brown under the grill.

Mainly Under the Grill

11. Fruit and Cheese Kebabs Put cubes of Cheddar cheese, cubes of banana and cubes of dessert apple on to metal skewers. Brush with melted butter or margarine. Heat under the grill until the cheese just begins to melt.

To make a change, coat the cheese in beaten egg and breadcrumbs, or crushed cornflakes, before putting on to the skewers.

12. Sausage Surprise Grill sausages until almost cooked. Cool enough to handle, split and fill with finely chopped dessert apple and chopped cheese or ham. Return to the grill pan and heat until golden brown. Serve with grilled tomatoes.

13. Delhi Chicken Brush 4 joints of young chicken with 2 oz. ($\frac{1}{4}$C) melted butter or margarine, mixed with a little curry powder. Cook under the grill until nearly tender, basting well as you do so. Remove from the grill and top one side only with a curry crumb mixture. To make this, cream 1 oz. butter or margarine with 1 teaspoon curry powder, then add about 2 oz. ($\frac{2}{3}$C) soft breadcrumbs. Return to the grill and cook until a crisp brown topping.

14. Speedy Pizza Halve large soft rolls (baps). Spread with plenty of butter or margarine, thickly sliced well seasoned tomatoes and sliced Gruyère or Cheddar cheese. Put under the grill and cook fairly slowly until the cheese melts. Top with anchovy fillets and serve at once.

15. Fish Twists Cut the rinds from streaky bacon rashers, twist round frozen fish fingers, then grill until the bacon is crisp and the fish fingers cooked. You need to turn once or twice during cooking. Serve with grilled tomatoes or canned spaghetti.

16. Kipper Toasts Grill kippers or kipper fillets and bacon. Put on slices of toast and top with sliced tomatoes. Return to the grill for about 2 minutes to heat the tomatoes.

Mainly in the Oven

Use a moderate to moderately hot oven, 375–400°F, Gas Mark 5–6 for all these, unless stated to the contrary.

17. Cottage Cheese and Ham Savoury Slice and fry 2 oz. ($\frac{1}{2}$C) mushrooms in 1 oz.

utter. Remove a few slices for garnish. Cut the flesh of 1 green pepper into rings, simmer in salted water for 5 minutes, drain. Save 2 rings for garnish. Chop the other rings finely. Beat 3 eggs with $\frac{1}{4}$ pint ($\frac{2}{3}$C) milk. Add $\frac{1}{2}$ oz. ($\frac{3}{8}$C) soft breadcrumbs, leave for about 10 minutes then add the mushrooms and pepper, 8 oz. (1$\frac{1}{4}$C) diced ham, 12 oz. (1$\frac{1}{2}$C) cottage cheese, seasoning and 1 teaspoon made mustard. Turn into an oven-proof dish and bake in the centre of a very moderate oven, 325–350°F, Gas Mark 3–4 for about 30 minutes. Add the garnish.

An even quicker snack is made if you cook the cottage cheese mixture, as above, over a *gentle* heat as you would scrambled egg. Stir as the mixture sets and serve immediately.

8. Beef Croustades Buy 4 good-sized rolls, cut a slice from the top of each roll and remove the crumb. Use this for breadcrumbs. Open a can of stewed steak, spoon into the empty cases, top with sliced tomatoes and put back the 'lid'. Bake for about 15 minutes just above the centre of the oven. (Illustrated on page 101.)

9. Hasty Beef Pie Put the contents of a can of stewed steak or steak and vegetables into a pie dish. Make about 4 oz. (1$\frac{1}{3}$C) breadcrumbs. Blend with 2 oz. ($\frac{1}{4}$C) melted margarine or butter and seasoning. Sprinkle or spread over the meat and heat for about 20 minutes in the centre of the oven. Lower the heat if the topping is browning before the meat is very hot. A little grated cheese may be sprinkled over the top of the crumbs about 5–10 minutes before serving the 'pie'. Garnish with sliced raw tomatoes and parsley.

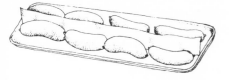

20. Baked Sandwiches This saves watching toasted sandwiches and you have much the same effect. Cut slices of bread, and sandwich together with some of the fillings on pages 102 or 103. Put into the oven and heat for about 10 minutes. If the outside of the bread is left unbuttered it is rather hard and crisp, but if you want a richer result, butter the top and bottom of the prepared sandwich before putting it into the oven.

21. Bean Hot Pot Open a medium-sized can of baked beans, add diced ham, chopped mushrooms and diced Cheddar cheese. The quantities depend upon personal taste. Put into a dish, cover and heat for about 25 minutes. Children enjoy this, for the cheese just melts, but keeps its shape.

22. Fish Whirls Spread fillets of plaice or whiting with anchovy fish paste and chopped parsley. Roll firmly. Put on a bed of sliced and well seasoned tomatoes. Brush with a little melted margarine or butter and bake for about 20–25 minutes. If you like the fish brown, leave uncovered. For a softer outside, cover the dish. Serve with potato crisps and green salad.

23. Crispy Fish Rolls Cut very thin slices of bread, remove the crusts. Spread with a little margarine or butter then with well seasoned flaked salmon, tuna or sardines. Roll firmly, secure with wooden cocktail sticks. Brush with melted butter or margarine. Heat for 15 minutes. Garnish with chopped parsley.

24. Bean and Egg Patties Cut 4 fairly thick slices of bread. Put on to a chopping board, cut out centres with a pastry cutter.

To freeze sausages so they are easily separated when frozen.

Put the sausages on a tray with a band of paper down the centre. When frozen wrap neatly.

Cottage cheese and ham savoury (below)

Arrange slices on oven-proof dishes, brush liberally with melted butter or margarine. Spoon baked beans into the centre of each slice and break an egg on top. Cover with a little butter or margarine and season. Bake for 15 minutes. The circles may be brushed with melted butter or margarine, rolled in grated cheese, blended with crushed potato crisps, and baked for the same time.

25. Mexican Frankfurters Cook about 3 oz. shell noodles in boiling salted water. Drain. Blend into a can of consommé or home-made consommé (see page 114) flavoured with a few drops chilli sauce. Add several sliced tomatoes and 6–8 Frankfurter sausages. Heat for about 20 minutes. Top with pineapple rings, tomato slices and parsley.

Corn paella

Take a pride in making interesting and varied salads. All too often a salad consists of the same mixture of vegetables; be adventurous and add fruits and nuts. We are told that 'salads are good for you', that is true, but they are also capable of being some of the most delicious dishes.

Blue Print

To Prepare Some Salad Ingredients

Beetroot Peel and dice or slice cooked beetroot. Put in seasoned vinegar. Grated raw beetroot makes a change.
Cabbage and similar greens Wash and shred finely.
Celery, Chicory and Seakale Wash, discard the very outer leaves or sticks. Chop neatly or as the particular recipe.

Cucumber Slice thinly, peel if wished, leave for a while in seasoned vinegar or lemon juice, or oil and vinegar or lemon juice.
Fruit Wash and slice if necessary. If adding the fruits that discolour easily (apples, peaches, avocado pears, etc.), then toss in lemon juice or well seasoned oil and vinegar or coat with mayonnaise.
Green Vegetables—Lettuce, Endive, Watercress and Cress Wash lettuce and similar vegetables, pull apart gently and then pat dry in a cloth or shake in a cloth or salad shaker. Use ice cold water for washing them. Shred or use the leaves whole. Watercress is sprigged and washed. Cress is cut with scissors, washed and the black seeds discarded.
Peppers (Capsicums) Cut the pulp or flesh into rings or dice. Discard cores and seeds. Some people like to 'blanch' peppers for a few minutes in boiling, salted water to soften slightly. Drain well.
Potatoes and Root Vegetables Cook in

skins where possible, and do not over-cook Skin when cooked, dice and toss in dressing while warm if possible, so the vegetable absorb the flavour. Add other ingredients t the salad while warm, but leave fresh her garnishes and any 'crisp' additions, such a celery until cold.
Radishes Wash, discard the green stalk slice or cut into shapes as page 105.
Rice Boil long grain rice, rinse well i sticky, but if boiled carefully this should no be necessary. I like to toss the *warm* rice i mayonnaise or oil and vinegar so it absorb the flavourings.
Tomatoes Skin if wished, slice or quarte or cut into 'water-lilies'.

● AVOID *Adding dressings to most green vegetables too early, otherwise they lose thei crispness. The more robust cabbage, used in coleslaw, is not spoiled by being coated with mayonnaise or oil and vinegar and left for some time before serving.*

Green Salad

Choose a selection of green ingredients only. These can be lettuce, endive, chicory, green pepper, celery, cucumber, cress and water-cress. Prepare the vegetables, it makes the salad more interesting if you mix more than one type of lettuce, then toss in well seasoned oil and vinegar. This is an ideal salad to serve with steaks and other cooked meats or fish.

Mixed Salad

You can use as many and varying ingredients in this salad as wished.
Choose a lettuce or other similar green vegetable. Add sliced or diced cucumber, sliced tomatoes, radishes (whole or sliced), green or red pepper, cut into strips or dice, chopped celery or leaves of chicory, cress, spring onions and sliced hard boiled egg. To make the mixed salad more interesting, add chopped nuts, diced dessert apples and cooked sweet corn. Avoid too many solid vegetables, such as potatoes if the salad is being served with a fairly substantial dish. Obviously you can change the 'emphasis' of the mixed salad according to the type of food with which it is being served. If serving with fish I would be very generous with cucumber, and use chopped fresh tarragon in the dressing.

Quantities to Allow

Obviously the quantities allowed depend upon the quantity of other vegetables used, but this may be a guide to buying salads.
Beetroot 1 large one serves 4–6 (unless being served by itself, when it is enough for about 3 people).
Cabbage—a small cabbage cuts up to make coleslaw for about 6–8 people.
Celery—a head serves about 6. A **chicory** head serves 2–3.
Cucumber—a medium-sized one is enough for about 6.
Green or red pepper—serves 4–6.
Lettuce or other green vegetable—allow 1 small to medium-sized lettuce for 4–6.
Potatoes and other root vegetables—allow about 4 oz. for each person.
Radishes—2–3 per person.
Rice—allow about 1 oz. rice before cooking for each person.
Tomatoes—1 medium-sized per person.

Storing and Freezing *Unfortunately salads do not store particularly well when once prepared. The salad ingredients keep well in covered containers in the refrigerator, but as soon as they are mixed together, particularly with dressing, they lose their crispness. Salads do not freeze.*

Endive

Chicory

Emphasis on Vegetables

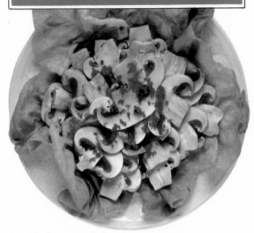

Mushroom salad

The recipes for two 'basic' salads are given on the left, but remember you can serve one vegetable alone for a salad, or mix two or three. These simple salads are excellent as an hors d'oeuvre as well as an accompaniment to hot or cold meats.

For Family Occasions

Chicory and Pepper Salad

There is often confusion about the word 'chicory'. In Britain this means the white vegetable which looks like a delicate head of celery and has a slightly similar flavour. In many countries this is called 'endive' and chicory means the vegetable that looks like a curly lettuce, see sketches.
Wash and separate the chicory leaves. Cut a raw red pepper into narrow strips. Wash and slice a few button mushrooms. Toss the pepper and mushrooms in a little oil and vinegar dressing, put into a bowl and arrange the chicory leaves round. Serve this salad with cold meats, or cheese.

Coleslaw

This salad is based on shredded cabbage. Choose white (often called Dutch) cabbage or use the heart of cabbage, not the tougher outer leaves. Wash and shred the cabbage very finely. Blend with mayonnaise.
This is a very basic coleslaw. It can be varied by adding grated raw carrots, chopped celery, chopped apple, raisins, green and/or red pepper and chopped nuts. It can be tossed in soured cream or oil and vinegar rather than mayonnaise. Serve this with cold meats, cheese or with grilled meats and fish.

Mushroom Salad

Raw mushrooms are delicious in a salad. Choose firm small button mushrooms, wash and trim the stalks, but do not peel. Slice

neatly and season or toss in an oil and vinegar dressing. Put on to crisp lettuce and top with chopped parsley or a mixture of fresh herbs. Serve this salad with hard boiled eggs or cheese, or as part of a mixed hors d'oeuvre.

For Special Occasions

American Salad

The salad illustrated on this page is typically an American one, for it has a colourful and delicious variety of ingredients, including sweet corn.
Mix cooked green beans, cooked or canned sweet corn, finely diced red pepper, sliced raw mushrooms, sliced firm tomatoes, and black olives. Toss in oil and vinegar. Put into a dish and top with rings of raw onion. Serve this salad with cold chicken or turkey.

Oil and Vinegar (French) Dressing

The proportions of oil and vinegar can be varied according to personal taste, but the most usual quantities are as follows:
Put a little salt, pepper, pinch dry mustard or little made or French mustard and a pinch sugar on to a plate. Gradually blend in 2 tablespoons olive or other first-class salad oil. Add 1 tablespoon white wine, white malt, red wine or brown malt vinegar. The choice of vinegar can be varied according to the type of salad. You can add chopped herbs or part of a crushed clove of garlic if wished.
It is sensible to make up large quantities of this dressing (mix in the liquidiser goblet), then store it in screw-topped jars. Shake just before use.

Storing and Freezing *See comments about storing on the left. I find peppers freeze well. Freeze without wrapping, wrap when very hard. Use in salads when only just defrosted.*
To use any left over *Cover, store in a refrigerator or cool place and use as soon as possible.*

American salad

Fruit blends with most other ingredients. You can use fresh, canned or defrosted frozen fruit. Choose citrus fruits to serve with rich foods, for example orange with duck, grapefruit with boiled bacon. Fruit blends well with all types of cheese salads, but particularly with cottage cheese. Dried prunes are an excellent accompaniment to cold beef or pork, so add these with raw apple to a green salad.

For All Occasions

Orange Salad

Lettuce; large oranges; oil and vinegar dressing; chopped parsley.

Arrange the lettuce on a dish, cut away the peel from the oranges and cut into segments. Moisten with dressing and top with chopped parsley if wished. Serve with duck, pork or goose.

You can add a little chopped green pepper, chicory or celery, but do not make this salad too elaborate, as the oranges are very important to counteract the richness of the meat.

Carrot and Apple Salad

Top prepared lettuce and watercress or other green salad vegetable with coarsely grated carrot, as shown in the picture. Arrange segments of apple, dipped in oil and vinegar dressing, as a garnish. This salad can be made more interesting if finely chopped apple and chopped nuts are mixed with the carrot. Serve with cooked sausages, pork, goose or other fairly rich meats or with cheese.

Emphasis on Fruit

Chicken peach salad (top)
Carrot and apple salad (below)

For Special Occasions

Avocado Pear Salad

2 avocado pears; oil and vinegar dressing; lettuce; 1–2 oranges; 2 tomatoes; cucumber. Halve the avocado pears, remove the stones, then peel away the skin from the pears. Slice and put into the dressing immediately, so the fruit does not discolour. Arrange a bed of lettuce on a dish. Cut the peel from the oranges, then cut into segments, and slice the tomatoes. Arrange the pears, oranges and tomatoes on the lettuce. Garnish with twists of cucumber. Serve this salad with cold poultry or meat or with hot roasts. (Illustrated on page 101.) *Serves 4–6.*

Chicken Peach Salad

Cooked chicken has a very delicate flavour and a salad has to compliment this. The salad shown on this page is an ideal blending of flavours. Arrange the prepared lettuce, watercress and chicory in a bowl. Top with neatly diced pieces of cooked chicken, sliced fresh pear, dipped in oil and vinegar dressing, sliced canned peaches and fresh or dried dates. Serve with mayonnaise or oil and vinegar dressing and garnish with lemon.

Storing and Freezing *Store as other salads. Frozen chicken can be used, but do not freeze the completed salad. Ripe avocado pears freeze well, but use immediately they are defrosted.*

To use any left over *Cover, store in a refrigerator and use as soon as possible.*

Practically every kind of cheese can be served in a salad. The cheese may be sliced, diced, grated or cut into neat wedges. Cottage cheese should be piled neatly on the bed of salad, or used as a filling for ham, as in the pictures on this page.

Eggs are generally hard boiled for salads, but scrambled egg, mixed with mayonnaise and finely chopped chives or other fresh herbs is delicious. The scrambled egg can be put on top of the salad ingredients or used as a filling for tomato cases or tiny boat shapes of well seasoned cucumber, see the sketches.

Hawaiian Salad

1 lettuce; 1–2 heads chicory; about 8 oz. (1C) cottage cheese; fresh or canned pineapple rings; 2–3 oranges; 1 apple; piece cucumber; oil and vinegar dressing.

Prepare the lettuce, put on a flat dish. Wash and separate the chicory leaves, arrange at either end of the dish. Spoon the cottage cheese into the centre of the lettuce, garnish with halved pineapple rings, orange segments, apple and cucumber slices (both dipped in oil and vinegar). *Serves 4.*

Note About 2 tablespoons mayonnaise can be blended into the cheese if wished.

Californian Cottage Cheese Salad

Arrange lettuce on individual plates. Top with cottage cheese, halved walnuts, cooked, well drained prunes and radish slices.

This salad can be served on buttered bread or crispbread as an open sandwich.

Stuffed Ham Rolls

1 lettuce; 6 large slices lean ham or mortadella; about 8 oz. cottage cheese; 1–2 tablespoons chopped nuts; 1–2 tablespoons chopped gherkins. *To garnish:* 4–6 slices of cucumber.

Prepare the lettuce and arrange on 4 or 6 small dishes. Halve the ham or mortadella slices. Blend the cottage cheese with the nuts and gherkins, spread over the ham and roll neatly. Put 2–3 rolls on each plate, garnish

Hawaiian salad (right)
Californian cottage cheese salad, Stuffed ham rolls and Cheese and mushroom salad (below)

Cheese and Eggs in Salads

with watercress and twists of cucumber. *Serves 4–6.*

This salad can be served on buttered bread or crispbread as an open sandwich.

Cheese and Mushroom Salad

Arrange slices of cucumber on a dish, top with cottage cheese, then arrange sliced raw mushrooms over the cheese. Garnish with parsley.

This salad can be served on buttered bread or crispbread as an open sandwich.

Egg and Carrot Salad

3 hard boiled eggs; 2 medium-sized carrots; 3–4 tablespoons salted peanuts; 2 teaspoons chopped parsley; mayonnaise; lettuce.

Chop the eggs coarsely, peel and grate the carrots. Mix with the peanuts, chopped parsley and mayonnaise to moisten. Use the larger lettuce leaves as cups and spoon some of the egg mixture into the centre of each cup. Serve the lettuce heart in the middle of the dish of filled lettuce leaves. *Serves 4.*

To vary

Egg and Prawn Salad Use shelled prawns instead of peanuts.

Egg and Potato Salad Use diced cooked new potatoes instead of grated carrots, add chopped chives and chopped parsley.

Egg and Corn Salad Omit the nuts and use cooked corn in the salad.

Storing and Freezing *See comments on other salads. Cottage cheese can be stored for several days in a refrigerator or for a limited time in a freezer—it tends to dry-out if kept for too long.*

To use any left over *Cover, store in a cool place and use as quickly as possible.*

1. Use scrambled egg in salads to fill tomato cases.

2. Scrambled egg also makes an interesting filling for cucumber 'boats'.

One of the most appetising ways to serve cold meat and fish is mixed with other ingredients in a salad, rather than just having sliced meat or a piece of fish on a plate.

By mixing the meat or fish with other foods you make it look more appetising, often it gives added moistness and it can make the meat or fish 'go further'. Our traditional meat pie (opposite) is a perfect accompaniment to salads.

Ways to Serve Meat in Salads

Cut the meat into neat pieces (as the chicken on page 110) and mix with the salad.
Cut the meat thinly, roll round a stuffing and serve on a bed of salad.

Beef Rolls

Mix horseradish cream with cream cheese or mayonnaise. Spread on slices of cooked beef and roll. Or blend chopped mustard pickle and a little mayonnaise, spread over the beef and roll.

Pork or Ham Rolls

Cottage cheese is an excellent filling for these meats, since it is not too rich. Flavour the cheese with a little chopped onion and freshly chopped sage. Spread over the meat and roll.
Cover the pork or ham with diced raw apple, mixed with diced cooked prunes, roll firmly. Blend cottage, cream or Demi-sel cheese with a little curry powder. Spread on the meat and roll firmly.

Tongue Rolls

Blend mayonnaise with chopped gherkins and capers. Spread over the tongue and roll. A sweet chutney also blends well with tongue. Spread thinly, top with chopped cucumber and roll.
Some meats, lamb and veal for example, have the wrong texture to roll neatly.

Meat and Fish Salads

Ham and Pâté Cones

8 good-shaped slices ham; 8 cooked or canned asparagus tips; about 4 tablespoons coleslaw (see page 109); approximately 2–3 oz. ($\frac{1}{2}$C) canned or home-made pâté; stuffed olives. *To garnish*: lettuce; radishes.
Spread a slice of ham on a board and lay an asparagus tip diagonally on the meat. Add the coleslaw. Roll into a cone. Put the pâté into a piping bag with a $\frac{1}{4}$- or $\frac{1}{2}$-inch rose (potato) pipe. Press out rosettes at the top of each ham cone and top with a slice of stuffed olive. Serve on a bed of lettuce and garnish with radishes. *Serves 4*.
Note If the pâté is rather firm blend with a little mayonnaise or cream.

Mixed Meat Rolls

A good mixture of meats to serve would be pressed beef filled with asparagus, mortadella filled with coleslaw (see page 109) and the ham and pâté cones above.

Ways to Serve Fish in Salads

Flaked white fish or shell fish may be mixed with other ingredients in a salad. The fish and potato salad below is a good basic recipe that can be varied in many ways.

Fish and Potato Salad

About 1–1$\frac{1}{4}$ lb. white fish; about 1 lb. potatoes, preferably new; seasoning; piece cucumber; few radishes; few capers; 1 dessert apple (optional); mayonnaise. *To garnish*: lettuce; tomatoes; 1 lemon.
Cook the fish and the potatoes in well seasoned water. Dice the potatoes neatly when cooked and flake the fish. Blend with the diced cucumber, sliced radishes, capers and diced apple. Add just enough mayonnaise to bind, about 4–5 tablespoons. Put into a plain mould or basin and leave until ready to serve. Turn out on to a bed of lettuce and garnish with sliced tomatoes and lemon. *Serves 4–6*.
To vary Chopped hard boiled eggs can be added to the above ingredients and white and shell fish can be mixed together.

Prawn and Rice Salad

6 oz. ($\frac{3}{4}$C) long grain rice; nearly $\frac{3}{4}$ pint (nearly 2C) water; seasoning; 4–5 tablespoons oil and vinegar dressing; little chopped parsley; little chopped rosemary (optional); about 8 oz. (1$\frac{1}{2}$–2C) shelled prawns; about 8 oz. (1$\frac{1}{4}$–1$\frac{1}{2}$C) diced cooked chicken; few mushrooms; 1–2 dessert apples; lettuce. *To garnish*: few prawns.
Put the rice, water and seasoning into a saucepan. Bring the water to the boil, stir briskly, cover the pan, lower the heat and cook for 15 minutes. By this time the liquid should have evaporated and the rice cooked, without being sticky. Toss the rice in dressing while hot. Cool and add the herbs, prawns, chicken, chopped mushrooms and diced apples. Shred the lettuce finely, put at the bottom of a salad bowl. Add the rice salad, and garnish with prawns. *Serves 4–6*.

Storing and Freezing *Although meat and fish may be frozen or stored, the salad ingredients on this page, including rice, do not freeze well.*
To use any left over *Cover, store in the refrigerator and use as quickly as possible.*

Prawn and rice salad

The term 'raised pies' refers to the fact that the traditional way of making these was to mould (or raise) the pastry dough, rather like a sculptor moulds clay. The sketches indicate how this is done, but if preferred you can make and bake the pie in a cake tin. If possible choose a tin with a loose base or a side lock so the pie may be removed without fear of the pastry breaking. The Blue Print gives the correct pastry for this type of pie, but short crust could be substituted.

Blue Print Recipe

Hot Water Crust Pastry

4 oz. ($\frac{1}{2}$C) fat, preferably lard · $\frac{1}{4}$ pint ($\frac{2}{3}$C) water · 12 oz. (3C) flour, preferably plain · good pinch salt · 1 egg yolk (optional).

To make Put the fat and water into a saucepan, heat until the fat has melted. Sieve the flour and salt into a mixing bowl, add the melted lard and water, knead lightly, add the egg yolk. This is not essential, but gives a better colour to the pastry and helps it to crisp. If omitting the egg yolk you may need just a little more water, for the dough should be a soft rolling consistency. Keep warm and use as shown in the sketches.

● **AVOID** *Letting the pastry cool, it is called a 'hot water crust' because the fat and water are heated, but the dough should be used while warm, soft and pliable.*
● **TO RECTIFY** *If the dough does become cold, put it into a warm place for a short time.*

Pork Pie

Ingredients as Blue Print PLUS $1\frac{1}{2}$–$1\frac{3}{4}$ lb. pork (choose about $1\frac{1}{4}$–$1\frac{1}{2}$ lb. fillet and the rest belly of pork, to give a little fat), seasoning, 1–2 teaspoons grated lemon rind, good pinch chopped fresh or dried sage, about 6 tablespoons stock and 1 teaspoon powdered gelatine. *To glaze:* 1 egg.
Dice or mince the meat, add the flavourings and 2–3 tablespoons stock. Make the pastry case, as the Blue Print. Mould or cut out. Put the filling into the pastry case, place the lid in position; *do not press down too firmly* as you must leave room for the jelly. Make a slit on top, decorate with leaves and fork the edge as in the picture. Beat the egg and brush the top, or top and sides in the moulded version of the pie. Bake in the centre of a moderate oven, 350–375°F, Gas Mark 4–5, for 1 hour. Lower the heat to very moderate, 325–350°F, Gas Mark 3–4, for a further 1–$1\frac{1}{4}$ hours. Take the pie out of the oven, allow to cool. Meanwhile soften the gelatine in the cold stock, stand over hot water and allow to dissolve. Let the jelly mixture cool and begin to stiffen *very slightly*. Put a plastic funnel or

cone of foil or greaseproof paper into the slit on top of the pie and pour the jelly through this. Leave in a cold place until set. *Serves 6.*
Note In the traditional Melton Mowbray pork pie, 6–7 chopped anchovy fillets are added to the pork.

A home-made veal and ham, or chicken and ham pie is an excellent choice for summer. Follow the directions in the Blue Print for the pastry and the proportions and flavourings for the filling as the pork pie but use.

Veal and Ham Pie

$1\frac{1}{4}$ lb. diced fillet veal and 4–8 oz. diced or minced ham or gammon in place of the pork and 2–3 hard boiled eggs.

Chicken and Ham Pie

12 oz. diced breast chicken, 8 oz. diced or minced dark meat and 4–8 oz. diced or minced ham or gammon in place of the pork and 2–3 hard boiled eggs.
Put half the filling in the pastry case, add the shelled eggs, then the rest of the filling and bake as the pork pie.

Storing and Freezing *This type of pie cannot be reheated and must be used when fresh. If freezing use as soon as the pie is defrosted.*

To Mould a Pie
1. Use about $\frac{3}{4}$ of the dough, flatten this slightly with your hand. Keep remaining dough in a warm place.
2. Now place a round or oval mould or tin on this and gradually pull and mould the dough round this to give the right shape,

and an even thickness. Remove the mould or tin.
3. Put the filling into the pastry case, see recipes, then damp the top edges of pastry.
4. Mould a lid of pastry, place on to the top of the pie, make a slit, decorate and bake as pork pie.

To Make a Pie in a Tin
5. Roll out the pastry and cut 2 rounds the size of the cake tin. Put one into the base of the greased tin; damp the edges. Keep the second round warm.
6. Roll the remaining pastry into a band, the circumference and

depth of the tin. Insert into the tin.
7. Put in the filling, pull the side band of pastry gently up as you do so to give a neat appearance.
8. Damp the edges of the pastry, place the 'lid' into position, make a slit, decorate and bake as pork pie.

Making Soups

Meat soups, some of which are covered on this page, are among the easiest to make. Meat has such a pronounced flavour, that it not only gives an excellent stock, but makes a complete soup with few additional ingredients, see Blue Print 2, Consommé. Of course there are many meat soups where other ingredients are added to give a more filling dish.

Blue Print Recipes

1. To Make Stock

The term 'stock' is used when making many soups, also in stews and other savoury dishes.

A **brown stock** is made from beef or game bones. A marrow bone gives the finest stock of all.

A **white stock** is made from veal, chicken or turkey bones. If you add the giblets of the poultry you darken the stock, although you do give additional flavour.

To make   Cover the washed bones with cold water.

To cook   Bring the water to the boil, remove any grey 'scum' if this has formed. Add seasoning, a *bouquet garni* of herbs and simmer in a tightly covered pan for 2–3 hours, or allow at least 40 minutes, at 15 lb. in a pressure cooker.

Various vegetables can be added to give flavour, but remember that a stock that has had vegetables in it does not keep as well as one without.

● **AVOID** *Adding too much liquid, other-wise the stock has little flavour.*

● **TO RECTIFY** *If the stock is lacking in flavour, remove the saucepan lid and let the liquid evaporate and become more concentrated.*

● **SHORT CUT** *Use stock cubes instead of making stock.*

● **TO SLIMMERS** *Good clear, unthickened stocks are ideal for low calorie soups.*

2. Consommé

1 lb. shin of beef · 2½ pints (6⅔C) beef stock (see Blue Print 1) · 1 carrot (optional) · 1 onion (optional) · bay leaf · seasoning · 2 egg whites plus shells · sherry to taste · To garnish: as individual recipes.

To make   Cut the meat into neat pieces. Put into the pan with the stock.

To cook   Bring to the boil. Add the whole vegetables (if the stock is well flavoured these should not be necessary). Put in the bay leaf and a little seasoning. Simmer steadily for about 1½ hours. Strain the consommé, return to the pan, add the egg whites and shells and simmer very gently for about 10 minutes. The egg whites and shells 'gather-up' any tiny partickles of meat etc., and give a perfectly clear soup. Strain and add a little sherry before serving.

To serve   Hot, lightly frozen or jellied. The consommé may set lightly without gelatine, but if it will not, then dissolve about 1 teaspoon softened gelatine in each 1 pint (2⅔C) warm consommé. Allow to set lightly, whisk and serve in chilled soup cups. *All recipes based on this serve 4–6.*

Garnishes for Consommé
The garnish gives the name to the particular consommé. Add tiny cubes of cooked vegetables, the soup is then **Consommé Jardinière**; add match-stick shapes of cooked vegetables for **Consommé Julienne**.

Here are some more versions of consommé.
Consommé à l'Africaine   Garnish with cooked rice; flavour with curry powder and sliced canned or cooked artichoke hearts.
Consommé Epicurien Garnish with shredded blanched almonds and chopped chervil.
Consommé Nouilles Garnish with noodles. This may be made more interesting by adding clear, very well sieved, tomato pulp or a little concentrated tomato purée.

Argentine Beef Soup
2 tablespoons olive or other oil; 2 large onions; 2–3 rashers streaky bacon; 1 oz. flour; about 4 large skinned tomatoes plus 2–3 tablespoons water or medium-sized can tomatoes; 1½ pints (4C) beef stock (see Blue Print 1); 8 oz. chuck steak; 4 oz. (nearly ¾C)

Argentine beef soup

fresh or frozen peas; 2–3 large carrots; *bouquet garni*; seasoning.
Heat the oil in a large pan, fry the peeled chopped onions for several minutes, add the chopped bacon and cook for a further few minutes. Stir in the flour, cook until a thickened 'roux'. Stir well. Add the chopped fresh tomatoes and water, or the canned tomatoes, and the stock. Bring to the boil, put in the diced beef, peas, peeled diced carrots, *bouquet garni* and a little seasoning. Cover the pan and simmer gently for about 2 hours. Serve with hot toast. *Serves 6.*
A little pasta can be added to the soup 30 minutes before the end of the cooking time.
Storing and Freezing   *Stock is a highly perishable liquid so store in a cool place or in the refrigerator. Even so it will need boiling every 2–3 days. You can freeze stock. Remember the container should not be too full as the stock will expand in freezing. Leave about ¾-inch 'head-room'. Treat consommé in the same way, but try to freeze without the sherry and add this when defrosted. The reason is that alcohol loses flavour in freezing.*
To use any left over   *Never waste good stock, add it to a gravy, stew or casserole.*

Making stock

Poultry and Game Soups

These soups can be extremely economical, for the basis of many poultry or game soups is the carcass. Do not discard poultry or game bones. There is a great deal of flavour to be obtained by simmering these. The giblets should be used for this purpose also, although you may like to omit the liver, as it tends to give a bitter flavour. Naturally part of a chicken or a less tender game bird could be used instead of the carcass. This produces a stock with more flavour and the flesh of the poultry may be sieved or chopped and added to the soup.

Blue Print Recipe

Chicken Soup

The carcass of a chicken · about 2½–3 pints (7–8½C) water to cover · seasoning · 1–2 onions · 1–2 carrots · *bouquet garni* · 1 oz. flour. To garnish: fried croûtons (see page 117).

To make Put the chicken carcass, plus the giblets (less the liver) if available, into a saucepan. Cover with water, add seasoning, vegetables and herbs.
To cook Bring the liquid to the boil, cover the pan and simmer for at least 2 hours or allow about 40 minutes at 15 lb. pressure. Strain the stock. Any small pieces of chicken can be chopped or sieved and added to the stock. Blend the flour with a little stock, put into the pan with the remainder of the stock and cook until slightly thickened, stirring well.
To serve Hot topped with croûtons. *All recipes based on this serve 5–6.*

● **AVOID** *Using too much liquid, otherwise the soup lacks flavour.*
● **TO RECTIFY** *If too much liquid has been added, lift the lid of the pan so the liquid evaporates.*
● **SHORT CUT** *Shorten the cooking time and add 1–2 chicken stock cubes to flavour.*
● **TO SLIMMERS** *Do not thicken.*
Storing and Freezing *Keep for 2–3 days only in the refrigerator. All these soups freeze well, with the exception of the noodle variety; pasta in a soup is over-softened and is spoiled by freezing.*
To use any left over *Heat as the recipe. Avoid boiling the soup when cream and egg yolks are already added.*

Tomato Chicken Soup

Ingredients as Blue Print PLUS 2–3 tablespoons concentrated tomato purée.
Make the soup as the Blue Print, add the tomato purée gradually. Taste after adding some of the purée to check that the flavour is not too strong.

Chicken Noodle Soup

Ingredients as Blue Print PLUS 3–4 tablespoons shell noodles.
Make the soup as the Blue Print, add the noodles and cook steadily for about 15 minutes until tender.

and egg yolks and whisk into the soup. A little dry sherry or white wine can be added for extra flavour.
Garnishes Top the soup with lightly browned almonds, asparagus tips, parsley, paprika and/or croûtons (see page 117).

Game Soup

Method as Blue Print but use the carcass of a small hare or 1–2 pheasants or other game birds, such as partridge, grouse, quail or wild duck in place of chicken.
Flavour the completed soup with a little red wine and 1 tablespoon red currant jelly.

To vary Add about 2 tablespoons concentrated tomato purée to the soup, blend thoroughly, *then* add the noodles. If desired diced carrots, chopped onions and peas may be added to the soup *with* the noodles.

Cream of Chicken Soup

Ingredients as Blue Print PLUS ¼–½ pint (⅔–1⅓C) thin or thick cream and 1–2 egg yolks.
Make the soup as the Blue Print, when thickened draw the pan on one side so the soup is no longer boiling. Blend the cream

Chicken noodle soup

Chicken Broth

Ingredients as Blue Print PLUS about 12 oz. (1½–2C) diced vegetables.
Make the soup as the Blue Print. Add the vegetables to the strained stock *before* thickening and cook for about 15 minutes. Thicken as the Blue Print or thicken and *then* add a little cream or cream and egg yolks, as the Cream of Chicken Soup.
To vary Add 1 oz. rice or pearl barley. Add a few cooked prunes.

Fish Soups

It is surprising just how rarely one is given fish soup in a private home, although many restaurants specialise in this. Fish soups are so varied, ranging from delicate creamy flavours to highly spiced soups and the luxurious shell fish bisques. In many cases you need fish stock for the soup and the Blue Print deals with making this.

Blue Print Recipe

Fish Stock

To make Use the skins and bones from fish or, if insufficient to give a good flavoured stock, buy a fish head too. When using lobster or similar shell fish, simmer the shells in liquid. This produces a very delicate pale pink stock, which enhances the colour of the soup.

To cook Put the bones, skin, head or shells into a pan. Cover with cold water, or use partially water and partially white wine. Add seasoning and a *bouquet garni*. Bring the liquid to the boil, remove any grey scum, simmer steadily for about 30–40 minutes in a covered pan, or allow about 10–15 minutes at 15 lb. in a pressure cooker. Sliced onions, carrots and celery may be added. Strain the stock carefully.

● **AVOID** *Over-cooking fish stock, it does not improve the flavour.*
● **SHORT CUT** *It may sound unusual, but chicken stock, or water and a chicken stock cube can be used in fish soups, or use water and a little anchovy essence.*
● **TO SLIMMERS** *Fish is a low calorie food and some of the unthickened fish soups would be a very wise choice.*

Creamed Fish Soup

About 8–12 oz. white fish; 1½ pints (4C) fish stock (see Blue Print); 1 oz. cornflour; 1–2 oz. butter; seasoning; grated rind 1 lemon; ¼ pint (⅔C) milk; ¼ pint (⅔C) thick cream. *To garnish*: chopped parsley or dill and/or cooked peas; paprika.
Put the fish into about ½ pint (1⅓C) of the fish stock. Simmer gently until just tender. Strain the fish from the liquid and put the stock into a saucepan. Blend the rest of the

fish stock with the cornflour, put into the saucepan, add the butter, a little more seasoning if required and the lemon rind. Bring to the boil, cook until slightly thickened, stirring well. Add the milk and cream and the flaked fish. Heat for a few minutes only, *without boiling*. Top with the garnish and serve. *Serves 4–6*.
To vary To make a thicker soup, either decrease the amount of fish stock (which gives a creamier result) or increase the amount of cornflour to 1½–2 oz. (up to ½C).
Creamed shell fish soup Use prepared or canned mussels, shelled prawns or flaked crabmeat instead of white fish.
Slimmers Soup Cook the fish as above. Add to *very well flavoured* fish stock and blend in a little yoghourt instead of milk and cream.

Spiced Fish Soup

2 tablespoons oil; 1–2 cloves garlic; 1 large onion; 3 large tomatoes; 1½ pints (4C) fish stock (see Blue Print); ½ teaspoon paprika; pinch allspice; good pinch saffron*; pinch turmeric; about 12 oz. white fish; seasoning. *To garnish*: croûtons or garlic croûtons (see page 117); parsley.
*If using a few saffron strands instead of saffron powder infuse this in the stock for about 30 minutes, then strain and use the stock.
Heat the oil in a pan, fry the crushed garlic, the chopped onion and skinned chopped tomatoes until a thick purée. Blend the fish stock with all the flavourings, add to the purée, together with the finely diced, skinned raw white fish. Simmer until the fish is tender. Season to taste and garnish with the croûtons and parsley just before serving. *Serves 4–6*.

Genoese Fish Soup

Follow the recipe for the Spiced Fish Soup and add a few shelled prawns and mussels just before serving.

Crab Bisque

1 medium-sized cooked crab; ¾ pint (2C) fish stock (see Blue Print) or water; 1 lemon; seasoning; *bouquet garni*; 1 onion; 2 oz. (½C) mushrooms; 2 oz. (¼C) butter; ½ pint (1⅓C) thin cream; 2 egg yolks; 2 tablespoons sherry.
Remove all the meat from the crab, put on one side. Put the crab shell into a pan with the stock or water, the pared lemon rind, a little lemon juice, seasoning and *bouquet garni*. Cover the pan tightly and simmer for about 30 minutes. Chop the onion, slice the mushrooms and toss in the hot butter. Add the strained crab stock and crabmeat and heat gently. Blend the cream with the egg yolks, add to the crab mixture and heat, *without boiling*. Stir in the sherry, heat for 1–2 minutes and serve. (Illustrated on page 101.) *Serves 4–5*.

Lobster Bisque

1 medium-sized cooked lobster; ¾ pint (2C) water; 1 onion; 1 lemon; small piece celery;

seasoning; ½ pint (1⅓C) thin cream; 2 egg yolks; 2 tablespoons dry sherry or brandy.
Remove all the flesh from the lobster and put on one side. Put the crushed shell into a pan with the water, chopped onion, pared lemon rind and a little juice and chopped celery. Season, cover the pan tightly and simmer for 30 minutes. Strain the lobster stock into a pan, add the flaked lobster and the cream, blended with the egg yolks, and heat *without boiling*. Add the sherry or brandy, heat for about 2 minutes and serve. Garnish with the tiny claws. *Serves 4–6*.
To vary Prawns, shrimps, scallops or oysters may be used instead of lobster. Scallops need cooking, so slice or dice and simmer in the strained fish stock for about 8 minutes before adding the cream.

Storing and Freezing *Fish is highly perishable so do not store any of these soups. Frozen fish may be used in making the soup, but I find the flavour of fish rather disappointing if frozen.*

Chicken chowder

Chowders

The term Chowder is used to describe a really thick soup, which is very like a rather liquid stew, full of interesting ingredients. Chowders make excellent light meals. Serve with toast or fresh rolls.

Blue Print Recipe

Salmon Chowder

1 pint (2⅔C) milk · medium-sized can sweet corn · medium-sized can salmon · 1 oz. butter · seasoning · chopped parsley

To cook Put the milk and sweet corn into a pan. Bring almost to the boil. Add the

To make croûtons
1. Either dice toasted bread or dice bread and fry in hot oil or fat until crisp and golden brown.
2. Drain on absorbent paper.

To make garlic croûtons
3. Fry as above, then roll in garlic salt.

flaked salmon, butter, seasoning and parsley. Heat gently for a few minutes. *All recipes based on this serve 4.*
To vary Use tuna, crabmeat, chopped prawns or flaked white fish in place of salmon.
Omit the corn and add raw diced vegetables (potatoes, onions, peas, carrots) to the milk. Simmer steadily for about 15 minutes. Add a little extra milk or white stock, then the remaining ingredients.

Chicken Chowder

2 or 3 rashers bacon; 1 onion; ¾ pint (2C) chicken stock; about 12 oz. (1½C) diced raw root vegetables; ½ pint (1⅓C) milk; about 6 oz. (nearly 1C) diced cooked chicken; 3–4 tablespoons sweet corn; seasoning. *To garnish:* chopped parsley; paprika.
Chop the bacon and the peeled onion. Fry the bacon for a few minutes, add the onion then cook together until the bacon is crisp. Add the stock. Bring to the boil, put in the vegetables and cook until just tender. Add the milk, chicken, sweet corn and seasoning.

Salmon chowder

Simmer for a few minutes then serve, topped with parsley and paprika. *Serves 4–6.*

To vary
Lobster Chowder Use the recipe above, but add flaked lobster in place of chicken. You can make the chowder with chicken stock or simmer the lobster shells to give a fish stock.
Ham Chowder Use stock from boiling bacon or ham in place of chicken stock. Increase the amount of bacon slightly and reduce the amount of chicken.
Clam Chowder Use fish stock in place of chicken stock and use about 8 oz. bacon. Add a medium-sized can clams instead of chicken.

Storing and Freezing *Store in the refrigerator and reheat gently. These chowders freeze well but should be used within several weeks.*
To use any left over *Heat for a short time only, do not over-cook.*

There are three basic ways in which one can make a vegetable soup.

The first is to chop, shred or grate the vegetables and cook them in clear stock (or water, if the vegetables have sufficient flavour). Most vegetables are suitable for this type of soup, either by themselves or mixed with others, see Blue Print 1.

The second type of vegetable soup is a purée. Cook the vegetables in stock or water until tender, then emulsify in the liquidiser goblet, or sieve. The 'starchy' vegetables, such as potatoes, give a thick purée soup, other vegetables a thinner purée. Blue Print 2 describes this type of soup.

In Blue Print 3 you have a creamed vegetable soup. Here the vegetables are blended with a creamy white sauce and cream if wished.

Blue Print Recipes

1. Onion and Capsicum Soup

2 large onions · 1–2 cloves garlic (optional) · 2 tablespoons oil or 2 oz. ($\frac{1}{4}$C) butter or margarine · 1 large green and 1 large red pepper (capsicums) · 1$\frac{1}{2}$ pints (4C) brown or white stock or water · 2 large tomatoes · 2–4 oz. ($\frac{1}{2}$–1C) mushrooms · seasoning. To garnish: chopped herbs, grated cheese or croûtons (see page 117).

To make   Peel the onions and cut into narrow strips. Peel and crush the garlic cloves.
To cook   Heat the oil or butter and toss the onion and garlic in this until nearly transparent. Take care the onions do not brown. Discard the cores and seeds from the peppers and cut the pulp, or flesh, into small strips. Blend with the onion but do not fry if you like a firm texture. Add the liquid, bring steadily to the boil, add the skinned chopped tomatoes and sliced mushrooms. Continue cooking until the vegetables are soft. Season well.
To serve   While very hot. Garnish with chopped fresh herbs, grated cheese or croûtons. *All recipes based on this serve 4–6.*
To vary   Use all onions and brown stock. Use all mushrooms and brown stock.

2. Green Pea and Potato Soup

2 large old potatoes · 1 large onion · 2 oz. ($\frac{1}{4}$C) margarine or butter · 1$\frac{1}{2}$ pints (4C) white stock or water · 8 oz. (1$\frac{1}{4}$C) shelled peas or frozen peas · *bouquet garni* · sprig mint or pinch dried mint · seasoning · little cream (optional). To garnish: parsley, mint, watercress or chives.

To make   Peel and dice the potatoes and onion.

Cream of mushroom soup

To cook   Toss the vegetables in the hot margarine or butter for a few minutes, take care they do not brown. Add the stock, bring to the boil, simmer for about 15 minutes. Add the peas, herbs and seasoning. Continue cooking gently for 30 minutes. Remove the *bouquet garni* and either emulsify in a warmed liquidiser or sieve the soup. Reheat, stir in the cream, if liked.
To serve   Top with chopped and/or sprigged herbs. *All recipes based on this serve 4–6.*
To vary   Use 3–4 potatoes and 2 onions.

Lentil Soup

Method as Blue Print 2. Put 6 oz. ($\frac{3}{4}$C) lentils into a pan with 2 pints (5$\frac{1}{3}$C) stock, preferably from simmering a ham bone or boiling bacon. Add 1–2 chopped onions, a little chopped celery (optional), 1–2 chopped tomatoes, a *bouquet garni* and seasoning.

Simmer steadily for about 1$\frac{1}{2}$ hours or allow 15 minutes at 15 lb. in a pressure cooker. Remove *bouquet garni* and either emulsify in a warmed liquidiser or sieve. Return to the pan, add 1–2 oz. butter or margarine and/or a little cream. Taste and season well, if necessary. Reheat and garnish with chopped parsley.

Leek and Potato Soup

Follow Blue Print 2, but use 1 lb. leeks in place of the onion. Wash the leeks, cut into rings and cook with the potatoes as the Blue Print. Top with paprika and a few pieces of reserved leek before serving.

3. Cream of Mushroom Soup

4–6 oz. (1–1$\frac{1}{2}$C) mushrooms · 1 onion · $\frac{1}{2}$ pint (1$\frac{1}{3}$C) white stock · *bouquet garni* · 2 oz. ($\frac{1}{4}$C) butter or margarine ·

2 oz. ($\frac{1}{2}$C) flour · 1 pint (2$\frac{2}{3}$C) milk · seasoning · 3–4 tablespoons thick cream (optional). To garnish: chopped parsley.

To make   Wash and slice the mushrooms, do not peel if good quality. Peel, but do not chop, the onion.
To cook   Put the vegetables into a saucepan with the stock and *bouquet garni*. Simmer for 15 minutes. Meanwhile heat the butter or margarine in another pan, stir in the flour, cook for 2–3 minutes, stirring well. Gradually add the milk, bring to the boil and cook until a thickened sauce.

For a delicate mushroom soup, strain just the liquid from cooking the mushrooms into the sauce, then add seasoning, some of the cooked mushrooms and the cream. For a soup with more flavour emulsify *all* the mushrooms, onion and stock in the warmed liquidiser goblet, or sieve and add to the sauce, together with seasoning and cream. The third version is to remove the onion, then add *all* the cooked mushrooms, and stock to the sauce with seasoning and cream.
To serve   Top with chopped parsley. *All recipes based on this serve 4–6.*
To vary   Use Jerusalem artichokes, celery, spinach, etc. If using 'starchy' vegetables, such as potatoes, in a creamed soup reduce the flour to 1–1$\frac{1}{2}$ oz.

Tomato Soups

Tomatoes are extremely versatile in soup. You can make a clear tomato soup as Blue Print 1; use about 1 lb. additional tomatoes in place of peppers and mushrooms. On the other hand a creamed tomato soup is delicious. Use Blue Print 3. Simmer 1 lb. tomatoes, 1–2 onions and $\frac{1}{2}$ pint (1$\frac{1}{3}$C) white stock with a *bouquet garni* of herbs. Sieve or emulsify, reheat then blend the very hot tomato purée into the very hot white sauce (as Blue Print 3), season well.

Tomato and Pasta Soup

1$\frac{1}{2}$ lb. tomatoes; 2 onions; 2 oz. ($\frac{1}{4}$C) margarine or butter; 1$\frac{1}{2}$ pints (4C) white stock; *bouquet garni*; seasoning; 1 tablespoon concentrated tomato purée; 1–2 diced carrots; 2–3 tablespoons uncooked pasta.
Chop the tomatoes and onions. Toss the onions in the hot margarine or butter for 2–3 minutes. Add the tomatoes, stock, *bouquet garni* and seasoning. Simmer for 20 minutes, sieve or emulsify, return to the pan with the rest of the ingredients. Cook for 15 minutes. Add extra liquid if the soup becomes too thick. *Serves 6.*

Storing and Freezing   *Store soups for 2–3 days only in the refrigerator. The purée soups freeze best.*
To use any left over   *Heat; this can be done quickly unless there is cream in the soup. A creamed soup with tomatoes must be heated gently to prevent the soup curdling.*

Leek and potato soup

A cold soup should be refreshing in flavour, so it sharpens one's appetite for the rest of the meal.

A cucumber soup is excellent cold, and ideal when these vegetables are plentiful and inexpensive, see Blue Print 1.

Fruit soups are popular in several European countries. These are unusual, but very suitable for the first course of a meal, providing a sharp-flavoured fruit is chosen and it is not over-sweetened in cooking.

Blue Print Recipes

1. Cucumber Soup

2 small or 1 large cucumber · 1 onion · 2 oz. ($\frac{1}{4}$C) butter · 1$\frac{1}{2}$ pints (4C) white stock · seasoning · $\frac{1}{4}$ pint ($\frac{2}{3}$C) thick cream

To make Peel and chop nearly all the cucumber. Put a small piece on one side to slice for garnish and retain a small portion of the peel to give colour and additional flavour to the soup; too much peel gives a bitter taste. Peel and chop the onion.

To cook Toss the vegetables in the hot butter for a few minutes, take care they do not brown. Add the stock, the piece of cucumber peel and a little seasoning. Simmer for 20 minutes, then emulsify in a liquidiser

Cucumber soup (left)
Savoury apple soup (right)

Cold Soups

or sieve. Cool, then blend in the cream.

To serve Chill well and top with sliced cucumber. *All recipes based on this serve 4–6.*

To vary Add a pinch curry powder to the soup.

Use a little white wine in place of some of the stock.

Blend 2–3 oz. ($\frac{1}{2}$–$\frac{3}{4}$C) grated Cheddar cheese with the hot cucumber purée, immediately after sieving or emulsifying. Cool and continue as the Blue Print.

Use 2–3 large leeks instead of the cucumber.

Use 4 onions instead of the cucumber.

Use 1 lb. tomatoes and 1 large old potato instead of the cucumber.

2. Savoury Apple Soup

1 pint (2$\frac{2}{3}$C) water · 1 lemon · 2 oz. ($\frac{1}{4}$C) sugar · 1 lb. cooking apples · 1–2 pickled

gherkins · $\frac{1}{4}$ pint ($\frac{2}{3}$C) cider or white wine $\frac{1}{4}$ pint ($\frac{2}{3}$C) thin cream. To garnish: littl cream cheese or soured cream · paprika watercress.

To make Put the water, sliced lemon an sugar into a pan.

To cook Bring the liquid to the boil. Pe and core the apples, add to the liquid the simmer for 15 minutes or until tender. Eithe remove the lemon and emulsify the apple or sieve the fruit. Add the sliced gherkins the warm soup with the cider or wine. Allo to cool and blend in the cream. Remove th gherkins if wished.

To serve Garnish with the cream cheese o soured cream, paprika and watercress. A *recipes based on this serve 4–6.*

To vary Remove several apple slices befor the fruit becomes a pulp and use as a garnish Add about 3–4 oz. (generous $\frac{1}{2}$C) raisins o sultanas to the apples as they cook.

Use a little more water and thicken the sou with a few tablespoons wholemeal or ry breadcrumbs.

Use sharp plums or cooking cherries instea of apples.

Storing and Freezing *Keep for 1–2 days in the refrigerator. The soups freeze well, ad wine and cream* after *defrosting if possible.*

seven
INTERNATIONAL DISHES

We often hear the expression that 'the world is getting smaller', for communications make it relatively easy to keep in touch with most countries and this is certainly true in the field of cookery.

Each country has its traditional recipes, created to make the best use of the natural foods available, or the foods imported regularly and easily. Holidays spent abroad enable us to eat these dishes and to form an idea of the typical meals enjoyed by the population and when we return, we can try to make these dishes in our own homes. Sometimes, of course, it is not very easy, for the essential local ingredients may not be available. In this part, therefore, I always suggest an alternative if I feel you may have problems in obtaining the authentic ingredient.

Obviously it is impossible to give a vast selection of world dishes in a limited space, but I have included the recipes that I think are outstanding and very typical of a particular country. In many countries one can learn of foreign food by eating in a Chinese, Italian, French, or other national restaurant. I am sure I speak for many other enthusiastic travellers when I say that each country, or typical national restaurant, I visit teaches me something new.

From France I learned many years ago the wise use of wine in cooking, and that perfect sauces can turn a *good* dish into a *superb* one. From Italy, that pasta does not consist only of macaroni cheese, or spaghetti with a meat or tomato sauce, but that there is a vast range of pasta and accompaniments.

There are probably no finer cakes in the world than those produced by the Austrians, as they are so imaginative, making use of fruits and nuts to create light tortes. While on the subject of cakes, you will find on page 140 the dark, rich, special occasion fruit cake of Britain, which is enjoyed in many countries today. In addition, on the same page, is the fondant icing I admire so much and which is a feature of special cakes in Australia.

Most parts of Britain, and indeed many other countries, have Chinese restaurants, so that even if you have never visited the Far East you can appreciate Chinese food. I think the lesson their cooks have taught me is that food should not be over-cooked; Chinese vegetables, and indeed all their food, retains the maximum flavour and texture.

Danish Weinerbrød (Danish pastries) may sound unusual for breakfast, and I have been offered them at that time of the day in Denmark, but the genuine pastries are so light and delicate that really one can eat them at most meals.

You will find quite luxurious desserts in this part, but when fresh fruit is plentiful try Rødgrød one of simplest of all cold puddings from Scandinavia.

Soups

Practically every country produces soup of some kind and the Blue Print gives an insight into the kinds of soup famous in some parts of the world.

Blue Print
World Soups

A soup is one of the best ways of taking the 'edge off one's appetite' and countries vary in the way they do this.

Argentine, with its abundance of beef, concentrates on meat soups, which make a light meal. A typical recipe is given on this page. Do not over-cook this soup, for the meat should be just tender but never lose its shape.

France specialises in delicious soups, but one of the finest is the onion soup, topped with cheese, given opposite. Choose a fine Gruyère cheese for the topping.

Russian cooks specialise in a delicious Borshch, which can be made with beetroot or cranberries, and is equally good served hot or cold. A less well known, but equally excellent soup is Okrochka; try this in hot weather.

Hungary's famous goulash was originally meant as a soup, and you will find a soup-like adaptation of the more substantial meat dish, which carries this name, on page 131.

One of the simplest soups is the *Greek* egg and lemon soup, which is generally served hot, but is excellent if lightly iced. This reflects the generous use of lemons in Mediterranean cooking.

Minestrone soup combines the *Italians'* liking for vegetables and pasta and I doubt if you would want a substantial main dish after a bowl of this filling soup.

Storing and Freezing *All the soups keep in the refrigerator for a day or so. The onion soup freezes well, even with the topping (this softens of course). I find the other soups freeze for only a very short time, the beans seem to lose texture and the other ingredients lose flavour.*

Soupa Avgolemono
Greek egg and lemon soup
2 pints (5⅓C) chicken stock (if this is lacking in flavour add a chicken stock cube); seasoning; 2 oz. (nearly ¼C) long grain rice; 2 eggs; 1 lemon.

Put the stock into a pan, add the stock cube if necessary, but since this gives a fairly salt flavour be sparing with the seasoning. Bring the stock to the boil, add the rice, stir well and cook for approximately 15 minutes, until the rice is tender. Break the eggs into a basin, whisk in the juice of the lemon, then add about 4–5 tablespoons of the hot stock gradually. Add the egg mixture to the very hot stock and rice just before serving. Heat gently, but do not allow the soup to boil. *Serves 4–6.*

Psarosoupa me Avgolemono
Fish soup with egg and lemon
This is a similar soup to the recipe above, in that the egg and lemon mixture are added to the soup.

Cook 1–2 diced onions, 2 diced carrots and 1–2 sticks celery (chopped into neat pieces) in about 3 pints (8C) salted water or fish stock. When the vegetables are tender, this takes about 20 minutes, add 1 lb. white fish, cut into small pieces, and seasoning. Continue cooking for a further 10 minutes. Add a tablespoon olive oil, then the eggs and lemon, blended with a little of the stock from the pan. Heat, but do not boil. Garnish with celery leaves or parsley. *Serves 4–6.*

Borshch
Russian beetroot soup
2 oz. (¼C) butter or 2 good tablespoons oil; 1 large onion (optional); 1 very large raw beetroot; 2 pints (5⅓C) brown or white stock; seasoning. *To garnish*: chopped parsley or chives and/or soured cream or yoghourt.

Heat the butter or oil. Add the very finely chopped or grated onion and the chopped or grated raw beetroot. Toss the vegetables in the butter or oil for about 5 minutes, taking care they do not discolour. Add the stock and seasoning. Cover the pan and simmer for about 45 minutes. Serve hot, topped with parsley or chives. If preferred, allow to cool and top with soured cream or yoghourt. *Serves 4–6.*

To vary Add a little shredded cabbage and a few sliced tomatoes to the stock during cooking.

Cooked beetroot may be used, in which case reduce the amount of stock to 1½ pints (4C) and cook for about 20 minutes only.

Use about three-quarters stock and a quarter white wine in the recipe.

Omit the beetroot and use about 8 oz. (1C) cranberries. These are very sharp in flavour and it is advisable to add a little sugar to the soup.

Okrochka
Russian cucumber summer soup
1 large cucumber; 1 salted cucumber or 2–3 small pickled gherkins; about 8 oz. (1¼C) cooked chicken or meat; 3–4 spring onions; 2 hard boiled eggs; 1 teaspoon French mustard; good pinch sugar; seasoning; ¼ pint (⅔C) soured cream or yoghourt; 1½ pints (4C) kvass (see recipe below) or use half chicken and half beef stock or partially stock and partially white wine (flavoured with mint). *To garnish*: chopped dill.

Peel and dice the fresh cucumber and dice the salted cucumber or gherkins. Put into a basin with the finely diced chicken or meat, chopped spring onions (use some of the green stalk) and the chopped hard boiled eggs. Blend the mustard, sugar and seasoning with the cream or yoghourt and add to the chopped ingredients. Stir in the kvass, stock or stock and wine. If not using kvass, put a bunch of mint in the soup, remove before serving. Chill the soup. Top with chopped dill just before serving. If fresh dill is not obtainable, add a good pinch of the dried herb to the soup. *Serves 6–8.*

Kvass
Russian fermented rye bread
This lightly alcoholic drink is used a great deal in Russian soups. It is troublesome to prepare, and I find I obtain a similar flavour

by mixing white and brown stock and white wine. However if you would like to make your own this is what you do.

Buy about 1 lb. very dark rye bread. Slice and bake in a very moderate oven until crisp. Put into a container, add about 6 pints boiling water and leave undisturbed for about 4–5 hours. Strain the liquid on to 1 oz. yeast, then add about 8 oz. (1C) sugar and a good bunch mint; bruise the leaves to extract the maximum flavour. Leave to ferment in a warm place for about 6 hours, then strain off the liquid on to 2–3 oz. (nearly ½C) raisins. Keep in bottles for 3–4 days before use.

Locro de Trigo
Argentine beef stew with beans and corn
4 oz. (about ¾C) dried butter beans (soaked overnight) or use canned beans*; 2 onions; 1 large red pepper; 1½ lb. chuck steak; 2 tablespoons olive or other oil; 2 pints (5⅓C) brown stock; 2 teaspoons paprika; few bacon rashers**; 8 oz. red or garlic sausage; seasoning; about 8 oz. (just over 1C) canned or cooked sweet corn.

*If using canned beans, drain and add with the sweet corn, you need a 1–1¼ lb. can.

**Green (mild) bacon if possible.

Drain the soaked beans, peel and chop the onions and dice the pepper (discard core and seeds). Cut the meat into small neat pieces. Heat the oil in a large pan, toss the onion, pepper and beef in this for a few minutes. Blend the stock with the paprika, add this to the pan together with the butter beans, diced bacon, sliced sausage and seasoning. Bring the liquid just to boiling point, lower the heat, cover tightly and simmer gently for about 2 hours. Add the drained sweet corn and any extra seasoning desired. Simmer for a further 30 minutes. This is a filling soup that makes a complete meal with bread. *Serves 6.*

Minestrone
Italian thick vegetable soup
2–3 oz. (just over ¼C) dried haricot beans; 1½ pints (4C) white stock or water and chicken stock cubes; 1–2 onions; 1–2 cloves garlic; 2 tablespoons olive oil; 1–2 rashers bacon; about 2 large tomatoes; 2 medium-sized carrots; seasoning; 2 oz. macaroni; small piece cabbage; about ¼ pint (⅔C) white wine. *To garnish*: chopped parsley; grated Parmesan cheese.

Okrochka (above)
Soupe à l'oignon gratinée (far left)
Locro de trigo (below left)

Put the beans to soak in the stock or water and stock cubes, leave overnight. Peel and cut the onions into neat pieces and slice the garlic finely. Toss in the oil, take care they do not discolour. Add the beans and stock, the neatly diced bacon, skinned sliced tomatoes and peeled and sliced carrots. Add a little seasoning, if necessary. Cover the pan and simmer gently for about 1½ hours. Add the macaroni and the finely shredded cabbage and continue cooking for a further 15–20 minutes, or until just soft. Add the wine towards the end of the cooking time, together with more seasoning, if desired. Top with the parsley and leave everyone to help themselves to cheese. *Serves 4–6.*

Soupe à l'oignon
French onion soup
4 large good strong onions; 1–2 cloves garlic (optional); 2 oz. (¼C) butter or use 1 oz. butter and a good tablespoon olive oil; 1½–2 pints (4–5⅓C) (depending upon thickness desired) very good strong brown stock; seasoning.
Peel the onions, cut into thin rings then divide each ring into pieces. Save a few whole rings for garnish if wished. It is worth while cutting the onions neatly, for it makes a difference to the look of the soup. Peel and crush the garlic cloves (these are not essential, but strangely enough onions lose so much flavour when cooked that I find I need the garlic to give a definite flavour). Toss the onions and garlic in the hot butter or butter and oil until pale golden. Add the stock and seasoning to taste. Cover the pan and simmer steadily for about 20–30 minutes. *Serves 4–6.*

Soupe à l'Oignon Gratinée
French onion soup with cheese
Make the soup as above, put into one large or several individual heat-proof serving dishes. Top with rounds of French bread or toast and grated Gruyère cheese and brown under the grill for just a few minutes.

123

Fish Dishes

There are many countries in the world where the fish dishes are superb, and where you have an excellent choice of fish. In addition to the recipes described on this page you will find many more on pages 162–171.

Blue Print
World Fish Dishes

France has innumerable dishes using sole, which can be adapted for the less expensive plaice and whiting.
Norway has some of the finest fish in the world and their cooks create simple but superb dishes. Never despise cod, Norwegians will prove it to be a superb fish when really fresh and well cooked.
Portugal, like so many Catholic countries specialises in salt cod dishes, i.e. Bacalhau, but since this is not easy to obtain I have selected a very simple, but original dish that can be made with most white fish and which uses cockles too.
The *Italian* Fritto Misto, pictured on this page could be prepared in most countries, just take a selection of fish, coat it in light batter and fry until crisp.

Storing and Freezing. *Fish is a highly perishable food, so store for the shortest time possible. Uncooked fish freezes well. The recipes on this page can be made with frozen fish, there is no need to defrost before cooking.*

Sole Bonne Femme
French sole with mushrooms
8 fillets sole; 1 small onion or shallot; ½ pint (1⅓C) fish stock; seasoning; lemon juice; 4 oz. (1C) mushrooms; 2 oz. (¼C) butter; 1 oz. flour; about ¼ pint (⅔C) thin cream or milk; 1 egg yolk. *To garnish*: creamed potato; parsley.
Fold the fillets or lay flat in an oven-proof dish, add the chopped onion or shallot, stock, seasoning and a squeeze lemon juice (save the rest of the lemon for garnish). Bake for about 15–20 minutes in a moderate oven, until the fish is tender but unbroken. Meanwhile, slice and fry the mushrooms in the butter, add the flour and cook for 2–3 minutes. Gradually add the strained fish stock (keep the fish warm in the dish), most of the cream or milk and a little seasoning. Cook until thickened. Blend the egg yolk with the remaining cream or milk. Add to the sauce and heat, but do *not boil*. Lift the fillets on to a very hot serving dish, coat with the sauce. Pipe a border of creamed potatoes round the dish. Garnish with parsley and lemon. *Serves 4.*

To vary The dish may be put under the grill for 2–3 minutes until the sauce browns very lightly.

Fisk På Fat
Norwegian fish on a platter
About 1½ lb. fresh cod fillet; 1 egg white; 2–3 tablespoons fine biscuit crumbs; 3 oz. (⅜C) butter; 1 oz. flour; ¾ pint (2C) fish stock; seasoning; 2–3 tablespoons thick cream; 1–2 tablespoons sherry; 1–2 lemons. *To garnish*: dill or parsley.
Cut the fish into about 12 small portions. Coat in egg white and then crumbs. Fry in 2 oz. (¼C) hot butter until just golden. Meanwhile make a sauce with the remaining 1 oz. butter, flour, fish stock and seasoning.

When the sauce is cooked, add the cream and sherry. Put half the fish portions into an oven-proof dish, cover with a layer of thinly sliced lemon and half the sauce. Add the rest of the fish, a layer of lemon, then the sauce. Bake for about 20–25 minutes in a moderate oven. Serve at once topped with dill or parsley. *Serves 4–6.*

Pescado Madeira
Portuguese fish in Madeira wine
4 large or 8 small fillets whiting or cutlets of hake; seasoning; 1 lemon; about 1 tablespoon flour; 2 oz. (¼C) butter or 2 tablespoons olive oil; about ¼ pint (⅔C) Madeira wine; 8 oz. (1C) cockles.
Dry the fish well. Season lightly and flavour with very finely grated lemon rind and juice, then dust with flour. Fry in the hot butter or oil until golden. Leave in the pan, add the wine and cockles. Warm for a few minutes and serve. *Serves 4.*

Fritto Misto
Italian fried fish
Buy the widest selection of fish possible, white fish of various kinds, shell fish—large prawns, mussels, scallops etc. In Italy they would use fresh anchovies or tiny fish, often mistaken for sardines, but really the fry of the shad. If you wish to provide variety to the dish, use well drained canned anchovy fillets and sardines.

For about 1¼–1½ lb. mixed fish, make a batter with 4 oz. (1C) flour, pinch salt, 2 egg yolks, ¼ pint (⅔C) milk, 2 tablespoons water and 2 stiffly beaten egg whites. Coat the fish in a very little seasoned flour, then in the batter. Fry until the fish is crisp, golden brown and cooked. Drain on absorbent paper and serve with tomato or tartare sauce. *Serves 4–6.*

Fritto misto

Paella

Spanish rice dish

The word 'Paella' means 'cooked in a pan'. The true Spanish dish is always cooked and served in the same pan, so it is very hot as it comes to the table; the variations are endless, see below and page 76.

3 tablespoons oil; 2–3 tablespoons pine nuts; 2–3 cloves garlic; 2–3 onions; 8 oz. (1C) long grain rice; good pinch saffron or few strands saffron*; 1 pint (2⅔C) chicken stock; 1 green pepper; few cooked green beans; 3–4 tomatoes; few cooked peas; 1 red pepper; seasoning.

*If using saffron strands infuse in the stock for a while, then strain.

Heat the oil in a large pan. Add the pine nuts and brown, then lift out. Crush the garlic and chop the onions, fry steadily in hot oil. Add the rice and mix with the onions and garlic. Add the saffron to the stock, pour into the pan and cook for about 10 minutes, stirring once or twice. Put in the diced green pepper, beans, coarsely chopped, skinned tomatoes, peas, diced red pepper and seasoning. Stir gently into the rice mixture and continue cooking until the rice is tender and moist, but has absorbed all the surplus stock. Top with pine nuts. *Serves 4.*

Note Crisp spring onions make an unusual but interesting accompaniment.

To vary The above recipe is a very simple Paella. The really exciting ones use slightly less rice (4–6 oz.—½–¾C) to a little more liquid. Diced raw chicken is fried in the oil before the rice, then the rice is cooked as above. Towards the end of the cooking time, add some or all of the following ingredients: diced garlic sausages, prawns, mussels and pieces of lobster or crab. Heat and serve. Obviously the number of servings depends upon the quantity and variety of extra ingredients.

Risotto

Italian rice

A risotto is some kind of rice dish which can be varied in many ways.

2 oz. (¼C) butter or use 1 oz. butter and 1 tablespoon oil; 1 small onion; 1 clove garlic (optional); 8 oz. (1C) long grain rice; 1 pint (2⅔C) chicken stock; good pinch saffron or few strands saffron*; seasoning; little grated nutmeg; 1 tablespoon tomato purée; little grated Parmesan cheese. *To garnish*: sprigs of watercress.

*If using saffron strands infuse in the stock for a while, then strain.

Heat the butter or butter and oil in a pan. Add the finely chopped onion and crushed garlic or, if a more delicate flavour is preferred, put the whole clove of garlic into the hot butter for a few minutes only, then remove. Add the rice, and turn in the butter or butter and oil until every grain is separate. This prevents the rice from becoming sticky. Blend the stock with the saffron, seasoning, nutmeg and tomato purée, then add to the rice, stir well. Cook steadily until the rice has absorbed the liquid. A risotto should be pleasantly moist. Top with the cheese and serve. *Serves 4.*

To vary This particular, very simple, risotto is often made to serve with cooked meat, fish or other ingredients. In the picture are hard boiled sliced eggs, cooked or canned red peppers, chickens' livers, cooked in hot butter, and prawns. All of these can be added to the rice mixture, and heated gently, or served with it.

Risi e bisi—Italian rice and peas. Add 8 oz. (1C) cooked peas or red beans half way through cooking.

Rice Dishes

Rice is a food that is used throughout most of the world and has been the staple diet in many countries of the East. However you serve rice, it is important to cook it correctly and choose the right type of rice. For sweet puddings round grain rice is best, for it produces a more creamy texture. A medium grain rice, which is quite difficult to obtain, can be used for savoury or sweet dishes. A long grain rice is ideal for savoury dishes, since it keeps a better shape.

Blue Print
To Cook Rice

Choose the right type of rice, see above. In addition there is the natural brown rice, which although it may look less attractive, retains more of the food value of the grain. Wild rice, which is delicious and very expensive, is not a true rice, but the grain from a special grass. Italian rice, used for risotto, cooks with a translucent appearance, but long grain is a good alternative.

There are many ways of cooking rice. You can cook the rice in a large quantity of salted water, as for pasta (see page 128), drain, then rinse under cold water. Allow the rice to dry out on flat trays, or put it into a sieve or steamer over boiling water to reheat. A simpler way is to use a definite proportion of water to rice and avoid rinsing.

To each 1 cup of rice use 2 cups of water for quick-cooking rice or 2½ cups for rice that takes a little longer. This means to each 1 oz. rice use 2 or 2½ fluid oz. water. Put the rice with the cold water and a little salt into a saucepan. Bring the water to the boil as quickly as possible, stir briskly, cover the pan and lower the heat. Simmer steadily for about 15 minutes; at the end of this time the rice is tender, but not sticky, and the liquid absorbed. Some recipes, however do need longer cooking and slightly different proportions of liquid.

Storing and Freezing *Cooked rice or rice dishes keep well, cover to prevent hardening. Rice loses flavour and texture when frozen.*

To use any left over *Tip cooked rice into cold water, add salt if wished. Bring to the boil as quickly as possible, strain and use. If reheating rice dishes, add a little extra stock.*

A pâté is not only an excellent hors d'oeuvre, but it can be used as a filling for sandwiches or the basis for cocktail and party savouries.

Blue Print
Some World Pâtés

I have chosen four pâtés. since they seem to me to cover the most interesting approach to this particular dish.

From *France* one of the many delicious liver pâtés. Each region in France seems to produce a slightly different pâté; some creamy and soft, others coarsely minced and full of the flavour of garlic and herbs. The pâté given on this page is the latter type.

Although I have attributed the smoked cod's roe pâté to *Greece*, this is found in other Mediterranean countries too. Smoked cod's roe is not always obtainable so I give a variation using freshly cooked cod's roe— not the authentic recipe of Taramasalata, but very good. When buying smoked cod's roe make sure it is not stale, for it becomes very dry. The red roe should be soft to the touch and it should be relatively easy to remove the roe from the skin.

Aubergines (egg plants) are now being used a great deal in many countries and one of the most excellent pâtés is made with this vegetable. It often is called caviare, I must confess I find the flavour of this pâté delicious, but not like caviare. The recipe is found in *Turkey*, and other countries too.

I have also included a pâté, made with a famous *British* ingredient *Scotch* smoked salmon. This is a luxury ingredient but it does enable you to use small 'untidy' pieces which can be bought considerably cheaper than elegant slices of the fish.

Finally I have added two very quick and easy savouries from *Sweden*, which make use of home-made or commercial pâté.

Taramasalata
Greek smoked cod's roe pâté
This is only one of many recipes for this pâté. About 8 oz. smoked cod's roe; 2 oz. (up to ¼C) butter or 2 tablespoons olive oil; 1 lemon; pepper; 1 clove garlic (optional); little chopped parsley.
Remove all the skin from the roe. Blend the roe with the butter or oil, lemon juice to taste, pepper and a finely crushed clove of garlic. Put into a bowl and top with chopped parsley. Serve with hot toast, lemon and butter. *Serves up to 6 as a pâté.*

To vary Blend the mixture above with about 2 tablespoons very fine soft crumbs. Blend with 1 very smooth mashed potato; this makes a less rich pâté.
Halve the butter or oil and gradually whisk in 2–3 tablespoons warm water and the same amount of thin cream, flavour with chopped chives. This gives a mousse-like texture.
The liquidiser can be used to make this pâté.

Pâtés of the World

Use freshly cooked or canned cod's roe. Use the recipe above, but flavour with a little anchovy essence and tomato purée to give both the colour and the salt flavour of smoked cod's roe.

Smoked Salmon Pâté
Follow the directions for the first Taramasalata, then blend in thin cream to give a soft consistency. Serve topped with olives, gherkins and lemon. The smoked salmon can be minced, or chopped and pounded, before adding the other ingredients.

Patlican Salatasi
Turkish aubergine (egg plant) salad or pâté
2 large aubergines; about 2–3 tablespoons olive oil; 1 lemon; seasoning. *To garnish (optional)*: tomatoes; onions; olives; peppers.
Halve the aubergines and bake or grill until the skins turn black and the pulp is soft. This takes about 25–30 minutes under a low grill or at least 1–1¼ hours in a very moderate oven. Remove the skin, then mash the pulp in a basin. Gradually stir in the oil (often much more oil than this is used, but that does make the pâté very 'oily'). Add lemon juice and seasoning to taste. Shape neatly and serve as a pâté with hot toast and butter, or garnish with sliced tomatoes, rings of onion, or olives or rings of green pepper. If pre-

Taramasalata (right)
Pâté de grillotin (below)

ferred, serve as a salad with all these other ingredients. (Illustrated on page 121.) *Serves up to 8 as a pâté.*

Lefverkorf
Swedish liver sausages
4 oz. (about ½C) liver sausage or liver pâté; 3 tablespoons (¼C) thick cream; 1–2 tablespoons finely chopped olives; seasoning; chopped parsley. *To garnish*: lettuce; 1 lemon.
Blend the liver sausage or pâté with the cream, olives and seasoning. Form into about 12 finger shapes, roll in chopped parsley. Serve on a bed of lettuce and garnish with lemon. Serve with hot toast and butter. *Serves 4–6.*

Pâté Med Ostbuller
Swedish pâté and cheese balls
Follow the directions for the recipe above, but omit the cream and add about 4 oz. (½C) soft cream cheese. Add a little dry sherry to flavour if wished. Form into about 18 balls and roll in parsley. Serve with hot toast and butter. *Serves 4–6.*

Pâté de Grillotin
French pork pâté
1 lb. pig's liver; 8 oz. lean pork meat; 8 oz. fat belly of pork; 1–2 cloves garlic; 1 shallot or small onion; 2 oz. (¼C) lard or butter; 1 oz. flour; ¼ pint (⅔C) brown stock; 1–2 teaspoons freshly chopped herbs; seasoning; little grated nutmeg; 2–3 sage leaves; about 1 lb. fairly fat rashers bacon.
Chop the liver, pork and belly of pork separately. If preferred put through a coarse mincer. Crush the garlic, chop the shallot or onion. Toss for a few minutes in the lard or butter, stir in the flour and blend the stock gradually into the mixture. Bring to the boil and thicken. Add the herbs, seasoning and nutmeg. Put in all the meat. If you wish the meat in the pâté to be clearly defined stir *very little*. Put a few sage leaves at the bottom of a tin or oven-proof dish, then line the bottom and sides with the bacon. Spoon in the pâté. Cover with greased foil or paper. Stand in a container of water and bake in a slow to very moderate oven, 300–325°F, Gas Mark 2–3 for about 1¼ hours. Allow to cool in the tin and place a small weight on top (this makes it easier to slice the pâté). Serve with hot toast and butter. *Serves 8–10.*
To vary For a more luxurious pâté add 1–2 tablespoons brandy and a few skinned pistachio nuts.
For a creamier, smoother pâté use half pork and half calf's liver and thin cream or milk instead of stock. Put the meat through a mincer two or three times.

Storing and freezing *All the pâtés given store for several days in the refrigerator; keep well covered so they do not dry. They all freeze well for a very limited period.*
To use any left over *Excellent for a sandwich filling.*

Lasagna al Forno

Italian baked lasagna (with yoghourt topping)

For the meat sauce: 1 .tablespoon oil; 1 medium-sized onion; 1 clove garlic (optional); about 4–5 large tomatoes plus ¼ pint (⅔C) brown stock or use canned tomatoes with the liquid from the can; 1–2 teaspoons chopped mixed fresh herbs; 1 lb. lean minced beef; seasoning. *For the cheese sauce:* 1 oz. butter; 1 oz. flour; ½ pint (1⅓C) milk; ¼–½ level teaspoon dry mustard; seasoning; about 2–3 oz. (⅔–1C) grated Gruyère or Cheddar cheese. *For the pasta:* 4–5 oz. lasagna; at least 2 pints (5–6C) water; 1 teaspoon salt. *For the yoghourt topping:* 5 oz. (⅝C) yoghourt; 1 egg; ½ oz. flour; approximately 2 tablespoons Parmesan cheese.

First make the meat sauce, heat the oil and fry the chopped onion and crushed garlic for a few minutes. Add the skinned chopped tomatoes and stock or the canned tomatoes and liquid. Stir until a fairly smooth purée, then add the herbs and the meat. Cook gently, stirring from time to time to break up the lumps of minced beef. Season well. Allow to simmer gently for about 45 minutes. Meanwhile make the cheese sauce, heat the butter, stir in the flour and cook for 2–3 minutes. Blend in the milk, bring to the boil and cook gently until thickened. Stir in the mustard, seasoning and cheese. Do not cook again after the cheese is added. Put the lasagna into the boiling salted water, cook until tender, drain. Lasagna is often dried, as Sketch 3 below, so that you do not use damp pasta in the dish, and this gives a better result. Cut the pasta into neat pieces, put in layers with the meat and cheese sauces, but end with lasagna. Top with the yoghourt layer, made by blending the yoghourt, egg and flour. Spread over the lasagna and sprinkle with the grated Parmesan cheese. Bake in the centre of a moderate oven, 375°F, Gas Mark 4–5, for about 30 minutes. If you have allowed the pasta, meat and cheese sauces to cool, allow about 45 minutes at a slightly lower temperature. Serve at once. *Serves 4–5 as a main dish or about 8–10 as an hors d'oeuvre.*

To vary The meat sauce may be thickened with a little cornflour if wished, although I prefer an unthickened sauce. To make a more interesting meat sauce, add a little red wine instead of stock or tomato liquid, a finely chopped green or red pepper and a few chopped mushrooms. You can also flavour the sauce with a little Worcestershire sauce.

1. Hold the spaghetti in one hand until the bottom part softens.

2. Twist the spaghetti so the softened ends turn into the water, allowing remaining pasta to drop into the pan.

Pasta Dishes

There is an almost bewildering selection of pasta from which to choose, but some of the most interesting are the wide ribbon lasagna and big cannelloni tubes. Lasagna dishes can be served with a variety of sauces and cheeses and almost any stuffing can be used for cannelloni. Whichever pasta you choose, the rules for cooking are the same.

Blue Print
Cooking Pasta

Allow 2 pints (5–6C) water to each 4 oz. pasta—this is an absolute minimum. Season with about 1 teaspoon salt. Bring the water to the boil *before* adding the pasta. Add the pasta to the boiling water. If cooking long pasta, such as spaghetti, see the sketches, for they explain how to insert the strands into the pan so they do not break. Time the cooking carefully. Approximate cooking time is generally given on the packet. The quick-cooking macaroni for example takes about 7–8 minutes from the time the water returns to the boil, after adding the pasta. Do not over-cook. Strain the pasta as soon as it is cooked.

● **AVOID** *Over-cooking the pasta, otherwise it loses both texture and flavour; the Italians use the expression 'al dente', which means that it is still slightly nutty. To test, press a piece against the side of the pan with a fork. It should need quite firm pressure to break the pasta: The pasta sticking together, while cooking.*

● **TO RECTIFY** *Lift the pasta once or twice with two forks during cooking, so you separate the strands.*

● **TO SLIMMERS** *The starch content is reduced a little if the pasta is rinsed in boiling water after straining.*

Spaghetti Bolognese

Lasagna Verdi Try the green spinach-flavoured lasagna. Use as the recipe above, or make about double the quantity of cheese sauce and put layers of lasagna and layers of cheese sauce.

Another delicious version of the lasagna dish, above, is to make just the meat sauce and instead of a cheese sauce to use layers of three kinds of cheese, grated Parmesan, Ricotto (the Italian cream cheese) and Mozzarella, an excellent cooking cheese.

Spaghetti Bolognese

Italian spaghetti with meat sauce

6–8 oz. spaghetti; 3–4 pints (8–11C) water; 1½ teaspoons salt; Bolognese sauce (see meat sauce under Lasagna al Forno); grated Parmesan cheese.

Cook the spaghetti as the Blue Print and Sketches 1 and 2. Drain and top with the cooked sauce. Serve with grated Parmesan cheese. *Serves 4.*

Macceroni al Pomodoro

Italian macaroni with tomatoes

For the tomato sauce: 1 lb. tomatoes; 1 tablespoon oil; 1 oz. butter; 1–2 onions; 1 teaspoon chopped basil; ¼ teaspoon chopped oregano; 1 teaspoon chopped parsley; seasoning. *For the pasta:* 6–8 oz. macaroni; 3–4 pints (8–11C) water; 1½ teaspoons salt; 1–2 oz. butter; grated Parmesan cheese.

3. Drape cooked lasagna over the sides of a saucepan to 'dry out'.

Cannelloni Ripieni

Italian pancakes, filled with a savoury ham mixture, topped with cheese sauce

For the stuffing: 1 tablespoon oil; 1 oz. butter; 1 onion; 4 oz. (1C) mushrooms; small portion green pepper (optional); 2–4 oz. (about ¼–½C) chopped ham; 1 egg; 1–2 oz. grated Parmesan cheese; seasoning. *For the sauce:* 1½ oz. butter; 1½ oz. flour; ¾ pint (2C) milk; seasoning; 1 oz. (⅓C) grated Parmesan cheese; 2 oz. (⅔C) grated Gruyère or Cheddar cheese. *For the pasta:* 6–8 tubes cannelloni*; 3–4 pints (8–11C) water; 1 teaspoon salt.
*Small pancakes can be used instead.

To make the stuffing, heat the oil and butter, add the finely chopped onion and chopped mushrooms. Cook gently until tender, then add the chopped green pepper and chopped ham and blend well. Stir in the egg, cheese and seasoning, do not cook again. To make the sauce, heat the butter in the pan, stir in the flour and cook for several minutes, stirring well. Gradually blend in the milk. Bring to the boil and stir until thickened. Add the seasoning. Stir in the cheeses, but do not cook again. Cook the cannelloni in the boiling salted water until tender. Drain, allow to cool, then put the filling into each 'tube' or pancake. If using pancakes roll firmly. Spoon 2–3 tablespoons of the cheese sauce into an oven-proof dish, add the filled cannelloni, top with the remainder of the sauce. Heat for about 25 minutes, until the cheese sauce is delicately brown. *Serves 3–4 as a main dish or 6–8 as an hors d'oeuvre.*

Crisp Fried Noodles

A Chinese speciality

Boil the noodles in salted water, as the Blue Print, but drain before they are quite tender. Lay on absorbent paper for a while to absorb any surplus water. Lower into very hot fat or oil and fry steadily until crisp and golden.

Storing and Freezing *The pasta dishes can be stored before being heated; they tend to become drier, so be generous with the quantity of sauce. They freeze quite well for a limited time.*
To use any left over *Put into cold salted water, bring to the boil as quickly as possible, drain and use.*

Skin and chop the tomatoes. Heat the oil and butter and fry the finely chopped onions. Add the tomatoes, herbs and seasoning and simmer gently in a covered pan until a thick purée. Sieve and reheat if wished. Meanwhile cook the macaroni in the boiling salted water. Drain and put into a dish, top with the extra butter and tomato sauce and serve with the Parmesan cheese. *Serves 4.*

Cannelloni al Pomodoro

Italian filled pancakes with tomato sauce

For the stuffing: about 8 oz. (1C) cooked spinach; 1 oz. butter; 4 oz. (½C) cream cheese; 2–3 tablespoons grated Parmesan cheese; seasoning. Tomato sauce (see recipe under Macceroni al Pomodoro). *For the pasta:* 6–8 large cannelloni 'tubes'*; 3–4 pints (8–11C) water; 1 teaspoon salt; grated Parmesan cheese.
*Small pancakes can be used instead.

Prepare the stuffing, by blending the sieved or chopped spinach with the other ingredients. Prepare the tomato sauce. Cook the cannelloni in the boiling salted water until just tender. Do not over-cook, otherwise it is very difficult to insert the stuffing. Drain and cool slightly, then spoon the stuffing into each cooked 'tube' or pancake. If using pancakes roll firmly. Put into a greased dish, top with the tomato sauce and heat through for a short time. Serve with grated Parmesan cheese. *Serves 3–4 as a main dish or 6–8 as an hors d'oeuvre.*

To vary

Cannelloni Roma Add chopped cooked ham to the tomato sauce when cooked.

For a meat filling, follow the recipe for Bolognese sauce (see meat sauce under Lasagna al Forno), but simmer uncovered towards the end of cooking until very thick.

Lasagna al forno

On this page and page 131 are some of the interesting meat dishes from various parts of the world.

Blue Print
Some World Meat Dishes

Many European countries produce good veal, but *Holland* specialises in rearing animals to give the tenderest of meat. Dutch cooking is simple and uncomplicated, but the particular veal dish given keeps the veal pleasantly moist, while the sauce enhances the delicate flavour.

Hungary and the countries immediately adjoining, all make generous use of soured cream and paprika in meat cookery. Goulash is the best known of all paprika meat dishes and justifiably so, for the sweet spice (do not fear it is too hot) gives flavour and colour to the interesting blending of meat and vegetables.

In most Mediterranean countries, as well as *Russia*, you will find a variety of meats cooked with vegetables on skewers, although the name of the dish may vary, according to the particular country. Choose young tender meats for this purpose for the kebabs are cooked very quickly.

Arabic meat cookery is full of surprises. You have nuts, spices and lemon added to lamb in the *Moroccan Tajine Tfaia*.

Chickens are eaten in most countries and there are new recipes here for you to try. An adaptation of Goulash is made with chicken, and an interesting but very simple dish from *Russia* is given, where the chicken is cooked with walnuts.

Shisk Kebab or Shashlik
Meat on a skewer

8 oz. (1C) long grain rice; 2 tablespoons oil; 1 pint (2⅔C) stock; approximately 1–1¼ lb. lean, tender meat—this can be lean lamb or pork or a mixture of these meats; good pinch allspice; seasoning; 4 onions; 8 tomatoes; 2–3 green peppers; oil for cooking the meat. Toss the rice in the hot oil, add the stock, then cook as the risotto on page 125. Cut the meat into neat cubes, roll in allspice and seasoning. Quarter the onions (if you like them very tender they can be boiled for about 10 minutes in salted water, then

drained and quartered). Halve or quarter the tomatoes, roughly dice the green peppers. Put the meat and vegetables on to long metal skewers, brush with oil and cook over a barbecue or charcoal fire in the authentic fashion or cook under a pre-heated gas or electric grill. Turn the skewers to make sure the meat is evenly browned and baste well with oil during cooking. Serve on the bed of cooked rice. *Serves 4.*

To vary To give a more interesting flavour, the cubes of meat may be coated with grated lemon rind or lemon juice and crushed peppercorns.

Sliced aubergines are often used for this dish, make sure the vegetables are well coated with oil and seasoned.

Kalfsoesters met Kaas
Dutch veal with cream sauce

4 fillets veal; seasoning; 2 oz. (¼C) butter; 2–3 teaspoons oil; 4 slices Dutch cheese (Gouda is a good choice); 4 rashers bacon; ¼ pint (⅔C) thick cream; pinch grated lemon rind; pinch curry powder; 2 teaspoons tomato purée. *To garnish*: lemon; parsley. Beat the fillets of veal until very thin, season lightly. Heat the butter and oil (the oil prevents the butter discolouring) in a large frying pan. Fry the veal on both sides until nearly tender. Put into an oven-proof dish. Top each fillet of meat with cheese and bacon and heat for about 15 minutes towards the top of a moderate to moderately hot oven, 375–400°F, Gas Mark 5–6. Do not over-cook. Put the cream with the other ingredients into the frying pan, stir well to absorb any meat juices, heat gently and pour over the veal just before serving. Garnish with lemon and parsley. *Serves 4.*

Tajine Tfaia
Moroccan lamb dish

1¼–1½ lb. lean lamb (cut from the top of the leg if possible); good pinch cumin; pinch powdered saffron; pinch ginger; seasoning; finely grated rind 1–2 lemons; 2 oz. (¼C) butter; 1–2 tablespoons oil; 2 onions; 1 clove garlic; little water or stock; about 1 tablespoon lemon juice; 4 oz (⅔C) blanched almonds.

Cut the lamb into small cubes, about 1–1½-inches in size. Mix the spices with seasoning and lemon rind and roll the meat in this. Heat the butter and oil in a tajine (the sketch on page 131 shows what this looks like) or in a heat-proof dish or strong pan with a lid. Cook the lamb until it turns golden brown on the outside. Add the finely chopped onions, crushed garlic and just enough water or stock to prevent the mixture becoming dry. Cover the cooking utensil and simmer for about 10–15 minutes, until the meat and vegetables are tender and moist (there should be no surplus liquid). Add the lemon juice, any extra seasoning required and the almonds. Heat for a few minutes and serve. This is excellent with rice or the coarse semolina known as cous-cous. *Serves 4–6.*

Goulash (Gulyas)

Hungarian paprika stew

12 oz. lean beef (choose good quality chuck steak); 12 oz. stewing veal or lean pork; 2–3 onions; 2 oz. (¼C) butter; seasoning; about 3 teaspoons paprika (use less the first time to make sure you enjoy the flavour); 1–1½ lb. tomatoes; little water or white stock. *To garnish*: soured cream; parsley.

Cut the meat into neat pieces, peel and slice the onions neatly. Heat the butter in a pan with a tightly fitting lid (this is important for a goulash is a thick stew with little extra liquid). Fry the meat in the hot butter until golden coloured, add the onions, seasoning and paprika, stir well to blend. Skin and slice the tomatoes, put into the pan with a few tablespoons water or stock. Cover the pan and simmer very gently until the meat is tender. This will be about 1½–2 hours. If necessary, add a little liquid during cooking. Turn into a serving dish and top with soured cream and parsley. Serve with boiled potatoes or noodles. *Serves 4–6.*

To vary Sliced potatoes may be added half way through cooking.

To turn this into a soup, rather than a meat dish, use the ingredients above but only 8–10 oz. meat and add 1 pint (2⅔C) stock. Simmer for 1 hour, then add 2 peeled diced old potatoes. Continue cooking for a further 1 hour, then beat the potatoes well, so they thicken the soup. Add stock if too thick. Serve topped with soured cream and parsley.

Satzivi

Russian chicken and walnuts

4 joints young frying chicken; 3 oz. (⅜C) butter; 1–2 onions; 6 oz. (1C) fresh or halved walnuts; ¼ pint (⅔C) red wine; 2–3 tablespoons malt or red wine vinegar; 1 red chilli pepper (the small hot pepper); seasoning.
Fry the chicken in the hot butter in a large frying pan until golden. Remove and put into a casserole. Add the finely chopped onions to the remaining butter and cook for a few minutes. Spoon over the chicken. Heat the nuts, wine, vinegar and finely chopped chilli pepper in the frying pan until the liquid comes to the boil. Add a little seasoning and add to the chicken. Cover the casserole and cook for about 1 hour in the centre of a very moderate to moderate oven, 325–350°F, Gas Mark 4–5. Serve hot, or preferably cold with a green salad. (Illustrated on page 121.) *Serves 4.*

Paprikascsirke

Hungarian paprika chicken

1 chicken; 1 onion; little grated lemon rind; 1½ pints (4C) water; 4–5 peppercorns; little salt; *bouquet garni. For the sauce*: 3 oz. (⅜C) butter; 4 oz. (1C) button mushrooms; 1 oz. flour; 1–2 tablespoons paprika; 1 pint (2⅔C) stock (see method); ¼ pint (⅔C) thick cream; seasoning.

Joint the chicken (or buy 4 joints of chicken). Chop the onion. Put the lemon rind, chicken, water and onion into a pan with the peppercorns, salt and *bouquet garni*. Simmer until the chicken is tender. This takes about 45 minutes to 1 hour if young. Lift the chicken from the stock, strain the stock and keep 1 pint (2⅔C) for the sauce. Either dice the chicken or keep in the 4 joints. Heat the butter in a pan. Toss the mushrooms in the hot butter for a few minutes, lift out on to a plate. Add the flour and paprika, stir well for 2–3 minutes over a low heat, then gradually blend in the stock, bring to the boil and cook, stirring, until thickened. Put the pieces or joints of chicken and mushrooms into the sauce. Simmer until thoroughly heated. Add some of the cream and seasoning, and simmer for 4–5 minutes; do not boil. Top with the remainder of the cream. *Serves 4–6.*

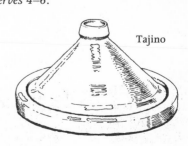
Tajino

Cooked meats from a number of countries are found in most supermarkets and I thought you would find it helpful to have these identified.

1. Cervelat. *German.* Non-garlic salami, made of well seasoned pork. Excellent cold.
2A. Pork Ring. *Polish.* A smoked sausage, flavoured with garlic. Excellent sliced and added to chicken or other casseroles, or simmer in stock for about 15 minutes. Serve hot.
2B. Black Pudding. *British.* Slice and fry, excellent with bacon. Many countries produce Black Pudding.
3. Chorizos. *Spanish.* Garlic sausage, excellent sliced and added to the other ingredients in Paella.

Some Interesting Cooked Meats

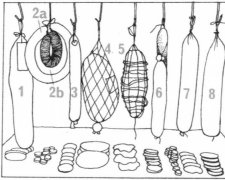

4. Mortadella. *Italian.* Salami sausage flavoured mildly with garlic. Excellent cold as an hors d'oeuvre.
5. Coppe. *Italian.* A smoked ham. Cut very thinly and serve as an hors d'oeuvre by itself or with sliced melon, ripe figs or ripe pears.
6 upper. *Saucesson.* French. A garlic sausage made of pork and ham. Serve cold.
6 lower. Cervelat. *German* (see No. 1)—can also be simmered for 15 minutes in stock or water and served hot.
7. Kalbfleischwurst. *German.* A veal sausage, mild in flavour, excellent for sandwiches or with salad, eaten cold.
8. Schinkenrotwurst. *German.* This is rather 'peppery' in flavour. Slice and eat cold.

Chinese food is interesting and wholesome, for vegetables are given the minimum cooking time and therefore retain both texture, flavour and vitamins. Some recipes on this page are authentically Chinese, the other dishes have Chinese 'touches', and make use of every-day ingredients, readily available. With the popularity of Chinese dishes you will be able to buy ingredients such as bean sprouts, water chestnuts and bamboo shoots in good grocery shops and some supermarkets.

Blue Print
Chinese Food

Choose *tender* cuts of meat (steak, lean fillet of pork, young chicken, etc). The meat is cut in small pieces so it may be cooked within a short time.

Choose *young* vegetables which will be pleasant if lightly cooked.

Make use of the dry flavour of sherry to take the place of Chinese saké (a wine used a great deal in cooking), and soy or soya sauce. Try the popular Chinese blend of savoury sharp flavours, mixed with the sweetness of sugar and honey. Most people are becoming very fond of the sauce we know as 'sweet and sour'.

Serve several dishes for a real Chinese meal, plus boiled or fried rice and/or fried noodles (see page 129). The portions given under each recipe assume this is the only dish being cooked.

Cha yu Chuan
Fried fish rolls

8 oz. white fish fillet (weight without skin or bone); good pinch salt; 1 teaspoon saké (or use sherry); 1 teaspoon syrup from a jar of preserved ginger*; 8 walnut halves; 2 oz. ham. *For the batter*: 2 egg whites; pinch salt; 1 oz. cornflour. *For frying*: oil.

*Or use extra sherry with a pinch of ground ginger.

Cut the fish into 8 strips, season with the salt, the saké or sherry and ginger syrup. Put a halved walnut in the centre of each strip of fish, top with finely chopped ham, then roll firmly. Whisk the egg whites stiffly, blend the salt and cornflour into the egg whites. Put a small wooden skewer into the fish rolls. Dip the rolls into the egg white mixture; do this carefully, so the filling does not come out. Fry for about 5 minutes in hot oil. Serve with the sweet and sour sauce below. *Serves 4.*

Sweet and Sour Sauce

2 tablespoons sugar; seasoning; 1½ level teaspoons cornflour; 3 tablespoons brown malt vinegar; 2 teaspoons soy sauce; ¼ pint (⅔C) chicken stock; 2 tablespoons mixed vinegar pickles.

Blend the sugar, seasoning and cornflour with the vinegar, soy sauce and stock. Put in-to a saucepan and cook until thickened, stirring well. Add the chopped pickles.

If preferred use pineapple syrup instead of the stock and chopped pineapple instead of pickles. *Serves 4.*

Chao Niu Jou Szu
Beef shreds

8 oz. tender lean beef (use fillet or rump steak); 1 or 2 sticks celery; 2 small carrots or piece swede; small piece cucumber; 2 or 3 spring onions; 1 egg white; 2 teaspoons cornflour; 2 tablespoons oil; 2 tablespoons water; 1 tablespoon soy sauce; 2 tablespoons saké (or use sherry); seasoning; good pinch sugar; little ground ginger.

Cut the beef in thin strips, in the picture the beef is in larger pieces than would be served in a Chinese household. Slice the celery and the peeled carrots or swede finely. Leave the peel on the cucumber and cut into narrow strips. Chop the spring onions very finely indeed. Coat the beef with the egg white blended with half the cornflour. Heat the oil and fry the beef for a few minutes only, add the vegetables and toss in the oil. Blend the remaining cornflour with the rest of the ingredients. Pour over the meat and vege-tables and cook for a further 5 minutes. Stir well as the sauce thickens. Serve in a

From left to right:
Sweet and sour
vegetables, Jou szu
chao ching chiao and
Chao niu jou szu.

deep bowl with the sauce and most of the vegetables at the bottom of the bowl and the meat on top, garnished with a few pieces of vegetable. *Serves 4.*

To vary The meat can also be garnished with small pieces of lemon.

Jou Szu Chao Ching Chiao
Green pepper and meat

6 oz. lean tender pork; 2 small green peppers; little dark green cabbage; small piece swede; 2 tablespoons oil; 1 level teaspoon corn-flour; 3 tablespoons water or chicken stock; up to 1 tablespoon soy sauce; 2–3 tablespoons saké (or use sherry); seasoning; 1 teaspoon sugar.

Dice the pork, cut the peppers into tiny pieces and discard the core and seeds. Cut the cabbage into shreds and dice the peeled piece of swede. Heat the oil in a large shallow pan, toss the pork in this, then add the vegetables for a few minutes only, until the meat is nearly tender. Blend the cornflour with the rest of the ingredients. Pour over the meat and vegetables and stir as the sauce thickens. *Serves 4.*

The peppers can be omitted and diced young marrow (courgettes or zucchini) used instead, as shown in the picture. *Serves 4.*

Sweet and Sour Vegetables

The bowl on the left of the picture shows diced vegetables (again they must be diced most finely if serving with chopsticks), cooked lightly in salted water or tossed in a little oil as the recipe above. These are served with the sweet and sour sauce.

Fried Rice

Boil rice until *just* tender, do *not* over-cook. Rinse in boiling or cold water, then drain the rice and spread on flat trays to dry. Put into a fine meshed frying basket and fry in deep, very hot oil, for about 2–3 minutes until golden. Drain and serve. If preferred, fry the rice in a little very hot oil in a frying pan.

These dishes are not truly Chinese, but the Oriental touches make them very pleasant.

Bean Sprouts and Prawns

Mix drained canned bean shoots with prawns. Heat in a little oil, flavour with soy sauce.

Sweet and Sour Pork

Cook diced tender pork in oil until tender, or coat in batter (as the fish rolls) and fry. Serve with the sweet and sour sauce; add diced pineapple and red pepper to the sauce.

Chicken and Rice

Add a pinch saffron powder to the water in which the rice is being cooked, together with diced chicken and green pepper. Allow the liquid to evaporate and flavour with soy sauce, pinch ginger and seasoning.

Storing and Freezing *Chinese dishes should not be stored or frozen; they lose so much of their crisp texture.*

Interesting Desserts

The desserts on these two pages are all outstanding in their particular country.

Blue Print
Some World Desserts

The *French* take 'ordinary pancakes' and turn them into a gourmet's delight in the very famous Crêpes Suzettes. The fritters made of light choux pastry and served with a cherry sauce come from *France* too, and so does the Savarin (page 137), which is equally good as a gâteau for tea or coffee time. The simple Rødgrød from *Scandinavia* enables one to enjoy the flavour of summer fruits in an easily served form. Blintzes are attributed to several countries, be adventurous in your choice of fillings for these.

Savoury and highly spiced foods are a feature of *Spanish* cooking, but the cool, refreshing Coffee Sorbet is a perfect hot weather dessert.

Storing and Freezing   *The filled Crêpes Suzettes may be stored or frozen and the sauce freezes (it may not become very hard because of the high percentage of sugar).*
The Beignets Soufflés, Churros and Waffles neither store nor freeze well, they need to be made freshly.
Rødgrød should be stored in a refrigerator so it can be served very cold. It freezes, but can separate slightly in storing.

Crêpes Suzettes
French citrus pancakes

6 oz. (1½C) plain flour; pinch salt; 2 eggs; ¾ pint (2C) milk; oil or fat for frying. *For the filling*: 2–3 oz. (¼–⅜C) butter; finely grated rind 2 oranges or 4 tangerines; 3 oz. (nearly ¾C) icing sugar; little orange or tangerine juice. *For the sauce*: 2 oz. (¼C) caster or granulated sugar; juice 2 oranges or 4 tangerines; juice 1 small lemon; 2–3 tablespoons Curaçao or Cointreau.

Make the pancake batter by beating all the ingredients together. Fry spoonfuls of the batter in a very little hot oil or fat to give about 12 thin pancakes. Blend all the ingredients for the filling together, add just enough fruit juice to give the consistency of a thick cream. Put some of the filling into the centre of each cooked pancake, then fold in four, as in the picture. Put the sugar into a large pan and heat over a low heat until it just begins to turn golden brown. Add the fruit juice and blend with the sugar. Heat the pancakes very gently in the hot sauce. Add the Curaçao or Cointreau just before serving. Ignite if wished. *Serves 6.*

To vary   Although oranges or tangerines are the accepted filling, orange marmalade or red currant jelly could be put into the pancakes.
Thin shreds of peel can be soaked, then heated in the sauce with the pancakes.
Although not really part of the dish, you can decorate with slices of orange.

Blintzes (Bliny)
Russian filled pancakes

Make the pancakes as the Crêpes Suzettes, then fill with:
Sweetened cottage cheese, flavoured with lemon or vanilla.
Sweetened cottage cheese and strawberries.
Soured cream and cooked fruit.
(Illustrated on page 121.)

Crêpes Suzettes

Granizado de Café
Spanish coffee sorbet

1 pint (2⅔C) really strong coffee; about 2 oz. (¼C) sugar; 2 tablespoons Bénédictine; vanilla ice cream.

Blend the coffee, sugar and liqueur. Pour into a freezing tray or utensil and freeze until *lightly frozen*. Serve portions of vanilla ice cream in sundae glasses, top with the sorbet. *Serves about 6.*

Beignets aux Cerises
French cherry fritters

For the sauce: 1 lb. black or Morello cherries; ¼ pint (⅔C) water; 2–4 oz. (¼–½C) sugar; 1 teaspoon arrowroot; 3–4 tablespoons cherry brandy. *For the choux pastry*: ¼ pint (⅔C) water; 1 oz. butter; 3 oz. (¾C) flour, plain or self-raising; pinch sugar; 2 eggs; 1 egg yolk. *To fry*: oil.

Put the cherries, water and sugar into a pan and simmer for about 5 minutes. Blend the arrowroot with the cherry brandy, stir into the cherry mixture, boil steadily, stirring well, until thickened. Keep hot. Heat the water and the butter in a saucepan. When the butter has melted add the flour, sieved with sugar. Stir the mixture over a low heat

Gaufres à la flamande

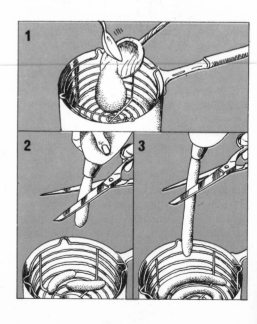

until it forms a firm ball. Remove the pan from the heat and gradually add the beaten eggs and egg yolk. Heat the oil to about 365°F, i.e. until a cube of day-old bread turns golden brown in about 30 seconds. Either put spoonfuls of the mixture into the hot oil, Sketch 1 or put the choux pastry into a cloth bag with a 1-inch plain pipe. Squeeze the choux pastry through the pipe with your left hand and cut off 1–1½-inch lengths with kitchen scissors, see Sketches 2 and 3. Fry steadily for about 6–8 minutes until golden brown, lift out of the oil, drain on absorbent paper. Keep hot on a flat dish in a low oven. To serve, pile into a pyramid and serve with the hot sauce. *Serves 6–8.*

Churros
Spanish fried choux pastry
Make the choux pastry as the beignets above. Put into the piping bag with a ½-inch plain pipe and pipe out lengths of several inches, see Sketch 3. Fry as the beignets, drain and coat with 2–3 oz. (nearly ½C) icing sugar.

Beignets à la Confiture
Jam fritters
Make the fritters as the beignets above. Heat 8 oz. (generous ½C) jam and serve as a sauce.

Rødgrød
Danish red pudding
8 oz. (1C) red currants; 8 oz. (1C) raspberries or loganberries; 1 pint (2⅔C) water; 4 oz. (½C) sugar*; 1½ oz. (nearly ⅓C) cornflour, *or to taste.
Cook the fruit in nearly all the water, and the sugar until soft. Blend the cornflour with the remainder of the water. Add to the fruit mixture and stir over a low heat until thickened. If preferred, sieve the fruit mixture then thicken with the cornflour. This should not be too solid, but like a fruit porridge. Serve cold with cream, or it is delicious with ice cream. *Serves 4–6.*

Gaufres à la Flamande
Flemish waffles
¼ oz. yeast; 2 teaspoons sugar; 3 tablespoons tepid water; 8 oz. (2C) plain flour; pinch salt; 4 eggs; 1 oz. butter; 1 tablespoon brandy; ¼ pint (⅔C) thin cream; little oil. *To serve:* sugar.
Cream the yeast with a teaspoon sugar, add the tepid water and a sprinkling of flour, leave until the surface is covered in bubbles. Sieve the flour and salt. Add the eggs and remaining sugar; beat well then add the yeast mixture, melted butter, brandy and cream. Beat very well until smooth. Cover the basin and leave for 1½–2 hours at room temperature until a light mixture. Brush a waffle iron with very little oil and heat thoroughly. Spoon some of the batter into the iron. Cook for several minutes. Serve hot with plenty of sugar. These are also delicious with hot jam, syrup or fruit purée and ice cream. *Serves 4.*

Beignets aux cerises

Yeast is used in most countries for making breads of all kinds, and delicious cakes and buns.

World Yeast Recipes

Britain has a tradition of excellent yeast buns and cakes. The most famous of all buns made in Britain is the Hot Cross Bun served on Good Friday. *France* specialises in the rich textured cakes soaked in rum. Savarin and Babas au Rhum are really very simple to make and yet produce a most impressive result.

Yeast Mixtures

Denmark's yeast pastries have become famous throughout the world, they are delicate in texture and the fillings provide interesting variety.

● **AVOID** *Making any yeast mixture too dry, even when it has to be handled: Overhandling the dough: 'Proving' too quickly: Baking too slowly.*
● **TO RECTIFY** *If the dough is too dry, blend in a little extra* warm *liquid: If the dough is rising (proving) very quickly move to a cooler place:*

If the dough is baking too slowly raise the oven temperature or move to a hotter place in the oven.

Storing and Freezing *Yeast mixtures rarely store for any length of time, they become stale and the recipes on this page are no exception. If you keep them for a day or so they can be freshened by warming in a warm oven, then adding more syrup to the Savarin and Babas. They freeze splendidly and can be put into the oven for a few minutes to thaw out quickly, take care the icing does not scorch, or they can be left at room temperature to thaw out.*

Weinerbrød and Hot cross buns

Savarin

French rum gâteau

Generous $\frac{1}{4}$ oz. yeast; 1 teaspoon sugar; 12 tablespoons (1C) tepid milk; 6 oz. ($1\frac{1}{2}$C) plain flour; 3 oz. ($\frac{3}{8}$C) butter; 3 eggs. *For the syrup*: nearly $\frac{1}{2}$ pint ($1\frac{1}{4}$C) water; 4 oz. ($\frac{1}{2}$C) sugar; juice 1–2 lemons; 2–3 tablespoons rum. *For the filling*: fresh fruit.

Cream the yeast with the sugar, add the milk and a sprinkling of flour. Put into a warm place for 15–20 minutes until the surface is covered with bubbles. Add the sieved flour, melted butter and beaten eggs. Mix thoroughly. Pour into a well greased and warmed 7–8-inch cake tin or a 9–10-inch ring tin (this should be 3–4-inches deep). Cover lightly and allow to 'prove' for about 40–45 minutes, until the dough begins to rise. Bake in the centre of a hot oven, 425–450°F, Gas Mark 6–7. Allow a total cooking time of 35–40 minutes for the cake, but 25–30 minutes for the ring tin. Reduce the heat to very moderate after 15 minutes. Meanwhile heat the water, sugar and lemon juice until a syrup-like consistency. Add the rum. Turn the cake out on to a wire cooling tray, with a plate underneath. Prick with a fine skewer and pour the hot syrup over carefully. When cool, lift on to the serving dish. Fill the centre of the ring, or cover the top of the cake with fresh fruit, i.e. oranges, apples, pears, bananas, grapes, peaches, cherries. The sides can also be decorated as in the picture. *Serves 6–8.*

To vary To make a smaller size, i.e. an 8–9-inch shallow ring, or 6–7-inch cake, use only $\frac{1}{4}$ oz. yeast, 1 teaspoon sugar, $\frac{1}{4}$ pint ($\frac{2}{3}$C) milk, 4 oz. (1C) flour, 2 oz. ($\frac{1}{4}$C) butter and 2 eggs. Use just over half the amount of rum syrup.

Weinerbrød

Danish yeast pastries

$\frac{3}{4}$ oz. yeast; 2 oz. ($\frac{1}{4}$C) sugar; $\frac{1}{2}$ pint ($1\frac{1}{3}$C) tepid milk or milk and water; 1 lb. (4C) plain flour; 6–8 oz. ($\frac{3}{4}$–1C) butter or margarine; 1 egg. *Fillings*: (see method). *To ice*: 8 oz. (nearly 2C) icing sugar; little water; glacé cherries and/or chopped nuts.

Cream the yeast with a teaspoon sugar, add the tepid milk or milk and water and a sprinkling of flour. Leave in a warm place for 15–20 minutes until the surface is covered with bubbles. Meanwhile put the rest of the flour into a bowl. Rub in 2 oz. ($\frac{1}{4}$C) butter or margarine, add the rest of the sugar. Divide the remaining butter or margarine into two portions and leave at room temperature so it softens to a spreading consistency. Add the yeast liquid to the flour, then stir in the egg. Mix well, turn on to a floured board and knead until smooth. Return the dough to the mixing bowl, cover with a cloth and leave for about 1 hour to 'prove'. The dough should rise to about double its original size. Turn out of the bowl. Knead again and roll out to form an oblong shape, about $\frac{1}{2}$-inch in thickness (no thicker). Spread with half the softened butter or margarine, fold in 3, turn at right angles, then roll out once more. Spread with the last of the butter or margarine, fold in 3, turn at right angles, roll again, then fold and turn. The yeast dough is now ready to use and can be made into many different shapes. The picture illustrates one of the most popular, i.e. an envelope.

Envelopes Make the yeast dough above. Roll out until very thin (about $\frac{1}{4}$-inch). Cut into 4-inch squares. Put a little filling in the centre of each square. This can be jam, honey, lemon curd, thick apple purée, marzipan or chopped preserved ginger, see Sketch 1. Fold the dough so the corners come into the centre, covering the filling, see Sketch 2.

Lift the pastries on to warmed flat baking trays. Allow to 'prove' for 20 minutes in a warm place. Bake for approximately 12 minutes above the centre of a hot oven, 425–450°F, Gas Mark 6–7. Allow to cool. Blend the icing sugar with enough water to give a thin coating. Spread over each pastry. Top with glacé cherries and/or finely chopped nuts.

Savarin

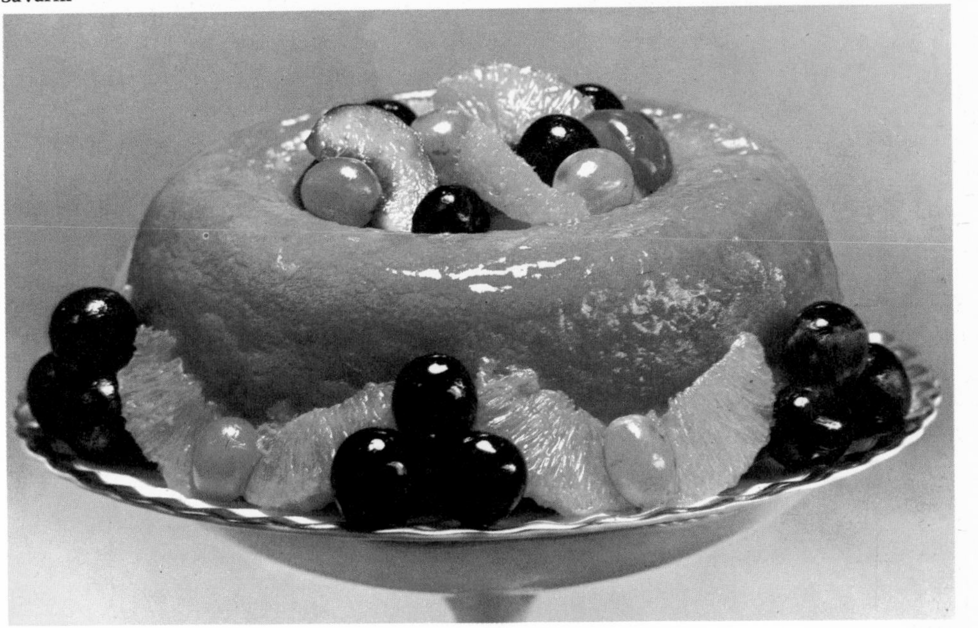

Hot Cross Buns

Generous $\frac{1}{2}$ oz. yeast; 3 oz. ($\frac{3}{8}$C) sugar; just under $\frac{1}{2}$ pint (generous 1C) milk or milk and water; 1 lb. (4C) plain flour; pinch salt; $\frac{1}{2}$ teaspoon allspice; $\frac{1}{2}$ teaspoon powdered cinnamon; 2 oz. ($\frac{1}{4}$C) butter or margarine; about 3 oz. ($\frac{1}{2}$C) dried fruit. *To glaze*: 2 oz. ($\frac{1}{4}$C) sugar; 2 tablespoons hot water.

Cream the yeast with a teaspoon of the sugar. Add the milk or milk and water, together with a sprinkling of flour. Put in a warm place for 15–20 minutes until the surface is covered with bubbles. Meanwhile sieve the flour, salt and spices together. Rub in the butter or margarine, add the remainder of the sugar, the dried fruit, then the yeast mixture. Knead lightly but well. Cover and leave in a warm place to 'prove'. This takes at least 1 hour. Knead again, cut into 12–16 pieces, form into rounds. Put on to warmed, lightly greased baking trays, mark a cross on each bun with a knife. Leave to 'prove' for about 15 minutes, then bake as the Danish pastries above. Blend the sugar and water. Brush the buns with this glaze as soon as they come from the oven. *Makes 12–16.*

To vary To make more prominent crosses, pipe on a cross of thick batter before baking.

To use dried yeast

1. Put the tepid liquid and sugar into a basin

2. Sprinkle the dried yeast on top

3. Wait for about 10 minutes then mix well and continue as for fresh yeast

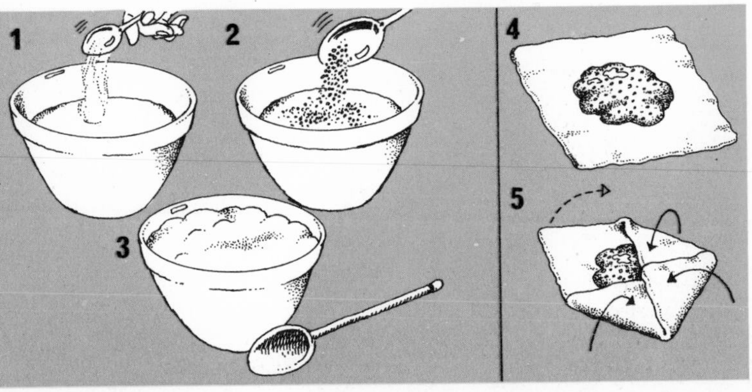

Babas au Rhum

French individual cakes

Make the mixture as the Savarin above with 6 oz. ($1\frac{1}{2}$C) flour, etc., but use only 6 tablespoons milk. Grease, flour and warm Baba tins (these look like small sponge flan tins), or use really deep patty tins. Half fill the tins with the yeast mixture, allow to 'prove' for 20–25 minutes, then bake in a hot oven for 10 minutes only. Turn out, prick, then coat with the syrup as above. Cool and top with whipped cream and glacé cherries. *Makes about 12.*

Some Interesting Cakes

I have chosen five of the most interesting cakes on this and the next two pages. They vary tremendously in texture as well as flavour.

Blue Print
Some World Cakes

From *Austria* comes the delicious Sacher Torte. There are many recipes for this famous chocolate cake, so I give several variations.

The Walnut Layer Cake is only one of the many *American* specialities, so I have given suggestions for similar textured cakes underneath.

The classic *French* Genoese Pastry forms the base for many elaborate gâteaux.

The *British* Simnel (fruit) cake, with the filling and topping of marzipan is generally served at Easter time. Once though it was the traditional cake for Mothering Sunday.

Each country has its own celebration cake for weddings or other very special occasions. In many parts of the world a rich fruit mixture is popular. The cake on page 140 makes a perfect wedding cake or can be used for christenings. The icing is one you will find in *Australia* and this enables you to plan the most artistic moulding. It is far more simple than it might appear.

Storing and Freezing *Keep the cakes in an airtight tin, away from pastry, biscuits and bread. There is little point in freezing the Simnel cake, it improves by maturing in a tin. The chocolate cake and the layer cakes on these pages can be frozen, but personally I always feel they lose some of their moist texture.*

To use any left over *There are no problems about left over cakes in any of these recipes for they remain in good condition for some days or weeks in the case of the fruit cake.*

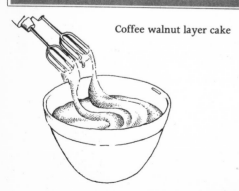

Coffee walnut layer cake

Sacher Torte
Austrian chocolate cake

6 oz. plain chocolate or chocolate couverture; 6 oz. (¾C) butter; 5–6 oz. (up to ¾C) caster sugar; 6 eggs; 6 oz. (1½C) self-raising flour (or plain flour and 1½ level teaspoons baking powder). *For the filling and decoration:* 2–3 tablespoons apricot jam; about ½ pint (1⅓C) thick cream; about 6 oz. plain chocolate or chocolate couverture.

Melt the chocolate in a basin over hot, but not boiling water. Cool slightly. Cream the butter and sugar until soft and light, add the chocolate and beat well. Separate the eggs, beat the egg yolks gradually into the creamed mixture. Sieve the flour or flour and baking powder, fold into the chocolate mixture. Lastly fold in the whisked egg whites. These should not be quite as stiff as for meringues, otherwise the cake becomes too dry and is inclined to break. Grease a 9-inch cake tin and flour lightly. Spoon in the mixture. Flatten on top and bake for about 1¼ hours in the centre of a slow to very moderate oven, 300–325°F, Gas Mark 2–3. Test, and the cake should be just firm to a gentle touch. Cool carefully in the tin for a time, then invert on to a wire cooling tray. When quite cold, split and fill with jam and half the whipped cream. Top with melted chocolate and, when quite firm and set, decorate with whipped cream.

To vary Omit the flour and use the same weight of ground almonds or hazel-nuts, i.e. (1½C). Add 1 tablespoon cornflour with the nuts.

Use half flour (¾C) and half fine soft breadcrumbs (¾C).

Flavour the whipped cream with a little sieved cocoa or *cooled* melted chocolate. Allow to stiffen sufficiently for piping and decorate as the picture on this page.

Bake the cake in a larger, more shallow tin for about 50 minutes. Do not split. Spread with apricot jam, whipped cream and cooled melted chocolate. The icing layer should be almost as thick as the cake.

Use thick cherry purée (from cooking black cherries) in place of jam.

Walnut Layer Cake

6 oz. (¾C) butter or margarine; 6 oz. (¾C) caster sugar; 3 large eggs; 1 egg yolk; 1 tablespoon milk; 6 oz. (1½C) self-raising flour (or preferably plain flour and 1 level teaspoon baking powder); 3 oz. (¾C) finely chopped walnuts. *For the filling:* 4 oz. (½C) butter; 8 oz. (almost 2C) icing sugar; 1 tablespoon milk. *For the frosting:* 8 oz. (1C) granulated sugar; 4 tablespoons water; pinch cream of tartar; 1 egg white; few walnut halves.

Cream the butter or margarine and sugar until soft and light. Gradually beat in the eggs, plus the egg yolk and the milk. Fold in the sieved flour or flour and baking powder and the chopped walnuts. Grease and flour two 7–8-inch sandwich tins (or line the bases with greased greaseproof paper). Divide the mixture between the tins and smooth flat on top. Bake just above the centre of a moderate oven, 350–375°F, Gas Mark 4–5 for approximately 25 minutes, until firm to the touch. Turn out carefully and cool.

Cream the butter and icing sugar together, add the milk. Split each cake through the centre to give four layers, spread with the butter icing and put the cake together again. Put the sugar and water into a strong saucepan, stir until the sugar has dissolved. Boil steadily, without stirring, until the mixture reaches 238–240°F, i.e. it forms a 'soft ball' when tested in cold water. Add the pinch cream of tartar and beat hard until cloudy, then pour steadily on to the stiffly whisked egg white. Continue beating until the icing thickens, then spread over the top and sides of the cake. Decorate with walnut halves.

Coffee Walnut Layer Cake

Ingredients as Walnut Layer Cake, but substitute 1 tablespoon strong coffee for the milk in the cake recipe. You can also *omit* 1 oz. caster sugar and use the same amount of brown sugar, which gives a very pleasant flavour and colour to the cake (this is shown in the picture).

Walnut Frosted Layer Cake

Ingredients for the cake as the Walnut Layer Cake or the Coffee Layer Cake. Omit the butter icing filling. Make double the amount of frosting and use half of this to sandwich the layers together.

Simnel Cake

Ingredients as the rich fruit cake on page 140, but use caster instead of soft brown sugar to give the golden coloured cake in the picture. If making the 7-inch round cake you need marzipan made with 8 oz. (2C) ground almonds, 4 oz. (½C) caster sugar, 4 oz. (nearly 1C) icing sugar, 2 egg yolks and a few drops almond essence, also a little sieved apricot jam and/or egg white or whites.

Make the cake mixture. Mix the ground almonds with all the other ingredients for the marzipan. Roll out just under half the marzipan to a 7-inch round and use as a filling for the cake. Put half the cake mixture into the prepared tin, add the round of marzipan, then the rest of the cake mixture. Bake as the table on page 140, but allow about 15–20 minutes extra for the marzipan through the centre. Allow the cake to cool. Roll out most of the remaining marzipan into a 7-inch round. Brush the top of the cake with a little egg white, or melted apricot jam. Put the round of marzipan on top. Make small balls of the rest of the marzipan. Press on top of the cake. Brush with egg white and brown

under the grill with the heat turned very low. Decorate with Easter eggs and chicks as shown in the picture.

To vary Do not bake the marzipan *with* the cake. Instead split the cake when quite cold, brush with a little egg white or apricot jam and put the round of marzipan through the middle (as shown in the picture). Top with the rest of the marzipan and brown slightly as the recipe above.

Pâte à Genoise

Genoese pastry

Although given the name of 'pastry', this has the texture of a light sponge cake. Indeed it is very similar to a 'true' sponge, in that the eggs and sugar are whisked until light and fluffy. The important difference is that melted butter is folded into the mixture. This gives a pleasantly moist texture and makes Genoese pastry a perfect basis for light gâteaux and small fancy cakes. The mixture keeps well for several days or even longer when coated with icing.

3 large eggs; 4 oz. (½C) caster sugar; 3–4 oz. (⅜–½C) butter; 3 oz. (¾C) self-raising flour (or plain flour with ½ level teaspoon baking powder); *To fill:* ¼ pint (⅔C) thick cream; 2–3 tablespoons jam; little sieved icing sugar.

Put the eggs and sugar into a bowl and whisk until thick. You should be able to see the trail of the whisk in the mixture, see sketch. Melt butter, allow to cool. Sieve the flour or flour and baking powder very well. Fold the flour into the eggs and sugar with a metal spoon, then fold in the butter. Do this gently, but carefully and thoroughly. The mixture is then

Simnel cake (below)
Sacher torte (top)

ready to bake. Genoese pastry can be baked in Victoria sandwich tins or in a flat tin to cut into small cakes. To bake in sandwich tins, grease and flour two 7-inch tins, divide the mixture between these and bake for approximately 15–18 minutes above the centre of a moderate oven, 350–375°F, Gas Mark 4–5. Sandwich the cakes with whipped cream and jam and top with sieved icing sugar or decorate as desired. If baking in a small Swiss Roll tin allow about the same time. Cool, cut into small shapes and coat with icing or decorate as wished.

Rich Cake

The table below gives the proportions for making a very rich fruit cake.

The baking temperature for this cake should start at about 300–325°F, Gas Mark 2–3. I allow about 1 hour at this temperature, then reduce to 275–300°F, Gas Mark 1–2 for the remainder of the cooking time. As ovens vary so much though, check and test after the suggested period. The cake is done if firm to the touch and silent. An *uncooked rich fruit cake has a distinct humming sound.*

Always line the tin with double-greased greaseproof paper and have rounds of brown paper under the greaseproof paper at the base. I tie a deep band of brown paper round the outside of the tin to prevent the mixture darkening too much.

Always allow a very rich fruit cake to cool in the tin. The weight of the fruit could cause the cake to crack (or even break) if handled when hot.

If desired, you can prick the cooked cake at intervals of a week to 10 days and spoon sherry, brandy or rum over to keep it moist. *If using a cup measure for fruit* remember that if lightly packed it holds between 5–6 oz. If you press the fruit down it is about 8 oz.

1 Cup (C) flour = 4 oz.
1 Cup (C) butter = 8 oz.
1 Cup (C) moist brown sugar = 7 oz.
1 Cup (C) glacé cherries = 7 oz.
1 Cup (C) chopped candied peel = 4 oz.

Method of Making a Rich Fruit Cake

1. Ensure the fruit is dry.
2. Sieve the flour and spices.
3. Cream the butter and sugar with grated lemon rind and treacle, if used.
4. Gradually beat in the eggs, plus any liquid.
5. Add the sieved flour and spices to the egg mixture.
6. Add the dried fruit, halved or quartered glacé cherries, nuts, ground almonds, if used, and peel.
7. Put into the prepared tin.
8. Bake as the table.
9. Cool in the tin, turn out when cold.
10. Store in an airtight tin or wrapped in foil.
11. Prick regularly, as suggested above, and soak with brandy, sherry or rum.

Celebration Cake

The cake in the picture was made as the 8-inch square cake in the table. It was then coated with marzipan, using 1¼ lb. ground almonds, etc. (see page 139). After coating with marzipan the cake was finished with the Australian type fondant (plastic) icing, decorated with this and Royal icing piping. *To coat the cake and give some icing for the decorative shapes:* ¾ oz. powdered gelatine; 3 fl. oz. (¼C) water or water and lemon juice; 4 oz. (just over ¼C) liquid glucose; generous 1 oz. (good tablespoon) glycerine; 3 lb. (about 11C) sieved icing sugar; few drops cochineal; little cornflour; sieved apricot jam. *For the*

Celebration cake

piping: 2 egg whites; 1 tablespoon lemon juice; 1 lb. (good 3½C) sieved icing sugar; few drops cochineal.

To make the plastic icing, soften the gelatine in the water, or water and lemon juice. Dissolve over hot water. Put the glucose and glycerine into a large pan, heat gently, add the dissolved gelatine and heat together. Stir in nearly all the icing sugar and colouring, mix with a wooden spoon. Turn on to a board dusted with icing sugar and the cornflour. Knead until smooth and free from cracks. Take just over three-quarters of the mixture, roll out to a square sufficiently large to cover the cake. Put over the cake, press gently to make 'it fit'; it is advisable to brush the marzipan first with sieved apricot jam to help the icing adhere. Neaten the bottom edges. Roll out the rest of the icing very thinly, cut into the shapes shown in the picture, i.e. small halved circles. Lay on waxed paper.

Make the Royal icing for piping. Whisk the egg whites lightly, add the lemon juice and icing sugar, beat hard until smooth. Tint very pale pink. Put some of the icing into paper or cloth bag or syringe with a 1, 0'or even 00 (very fine) writing pipe. Pipe the design round the little half circles. Leave for 24 hours until very firm. Pipe a narrow line of Royal icing round the edge of the top of the cake, press the little shapes into position. Continue round the side. When all the shapes are on the cake, neaten with piping.

Amounts of ingredients for different sized tins

Size of cake tin:	6-inch square 7-inch round	8-inch square 9-inch round	10-inch square 11-inch round
Currants	10 oz.	1 lb. 4 oz.	1 lb. 14 oz.
Sultanas	8 oz.	1 lb.	1 lb. 8 oz.
Raisins	6 oz.	12 oz.	1 lb. 2 oz.
Glacé cherries	4 oz.	8 oz.	12 oz.
Mixed peel	4 oz.	8 oz.	12 oz.
Blanched chopped almonds	4 oz.	8 oz.	12 oz.
Plain flour	6 oz.	12 oz.	1 lb. 2 oz.
Ground cinnamon	¼ teaspoon	½ teaspoon	1 teaspoon
Ground mace	¼ teaspoon	½ teaspoon	1 teaspoon
Butter	6 oz.	12 oz.	1 lb. 2 oz.
Soft brown sugar	6 oz.	12 oz.	1 lb. 2 oz.
Lemon rind	½ lemon	1 lemon	1½ lemons
Eggs—large	3	6	9
Brandy (or milk), sweet sherry or rum	1 tablespoon	2 tablespoons	3 tablespoons
COOKING TIME	2¾–3 hours	4–4½ hours	6½–7 hours
TEST AFTER	2½ hours	3¾ hours	5 hours

Additional ingredients you may add:

Grated orange rind—as lemon.
Allspice or mixed spice—as mace or reduce cinnamon slightly and use more spice.
Ground almonds—add 1 oz. to small, 2 oz. to medium-sized, and 3 oz. to large cake.
Black treacle—helps to make the cake very moist and slice well. Use 1 tablespoon in small, 2 tablespoons in medium-sized, and 3 tablespoons in large cake; cream with the butter and sugar.

eight
DRINKS, PRESERVES & SWEETMEATS

This section covers a wide range of recipes. I think it might be said to cover the kind of cooking and preserving that can make our catering so much more individual and interesting.

The first part, i.e. pages 142–146, deals not only with making your own wine but with interesting drinks for special occasions, fruit cups for children, wine cups and punches for adults. For many generations home wine-making has been a popular hobby. It is an interesting fact that most edible fruits and vegetables and quite a number of flowers, as well as ingredients such as rice, make good wines.

Sweet making is a fairly complex form of cookery for the mixture has to be boiled to exactly the right temperature, but as long as this is done you should have no problems in following the recipes on 160. There are also several recipes on page 159 that need no cooking, but which make

equally delicious sweets and are very suitable for children to make.

There is no preserve more pleasant than home-made marmalade for breakfast, or any other time of the day. The range of citrus fruits available means that marmalade can be made throughout the year, although bottling and freezing enable one to preserve the bitter Seville oranges and to use them when convenient. You will

find a wide range of recipes for jams and jellies on pages 148–149 and page 152. As well as the usual strawberry, apricot and raspberry, I have also included rather more unusual fruits, such as mango, fig and passion fruit.

Bottling is still very popular, despite the advent of freezing and to give it a touch of 'luxury' I have also added a recipe for bottling various fruits in liqueur, which are really delicious. Many people enjoy making their own pickles and chutney and you will find recipes for these on pages 156 and 157.

Most of the pages carry a Blue Print and you will find this your guide to many other preserves and wines.

Freezing is becoming so much a part of home preservation that I have included some special tips on freezing fruits and vegetables, although in such a small space it is impossible to give detailed instructions.

Wine Making

On this and the next two pages you will find wines made from fruits, flowers, vegetables and cereals, such as rice. If you do not find exactly the fruit or vegetable you wish to use, then follow the recipe for a similar type, i.e. red currants could be used in the same way as blackcurrants.

Blue Print

The Process of Making Wine

When making wine this is basically what happens:

1. The fruit, vegetables, etc., are placed in the container and water (generally boiling) is added. In addition yeast is put in to cause fermentation. Chemists, or other shops selling wine-making equipment, also sell wine-making yeast and this gives a considerably better flavour to the wine than ordinary baker's yeast.
2. In addition to the liquid and yeast, sugar and some additional flavourings are added. The fruit or vegetables should be pressed to extract the juice.
3. The liquid is then left in the container, which should be covered either with a lid or a cloth to keep it clean, so that fermentation may begin. In order to have good fermentation the temperature is very important. The ideal temperature is about 70°F and the atmosphere should be dry.
4. After fermentation (bubbling) begins stir the mixture well.
5. Leave the wine in the container for a further 2 days. This allows it to settle and

any sediment to drop to the bottom of the liquid.
6. Strain very carefully into the cask or other large container. You must fill this container, otherwise if air is present the wine will not continue the process of fermentation but will be spoilt, so measure carefully and have a little extra wine left over for refilling, see point 8. Keep left over wine in a covered jar or other container.
7. As the wine continues to ferment some will probably overflow into the tray. As this has been in contact with the air do not use it.
8. As the liquid overflows you will need to top up with a little fresh so that the cask or bottle is always kept full.
9. The time that the wine should be left in the large container varies appreciably. If in doubt a good average time is six months, but some wines are better for a slightly longer period, others for a shorter period.
10. Ideally the wine should be quite clear at the end of this period. If it is not clear then it must be strained before bottling.
11. If the wine still looks slightly cloudy:
   a) allow one stiffly whisked egg white to each 3 gallons of wine. Put the whites into the liquid, leave for 24 hours and then strain.
   b) add ¾ oz. isinglass to each 3 gallons of liquid. This takes longer to clear the wine so leave for 2–3 weeks and then strain.
   c) the more professional way of straining is to use a wine syphon to remove the liquid, and this leaves any sediment in the bottom of the cask or other container.
12. Strain the wine carefully into the bottles. Make sure they are filled and close with the corks.
13. Store in a cool, dry place for a minimum of 2–3 months, unless stated otherwise, before drinking.

● **AVOID** *Using equipment that is not 100% clean and free from bacteria.*

● **TO RECTIFY** *The easiest way to clean equipment is as follows: Dissolve 2 Camden tablets and ½ tablespoon citric acid in each gallon of cold water. Pour into the containers. Leave for a minimum of 3 days, pour out, fill with boiling water as a final precaution. If using glass jars warm these before adding boiling water to make sure that they do not crack.*

FRUIT WINES

Choose fruit that is just ripe, but not over-ripe. There is no need to peel the fruit or remove the flower ends, as in gooseberries. Wash and dry the fruit, cut away any bruised parts. In order to extract the maximum juice

EQUIPMENT

In order to make wine you need a certain amount of equipment and most large chemists sell wine-making equipment. These are the basic needs, you can, of course, have more elaborate equipment if you desire.

Knives and a good surface for cutting the vegetables or fruit.

A large container in which to put the fruit, vegetables, etc., plus the water—large glass bottles, plastic containers or *perfect* enamel pans. The only metal you can use is very good stainless steel. During this process you will need to press the fruit etc., to extract the maximum amount of juice so you need a really strong wooden spoon or presser.

The juice needs to be strained from the solid matter so you must have some

Fruit Wines

Fruit	Weight	Boiling water See Stage 1	Sugar and flavouring to each 8 pints water. See Stage 2	Yeast to each 8 pints water. See Stage 2	Time to mature in cask or jar. See Stages 6–9	Flavour
Apple	4 lb.	8 pints	2 lb.	½ oz.	6 months	dry white wine
Apple—crab	4 lb.	8 pints	3 lb. plus juice 2–3 lemons	½ oz.	12 months	dry white wine
Apricot	5 lb. stoned	8 pints	3 lb. plus juice 2–3 lemons	½ oz.	6 months	sweet white wine
Blackberry	6 lb.	6 pints	2½ lb.	¼ oz.	4 months	moderately sweet red wine
Blackcurrant	5 lb.	7 pints	3 lb.	¼ oz.	9 months	port wine
Cherry—preferably black	7 lb.	8 pints	2½ lb. plus juice 2 lemons	¼ oz.	5 months	claret
Damson	4 lb.	8 pints	3 lb. plus juice 1–2 lemons	¼ oz.	6 months	really dry red wine
Elderberry	4 lb.	9 pints	2½ lb. plus 8 oz. raisins	¼ oz.	8 months	port wine
Grape—black	4 lb.	5 pints	2 lb.	¼ oz.	6 months	very dry white wine
white	4 lb.	8 pints	3½ lb.	¼ oz.	6 months	sweet white wine
Haw	5 lb.	6 pints; leave for 1 week to infuse	3 lb. plus juice 2 lemons	¼ oz.	4 months	not quite as dry as rose hip
Orange—do not peel, slice thinly	6 lb.	8 pints	3 lb. plus juice 2 lemons	¼ oz.	6 months	light, moderately dry sherry
Pear—you can use moderately firm pears	4 lb.	8 pints	3 lb. plus juice 2 lemons	½ oz.	3 months	light, fairly sweet white wine
Plum—ripe red For firm red (not Victoria) use 6 pints water	4 lb.	5 pints	2½ lb., but 1 lb. of this sprinkled over fruit before adding water, plus juice 1 lemon	¼ oz.	8 months	moderately sweet red wine
Rose hip—mince these	5 lb.	6 pints; leave for 1 week to infuse	3 lb. plus juice 2 lemons	¼ oz.	4 months	very dry white wine
Rhubarb	4 lb.	6 pints	2½ lb. plus juice 2 oranges	¼ oz.	8 months	dry white wine

from the fruit, chop it into small pieces before putting into the container. Do not grate fruit, otherwise it forms a pulp, which does not produce a good wine. If the fruit contains stones remove these, unless you like the slight almond taste they will give.

The measure of water used in these and other wines is the Imperial pint, i.e. 8 pints = 1 gallon. 1 lb. raisins is a very generous 2½C.

VEGETABLE WINES

Choose very good quality, fresh vegetables to provide first-class wine. The vegetables should be fairly mature. Wash vegetables, remove any damaged parts, but do not peel. Chop or slice, but do not grate the vegetables.

method of straining this. Flannel (as used in jelly bags) is ideal, or several thicknesses of muslin which should be placed over a large sieve or strainer.

The juice then has to be placed in a large container for fermentation. In the old days crocks were used but today these are very difficult to obtain. You can buy special bottles or you may be able to obtain wooden casks; the container must have a lid. If you intend to make an appreciable amount of wine it is worthwhile having an air-lock. This fits into the cork and allows you to control the air bubbles while the juice ferments to make the wine (as in the picture).

You also need a tray under the container for during the process of fermentation the juice often overflows.

Wine bottles and corks.

Vegetable Wines

Vegetable	Weight	Boiling water See Stage 1	Sugar and flavouring to each 8 pints water. See Stage 2	Yeast to each 8 pints water. See Stage 2	Time to mature in cask or jar. See Stages 6–9	Flavour
Beetroot—uncooked	4 lb.	6 pints plus 2 oz. bruised root ginger	2 lb. plus juice 2 lemons	½ oz.	9 months	port wine
Carrot	4 lb.	7 pints	2 lb. plus juice 1–2 lemons	½ oz.	8 months	dry sherry
Parsnip—best when used after mild frost or Potato	4 lb.	6 pints plus 1½ oz. bruised root ginger	3 lb. plus 4 oz. raisins, 8 oz. pearl barley, juice 1–2 lemons	½ oz.	8 months	Parsnip—moderately sweet white wine Potato—dry white wine
Swede or Turnip	4 lb.	6 pints	2–2½ lb. plus juice 2 lemons, 1 orange	½ oz.	6 months	Swede—golden dry white wine. Turnip—light dry white wine.
Tomato	8 lb.	2 pints	2 lb. plus juice 2 lemons	½ oz.	6 months	moderately dry rosé wine

Cold Drinks

On this and the next page are a variety of drinks, both alcoholic and non-alcoholic. A wine cup or hot punch are delicious drinks to serve at a special party and they have the added advantage of being comparatively inexpensive. Children will enjoy their fruit cup, which has a sophisticated 'adult look'. Homemade lemonade, and the various drinks based upon this, make excellent use of refreshing citrus fruit, with its high Vitamin C content.

Blue Print Recipes

1. Lemonade

6 lemons · 1 pint (2⅔C) water · about 4 oz. (about ½C) sugar · ice cubes · iced water or soda water. To decorate: slices of lemon and/or sprigs of mint.

To make Grate the rind from the lemons, be careful to take just the top 'zest', i.e. the yellow part of the skin. Avoid using the white pith. Squeeze out the juice. Put the water and sugar into a large saucepan. Add the lemon rind. Stir until the sugar has dissolved then boil for a few minutes. Cool, add the lemon juice.

To serve Strain a little lemonade into glasses or some of the lemonade into a jug. Add crushed ice and fill up with ice cold water or soda water. Decorate with slices of

Lemonade

lemon and/or sprigs of mint. *All recipes based on this make 8–10 glasses.*

To vary

Orangeade Use 6 oranges and 2 lemons and proceed as above.

Pineappleade Use 4 lemons and 1 medium-sized peeled sliced pineapple. Make the syrup with the lemon rind and finely chopped pineapple. Decorate with thin slices of pineapple and a few pineapple leaves.

2. Wine Cup

2 lemons · 1–2 oranges · ½ pint (1⅓C) water · 2–3 oz. (¼–⅜C) sugar · ice cubes · 2 bottles white wine · miniature bottle or wineglass brandy. To decorate: cucumber slices · orange slices · sprigs borage or mint (optional).

To make Pare the rind from the lemons and oranges very thinly. Squeeze out the juice and put on one side. Simmer the peel in the water for about 5 minutes. Add the sugar and stir until dissolved. Strain and allow to cool, then blend with the fruit juices.

To serve Put the ice into a serving bowl, add the fruit mixture, wine and brandy. Stir gently to mix, then decorate with the cucumber, orange slices and herbs, when these are available. *All recipes based on this make about 16 glasses unless stated otherwise.*

Flower and Leaf Wines

Flower	Quantity	Boiling water See Stage 1	Sugar and flavouring to each 8 pints water. See Stage 2	Yeast to each 8 pints water. See Stage 2	Time to mature in cask or jar. See Stages 6–9	Flavour
Broom	5 pints	8 pints plus rind 3 oranges, 3 lemons	3 lb. plus juice 3 oranges, 3 lemons	½ oz.	6 months	dry white wine
Clover— use purple	6 pints	8 pints plus rind 3 oranges, 3 lemons	3 lb. plus juice 3 oranges, 3 lemons	½ oz.	6 months	dry white wine
Cowslip	6 pints	8 pints plus rind 3 oranges, 3 lemons	3 lb. plus juice 3 oranges, 3 lemons	½ oz.	6 months	very light, moderately dry white wine
Dandelion	5 pints	8 pints plus 1 oz. ginger *or* 8 oz. raisins	3 lb. brown sugar plus juice 2 oranges, 1 lemon	½ oz.	6 months	very light, moderately dry white wine
Elderflower	1 pint	8 pints	3 lb. plus juice 1 orange	½ oz.	6 months	dry white wine
Parsley	4 pints	8 pints plus rind 3 oranges, 3 lemons	3 lb. plus juice 3 oranges, 3 lemons	½ oz.	6 months	dry white wine
Rose petal*	4 pints	8 pints	3 lb. plus juice 2 lemons, 1 orange	½ oz.	6 months	light dry wine or light rosé wine

*Choose fragrant roses—the dark red are best as they produce a rosé wine.

Wines from Flowers & Leaves

Choose perfect flowers and pick them on a dry day. Wash the flowers in cold water, do not handle more than necessary for the blossoms bruise easily. The flowers are measured in Imperial pints.

To Make Cider

Each apple gives its own individual flavour to this famous drink, but you are wise to choose a crisp, fairly sharp and very juicy type of apple. Wipe the fruit, do not peel, cut into small pieces and put into the container, described in Stage 1 in the Blue Print on page 142. To each 4 lb. apples allow 1 gallon boiling water and 1 lb. (2C) sugar. Pour over the fruit and leave for 3 days, stirring well each day. After 3 days add ½ oz. brewer's yeast. Leave in the container to ferment, then continue as Stages 3–17 of the Blue Print. Cider matures in the cask, or substitute, in 6 months.

To vary Use only $\frac{1}{4}$ pint ($\frac{2}{3}$C) water with the fruit rinds.
Use weak, well strained China tea in place of water.
Use a rosé wine and Maraschino instead of white wine and brandy, top with sliced peaches and cherries.
Use only $\frac{1}{4}$ pint ($\frac{2}{3}$C) water, then add $\frac{1}{2}$ pint ($1\frac{1}{3}$C) soda water just before serving.

Cider Cup

As Blue Print, but use cider in place of white wine. This cup can be topped with apple rings and strawberries.

Champagne Cup

As Blue Print, but use non-vintage champagne in place of white wine, top with sliced peaches, strawberries and borage.

Fruit Cup for Children

As Blue Print, but use 2 pints ($5\frac{1}{3}$C) pineapple juice and $\frac{1}{2}$ pint ($1\frac{1}{3}$C) ginger-ale or lemonade in place of wine. Top with sliced fruit. *Makes about 12–13 glasses.*

Wine cup

Sweet Cider

Method as above, but to each 4 lb. apples allow 1 gallon boiling water, 8 oz. raisins and 2 lb. (4C) sugar. Continue as above.

Cereal Wines

These grains need more yeast than flowers, fruit and vegetables.

Cereal	Quantity	Boiling water See Stage 1	Sugar and flavouring to each 8 pints water. See Stage 2	Yeast to each 8 pints water Stage 2	Time to mature in cask or jar. See Stages 6–9	Flavour
Barley— pearl barley preferably	1 pint	8 pints	$3\frac{1}{2}$–4 lb. brown sugar plus 2 lb. raisins	2 oz.	6 months	light port
Maize	1 pint	8 pints	$3\frac{1}{2}$–4 lb. brown sugar plus 2 lb. raisins	2 oz.	6 months	light port
Rice— long grain	1 pint	8 pints	$2\frac{1}{2}$ lb. plus 1 lb. raisins	2 oz.	6 months	almost like white port
Rice— round grain	1 pint	8 pints	3 lb. plus 1 lb. raisins	2 oz.	6 months	sweeter white port
Wheat	1 pint	8 pints	$3\frac{1}{2}$–4 lb. brown sugar plus 2 lb. raisins, 2 sliced oranges	2 oz.	6 months	light port

Blue Print Recipe

Red Wine Punch

2 oranges · cloves (amount according to personal taste) · 2 bottles red wine (claret is ideal) · 1 cinnamon stick.

To make Stud the oranges with cloves. Bake in a moderate oven for about 25 minutes until golden coloured. This enhances the flavour of the fruit. Cut into slices with a sharp knife. Put the orange slices and wine into a pan with the cinnamon. Bring steadily to boiling point, but do not boil.
To serve In a heated punch bowl. Remove the cinnamon stick. *All recipes based on this make about 12 glasses.*

To vary Top with grated nutmeg and omit the cinnamon stick.
Add ½ pint (1⅓C) strained China tea to the wine together with a miniature bottle or wineglass of rum. Top with grated nutmeg.
Add 1–2 tablespoons sugar to the wine, stir well as it heats to dissolve the sugar.

Ginger Punch

Follow the Blue Print recipe, but use ginger-ale instead of red wine.

Mulled Wine

Ingredients as the Blue Print PLUS ½ pint (1⅓C) water and 2 oz. (¼C) sugar.

Hot Drinks

Bake the oranges as the Blue Print and slice. Put into a saucepan with the water, sugar and cinnamon and heat. Add the wine and bring almost to boiling point. Ladle into heated glasses.

Mulled Ale

2 oranges; few cloves; 1 lemon; 3 pints ale; miniature bottle or wineglass brandy; 1–2 tablespoons sugar; 1–2 sticks cinnamon; grated nutmeg; good pinch allspice.

Stud the oranges with the cloves and bake as the Blue Print. Slice the oranges and the lemon and put into a pan with the ale, brandy, sugar and cinnamon stick. Heat steadily, stirring well to dissolve the sugar. Remove the cinnamon stick. Pour into a hot punch bowl. Top with the nutmeg and allspice. Put a hot poker (if available) into the hot drink just before ladling into well heated glasses.

To vary
Cream Mull Top each portion of mulled wine or mulled ale with a little thin or thick cream. Serve at once.

Gaelic Coffee (Irish Coffee)

Serve this in warmed glasses. It takes the place of ordinary coffee at the end of a meal. Put a measure of Irish whiskey into the glasses, then add black coffee and sweeten to taste. Pour thick cream on top, over the back of a spoon, see the sketches.

The pages that follow give recipes for jams, jellies, marmalades and other home preserves. Below is the recipe for one of the most delicious of all preserves, lemon curd, with suggestions to vary this which you may like to try.

Blue Print Recipe

Lemon Curd

8 oz. (1C) caster or loaf sugar · 2 large lemons · 4 oz. (½C) fresh butter · 2 large eggs.

To make If using caster sugar, grate the rind from the lemons very carefully so you do not remove the white pith. You need just the yellow 'zest' of the fruit. If using loaf sugar, rub the lumps over the lemons until they have removed the yellow 'zest'; this is the better method. Put the sugar, lemon rind and butter into the top of a double saucepan, or into a basin, over hot, but not boiling water. Add the strained lemon juice.

To cook Heat until the butter has melted, stir from time to time. Add the well beaten eggs and continue cooking, stirring all the time until the mixture coats the back of a wooden spoon. Pour into pots and seal down as Stage 12 in the Blue Print on page 148.

To serve With bread and butter or as a filling for tarts, Pavlova, sponges etc. *All recipes based on this make about 1 lb.*

To vary Use 1 lemon and 1 orange.
Add the rind of 1 extra lemon for more flavour.
Use 3–4 tangerines in place of lemons.

All edible fruits can be used for jam, and some vegetables as well, i.e. marrow and tomatoes.

Fruits vary in the amount of pectin (natural setting quality) they contain and it is important to appreciate this point and adjust the amount of sugar accordingly. The less natural setting quality present in the fruit, the less sugar it will set. When making jam with low pectin fruit, dessert cherries and strawberries are good examples, it is therefore advisable to add lemon or red currant juice, both of which have a high acid and pectin content.

Sugar is the preservative in jam making and sufficient must be used to prevent the jam fermenting or forming mould. Many of the points given in the Blue Print also apply to jellies and marmalade.

Blue Print

Making Jam

1. Warm the well washed jars.
2. Prepare the fruit. Wash in cold water, or wipe, halve or chop if wished. The fruit should be *just* ripe.
3. Put the fruit into the preserving pan, with water if used (see opposite).
4. Simmer slowly until the fruit is soft. This slow cooking extracts the maximum amount of pectin from the fruit. The time varies according to the fruit.
5. Add the sugar, choose loaf or preserving sugar, which give the best result (they cause the minimum of scum). *Stir over a low heat until the sugar has thoroughly dissolved.*

Jam Making

6. If the recipe gives lemon or red currant juice, add this with the sugar or immediately the sugar has dissolved.
7. Bring the jam to the boil, boil as rapidly as possible but watch that it does not boil over. Stir occasionally, but not too often, as continual stirring lowers the temperature and the quicker the jam sets the better the colour and flavour.
8. Test early for setting point. Always turn off the heat and pull the pan carefully off the hotplate as you test. Jam has reached setting point when:
a) a little, put on a saucer and cooled, wrinkles when pushed with a finger as in the picture on this page.
b) any cooled jam left on the spoon hangs in a 'flake', as shown in the sketch.
c) the jam reaches 220°F when tested with a sugar thermometer.
9. When the jam has reached setting point, remove any scum from the top of the preserve. It may be possible to disperse this if you stir carefully and slowly.
10. If the jam contains whole fruit (or peel as in marmalade) allow it to cool and begin to stiffen, stir to distribute the pieces of fruit or peel, then pour into the hot jars. If the jam is an even purée put into the jars at once. Either ladle in with a large spoon, or dip a strong jug into the jam and pour from this into the jars.
11. Fill the jars to within $\frac{1}{4}$-inch of the top. The less room left in the jar for air space, the less the possibility of mould developing on top of the jam.
12. Put the waxed cover on the jam, then cover with the cellophane round as in the picture. Moisten this slightly on the outside so you have a taut covering.
13. Label neatly.
14. Store in a cool, dry place. If you have central heating, I find it better to put the jam into bottling jars and to seal down with the tops of the jars. This prevents the jam 'drying out' or becoming 'sugary'.

Yield

Every 1 lb. sugar should produce $1\frac{2}{3}$ lb. completed jam, jelly or marmalade.

● **AVOID** *Using over-ripe fruit: Adding the sugar too early to fruit with tough skins, e.g. blackcurrants. The skin does not soften after the sugar has been added: Boiling the jam too quickly to soften the fruit, or too slowly once the sugar has dissolved.*

Proportions for Jam

I have divided the fruits into various groups, so you can see easily which fruits need other additions, such as water and lemon juice. The amount of sugar, water and lemon juice recommended *refers to 1 lb. fruit (weight after peeling, etc.).* 1 lb. sugar is 2C.

Group 1

These fruits have a particularly high setting quality so can set a high amount of sugar. They need an appreciable amount of water, otherwise the jam is too stiff. Simmer the fruit in water, see Stages 1–4. Add sugar as Stage 5, continue to Stage 13 in the Blue Print.

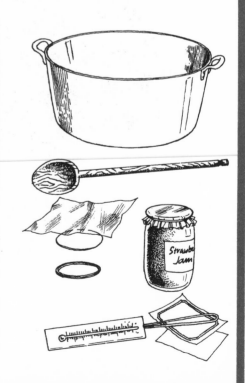

Fruit	Water	Sugar and Lemon Juice
Apples	¼ pint	1 lb. flavour with ground ginger, or orange juice in place of some of the water
Blackcurrants	½–¾ pint	1¼ lb.
Damsons	¼–½ pint	1¼ lb.
Gooseberries	¼–½ pint	1¼ lb.
Quinces	¼–½ pint	1¼ lb. 1 tablespoon lemon juice

Group 2

These fruits set reasonably well, but are juicy so need less water or no water. You rarely need lemon juice with fruits in this group. Any fruits not mentioned on this page can be treated as this group. If no mention is made of adding water, mash the fruit in the pan to extract some juice. Simmer gently until a smooth purée, add the sugar as Stage 5, continue to Stage 13 in the Blue Print.

Fruit	Water	Sugar and Lemon Juice
Blueberries (Whortleberries)	no water	1 lb.
Cherries— Morello cooking	2–3 table- spoons	14 oz. to 1 lb. stoned or 1¼ lb. with stones
Gooseberries —fairly ripe	no water	1 lb.
Greengages	no water but *up to* ¼ pint if firm	1 lb.

Group 2 cont.

Loganberries	no water	1 lb.
Passion fruit	no water	1 lb.
Plums	as greengages	
Raspberries	no water	1 lb.
Rhubarb	no water	1 lb.

Group 3

These fruits are deficient in pectin so need lemon or red currant juice to obtain a good set. To make red currant juice, mash then strain the fruit through a jelly bag. If no mention is made of water, mash the fruit in the pan to extract the juice then simmer, or simmer the fruit *with* the water as Stages 1–4. Add the sugar and lemon or red currant juice, then continue as Stages 5–13 in the Blue Print.

Fruit	Water	Sugar and Lemon Juice
Apricots— fresh	2 table- spoons water	1 lb. juice 1 large lemon
Apricots— dried	3 pints (soak for 12–24 hours)	3 lb. juice 2–3 lemons
Blackberries	no water	1 lb.
Blackberries and apples 1 lb. each	¼ pint simmer apples in this, then add black- berries	2 lb.
Cherries— dessert	no water 2–3 table- spoons if firm	14 oz. to 1 lb. stoned or 1¼ lb. with stones. Juice 1 lemon

Group 3 cont.

Figs	as apricots (fresh or dried)	
Guava	3–4 table- spoons	1 lb. juice 1 lemon
Lychee	no water	15 oz. juice 1 lemon
Mango	as guava	
Melon	no water	1 lb. juice 2 lemons
Peaches	as apricots (fresh or dried)	
Pineapple	as lychee	
Strawberries	no water	14 oz. juice 1 lemon or 6 tablespoons red currant juice
Tomato	as lychee, flavour with ginger	

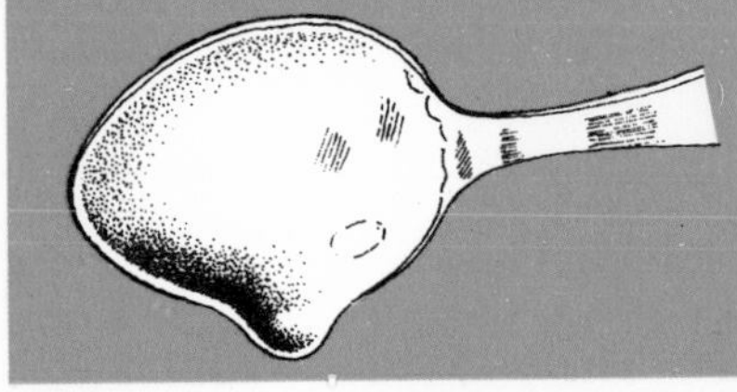

Group 4—Conserves

In these preserves the fruit is kept whole in a thick syrup. There are two ways of preparing this: A. With no water. B. With a syrup, made of sugar and water.

The fruits and vegetables most suitable for Method A are: diced cooking apples, diced pears, peeled diced pumpkin or marrow, diced fresh pineapple, black cherries, strawberries, halved Victoria plums, sliced guavas, sliced mangoes.

Use the amount of sugar given in the jam recipes. Pumpkin and marrow (not included above) need 1 lb. (2C) sugar to each 1 lb. diced vegetable. Sprinkle the sugar over the fruit and leave for several hours. Tip into a pan and stir over a gentle heat until the sugar dissolves. Add lemon juice, if included in the recipes above (pumpkin and marrow need the juice of 1 lemon to each 1 lb. fruit). Cook fairly rapidly until lightly set. See Stages 7–13 in the Blue Print.

Diced preserved ginger or crystallised or ground ginger may be added to apple, marrow and pear. Add towards the end of the cooking time. A few raisins may be added to plums. Add towards the end of the cooking time. 2 tablespoons Kirsch is delicious with pineapple and cherries. Add to the fruit with the sugar.

The fruits most suitable for Method B are: fresh green figs, whole apricots, small plums, cranberries, halved peaches.

Allow 1 lb. (2C) sugar and ¼ pint (⅔C) water to each 1 lb. prepared fruit. Add the juice of 1 lemon. Simmer the sugar, water and lemon juice over a low heat until the sugar has dissolved. Add the fruit and cook steadily until the syrup is thick and the fruit just tender.

Group 5—Fruit Cheeses

These are an excellent way of dealing with the fruits that contain a high percentage of pips and stones, e.g. blackberries, damsons, etc. Cook the fruit as though making jam. Rub through a sieve. Measure the pulp and allow 1 lb. (2C) sugar to each 1 pint (2⅔C) pulp. Add the sugar and lemon juice (if given in the recipe for jam). Continue as Stages 5–13 in the Blue Print.

Marmalade has been a favourite preserve for many centuries and the term originally described a preserve prepared from quinces. Today quince marmalade is a rarity (it is so delicious that a recipe is included on page 151) and one assumes that marmalade is made from citrus fruits, especially Seville or bitter oranges.

There are many recipes for orange marmalade. I give two basic Blue Prints, the first covers the type of marmalade where the fruit is shredded to give a 'fine cut' peel, the second describes the method where the fruit is boiled whole, to give a 'chunky' type.

Blue Print 1

Making Marmalade

1. Wash the fruit, halve and squeeze out all the juice, put the juice in a small container.
2. Remove the pips and put them on one side.
3. Shred the peel, together with the pith and pulp. This can be done by hand, or by using a shredding attachment or mincer.
4. Put the shredded peel into a bowl and

Making Marmalade

cover with the amount of cold water given in the recipe.
5. Tie the pips in a piece of muslin and put into the bowl with the peel and water.
6. Soak for 12 hours.
7. Tip the peel, liquid and bag of pips into the preserving pan. Simmer gently until the peel is tender, approximately 1½ hours. Test by feeling a piece of peel with your forefinger and thumb.
8. Add the sugar, the orange juice and lemon juice (if included in the recipe). Continue as Stages 5–9 under jam making Blue Print on page 148. Remove the bag of pips and continue as Stages 10–13 under jam making.

Making Marmalade

1. Wash the fruit, put into a saucepan with the cold water.
2. Simmer gently until the fruit is tender, approximately 1½–2 hours. Test by trying to insert a wooden skewer into the fruit, if it goes in easily the fruit is ready to be chopped.
3. Lift the fruit from the liquid, cool enough to handle.
4. Halve the fruit, remove all the pips.
5. Put these into the liquid and simmer gently for 15 minutes; there is no need to tie the pips in muslin.
6. Strain to remove the pips.
7. Meanwhile chop the oranges into strips.
8. Add to the liquid, after removing pips.
9. Heat until boiling, then add the sugar. Continue as Stages 5–13 under jam making Blue Print on page 148.

Equipment

As jam making, plus a mincer, sharp knife or shredder for mincing, chopping or shredding the fruit.

The proportions of sugar, water and lemon juice *are for each 1 lb. fruit*, so weigh the fruit before calculating. If using cup measures 1 lb. sugar = 2C, 1 pint water = $2\frac{2}{3}$C.

Proportions for Marmalade

Fruit	Type of marmalade	Additional ingredients
Bitter or Seville oranges	A. To give sweet marmalade. Blue Print 1	3 pints water 3 lb. sugar 2 tablespoons lemon juice
As above	B. Less sweet marmalade. Blue Print 1	2 pints water 2 lb. sugar no lemon juice
As above	C. Chunky marmalade. Blue Print 2	2 pints water 2 lb. sugar no lemon juice
Sweet oranges	As B.	Plus 3 tablespoons lemon juice
Bitter and sweet oranges	As B. or C.	Plus 2 tablespoons lemon juice
Lemons	As B.	no lemon juice
Grapefruit	As B.	no lemon juice
Tangerines or similar	As B.	Plus 4 tablespoons lemon juice
Three fruit made from grapefruit, bitter oranges, lemons	As A. or B.	no lemon juice
Four fruit made from grapefruit, bitter oranges, lemons, sweet oranges or tangerines	As B.	Plus 2 tablespoons lemon juice

Quince Marmalade

Wash, peel and slice or shred quinces neatly. Put into a saucepan. To each 1 lb. prepared quinces allow $\frac{1}{2}$ pint ($1\frac{1}{3}$C) water, the grated rind 2 lemons, 1 lb. (2C) sugar and 2 tablespoons lemon juice. Simmer the fruit and lemon rind in the water until tender. Add the sugar and lemon juice, stir until dissolved. Continue as jam making Blue Print on page 148, Stages 5–13.

To keep the pieces of quince firmer, heat the sugar, water and lemon rind for a few minutes, add the peeled sliced quinces. Simmer until nearly tender, add the lemon juice and continue as Stages 7–13 under jam making.

Jelly Marmalade

Choose the fruit required. Follow the proportions of water and sugar in the table above. Prepare the fruit as follows:

1. Halve, remove the juice and pips.
2. Remove all the pulp and white pith, leaving very thin fruit peel.
3. Tie pulp, pith and pips in muslin.
4. Shred the peel finely.
5. Soak the peel as Blue Print 1 with the muslin bag.
6. Cook as Blue Print 1, removing the bag of pips, pulp and pith when setting point is reached.

A clear fruit jelly is a delicious preserve and one that is often served with meat (e.g. red currant jelly with game or mutton, cranberry jelly with turkey, etc.).

Jellies are also excellent for glazing fruit flans and filling sponge cakes. A perfect jelly is crystal clear and firmly set, but never over-solid.

Blue Print

Making Jellies

1. Prepare the fruit. There is no need to peel fruits, such as apple, or remove the cores. These play an important part in giving flavour and making the jelly set. Simply wash and chop fruit into convenient-sized pieces.
2. Put the fruit into the preserving pan with the water.
3. Simmer gently until a pulp, this will take from 10 minutes minimum time, depending upon the fruit.
4. Strain through the jelly bag or substitute, see under Equipment. This takes some hours.
5. Measure the juice and calculate the amount of sugar needed.
6. Put the juice back into the preserving pan and bring to the boil. Continue as Stages 5–9 under jam making Blue Print on page 148. The method of testing jelly is exactly the same as for jam.
7. Pour the very hot jelly into the warmed jars, tap the jars gently and tilt slightly as you begin to fill them. This makes sure there are no air bubbles to spoil the clarity of the jelly. Cover and store as for jam, see Stages 11–13.

Equipment

As jam making, plus a jelly bag. If you have no jelly bag, then put several layers of muslin over a large sieve and strain the pulp through.

● **AVOID** *Pushing the pulp through the bag or muslin, otherwise you have a cloudy jelly.*

Proportions for Jelly

The amount of water given is for each 1 lb. fruit. The amount of sugar and lemon juice is for each 1 pint ($2\frac{2}{3}$C) juice *after* straining.

Fruit	Water	Sugar and Lemon Juice
Apple— cooking or crab apple	$\frac{1}{2}$ pint	1 lb. no lemon juice
Apricot	$\frac{1}{4}$ pint	1 lb. 2 tablespoons lemon juice
Blackberry	4 tablespoons	14 oz. 2 tablespoons lemon juice
1 lb. blackberries *and* 1 lb. cooking apples, i.e. 2 lb. fruit	12 tablespoons	15 oz. lemon juice not essential
Cranberry	$\frac{1}{2}$ pint	1 lb. 1 tablespoon lemon juice
Gooseberry— firm, cooking	$\frac{1}{2}$ pint	1 lb. no lemon juice
—dessert	$\frac{1}{4}$ pint	1 lb. 2 tablespoons lemon juice
Guava	$\frac{1}{4}$ pint	14 oz. 3 tablespoons lemon juice

Mint jelly—
As apple or gooseberry plus 2 tablespoons vinegar or lemon juice and 1–2 tablespoons chopped mint to each 1 pint juice. Add vinegar after sugar has dissolved and mint just before setting point.

Quince—or mixed quince and apple	$\frac{1}{2}$ pint	1 lb. no lemon juice
Red currant	$\frac{1}{2}$ pint	1 lb. no lemon juice

Using a jelly bag

Using muslin and a large sieve

Although in many homes freezing has taken the place of bottling, there are certain fruits which are better bottled and, of course, many people do not have the desire or space for a home freezer and still wish to have summer fruits in the middle of winter.

Blue Print

Steriliser Method of Bottling

1. You can bottle the fruit in water but it is infinitely better to use a sugar syrup. Prepare this first so that it can cool. The amount of sugar used is very much a question of personal taste. If you wish to use the minimum of sugar then allow 2 oz. to 1 pint water, i.e. $\frac{1}{4}$C to $2\frac{2}{3}$C. A heavy syrup can be as much as 10 oz. sugar to 1 pint water, i.e. $1\frac{1}{4}$C to $2\frac{2}{3}$C. Most people, however, find the latter too sweet and choose an amount in between the minimum and maximum. Put the sugar and water into a pan, stir until the sugar has dissolved, allow to cool.
2. Prepare the fruit, see below.
3. Pack the fruit into the jars. Push gently with hard fruit so this fits well, tap the jars gently if packing soft fruit so the fruit will settle into position.
4. Pour the syrup over the fruit, tap the jars gently as you do so to make certain you get rid of any air bubbles. Fill to within $\frac{1}{4}$-inch of the top of the jar.
5. Put on the tops:
a) if using screw-bands put the rubber ring, glass top and band in position then loosen the band slightly to allow for expansion.
b) put the tops and clips in position.
6. Fill the steriliser or deep pan with cold water. Ideally one should cover the jars. If that is not possible, then have as much water as you can and lay a cloth over the top of the container to keep in the steam.
7. Take $1\frac{1}{2}$ hours to bring the water up to 165–175°F, or the given temperature, and maintain for the period given below.
8. Lift the jars carefully out of the very hot water, tighten the screw-bands, if using.
9. Leave undisturbed overnight, or for 24 hours, then test to see if the jars have sealed. To do this, remove the screw-band or clip and make absolutely certain the lid is fast.
10. If the lid is not sealed check for a possible cause, i.e. a chip, a bent lid, a badly fitting rubber ring. Remedy this and re-sterilise. Naturally this is not ideal, since the fruit will be over-cooked.
11. Replace the clip or screw-band loosely; grease the inside of the screw-band.
12. Store in a cool, dry place.

● AVOID *Using jars that are not perfect:
Bringing the water to sterilising point too
quickly. It is essential that the full period is
allowed otherwise the fruits will be
inadequately heated. It is also essential to
maintain this heat for the full period: The
bottles touching each other.*
● TO RECTIFY *Check the temperature of the
water regularly: Put pieces of newspaper or
cloth between the bottles, so they do not touch.*
● SHORT CUT *Make a purée of the fruit
and preserve this way, which is much quicker.
Obviously the fruit purée has less uses.*
● TO SLIMMERS *Preserve the fruit in
water, not in a sugar syrup.*

To Prepare Fruit

Peaches Skin by lowering into boiling
water for a few seconds. Lift out, put into
cold water, leave until ready to pack, then
pull off the skins.

Apples and Pears Peel and slice, or halve
pears. Leave in cold water until ready to pack
or in a weak brine made by dissolving 1 *level*
tablespoon *kitchen* salt in 2 pints (5⅓C) cold
water. Rinse if wished.

Plums, Greengages and Apricots Wash
or wipe, halve and remove stones if wished.

Cherries and Damsons Wash, leave whole.

Timing for Fruits

Bring the water in the steriliser to 165–175°F.
Hold at this temperature for 10 minutes except when bottling:

Peaches Hold for 30 minutes.

Pears and Tomatoes Bring up to 180–
190°F, hold for 30 minutes.

Pulping Fruit

Simmer fruit with sugar to taste or add a
little salt to tomatoes. Meanwhile heat the
bottling jars. Put the boiling pulp into the
very hot jars, seal down, taking precautions
as Stage 5 in the Blue Print. Put into boiling
water.

For most fruits Hold at this temperature
for 8 minutes. **For tomatoes** Hold for 10
minutes. Lift out, tighten screw bands. Leave
and test as Stages 9 and 10 in the Blue Print.

Placing bottles in the steriliser

EQUIPMENT

Bottling jars. It is useful to choose various
sizes otherwise you may have too much
fruit opened if you have all large jars.
Keep the jars in a safe place before use.
After they have been used and the fruit
removed wash carefully and store so they
are not damaged. If using the type with
glass lids and rubber bands replace the
bands regularly. If using the type with
clip-on tops replace these tops regularly.
Wash jars thoroughly before use, rinse,
then *warm* and fill with boiling water to
sterilise.

Proper steriliser with a thermometer. This

has a rack upon which to stand the bottles.
If you do not wish to invest in a steriliser
then use a large, deep pan. Place a piece of
wood, folded cloth or folded paper (use
about 8 thicknesses) in the pan. This is
very important for the jars must *not* touch
the bottom of the pan.

A strong cloth to hold the hot jars when
removed from the steriliser.

A wooden board upon which to stand the
very hot jars when they come from the
steriliser.

Labels—not essential unless you wish to
give the date the fruit or vegetables were
bottled and amount of sugar added.

153

Bottling Vegetables

Never be persuaded to bottle vegetables other than in a pressure cooker at 10 lb. Your pressure cooker book will give full instructions for this, but this is the basic procedure.

Vegetable	Preparation	Blanching*	**Processing
Asparagus	Wash, trim off scales, cut in even lengths, tie in bundles, pack upright.	2–3 minutes	40 minutes
Beans—broad	Pod. Choose very young beans.	5 minutes	40 minutes
Beans—runner	Wash, string and slice.	5 minutes	40 minutes
Beetroot	Cut off tops. Blanch before slicing or dicing.	15–20 minutes	40 minutes
Carrots	Wash, scrape, slice or dice. Leave whole if young.	10 minutes	45 minutes
Celery	Wash, cut in even lengths.	6 minutes	40 minutes
Corn	Strip from cob.	2–3 minutes	50 minutes
Peas	Wash, shell and grade.	2–3 minutes	50 minutes
Potatoes—new	Wash, scrape carefully or peel thinly.	5 minutes	50 minutes

*Minutes to blanch in boiling water.
**Minutes to process at 10 lb. pressure.

1. Prepare the vegetables. Blanch in boiling water for the time given in the table, then strain.
2. Pack the vegetables into the bottling jars, leave 1-inch space in the jars.
3. Make a brine solution by boiling 1 teaspoon salt to each 1 pint (2⅔C) water.
4. Pour the boiling brine over the vegetables, leave 1-inch space at the top of the jars.
5. Put the lids on to the jars, give screw bands a half turn back to allow for the expansion of the glass.

6. Put 1 pint (2⅔C) boiling water into the pressure cooker, add 1 tablespoon vinegar, so the water does not darken the inside of the cooker.
7. Stand the jars on the rack in the cooker, make sure they do not touch each other or the sides of the pan.
8. Put on the lid and place on a low heat. Heat until all the air is expelled from the cooker, then heat for a further 5 minutes.
9. Place the 10 lb. weight in position then bring to pressure.

Apricot flan using bottled fruit

More Bottling

10. Maintain at this pressure for the time given in the table.
11. At the end of the time, move the cooker gently off the heat, do not touch the cooker until the pressure has dropped at room temperature.
12. Remove the jars and tighten the screw bands. Continue as Stages 9–12 in the Blue Print on page 152.
Note: Do not worry if some of the liquid boils out of the jars, this is quite normal.
When cooking bottled vegetables always heat for a minimum of 10 minutes.

Bottling Fruit in Liqueur

Fruit, bottled in brandy or other liqueur, is delicious to serve as a dessert. Many fruits can be preserved in this way, e.g. fresh peaches, pineapple, apricots, black and red dessert cherries, peeled oranges, perfect Victoria or other plums, firm, but ripe greengages, damsons and tangerines. Choose brandy, Curaçao, Kirsch or Maraschino.
Make a syrup by boiling together 4–8 oz. (½–1C) sugar with ¾ pint (2C) water. Strain and cool then add about ¼ pint (⅔C) brandy or other liqueur to ¾ pint (2C) or 1 pint (2⅔C) syrup.
Prepare the fruit as instructions on page 153. The fruit looks more impressive if bottled whole. Prick the skins of plums, damsons etc. so the syrup soaks in. Pack into the jars and cover with the flavoured syrup. Continue as Stages 5–12 in the Blue Print on page 152. Do not use for 2–3 months, so the flavour of the syrup impregnates the fruit.
When sterilising oranges and tangerines, which normally are not bottled, allow 1½ hours to bring the water to 165–175°F and maintain at this temperature for 15 minutes.

To use Bottled Fruit

Bottled fruit has been softened in the process of sterilisation so do not over-cook when you open the jar.
To use the fruit in a flan as shown on this page, lift the fruit out of the liquid. Pack the *well drained* fruit into the cooked flan case. Boil the liquid, if too large a quantity for glazing then continue boiling until you have the amount required: a 7-inch flan needs about ¼ pint (⅔C) syrup; an 8-inch flan about 12 tablespoons (1C) syrup.
Blend 1–1½ teaspoons arrowroot or cornflour with 1–2 tablespoons cold water. Add to the liquid in the pan. Stir well as the liquid boils, until thickened and clear. Cool slightly then coat the fruit.

Bottling Tomatoes

Skin tomatoes if wished. Naturally tomatoes are not covered with syrup, sprinkle with a little salt and sugar. Fill the jars with cold water or omit the water and bottle the tomatoes in their own juice.

Soft fruits can also be bottled with sugar to taste, rather than in syrup.

154

Fruits bottled in liqueur

Making Pickles and Chutneys

Pickles can be sweet or hot, they can be made with almost any type of vegetable and it also is possible to pickle fruit.

The Blue Print gives the important points on making chutney, but many of the points (particularly those dealing with the choice of vinegar and covering) are equally as important for pickles.

Blue Print
Making Chutney

1. Read the points about equipment carefully.
2. Buy good quality *malt* vinegar, it may be white or brown, and use the full quantity in the recipe. Put the prepared fruit and other ingredients into the pan (see Blue Print Recipe for Tomato Chutney). Add vinegar *gradually* as the fruit and vegetables soften. Remove the pickling spices before adding the sugar.
3. Stir the sugar until dissolved.
4. Cook until the consistency of jam in an open pan.
5. Put into warm jars, fill to within ½-inch of the top.
6. Cover carefully, do not allow metal caps to cover chutney (or pickles) since the vinegar will cause this to rust. Put a waxed circle over the chutney then a round of card, then a metal cap or use jars described under equipment.
7. Store in a cool, dry place, away from bright lights.

● **AVOID** *Using the* wrong type of pan, *this could cause the chutney to discolour and have a very unpleasant taste: Reducing the proportions of vinegar and sugar.*

Equipment

A large preserving pan or saucepan. Do not use copper, iron or brass. Aluminium or unchipped enamel may be used.

Jars, those with glass lids are excellent; if using metal tops read Stage 6 in the Blue Print. If using cellophane, as for jam, put a thick white or brown paper covering over; this prevents the chutney drying.

Green tomato chutney

Proportions to use for Chutney

The recipe below is a fairly standard one that you may adapt with other fruits and vegetables. If in doubt use the following proportions. To 2 lb. fruit or fruit and vegetables allow 8 oz. (1C) sugar (brown or white) and ½ pint (1⅓C) vinegar plus flavourings that blend with the particular fruit or vegetable.

Blue Print Recipe
Tomato Chutney

2 lb. red or green tomatoes · 1 large onion · 1 large apple · 1 clove garlic (optional) · ½ pint (1⅓C) white or brown malt vinegar · 1–2 teaspoons mixed pickling spices · 2–3 oz. (nearly ½C) sultanas or raisins · ½ teaspoon salt · 10 oz. (1¼C) white sugar.

To make Chop the tomatoes and the peeled onion. The tomatoes may be skinned, but this is not essential. Peel, core and chop the apple, crush the clove of garlic. Put the fruit and vegetables into the pan with about half the vinegar and the pickling spices (tied up in muslin).

To cook Simmer steadily until becoming soft. Add the remainder of the vinegar gradually. Remove the pickling spices. Put in the rest of the ingredients, and continue cooking as Stages 3–7 in the Blue Print.

Flavourings to Add

A little chopped preserved, green or ground ginger may be added.

Flavour with allspice or cinnamon, use about 1–2 teaspoons to the quantities above.

Add thin strips of red pepper (the sweet capsicum) with the sugar. This is shown in the green tomato chutney in the picture.

You can also add a *small* quantity of chopped red or green chilli pepper, but this is very hot.

Add chopped dates instead of raisins; the amount of dried fruit may be increased if desired.

Rhubarb, plums, apples, apricots, marrow, sliced aubergines (egg plants) and damsons may all be used in place of tomatoes.

Brine for Pickles

It is important that vegetables are salted before pickling, for this helps to keep them a good flavour and texture. Some vegetables are better put in salt and water (wet brine), others in a generous sprinkling of salt (dry brine). Use kitchen, rather than refined table salt and allow 2 oz. (2 very slightly rounded tablespoons) salt to each 1 pint (2⅔C) cold water for wet brine.

Spiced Vinegar

Add 1 tablespoon mixed pickling spices, either buy these or make your own (see below), to each 1 pint (2⅔C) vinegar used. Boil the vinegar for 15 minutes; this allows the vinegar to absorb the flavour of the spices, and also sterilises the vinegar. Strain and use in the recipes. Many recipes need cold vinegar, so allow time for this to cool.

If you cannot buy mixed pickling spices

Red tomato chutney

make up your own. Blend 1–2 dried chillis (very hot) with mustard seed, peppercorns, dried mace, 2–3 cloves, celery seeds and dried ginger.

Pickled Beetroot

Use cooked beetroot for this. Skin and slice or dice the beetroot. Cook again for 10 minutes in boiling salted water, drain and pack into hot jars. Pour over the hot strained spiced vinegar and cover.

Pickled Cabbage

Choose red cabbage, discard the very outer, rough leaves. Shred the cabbage neatly. Put a layer into a bowl, then a layer of salt. Continue like this ending with salt. Leave for 24 hours. Drain off the surplus moisture, rinse the cabbage in cold water if wished, but it remains a better texture if left without rinsing. Pack into jars and pour over the cold spiced vinegar.

Pickled Cucumbers

Method as pickled onions.

Pickled Mushrooms

Skin the mushrooms and boil in salted water for 5 minutes only. Make up the spiced vinegar and add a generous amount of peppercorns to this or season with a little black pepper. Drain the mushrooms, pack into hot jars, pour over the hot strained spiced vinegar and cover.

Pickled Onions

Use small onions or shallots. Peel with a stainless steel or silver knife. Put into wet brine for up to 48 hours. Rinse under the cold tap and shake dry if you do not like the slightly salty flavour. Put into jars, add cold spiced vinegar and cover.

Mixed Vinegar Pickles

If using mixed vegetables it is better to use wet brine, as for pickled onions. Choose onions, beans, sprigged cauliflower, tiny cucumbers, green or firm red tomatoes. Divide or cut into neat pieces. Leave for up to 48 hours in the wet brine. Drain, pack into jars and add the cold spiced vinegar.

Sweet vinegar pickles If you like a slightly sweet flavour, simmer 1 oz. sugar with the vinegar and pickling spices and use in the recipes.

Fruit vinegar and plum chutney

Mustard Pickle

For this pickle the vegetables do not need soaking for so long in the brine, as they are cooked in the mustard flavoured sauce. Select a good mixture of vegetables, see Vinegar Pickles left. Prepare and leave in wet brine for about 12 hours only. Drain and rinse in cold water, allow to dry.

To make the sauce, put 1 tablespoon dry English mustard with 2 teaspoons turmeric and 1–2 teaspoons paprika into a basin. Add 2 oz. ($\frac{1}{4}$C) brown or white sugar and 1 tablespoon flour. Blend in 1 pint ($2\frac{2}{3}$C) spiced vinegar. Put into a saucepan, bring slowly to the boil, stirring all the time. Put in the vegetables and simmer for 4–5 minutes only. Taste the sauce and add flavourings as required, i.e. a little pepper, ginger or even a little salt. Spoon into hot jars and seal down.

Salted Beans

This is a simple and very efficient way of preserving runner, French or green beans (often called haricots verts).

Choose young beans and kitchen salt. Allow approximately 3 lb. beans to 1 lb. salt. Prepare the beans as though for cooking. Put a good layer of kitchen salt into a glass or earthenware jar, then add a layer of beans. Continue like this ending with salt. Press down firmly. Keep covered with a cloth or several thicknesses of paper.

To use the beans Remove as many beans as required and wash in plenty of cold water. Soak for 2 hours in warm water, then cook as usual, but do not add salt.

Flavoured Vinegars

Vinegar can be flavoured in many ways to add interest to cooking.

Herb Vinegar

Put sprigs of fresh sage, mint, tarragon or rosemary into bottles of white or brown malt, or wine vinegar. Leave in the vinegar and use as required.

Fruit Vinegars

Add sliced fruit to the vinegar (this is delicious vinegar for a sweet salad dressing). The picture shows plum vinegar, i.e. a few sliced red plums were infused in the vinegar for about 4 days. The liquid was then strained from the fruit and boiled with sugar. Allow about 4–8 oz. ($\frac{1}{2}$–1C) sugar to each 1 pint ($2\frac{2}{3}$C) vinegar. Boil until thick and syrupy. Put into hot bottles and seal down. This is also excellent with very hot water as a soothing drink. Other fruits may be used.

Pickled Fruits

Some fruits are excellent in a sweetened vinegar. Choose crab apples (these do not need peeling), halved skinned peaches, peeled halved or whole pears, damsons, apricots, etc. Choose white vinegar and boil with the pickling spices, then strain.

To each 1 pint ($2\frac{2}{3}$C) vinegar allow 2 lb. (4C) sugar and just under 2 lb. prepared fruit. Simmer the sugar and vinegar until the sugar has dissolved, stir well. Add the fruit and simmer for a short time, until tender, but unbroken. Spoon into hot jars and seal down.

Home Freezing

There are many ways of preserving foods, and freezing is certainly among the best. This page gives hints on freezing fruit and vegetables.

Freezing Fruit

1. Wash and prepare the fruit, i.e. peel and core or halve and stone.
2. Make a syrup for firm fruit such as plums, see Stage 1 in bottling Blue Print on page 152.
3. Pack the fruit in waxed containers or heavy gauge polythene bags.
4. Freeze soft fruit with a sprinkling of sugar, or without sugar, seal containers and freeze.
5. Cover hard firm fruit such as plums and apricots with syrup, seal containers and freeze.
6. Prepare strawberries by putting in lines on flat trays, freeze, then pack. Or make a purée of strawberries, pack and freeze.
7. *Remember* that fruit *contains a high percentage of water* so expands in freezing. It is therefore important to leave about $\frac{1}{2}$–$\frac{3}{4}$-inch 'head-room' in the containers to allow for this expansion.
8. Use frozen fruit as soon as it 'thaws out', otherwise it loses appearance and flavour. Frozen fruits will last up to a year.

The most successful fruits to freeze are: apples, blackcurrants, loganberries, raspberries, red currants, rhubarb.

Packing fruit for freezing

Freezing Vegetables

If you grow, or buy, first class vegetables it is well worth freezing them. Choose vegetables in peak condition and freeze as soon as possible after buying or picking. This is important as many of the vitamins and mineral salts in the vegetables will be lost if they are left for a long time before freezing. Your instruction book will give full details on this but the basic procedure is as follows:
1. Prepare the vegetables as though for cooking.
2. Blanch them in boiling water for a few minutes, your freezer book will give definite times, but an average time is about 2–3 minutes. Small quantities of vegetables are blanched at one time so the water continues to boil. Blanching destroys certain enzymes, and ensures that the vegetables retain colour, flavour and texture.
3. Cool rapidly, by plunging the vegetables into ice cold water.
4. Pack in heavy gauge polythene bags or waxed containers.
5. Expel the air and seal.
6. Freeze as quickly as possible.
7. As frozen vegetables have been 'blanched' you will find the cooking time is shorter than when cooking fresh vegetables. The vegetables keep for about a year.

The most successful vegetables to freeze are: asparagus, beans—broad, French or sliced runner, broccoli, Brussels sprouts, carrots (diced) or small whole ones, cauliflower, mixed diced root vegetables, peas, potatoes (made into croquettes), spinach.

Salad vegetables, lettuce, cucumber etc. do not freeze well. Tomatoes can be pulped and frozen.

Blanching beans

Home-Made Sweets

Many recipes for sweets can be made very simply, so a child could produce them. In making the cooked sweets on the following page, make sure the children are supervised carefully, for the temperature to which the sugar mixtures have to be boiled are very high, and could cause a very bad accident if some of the mixture was spilled. The sweets that do not require cooking are on this page. To produce professional looking shapes for many sweets you need rubber moulds which can be obtained from good ironmongers, see the sketches.

Fondant

This is made like Royal icing and flavoured and coloured to produce a variety of sweets.
2 egg whites; 1 lb. (good $3\frac{1}{2}$C) sieved icing sugar; flavourings (see below).
Whisk the egg whites lightly, gradually beat in the sugar then add the flavouring and colouring. Knead very well to blend flavouring and colouring. If using the fondant to make just one kind of sweetmeat add the flavouring and colouring to the egg whites before the icing sugar. Allow the sweetmeats to 'dry out' and harden before packing.

Peppermint creams Take some of the fondant and work a few drops of oil of peppermint or peppermint essence into the mixture. If you like a soft creamy-type fondant, work in a very little full cream evaporated milk. Knead the mixture well, roll out and cut into small rounds. Leave to harden.

Chocolate peppermint creams Melt plain chocolate in a basin over hot, but not boiling water. Dip the peppermint creams in this, leave on trays to harden.

Crème de menthe fondant As peppermint creams, but work a little crème de menthe and green colouring into the fondant.

Assorted fondants Divide the fondant into three and add a few drops orange colouring and orange juice; raspberry essence and cochineal; almond essence and mauve colouring. Add a little evaporated milk if you wish to soften the fondant. Press into sweet moulds and allow to harden, then remove from the moulds.

Cherry fondants Add chopped glacé cherries to the fondant and roll in balls.

Coconut fondant Soften the fondant with a very little evaporated milk or use a little sweetened condensed milk. Work some desiccated coconut into the mixture. Roll out, cut into rounds as peppermint creams. Press a piped flower or similar decoration on top (see picture page 160), leave to harden.

Marzipan

Blend 8 oz. (2C) ground almonds, few drops almond essence, 4 oz. (nearly 1C) sieved icing sugar, 4 oz. ($\frac{1}{2}$C) caster sugar and bind with a whole egg. Roll out the marzipan, work in colouring, nuts, etc. as the individual recipes.

Marzipan dates Stone dates, fill with a little marzipan and blanched almonds. Tint marzipan pale green, roll out into narrow strips. Wrap round the bottom of the dates (see the picture). Roll in a little sieved icing sugar.

Marzipan rolls Make a 'tube' of natural coloured marzipan, then tint some marzipan green. Roll out thinly, wrap round the 'tube', roll in a very little sieved icing or caster sugar and leave to harden. Cut into $\frac{1}{2}-\frac{3}{4}$-inch lengths (see picture page 160).

Marzipan and coconut truffles Make the marzipan slightly softer than usual; add a little extra egg, sherry, orange or lemon juice. Work a small quantity of desiccated coconut into the marzipan. Form into balls, flatten slightly, roll in coconut or sugar. Top with glacé cherries or halved walnuts.

Harlequin squares Tint some marzipan pink, some green and leave the rest natural. Roll each portion out neatly, place on top of each other. Leave to harden and cut into small squares or diamonds. This can be varied by adding chopped nuts with one portion, raisins with the second and chopped glacé cherries with the third.

Chocolate Truffles

$\frac{1}{4}$ pint ($\frac{2}{3}$C) sweetened condensed milk; 2 tablespoons sieved apricot jam; 1 oz. sieved cocoa; few drops rum essence; 4 oz. (1$\frac{1}{3}$C) fine biscuit or plain cake crumbs. *To coat:* chocolate vermicelli.

Mix all the ingredients, except the vermicelli, together. Form into about 18–24 balls, roll in the chocolate vermicelli.

To vary Add chopped raisins, sultanas or nuts.

Press the fondant into the sweetmeat rubber mould

Leave to harden and remove

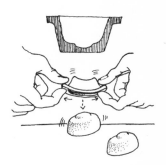

More Sweets

When making cooked sweets choose a *strong* pan, *stir well* until the sugar has dissolved then stir as little as possible, except with sweets containing cream or milk. Test with a sugar thermometer or by dropping ½ teaspoon of the mixture into cold water. Brush the sides of the pan with a pastry brush, dipped in cold water, as the mixture cooks. This saves some of the mixture crystallising on the sides of the pan. *It is important to beat, when stated in the recipe.*

Nougat

4 oz. (1C) blanched chopped almonds; 2 oz. (½C) chopped walnuts; 3 oz. (nearly ½C) chopped glacé cherries; 1 lb. (2C) granulated sugar; ¼ pint (⅔C) water; few drops vanilla or almond essence; 3 level tablespoons golden syrup; pinch cream of tartar; 3 level tablespoons honey; 4 egg whites.

Mix the nuts and cherries together. Put the sugar, water and essence into a strong saucepan, stir well until the sugar has dissolved, then boil steadily for a few minutes. Add the syrup, stir again and allow the mixture to reach nearly 270°F, so it forms a 'very firm ball' when tested in cold water, then beat in the cream of tartar. Remove from the heat. While the syrup is boiling, melt the honey in a basin over hot water. Whisk the egg whites until very stiff in a good-sized bowl, then stand this over a pan of hot water.

Gradually blend the mixture from the saucepan and the nut mixture into the egg whites. Stir all the time. Finally blend in the warm honey. Test once again and the mixture should form a 'firm ball' in cold water. If it seems a little soft, continue stirring over the pan of hot water until the right stage is reached. Brush a tin with a very little oil, pour in the mixture and leave to set. Cut into squares with a knife dipped in very hot water.

Cooked Fondant

1 lb. (2C) granulated sugar; 12 tablespoons (1C) water; 1 good pinch cream of tartar.

Stir the sugar and water over a low heat until the sugar has dissolved, then boil steadily, without stirring more than once or twice until the mixture reaches 238°F, or forms a 'soft ball' when tested in cold water. Add the cream of tartar, beat hard until cloudy, then cool enough to handle and use as the uncooked fondant on page 159.

Coconut ice Put 4 oz. (1⅓C) desiccated coconut on one side while making the fondant. When the fondant has reached the 'soft ball' stage add the desiccated coconut and 1 tablespoon thick cream. Beat until cloudy. Pour half into an oiled tin. Tint the remainder with a few drops of cochineal and pour carefully over the white layer. Allow to harden then cut into small portions or bars.

Fudge

2 tablespoons water; 2 oz. (¼C) butter; 1 lb. (2C) granulated sugar; ½ pint (1⅓C) full cream unsweetened evaporated milk; about ½ teaspoon vanilla essence.

Put the water and butter into a strong pan, allow the butter to melt, add the sugar and milk, stir over a low heat until the sugar has dissolved, add the essence. Boil steadily, stirring fairly frequently until the mixture reaches 238°F, i.e. forms a 'soft ball', when tested in cold water. Beat until the sweet mixture turns cloudy, then pour into a well oiled or buttered tin. Allow to set, cut into squares with a sharp knife. Wrap to store or put into a tin, otherwise the fudge hardens and loses its creamy texture.

Chocolate fudge Add about 6 oz. plain chocolate or 1 oz. sieved cocoa powder after the sugar mixture has dissolved. Continue as recipe.

Coffee fudge Add about 2–3 level teaspoons instant coffee powder to the mixture after the sugar has dissolved. Continue as recipe.

Fruit and nut fudge Add about 4–5 oz. (about ¾C) dried fruit and/or 2–4 oz. (½–1C) chopped nuts to the fudge mixture just before it reaches the 'soft ball' stage.

Turkish Delight

½ pint (1⅓C) water; 1 lb. (2C) granulated sugar; 1 oz. gelatine; 4 tablespoons lemon juice; ½ level teaspoon tartaric acid; little sieved icing sugar; cochineal.

Put most of the water and the sugar into a strong saucepan and stir until the sugar has dissolved. Soften the gelatine in the remaining cold water, then add to the sugar mixture and stir until blended. Add the lemon juice and acid. Boil steadily, stirring once or twice, for 8 minutes then pour half into a tin, dusted liberally with sieved icing sugar. Tint the remaining mixture a pale pink, then pour into a tin, dusted with sieved icing sugar. Allow the mixtures to cool and set, cut with a knife, dipped in hot water, then roll in more sieved icing sugar. Although not essential, it is advisable to store this in an airtight tin.

Nut Brittle

¼ pint (⅔C) water; ½ oz. butter; 1 lb. (2C) granulated sugar; 6 tablespoons golden syrup; about 8 oz. (2C) chopped nuts; pinch cream of tartar.

Put the water and butter into a strong pan, heat for 2–3 minutes until the butter has melted, then add the sugar and syrup. Stir over a low heat until the sugar has dissolved, boil steadily until the mixture reaches the 'crack stage', 290°F, i.e. when tested in cold water it forms a thread that cracks easily. Add the nuts and cream of tartar and heat for 2–3 minutes, stirring well. Either pour into a flat buttered tin and break in pieces when set or drop in small spoonfuls on to a buttered tray and allow to set. Store in an airtight tin or wrap in waxed paper so the mixture does not become sticky.

This part covers three very important groups of food, fish of all kinds, poultry, and game, together with the basic methods of cooking these and some new recipes and ideas.

Fish is not only an important protein food but a very adaptable one. There are so many different kinds of fish from which to choose and such a variety of ways in which fish may be cooked, that it should never be monotonous. If you are following a slimming diet, fish, if served without rich sauces or high calorie garnishes, is relatively low in calories, particularly if you choose the white or shell variety. White fish is very easily digested, shell fish and oily fish are more indigestible.

Fish is a highly perishable food, so choose it wisely. Fresh white fish is firm in texture, with bright eyes and a pleasant smell. If it has a strong smell of ammonia, it is *stale*. Shell fish is of good quality when it has a firm-looking shell. The tails of lobster or prawns should 'spring back' again after being pulled out and both crab and lobster should feel heavy for their size. If they are surprisingly light it is because they are 'watery' and are, therefore,

nine
FISH AND POULTRY

not a good buy. Oily fish, such as mackerel and herrings, should have bright silver scales and bright eyes. If the scales and eyes look dull, then be critical about buying the fish. Store fish carefully, put it as near the freezing compartment in the refrigerator as possible and use quickly. Most fish freezes well and you can substitute frozen fish for fresh in many recipes.

From page 172 onwards are methods of cooking all kinds of poultry and game, with particular emphasis on chicken. Young chickens have become both plentiful and comparatively inexpensive.

Chicken can be cooked in many different ways, but choose the right kind of chicken for each cooking process. A large roasting chicken, when jointed, would take too long to fry so could be over-cooked on the outside before being cooked through to the centre. Very young chickens are better cooked in a simple manner, such as frying and grilling, or poached and served in a cream sauce. This ensures that the delicate flavour is not lost and the young flesh does not become dry. Young chickens (often called 'broilers') have firm legs and plump breasts. The skin should be dry and firm looking.

Roasting chickens should have a flexible 'wish-bone', firm, but not 'sinewy' looking legs and a really firm plump breast. If untrussed, the eyes should be bright and the comb firm and bright in colour. A boiling fowl should have a reasonable amount of fat, but do not buy if there is an excessive amount of pale creamy-yellow fat, for the bird will be wasteful.

A good turkey is broad-breasted with firm legs. Avoid turkeys where the legs seem deficient in flesh. Duck and goose rarely have very plump breasts, but check that there is a fairly generous amount of meat and not too much fat.

Fish dishes are often very under-rated. They can be quite outstanding. It is, of course, very important to choose fresh fish and the points to look for are given on page 161. Careful cooking is essential if the fish is not to be spoiled.

Sometimes you will wish to bone the fish, unless the fishmonger has done this for you. The pictures on this page show how to bone herrings, but other fish, of a similar shape, can be dealt with in the same way. If you wish to fillet and skin flat fish, see the sketches on page 164.

Blue Print

To Cook Fish

The following points apply whichever method of cooking the fish is chosen.

1. Wash and dry the fish.
2. Season it lightly.
3. Choose any other flavouring desired. Remember most fish has a delicate flavour and this is easily lost if very strong tasting ingredients are added. The most successful flavourings with fish are:

Fresh or dried herbs lemon thyme, dill, chervil, parsley, chives.
Fruits lemon, orange, apple (particularly with herrings and mackerel), gooseberries (make a purée to serve with mackerel).
Vegetables tomatoes, mushrooms, peas and other green vegetables, onions (use sparingly), garlic (use sparingly).
Other flavourings horseradish (particularly with smoked fish), spices (particularly with oily fish), nutmeg, tomato ketchup or

concentrated tomato purée, mustard (particularly with herrings).
Liquids milk, cream, wines of all kinds (but white are better), cider, vinegar.
Stuffings many stuffings blend well with fish and you will find a number of suggestions opposite.
4. Choose your method of cooking and prepare as the particular Blue Print or recipe.
5. Cook for the recommended time, but always test before serving since the thickness of fish fillets, steaks, etc., varies so much. The fish is cooked if it *just* flakes from the skin or bone when tested with the tip of a knife.
6. Have any sauces all ready by the time the fish is cooked, unless you need the stock in which the fish has been cooked. Fish spoils if kept waiting for too long.
7. In order to enjoy a fish dish, choose the rest of your menu carefully. Do not precede a delicately flavoured sole dish with a very strong flavoured pâté or soup which would make the fish seem tasteless by comparison.

● **AVOID** *Handling the fish carelessly, support it with a fish slice, for fish breaks easily and this can spoil the appearance: Either under or over-cooking the fish: Serving fish that may not appear 100% fresh.*
● **TO RECTIFY** *If the fish does break, arrange neatly on the serving dish or plate and garnish or coat carefully with sauce to 'mask' the broken pieces.*
● **SHORT CUTS** *Use frozen fish for quick dishes or make use of canned fish: Choose the quick cooking methods, i.e. grilling and frying.*
● **TO SLIMMERS** *You are fortunate in that fish is low in calories; choose the methods that do not add extra calories to the dish—grilling, baking (without fattening garnishes or sauces), poaching or steaming.*

Quantities

Allow per person:
1 medium-sized sole or similar fish, 1 medium-sized to large trout or similar fish.
4–6 oz. fish fillet, without bone or thick skin, rather more if there are large bones and heavy skin, as on cutlets of fish (often called steaks).

½ medium-sized, or 1 small lobster or crab (if served in a sauce the fish can be used more economically).
1 pint mussels.
Minimum about 2 oz. shelled prawns or ½ pint with shells.
1 large or a pair of smaller kippers.
2–3 oz. roe for a savoury, up to 6 oz. for a main dish.

Storing and Freezing *In order to avoid continual repetition the points here apply to most fish, but where there is a particular point of importance you will find this given on the relevant page.*
Store fresh fish with the greatest care. Even in a refrigerator it should be kept for the minimum period. Read your manufacturer's instructions about freezing fish and use within the suggested period.
Put the fish as near the freezing compartment as possible in the refrigerator. Often one can use ready-frozen fish to take the place of fresh fish in a recipe. The general recommendations about defrosting are as follows, you can cook from the frozen state if the pieces of fish are small, but when cooking large fish I find it better to let them defrost before cooking, otherwise the outside tends to become over-cooked before the centre is tender.
To use any left over *Cooked fish must be used quickly, unless you wish to freeze this. It can be put into fish pies, fish cakes, etc. There are certain methods of cooking which enable you to make better use of cooked fish, i.e. poached and baked are better than fried or grilled fish.*

1. Cut the head off the fish, remove the intestines and wash well. Save the roe to use with the fish. Wash in cold water.
2. Split the fish along the belly.
3. Open out and lay on a wooden surface with the cut side downwards, run your fingers firmly along the back bone.
4. Turn the fish over and you will find you can remove the bones very easily.

This is one of the most adaptable ways of cooking fish, for the fish can be placed into a suitable dish in the oven with a little margarine or butter, with milk, with vegetables or with a sauce, and cooked until tender.

The fish may be stuffed before baking and recipes for stuffings, suitable for most fish, are given on this page.

Blue Print

To Bake Fish

This method is suitable for all white, oily, smoked and fresh water fish, but is less successful with shell fish, except in a sauce.

If Baking With No Additional Ingredients

Set the oven to moderate to moderately hot, 375–400°F, Gas Mark 5–6. Rub the bottom of an oven-proof dish with a little butter or margarine. Put the prepared fish on this, top with a little more butter or margarine and seasoning to taste or any other flavouring, i.e. a little chopped parsley, squeeze lemon juice, etc.

If you wish to have a slightly golden coloured look to the fish *do not cover*. If you wish the fish to remain very moist, *cover* the dish with a lid, foil or transparent cooking wrap.

Put, unless stated to the contrary, fillets of fish towards the top of the oven, but thicker steaks (cutlets) or whole fish should be put in or near the centre of the oven. This makes certain the outside of the fish is not over-cooked before the centre is tender.

Timing

Thin fillets take about 12 minutes, or about 15 minutes if covered.
Folded fillets take about 16 minutes, or about 20 minutes if covered.
Whole flat fish, e.g. sole, thick steaks (cutlets) or very thick fillets take about 25 minutes, or about 30 minutes if covered.
Thick whole fish, e.g. trout, take about 30–35 minutes, or about 40 minutes if stuffed *or* covered, or a little longer if both stuffed and covered.

Baking with Additional Ingredients

Baking with liquid You can omit the butter or margarine, although this can be added. The cooking times are the same as above.

Baking with vegetables i.e. sliced tomatoes, mushrooms and onions. Always slice onions *very thinly* or chop finely, since they take longer to cook than most fish. The cooking times will be a little longer than those given above.

Wrapping in foil Allow an extra 5–10 minutes cooking time.

Baking Fish

Quick Ways to Give Flavour to Baked Fish

Add a little cider or wine to the fish.
Put the fish on a bed of sliced tomatoes, season and top with sliced tomatoes, season well.
Blend a little paprika (sweet pepper) with thin cream, pour over the fish and bake.
Add tiny pieces of lemon flesh, chopped parsley and plenty of melted butter to the fish.

Sole and Lemon

4 small to medium-sized sole or other white fish; seasoning; 2 oz. (¼C) butter or margarine; 2 small onions; 2 lemons. *To garnish:* parsley.

The fish may be cooked whole or divided into fillets for this dish. Season lightly. Cut 4 large pieces of aluminium foil, sufficient to wrap round the fish. Grease with half the butter or margarine and place the fish in the centre. Peel the onions and cut into thin rings. Put over the fish. Slice the lemons thinly, remove any pips (which would give a bitter flavour to the fish). Put over the onions and top with the remaining butter. Wrap the foil round the fish, put on flat baking trays and bake as the Blue Print. Open the foil and tip on to the hot serving dish or plates. Garnish with parsley. *Serves 4.*

Note Cooked lemons have a delicious but unusual flavour, obviously you may not like this, in which case add the lemons as garnish afterwards.

Some Stuffings for Fish

While you can use most stuffing recipes the following are particularly suitable. The amounts below give enough stuffing for 4 generous portions.

Asparagus and onion Chop the stalks from a small can of asparagus or a small bunch of cooked asparagus (save the tips for garnishing the finished dish). Blend with 2 oz. (⅔C) soft breadcrumbs, 1 small grated onion, seasoning and 2 oz. (¼C) melted butter or margarine. This is suitable for most fish, but particularly fish with a delicate flavour.

Celery and apple Chop several sticks celery, blend with 2 peeled chopped dessert apples, 2 teaspoons chopped onion, seasoning, 1 teaspoon sugar (optional) and 1 tablespoon raisins. This is a difficult stuffing to handle as it has no crumbs, etc., so is suitable for baking separately and serving with the fish, or putting into whole fish. It can be varied by adding chopped parsley. This is suitable for mackerel and fairly strongly flavoured fish.

Mushroom and tomato Chop 4 oz. (1C) mushrooms, mix with 2 large skinned chopped tomatoes, a little chopped parsley, 1 oz. melted butter or margarine, and plenty of seasoning. This is suitable for all fish.

Sage and onion See page 173. This is suitable only for fish with a strong flavour.

Parsley and thyme (veal) stuffing See page 173. This is suitable for most fish.

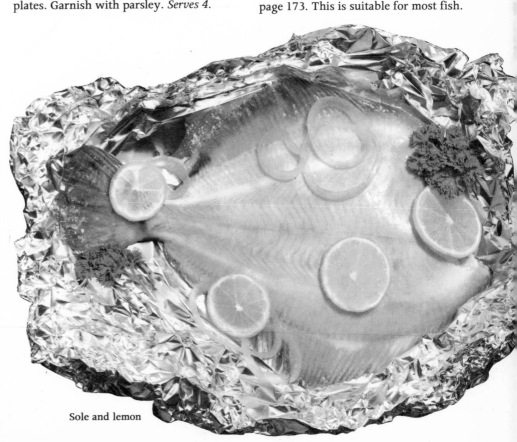

Sole and lemon

The following fish dishes, although entirely different in flavour and appearance, are based on the process of baking fish described on page 163.

Somerset Fish

This is suitable for fish with a fairly good texture and flavour, such as trout, herring and mackerel.

4 portions or whole fish; 2–3 small onions; seasoning; 2 dessert apples; about $\frac{1}{2}$ pint (1$\frac{1}{3}$C) cider; 2–3 bay leaves. *To garnish:* 1 lemon.

Wash and dry the fish. Peel and cut the onions into thin rings. Season the fish and put into an oven-proof dish with most of the onions, separated into rings, the peeled, finely chopped apples and the cider. Put the bay leaves into the liquid (the flavour of this herb is very strong, so add 1 leaf only if you are not fond of it). Top with the few remaining onion rings. Bake as the Blue Print on page 163. Garnish with the lemon and serve in the baking dish.

For Special Occasions

Sole with White Wine Sauce

4 large or 8 smaller fillets of sole (or use other white fish, whiting is excellent for this dish); seasoning; about 2 oz. ($\frac{1}{4}$C) butter; about $\frac{2}{3}$ pint (nearly 2C) white wine; $\frac{1}{2}$ oz. flour; $\frac{1}{4}$ pint ($\frac{2}{3}$C) milk; 2–3 tablespoons thick or thin cream. *To garnish:* paprika; 1 lemon.

Roll or fold the fillets of fish, put into a baking dish and season lightly. Top with nearly half the butter and the white wine. Cover the dish and bake in a moderate oven, 350–375°F, Gas

Mark 4–5, for about 20 minutes or a little less, since the fish has to be kept waiting while finishing the sauce. Meanwhile heat the remainder of the butter in a saucepan, stir in the flour and continue stirring over a low heat for a few minutes. Gradually blend in the milk and bring to the boil, stir until a very thick sauce. Lift the fish on to a very hot serving dish, strain the liquid from cooking the fish gradually into the thick sauce, then stir gently until smooth. Stir in the cream, heat without boiling. Pour over the baked fish, top with paprika and garnish with sliced lemon.

To vary

Sole Veronique Add a few de-seeded grapes (peel if wished) to the wine and fish. Garnish with more grapes and lemon.

Sole Sevilla Place slices of orange under each rolled fillet when cooked and proceed as the recipe above. Garnish with de-seeded grapes; peel if wished.

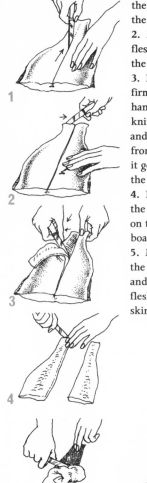

1. Cut the fish down the centre and round the edges.
2. Make a cut in the flesh at the tail end of the fish.
3. Hold the tail firmly with your left hand and insert the knife under the flesh and cut one fillet away from the bone, easing it gently as you cut the fish.
4. Lay the fillets with the skin underneath on to a chopping board.
5. Make a cut across the tip of the fillet and gently cut the flesh away from the skin.

Sole Sevilla (above)
Somerset trout (below)

Grilling Fish

Grilling is not only a quick method of cooking fish, but a very wise one too. Fish that is grilled is more easily digested and certainly less fattening than fried fish.

Blue Print

To Grill Fish

This method is suitable for most fish except some smoked fish.

Heat the grill before placing the fish under the heat, for it is important the fish is cooked quickly. Thin fillets do not need turning over, but thicker pieces of fish should be turned. Lift the fish carefully, for it can easily be broken.

Always brush the fish with melted butter or other fat before cooking, so it does not become dry and 'baste' with a little more butter or fat during cooking or when turning the fish; if cooking the fish on the grid cover this with buttered foil or grease the grid so the fish does not stick.

Vegetables such as mushrooms or tomatoes may be cooked on the grid of the grill pan or in the grill pan itself. Season the vegetables lightly and brush or coat these with a little butter or fat.

Timing

Thin fillets take about 5 minutes. Thicker fillets take about 8–9 minutes. Thick steaks (cutlets) or whole fish take about 10 minutes.

Lift the fish from the grill pan or grid with a fish slice and put on to a serving dish. There is no need to drain grilled fish on absorbent paper. Garnish with parsley and lemon or cooked tomatoes and mushrooms. Tartare sauce or other sauces may be served with the fish if desired.

● **AVOID** *Over-cooking and cooking too slowly: Allowing the fish to dry.*
● **TO RECTIFY** *The grill should be pre-heated and the heat may be lowered after browning the outside of the fish: Keep well basted with melted butter.*

Storing and Freezing   *See page 162. Fish can be grilled from the frozen state.*
To use any left over   *Any grilled fish can be used in salads, or in fish cakes or fish pies, see page 170.*

Quick Ways to Give Flavour to Grilled Fish

The following flavourings can be added to the melted butter, or other fat, used to brush the fish before grilling.

Grated lemon rind and lemon juice.
A little tomato ketchup or fresh or canned tomato purée.
A crushed clove garlic and seasoning.
A little curry powder and a few drops Worcestershire and/or chilli sauce.

The following toppings can be put on to the fish when it is nearly tender.
Fine soft breadcrumbs, blended with melted butter and seasoning.
Grated cheese, blended with breadcrumbs.
Slices of Cheddar cheese.
Cottage cheese, mixed with chopped parsley and chopped chives.

For Special Occasions

Savoury Grilled Turbot

3 oz. ($\frac{3}{8}$C) butter; 1 tablespoon lemon juice; $\frac{1}{2}$–1 teaspoon paprika; seasoning; 4 steaks (cutlets) turbot or other white fish. *To garnish:* parsley; lemon.

Heat the butter in a pan until it turns golden brown, this gives a delicious flavour to the fish, but it is essential the butter does not become too dark. Add the lemon juice, paprika and seasoning. Brush one side of the fish with some of the butter mixture and put on the greased grid or on buttered foil. Cook as the Blue Print, turning once. Serve topped with any hot butter and garnish with parsley and lemon. Serve with new potatoes. *Serves 4.*

Chablis Halibut

About 2 wineglasses Chablis or other dry white wine; 4 steaks (cutlets) halibut or other white fish; seasoning; 2 oz. ($\frac{1}{4}$C) butter. *To*

garnish: cooked or canned sweetcorn; red pepper; parsley.

Put the wine in a shallow dish and leave the fish soaking in this for 1 hour. Turn the fish after 30 minutes. Lift the fish out of the wine, season lightly. Melt the butter, brush the fish with this and grill as the Blue Print, turning once. Serve with the hot sweet corn, topped with red pepper and garnish with parsley. Heat any wine left in the dish and spoon over the fish before serving. *Serves 4.*

Grilled Lobster

Split a cooked lobster, remove the intestinal vein, crack the large claws and remove the flesh. Lay this on top of the flesh in the body of the fish. Brush with well seasoned butter and grill steadily until warmed through and the top is golden coloured. This can be done over a barbecue fire for a luxury dish. Serve with green salad. *1 medium-sized lobster serves 2.*

Grilled Prawns

Do not shell the prawns. Naturally for this dish they need to be the very large type. Lay the prawns on foil on the grid of the grill pan, brush with a little oil, then grill until the shells are brown. Live prawns may be grilled this way instead of boiling them. They also may be cooked over a barbecue fire. Serve with lemon and cayenne pepper.

Pacific Cutlets

Grill 4 portions of white fish as the Blue Print. Top with grated or sliced cheese and melt under the grill. Meanwhile toss 2–4 oz. ($\frac{1}{4}$–$\frac{1}{2}$C) chopped shelled large Pacific prawns or smaller prawns in a little butter for 2–3 minutes, add 2 teaspoons lemon juice and a good shake of pepper. Spoon on top of the fish and serve at once. Garnish with wedges of lemon or whole unshelled prawns. *Serves 4.*

Frying Fish

Frying is undoubtedly one of the, if not the, most popular forms of fish cookery. It is an excellent method, for the coating ensures that the moisture and flavour are 'sealed in' the fish.

Blue Prints

1. To Fry Fish

Fish can be fried in two ways.
In shallow fat, this can be butter or margarine, cooking fat or oil.
In deep fat or oil.
Although fish can, and often is fried without coating, see Fish Meunière, it is frequently coated before frying. The coating gives a pleasant crispness to the outside as well as keeping the fish moist.
There are several ways of coating fish.
1. With seasoned flour. Allow about $\frac{1}{2}$ tablespoon flour to each portion of fish.
2. With seasoned flour and then with beaten egg and fine crisp breadcrumbs (you can use fine soft crumbs if preferred). It is a good idea to coat the fish with a very thin layer of flour (about $\frac{1}{4}$ tablespoon per portion) before the egg, as this helps the final coating to adhere to the fish. 1 egg plus about 2 oz. (1C) crisp breadcrumbs should coat 4 portions.
3. With a batter, this is described opposite.
4. With more unusual coatings, such as oatmeal.

2. To Fry Fish in Shallow Fat

This method is suitable for all white and oily fish and some shell fish (such as shrimps and prawns), but is unsuitable for smoked fish and most shell fish.
It is excellent for fillets of fish, but deep frying is preferable for thick portions of fish for you have better overall browning, although they *can* be cooked in a small amount of fat.
Heat enough oil or cooking fat in a frying pan to give a depth of about $\frac{1}{4}$ inch, or preferably $\frac{1}{2}$ inch. Put in the prepared fish and fry quickly until crisp and brown on the under side, turn and fry on the second side, lower the heat and continue cooking until tender.

Timing

Thin fillets take about 4 minutes.
Thicker fillets take about 5–6 minutes.
Thick steaks (cutlets) or whole fish take about 10 minutes.
Lift the fish from the fat with a fish slice and drain on absorbent paper before serving. Fried fish can be served without a sauce, just garnished with lemon and parsley, but tartare sauce is the usual accompaniment, see opposite.

● **AVOID** *Too cool fat which would make the fish greasy or too hot fat which would over-cook the outside before the centre is cooked.*

Quick Ways to Give Flavour to Fried Fish

Mix the juice of a small lemon with each egg used for coating the fish and blend the finely grated lemon rind with the crumbs. Add a small quantity of grated cheese to the crumbs used in coating the fish. *It is important that this cheese coating is used only on thin fillets. Cheese is spoiled if over-cooked and thicker portions of fish take too long to cook.*
Add a little chopped parsley or chives to the crumbs used in coating the fish.

Herrings in Oatmeal

Cut off the heads from fresh herrings, remove the intestines and clean. Remove the back bone (see pictures page 162). Fillet if wished. Wash and dry the fish. Mix fine or medium oatmeal with a little seasoning and coat the fish in this. Fry as Blue Print 2 on this page.

For Special Occasions

Fish Meunière

Choose fillets of white fish, small whole white fish, trout or shelled prawns.
4 portions fish or the equivalent in prawns; seasoning; 3 oz. ($\frac{3}{8}$C) butter (even a little more if you like rather rich food); 1–2 tablespoons lemon juice; little chopped parsley; few capers (optional). To garnish: lemon.
Wash and dry the fish and season lightly. Heat the butter in a large pan and fry the fish until just tender. Lift the fish on to a very hot dish. If there is very little butter left in the pan you will need to add more. Heat the butter until it turns golden brown, add the lemon juice, parsley and capers and pour over the fish. Garnish with sliced lemon and serve at once. *Serves 4.*

Fish Belle Meunière

Cook the fish as above, but omit the parsley and capers. Instead fry a few soft roes and prawns in the browned butter.

Trout Woolpack

Although trout is shown in the picture, this recipe is suitable for most other fish. You will need about 5 oz. ($\frac{5}{8}$C) butter for 4 portions fish or whole fish. Fry the fish, remove from the pan, but do not allow the butter to turn too brown. Fry 4 oz. (1C) sliced button mushrooms and a generous amount of small prawns or shrimps in the butter, add 1–2 tablespoons lemon juice as the recipe above, together with extra seasoning. Spoon over the fish and garnish with parsley and lemon. *Serves 4.*

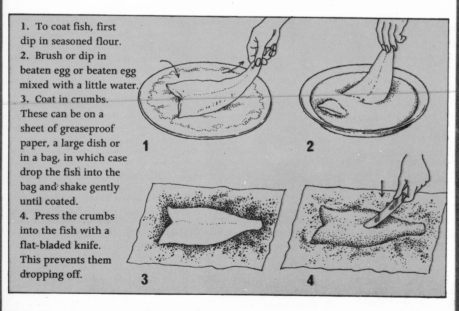

1. To coat fish, first dip in seasoned flour.
2. Brush or dip in beaten egg or beaten egg mixed with a little water.
3. Coat in crumbs. These can be on a sheet of greaseproof paper, a large dish or in a bag, in which case drop the fish into the bag and shake gently until coated.
4. Press the crumbs into the fish with a flat-bladed knife. This prevents them dropping off.

Trout woolpack

Rolled Fillets of Fish

Roll fillets of skinned white fish and secure with wooden cocktail sticks. Dip in the coating, remove sticks before frying. Use an egg and breadcrumb or batter coating, fry as the Blue Print on this page. If the fillets are rolled they take slightly longer to cook.

Stuffed Rolled Fillets of Fish

Spread the fillets with a fairly firm stuffing, i.e. parsley and thyme (page 173), mushroom and tomato (page 163). Roll, then coat and fry.

Goujons (Ribbons) of Fish

This is a way of making the more expensive white fish, such as sole, 'go further'. Divide the fish (sole, plaice, whiting or small pieces of pilchard can be used) into neat strips, coat in egg and crumbs or batter and fry as the Blue Print. Small sprigs of raw or lightly cooked cauliflower can also be coated with batter and fried with the fish as in the picture. Garnish with lemon.

This is another advantage of deep frying, the flavours do not intermingle or impart flavour to the fat or oil. Potato chips or other vegetables, such as onion rings, can be fried immediately before the fish and kept hot. Traditional fish and chips are illustrated on page 161.

Tartare Sauce

¼ pint (⅔C) mayonnaise or Hollandaise sauce; 2 teaspoons each chopped parsley, chopped gherkins and capers; few drops tarragon vinegar (optional).
Mix all the ingredients together. If using mayonnaise as a basis for this sauce you can make a large quantity and store the remainder in a screw-topped bottle in the refrigerator.

Storing and Freezing *Ready frozen fish may be used, without waiting for it to thaw out, although it is difficult to coat frozen fish. Remember though you can buy ready-coated portions of frozen fish for shallow or deep frying. The cooking time is only a few minutes longer.*
To use any left over *Fried fish is not very suitable for using in other ways. It could be frozen, ready to reheat, but take care it is not over-cooked.*

Do not imagine that frying fish in deep fat (or oil) is more extravagant than shallow frying. If the temperature of the fat or oil is correct it is surprising just how *little* is absorbed by the fish coating.

Blue Print

To Fry Fish in Deep Fat

This method is suitable for white fish and for large prawns. It is rarely used for oily fish and other shell fish and never for smoked fish. It is better to coat the fish when using this method of cooking. Choose either egg and crumbs, i.e. **2** on the Blue Print opposite or the batter coating below.
To make a batter to coat 4 portions of fish (or equivalent in large prawns—scampi), sieve 4 oz. (1C) flour, plain or self-raising, with a pinch salt. Add 1 egg and about 12 tablespoons (1C) milk or milk and water. When coating in batter, dip the fish in seasoned flour first (allow about ¼ tablespoon per portion), this encourages the batter to adhere to the fish. Dip in the batter, allow any surplus batter to drop back into the basin so you do not have too thick a coating.
Make sure the pan of fat or oil is not overfilled, for naturally the level will rise when the fish is placed into the pan. *Test the temperature of the fat or oil*, it should be 365°F, or a cube of day-old bread should turn golden brown within under 1 minute. Place the frying basket into the

hot fat or oil so this becomes coated, which prevents the fish sticking to the mesh. Lift the warmed basket from the fat or oil, lower the coated fish into this.

Timing
Thin fillets take about 3 minutes.
Thicker fillets take about 4 minutes.
Thick steaks (cutlets) or whole fish take about 5–6 minutes.

Lift the fish from the fat or oil, allow the basket to remain over the top of the pan for a few seconds for any surplus fat to drop back into the pan. Drain on absorbent paper and serve. Deep fried fish can be served without a sauce, but a tartare sauce is the usual accompaniment.

● **AVOID** *Too hot fat or oil which will scorch the outside: Too cool fat or oil which will cause the coating to become greasy or even 'drop off' the fish.*
● **TO RECTIFY** *Test the temperature of the fat before frying (see Blue Print).*

AVOID ANY DANGER OF FIRE—NEVER LEAVE A PAN OF FAT OR OIL UNATTENDED AND ALWAYS TURN THE HANDLE TOWARDS THE CENTRE OF THE COOKER SO IT CANNOT BE KNOCKED AGAINST.

Goujons of fish (above left). Rolled fillets of fish (above).

Poaching Fish

I have used the term 'poach', rather than 'boil', for it describes the method that should be used for cooking fish. If fish really is boiled in liquid, it is cooked too rapidly and the outer flesh can, and probably will, break badly and become 'watery'. Poaching means cooking gently in simmering liquid.

Blue Print

To Poach Fish

This is suitable for all kinds of fish including shell fish.
The liquid in which the fish is poached can be.
1. Seasoned water or when 'boiling' crab, lobster, etc. many people like to use sea water.
2. Wine, cider or wine and water.
3. Milk or milk and thin cream.
4. A court-bouillon. This is made by using either fish stock (made by boiling the head, skins and bones of fish) or fish stock blended with white wine, a *bouquet garni* and seasoning.
The amount of liquid varies according to the thickness of the fish. Some people like to put the fish into cold liquid, bring the liquid to simmering point and continue, others like to put the fish into the simmering liquid. If putting into warmed liquid shorten the cooking times below by about 2 minutes.

Timing

Thin fillets take about 7–8 minutes.
Thicker fillets, steaks (cutlets) or small whole fish take about 10–12 minutes.
Whole fish—allow 7–8 minutes per lb. or up to 10 minutes per lb. for solid type fish, i.e. salmon.

Lift the fish out of the liquid with a fish slice, drain for a moment over the pan, then put on to a heated serving dish. If serving cold, allow to cool in the liquid; the cooking time should therefore be reduced by about 5 minutes. Poached fish is generally served with a sauce and the easiest and most simple sauces are on this page.

● **AVOID** *Over-cooking: Failing to season the liquid which produces rather tasteless fish.*
● **TO SLIMMERS** *An ideal method of cooking.*

SAUCES TO SERVE WITH POACHED FISH

White Sauce
1 oz. butter or margarine; 1 oz. flour; ½ pint (1⅓C) milk or use half milk and half liquid from cooking the fish; seasoning.
Heat the butter or margarine in a saucepan. Stir in the flour and continue stirring over a low heat until the 'roux' forms a dry mixture. Gradually add the milk or milk and other liquid, bring to the boil, cook until thickened, stirring all the time. Add seasoning to taste.
Anchovy sauce   Use no salt in the sauce, add a few drops of anchovy essence.
Cheese sauce   Add 3–4 tablespoons grated cheese to the thickened sauce, stir over a low heat, do not boil again. A little mustard can be added, if liked.
Cream sauce   Add 2–3 tablespoons thick cream to the thickened sauce, heat gently.
Lemon sauce   Add the grated rind of 1 lemon to the flour. Add 1–2 tablespoons lemon juice to the thickened sauce, do not boil again and heat very gently.
Parsley sauce   Add 1–2 tablespoons chopped parsley to the thickened sauce. Allow the parsley to cook for 2–3 minutes in the sauce for a milder flavour.
Shrimp or prawn sauce   Add a few tablespoons whole shrimps or chopped prawns to the sauce, heat gently so the shell fish is not toughened.

More Fish Dishes

On this page are a variety of fish dishes, including two other Blue Prints for simple methods of cooking fish.

Haddock and Mushroom Scallops
Little butter and cream; 1 lb. (2C) cooked potatoes; about 8 oz. fresh haddock; about 8 oz. smoked haddock; 1 pint (2⅔C) milk; 1½ oz. butter; 1 oz. flour; 4 oz. (1C) mushrooms; seasoning; 1 small can sweet corn. *To garnish*: 4 tomatoes; parsley.
Blend a little butter and cream into the mashed potatoes. Put into a piping bag with a ½-inch rose and pipe a border round the edge of 6 scallop shells or individual heat-proof dishes. Brown gently under a very low grill or in a very moderate to moderate oven while making the fish mixture. Put the fish into the milk with about one third of the butter. Simmer steadily until tender, i.e. about 10–12 minutes. Lift the fish out of the milk on to a flat dish, allow to cool slightly, then skin and flake. Meanwhile heat the remaining butter in a pan, stir in the flour and cook for several minutes, stirring all the time. Strain the milk, used in cooking the fish, into the 'roux'. Bring gradually to the boil and cook until thickened, stirring all the time. Put in the whole mushrooms and simmer for about 5 minutes, then add the flaked fish. Season to taste, add some of the sweet corn. Put the sauce mixture into the border of potato and top with hot sweet corn. Garnish with wedges of tomato and parsley. *Serves 6.*
Note   Other white and smoked fish can be used in this recipe.

Blue Prints

1. To Roast Fish

This method is suitable for white and oily fish.
It is similar to baking fish, as the instructions on page 163, but a more generous amount of butter or other fat is used. The fish is basted in the hot butter or fat as it cooks in a moderately hot to hot oven, 375–400°F, Gas Mark 5–6, so the outside skin becomes crisp and brown. The cooking time is similar to that given for baking. It is very suitable for whole fish or thick pieces of cod, fresh haddock, etc.

2. To Steam Fish

This method is suitable for white fish, preferably whiting, sole, plaice and similar fish. It is an excellent way of cooking fish for small children, older people or invalids as it is the

Haddock and mushroom scallops

most easily digested form of cooked fish. The easiest method of steaming fish is to put the lightly seasoned fish on a buttered plate and top with a little butter. Sometimes this must be omitted if people are on a fat-free diet, but obviously it makes the fish more interesting. Top with a small quantity of milk. Put the plate over a pan of boiling water and cover with another plate, foil or a saucepan lid. Keep the water boiling and allow the following times.

Timing

Thin fillets take about 8–10 minutes.
Thicker fillets or thin steaks take about 12–15 minutes.
The liquid left on the plate can be added to a white, cheese or anchovy sauce (see opposite) to serve with the fish.

Fish Milanaise

4 portions white fish (preferably large fillets sole, whiting, plaice, etc.); seasoning; 2–3 tablespoons white wine; 2 oz. ($\frac{1}{4}$C) butter; about 6 oz. ribbon noodles; 2–4 oz. ($\frac{1}{2}$–1C) button mushrooms; few cooked peas. *To garnish*: paprika; lemon.
Put the fish on to a large plate, add the seasoning, wine and about $\frac{1}{2}$ oz. only of butter. Steam as the Blue Print. Meanwhile boil the noodles in plenty of well seasoned water and fry the mushrooms in the remaining butter. Drain the noodles, return to the saucepan with the peas and mushrooms. Heat gently for a few minutes, then put on a hot dish. Lift the fish on top of the noodles and garnish with paprika and lemon. This can be served with any of the sauces opposite. *Serves 4.*

Normandy Herrings

4 large herrings; seasoning; 1 oz. flour; 3 oz. ($\frac{3}{8}$C) butter or margarine; 1 large onion; 2–3 dessert apples; 1 tablespoon lemon juice. *To garnish*: parsley.
Remove the heads from the fish, clean and remove the back bone, if wished, as instructions on page 162. Season the flour and roll

Normandy herrings

Fish Milanaise

the fish in this. Heat about 2 oz. ($\frac{1}{4}$C) of the butter or margarine in a large pan. Peel and chop the onion. Core the apples, slice 1 apple for garnish, as in the picture, and chop the remainder. Fry the apples and onions in the pan until the apples are soft and the onion is transparent. Add the lemon juice. Put the chopped onions and apples into a hot serving dish and keep warm; keep the apple slices separate. Heat the remaining butter or margarine in the frying pan and cook the fish until tender. Put on top of the mixture in the serving dish and garnish with the apple slices and parsley. *Serves 4.*
To vary Use shelled prawns in place of the apples and onion. Fry the fish first, remove and keep warm, then fry the prawns in the cleaned pan in a little extra butter. Add 1–2 tablespoons Chablis or Calvados and spoon over the fish.

Fish Pies and Patties

Although ready-cooked fish can be used in fish pies and patties, it is obviously better to choose the right fish and cook or prepare it specially for these economical and interesting dishes.

Seafood Pie

1½ lb. white fish (inexpensive kind); about ½ pint (1⅓C) fish stock or water; seasoning; 1 pint (2⅔C) white or other sauce (see page 168); few prawns; about 1 lb. (2C) creamed potato; little butter or margarine.

Bake or poach the fish as the Blue Prints on pages 163 and 168, using the fish stock or water and seasoning. Drain and flake the fish, use the liquid as part of the sauce if wished. Mix the sauce and fish, add the prawns. Put into a pie dish and top with the creamed potato and a little butter or margarine. Bake for approximately 30 minutes just above the centre of a moderate to moderately hot oven, 375–400°F, Gas Mark 5–6. *Serves 4–5.*

Salmon Pie

Use cooked fresh or canned salmon in place of white fish in the recipe above. Mix with the sauce, then add a few sliced cooked carrots, 2 chopped hard boiled eggs and about 3–4 tablespoons grated cheese. Top with the creamed potato or a puff pastry crust (made with 5–6 oz. (1¼–1½C) flour, etc.). If using potato, bake as the recipe above. If using puff pastry, bake as the recipe below for Fish in a Jacket.

Fish Pie Americaine

Fry 2–3 rashers chopped bacon with 1–2 chopped onions, then add about 3 chopped and skinned tomatoes. Stir in 1 oz. flour and cook for several minutes, stirring all the time. Gradually blend in ¾ pint (2C) chicken or fish stock. Bring to the boil, cook until a thickened mixture. Stir well as the mixture thickens. Add about 1–1½ lb. flaked cooked white fish, season well. Put into a pie dish, top with creamed potato and bake as the Seafood Pie.

Fish in a Jacket

1 lb. frozen puff pastry or puff pastry made with 8 oz. (2C) flour, etc.; 4 very large or 6 smaller fillets white fish; seasoning; 1 oz. butter; 1 oz. flour; ¼ pint (⅔C) milk; about 4 oz. (1C) mushrooms. *To glaze:* 1 egg; 1 tablespoon water. *To garnish:* sliced lemon and parsley.

Prepare the pastry and roll out thinly, then cut into 4 or 6 squares, large enough to cover the fish. Lay the fillets flat on a board, season lightly. Make a thick sauce with the butter, flour and milk as the method on page 168. Add the chopped uncooked mushrooms and season well. Spread over half of each fillet, see Sketch 1. Fold the other half of the fish over the sauce, see Sketch 2. Lay on the squares of pastry, moisten the edges, fold over in triangles and seal the edges, see Sketches 3 and 4. Lift on to a baking sheet, brush with a little beaten egg, blended with water. Bake for 10 minutes just above the centre of a very hot oven, 475°F, Gas Mark 8, then lower the heat to moderate and cook for a further 20–25 minutes until golden brown and well risen. Garnish with lemon and parsley and serve hot. *Serves 4–6.*

To vary If preferred, blend flaked cooked fish with a thick sauce and chopped mushrooms and use as a filling for the pastry.

Fish Cakes

8 oz. cooked fish*; 8 oz. (1C) creamed potatoes; 1 egg; seasoning. *To coat:* ½ oz. flour; 1 egg; approximately 2 oz. (1C) crisp breadcrumbs. *To fry:* about 2 oz. (¼C) fat or 2 tablespoons oil.

*white fish, herrings, kippers, tuna (canned or fresh) or salmon (canned or fresh) may be used.

Flake the cooked fish finely, blend with the potatoes, the egg and seasoning. Form into 8 flat cakes. Coat in the flour, blended with a little seasoning, then the egg and breadcrumbs. Pat into a good shape with a flat-bladed knife. Heat the fat or oil in a frying pan and fry the fish cakes until crisp and brown on both sides. Drain on absorbent paper and serve hot with lemon or with a sauce (see page 168). *Serves 4.*

To vary Bind with a thick white sauce (as the recipe for Fish in a Jacket) instead of the egg.

Add 1–2 tablespoons chopped parsley to the fish mixture.

Bind the fish cakes with about 4 tablespoons fresh, well seasoned tomato puree instead of egg.

Flavour with 2–3 teaspoons chopped chives.

Storing and Freezing *Fish cakes freeze splendidly and can be cooked from the frozen state.*

    Fish in a jacket

Traditional Fish Dishes

Some of the most interesting fish recipes are old-fashioned favourites.

Creamed Haddock

Finnan haddie is one of the most famous Scottish fish for it is prime haddock, delicately smoked. It can be poached in water and topped with butter or poached egg, but this way is both nutritious and less well known.

Enough smoked haddock for 4–6 people; ½ pint (1⅓C) milk; ¼ pint (⅔C) thin cream; 1 oz. butter; pepper.

Either cut the haddock into neat pieces or cut into small portions. Put into a dish. Warm the milk, cream and butter and add plenty of pepper. Pour over the fish. Cover the dish and bake for about 25 minutes in a moderate oven, 350–375°F, Gas Mark 4–5. Serve with fresh rolls and butter for breakfast or supper. *Serves 4–6.*

Scallops Poached in Wine

Enough scallops for 4 people—these vary in size from the large scallops shown in the picture (where 1 per person is a good portion) to the very small scallops of Australia or the tiny 'Queenies' from the Isle of Man; 1 oz. butter; just about ½ pint (1⅓C) white

Creamed haddock (top)
Scallops poached in wine (above)

wine; seasoning. *For the base of the dish:* about 3 oz. (1½C) crisp breadcrumbs; 1½ oz. butter. *To garnish:* parsley..

Remove the scallops from their shells, save the tiny amount of liquor. Heat the butter in a large frying pan, toss the scallops in this for about 2 minutes, then add the wine, liquor and seasoning. Simmer steadily until tender. Do not over-cook. Meanwhile toss the bread-crumbs in melted butter in a second frying pan. Put the crisp crumbs into scallop or individual dishes, top with the cooked scallops, garnish with parsley and serve. This dish will appeal to people who do not like creamy sauces. *Serves 4.*

To vary Proceed as above, then use any white wine left to add to a white, cream or cheese sauce (see page 168). Top the scallops with the sauce and serve.

Storing and Freezing *Smoked fish keeps rather better than fresh, but the flavour of smoked haddock is at its finest when freshly smoked. Frozen smoked haddock is excellent and can be cooked from the frozen state, although you must allow it to thaw out to cut into tiny pieces as the picture on this page. Scallops should be eaten when fresh. They freeze very well. I find the best way is to cover the scallops with water and freeze in a cube of ice. Wrap and store, then drop them into boiling water to melt the ice and cook as usual.*
To use any left over *Kedgeree—Left over smoked haddock may be heated with cooked rice, butter and a little cream if wished. Add chopped hard boiled egg whites and seasoning to taste. Pile on to a hot dish and top with chopped hard boiled egg yolks.*

In most families the traditional bird at Christmas time is a turkey, and indeed roasted poultry or game is an ideal choice for a celebration meal. The points about selecting poultry will be found on page 161. Choose quick roasting for prime birds and slower roasting for poorer quality, or when the bird has been frozen. *Always allow frozen poultry to thaw out before cooking, this takes up to 48 hours with a very large turkey.*

Blue Print Recipes

1. To Roast Chicken and Turkey

A large roasting fowl or capon serves 6–8. A medium-sized chicken can be cut into 4 portions and small spring chickens halved, or if very small, left whole as a portion for one. Guinea fowl is cooked and served as chicken. When buying turkey, remember there is a considerable weight of bone, so allow at least 12 oz. per person, i.e. a 12 lb. bird (weight when trussed) would provide portions for 14–16 people.

These are dry-fleshed birds and must be kept moist during cooking, so cover the bird, particularly the breast, with a generous amount of fat bacon or fat. Put stuffing inside the bird as it helps to keep it moist. Always weigh the bird after stuffing to calculate the cooking time. Baste the bird from time to time to keep it moist.

Timing

For quick roasting Set the oven to hot,

Roasting Poultry

425–450°F, Gas Mark 7–8, the heat may be reduced to moderately hot after 15 minutes if roasting a small chicken and 30 minutes for a larger bird.

Chicken 15 minutes per lb. and 15 minutes over.

Turkey 15 minutes per lb. and 15 minutes over for a bird up to 12 lb. in weight. After this add an additional 12 minutes per lb. up to 21 lb., after this allow only 10 minutes for each additional 1 lb. If the bird is exceptionally broad breasted be a little generous with the cooking time.

For slower roasting Set the oven to moderate, 350–375°F, Gas Mark 4–5, only.

Chicken 25 minutes per lb. and 25 minutes over.

Turkey 25 minutes per lb. and 25 minutes over for a bird up to 12 lb. in weight. After this add an additional 20 minutes per lb. up to 21 lb. then allow 15 minutes for each additional 1 lb. If the bird is exceptionally broad breasted then allow an extra 5 minutes per lb.

If using a covered roasting tin or foil allow an extra 15–20 minutes cooking time. Lift the lid of the tin or open the foil for about 30 minutes before the end of the cooking period so the skin may brown and crisp. Extra cooking time is *not* necessary when using cooking film or roasting bags.

Accompaniments

The traditional accompaniments with both these birds are: bread sauce (or cranberry sauce with turkey); parsley and thyme (veal stuffing and/or chestnut stuffing; roasted sausages and bacon rolls; thickened gravy There are however more unusual accompaniments which may be served and these are given opposite and on page 174.

When roasting a chicken or turkey, prepare the bird, i.e. put in stuffing, see the sketches. Heat the oven, cover the bird with fat or fat bacon. Cook for the time calculated. Add the sausages about 30 minutes before the end of the cooking time and the bacon rolls about 10–15 minutes before 'dishing-up'. Lift the bird on to the hot serving dish and use a little of the fat in the tin to add to the gravy. Hints on making gravy will be found on page 23.

1. Insert the stuffing under the skin of the neck.
2. Pull the skin right over the stuffing and

secure with a skewer.
3. Put any remaining stuffing (or if using two kinds, the second one) inside the bird.

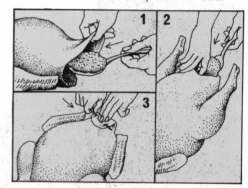

2. To Roast Duck and Goose

Duck and goose are birds that contain a high percentage of fat. I find I obtain a really 'fat free' bird, with deliciously crisp skin if I cook the bird for about 30 minutes then take the roasting tin out of the oven. Prick the skin carefully, do not prick too deeply, with a fine skewer and the excess fat 'spurts out'. Do this once or twice for duck but at least twice more for a goose. Do not add extra fat when cooking duck or goose. The cooking times are the same as for chicken and turkey.

Quantities

A large duck can be cut into 4 joints, but a small duckling should be halved.

Goose is a very extravagant bird, for it has very large bones and relatively little meat, so you should allow at least 1 lb. weight per person (after the bird is trussed).

Accompaniments

The traditional accompaniments with both these birds are apple sauce; sage and onion stuffing and thickened gravy. Less usual accompaniments are given opposite and on page 174. Duckling always looks more interesting if garnished with slices of orange.

Roast turkey

Young game can be roasted in the same way as poultry. Although it is not necessary to stuff this, I find that one can use some kind of stuffing for pheasant and grouse and suggestions are given below.

Blue Print

To Roast Game

Choose young pheasant, partridge, grouse or other young game birds, saddle (the back joints) of hare or a whole leveret (a very young hare), rabbit (this must be very young and a tame rabbit is better than a wild one) or a joint of venison.

Quantities

A small bird is generally served to one person; a medium-sized grouse or other bird is halved, but there is a surprising amount of flesh on good pheasants and these can be carved like chicken.

Roast the bird as the Blue Print opposite for chicken and turkey. Game is also dry-fleshed, so must be covered with plenty of fat or fat bacon. The cooking times are the same as for chicken and turky. Roast pigeons are illustrated on page 161.

Accompaniments

Serve most game with bacon rolls, bread sauce or red currant jelly, fried breadcrumbs and game chips. The gravy should not be too thick, and can be flavoured with wine. Garnish with watercress. Venison can be served with a wine sauce and hare or rabbit is served with sage and onion stuffing.

SOME INTERESTING STUFFINGS

Never make a stuffing too dry, it should be pleasantly moist. All stuffings given serve 5–6 if only one stuffing is made, but double that number if making two stuffings.

To Serve With Chicken, Turkey and Guinea Fowl

Parsley and thyme (veal) stuffing Blend together 4 oz. (1⅓C) soft breadcrumbs, 1–2 tablespoons chopped parsley, 2 oz. (¼C) shredded suet, or melted margarine or butter, or chicken or turkey fat, 1–2 teaspoons chopped fresh thyme or good pinch dried thyme, grated rind and juice of 1 lemon and 1 egg. Season well.

Forcemeat stuffing Blend 4 oz. chopped lean ham with 8 oz. sausagemeat, 1–2 teaspoons chopped parsley, grated rind 1 lemon, 2 oz. (nearly ⅓C) sultanas and 1 egg.

Liver stuffing Blend about 8 oz. minced raw liver (this can be calf's liver, chickens' livers, turkey or a mixture) with 2 rashers chopped bacon. Heat 2 oz. (¼C) butter and toss the liver and bacon in this, then add 1 finely chopped onion, do not cook again. Blend with about 8 oz. (1C) very smooth mashed potato, 2 eggs, 1 teaspoon freshly chopped mixed herbs or a pinch dried herbs

and seasoning. This is also very good with duck, goose or pheasant.

Giblet stuffing Cook the giblets until just tender. Remove all the flesh from the neck bone and chop this with the heart and liver. Blend with 2 oz. (⅔C) soft breadcrumbs, 1 tablespoon chopped parsley, 1 tablespoon chopped nuts, 2 tablespoons raisins, seasoning and 1 egg. Finally chop a small onion, toss in 1 oz. butter or chicken fat and blend with the other ingredients. If using turkey giblets *double* all the other ingredients in this recipe. This is also good with duck or goose.

Chestnut stuffing Slit 1 lb. chestnuts and boil in water for 5–10 minutes, remove the skins while still warm. Put the chestnuts into ½ pint (1⅓C) chicken, ham or turkey stock and simmer until tender and nearly all the stock is absorbed, then chop or sieve. Blend with 4 oz. diced ham, 8 oz. pork sausagemeat, seasoning and a little stock. If preferred, the chestnuts may be left whole and blended with the other ingredients.

To Serve With Duck and Goose

Sage and onion stuffing Peel, chop and cook 2–3 large onions for 10 minutes in ¼ pint (⅔C) water, season well. Strain, then blend with 3 oz. (1C) soft breadcrumbs, 1–2 teaspoons chopped fresh sage or ½ teaspoon dried sage and 2 oz. (¼C) shredded suet or melted margarine. Bind with the onion stock and/or an egg.

Orange rice stuffing Grate the rind from 3 oranges and squeeze out the juice. Measure the juice and add enough water to give ¾ pint (2C) liquid. Chop 1 large onion finely and toss in 2 oz. (¼C) margarine or butter, then add 6 oz. (¾C) long grain rice, the orange rind and juice and ½ teaspoon chopped fresh sage. Simmer until the rice is nearly tender, season well, then add 2 oz. (⅓C) raisins. Do not overcook the rice, otherwise it becomes too 'solid' when put into the bird and cooked again.

Celery and nut stuffing Chop the heart of a good-sized head of celery, do not use the outer sticks. Add the tender leaves, chopped finely. Mix with about 4 oz. (1C) chopped walnuts, 4 oz. (about ⅔C) sultanas, 2 oz. (⅔C) soft breadcrumbs (preferably brown), the grated rind and juice of 1 lemon or orange and 2 oz. (¼C) melted butter or margarine. Season well.

To Serve With Game

Soak white grapes in a little red wine and put into the bird before roasting.

Blend cream cheese with a little brandy and put into the bird.

Blend 2 oz. (¼C) butter with the cooked chopped liver of the game bird, season well and use as stuffing inside the bird.

Fried crumbs Make fairly coarse white breadcrumbs. Fry in hot butter or margarine until crisp and golden brown. Drain on absorbent paper and serve with roasted game.

Game chips Slice peeled potatoes thinly. Fry in very hot deep fat until crisp and brown. Drain on absorbent paper.

Storing and Freezing *Roasted poultry and game should be stored in a refrigerator. If freezing poultry or game it is advisable to freeze the stuffing in separate containers.*

Roast pheasants

Roasted poussins

A New Look at Roasted Poultry

The recipes on this page are based on the Blue Prints on page 172, but slightly unusual accompaniments and flavourings make a familiar roasted chicken or duck into a very special dish.

Chicken Bordelaise

Roast the chicken as the Blue Print on page 172, but add about 20 very small peeled onions or shallots to the fat in the roasting tin. Roast the chicken for about 30 minutes, then pour about $\frac{1}{2}$ pint (1$\frac{1}{3}$C) red wine over the chicken. Add 4–8 oz. (1–2C) small button mushrooms to the tin about 20 minutes before the chicken is cooked. Baste once or twice more with the wine. Serve the chicken with the well drained onions or shallots and mushrooms round. Use most of the liquid from the roasting tin in the gravy.

Apricot Chicken

Stuff the inside of the chicken with halved canned or cooked apricots. If this is too sweet for you, then follow the recipe for parsley and thyme stuffing, but omit the thyme and add about 8–10 chopped cooked or canned apricot halves to the other ingredients in the stuffing. Baste the chicken with a few tablespoons of the apricot syrup towards the end of the cooking time. Serve garnished with more halved apricots. Make gravy in the usual way, but add a few tablespoons apricot syrup to the thickened gravy.

Roasted Poussins

Stuff 4 small spring chickens with well drained cooked or canned sweet corn, blended with a very small amount of chopped chives or spring onions and a little butter. Pour melted butter over the chickens and roast until tender. Lift the small chickens on to a hot serving dish and keep hot. Spoon 1 tablespoon of the fat from the roasting tin into a saucepan. Blend 1 level tablespoon cornflour and a good pinch paprika with the fat, cook for 2–3 minutes, stirring all the time. Gradually blend $\frac{1}{2}$ pint (1$\frac{1}{3}$C) thin cream, or cream blended with chicken stock, into the 'roux'. Bring slowly to the boil, stirring until thickened. Remove from the heat and add an egg yolk, blended with 2 tablespoons cream and 1 tablespoon sherry. Return to a very low heat and cook, without boiling, for a few minutes. Season well. Spoon the sauce over the spring chickens, garnish with red pepper and serve. *Serves 4 or 8 depending upon the size of the spring chickens.*

The poussins in the picture are served on a bed of ratatouille, which makes a delicious and unusual accompaniment.

Duck with Cherries

Roast 1 large duck or 2 smaller ducklings in the usual way. About 10 minutes before the duck is cooked, lift the roasting tin from the oven. Remove the duck on to a plate and pour the fat from the tin into a basin. Return the duck to the tin with a medium-sized can of black cherries and the liquid from the can and continue cooking until the duck is tender. Baste the duck once or twice with the cherry liquid. Lift on to a hot dish. Blend 1 tablespoon cornflour or arrowroot with $\frac{1}{4}$ pint ($\frac{2}{3}$C) very well strained stock (made by simmering the duck giblets). Put into a saucepan with the strained cherry stock. Bring to the boil, cook until thickened, stirring all the time. Then add the cherries and a little cherry brandy. Taste the sauce, and if it is too sweet, add a squeeze of lemon juice. Serve the sauce round the duck. Garnish with watercress. *Serves 4.*

Some Sauces for Poultry and Game

Apple sauce Simmer peeled sliced apples in a very little water until soft, sieve or beat until smooth or emulsify in the liquidiser, sweeten to taste. This is particularly good if chopped cooked prunes and cinnamon are added to the sauce just before serving.

Bread sauce This is a slightly richer recipe than often given, but it is much nicer. Put 3 oz. (1C) soft breadcrumbs into a pan with $\frac{1}{2}$ pint (1$\frac{1}{3}$C) milk, $\frac{1}{2}$ oz. butter, 1 onion (stuck with 2–3 cloves), seasoning and 2 tablespoons thick cream. Heat very slowly until thickened and keep in a warm place until ready to serve. I generally put this into the top of a double saucepan over boiling water then it cannot burn. Remove the onion and cloves and stir well before serving.

Cranberry sauce Make a syrup of $\frac{1}{4}$ pint ($\frac{2}{3}$C) water and 2–3 oz. ($\frac{1}{4}$–$\frac{3}{8}$C) sugar. Add 8 oz. cranberries and 2 oz. ($\frac{1}{3}$C) sultanas and cook until tender. Add 1 tablespoon port wine if wished. The sauce can be put into the liquidiser goblet and emulsified to give a smooth mixture.

Seville orange sauce Grate the rind of 2 Seville or bitter oranges, put into a pan with $\frac{3}{4}$ pint (2C) duck or goose stock. Simmer for 10 minutes in an open pan so some of the liquid evaporates. Blend the orange juice with $\frac{1}{2}$ oz. cornflour, 2 teaspoons sugar and seasoning. Put into the giblet stock in the pan and stir over a gentle heat until thickened and clear.

Wine sauce Heat 2 tablespoons fat from roasting game in a pan, stir in 1$\frac{1}{2}$ oz. flour and cook for several minutes, stirring well. Add $\frac{1}{2}$ pint (1$\frac{1}{3}$C) brown stock, $\frac{1}{4}$ pint ($\frac{2}{3}$C) port or red wine, 1–2 tablespoons red currant jelly, seasoning and a clove of garlic. Bring to the boil and remove the garlic. Stir over a medium heat as the sauce thickens.

Special Poultry & Game Dishes

Although there are a large variety of pies made with poultry and game, the Terrine en Croûte on this page is particularly delicious.

Blue Print Recipe

Terrine of Chicken

1 roasting chicken, about 3½ lb. when trussed · the chicken giblets · about ¾ pint (about 2C) water · 1 onion · *bouquet garni* · seasoning · 6–8 oz. lean pork or veal (cut from the top of the leg) · approximately 12 oz. thin rashers bacon · 8 oz. pork sausagemeat · 1–2 tablespoons chopped parsley.

To make Cut all the meat from the bones of the chicken. Take great care when removing the breast meat as this needs to be cut later into neat slices. Put the chicken bones and the giblets with the water, whole onion and herbs into a pan. Season well. Put the lid on the pan and simmer for about 30 minutes. Remove the lid and allow the liquid to boil rapidly to give 4 tablespoons really strong stock. Remove the liver. Put the cooked chicken liver, all the dark meat (leave just the breast), the pork or veal and 2 rashers of bacon through a mincer, season well and blend with the sausagemeat and 2 tablespoons of the stock. Slice the breast neatly, put on a dish, add the remaining stock and the chopped parsley, season lightly. Line the bottom of an oval or oblong oven-proof dish with half the bacon rashers. Put a layer of the minced meat mixture over the bacon, then add some of the sliced chicken breast. Continue filling the dish like this, ending with minced meat. Cover with bacon rashers. Put a well-fitting lid on the dish, if available, and wrap foil round the outside, so no steam escapes.

To cook Stand the dish in a tin of cold water. Cook for 1½ hours in the centre of a very moderate oven, do not exceed 325°F, Gas Mark 3. Remove from the oven. Lift the lid carefully (as there is a lot of steam 'trapped' inside the dish). Put a light weight over the terrine, so it is pressed into a neat shape as it cools. Turn out when ready to serve.

To serve Cold with toast and butter or with salad. *All recipes based on this serve 8–12 as an hors d'oeuvre or 4–6 as a main dish.*

Terrine en Croûte

Ingredients as the Blue Print, but omit the bacon for the top and bottom of the dish, just use the 2 rashers of bacon to mince with the chicken meat, etc. Make either a short crust pastry or raised (hot water crust) pastry with 12 oz. (3C) flour, etc. Roll out about three-quarters of the pastry and line a 2-lb. loaf tin. Fill with the terrine as outlined above. Cover with a 'lid' of pastry. Seal the edges, brush with beaten egg and decorate with pastry leaves, also brushed with egg. Bake for approximately 30 minutes in the centre of a moderately hot to hot oven, 400–425°F, Gas Mark 6–7, to set the pastry, then reduce the heat to very moderate, 325°F, Gas Mark 3 for a further 1 hour. Although it is not usual to serve this hot I think it is delicious. If planning to serve hot, use short crust pastry. (Illustrated on Menu Maker 33.)

To vary To make a more exotic terrine or terrine en croûte of poultry, use only 2 tablespoons stock and add 3 tablespoons brandy to this. Use to blend with the minced ingredients and the chicken breast. Omit the parsley and add 2–3 tablespoons chopped, skinned pistachio nuts.

Terrine of Game

Ingredients as the Blue Print, but use young pheasant or grouse in place of chicken. Pheasant has a good breast, but if the breast of grouse is not very plump, add a little chicken breast.

Pheasant Mould

1 pheasant, preferably a hen bird; 4 tablespoons strong game stock (made from simmering the giblets and bones, see method); 8 oz. lean ham; grated rind 2 large oranges; 2 teaspoons chopped chives or 1 teaspoon grated onion; 2 eggs; 4 tablespoons thick cream; 2 tablespoons brandy or extra stock; seasoning.

If using a young pheasant prepare as the Blue Print, i.e. cut the flesh from the bones. If using an older bird then simmer gently for about 45 minutes, cool enough to handle, and remove the bones from the flesh. In either case, simmer the giblets and bones with water and herbs in an open pan so the liquid is reduced to the small quantity given in the ingredients, as in the Blue Print. Mince the pheasant flesh and ham, mix with the other ingredients and season well. If you find game flavour fairly strong, you may care to add about 2 teaspoons honey to the other ingredients. This will not be 'detected', but gives a pleasant blending of flavours. Butter a 2–3-pint mould well. Put in the mixture and cook as the Blue Print. This can be served cold with salad or hot with vegetables and a wine sauce, opposite. *Serves 4–6.*

Chicken Aspic Mould

To a 1 pint (2⅔C) packet aspic jelly powder, use about 8–12 oz. diced cooked chicken, 3–4 cooked carrots, and 3–4 tablespoons cooked peas.

Make up the aspic jelly to give just 1 pint (2⅔C) liquid, do not exceed this amount. It is a good idea to use strained chicken stock instead of water to make the jelly. Blend the diced chicken with diced cooked carrots and peas, add to the aspic jelly and allow to set.

Storing and Freezing *The terrines, moulds and aspic keep for 1–2 days only in a refrigerator but can be frozen. They tend to 'dry out' slightly so use within a few weeks.*

To use any left over *Store carefully and use instead of pâté as an hors d'oeuvre.*

Terrine of chicken

Poultry & Game Casserole Dishes

Do not imagine a stew or casserole of chicken must take a very long time to cook, the small young frying (broiler) chickens can be used and the dish will be ready in a comparatively short time. A stew or casserole is, however, an excellent way of cooking poultry and game not sufficiently tender for quick or even slow roasting.

Oriental Chicken

1 large roasting chicken*. *For the stuffing and sauce:* small can bean sprouts; 4 oz. lean ham; small can water chestnuts; 2 oz. ($\frac{1}{2}$C) chopped nuts; seasoning; 2 tablespoons chopped preserved ginger; $\frac{3}{4}$ pint (2C) chicken stock; 2 *level* tablespoons cornflour; 2 tablespoons sherry; little oil.
*A boiling fowl is unsuitable for this particular dish.
Wash and dry the chicken. Drain the bean sprouts, mix half with the diced ham. Drain and chop half the water chestnuts and add to the ham and bean sprouts together with the chopped nuts, seasoning and half the ginger. Stuff the chicken with this mixture. Blend the stock with the cornflour. Put into a pan and heat until thickened, stirring well. Add the remainder of the bean sprouts, sliced water chestnuts and ginger, together with a little seasoning and sherry. Pour this mixture into a large casserole. Place the chicken in the casserole. Brush the breast of the bird

with oil and cover the casserole with a lid. Cook for 2 hours in the centre of a very moderate to moderate oven. (Illustrated on page 161.) *Serves 6–8.*

Chicken Espagnole

8 joints young chicken; 1 oz. flour; seasoning; 2 oz. ($\frac{1}{4}$C) butter; 1 tablespoon olive oil; 2 large onions or about 8 small onions; 1–2 cloves garlic; 1 lb. tomatoes; $\frac{1}{2}$ pint (1$\frac{1}{3}$C) chicken stock or water and a chicken stock cube; 4 oz. (1C) small mushrooms. *To garnish:* chopped parsley.
Wash and dry the chicken, roll in flour, blended with a generous amount of seasoning. Heat the butter and oil in a pan, toss the chicken in this until golden brown. Put on a plate, then toss the thinly sliced or whole onions in the remaining butter and oil for 5 minutes. If you like a strong garlic flavour, crush the cloves of garlic and fry *with* the onions; if you do not like this flavour to be too strong, add the whole cloves of garlic with the onions but remove after 2–3 minutes. Skin the tomatoes, chop if very large, add to the onions, together with the stock or water and stock cube. Bring to the boil, then add the mushrooms and season well. Put the chicken joints into the pan, but keep them above the level of the liquid if possible. If you like plenty of sauce cover the pan, so the liquid does not evaporate. If you prefer dishes less moist, then leave the lid off the pan for the last 15 minutes. Cook over a low heat for 30–35 minutes, then serve topped with chopped parsley. If preferred, transfer the mixture to a casserole to cook. Cover and allow about 45 minutes to 1 hour in a very moderate to moderate oven, 325–350°F, Gas Mark 3–4. *Gives 4 generous portions.*

To vary Add 1–2 sliced green or red peppers to the ingredients above. If wishing the peppers to remain fairly firm in texture add about 10 minutes before chicken is cooked.

Casserole of Duck

1 large duck; stuffing (see method); about 12 very small onions; 1–2 cloves garlic; 4–5 carrots; $\frac{3}{4}$ pint (2C) duck stock (made by simmering giblets); seasoning; 1 oz. flour; 4 large potatoes. *To garnish:* parsley.
This is an excellent way of cooking a rather fat duck. The duck can be stuffed with sage and onion, chestnut stuffing, or with whole peeled apples and soaked, but not cooked, prunes. Roast the duck in a hot oven for about 30 minutes, until really crisp and brown and until much of the fat has run out. While the duck is cooking, simmer the peeled onions, crushed garlic and halved or quartered carrots in $\frac{1}{2}$ pint (1$\frac{1}{3}$C) stock for 30 minutes, season well. Blend the flour with the remaining stock, stir into the pan, then cook until a smooth thickened sauce. Transfer to a casserole with the peeled and roughly sliced potatoes. Place the duck on top, cover the casserole and cook for 1$\frac{1}{2}$ hours in the centre of a very moderate to moderate oven. Garnish with parsley. *Serves 4.*

To vary Omit the carrots and potatoes and add about 8 oz. whole peeled chestnuts and 12 soaked, but not cooked, prunes.

Country Chicken Casserole

Use the recipe for casserole of duck, but use a boiling fowl. Stuff the fowl with a large bunch of mixed fresh herbs, then continue as for the casserole of duck. If the bird seems fairly tough, allow 2 hours in the casserole in a slow to very moderate oven.

Casserole of duck (left)
Chicken Espagnole (right)
Hare in Madeira sauce (right, above)

Duck and Pineapple

1 large duck; $\frac{1}{4}$ pint ($\frac{2}{3}$C) duck stock (made by simmering giblets); 1 large can pineapple rings; 12 small onions; 2 tablespoons soy sauce; 1 tablespoon white wine vinegar; seasoning; 1 oz. flour.

Roast the duck for 30 minutes, as described in the casserole of duck. Do not stuff the duck in this recipe. Blend the duck stock with enough syrup from the can of pineapple to give $\frac{3}{4}$ pint (2C). Simmer the onions in $\frac{1}{2}$ pint ($1\frac{1}{3}$C) of this liquid for 30 minutes. At the end of this time add the soy sauce, vinegar, seasoning and flour, blended with the remaining liquid. Stir until thickened. Put most of the pineapple, cut into neat pieces, into the liquid. Pour into a deep casserole, lift the well drained duck on top. Cover the casserole and cook for $1\frac{1}{2}$ hours in the centre of a very moderate to moderate oven, 325–350°F, Gas Mark 3–4. Lift the lid and garnish the duck with the remaining rings of pineapple. *Serves 4.*

Pheasant in Madeira Sauce

Although this recipe can be used for a young bird, it is a very good way of using an older or casseroling bird.

1 good-sized pheasant; 2 rashers rather fat bacon (about $\frac{1}{4}$-inch in thickness); $\frac{1}{2}$ oz. flour; the pheasant giblets; 1 tiny orange or tangerine; 3 oz. ($\frac{3}{8}$C) butter or cooking fat; 4 oz. (1C) button mushrooms; 12 tablespoons (1C) Madeira wine; good pinch dried or $\frac{1}{2}$ teaspoon freshly chopped herbs; seasoning. Slit the skin over the breast of the pheasant,

lay the bacon over the breast, then replace the pheasant skin. Dust lightly with flour. Put the pheasant liver and the peeled orange or tangerine inside the bird. Heat half the butter or fat and brown the pheasant in this. Lift out of the pan and put into a casserole. Heat the rest of the butter or fat and cook the mushrooms in this. Add to the casserole with the wine, herbs and seasoning. Cover the casserole. Allow 1 hour for a young bird in a moderate to moderately hot oven, 375–400°F, Gas Mark 5–6, or 2 hours in a very moderate to moderate oven, 325–350°F, Gas Mark 3–4, for an older bird. If using the longer cooking time you may like to add a little extra wine or stock made by simmering the rest of the giblets from the pheasant.

To vary Use other game birds.

Tiny or sliced onions and/or peeled chestnuts may also be added to the casserole.

Hare in Madeira sauce Use jointed *young* hare instead of pheasant. Sprinkle the saddle (back) joints of hare with flour, mixed with a little chopped sage, fry in half the fat then continue as above. Allow 1 hour cooking time. Omit the liver and orange or tangerine.

Chicken and Almonds

3 oz. (well over $\frac{1}{2}$C) blanched whole almonds; 3 tablespoons olive oil; 4 joints young chicken; seasoning; $\frac{1}{2}$ oz. flour; $\frac{1}{2}$ pint ($1\frac{1}{3}$C) white wine or white wine mixed with chicken stock; pinch saffron*; $\frac{1}{2}$ level tablespoon cornflour or 1 level tablespoon flour; about 12 cocktail onions; few whole small pickled gherkins.

*If using saffron strands infuse in the wine or wine and stock for 30 minutes, then strain.

Fry the almonds in 1 tablespoon oil, lift out of the pan. Coat the chicken in seasoned flour and fry in the remainder of the oil, until golden. Remove from the pan. Blend the wine or wine and stock with the saffron and cornflour or flour. Pour into the pan, cook until thickened slightly. Add the pieces of chicken, cover the pan and simmer for 25 minutes. Put in the onions and gherkins. Heat for 5 minutes. Serve in a border of boiled rice or creamed potatoes, and top with the browned almonds. *Serves 4.*

To vary Use pine nuts.

Frying and Grilling Chicken

I have headed this page as two methods of cooking chicken, for young chickens are very plentiful and inexpensive. Neither duck nor goose are suitable for frying or grilling and joints of turkey are too large. Certain recipes on these pages can be used with very young game.

Blue Print

1. To Fry Chicken

Choose young frying (broiler) chickens. If not ready-jointed, then cut the chicken into neat joints, with a very sharp knife.

If the chickens are frozen, they can be cooked without defrosting, but I find I get a better coating if I allow the chickens to defrost, dry the joints, then coat them.

Coat the chicken joints with seasoned flour, or egg and crumbs, or batter, in exactly the same way as described under frying fish on pages 166 and 167; the coating clings better if the skin is removed from the joints.

The chicken joints may be cooked in shallow or deep fat.

Timing

The cooking times will be about 15 minutes in shallow fat, turning the joints regularly or about 10–12 minutes in deep fat or oil.

Drain on absorbent paper and serve with salad, or with cooked rice, as shown in the pictures, or with mixed vegetables.

● **AVOID** *Having the fat too hot or too cold. See the Blue Print on page 167.*

Fried chicken Italienne

2. To Grill Chicken

Choose young chickens (broilers). Joint as described under Blue Print 1. They may be grilled from the frozen state or defrosted, dried well then grilled.

Make sure the grill is very hot before putting the chickens under the heat. Brush the grid of the grill pan with melted butter, margarine or fat, to prevent the joints sticking.

Brush the joints of chicken with melted fat of some kind, season if wished. Cook for approximately 15 minutes, turning several times and basting with the fat. When the outside of the chicken joints are brown and crisp, the heat may be reduced so the chicken is cooked through to the centre. Mushrooms and tomatoes may be cooked on the grid of the grill pan, or in the grill pan itself at the same time. Season the vegetables, brush with melted butter, margarine or oil before cooking, so they do not dry.

● **AVOID** *Cooking the chicken too slowly: Cooking the chicken without fat (unless counting calories), for it will become very dry.*

● **TO SLIMMERS** *Grilling is an excellent method of cooking any food and young chicken is relatively low in calories. You can try 'basting' the chicken with fruit juice, rather than fat.*

Storing and Freezing *Young chickens keep relatively well in a cool place or refrigerator. Frozen joints may be stored in the freezing compartment of the refrigerator for the time stated on the package. You can freeze your own young chicken joints.*

To use any left over *Use in salads or sandwiches. Do not cook again as the delicate flavour and texture is easily spoiled.*

Fried chicken and oranges

For Family Occasions

Fried Chicken and Oranges

4 portions chicken; 1 oz. flour; seasoning; 2 oz. ($\frac{1}{4}$C) butter; $\frac{1}{2}$ tablespoon oil; 3 large oranges.

Dry the portions of chicken and coat in seasoned flour. Heat the butter and oil in a pan. Fry the chicken as Blue Print 1 until nearly tender. Squeeze the juice from 2 oranges, pour over the chicken and finish cooking. Serve the chicken joints on a bed of boiled rice and garnish with the remaining orange, peeled and cut into rings. *Serves 4.*

To vary This is even more delicious if 2–3 tablespoons halved walnuts are added to the pan with the orange juice. The combination of crisp nuts and orange juice is very pleasant.

Fried Chicken Italienne

8 drumsticks of young chicken; 1 level tablespoon flour; seasoning; 1 or 2 eggs (depending upon the size); 2–3 oz. (1–1$\frac{1}{2}$C) crisp breadcrumbs; 2 tablespoons grated Parmesan cheese. *To fry:* deep fat or oil. *For the rice*

mixture: 2 oz. (¼C) butter or margarine; 1 green and 1 red pepper; 8 oz. (1C) long grain rice; 1 pint (2⅔C) chicken stock or water and 1 or 2 stock cubes; seasoning; few cooked peas; little cooked or canned sweet corn. *To garnish:* watercress or cooked spinach or other green vegetable.

Coat the drumsticks with the flour mixed with seasoning, the beaten egg, then the crumbs, blended with the cheese. If possible chill for a while so the coating sets well. Meanwhile heat the butter or margarine in a pan. Dice the peppers, removing the cores and seeds and toss in the butter for a few minutes. Add the rice and mix with the butter and peppers. Put the stock or water and stock cubes into the pan, bring to the boil, stir, season well and cook until the rice is nearly tender. Add the peas and sweet corn and finish cooking until the rice is tender and the liquid absorbed. Meanwhile deep fry the drumsticks as Blue Print 1; take particular care that the fat or oil is not too hot, otherwise the cheese will scorch. Drain on absorbent paper. Pile the rice mixture on to a very hot dish. Arrange the drumsticks around and garnish with the watercress or alternative. *Serves 4.*

Stuffed Chicken Cutlets

4 joints chicken, preferably breast joints; 8 oz. pork sausagemeat; 1 tablespoon chopped parsley; 2 oz. (½C) mushrooms; butter or chicken fat for frying or grilling. *To garnish:* cooked tomatoes.

Remove the bones from the chicken joints. Blend the sausagemeat, parsley and finely chopped mushrooms together. Divide this mixture into 4 portions and press each portion against the joints of chicken. Do this on the underside where the bones were removed. Fry or grill the joints as Blue Prints 1 or 2, frying in or basting with the butter or chicken fat. Serve with fried or grilled tomatoes. *Serves 4.*

For Special Occasions

Spatchcock of Chicken

4 very small young chickens or 2 larger ones; seasoning; 2 oz. (¼C) butter; grated rind 1 lemon. *To garnish:* watercress; lemon.

Split the chickens right down the backbone, so they open out quite flat, see the sketches. Mix the seasoning with the melted butter, add the lemon rind. Grill the chickens as described under Blue Print 2, basting with the butter as they cook. Garnish with watercress and sliced lemon. *Serves 4.*

To vary Very young pigeons or partridges may be cooked in the same way. Omit the lemon if wished and flavour the butter with a few drops Worcestershire sauce and a pinch curry powder.

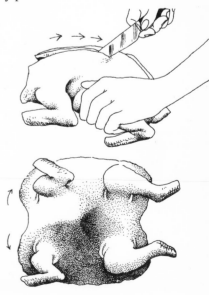

Using Cooked Poultry and Game

The recipes on this page make good use of cooked poultry and game. Read the points outlined in the Blue Print before preparing the recipes.

Blue Print

Using Cooked Poultry and Game

Never waste the carcass of a bird, simmer in water to give a good stock, flavour the liquid with herbs and vegetables and season well.

Choose recipes where the meats are given the minimum heating time. Both poultry and game (with the exception of duck and goose) tend to have a dry flesh which will be spoiled by a second long cooking. Remember a certain amount of flavour is lost when food is cooked a second time, so compensate for this by adding herbs, cooking fresh vegetables in the sauce or using spices. Serve the dish as soon as possible after cooking and make sure the accompaniments are interesting and freshly cooked; crisp salads are splendid with any of these dishes.

Creamed Turkey Duchesse

1–1¼ lb. (2–2½ C) mashed potatoes; 2 eggs or 2 egg yolks; 2 oz. (¼ C) butter or margarine; seasoning; 4 oz. (1C) button mushrooms; 1 green pepper; ½ pint (1⅓ C) turkey stock (made by simmering the carcass or giblets); 1 oz. flour; ¼ pint (⅔ C) milk; few drops Tabasco sauce; about 1 lb. diced cooked turkey plus any small pieces of stuffing (optional); 2–3 tablespoons top of the milk or thin cream. *To garnish:* parsley.

Blend the mashed potatoes with 1 egg or egg yolk and half the butter or margarine, season well. Form into a border round the edge of an oven-proof dish. Brush with the second egg or egg yolk, diluted with a few drops of water and brown in a moderate oven, 350–375°F, Gas Mark 4–5. Meanwhile simmer the mushrooms and diced green pepper (discard the core and seeds) in the stock for 10 minutes. Strain the liquid from the mushrooms and pepper, put this on one side for the sauce. Heat the remainder of the butter or margarine in a saucepan, stir in the flour, cook for several minutes, stirring all the time, add the milk gradually, then the stock. Bring to the boil, and cook until thickened, stirring briskly, season well. Flavour with the Tabasco. Taste and add a little more Tabasco, if desired. Put the vegetables and turkey into the sauce and heat gently for a few minutes. Add the stuffing and cream towards the end of the heating period. Bring the dish out of the oven. Pile the turkey mixture into the centre and garnish with parsley. *Serves 4–6.*

To vary Cooked pheasant or chicken may be used instead of turkey. If using pheasant, simmer 1–2 diced onions in the stock to give more flavour.

Chicken Pilau

2 onions; 1 clove garlic (optional); 2 tablespoons chicken fat or oil; 8 oz. (1C) long grain rice; 1 pint (2⅔ C) chicken stock (made by simmering chicken carcass or giblets); 1–2 oz. sultanas; few pine or other nuts (optional); 12 oz. diced chicken; seasoning. *To garnish:* few nuts or crisp breadcrumbs.

Peel and chop the onions, crush the garlic. Fry in the hot fat or oil for a few minutes, then add the rice, turn in the fat or oil. Add the stock, bring to the boil, stir, then simmer in an open pan for about 10 minutes. Add the rest of the ingredients and cook for a further 10–15 minutes until the liquid has just been absorbed. Pile on to a hot dish and top with the nuts or crumbs. *Serves 4–5.*

Duck and Chestnuts

8 oz.–1 lb. chestnuts; about 12 small onions or shallots; 2 oz. (¼ C) duck fat or margarine; 1 oz. flour; ½ pint (1⅓ C) duck stock (made by simmering the carcass or giblets); ¼ pint (⅔ C) red wine; seasoning; 1 small dessert apple; 8–12 oz. diced cooked duck plus any skin; little fat to fry the skin. *To garnish:* 1 dessert apple; little lemon juice.

Slit the chestnuts, boil for 5–10 minutes, remove the skins while warm. Peel the onions. Toss the onions in the hot duck fat or margarine until golden. Lift out of the pan, stir in the flour and cook the 'roux' for several minutes. Add the duck stock gradually, bring to the boil, cook until thickened, stirring all the time. Add the wine. Put the chestnuts and onions into the sauce, season well. Cover the pan, simmer for 20–25 minutes. Peel, core and dice the apple, put into the sauce with the duck and heat for a few minutes. To many people the skin of a duck is almost the most delicious part, so cut any pieces of skin left into neat dice. Put a little fat in a small frying pan, heat and fry the diced skin until very crisp. Put the duck mixture into a hot serving dish. Garnish with rings of apple, dipped in lemon juice and top these with the very hot crisp skin. *Serves 4–5.*

Creamed turkey duchesse

VEGETABLES AND MEALS WITHOUT MEAT

In this section you will find a great number of dishes using vegetables. Some of the recipes treat them as an accompaniment to the main dish, in others the vegetables themselves are the basis of the meal.

With modern freezing, canning and drying, it is now possible to obtain almost every vegetable at any time during the year. Frozen vegetables are always very young and tender, so do not over-cook them, follow the directions carefully on the package.

Canned vegetables have been cooked in the process of canning, so should be heated only. Prolonged cooking spoils much of their flavour and texture. Dehydrated vegetables are of two types, firstly the modern Accelerated Freeze Dried variety (i.e. the type that are first frozen and then dried), these need very little soaking and a short cooking time. Secondly there are the more traditional dried vegetables which should be soaked well and/or given a long cooking period.

It is surprising how often beautifully fresh vegetables are spoiled by overcooking and this applies particularly to green vegetables. They contain essential mineral salts and Vitamin C (the vitamin that helps to build up resistance to colds, and give a clear healthy skin). Unfortunately this vitamin is lost if the vegetables are stale (so shop critically), or if the vegetables are over-cooked. Page 182 gives the correct *modern* method of cooking green vegetables, known as the Conserved Method. Please do not consider this only as a method of cooking to preserve food values. It also ensures you have vegetables that are full of flavour, a good colour and an interesting texture.

Onions, leeks and garlic are bulb vegetables (although garlic is often classed as a herb). Although these are used frequently to provide additional flavour to other dishes, both onions and leeks can be the basis of interesting meals.

Most people, young and old, are fond of fried potatoes—but how often are these disappointing? The perfect fried potato should be dry, not greasy, crisp, not 'soggy' and an even golden brown in colour. Page 188 deals with the '8 secrets' of successful fried potatoes and gives some new ways of shaping and presenting fried potatoes too.

The usual protein foods, meat, fish and poultry are expensive and there may be times when you wish to serve a sustaining meal without using them. You will find a great number of the dishes, especially in the latter part of this section, give a really good meal, based upon vegetables.

Although the list of green vegetables is very long and cooking times vary, the basic principles of cooking practically every variety are covered in the Blue Print. This page deals with the 'homely' green vegetables and the methods of dealing with the more luxurious ones are given on page 185.

Buying Green Vegetables

In order to ensure you have the very *best* green vegetables available, check on the following points when buying.

Broccoli—green or purple—should have very green leaves (if they have the slightest yellow tinge, they are stale); the flower should be firm.

Avoid cabbage or greens with slightly yellow leaves, these indicate a stale vegetable. Feel the vegetables, they should be heavy for their size, if surprisingly light this indicates there is little heart to the cabbage.

The outer leaves of cauliflower should be green and firm looking and the flower firm and white.

If spinach or greens look limp do not buy if possible—they could 'revive' when put into cold water, but they may be too stale to be good.

Storing Green Vegetables

Unpack as soon as possible. If you have a very large refrigerator you can pack the vegetables into covered containers, but as this is unlikely for most people, this is the way to store:

Keep as much air circulation as possible around the vegetables.

Store away from bright light if possible.

Keep in the coolest place possible.

If storing cabbage, sprouts and firm greens for more than a day, sprinkle lightly with cold water.

If storing spinach, greens or broccoli for more than a day (which is not advisable) then keep dry, if sprinkled with water they are inclined to become 'slimy'.

Preparing Green Vegetables

Do not wash, soak, cut or shred the vegetables until ready to cook. Mineral salts are soluble in water and will be 'lost' by soaking. Vitamin C is destroyed by leaving cut surfaces exposed to the air.

Wash the vegetables in cold water, leave in the water for the shortest time possible.

If you add a little salt to the water it makes sure that tiny insects, that often are found in green vegetables, will be 'drawn out'.

Cabbage and Similar Green Vegetables Shred as finely as possible, with a sharp knife, to shorten cooking time.

Sprouts Remove only the very outer leaves, all too often much of each sprout is wasted by excess removal of leaves. Make a cross at the base of each sprout, this helps to shorten cooking time.

Cauliflower The stems and green leaves are delicious, so remove these and trim ready for cooking. Discard only the imperfect outer stems and leaves. You can trim the thick part of the stems, but if these are placed into the boiling water a few minutes *before* the flower, they become tender when ready to 'dish up' the vegetable.

Spinach There are two types, the small leafed (New Zealand) and the large leafed (Beet) spinach. When preparing the small leafed spinach just break away any surplus stalks at the base. When preparing the large leafed spinach I pull the green leaves away from the stems, then trim the stems and cook as a separate vegetable. These are delicious when cooked in boiling salted water, strained and topped with melted butter and chopped chives or parsley.

Broccoli Remove the very outer leaves. Keep the flower heads and the small leaves surrounding these intact. Choose a large saucepan, so the flowers and stalks may be laid flat in the boiling salted water in the pan.

Blue Print
The Conserved Method of Cooking

1. Prepare the vegetables as this page.

2. Put only enough water into the pan to give a depth of $1-1\frac{1}{2}$ inches—except for cauliflower and spinach, see below. Add a good pinch salt.

3. Make sure the saucepan has a tightly fitting lid.

4. Bring the water to the boil.

5. Remove the vegetables from the water in which they were washed, drain—except for spinach, see below.

6. Take the prepared vegetables over to the cooker in a colander or bowl.

7. Add the vegetables *gradually to the boiling water*. This is important for the water should continue to boil and it will do this if the vegetables are added steadily, rather than all at once.

8. When all the vegetables have been added to the water, put on the lid and time the cooking.

Shredded Cabbage can be ready in 2–3 minutes, tougher types of cabbage take a minute or so longer.

Sprouts, if small, will take only 5–6 minutes.

Broccoli about 8–10 minutes.

Cauliflower As this vegetable does take longer to cook than cabbage, allow about 3 inches of water. Follow points 1–7 above, place the flower or flower sprigs downwards in the boiling salted water.

Allow about 15–20 minutes for a whole cauliflower but 10–15 minutes for sprigged cauliflower, until the stems are just tender but the flower unbroken.

Cauliflower with brown sauce topping

Spinach This contains a high percentage of water, so wash well (often spinach has a lot of sand and soil sticking to the leaves, so may need washing in 2–3 changes of cold water), do not drain. Simply put into the pan with *no extra water*, just the water adhering to the leaves. Add a little salt. Cook steadily for 2–3 minutes, so the water runs off the leaves, then raise the heat slightly and continue cooking until tender.

The very young small leafed spinach takes only about 7–8 minutes. The larger leafed spinach rather more. If you are worried about the spinach sticking to the pan, put in ½ inch water, bring to the boil, then add the damp vegetable.

9. Strain the vegetables *as soon as they are cooked*, top with a little butter or margarine and serve as quickly as possible.

Use the vegetable water if possible to add to gravy, soups and stews. Some people like to drink it, but that, I must confess, is an acquired taste.

Toppings for Green Vegetables

Sprinkle the vegetables with freshly chopped herbs.

Top broccoli, cauliflower or cooked spinach with Hollandaise sauce (page 100), white or cheese sauce (see page 184—Cauliflower Basket). Always incorporate some of the vegetable liquid into the sauce.

Make a tomato sauce (see page 185—Artichokes Barigoule) or a brown sauce (see page 187—Parsnip Roast). Spoon over cooked cauliflower and top with chopped parsley.

● **AVOID** *Over-cooking green vegetables, or keeping them for any length of time before serving.*

● **TO RECTIFY** *Although you cannot 'revive' over-cooked vegetables, some of the toppings on this page give additional flavour.*

● **SHORT CUT** *The smaller the pieces of vegetable, the quicker the cooking time.*

● **TO SLIMMERS** *All green vegetables are low in calories, so when you are planning slimming meals serve as great a variety of green vegetables as possible.*

Storing and Freezing *Details of storing are given opposite. Raw spinach, cauliflower and broccoli freeze very well, cabbage is less successful.*

To use any left over *Page 200 gives many suggestions for using these.*

New Ways with Green Vegetables

Remember that firm Dutch white cabbage (excellent as the basis for Coleslaw) or red cabbage (often considered only for pickling) can be used instead of green cabbage or cabbage greens in any of the recipes. As the leaves of these are firmer than those of a tender green cabbage, allow 3–4 minutes longer cooking time than that given in the Blue Print. It is usual to cook red cabbage until quite tender and this can take a minimum of 30 minutes. You may, however, prefer its very firm (rather than crisp) texture if cooked for a shorter time.

Cabbage Pancakes

1 very small green cabbage, or use the *tender* outer leaves of a large cabbage and save the heart for another occasion; seasoning. *For the batter:* 4 oz. (1C) plain flour; pinch salt; 1 egg; ½ pint (1⅓C) milk and water. *For frying:* oil or fat.

Shred the cabbage and cook *very lightly* as in the Blue Print opposite, season well. Meanwhile make a pancake batter with the flour, salt, egg and milk and water. Strain the cabbage and mix with the batter. Heat a little oil or fat in a pan, pour enough of the mixture into the pan to give a thin coating. Cook until golden brown on the under side, turn and cook on the second side. Continue to make the rest of the pancakes. Serve topped with grilled or fried mushrooms. *Serves 4–6.*

Vichy Cabbage

1 small cabbage; 1–2 onions; at least 1 tablespoon chopped parsley; about 1 oz. margarine; ¼ pint (⅔C) beef or chicken stock; seasoning.

Shred the cabbage and chop the onion. Mix the onion and parsley together. Heat the margarine in a pan, toss the onion and parsley in this. Add the stock, bring to the boil, put in the cabbage gradually, as described in the Blue Print opposite. Cover the pan and cook for 2–3 minutes, lift the lid of the pan, add seasoning to taste, turn the cabbage round in the stock and allow this to boil for another 1–2 minutes until the mixture is still crisp and the liquid evaporated. This makes a pleasant alternative to the more usual way of cooking. (Illustrated on page 181.) *Serves 4–6.*

Viennese Cabbage

1 small red, green or white cabbage; seasoning; 2–4 teaspoons sugar (preferably brown); 2 oz. (¼C) butter; 1 small apple; ½ pint (1⅓C) chicken stock or water and ½ stock cube; 1 tablespoon vinegar; 1 level tablespoon flour.

Shred the cabbage finely, season lightly. Put the sugar and butter into a large saucepan and stir over a low heat. Continue cooking until the mixture turns golden brown, taking care it does not burn, stir once or twice. Add the peeled chopped apple and nearly all the stock or water and ½ stock cube. Bring to the boil. Add the cabbage gradually, so the liquid continues to boil, then stir in the vinegar. Cook for about 5–6 minutes with green cabbage, 10–15 minutes with white cabbage and 30 minutes with red cabbage. The vegetable should just be slightly crisp. Blend the flour with the rest of the liquid, stir into the cabbage, stir very well and continue stirring until the mixture thickens slightly. Test the cabbage and if sufficiently cooked serve, otherwise continue cooking for a few more minutes, adding a little extra stock or water if necessary. *Serves 4–6.*

Cauliflower Fritters

1 medium-sized cauliflower; salt. *For the batter:* 4 oz. (1C) flour, plain or self-raising; pinch salt; 2 eggs; ¼ pint (⅔C) water; 4 tablespoons milk. *For frying:* oil or fat.

Sprig the cauliflower and cook in boiling salted water as the Blue Print opposite; take particular care that the vegetable *is not overcooked*. Sieve the flour and salt, add the egg yolks, water and milk, then fold in the stiffly whisked egg whites. Strain the cauliflower carefully, so the sprigs are not broken. Heat the oil or fat. While you can fry these fritters in shallow fat it is easier and better to use deep fat. Dip the sprigs into the batter and fry for 1–2 minutes only in the hot fat. Drain on absorbent paper.

To make a light supper dish, toss in grated Cheddar, Gruyère or Parmesan cheese. *Serves 4–8.*

To vary Brussels sprouts or broccoli can be used instead of cauliflower.

Yoghourt fritters Use yoghourt or soured cream instead of water and milk.

Tomato and cauliflower fritters Use tomato juice instead of water and milk.

Cauliflower Pancake Gâteau

Pancake batter (see Cabbage Pancakes). *For frying:* oil or fat. *For the filling:* 1 cauliflower; salt; little butter and thick cream; chopped chives and chopped parsley (optional). *To serve:* melted butter.

Make a pancake batter as the recipe for Cabbage Pancakes. Cook the pancakes in hot oil or fat. Keep hot while the sprigged cauliflower is cooked in salted water, as the Blue Print. Strain the cauliflower, tip into a hot basin and mash roughly with a fork. Blend with a little melted butter and cream. Spread each pancake with this mixture, pile one on top of the other. Top the pile with the chopped chives and parsley, if liked. Pour a little melted butter on top and serve at once. Serve with poached or baked eggs. *Serves 4–6.*

To vary Cooked creamed spinach (see page 184—Spinach Niçoise) can be used instead of cauliflower, or spinach and cauliflower can be used alternately. (Illustrated on page 181.)

The following recipes make excellent light luncheon or supper dishes.

Cauliflower Basket

1 medium-sized cauliflower; salt. *For the cheese sauce*: 1 oz. butter or margarine; 1 oz. flour; $\frac{1}{4}$ pint ($\frac{2}{3}$C) milk; $\frac{1}{4}$ pint ($\frac{2}{3}$C) liquid from cooking the cauliflower; seasoning; 4 oz. (1C) grated Cheddar cheese; 2 eggs; 1 tablespoon chopped gherkins; 1 teaspoon capers; 1 tablespoon chopped parsley; 1 tablespoon chopped chives.

Prepare the cauliflower as page 182, keeping it whole. Cook in boiling salted water until just tender, drain. While the cauliflower is cooking, prepare the sauce. Heat the butter or margarine in a pan, stir in the flour and cook over a gentle heat for 2–3 minutes, stirring well. Gradually add the milk, bring to the boil, then add the cauliflower liquid and stir as the sauce thickens over a medium heat. Add seasoning and nearly all the cheese. Hard boil the eggs, shell, chop and blend with the hot cheese sauce together with the gherkins, capers and herbs. Scoop out the centre part of the cauliflower. Put this on to a plate, chop coarsely and add to the sauce. Stand the cauliflower in a hot serving dish. Pile the cheese mixture into the centre. Top with the remainder of the cheese and brown for 1–2 minutes under a very hot grill. *Serves 4–6.*

Outlaw Cabbage

1 lb. cooked minced beef; $\frac{1}{2}$ pint (1$\frac{1}{3}$C) milk; 2 oz. ($\frac{1}{2}$C) soft breadcrumbs and seasoning (or use a packet of bread sauce mix); 1 tablespoon tomato purée; pinch mixed dried herbs or 1 teaspoon freshly chopped herbs; 1 small to medium-sized cabbage; salt; 1 oz. butter

Main Dishes with Green Vegetables

Outlaw cabbage

or margarine; black pepper.

Put the beef into a basin. Blend the milk with the crumbs and seasoning (or the bread sauce mix), add to the beef with the tomato purée and herbs. Mix thoroughly and put into an oven-proof dish. Cover the dish with foil and bake for approximately 25 minutes in the centre of a moderate oven, 350–375°F, Gas Mark 4–5. Meanwhile cook the shredded cabbage in salted water, as the Blue Print on page 182, for a very few minutes only. Strain, mix with the melted butter or margarine and pepper. Put on top of the hot beef mixture and return to the oven for about 8–10 minutes. *Serves 4–6.*

To vary Use 8 oz. (2C) diced Cheddar or Gruyère cheese or 4–6 hard boiled eggs in place of the meat.

Spinach Niçoise

1$\frac{1}{2}$–2 lb. fresh spinach or about 12 oz. frozen spinach; salt; 3 oz. ($\frac{3}{8}$C) butter or margarine; 2–3 tablespoons thick cream; pepper; 4 large tomatoes; 2 onions; 4 oz. (1C) grated Cheddar, Gruyère or Emmenthal cheese.

Cook the spinach with a little salt as described in the Blue Print on page 182 or as on the packet of frozen spinach. Strain, either sieve or chop finely. Return to the pan with half the butter or margarine and the cream. Heat gently until a creamy consistency. Add pepper to taste. While the spinach is cooking, prepare the tomato layer. Skin and chop the tomatoes and onions. Heat gently in the remaining butter or margarine until soft. Add the cheese, season with salt and pepper, do not heat again. Put the creamed spinach into a shallow, very hot, heat-proof dish, top with the hot tomato and cheese mixture. Heat for a few minutes under the grill and serve at once. *Serves 4–6.*

To vary A few seedless raisins may be added to the tomato layer if wished.

Use cooked sprigged cauliflower or cooked sliced courgettes instead of spinach.

Spinach niçoise

A Touch of Luxury

Some green vegetables are frankly a luxury and deserve to be served as a separate course. Three of the most interesting are globe artichokes, asparagus and courgettes (often called zucchini).

Globe Artichokes

The green globe artichokes make an excellent hors d'oeuvre; Jerusalem artichokes are described on page 186.

To prepare artichokes Wash in cold salted water. Cut away any stalk and pull off any rather tough outer leaves. You can cut the leaves in a straight line with scissors, if wished.

To cook artichokes Cook the whole artichokes in boiling salted water until tender. The time varies, small very young artichokes take about 25 minutes, very large ones take about 40 minutes. Test to see if you can pull away a leaf. Drain, remove the 'choke' with the centre leaves and serve with melted butter.

To eat artichokes, pull away each leaf, dip the base in the butter and eat the tender part. The base of the artichoke, often called the heart, is eaten with a knife and fork.

Artichokes Vinaigrette

Prepare and cook the artichokes as above. Allow to cool. Remove the centre 'choke' as above, if wished. Make an oil and vinegar dressing, season well and either spoon into the centre of each artichoke or serve separately.

Artichokes Barigoule

4 large globe artichokes; salt. *For the stuffing:* 6 oz. (1½C) button mushrooms; 2 medium-sized onions; 2 oz. (¼C) margarine or butter; 2 oz. (½C) soft breadcrumbs; 1 teaspoon chopped parsley; 1 teaspoon chopped chives; seasoning. *For the tomato sauce:* 2 oz. (¼C) margarine or butter; 1 onion; 4 large tomatoes; ¼ pint (⅔C) white stock; 1 tablespoon flour; 1 tablespoon tomato purée.
Prepare and cook the artichokes as above in boiling salted water. While the vegetables are cooking, wash and chop the mushrooms, peel and chop the onions finely. Toss in the hot margarine or butter. Add the crumbs, herbs and seasoning. Drain the artichokes, remove the 'chokes' and centre leaves, pack the filling in the centres and put into an oven-proof dish. Pour the thick tomato sauce round the vegetables. To make the sauce, heat the margarine or butter in a pan, add the peeled and chopped onion and tomatoes, cook for a few minutes. Blend the stock with the flour, pour into the pan. Add the tomato purée and seasoning. Stir over a moderate heat until the sauce thickens. Cover the dish with a lid or foil and bake for 25 minutes in the centre of a moderate oven, 350–375°F, Gas Mark 4–5. *Serves 4.*

Asparagus

To prepare asparagus Scrape the base of the stems gently with a knife. Cut the ends off the asparagus. Tie in bundles with raffia or thin string.
To cook asparagus Stand upright in a deep pan of boiling salted water; it is possible to buy special asparagus pans.
Cover the pan with a lid, or if the asparagus is too long and protrudes above the level of the pan, put foil over this. You must keep the steam in, so that the whole stem cooks evenly. Allow 15–20 minutes for fairly thin stems but up to 25 minutes for thicker ones. Lift out of the pan, drain and serve hot with plenty of melted butter.

Eat asparagus with your fingers. Asparagus can be served cold with oil and vinegar as the globe artichokes above or hot or cold with Hollandaise sauce (see page 100).

Courgettes

To prepare courgettes Wash well, do not peel. Remove the rather hard stalk end. Either cut each courgette in half lengthways or cut into thin slices.
To cook courgettes Cook in boiling salted water as the Blue Print on page 182 for about 5–8 minutes, drain and top with melted butter. Alternatively season the courgettes and steam for approximately the same time.

Courgettes in Butter

4 courgettes; 2–3 oz. (¼–⅜C) butter; seasoning; 2–3 tablespoons water or white stock.
Prepare the courgettes as above. Heat the butter with a little seasoning and the liquid in a large pan. Put in the vegetables and cook for 8–10 minutes, until the liquid has evaporated. *Serves 4.*
To vary Cook the courgettes in boiling salted water for 2–3 minutes. Drain thoroughly. Heat 2–3 oz. (¼–⅜C) butter or margarine in a pan. Put in the courgettes and cook in a covered pan for another 8–10 minutes, turning or shaking the pan to prevent them from sticking.

Fried Courgettes

Prepare and slice the courgettes as above Coat with well seasoned flour or with flour then beaten egg and crisp breadcrumbs or with batter (see the batter under Cauliflower Fritters, page 183). Fry in hot fat or oil until crisp and golden brown on either side and quite tender. Either shallow or deep fat or oil may be used. Drain on absorbent paper before serving.

Storing and Freezing *Globe artichokes and courgettes keep well for 2–3 days if stored in a cool place. Asparagus should be used within 1–2 days, otherwise it becomes dry. Asparagus freezes excellently. Courgettes only freeze as part of a cooked dish, for example in Ratatouille, page 198. Globe artichokes do not freeze well.*

Cooking Root Vegetables

Root vegetables are not only an excellent addition to soups and stews and a splendid basis for Russian salad, but they are well worth cooking in various ways to serve with fish and meat, or as a dish by themselves. Leeks and onions are not included here, but will be found on pages 191 and 192. Potatoes are covered on pages 188–190.

Blue Print

To Cook Root Vegetables by Boiling

1. Prepare the vegetables as this page.
2. Since most root vegetables take longer to cook than green vegetables, put about 3 inches of water into the pan.
3. Bring the water to the boil, add salt to taste.
4. Add the vegetables steadily (see the Blue Print on page 182) and cook until tender. This will vary according to the size but an indication is given below.
Artichokes—Jerusalem 25 minutes, add 2 teaspoons lemon juice to the water.

Beetroot Allow 1½–2 hours, according to size. Do not add salt.
Carrots Young whole baby carrots, 15 minutes. Sliced older carrots, 20–30 minutes. Whole old carrots, 45 minutes.
Celeriac (celery root) As turnips, add 2 teaspoons lemon juice to the water.
Celery, Fennel and Seakale (oyster plant) Diced will take 10–15 minutes.
Chicory As celery, add 2 teaspoons lemon juice to the water.
Parsnips, Swedes and Turnips If young and sliced, about 15 minutes. If old and diced into ½–¾-inch cubes, 20 minutes, if sliced about 30 minutes.
5. Cook the vegetables until tender, boil steadily *not* too rapidly otherwise the vegetables often break on the outside.
6. Strain then return to the pan with a little butter or margarine and toss in the pan as the fat melts.
7. Add chopped fresh herbs if desired, then serve.

● **AVOID** *Over-cooking these vegetables, naturally they must be tender when served hot, but they must retain a little of their firm texture to be interesting.*
● **TO RECTIFY** *If over-cooked, mash the vegetables as potatoes (see page 188).*
● **TO SLIMMERS** *Although some of the vegetables in this group are higher in calories than green vegetables, i.e. swedes and turnips, small portions will be allowed in most slimming diets. Celery and chicory are very low in calories.*

Preparing Root Vegetables

These vary in character a great deal.
Artichokes Scrape or peel. Keep in cold water with a little lemon juice until ready to cook as they darken in colour.
Beetroot Remove stalks and leaves. Wash, do not cut otherwise the vegetable bleeds.
Carrots, Turnips, Swedes, Parsnips Remove stalks and leaves. If very young, scrub well or scrape gently. If old, peel thinly.
Celeriac (celery root) Peel and slice or dice. Treat as artichokes before cooking.
Celery and Seakale (oyster plant) Wash in cold water and divide into neat pieces.
Chicory Needs just the outer leaves removing.
Fennel Remove the leaves, these can be chopped and added to white or other sauces instead of parsley. Wash and slice the root.

Buying Root Vegetables

Check to see they are unblemished. If you buy ready washed root vegetables use fairly quickly as the soil adhering to vegetables acts as a protection.

New Ways to Cook and Flavour Root Vegetables

Cook in chicken stock instead of water. Use only enough stock to keep the vegetables from burning. Lift the lid of the pan for the last few minutes so the excess liquid evaporates. This method is excellent with *all* root vegetables.
Cook the vegetables as the Blue Print, then toss in butter or margarine, mixed with a very *little sugar*; excellent with carrots, turnips, parsnips and swedes.
Mash some root vegetables as potatoes, see page 188.
Roast or fry some root vegetables as potatoes, see page 188. The most successful to roast are parsnips and swedes. Parsnips should be parboiled for 10–15 minutes before roasting. The most successful to fry are artichokes, carrots, parsnips and swedes.

Chinese Style Vegetable Soup

1 tablespoon corn or olive oil; 3 tablespoons long grain rice; 2 pints (5⅓C) chicken stock or water and 2–3 chicken stock cubes; seasoning; 1 small carrot; 1 small turnip; small piece swede; 1–2 sticks celery. *To garnish*: chopped parsley.
Heat the oil in a saucepan. Add the rice and turn in the oil for several minutes. Pour the stock into the pan, or the water and stock cubes, bring to the boil. Stir briskly, add seasoning. Lower the heat and cover the pan. Simmer gently for 20 minutes, until the rice is *just* tender. Grate the vegetables finely or coarsely according to personal taste, add to the soup and heat for a few minutes only so the vegetables retain their firm texture. Add extra seasoning if required. Serve topped with parsley. *Serves 4–6.*
To vary Add yoghourt to the soup just before serving.

Chinese style vegetable soup

Macedoine of Vegetables

Dice carrots, turnip, swede and parsnip (use a smaller proportion of parsnip and turnip than carrots or swede as they have a very strong flavour). Add chopped celery when in season. Cook as the Blue Print until tender. Strain, toss in a little butter or margarine and garnish with chopped parsley. This colourful selection of vegetables is an excellent garnish to dishes.

To turn into a complete meal, top with grated cheese or a cheese sauce or blend with the protein vegetables—cooked peas, beans or lentils.

Storing and Freezing *Store root vegetables in a cool dry place, away from bright light. Old mature carrots and turnips can be kept for several weeks. Younger vegetables should be eaten when fresh. Celery and similar vegetables should be used within 2–3 days maximum. Raw or cooked carrots and turnips freeze well, particularly when diced. The vegetables which contain a high percentage of water, e.g. celery, do not freeze.*
To use any left over *Add to salads and soups.*

Dutch vegetable flan

Main Dishes with Green Vegetables

Most root vegetables are fairly substantial so are an excellent basis for satisfying dishes.

Dutch Vegetable Flan

For the pastry: 6 oz. (1½C) flour, preferably plain; good pinch salt; shake pepper; ¼ teaspoon dry mustard; 3 oz. (⅜C) butter or margarine; water, or 1 egg yolk and water, to mix. *For the filling:* 1 medium-sized onion; 3 medium-sized carrots; 4 oz. (1C) mushrooms; 1 oz. butter; 2 eggs; ¼ pint (⅔C) milk; 4 oz. (approximately 1C) grated Dutch Gouda cheese; seasoning.

Sieve the flour with the seasonings, rub in the butter or margarine and bind with water, or egg yolk and water, to a firm rolling consistency. Roll out the pastry and line an 8-inch flan ring, on an upturned baking tray, or a sandwich tin or flan dish. Peel and chop the onion and carrots, wash and slice the mushrooms. Heat the butter and toss the vegetables in this for a few minutes, stir as you do so. Allow the vegetables to cool then put into the pastry case. Beat the eggs, add the milk, grated cheese and seasoning. Pour over the vegetables. Bake in the centre of a moderate to moderately hot oven, 375–400°F, Gas Mark 5–6, for 25–30 minutes until the pastry has set and is beginning to brown. Lower the heat slightly and cook for a further 15 minutes until the cheese filling is set. If using a flan ring remove this for the final 15 minutes, so the pastry may brown well on the sides. Serve hot or cold with salad. *Serves 4.*

To vary

Onion Flan Use 4 onions and omit the root vegetables and mushrooms. Cut the onions into rings and cook in the butter as the recipe above. Make the cheese custard mixture, add the onions to this; 2–3 tablespoons diced ham may also be added. Spoon into the pastry case and cook as the recipe above. Garnish with rings of fresh tomato and parsley. (Illustrated on page 192.)

Parsnip Roast

2 lb. parsnips; 2 onions; seasoning; 2 oz. (¼C) butter or margarine; 8 oz. (2C) grated Cheddar, Cheshire or other hard cheese; 2 eggs; 2 oz. (½C) soft breadcrumbs. *For the sauce:* vegetable stock; tomato juice; 1 oz. butter or margarine; 1 oz. flour; little yeast extract.

Peel and chop the parsnips and onions and cook in boiling salted water as the Blue Print opposite. Strain, but save the vegetable stock. Mash the vegetables with half the butter or margarine, add the cheese, the eggs and season well. Form into a neat shape on an ovenproof dish. Coat with breadcrumbs and the rest of the butter or margarine. Heat for a short time, about 15 minutes, in a hot oven, 425°F, Gas Mark 7, until golden brown. Serve hot with the sauce. To make this, measure the vegetable stock and add enough tomato juice to give just over ½ pint (1⅓C). Heat the butter or margarine, stir in the flour and cook for several minutes. Gradually blend in the liquid, bring to the boil and stir as the mixture thickens. Add enough yeast extract to give a fairly pronounced flavour. *Serves 4–6.*
To vary Use a mixture of parsnips and swedes.
Add a little chopped celery with, or instead of, the onions.

Carrot Walnut Loaf

1 lb. carrots; seasoning; 2 onions; 2 oz. (¼C) butter or margarine; 4 oz. (generous 1C) coarsely chopped walnuts; 6 oz. (1½C) soft breadcrumbs; 3 eggs; ½ pint (1⅓C) milk.

Peel and cut the carrots into ¼–½-inch pieces. Cook for about 5 minutes only in boiling salted water. If preferred the carrots may be cooked lightly in larger pieces then strained and chopped. Peel and chop or grate the onions, toss in the hot butter or margarine, add to the carrots with the rest of the ingredients, mix well and season. Grease a 2-lb. loaf tin, spoon the mixture into this. Cover with greased foil. Bake in the centre of a very moderate to moderate oven, 325–350°F, Gas Mark 3–4, for 1 hour. Cool for about 5 minutes then turn out and serve with a cheese sauce (see page 191—Leeks Mornay) or a tomato sauce (see page 200—Cabbage and Tomato Casserole). *Serves 4–6.*
To vary Use a mixture of diced root vegetables.

Storing and Freezing *These dishes are better eaten fresh. The flan stores well, but the other dishes tend to lose flavour.*

Cooking Potatoes

Potatoes may be cooked and served in dozens of different ways, but however interesting and unusual the recipe, it is based on the methods outlined here.

Blue Print

To Fry Potatoes

Although it is possible to fry raw potatoes in shallow fat, a better result is obtained by cooking in a deep pan of oil or fat.

To make Peel the potatoes, cut into the required shape, i.e. fingers (chips), slices, etc. Keep in cold water until ready to cook, then dry thoroughly in a cloth.

To cook Heat the oil or fat to 365°F. To test this, drop in one chip or slice; it should start to cook at once. If it drops to the bottom of the oil or fat, this is not sufficiently hot. Put the basket into the hot oil or fat (this makes sure the potatoes do not stick). Lift the basket from the oil. Put some of the prepared potatoes into this, lower into the hot oil or fat and cook until tender. Lift out of the pan. Continue cooking all the potatoes until tender. Reheat the oil or fat then fry the potatoes very quickly until golden brown, this takes approximately 2 minutes for each batch.

To serve Drain on absorbent paper and serve as soon as possible. The potatoes may be sprinkled with salt just before serving.

For perfect fried potatoes remember:
1. Dry the potatoes well.
2. Test the temperature of the oil or fat.
3. Heat the frying basket so they do not stick.
4. Do not cook too many potatoes at one time.
5. Cook until tender only.
6. Reheat the oil or fat.
7. Fry very quickly for the second time.
8. Drain on absorbent paper and serve.

To vary New potatoes may be washed, but not peeled, dried then fried as the Blue Print.

Ribbon potatoes Cut ribbons from the potatoes and fry as the Blue Print.

Allumette potatoes (match-sticks) Cut very thin fingers and fry as the Blue Print.

Potato balls Make balls with a vegetable scoop and fry as the Blue Print.

To Boil Potatoes

If you have never boiled potatoes with the skins left on, you are missing much of their good flavour. The skins may be removed after cooking and they pull off quite easily. This is an excellent method of cooking potatoes that tend to break in boiling.

If you wish to peel before cooking, cut away the peel from old potatoes, scrape away the skin from new potatoes. Keep in cold water until ready to cook, so the potatoes do not discolour. Put the potatoes into boiling salted water, lower the heat, so the potatoes cook steadily, rather than rapidly. Allow from 20–30 minutes according to size. Flavour new potatoes with a sprig of fresh mint during cooking, remove this before serving. Strain the potatoes and return to the pan with melted butter and chopped parsley.

To Roast Potatoes

I think nothing is more delicious than new potatoes, washed, dried then roasted in their skins. If roasting old potatoes, peel and divide large potatoes into convenient-sized pieces. Keep in cold water until ready to cook. Dry thoroughly.

Make sure the fat round the meat or in a separate roasting tin is *really* hot. There is no need to use more than 2 oz. ($\frac{1}{4}$C) fat to each 1–1$\frac{1}{2}$ lb. potatoes. Cooking fat, clarified dripping or lard are ideal. Roll the potatoes in the hot fat and roast in a hot oven, 425–450°F, Gas Mark 7–8. Allow 45–55 minutes for medium-sized potatoes. The potatoes may be turned once during cooking, but this is not essential.

To Steam Potatoes

Put well washed or peeled potatoes into a steamer over a pan of boiling water. Sprinkle with a little salt and cook as boiled potatoes but allow an extra 5–10 minutes cooking time.

To Bake Potatoes

Old potatoes bake better than new potatoes for they have a delicious 'floury' texture, but I have baked new potatoes. Wash and dry large potatoes. If you like a crisp skin, brush this with a little melted butter or margarine. Prick the potatoes with a fork so the skins will not burst. Put on to a baking tray.

For large potatoes, allow 1 hour in the centre of a moderate to moderately hot oven, 375–400°F, Gas Mark 5–6, or 1$\frac{1}{4}$–1$\frac{1}{2}$ hours in a very moderate oven. Lift the potatoes from the oven. Mark a cross on top and serve with butter.

Mashed or Creamed Potatoes

Boil old potatoes as the method above. Strain, return to the pan and break with a fork or masher until quite smooth. If you need *perfectly* smooth mashed potatoes, then sieve and return to the pan. To give a white fluffy texture add *hot* milk plus a knob of butter or margarine. Beat hard with a wooden spoon until very white. Pile into a hot dish and fork into shape.

Duchesse Potatoes

Sieve cooked and strained boiled potatoes. Add about 2 oz. ($\frac{1}{4}$C) butter or margarine and 1–2 egg yolks to each 1 lb. potatoes. As you wish the potatoes to hold a shape, omit the milk used in creamed potatoes. Duchesse potatoes are used for forming a border round a dish or to make a nest shape. Put the potatoes into a cloth piping bag with a $\frac{1}{2}$–1-inch potato rose. Pipe into the required shape and brown in a moderately hot oven, 400°F, Gas Mark 6.

Cheese and potato ring

On this page are some of the classic methods of cooking and serving potatoes, together with original ideas for you to try, including suggestions for sweet potatoes and yams.

Potatoes Dauphine

8 oz. (1C) sieved potatoes and seasoning (or use dehydrated (instant) potatoes, prepared as instructions on the packet). *For the choux pastry:* 2 oz. (¼C) butter; ¼ pint (⅔C) water; 3 oz. (¾C) flour, preferably plain; 2 eggs plus 1 egg yolk; seasoning. *For frying:* deep oil or fat.

Beat the sieved potatoes with seasoning until very smooth (or make up the dehydrated potatoes). Put the butter and water into a pan and heat until the butter has melted. Remove the pan from the heat, add the flour and stir over a low heat until the flour mixture forms a dry ball. Gradually beat the eggs and egg yolk into the choux pastry then blend in the potato purée. Taste, add more seasoning if required. Heat the oil or fat, to test see fried potatoes opposite. Either pipe or spoon small balls of the mixture into the oil or fat and fry for a few minutes until golden brown. Drain on absorbent paper and serve at once. *Serves 4–6.*

To vary The above recipe gives a particularly light version. You can use up to 1 lb. (2C) sieved potatoes to the amount of choux pastry given.

Add 2–3 tablespoons finely grated cheese (Parmesan, Gruyère, Cheddar) to the mixture, with or after adding the potatoes.

Flavour with chopped parsley and/or nutmeg.

Potato Cakes

Cream the potatoes as the recipe opposite, but to each 1 lb. potatoes add 1 tablespoon flour. Form into flat cakes, roll in seasoned flour and fry in shallow fat until crisp and golden brown. Drain on absorbent paper and serve at once.

Potatoes Almondine

Cream the potatoes or make Duchesse potatoes as the recipes opposite. Form into small balls. Roll in finely chopped almonds and fry for 2–3 minutes in deep fat or oil. Drain on absorbent paper and serve at once.

Cheese and Potato Ring

1 lb. old potatoes (weight when peeled); 12 oz. onions (weight when peeled); 2 oz. (¼C) margarine; 6 oz. (nearly 2C) *coarsely* grated cheese; seasoning; paprika. *To garnish:* parsley.

Either grate the potatoes and onions very coarsely or cut into small narrow and thin strips. Melt the margarine and toss the vegetables in this with half the cheese and plenty of seasoning and paprika. Put a well greased 8-inch ring tin into the oven to become very hot (this makes sure the mixture does not stick). Put the potato mixture into the tin, press down well. Cover with greased foil. Bake for approximately 45 minutes in the centre of a moderate oven, 350–375°F, Gas Mark 4–5. Turn out carefully on to a heated oven-proof dish. Spoon the rest of the cheese over the ring at intervals, return to the oven for 5–10 minutes until melted. Top with sprigs of parsley and serve. This makes a light main dish by itself or an accompaniment to a meal. *Serves 4–6.*

To vary To give the rather 'rough' look in the picture, use the recipe above, turn out on to the dish then gently 'pull out' the vegetables from their neat round.

Dauphine potatoes

Sweet Potatoes

These may be cooked in any of the ways suggested for ordinary potatoes. I think they are particularly good roasted. Be careful they do not burn in the hot fat, for they *are* sweeter than an ordinary potato. Sweet potatoes are often used as an ingredient in puddings. Yams are similar in flavour, but not appearance. Sweet potatoes are pink in colour and yams brown.

Potato Pancakes

2 large old potatoes; seasoning; 1 egg; 1 oz. flour, plain or self-raising; milk; 2–3 oz. (¼–⅜C) fat. *To serve:* chopped parsley.

Peel and grate the potatoes into a basin, add seasoning, the egg and flour and enough milk to make the consistency of a thick batter. Allow to stand for about 15 minutes. Heat the fat in a large pan. Drop in spoonfuls of the mixture and fry until golden brown on one side. Turn and cook on the second side, then lower the heat and allow a little extra cooking time. Serve topped with chopped parsley. *Makes about 8–10.*

Storing and Freezing *The recipes on this page, with the exception of Potatoes Dauphine and Cheese and Potato Ring, store well for 1–2 days and can be reheated or they can be frozen. Fried Potato Chips, opposite, freeze well if fried for the first time, drained well and separated on flat trays during freezing. They may then be packed in the usual way.*

To use any left over *Cooked boiled potatoes may be used in salads, or made into Sauté potatoes. Fry in a little hot fat until brown on both sides.*

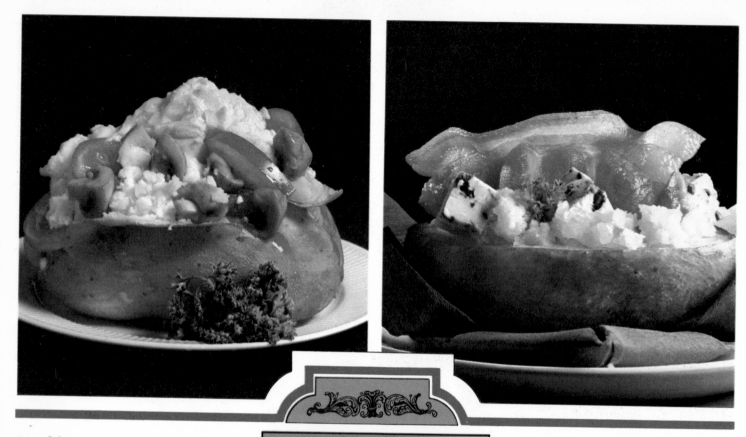

One of the most delicious and simplest main dishes is a stuffed potato and the suggestions on this page give you a wide variety of ways in which to turn a jacket potato into a main dish.

Potato Nests

1 lb. (2C) mashed potatoes; 2 oz. ($\frac{1}{4}$C) butter; 1–2 egg yolks. *For the filling:* $\frac{1}{2}$ pint (1$\frac{1}{3}$C) soured cream or yoghourt; 2–3 tablespoons cooked sweet corn; 8 oz. cooked chicken or diced cheese; 1 red pepper; seasoning.
Make Duchesse potatoes as page 188 and form into 6 individual flan shapes or nests. Brown and heat in a moderately hot oven, 400°F, Gas Mark 6. Meanwhile put the soured cream or yoghourt, sweet corn and chicken or cheese into the top of a double saucepan, or basin over hot water. Heat thoroughly. Add the diced red pepper (discard the core and seeds) and seasoning just before serving. Spoon into the centre of the crisp potato nests. *Serves 6.*

Ham and Potato Salad

2 oz. ($\frac{1}{4}$C) margarine or butter; 2 oz. ($\frac{1}{2}$C) mushrooms; about 8–12 oz. new or old potatoes; 4–8 oz. diced ham; some cooked peas; mayonnaise. *To garnish:* lettuce; tomatoes.
Heat the margarine or butter, fry the sliced mushrooms and allow to cool. Cook the potatoes by boiling or steaming, see page 188, dice and mix with the ham, peas, mushrooms and mayonnaise while warm. Allow to cool. Serve on a bed of lettuce with sliced tomatoes. *Serves 4–6.*
To vary This makes a delicious hot salad if crisply fried bacon or boiled ham is used instead of cold ham, make sure the peas and mushrooms are hot. Toss in the mayonnaise,

put on the lettuce, add the raw tomatoes and serve at once.
If you want a meatless meal, then increase the amount of peas, to add extra protein or add diced cheese and/or chopped hard boiled eggs.

Stuffed Baked Potatoes

First bake the potatoes as the instructions on page 188.
Corn and cheese stuffed potatoes Cut a slice from the top of the potatoes, scoop out the pulp and mash with seasoning and a little butter or margarine, then blend with a little

Farmhouse potatoes (above right)
Cheese and bacon boats (above left)

Main Dishes with Potatoes

grated cheese and yoghourt. Put back into the potato cases and top with cooked or canned sweet corn. Return to the oven for a short time to reheat.
Cheese and bacon boats Cut a slice from the top of the potatoes and remove the pulp very carefully. Dice this and blend with diced Danish Blue cheese, a little yoghourt or mayonnaise and chopped parsley. Put back into the potato cases. Return to the oven to heat and top with grilled or fried rashers of crisp bacon and a little more parsley just before serving.
Potatoes au gratin Halve the cooked potatoes spread with a little butter and grated cheese. Brown in the oven or under the grill and top with sliced tomatoes.
Eggs and potatoes Cut a slice from the top of the potatoes, scoop out the pulp and mash with seasoning and a little butter or margarine. Blend in chopped hard boiled egg whites. Put the mixture back into the potato cases and garnish with halved egg yolks, paprika and gherkin fans.
Soured cream potatoes Make a cross on the top of the potatoes and spoon in soured cream mixed with seasoning and chopped cucumber. Top with grilled bacon rolls.
Farmhouse potatoes Make a cross on top of the potatoes. Scoop out the pulp and mash with seasoning and a little butter or cream cheese. Put back into the potato cases and top with sliced cooked mushrooms and sliced tomatoes. Return to the oven to reheat and before serving top each one with a spoonful of cream cheese, mayonnaise, butter or scrambled egg.

To use any left over *The stuffed potatoes can be covered and reheated in the oven.*

Both leeks and onions can be cooked in a variety of ways and can form the basis of main meals.

To Prepare

Leeks Trim the green end and the root of the leeks. Wash thoroughly between the folds of the vegetables; these often are very dirty. Either cut into convenient lengths or thin slices, leave whole or halve lengthways.

Onions Remove the outer skin and trim the vegetable at both ends. Wash in cold water. Slice and separate the rings of onion, this is the method used for frying, or chop.

To Boil

Put the prepared vegetables into boiling salted water, see the Blue Print on page 186. Allow approximately 10–20 minutes for leeks (according to size).

Allow about 30 minutes for small whole onions, but up to 50–60 minutes for really large whole onions. It is important to boil the water steadily, rather than rapidly, so the whole onion becomes tender, not just the outside. Chopped onions will take about 5–10 minutes cooking time.

To Bake

Prepare the vegetables, then cut into thin slices. Put into a dish with a little milk, seasoning and margarine. Cover with greased foil or a lid. Bake in the centre of a very moderate to moderate oven, 325–350°F, Gas Mark 3–4, for approximately 45 minutes to 1 hour. Top with chopped parsley.

To Roast

Although leeks can be roasted in hot fat, they are less successful than onions. For 4 medium-sized onions or large leeks allow 2 oz. ($\frac{1}{4}$C) fat. Heat the fat in a roasting tin. Prepare the vegetables, dry thoroughly and turn in the hot fat. Roast towards the top of a moderately hot to hot oven, 375–400°F, Gas Mark 5–6. Allow about 45 minutes for medium-sized onions or leeks and a generous 1 hour for large onions or leeks.

To Fry

Fried leeks are served less often than fried onions, but they are very pleasant, if a trifle 'leathery' compared to the texture of an onion. Prepare the vegetables and cut into slices. You can separate the rings of leek, but I find it easier to fry them in lengths of about $\frac{1}{4}$–$\frac{1}{2}$ inch. Onion slices should be separated into rings.

For shallow frying, simply dry the vegetables, coat in a little seasoned flour if wished, then fry in hot fat or oil in a frying pan for approximately 5–6 minutes. Drain on absorbent paper.

If you want really crisply fried leeks, coat in seasoned flour then in batter (see the batter under Cauliflower Fritters on page 183) and deep fry.

Cooking Leeks and Onions

If you want really crisp onion rings, dip in milk then in seasoned flour. Put into a heated frying basket and lower into hot fat or oil and fry until crisp and golden brown. For a very crisp result fry as potatoes, i.e. cook steadily in the fat or oil until tender, but not quite brown. Remove from the pan. Reheat the fat or oil then fry for a second time for about 2 minutes. Drain on absorbent paper.

Leeks Mornay

8 good-sized leeks; seasoning; 1 oz. butter; 1 oz. flour; pinch dry mustard; $\frac{1}{2}$ pint ($1\frac{1}{3}$C) milk or use half milk and half stock from cooking the leeks; 4 oz. (1C) grated cheese; paprika.

*Dutch Gouda cheese gives a pleasantly mild flavour.

Prepare and boil the leeks as the instructions on this page. Season the cooking liquid well. Drain, put on to a heated serving dish and save $\frac{1}{4}$ pint ($\frac{2}{3}$C) of the stock unless using all milk. Heat the butter in a pan, stir in the flour and mustard and cook for several minutes. Gradually blend in the milk or milk and leek stock. Bring to the boil and stir as the sauce thickens. Stir in the cheese, add seasoning and heat for 1–2 minutes only. Pour over the leeks and top with paprika. This makes a light main dish by itself or an accompaniment to a meal. *Serves 4.*

Know Your Onions

The information on this page has assumed you are using large type onions (naturally these vary considerably in size). In addition there are the very small onions (often called pickling onions), that can be used in cooking and a similar vegetable known as a shallot. Shallots are used a great deal in Continental recipes, for they have a somewhat more defined flavour than an onion. They are sometimes slightly pink in colour.

Spring onions are used mainly in salads, but are excellent in cooking.

● **AVOID** *The strong smell of leeks or onions cooking by keeping the pan well covered.*

● **TO RECTIFY** *You can put in a slice of bread to absorb the smell, but this is not practical if you wish to use the leek or onion stock as it disintegrates in the liquid.*

● **SHORT CUT** *There are very useful dehydrated chopped onions which may be used for flavouring, but cannot be served as a main dish.*

● **TO SLIMMERS** *Both leeks and onions are low in calories.*

Storing and Freezing *Both leeks and onions store well, the latter will keep for some weeks in a cool dry place if mature. Young immature onions do not keep well. Both cooked leeks and onions can be frozen, but the raw vegetable when frozen, loses texture and taste.*

Leeks mornay

Main Dishes with Onions

Blue Print Recipe

Stuffed Onions

There are many ways in which onions may be stuffed to make a complete light meal.

4 large onions · 8–12 oz. cooked meat · 3 oz. ($\frac{3}{8}$C) margarine, butter or cooking fat · 3 oz. ($\frac{3}{4}$C) soft bread-crumbs · $\frac{1}{2}$ teaspoon chopped fresh sage or good pinch dried sage · 2–3 teaspoons chopped parsley · season-ing.

To make Peel the onions. Dice or mince the meat and blend with half the melted margarine, butter or cooking fat, the crumbs, herbs and seasoning.

To cook Put the onions into a pan of boiling water, season well and boil steadily for approximately 30 minutes, until the outsides are tender. Save some stock to make a sauce if wished. Lift out of the water, cool sufficiently to handle, then remove the centre of each onion. Chop fairly coarsely, as shown in the picture, and mix with the rest of the stuffing ingredients. Brush the bottom of an oven-proof dish or tin with some of the melted fat and put the onion 'shells' on this. Spoon the mixture into the onions, piling high to give an attractive appearance. Pour the rest of the melted fat over the top. Bake in the centre of a very moderate to moderate oven, 325–350°F, Gas Mark 3–4, for approximately 1 hour. If the stuffing is becoming too brown, cover the dish with foil or a lid.

To serve Hot with a sauce if wished.

All recipes based on this serve 4

To vary Use diced canned nutmeat instead of meat as above.

Use about 6 oz. (generous 1$\frac{1}{2}$C) chopped walnuts or other nuts in place of meat.

Stuffed onion

Onions à la King

About 24 tiny onions or shallots or about 36 spring onions; seasoning; 1 green pepper; 4 eggs; 1$\frac{1}{2}$ oz. butter or margarine; 1$\frac{1}{2}$ oz. flour; $\frac{3}{4}$ pint (2C) milk or milk and onion stock; 3–4 tablespoons cooked sweet corn. *For the croûtons:* 2 slices bread; 2 oz. ($\frac{1}{4}$C) fat or butter.

Prepare the onions (cut some of the stalk from spring onions, but leave about 1 inch green). Cook in well seasoned boiling water until just tender; do not over-cook. Cut the green pepper into narrow strips and add to the liquid for the last 5 minutes. Meanwhile boil the eggs until just firm, shell and slice. Make the white sauce with the butter or margarine, flour and milk or milk and onion stock. Add the sweet corn, sliced eggs and drained onions and pepper. Season well and serve topped with fried croûtons of bread. To make these, dice the bread and fry until crisp and brown in the hot fat or butter. *Serves 4.*

Cider Casserole

4 large onions or 4–5 medium-sized leeks; 3 oz. ($\frac{3}{8}$C) margarine; $\frac{1}{2}$ pint (1$\frac{1}{4}$C) cider; seasoning; pinch dried or fresh sage; 2–3 dessert apples; 4 thick rashers rather fat bacon or pork belly.

Peel and cut the onions into slices then separate into rings. If using leeks wash thoroughly and cut into $\frac{1}{2}$-inch lengths. Heat 2 oz. ($\frac{1}{4}$C) of the margarine in a large pan, toss the onion rings or leek slices in this until pale golden brown. Put into a casserole with the cider, seasoning and herbs. Cover with a lid and cook for approximately 40 minutes in the centre of a very moderate to moderate oven, 325–350°F, Gas Mark 3–4. Core and slice the apples, but do not peel, toss in the remaining margarine. Remove the casserole from the oven, arrange the apples over the top of the onion and cider mixture.

Top with the uncooked rashers of bacon or pork. Do not put the lid back on the dish. Return to the oven for a further 25–30 minutes. This is excellent served with baked potatoes (see page 188). *Serves 4.*

To vary Use white wine or stock in place of cider.

To make a meal, without using meat, add cooked haricot beans or a mixture of cooked beans and peas to the onion mixture with the apples.

Put the apples on top of the onions and cider as detailed in the recipe above. Cover the casserole and cook for 25–30 minutes. Remove the casserole from the oven and top with fairly thick slices of Gruyère or Cheddar cheese. Brown under the grill until the cheese melts, then serve at once.

Head of garlic   Clove of garlic

Using Garlic

Garlic is an invaluable flavouring, *if* you like it. Unfortunately its flavour is so pronounced that it can spoil dishes for some.

To use garlic discreetly, peel a clove and put it into the frying pan or saucepan for 1–2 minutes, then remove. Alternatively, halve the clove, rub round the pan, then remove. If you enjoy garlic, chop 1 or more cloves or crush with the tip of a knife. If you put a little salt on the board it helps to do this. Add to the dish as the recipe.

Storing and Freezing *Stuffed onions (when cooked) keep for a day or two and can be reheated. They freeze well for a limited period. Allow to defrost before reheating.*

Onion flan and cider casserole

Corn, Cucumbers and Marrows

Corn on the cob makes an excellent hot hors d'oeuvre. The younger generation in particular seem to enjoy the golden corn, dripping with melted butter.

Cucumber is surprisingly good as a cooked vegetable. Naturally it loses the firm crisp taste that is apparent when served in a salad.

To Cook Corn on the Cob

Choose corn with fresh looking pale green leaves and golden coloured kernels. If too pale the corn is under-ripe and will be lacking in flavour. Pull away the leaves before cooking and put the whole cob into boiling water. Cook for about 12 minutes until nearly tender, add a little salt and give an extra few minutes cooking. If the corn is salted at the beginning of the cooking period I find it tends to toughen it. Test the corn early, for over-cooking also toughens the vegetable.

Lift from the boiling water, drain well and serve with plenty of melted butter. If you wish to serve the corn off the cob pull the kernels away with the prongs of a fork, when it is just tender.

Frozen corn on the cob is cooked in the same way as fresh. The frozen corn kernels are not pre-cooked so need cooking until tender, see the directions on the packet. Canned corn is available as kernels off the cob. It is often mixed with diced red pepper (capsicum), or canned with a creamed sauce. It just needs heating. Do not over-cook for this causes the corn to darken in colour.

Corn Fritters

Corn fritters are an excellent accompaniment to chicken, meat or fish, they can be served topped with cheese to make a light main dish, or served with salad, as in the picture. Use cooked or canned sweet corn for the fritters and drain well before using.

8 oz. (2C) sweet corn; fritter batter as Cauliflower Fritters (page 183). *For frying:* oil or fat.

Mix the sweet corn with the batter. Blend thoroughly, then drop spoonfuls into hot deep or shallow oil or fat. Fry until crisp and golden brown on both sides. Drain on absorbent paper and serve. *Serves 4–6.*

Corn fritters

To vary Mix a little finely chopped ham, corned beef, fried bacon or cooked chicken with the batter and use only 4–6 oz. (1–1½C) sweet corn.
Add 2–3 oz. (½–¾C) grated Cheddar cheese to the batter, add the corn and cook as above.

Corn Risotto

1 medium-sized onion; 1 small green pepper; 1 small red pepper; 2 tablespoons corn or olive oil; 6 oz. (generous ¾C) long grain rice; 1 pint (2⅔C) water; *bouquet garni*; seasoning; 8 oz. (2C) canned or cooked sweet corn.
Chop the onion and dice the peppers, removing cores and seeds. Heat the oil in a pan. Toss the vegetables, with the rice, in this making sure the onion does not discolour. Add the water. Bring to the boil, stir well, add the herbs and seasoning. Cover the pan and simmer steadily for nearly 15 minutes. Lift the lid, stir the rice mixture, add the corn and heat for a few minutes, until the rice has absorbed all the liquid. Remove the *bouquet garni*. Serve as an accompaniment to main dishes or turn into a light dish by serving with big bowls of grated cheese. *Serves 4–6.*

To Cook Cucumber

If the cucumbers are forced they can be cooked *with* the skin, but the outdoor type tend to develop a rather tough, strongly flavoured skin and generally it is advisable to remove this.

To boil cucumber Cut into slices about ½-inch in thickness and boil as green vegetables on page 182 for 6–8 minutes. Drain and toss in butter and parsley or chopped chives or serve with a white or cheese sauce, see page 191 — Leeks Mornay.

To fry cucumber Cut into slices about ½-inch in thickness, then dip each slice in well seasoned flour. Fry in deep or shallow fat for about 4–5 minutes until golden brown. Drain on absorbent paper and serve. This is an excellent vegetable with cooked fish.

To Cook Marrow

The small marrows (courgettes or zucchini as they often are called) are described on page 185. The larger marrows may be cooked in the same way. When the marrows are young do not peel, simply slice or cut into segments. There may be no seeds to remove. When the marrow becomes older, remove both the skin and the seeds. Remember the big mature marrows, that look so impressive, are not very good for cooking. They are, however, excellent to use for jam and pickles.

To boil marrow Cook as the Blue Print on page 182; allow 7–10 minutes. Drain well and top with melted butter and chopped parsley or a white or cheese sauce, see page 191 — Leeks Mornay. Do not over-cook. Marrow can be steamed over boiling water for approximately the same time.

To roast marrow Put fairly large pieces into very hot fat and roast as potatoes, page 188. Allow approximately 40 minutes, turning once or twice. The marrow never becomes crisp and brown, but this method retains the maximum of flavour.

Stuffed marrow is one of the best ways of serving this vegetable. A recipe is given on page 194, and the stuffing used on page 199 is equally as good for marrow as for green peppers.

Storing and Freezing *All these vegetables store well. Keep cucumbers in a cool place. Corn freezes well but neither marrows nor cucumbers can be frozen in a raw state. Marrow can be frozen as part of a dish like Ratatouille.*

To use any left over *Corn can be added to soups and stews. Cucumber and marrow should be reheated for a few minutes.*

193

Mushrooms, like so many other vegetables, are invaluable for giving flavour to savoury dishes. They also make excellent light snacks and meals.

To Cook Mushrooms

To prepare mushrooms The cultivated mushrooms need not be skinned, in fact it is a mistake to do so, for the skin enhances the flavour. All that is required is to wash the mushrooms well and trim the base of the stalks. Wild, or less perfect mushrooms should be skinned before use.

To boil mushrooms If the mushrooms are put into boiling stock and simmered for about 5 minutes they are tender and you have added no fattening ingredients to these low calorie vegetables. If you have no stock, use water plus a little yeast extract and seasoning.

To fry mushrooms While mushrooms can be coated in seasoned flour or egg and crumbs or batter and fried in deep oil or fat, they are better if shallow fried. Heat enough margarine, butter, cooking fat, oil or, best of all, well clarified beef dripping in a frying pan to give a depth of about $\frac{1}{4}$ inch. Put in the mushrooms and turn in the fat until tender. This takes about 5 minutes.

To bake mushrooms Put the prepared mushrooms with plenty of margarine or butter or a little stock or milk into an oven-proof dish. Season well and cover with a lid or foil. Bake in the centre of a moderate to moderately hot oven, 375–400°F, Gas Mark 5–6, for 15–20 minutes.

Mushrooms

To grill mushrooms Put the prepared mushrooms in a generous amount of melted fat (see under frying) in the grill pan. Cook under the grill, spooning the hot fat over the vegetables once or twice.

Raw Mushrooms

Many people never try one of the best ways of serving mushrooms, i.e. raw. The picture opposite shows a simple but interesting hors d'oeuvre using uncooked mushrooms.

Tomatoes and mushrooms vinaigrette Skin and slice 4–6 really firm, but ripe tomatoes. Wash, dry and slice 4 oz. (1C) perfect button mushrooms. Blend $\frac{1}{2}$ teaspoon made mustard, a good pinch salt, sugar and shake of pepper with 3 tablespoons olive oil and $1\frac{1}{2}$ tablespoons lemon juice or white wine vinegar. Add a crushed clove of garlic or a little chopped onion if wished. Arrange the tomatoes in 4 individual dishes. Spoon the dressing over the top. Add the sliced mushrooms and top with chopped parsley. Mix well before eating. *Serves 4.*

Spinach and Mushroom Cream

1 lb. cooked spinach; 12 oz. (3C) button mushrooms; 1 medium-sized onion; 2 oz ($\frac{1}{4}$C) butter or margarine; 2 eggs; $\frac{1}{2}$ pint (1$\frac{1}{3}$C milk or use half milk and half single cream seasoning; 2 tablespoons soft breadcrumbs 2 tablespoons grated Parmesan cheese.

Chop or sieve the spinach to give a smooth purée. Slice the mushrooms and onion, toss in the hot butter or margarine. Arrange alternate layers of spinach and mushroom mixture in a pie or oven-proof dish. Beat the eggs with the warmed milk or milk and cream season well. Pour over the vegetables. Top with crumbs and cheese. Cover the dish with buttered foil and bake for 30 minutes in the centre of a very moderate to moderate oven 325–350°F, Gas Mark 3–4, remove the foil and cook for a further 10 minutes. *Serves 4–6*

Quick Dishes Using Mushrooms

Grill or fry mushrooms, top with cream cheese and grill for a few more minutes.

Grill or fry mushrooms, top with lightly scrambled eggs, blended with chopped parsley and chives.

Grill or fry mushrooms, top with soured cream, blended with chopped raw or fried onions and paprika.

Storing and Freezing *Mushrooms keep well in a covered container in the refrigerator for several days, but are best when eaten very fresh. They can be frozen after blanching or after frying or grilling.*

It would be difficult to visualise cooking without tomatoes, for they not only add flavour they give so much colour to dishes.

To Cook Tomatoes

To prepare tomatoes Skin the tomatoes, if wished, before cooking. Either put into boiling water for a very short time, then lift into cold water to cool rapidly and skin, or insert a fine skewer into the tomatoes and hold over a gas burner or electric hotplate until the skin 'pops'. Pull away the skin.

To boil tomatoes Put the tomatoes into a pan with a little liquid if wished. Season well and add a pinch of sugar if you like a fairly sweet flavour. Chopped herbs, chopped or grated onion or garlic may be added. Cook until hot or until a smooth purée.

To fry tomatoes Skin if wished and halve. Season lightly and cook in a little hot fat (see mushrooms above). They take about 4–5 minutes to become tender.

To grill tomatoes Put the halved or whole tomatoes in the grill pan or on the grid of the grill pan. Season lightly and top with a little hot margarine or butter. Cook for about 4 minutes under a hot grill.

To bake tomatoes Put the whole or halved well seasoned tomatoes into a greased dish. Top with a little margarine or butter and a lid if you wish them to be rather soft. Bake for approximately 15–20 minutes, depending upon size, towards the top of a moderate

Tomatoes

to moderately hot oven, 375–400°F, Gas Mark 5–6.

Cheddar Tomatoes

4 very large firm tomatoes; $\frac{1}{4}$ medium-sized cucumber; 4–6 oz. (1–1$\frac{1}{2}$C) grated Cheddar cheese; seasoning; mayonnaise; portion cooked cauliflower; paprika. *To garnish:* watercress.

Cut a slice off one end of the tomatoes. Scoop out the centre pulp, put into a basin and chop finely. Dice half the cucumber, slice the remainder. Mix the tomato pulp with half the diced cucumber, the cheese, seasoning and a little mayonnaise. Spoon into the tomato cases. Blend the rest of the diced cucumber with mayonnaise, put on top of each tomato with small sprigs of cauliflower topped with paprika. Serve in individual dishes with sliced cucumber and watercress. *Serves 4.*

Tomato Stuffed Marrow

1 medium-sized marrow; seasoning; 2 medium-sized onions; 2–3 oz. ($\frac{1}{4}$–$\frac{3}{8}$C) margarine or fat; 1 lb. tomatoes; 3 oz. (1C) soft breadcrumbs; 2 tablespoons chopped parsley or use a mixture of herbs.

Peel the marrow and slice lengthways. Remove the seeds. Sprinkle the marrow very lightly with seasoning and leave for about 30 minutes; the salt 'draws out' some of the water and makes it easier to brown the vegetable in the oven. Chop the onions and fry in half the margarine or fat. Add the skinned chopped tomatoes, crumbs and herbs. Season well. Put the stuffing into both halves of the marrow, then press together. Either tie or skewer the vegetable. Heat the rest of the margarine or fat. Pour over the marrow. Bake in the centre of a moderate oven, 350–375°F, Gas Mark 4–5, for 1 hour. Baste once or twice during cooking. *Serves 4–6.*

To vary To turn this into a more sustaining main dish add cooked lentils or haricot beans to the tomato mixture in place of crumbs.

Add 3–4 beaten eggs to the stuffing. This makes it rather soft when it first goes into the marrow, so handle carefully.

Add about 4 oz. (1C) chopped nuts to the stuffing.

Storing and Freezing *Store tomatoes in a cool place. If put in the refrigerator cover well. Tomato purée freezes excellently.*

Peas, Beans and Lentils

These vegetables are called 'pulses' and they have the great value of adding protein to our meals; they can be served in place of meat or fish. Once these vegetables were called 'second class proteins', but today that is considered incorrect. There is nothing 'second class' about them, they are simply vegetable rather than animal proteins.

Peas and beans of various kinds can be cooked as fresh vegetables. Lentils, of course, are dried and these need longer cooking. The modern Accelerated Freeze Dried peas and green beans can be cooked quite quickly. Remember you can obtain ordinary dried peas and beans and these do need longer cooking and preferably soaking. Frozen and canned peas and beans may be used in recipes when fresh vegetables are out of season.

To Cook Fresh Peas

All peas, with the exception of the mange-tout type, need removing from the pods. If you are fortunate enough to be able to buy the rather flat-looking mange-tout peas, simply wash, cut away the ends and cook the whole pods with the tiny peas inside. Peas are cooked in boiling salted water, as the Blue Print on page 182. Most people like a pinch of sugar and sprig of fresh mint added to the water. Cook for 10–15 minutes only when the peas are young. Over-cooking toughens them. Drain and toss in a little melted butter or margarine. Mange-tout peas cook in a few minutes only.

To Cook Fresh Beans

Beans vary in type a great deal.
Haricots verts Very thin green beans, which need just the ends removing.
French beans Medium-sized green beans, remove either end and string (cut away the very edges). Do not slice.
Runner beans Larger green beans, string the sides, remove either end, cut into thin slices. Put the beans into boiling salted water and cook for approximately 15 minutes, or until tender. Drain and toss in melted butter or margarine.
Broad beans A green bean, but it is the inside that is normally cooked. I find when these are very young that you can remove the beans from the pods, prepare, slice and cook the pods as runner beans. Cook the broad beans themselves in boiling salted water for about 15 minutes, drain, toss in melted butter or margarine.
Flageolets These are fresh haricot beans—cook as broad beans.

To Flavour Fresh Peas and Beans

Toss the cooked peas or beans in freshly chopped herbs or chopped or crushed garlic.
Mix the cooked peas or beans with tiny fried onions.
Mix the cooked peas or beans with a well seasoned fresh tomato purée or with sliced fried onions and/or fried mushrooms.

To Cook Dried Peas and Beans

Dried peas and dried haricot or butter beans are better if soaked overnight in cold water or pour boiling water over them and soak. Put into a pan with the same water and

Key
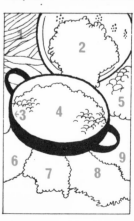

1. French beans
2. Red kidney beans
3. Dried haricot beans
4. Flageolets
5. Butter beans
6. Lentils
7. AFD peas
8. AFD beans
9. Split peas

seasoning. Simmer steadily until tender. This takes about 2 hours or a little longer with butter beans. Drain, toss in melted butter or margarine and chopped parsley, or serve in a white or cheese sauce, see page 191—Leeks Mornay.

Pressure cooking saves a great deal of time. Soak the dried vegetables as above. Put into the pressure cooker. Bring up to 15 lb. pressure and allow 15 minutes for peas and 30 minutes for haricot and butter beans. Allow the pressure to drop at room temperature.

Boston Baked Beans

1 lb. dried haricot beans; water to cover; 2 large tomatoes; 1–2 tablespoons black treacle; 1–2 teaspoons made mustard; seasoning; 12 oz. fat salt pork; 1–2 onions. *To garnish:* parsley.

Soak the beans overnight as described above. Simmer without seasoning in the water for 10–15 minutes. Strain the beans, but save a generous ½ pint (1⅓C) of the liquid. Simmer this with the tomatoes to make a thin sauce. Sieve. Add the treacle and mustard and a generous amount of seasoning. Dice the pork, slice the onions very thinly. Put the beans, pork and onions into a deep casserole. Pour over the tomato sauce and mix well. Allow plenty of space for the beans to swell during cooking. Put on the lid. Cover very tightly. If the lid does not fit well put foil round the dish. Cook in the centre of a very slow oven, 250–275°F, Gas Mark ½–1, for about 5 hours. Check the progress of the cooking after 2½ hours. If the beans are still very hard, raise the temperature slightly. If they are becoming a little dry, add boiling water to moisten, but do not make them too wet. Top with

parsley before serving. These can be served as a dish by themselves or an accompaniment. *Serves about 8.*

To vary   Omit the pork and add 1–2 crushed cloves of garlic with the tomato mixture. The tomatoes can be omitted and a little more treacle and mustard used for flavouring.

Lentil Vegetable Roast

12 oz. (1½C) lentils; water; seasoning; *bouquet garni*; 2 large onions; 1 clove garlic; 3 oz. (⅜C) margarine; 1 small dessert apple; few sticks celery; 1 small green pepper.

Put the lentils into a pan with only enough cold water to cover. Add the seasoning and herbs. Leave for 1–2 hours if possible, for this shortens the cooking time slightly. Simmer steadily for 1¼ hours until the water has evaporated and the lentils are tender. Remove the *bouquet garni*. Meanwhile chop the onions and crush the clove of garlic. Fry in 2 oz. (¼C) margarine until tender. Add to the warm lentil mixture in the pan, with the peeled diced apple, chopped celery and pepper (discard the core and seeds). Season well. Grease a 2-lb. baking dish or tin with half the remaining margarine. Put in the lentil mixture. Top with the remaining margarine. Do not cover if you want a crisp topping. Bake for 1 hour in the centre of a moderate oven, 350–375°F, Gas Mark 4–5. Turn out and serve with roast potatoes. (Illustrated on page 181.) *Serves 4–6.*

To vary

Crisp-coated roast   Coat the sides of the greased dish or tin with a thick layer of crumbs and top the lentil mixture with crumbs and margarine before baking.

Add a little curry powder and chopped herbs to flavour or 2–3 skinned tomatoes plus a

Mexican macaroni

pinch chilli powder. Add the tomatoes to the onions then blend with the cooked lentils. Use sieved cooked butter beans in place of lentils.

Mexican Macaroni

For the cheese sauce: 1 oz. margarine; 1 oz. flour; ½ pint (1⅓C) milk; 4 oz. (1C) grated Cheddar cheese; seasoning; pinch cayenne pepper (or use a packet cheese sauce mix with ½ pint (1⅓C) milk); 4 oz. macaroni; 1–2 teaspoons made mustard; 8 Frankfurter sausages; 4–6 oz. (1–1½C) cooked fresh peas.

Make the cheese sauce with the margarine, flour, milk and cheese. Season well and add the cayenne pepper (or make up the packet of cheese sauce mix). Meanwhile boil the macaroni in salted water, drain, add to the sauce. Stir in enough made mustard to give a fairly hot taste. Chop the Frankfurter sausages, add to the sauce with the peas. Heat for a few minutes then serve.

To vary   To make a meatless meal, increase the amount of sauce to ¾ pint (2C). Use twice the amount of peas or mix peas and cooked or canned haricot beans.

Country Style Beans

2 onions; 2 carrots; 2 oz. (¼C) margarine; ¾ pint (2C) water; seasoning; 1½ lb. French beans. *To garnish:* chopped chives.

Peel and grate both the onions and carrots. Toss in the hot margarine. Add the water. Bring to the boil and season well. Prepare the French beans, put into the flavoured liquid. Cook until tender in an open pan, so the liquid evaporates. Top with chopped chives. *Serves 4–6.*

To vary   Flavour the water with a little Worcestershire sauce.

This is an excellent way to serve ready cooked butter or haricot beans, or cooked dried peas. Reduce the amount of water to ½ pint (1⅓C) only for the beans or peas need heating only.

Storing and Freezing   *Peas and green beans should be eaten when fresh, they can be frozen with great success. Cut runner beans into fairly thick slices for freezing.*
To use any left over   *Add to salads, soups and stews.*

Boston baked beans

Nothing turns an ordinary meal into a special one more easily than an interesting selection of vegetable dishes. Some of the vegetables on these two pages can be served as a separate course.

Ratatouille

1 medium-sized to large aubergine (egg plant); about 8 oz. courgettes; seasoning; 1 lb. ripe tomatoes; 4 medium-sized onions; 1–2 cloves garlic; 1 green pepper; 1 red pepper; 3–4 tablespoons olive oil. *To garnish:* chopped or sprigged parsley (optional).

If you dislike the taste of the peel on an aubergine remove this, otherwise dice the vegetable neatly with the peel on. Slice the courgettes. These two vegetables can be put into a bowl, sprinkled lightly with salt and pepper and left for 30 minutes. This minimises the bitter taste from the aubergine peel and 'draws out' the water from the courgettes. Skin and slice or chop the tomatoes and onions; chop or crush the cloves of garlic. Dice the flesh from the green and red peppers, discard the cores and seeds. Heat the olive oil in a pan, add the tomatoes and onions and cook gently in the oil for a few minutes, for the juice to flow from the tomatoes. This makes sure the mixture will not stick to the pan. Add the rest of the vegetables, stir well. Season and cover the pan with a tightly fitting lid. Simmer gently until as tender as you would wish (about 30 minutes in all). The picture shows the vegetables clearly defined and retaining their individual textures. I

Special Occasion Vegetable Dishes

think this is delicious if serving hot, but if you wish this to be a cold hors d'oeuvre then I suggest cooking them a little longer. Top with parsley if wished before serving. *Serves 6–8.*

To vary The recipe above uses the minimum of oil, many people prefer to use rather more than this.

Add 3–4 tablespoons chopped parsley or parsley and chives to the vegetables before cooking. This gives a very pleasant flavour. Cook the mixture in a tightly covered casserole for about 45 minutes in a very moderate oven, or at least 1 hour in a slow oven.

The proportions of vegetables are entirely a matter of personal taste. You can add sliced

mushrooms if wished, omit the peppers or increase these. The recipe above though gives the generally accepted amounts of vegetables for a well balanced flavour.

Stuffed Aubergines

Aubergines, or 'little slippers' as I have heard them called, can be stuffed in a variety of ways. The method of preparing the aubergines is as follows:

Wash and dry the vegetables. If you wish to minimise the slightly bitter flavour, score the skins lightly, see sketch opposite, sprinkle with salt and leave for at least 15 minutes.

Cut the aubergines lengthways at the end of this time. Remove the centre strip of the vegetable. Chop this very finely. Brush the top of the halved aubergine with a generous amount of oil and cook under a low grill or in a moderate oven for about 15–20 minutes, until the pulp is softened. Remove the softened pulp, mix with the chopped core part and the selected stuffing. Put the halved aubergines in a well oiled dish in the oven to cook the stuffing. Allow approximately 30 minutes in a moderate oven, 350–375°F, Gas Mark 4–5. Do not cover the dish, unless stated in the recipe. The stuffing quantities below are enough to fill 8 halves, i.e. 4 medium-sized aubergines. *This would serve 4 as a light main dish.*

To vary

The aubergines may be boiled in salted water for 10–15 minutes then halved and filled. This gives a softer texture to the skin than cooking in the manner suggested above.

Espagnole Stuffing Chop 2 medium-sized onions finely, crush 1 clove garlic. Fry in 2 tablespoons oil until very soft. Add 3 skinned chopped tomatoes, 4 oz. (1C) chopped mushrooms and the aubergine pulp. Season well. Press into the aubergines, top with soft breadcrumbs and a little oil. Cook as above.

Cheese Filling Blend 4 oz. (1C tightly packed) cream cheese, 2–3 tablespoons grated Parmesan cheese, the aubergine pulp, 1 tablespoon chopped parsley, 1 egg and 2 oz. ($\frac{2}{3}$C) soft breadcrumbs. Press into the aubergine halves, top with more breadcrumbs and a little grated Parmesan cheese. Cook as above.

Ham Stuffing Fry 1 chopped onion in 1 oz. margarine or butter, add 2–3 tablespoons finely chopped celery, 8 oz. cooked diced lean ham and the aubergine pulp. Mix well, then stir in 1 egg, 1–2 tablespoons chopped parsley and seasoning. Press into the aubergine halves. Cover the dish to prevent the filling becoming too brown.

Nut Stuffing Follow the directions for the ham stuffing but substitute chopped nuts or nutmeat for the ham.

Stuffed Peppers

Although red peppers can be stuffed, the green (which are the under-ripe capsicums) have more flavour when cooked in this way. Cut the stalk end from the peppers, remove

Stuffed peppers (top)
Ratatouille (below)

the core and seeds carefully, so you do not break the flesh. Put the slices removed and the shells into boiling salted water and cook for approximately 10 minutes if you like the peppers firm, but over 15 minutes if you prefer them softer. Dice the slices removed, so these may be added to the selected stuffing or keep intact and use as 'lids' for the stuffing. Choose any of the stuffings suggested for aubergines or try the stuffing shown in the picture. Put the filled peppers into a well oiled dish in the oven and cook for approximately 30 minutes in a moderate oven, 350–375°F, Gas Mark 4–5. Do not cover the dish, unless stated in the recipe.

In addition to the fillings given opposite for aubergines try:

Speedy Herb Stuffing　Empty the contents of a packet of parsley and thyme stuffing, add 2–3 chopped mushrooms, a grated onion and about 12 oz. chopped corned beef or minced cooked meat. Bind with an egg and 2 oz. ($\frac{1}{4}$C) melted margarine. Season lightly. Mix the diced pepper slices with this. Press into 4 pepper cases and cook as above. This is excellent served with lightly cooked sliced carrots. *Serves 4.*

Vegetable Herb Stuffing　Omit the meat and add cooked haricot beans and 2 skinned chopped tomatoes to the ingredients in the Speedy Herb Stuffing.

Baked Avocado Pears

Although avocado pears are a fruit and not a vegetable I think they are delicious if baked round the joint. Halve the pears, remove the stones, sprinkle with lemon juice then season and brush with plenty of oil. Do not skin. Put round the joint and cook for approximately 30 minutes, until softened. They are particularly good with pork. If you want a meatless hot dish then try the following curry stuffed pears.

Avocado Pears Indienne

2 large ripe avocado pears; lemon juice; seasoning; 1$\frac{1}{2}$ tablespoons olive oil; 1 onion; 1 teaspoon curry powder; 4–6 oz. (1–1$\frac{1}{2}$C tightly packed) soft cream cheese; 3 oz. (1C) soft breadcrumbs; 2 tablespoons grated Parmesan cheese.
Halve the avocado pears, remove the stones. Sprinkle with lemon juice and seasoning. Brush with a little oil. Heat the remainder of the oil and fry the very finely chopped or grated onion until soft. Add the curry powder and mix well. Blend in the cream cheese and half the crumbs. Press into the centre of the pears, top with the rest of the crumbs and grated cheese. Bake for about 30 minutes in the centre of a moderate oven, 350–375°F, Gas Mark 4–5. *Serves 4.*

French Fried Fennel

1 fennel root; 2 oz. ($\frac{1}{2}$C) flour; 1 egg; 6 tablespoons milk; seasoning. *For frying:* oil or fat. Wash the fennel and slice the white root. Save the green leaves for garnish. Separate

French fried fennel

into rings. Mix the flour, egg and milk into a smooth batter. Season well. Dip the rings of fennel into the batter. Heat the oil or fat (deep oil or fat is better for frying this particular dish). Put in the coated rings and fry for 2–3 minutes only. This gives a cooked crisp outside without losing the natural firmness of the vegetable. *Serves 4 as an accompaniment to a main course.*

Red Cabbage with Apples

1 red cabbage; 2 oz. ($\frac{1}{4}$C) margarine; 2 dessert apples; 1 small onion; seasoning; 12 tablespoons (1C) red wine; little grated nutmeg. Shred the cabbage finely. Melt the margarine in a large pan, add the cabbage, the peeled chopped apples and onion and seasoning. Heat for a few minutes, turning the cabbage once or twice. Add the wine and nutmeg. Cover the pan tightly and cook steadily until the liquid has just evaporated and the cabbage is tender. This takes about 35 minutes. Naturally in this particular recipe the cab-

bage is softer than when using the Blue Print method on page 182. This is excellent with pork or goose. *Serves 4–6.*

Storing and Freezing　*Ratatouille stores well for several days, and freezes perfectly. The other vegetable dishes are better eaten fresh, but can be stored for 1–2 days or can be frozen, but the texture of the peppers and aubergines and stuffed avocado pears is not improved by freezing.*
To use any left over　*Ratatouille seems just as good when any left is reheated as when it is first made.*

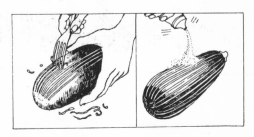

There is no great point in cooking more vegetables than you need for they *should* be freshly cooked for each meal. However, the following dishes provide interesting ways to use small amounts of left over vegetables.

Cabbage and Tomato Casserole

1 onion; 2 oz. ($\frac{1}{4}$C) margarine; 1 small apple; 4 large tomatoes; $\frac{1}{4}$ pint ($\frac{2}{3}$C) water; seasoning; about $\frac{1}{2}$ a small cooked cabbage; 3–4 oz. (1C) grated Cheddar cheese; 2 oz. (1C) crisp breadcrumbs.

Grate the onion. Toss in the hot margarine with the peeled and grated apple and skinned tomatoes. Add the water and seasoning. Simmer until a thick purée. Add the cooked shredded cabbage. Heat for a few minutes only. Put into a hot heat-proof dish. Top with the cheese and crumbs. Brown under the grill. *Serves 4.*

To vary Cauliflower, thickly sliced potatoes, etc. may be used in place of cabbage.

Bubble and Squeak

Mix equal quantities of cooked cabbage and mashed potatoes. Season well, add 1–2 tablespoons milk to make a fairly soft consistency. Heat 1–2 oz. ($\frac{1}{8}$–$\frac{1}{4}$C) fat in a large frying pan. Put in the vegetable mixture. Cook *steadily* until golden brown on the under side and piping hot. Fold like an omelette and serve at once.

Camp Fire Corn

3–4 rashers fairly fat bacon; about 8 oz. (1C) left over boiled or canned sweet corn; 4 eggs; seasoning; little butter or margarine; 4 slices bread or toast. *To garnish:* parsley or green pepper.

Remove the rinds from the bacon, chop in small pieces. Heat in a frying pan until crisp. Lower the heat, add the corn and stir the bacon and corn for a few minutes. Beat the eggs with seasoning. Pour into the pan. Scramble lightly. Serve on the buttered bread or toast and top with parsley or rings of green pepper. *Serves 4.*

Marrow Bake

Approximately 8 oz. cooked marrow; 1 oz. margarine; 1 tablespoon chopped chives or spring onion; 2 eggs; $\frac{1}{4}$. pint ($\frac{2}{3}$C) milk; seasoning; little grated nutmeg.

Mash the marrow with the softened margarine and chives or onion. Add the beaten eggs and warm milk. Season well. Pour into a pie dish and top with grated nutmeg. Bake in the centre of a very moderate oven, 325–350°F, Gas Mark 3–4, for 40 minutes, until just set. This is excellent with hot toast as a light supper dish.

Cabbage and tomato casserole

Ready Cooked Vegetables

Quick Ways to Use Left Over Vegetables

Many of the recipes in this section can be adapted to make good use of left over vegetables.

The Corn Risotto described on page 193 could be made with left over peas and corn, or with any other left over vegetables, such as beans, courgettes and aubergines.

Left over mashed potato can be made into Potatoes Dauphine or Potatoes Almondine, page 189.

Heat cooked diced vegetables in a little butter, add to well seasoned eggs and make Vegetable Scramble or a Vegetable Omelette. Blend cooked vegetables with a sauce and use as a filling for pancakes or omelettes.

Vegetable Pudding Make a pancake batter with 4 oz. (1C) plain flour, pinch salt, 1 egg and $\frac{1}{2}$ pint (1$\frac{1}{3}$C) milk. Heat 2 oz. ($\frac{1}{4}$C) margarine or fat in a Yorkshire pudding tin. Add left over vegetables, turn in the hot fat, then heat for a few minutes. Pour the batter over the hot vegetables. Bake for approximately 30 minutes above the centre of a hot oven. Lift out of the tin, top with freshly chopped herbs and/or grated cheese and serve. *This makes an excellent supper dish for 4.*

Storing and Freezing *Left over vegetables spoil quickly, so store in the refrigerator. Use as soon as possible. You can freeze left over vegetables but use the quickest method of reheating after you remove them from the freezer, otherwise they have little, if any, flavour.*

HORS D'OEUVRES, SAVOURIES & SAUCES

In this part of Perfect Cooking you will find the first course of a meal, the hors d'oeuvre, or 'meal starters', as they are often called today. This course is a very important one, for it can turn an every day meal into something special. It is a leisurely course, where everyone should relax, ready to enjoy their meal.

Although an hors d'oeuvre generally consists of a light cold or hot dish, and could be fruit juice only, the choice is important. If the hors d'oeuvre is too solid and·highly flavoured then it spoils one's appetite for the main course to ·follow. The hors d'oeuvre, like the dessert, should complement the main course. It should have a refreshing flavour, so that if your family and guests are not particularly hungry, the piquant flavour of this 'beginning to the meal' whets their appetites. In order to enjoy the first course, time the cooking carefully for your main dish, so you can linger over the start of a pleasant meal. Almost any kind of food could be served as an hors d'oeuvre and pages 202–211 give a very varied selection, together with ideas of *just when* that particular kind of meal starter would be ideal.

A savoury after, or instead of, the dessert is a very British taste. If you want a very special meal then add this course. If your family are not particularly fond of puddings and desserts then serve something savoury at the end of the meal. The recipes on pages 212–215 give you many suggestions. These savouries are ideal also to serve for light luncheon or supper dishes, particularly when you plan a 'meal on a tray'. They are easy to eat, quick to prepare and most important of all, are highly nutritious.

Can you make perfect sauces? All too often when I pose this question I am told that it is 'so difficult to make a smooth sauce'. That is not true. It takes both time and patience to achieve perfection in sauce making but it is *not* difficult. It is important to appreciate *why* sauces curdle or *why* they become lumpy and these points are dealt with in the last section of this part. It is also important to know *how* to put right an error when making a sauce, whether it is to correct seasoning, texture or consistency.

Interesting and well flavoured sauces can turn a simple dish into a superb one and mastering the art of sauce making is an important part of Perfect Cooking.

Fruit Plus

When you plan a really substantial main course and a rather creamy dessert, choose a 'fruity' hors d'oeuvre. The refreshing flavour will give everyone an appetite to appreciate the meat or fish course that follows.

Certain fruits and fruit juices are served so frequently that they could be dull. Melon, grapefruit, orange juice, all of these are very pleasant, but there are many occasions when they would be improved with a 'new look'.

Blue Print

Serving Fruit for an Hors d'Oeuvre

Never over-sweeten the fruit or fruit juice. If you do it makes it rather like a dessert.

Present it in an interesting way, i.e. melon should be cut as the sketches opposite, fruit juices should be served in frosted glasses and topped with mint leaves, which both smell and look attractive.

Try to have an unusual mixture of flavours when serving fruit, as the recipes on these pages.

● **AVOID** *Making your fruit hors d'oeuvre too sweet.*
● **TO RECTIFY** *Sprinkle a little lemon juice or dry sherry over the fruit if you have added too much sugar.*
● **SHORT CUT** *Use canned grapefruit segments and mix the liquid from the can with a little sherry or lemon juice.*
● **TO SLIMMERS** *An ideal hors d'oeuvre on most diets.*

Melon balls with lemon sauce

Melon

Throughout most of the year one is likely to be able to purchase some kind of melon. The most usual are Honeydew, Charentais, Cantaloupe and Ogen (the small melons that are generally served halved). The pink fleshed water melon is less suitable for a first course, except in the melon cocktail (page 207).

To buy melon, feel it and it should appear heavy for its size. Press gently but firmly and the melon should 'give' at either end, so indicating it is ripe.

Prepare by slicing or halving and removing the seeds. The usual accompaniments are sugar and ground ginger.

Although melons may not be kept in the refrigerator they are improved by being chilled before serving or serving on a bed of crushed ice.

Melon Balls with Lemon Sauce

1 melon (see below); 2 lemons; little water; 1–2 tablespoons sugar. *To garnish:* sprigs of mint; lemon twists.

Buy a ripe Honeydew, Charentais or Cantaloupe melon, or a rather large Ogen melon. Halve the melon, remove the seeds. Take a vegetable scoop and make balls of the flesh, see Sketch 4. Chill these. The rather untidy pieces of melon at the bottom of the fruit can be used for the sauce. Grate enough rind from the lemons to give about 2 teaspoons. Squeeze the juice, measure and add enough water to give ¼ pint (⅔C). Simmer the rind with the liquid and sugar for about 5 minutes. Pour over the odd pieces of melon, then sieve or emulsify in the liquidiser. Taste and add more sugar if wished. This is not really necessary, for the sauce should be both thick and fairly sharp. Spoon into the bottom of 4–6 glasses and top with the melon balls. Garnish with mint and lemon. *Serves 4–6.*

Melon and Crème de Menthe

Sprinkle balls of melon or a slice of melon with a little crème de menthe.

Melon and Pineapple

Freeze canned pineapple juice until lightly frozen; do not allow it to become too hard. Put at the bottom of glasses and top with diced melon or melon balls.

Melon and Parma Ham

Put slices of melon, this time with the skin removed, on plates with curls of Parma ham. Garnish with a slice of lemon and serve with paprika or cayenne pepper.

Grapefruit

This is one of the most refreshing hors d'oeuvre and particularly good if you are slimming. Grapefruit, like melon, should feel heavy for its size. Do not buy very light coloured fruit unless you can store them for a while, for they are inclined to be under-ripe and lacking in sweetness and flavour. Halve the grapefruit and separate the segments, discard the pith and seeds. Serve with sugar and decorated with cherries.

Jamaican Grapefruit

Halve the fruit, remove the segments, put into a basin. Blend with a little brown sugar and rum. Pile back into the grapefruit case, chill and serve very cold, or put back into the case, top with a little brown sugar and butter and heat under the grill.

Grapefruit and Avocado Pear

2 grapefruit; 2 avocado pears; 2 tablespoons oil; good pinch dry mustard; pinch salt; shake pepper; pinch sugar; 1 tablespoon white vinegar; lettuce.
Cut the peel away from the grapefruit, then cut into segments. Make the dressing before halving the avocado pears. Blend the oil with the seasonings and sugar, then the vinegar (this can be wine or malt). Halve the avocado pears, remove the stones and skin. Cut into slices. Put in the dressing, so they do not discolour. Arrange small lettuce leaves on 4 or 6 individual plates. Top with the sliced grapefruit and avocado pears. *Serves 4–6.*

Avocado Vinaigrette

2 ripe avocado pears (see method); lemon juice; dressing as above, but you need to make a little more. *To garnish:* lettuce.
To choose avocado pears, feel gently, not just at the tip but all over the fruit; it should yield to the gentlest pressure.
  Halve the pears, remove the stones, sprinkle lightly with lemon juice if there is even a slight delay in serving, as the fruit discolours badly. Fill the 'holes' where the stones were with the dressing. Garnish with lettuce leaves. *Serves 4.*

A New Look at Fruit

The recipes pictured and described on this page use fruits in unusual ways. The dishes are equally as suitable for an informal party as for an hors d'oeuvre. If serving as an hors d'oeuvre, pass each dish round the table with crisp biscuits, as shown in the picture, to counteract the rather rich flavour of the fillings.

Avocado Cream Dip

2 avocado pears; 2 tablespoons lemon juice; 3 tablespoons mayonnaise; 1 very small onion or 2–3 spring onions; 2 tablespoons soured cream; 2 tablespoons thick cream; seasoning. *To garnish:* shelled prawns or salted peanuts.
Halve the pears, remove the stones. Spoon the pulp into a basin; be careful not to break the skins, as these will be used for holding the filling. Add the lemon juice at once, so the pulp does not have an opportunity to discolour. Mash thoroughly, then blend in all the other ingredients; the onion or onions should be chopped very finely. Return the mixture to the 4 halved shells and top with prawns or nuts. *Serves 4, or 8–12 if part of a mixed hors d'oeuvre.*
To vary Add 2–3 oz. chopped prawns to the mixture.
Use cream cheese instead of thick cream and add finely chopped nuts to the mixture.

Kipper and Grapefruit Dip

2 rashers lean bacon; 1 small onion; 2 fairly large grapefruit; 12 oz. (1½C) cottage cheese; 6 tablespoons thick cream; 2 tablespoons chopped parsley; 1 can kipper fillets; seasoning.
Fry or grill the bacon until crisp, leave two larger pieces for garnish, then chop finely.

Chop or grate the onion. Remove the tops from the grapefruit and scoop out all the pulp. Press this through a sieve to extract the juice. Mix the juice with the cottage cheese, the chopped bacon and onion and the cream. Blend thoroughly, then add the parsley and the well drained flaked kipper fillets. Keep two pieces of kipper for garnish. Season the mixture very well, then pile back into the grapefruit cases. Garnish with the pieces of bacon and kipper. *Serves 4, or 8–12 if part of a mixed hors d'oeuvre.*

Melon and Pineapple Dip

1 Charentais or large Ogen melon; 1 lb. (2C tightly packed) cream cheese; 5 oz. (⅔C) natural yoghourt; 1 tablespoon concentrated tomato purée; 1 can pineapple pieces; 2 tablespoons chopped parsley; seasoning.
Cut the top off the melon, scoop the flesh from this slice. Remove the seeds then scoop out all the pulp; use a dessertspoon or a vegetable scoop, as shown in Sketch 4 opposite. If using a scoop, save a few melon balls for garnish. Blend the cream cheese, yoghourt and tomato purée until smooth. Stir in the melon pulp, well drained pineapple pieces and parsley. Mix thoroughly, add a little pineapple syrup from the can if the mixture is too stiff. Season well. Spoon back into the melon case and top with melon balls. *Serves 8, or 12–16 if part of a mixed hors d'oeuvre.*

Storing and Freezing *Grapefruit and melon store well for some time, although melons ripen quickly in hot weather. Put into a refrigerator for a short time before serving. Whole melons and whole grapefruit do not freeze well, but segments of grapefruit or melon balls, packed in sugar and water syrup, freeze very well for a limited time. Avocado pears also ripen quickly, so use soon after purchase. They can be kept for a few days in a refrigerator and can be frozen whole. Use as soon as they have defrosted. The avocado pear must be ripe when frozen.*
To use any left over *Left over fruit can be added to salads.*

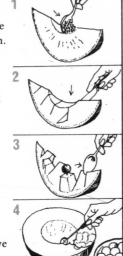

1. Cut a large melon into slices, remove the seeds, but not the skin.
2. Cut the slice into sections.
3. Pull the sections alternately to left and right so breaking the straight line of the slice. Garnish with a slice of lemon, or a grape or cherry on a cocktail stick.
4. To make melon balls. Insert the vegetable scoop into the melon, turn to give a ball.

Avocado dip, Kipper and grapefruit dip and Melon and pineapple dip

Practically every type of salad can be served as an hors d'oeuvre. The simplest salad can be delicious if the food is fresh and presented well.

Firm fresh tomatoes, sliced and topped with a little oil and vinegar and chopped onion, chives and parsley is an excellent beginning to the meal. Hard boiled eggs and tomatoes make a very satisfying as well as attractive salad. Slice firm tomatoes, as shown in the picture, season, and insert slices of hard boiled egg in between each cut. Serve on a bed of lettuce with mayonnaise to taste.

Stuffed hard boiled eggs (see also page 82) are another type of salad that can be prepared and served very easily.

Blue Print

Serving Salad for an Hors d'Oeuvre

Salads can be surprisingly filling and substantial, so let the salad you serve at the beginning of a meal be fairly light textured or allow small portions only. It should be well seasoned and flavoured to stimulate the palate.

A salad can be as varied or as simple as you like, but should not repeat the ingredients that follow in the main course. For example, if you are serving meat, fish or poultry with a tomato sauce, you should avoid adding tomatoes to the salad you present as the first course. You will find many salads suitable for a meal starter on pages 108–112. Some of the salads on these pages are based on pasta and these would be unusual and ideal if the main course was rather light, for they are very sustaining.

● **AVOID** *Too substantial salads, they should be light and interesting in both colour and texture.*

● **TO SLIMMERS** *Choose the low calorie ingredients, tomatoes, cucumber (fresh or pickled), green salad etc. where possible.*

Storing and Freezing *These salads are better eaten fresh. They can be covered and stored for a short time in the refrigerator.*

To use any left over *Serve in smaller dishes and with a fresh garnish.*

Smoked Salmon and Egg Salad

4 eggs; little mayonnaise; about 4 oz. very thinly cut smoked salmon; 1 lemon; cayenne pepper; seasoning; lettuce. *To garnish:* watercress; tomatoes.

Hard boil the eggs, remove from the boiling water, plunge into cold water and crack the shells. Remove the shells while the eggs are still warm, as it is easier to mash the yolks. Halve the eggs lengthways. Remove the yolks from the whites very carefully, put the yolks into a basin and mix thoroughly with enough mayonnaise to make a soft creamy consistency. Chop the smoked salmon finely and blend with a squeeze lemon juice and a shake cayenne pepper. Put into the white cases. Season the egg yolk mixture and put into a piping bag with a ¼-inch rose. Pipe the mixture on top of the smoked salmon and arrange on a bed of lettuce. Garnish with watercress and small wedges of tomato. *Serves 4, or 8 if part of a mixed hors d'oeuvre.*

Italian Salad

5 oz. pasta, preferably spiral shaped; seasoning; 5 oz. can Salata; 5 oz. can crushed pineapple; 1 oz. currants; 2 tablespoons olive oil; 1 tablespoon white wine vinegar.

Cook the pasta in well seasoned boiling water for about 8 minutes or until tender. Drain, rinse in cold water and drain again. Add the Salata, pineapple plus the juice from the can, and the currants. Stir in the oil, vinegar and a generous amount of seasoning. Pile into a dish. *Serves 6, or 12 if part of a mixed hors d'oeuvre.*

Pasta Slaw

3 oz. spaghetti rings; seasoning; ½ small white cabbage; 1 small green pepper; 1 medium-sized carrot. *For the dressing:* 4 tablespoons mayonnaise; 1 tablespoon soured cream; 1 tablespoon white or brown malt vinegar; 2 teaspoons sugar.

Cook the pasta in well seasoned boiling water for 10–12 minutes until tender. Drain, rinse in cold water and drain again. Shred the cabbage very finely, dice the green pepper (discard the core and seeds), grate the carrot coarsely. Mix the ingredients for the dressing together, add the pasta, then the remainder of the prepared ingredients. Chill well before serving. *Serves 6, or 12 if part of a mixed hors d'oeuvre.*

Summer Salad

4 oz. short cut macaroni; seasoning; 1 medium-sized can tuna; 1 oz. raisins; 1 oz. walnuts; 1 dessert apple; 2 sticks celery; 3 tablespoons mayonnaise; lettuce; chopped chives; lemon juice. *To garnish:* celery leaves.

Cook the macaroni in well seasoned boiling water for 8 minutes. Drain, rinse in cold water and drain again. Add the flaked fish, raisins, chopped nuts, cored and sliced, but not peeled, apple (reserve a few slices for garnish), chopped celery and mayonnaise. Mix thoroughly and season well. Line a dish with lettuce and pile the salad on top. Sprinkle with chopped chives and garnish with the reserved apple slices, dipped in lemon juice, and celery leaves. *Serves 4, or 8 if part of a mixed hors d'oeuvre.*

Garden Salad

4 oz. short cut macaroni; seasoning; 2 tablespoons olive oil; 1 tablespoon white or brown malt vinegar; pinch sugar; pinch dry mustard; 3–4 spring onions; 2 sticks celery; 1 small green pepper; 4 oz. Gruyère or processed cheese; 3 tablespoons mayonnaise. *To garnish:* 2–3 tomatoes.

Cook the macaroni in well seasoned boiling water for 8 minutes. Drain, rinse in cold water and drain again. Blend the oil, vinegar, sugar and mustard. Toss the macaroni in this. Add the chopped onions and celery, diced pepper (discard the core and seeds) and diced cheese. Mix with mayonnaise, season well and pile into a dish. Garnish with wedges of tomato. *Serves 4, or 8 if part of a mixed hors d'oeuvre.*

Maryland Salad

2 oz. shell pasta; seasoning; 3 oz. ($\frac{3}{4}$C) sweet corn; 1 small red pepper; 2–3 tablespoons mayonnaise; a little onion salt.

Cook the pasta in well seasoned boiling water for just about 10 minutes, drain, rinse in cold water, then drain again. Blend with the sweet corn, diced red pepper (discard the core and seeds), mayonnaise and seasoning. Allow to cool thoroughly then serve in a flat dish. *Serves 4 or 8 if part of a mixed hors d'oeuvre.*

To vary Add peas or mixed vegetables in place of the sweet corn. Add chopped ham.

Egg and tomato salad

Smoked salmon and egg salad

Italian salad, Summer salad, Pasta slaw and Garden salad

A selection of the dishes in this section would make a splendid hors d'oeuvre, but on this page are a wide variety of simple ingredients to give an ambitious looking tray from which to choose.

Select a mixed hors d'oeuvre if you have plenty of time to prepare the dishes and if your main course is fairly light. In the hors d'oeuvre tray opposite there is a good balance between vegetables and fish with a little meat. I doubt whether many people would have quite as large a selection as this so you will also find a choice of six ingredients with ideas to make them more exciting for special occasions and a very simple hors d'oeuvre consisting of just four dishes.

Blue Print

Perfect Mixed Hors d'Oeuvre

Plan a good mixture of different colours and textures.
Be adventurous about your mixture of ingredients, never mind adding fruit to

Mixed Hors D'Oeuvre

the vegetables, for example, balls of melon, slices of grapefruit and fresh orange.
keep a good balance between the amount of vegetables, fish and meat.
If you have separate hors d'oeuvre trays then serve each ingredient or prepared dish in an individual container, but if you do not possess these then I would arrange the basic mixed hors d'oeuvre on plates. Serve the ingredients really chilled, but if you add one hot dish, such as hot filled pancakes, fish cakes, hot prawns in sauce or browned butter, this adds to the interest of the meal starter.

● **AVOID** *Having all food in mayonnaise. It makes the first course too substantial and rich. Leave some vegetables, meat, or fish quite plain if you have others in a dressing. It is, however, usual to serve hors d'oeuvre ingredients in their dressings and not add these at the table.*

● **TO RECTIFY** *If your hors d'oeuvre selection seems rather rich then have bowls of lettuce, endive and watercress to counteract this.*
● **SHORT CUTS** *Use some of the ready prepared ingredients in addition to those given, i.e. pickled gherkins, walnuts, onions, canned anchovy fillets, flaked canned tuna or salmon. Use diced cooked vegetables, by themselves, or put into a dressing; this can be mayonnaise or oil and vinegar.*

● **TO SLIMMERS** *Concentrate on the plain vegetables, meat like salami and avoid the ingredients in sauces.*

Storing and Freezing *It is essential that a good hors d'oeuvre looks fresh, so prepare at the last minute. Keep the dishes covered and store in the refrigerator. The frosted cocktails are excellent for storing in the freezing compartment of a refrigerator or home freezer. Bring out some time before required, so the mixture is not too hard.*
To use any left over *Add any left over hors d'oeuvre to mixed salads. Return the cocktails to the freezer.*

Frosted tomato cocktail

An Hors d'Oeuvre Tray

Sliced celery—this could be blended with mayonnaise and chopped hard boiled eggs.

Pickled red cabbage.

Pickled herrings with onion rings.

Asparagus—cooked, tossed in seasoned oil and vinegar and topped with strips of red pepper.

Cottage cheese—mixed with chives. This could be blended also with diced ham and cooked vegetables for a most colourful dish.

Liver sausage—sliced.

Sweet corn—cooked or canned, with stuffed olives. This could be blended with chopped chicory, red and green peppers and a little well seasoned oil and vinegar.

Salami—sliced.

Coleslaw—this particular version was made with shredded cabbage and grated carrot, blended with well seasoned mayonnaise and a little lemon juice (or vinegar) to give a softer, more piquant sauce.

Sliced well seasoned tomato—topped with parsley (oil, vinegar and chopped chives could be added).

Flowerets of *partially* cooked cauliflower—topped with sieved egg yolk. The vegetable could be tossed in mayonnaise (the chopped egg white could be mixed with the peeled prawns—see below).

Halved pickled cucumbers.

Canned sardines on lettuce.

Rolls of boiled bacon or ham—these can be rolled round mixed vegetables in mayonnaise.

Peeled prawns in tomato mayonnaise (page 220).

Take Six Hors d'Oeuvre

1. Serve a variety of sliced salami and garlic sausage. Garnish with celery leaves.
Special occasion suggestion Dice and serve in walnut mustard sauce, i.e. mix mayonnaise with French mustard and chopped walnuts.
2. Canned artichoke hearts, tossed in well seasoned oil and vinegar.
Special occasion suggestion: Top the artichokes with cones of smoked salmon, wrapped round shelled prawns.
3. **Cheese and carrot salad** Mix equal quantities of coarsely grated cheese and carrot.
Special occasion suggestion Blend with shredded white cabbage, raisins, mayonnaise and chopped almonds.
4. **Potato and pepper salad** Toss diced cooked new potatoes, diced celery and red pepper (discard core and seeds) in well seasoned oil and vinegar or mayonnaise.
Special occasion suggestion Add diced gherkins, capers and chopped spring onions.
5. **Beetroot salad** Cut cooked beetroot into neat strips, blend with finely chopped onion, oil, vinegar and seasoning. Top with onion rings.
Special occasion suggestion Add chopped dessert apple and a very little diced cooked duck or chicken.
6. **Herring and onion salad** Cut Bismarck, cooked or rollmop herrings into neat pieces. Mix with diced apples, chopped onion and blend with natural yoghourt or soured cream. Garnish with sliced apple (dipped in lemon juice) and watercress.
Special occasion suggestion Add a small quantity of white wine to the yoghourt or soured cream, or use mayonnaise and wine blended together. Add diced pickled cucumber.

Four Simple Hors d'Oeuvre

Bean and salami salad Rub the salad bowl with a cut clove of garlic. Mix diced salami and cooked broad beans together. Toss in oil and vinegar. Season well.
To vary Diced Frankfurters, ham or garlic sausage may be used instead.
Orange herring salad Blend segments of fresh orange and soused or rollmop herrings together. Season well. Put on to a bed of lettuce.
To vary Use portions of smoked trout or smoked mackerel with orange or other fairly sharp fruit. Serve with horseradish cream.
Vegetable salad Niçoise Mix sliced or quartered tomatoes, tiny cooked whole or sliced new potatoes, diced cooked green beans and black olives. Toss in oil and vinegar and season well.
Mushroom rice salad Cook long grain rice in boiling salted water until just tender. Drain and toss in well seasoned oil and vinegar. Allow to cool then blend with strips of green pepper (discard the core and seeds), sliced raw button mushrooms and sultanas or raisins.

To vary Add chopped anchovy fillets. Add pine nuts or blanched almonds. Mix with cooked peas, flaked salmon and diced cucumber.

Frosted Tomato Cocktail

Although this cocktail can be served to everyone at the beginning of a meal, without the choice of an alternative, I occasionally have made it part of a mixed hors d'oeuvre, for it balances the rather rich flavour of foods in mayonnaise. In this case scoop out balls of the frosted mixture and serve on a bed of lettuce.

2 lb. ripe tomatoes; 4 tablespoons water; seasoning; good pinch sugar; little lemon juice; Worcestershire sauce to taste. *To garnish:* lettuce or mint.

Chop the tomatoes. Put into a saucepan with the water, seasoning and sugar. Heat for a few minutes only so you can extract the juice. Rub through a sieve, add lemon juice, Worcestershire sauce and any extra seasoning or flavouring required (celery salt, cayenne pepper and a few drops chilli sauce can be added). Put into the freezing tray and freeze lightly. Either spoon or scoop on to lettuce leaves and make part of a mixed hors d'oeuvre, or chop lightly (as the picture) and spoon into chilled glasses and top with mint leaves. *Serves 4–6, or 8–12 if part of a mixed hors d'oeuvre.*

To vary

Frosted melon cocktail The red fleshed water melon is ideal for this. Halve the melon, remove the seeds and scoop out the flesh. Mix with lemon juice, a little sugar, then taste. You may like to add seasoning to make it more piquant in flavour and/or a few drops chilli or Worcestershire sauce. Freeze and serve as the tomato cocktail above.

Four simple hors d'oeuvre

Fish Hors D'Oeuvre

Hors d'oeuvre, based upon fish, are an excellent choice. Fish is basically a light food and, as such, is ideal to start a meal.

Blue Print

Choosing Fish Hors d'Oeuvre

The fish dish may be cold or hot, but it should consist of a small portion only. Many fish dishes normally served for a main course could be offered as hors d'oeuvre, but allow half-sized portions. Some of the best fish dishes to choose are:
Fish cocktail, see below, and shell fish dishes.
Herrings, either rollmop or Bismarck with salad, or some of the canned savoury herring dishes.
Anchovy fillets, served with hard boiled egg.
Sole or other white fish, served in sauces or grilled or fried.
Light fish moulds, see below.

● **AVOID** *The rather substantial fish, such as turbot, unless used in a very small quantity as the Prawn and Turbot Salad.*
● **SHORT CUTS** *Use canned salmon, tuna or sardines in salads.*
● **TO SLIMMERS** *Choose fish salads with a low calorie dressing (see page 220).*

Haddock mousse

Prawn and turbot salad

For Family Occasions

Herring Salad

2 rollmop herrings; 1 dessert apple; 1 small onion; 2 medium-sized cooked potatoes; 2 hard boiled eggs; either ¼ pint (⅔C) soured cream or use thick cream plus 1 tablespoon lemon juice; seasoning. *To garnish:* lettuce; diced beetroot; chopped dill or parsley.
Cut the herrings into neat pieces. Mix with the diced apple (this need not be peeled), the grated or finely chopped onion, diced potatoes and eggs. Blend with the soured cream or thick cream and lemon juice. Season very well. Put into a plain basin or mould and leave in a cool place for several hours. Turn out on to a bed of lettuce, garnish with diced beetroot and dill or parsley. *Serves 4–6, or 8–12 if part of a mixed hors d'oeuvre.*

Potted Tuna Fish

Blend a medium-sized can well drained tuna fish with enough mayonnaise to make a smooth texture. Add 1–2 teaspoons chopped gherkins, 1–2 teaspoons chopped capers and 1 tablespoon chopped parsley. Season well. Form into a neat shape on a bed of lettuce and garnish with wedges of lemon and tomato. Serve with hot toast and butter. *Serves 4.*

For Special Occasions

Fish Cocktail

Although most fish can be used in a cocktail, it is usual to select shell fish. A mixture of different shell fish (cooked mussels, crab, prawns) makes a more interesting cocktail than if one variety only is used. Pay attention to the flavouring of the sauce, for this is very important; shred the lettuce finely, since the cocktail is eaten with a small spoon and fork and large pieces of lettuce can be difficult to manage.
For the sauce: 5–6 tablespoons mayonnaise; 1 tablespoon thick cream; ½ tablespoon lemon juice; 1 tablespoon fresh or canned tomato purée or use tomato ketchup if you like a slightly sweet flavour; few drops Worcestershire and/or Tabasco sauce and/or soy sauce; 1 tablespoon dry sherry (optional). Approximately 6 oz. (¾C) shelled prawns or other shell fish or a mixture of fish; ½ small lettuce. *To garnish:* 1 lemon; parsley; paprika.
Blend all the ingredients together for the sauce; this should pour easily, so if too thick add a little more cream. Blend most of the sauce with the fish, but save a little for the topping. Shred the lettuce finely, put into 4–5 glasses, top with the fish and sauce. Spoon the remaining sauce on top. Top with wedges of lemon, sprigs of parsley and paprika. Serve as cold as possible. It is ideal if the cocktail can be served on crushed ice. *Serves 4–5.*

Prawn and Turbot Salad

1 piece turbot, weighing about 6 oz.; seasoning; 3–4 oz. (generous ½C) shelled prawns; sauce as given in the Fish Cocktail or use mayonnaise with a little lemon juice; 1 small green pepper; 1 small red pepper; lettuce or watercress. *To garnish:* black olives.
Poach the fish in well seasoned water until just tender. Do not over-cook for the fish

continues to soften as it cools. Cut into small cubes, blend with the prawns. Prepare the sauce or mix mayonnaise with lemon juice. Add the diced flesh from the green and red peppers (discard the cores and seeds) and the fish. Put lettuce or watercress on to 4–6 individual dishes or use scallop shells, as shown in the picture. Spoon the fish mixture on top and garnish with olives. *Serves 4–6, or 8–12 if part of a mixed hors d'oeuvre.*

Haddock Mousse

1 lb. fresh haddock (weight without bones); ½ pint (1⅓C) water; seasoning; aspic jelly to set 1 pint (2⅔C); 2 eggs; 1 lemon; 1 tablespoon dry sherry; ½–1 teaspoon anchovy essence; ¼ pint (⅔C) thick cream. *To garnish:* sliced tomatoes; watercress or lettuce; sliced cucumber.

Poach the fish in the water with seasoning. Do not over-cook as the fish continues to become soft as it cools. Measure the liquid and make up to ½ pint (1⅓C) again. Soften then dissolve the aspic jelly in this. Separate the eggs. Beat the yolks in a basin with the grated rind and juice of the lemon, sherry and anchovy essence. Pour the warm aspic liquid over, whisking hard as you do so. Add the flaked fish and allow the mixture to cool and stiffen slightly. Whip the cream until it just holds its shape, do not over-whip, otherwise it is difficult to fold this into the jellied mixture. Fold the cream, then the stiffly whisked egg whites into the mixture. Put into a 7-inch deep plain mould or tin, brushed with a little oil. Leave to set, then turn out on to a serving dish and garnish with tomatoes, watercress or lettuce and twists of cucumber. *Serves 4–6, or 8–12 if part of a mixed hors d'oeuvre.*

To vary Omit the anchovy essence and add 1 tablespoon tomato purée to the aspic jelly.

Increase the amount of anchovy essence or add finely chopped anchovy fillets to the flaked white fish; be sparing with the salt if you do this.

Use flaked shell fish, simmer the shells in water to give a good flavour to the liquid. If using shell fish omit anchovy essence.

Smoked Fish Hors d'Oeuvre

Smoked fish makes a pleasing meal starter. There is no cooking or special preparation. Arrange on a plate with the garnishes suggested. Serve with thin brown bread and butter.

Smoked trout, mackerel, sprats and eel are served with horseradish cream, lemon wedges and cayenne pepper. Garnish with lettuce. Smoked salmon is served with lemon, cayenne pepper and garnished with lettuce. All these smoked fish can be served with lightly scrambled egg, which makes a pleasing contrast in colour and texture.

Allow 1 trout or *small* mackerel (or 2 fillets from a larger mackerel) per person or about 3–4 oz. smoked eel (a little less if boned fillet) or sprats or 2 oz. smoked salmon.

Hot Fish Hors D'Oeuvre

The dishes on this page are served hot; they would be a good choice when the main dish is a cold one.

For Family Occasions

Eskimo Risotto

4 oz. (½C) long grain rice; seasoning; about 8 oz. smoked haddock (weight without bones); ½ pint (1⅓C) milk; 2 eggs. *For the parsley sauce:* 1 oz. butter or margarine; 1 oz. flour; little extra milk if necessary and 1–2 tablespoons chopped parsley (or use a packet of parsley sauce mix); 2 large tomatoes; cayenne pepper.

Cook the rice in well seasoned water until tender, drain, unless all the water has been absorbed. Meanwhile poach the fish in the milk and hard boil the eggs. Lift the fish from the milk, save this for the sauce. To make the sauce, heat the butter or margarine in a pan, stir in the flour and cook over a low heat for 2–3 minutes. Gradually add the milk in which the haddock was cooked, bring to the boil and cook until thickened. Add a little extra milk, if necessary and the parsley (if using the parsley sauce mix follow the directions on the packet). Add the rice, flaked fish and most of the sliced egg to the sauce together with the diced tomatoes and a little seasoning, including cayenne pepper. Heat without boiling, then put into a hot dish and top with the remaining sliced egg. *Serves 4–6.*

For Special Occasions

Mussels in Mustard Brandy Sauce

5–6 pints mussels; 2 onions; 1–2 cloves garlic; 2 oz. (¼C) butter; ¼ pint (⅔C) water; seasoning; *bouquet garni*; scant 1 oz. flour; ¼ pint (⅔C) white wine; 2 teaspoons made mustard; 5 tablespoons brandy; ¼ pint (⅔C) thin or thick cream.

Eskimo risotto

Scrub the mussels well, remove any weeds on the side of the shells. Discard any mussels whose shells do not close when tapped sharply. Chop the onions and crush the garlic. Heat 1 oz. butter in a large pan, toss the onions and garlic in this, then add the mussels, water, seasoning and herbs. Heat gently until the mussels open, this takes only a short time, so watch the pan carefully. Strain, but keep all the liquid and onions. Remove the mussels from the shells. Heat the remaining butter in a pan, stir in the flour and cook gently for 2–3 minutes. Add the onions and liquid and the white wine. Bring slowly to the boil, stirring all the time. Stir in the mustard. Add the mussels, brandy and cream and heat *very gently without boiling.* Taste and add any extra seasoning required. Serve as soon as the mussels are hot. *This can serve up to 8 people, particularly if accompanied by crusty French bread.*

Salmon Mould

1 lb. uncooked salmon; 2 eggs; 1 oz. butter; 1 oz. flour; ½ pint (1⅓C) milk; 1 lemon; 2 tablespoons dry sherry; seasoning. *To garnish:* lemon; cucumber.

Put the fish through a fine mincer and pound until very soft and smooth. Add the eggs and beat well. Make a coating white sauce with the butter, flour and milk (see page 216). Add the finely grated lemon rind and juice and sherry to the sauce, when thickened, together with seasoning. Blend with the fish and eggs. Put into a well oiled mould, cover with oiled paper. Put into a steamer over hot, but not boiling, water and cook for 1 hour. Allow to stand for a few minutes then turn out on to a hot serving dish and garnish with lemon and rings of cucumber. Serve with tartare sauce (page 220). *Serves 4–6.*

To vary For a more economical dish use white fish plus a few drops anchovy essence.

Storing and Freezing *Cooked or uncooked fish must be stored in a refrigerator for the shortest time possible. Frozen fish can be chosen for most of the recipes. The Haddock Mousse and Salmon Mould freeze well. The salads and cocktails do not freeze, although defrosted shell fish is very satisfactory as the main ingredient.*

Fry the liver in the hot fat or butter until just tender. Hard boil the eggs. Mince or chop the liver with the onion. Add to the chopped hard boiled eggs and season well. Allow to cool, pile on to a dish and garnish with lemon and parsley. Serve with hot toast and butter. *Serves 4–5.*

Fried Garlic Sausage

Many garlic sausages can be served hot, particularly the Spanish Chorizo, and sliced black pudding makes an excellent hors d'oeuvre. It is important that the sausage is not dry so fry quickly.

Dip the slices of sausage into a very little flour and fry in hot fat for a few minutes. Serve garnished with tomatoes and lettuce.

For Special Occasions

Five Minute Pâté

8–10 oz. calves' liver; 2 oz. ($\frac{1}{4}$C) butter; seasoning; 2 tablespoons cream; 2 tablespoons sherry or brandy.

Cut the liver into small pieces. Heat the butter in a pan and fry the liver in this for several minutes only. Either mince or chop very finely while warm and blend with the other ingredients, or emulsify in the liquidiser with the seasoning, cream and sherry or brandy. Allow to cool and serve with hot toast and butter. *Serves 4–5.*

Note If the mixture seems too stiff for the liquidiser blades then add a very little extra hot liquid (cream, stock or brandy). If you add the liver gradually to the cream, etc. though it should emulsify easily.

To vary Add 1 crushed clove garlic to the liver when frying in the pan.

Add 1–2 gherkins to the mixture in the liquidiser.

Use chickens' livers instead. Pig's or lambs' liver could be used, but this needs slightly longer cooking.

Cover with a layer of melted butter to prevent it from drying.

Ham Mousse

Aspic jelly to set 1 pint (2$\frac{2}{3}$C); $\frac{1}{2}$ pint (1$\frac{1}{3}$C) chicken or ham stock; 2 eggs; 12 oz. lean ham; $\frac{1}{4}$ pint ($\frac{2}{3}$C) mayonnaise. *To garnish:* lemon; tomatoes; lettuce.

Soften and then dissolve the aspic jelly in the stock. Separate the eggs and beat the egg yolks for a few minutes. Add the warm aspic liquid, whisking hard as you do so. Cool, then add the minced or finely chopped ham and mayonnaise. Leave until the mixture stiffens slightly then fold in the whisked egg whites. Spoon into an oiled mould and allow to set. Turn out and garnish with wedges of lemon, tomato and lettuce. *Serves 4–6.*

To vary Add lightly whipped cream flavoured with sherry or lemon juice in place of mayonnaise.

Use tomato juice instead of stock in which to dissolve the aspic jelly.

Meat Hors D'Oeuvre

You will find that meat hors d'oeuvre are extremely popular, even when the main course consists of meat or poultry.

Blue Print

Choosing Meat Hors d'Oeuvre

With the very wide selection of garlic sausages, salami, etc. available, this can be a very simple course to prepare. Arrange the various kinds of salami (or choose all one kind) on a dish and garnish with lettuce and tomato. Serve with mustard or, to add a touch of originality, serve with Cumberland sauce (see page 119).

Parma or other smoked ham makes a luxurious meal starter. It can be served by itself or it blends well with melon, fresh figs, or dessert pears.

Undoubtedly pâté is popular with most people. Various recipes are to be found on page 126, but the recipe on this page is particularly quick and easy.

Small portions of some of the meat or chicken salads given on page 112 would also be very suitable. Modern food is often very informal and the slightly unusual version of sausage rolls would be a practical and inexpensive beginning to a meal.

Sausage twists and Sausage cheese savouries (above)

For Family Occasions

Sausage Twists

1 lb. small chipolata sausages. *Puff pastry made with:* 4 oz. (1C) plain flour; pinch salt; 4 oz. ($\frac{1}{2}$C) butter and water to mix (or buy 8 oz. frozen puff pastry). *To glaze:* little beaten egg.

Grill, fry or bake the sausages for about 6 minutes, until partially cooked. Allow to cool. Make the pastry and roll out until wafer thin. Cut into strips and roll round the sausages, as shown in the picture. Put on a baking tray. Brush with beaten egg. Bake for 15 minutes towards the top of a very hot oven, 450–475°F, Gas Mark 7–8. Reduce the heat after 7–8 minutes if necessary. Serve with mustard or one of the sauces below. *Serves 8 as an hors d'oeuvre.*

These sauces are all cold, but could be heated in the top of a double saucepan or basin over hot water.

Onion mustard sauce Blend $\frac{1}{4}$ pint ($\frac{2}{3}$C) mayonnaise with 2–3 tablespoons chopped spring onions (use the white part only) and 3–4 teaspoons French mustard or use half this quantity of made English mustard. Top with the chopped green stems of the onions.

Devilled tomato sauce Blend $\frac{1}{4}$ pint ($\frac{2}{3}$C) mayonnaise with 2 tablespoons tomato purée or ketchup and 2 tablespoons top of the milk or thin cream. Flavour with a few drops chilli and/or Worcestershire sauce. Top with parsley.

Pineapple sweet sour sauce Blend $\frac{1}{4}$ pint ($\frac{2}{3}$C) mayonnaise with 2–3 tablespoons syrup from a small can pineapple. Add 2–3 teaspoons vinegar, 1 teaspoon made mustard and the diced pineapple.

Chopped Liver

8–10 oz. calves' or chickens' liver; 2 oz. ($\frac{1}{4}$C) chicken fat or butter; 2 eggs; 1 small onion; seasoning. *To garnish:* lemon; parsley.

Many vegetables are served as an hors d'oeuvre, the most usual and appropriate being globe artichokes and asparagus. These vegetables can be served hot with melted butter or cold with a vinaigrette dressing. Many other vegetables are served as part of salads and these are described on pages 204–205.

Cheese is not often part of an hors d'oeuvre, but it is included in both the recipes pictured on this page. The cheese is used delicately so it does not make too substantial or too strongly flavoured a dish.

For Family Occasions

Vegetable Cheese Pie

2 oz. (¼C) butter or margarine; 4 large tomatoes; 2 onions; 2 oz. (½C) mushrooms; small can asparagus tips; seasoning; 12 oz. (1½C) mashed potatoes. *For the cheese sauce:* 1 oz. butter or margarine; 1 oz. flour; ½ pint (1⅓C) milk; 4 oz. (1C) grated Cheddar cheese. *To garnish:* 1–2 tomatoes.

Heat 1 oz. butter or margarine and fry the skinned chopped tomatoes, onions and mushrooms until softened. Mix with the drained asparagus tips and seasoning. Put into 4 individual dishes. Add the rest of the butter or margarine to the potatoes and season. Put into a piping bag with a ¼-inch rose pipe and pipe a border round the edge of the dishes. Make the cheese sauce as page 217. Spoon over the vegetables. Brown under the grill or in the oven and serve at once, garnished with sliced tomato. *Serves 4.*

To vary Use flaked cooked fish instead of the selection of vegetables.
Use one vegetable only instead of the selection in the recipe.
Use a béchamel sauce (see page 217) for the base rather than the white sauce given above.

Vegetable cheese pie

For Special Occasions

Cucumber Cheese Mould

1 lemon; ½ oz. powdered gelatine (enough to set 1 pint (2⅔C)); ½ pint (1⅓C) water; 1 large cucumber; ¼ pint (⅔C) mayonnaise; 8 oz. cream cheese; seasoning. *To garnish:* cucumber; watercress; lettuce; tomatoes.

Grate the rind from the lemon, use only the top 'zest'. Soften the gelatine in the lemon juice. Add the lemon rind to the water, heat and pour over the gelatine. Stir until the gelatine has dissolved. Strain, if wished, to remove the pieces of lemon rind. Allow to cool, but not set. Dice the cucumber finely, remove the peel if this is tough. Blend the cucumber with the mayonnaise and cream cheese. Gradually beat in the cool liquid gelatine mixture. Season well. Spoon into an oiled mould and allow to set. Turn out and garnish with cucumber, watercress, lettuce and sliced tomatoes. Serve with mayonnaise or tartare sauce (page 220). *Serves 6–8, or 12–16 if part of a mixed hors d'oeuvre.*

To vary Use a lemon flavoured jelly instead of powdered gelatine. This gives a slightly sweet flavour which is very pleasant. Add 2–3 tablespoons very finely chopped or grated onion to the gelatine liquid.

Mushroom Cocktail

4–6 oz. (1–1½C) button mushrooms; ¼ pint (⅔C) natural yoghourt; ½ tablespoon olive oil; 1 tablespoon lemon juice or white wine vinegar; 1 tablespoon chopped chives; 1 tablespoon chopped parsley; seasoning (optional); lettuce. *To garnish:* paprika.
Wash, dry and slice the mushrooms very thinly. Blend the yoghourt, oil, lemon juice or vinegar and herbs. Add seasoning if wished. Shred the lettuce very finely. Put into 4–6 glasses. Blend the mushrooms with the sauce. Spoon on top of the lettuce, garnish with paprika. *Serves 4–6.*

Cucumber cheese mould

Mainly Vegetable Hors D'Oeuvre

To vary Thin cream or mayonnaise may be used in place of yoghourt. The latter is rather thick, so blend with a little top of the milk.
Mix mushrooms and prawns in the recipe above.

Danish Cucumber Boats

1 medium-sized, but fairly thick, cucumber; 2 tablespoons oil; seasoning; 2 tablespoons lemon juice; 4 oz. smoked salmon; little horseradish cream; 3 eggs; 2 tablespoons thick cream; 1 oz. butter. *To garnish:* ½ red pepper; lettuce.
Remove the peel from the cucumber and slice lengthways. Cut into about 12 segments and remove the seeds, so giving small boat shapes. Chop the seeds and pieces removed very finely. Blend the oil, seasoning and lemon juice. Sprinkle the cucumber with this dressing and leave for about 20 minutes. Drain the cucumber. Fill each 'boat' with chopped smoked salmon, spread with a little horseradish cream. Season the beaten eggs, add the chopped cucumber and cream. Heat the butter in a saucepan. Scramble the eggs and spoon over the smoked salmon. Garnish with thin strips of red pepper and serve on a bed of lettuce. While the scrambled egg may be served cold, this is a very pleasant hors d'oeuvre with *cold* cucumber and salmon and *hot* egg topping. *Serves 4–6.*

Storing and Freezing *All these recipes should be served freshly cooked or freshly prepared.*

211

Toasted Savouries

There are many kinds of savouries that can be served at the end of a meal and on this, and the following pages, are some of the most interesting.

Blue Print

Choosing After Dinner Savouries

Cheese and other soufflés are ideal to end the meal – they *look* and *taste* exciting.

Egg, cheese, fish and other savoury mixtures may be served on toast or fried bread.

Small pastry shapes or cases made of choux pastry can be filled with a variety of fish, meat, vegetable or cheese mixtures.

Allow small portions only when you serve these savouries at the end of the meal; large slices of toast should be cut.

Toasted savouries
Toast the bread, remove the crusts and divide large slices of toast into two fingers, rounds or squares. Spread with butter or margarine then top with the other ingredients.

If keeping hot do not cover, otherwise the toast becomes soft. Put on a hot dish and keep in the oven with the heat turned very low.

Blue Print Recipe

Scotch Woodcock

4 large slices bread · 2 oz. ($\frac{1}{4}$C) butter · 6–8 eggs · seasoning · 2–3 tablespoons thick cream · 8 anchovy fillets · about 16–20 capers ·

To cook   Toast the bread, halve each slice if serving for an after dinner savoury and spread with half the butter. Heat the rest of the butter in a pan. Beat the eggs and seasoning with the cream. Scramble lightly, then spoon on top of the toast. Divide the anchovy fillets into thin strips. Arrange on top of the egg with the capers.
To serve   At once. *All recipes based on this serve 4 as a snack or 8 as a savoury.*

Canapés Brillat Savarin

Ingredients as Blue Print PLUS 2–3 oz. ($\frac{2}{3}$–1C) grated Gruyère cheese.
Mix the cheese with the eggs, and scramble as the Blue Print.

Asparagus Toasts

Ingredients as Blue Print PLUS cooked or canned asparagus and MINUS the anchovies and capers.
Chop the tender stalks of the asparagus, save the tips for garnish. Heat the stalks in the hot butter, add the beaten eggs and scramble as the Blue Print. Top with asparagus tips.

Devils on Horseback

2 large slices bread; $\frac{1}{2}$ oz. butter; 8 large cooked, but fairly firm prunes; 4 long or 8 short rashers streaky bacon.
Toast the bread, quarter each slice and spread with butter. Stone the prunes. Cut the rinds from the rashers of bacon, halve the long slices. Stretch the bacon as the sketch. Wrap round the prunes and secure with wooden cocktail sticks. Cook under a hot grill until the bacon is crisp and golden brown. Turn once or twice to ensure even cooking. Remove the cocktail sticks. Put on the toast and serve. *Serves 8.*
To vary   Fill the prunes with flaked almonds.

Fill the prunes with liver pâté.

Angels on Horseback   Use oysters instead of prunes. Season the oysters and sprinkle with lemon juice then wrap in the bacon and cook as above.

Sausage Cheese Savouries

Grill small sausages until just brown. Spread one side with French mustard and press a finger of Cheddar or Gruyère cheese against this. Wrap in halved or short rashers of bacon. Secure with wooden cocktail sticks. Grill as the Devils on Horseback above. Remove the cocktail sticks. Serve very hot. The savouries may be put on toast or fingers of fried bread if wished. (Illustrated on page 210).

To stretch bacon, hold one end of the halved rasher with your left hand, and 'stroke' the bacon with a knife to make it less rigid and longer.

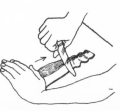

Crab and Tomato Toasts

4 small rounds bread; 2 oz. ($\frac{1}{4}$C) butter; $\frac{1}{2}$ lemon; small crab or can crabmeat; 2 tablespoons fresh or 1 tablespoon concentrated tomato purée; seasoning. *To garnish:* $\frac{1}{2}$–1 lemon; watercress or lettuce.

Toast the bread, spread with half the butter. Squeeze the juice from the $\frac{1}{2}$ lemon, blend with the flaked crabmeat, the tomato purée and the rest of the butter. Season well and spread on to the hot toast. Heat for a few minutes, then serve hot garnished with lemon and watercress or lettuce. *Serves 4.*

The best known of all cheese savouries is a Welsh Rarebit. The 'old fashioned' rarebit was of a sauce-like consistency, rather than the firmer texture we know today. I have given the softer mixture under Blue Print 2, for I find this particularly good when it is covering other ingredients, such as in the York Rarebit.

Blue Print Recipes

1. Welsh Rarebit

4 slices bread · 2 oz. ($\frac{1}{4}$C) butter or margarine · $\frac{1}{2}$ level tablespoon flour · $\frac{1}{4}$ teaspoon dry mustard · 3 tablespoons milk · 2 tablespoons ale (or use all milk) · 1 teaspoon Worcestershire sauce · seasoning · 6–8 oz. (1$\frac{1}{2}$–2C) grated cheese*. To garnish: parsley and/or sliced tomatoes.
* For a strongly flavoured mixture use mature Cheddar or Gruyère or add just a little Parmesan cheese. For a delicately flavoured mixture use mild Gouda or Edam cheese. Although it is not considered a cooking cheese, Double Gloucester makes a splendid rarebit, so does a golden Cheshire which cooks well.

To cook Toast the bread, halve each slice if required, spread with half the butter or margarine and keep hot, or toast while preparing the rarebit. Heat the rest of the butter or margarine in a pan, stir in the flour and mustard and cook for 2–3 minutes. Blend in the milk and ale, stir well as the mixture heats, as it is very thick. Add the sauce, seasoning and nearly all the cheese. Spread on the hot toast, sprinkle with the remainder of the cheese and brown under the grill.

To serve As hot as possible with mustard. Garnish with parsley and/or sliced tomatoes.
All recipes based on this give 8 small portions or 4 larger slices.
Note If wished increase the amount of Worcestershire sauce by up to 1 tablespoon, particularly if using all milk. The true rarebit should have a definite 'spicy' flavour.

2. Creamy Welsh Rarebit

To make Cream together 1 oz. butter, 1 egg or 2 egg yolks, seasoning, 1 teaspoon

made mustard and 6–8 oz. (1$\frac{1}{2}$–2C) grated Cheddar or other cheese. Gradually blend in 6 tablespoons milk or thin cream (or use partially ale and partially milk). Add a little Worcestershire sauce.

To cook Put this mixture into a pan, heat *gently* for 2–3 minutes only. Spread on toast as Blue Print 1, but keep well away from the edges, so it does not run off the toast when grilled. Grill until golden as Blue Print 1.

To serve Garnish and serve as Blue Print 1. If wished you can heat the mixture until a sauce-like consistency, put on to the toast and serve at once without placing under the grill.

York Rarebit

Ingredients as Blue Print 1 or 2 PLUS a little made mustard and 4 slices lean ham.
Toast the bread, spread with butter or margarine and a very little made mustard. Top with the ham, heat for 1 minute under the grill, then add the cheese mixture and brown.

Buck Rarebit

This is far too substantial for an after dinner savoury, although excellent for a light snack. It consists of a Welsh Rarebit topped with a poached egg, but if you wish to combine Welsh Rarebit and egg for a savoury use the following recipe.

Rarebit Scramble

Ingredients as Blue Print 2 PLUS 2–3 eggs, seasoning, 1 teaspoon chopped fresh herbs and an extra 1 oz. butter.
Prepare the toast and prepare, but do not cook, the rarebit mixture. Beat the eggs with the seasoning and herbs. Scramble lightly in the extra 1 oz. butter then spoon on to the hot toast. While the eggs are cooking heat the cheese mixture. Spoon over the scrambled eggs the moment they are set and grill quickly or serve without grilling.

Toasted Cheese

This has an entirely different texture from a Welsh Rarebit, but is very good. Slice Cheddar, Gruyère or other good cooking cheese. Put on to the hot buttered toast and heat until the cheese melts.

Grated cheese may be mixed with a good knob of well seasoned butter or margarine and spread on to the toast or blended with a little, very well seasoned, perfectly smooth creamed potato. It is then sprinkled with cheese and grilled until golden brown. This is both economical and interesting in texture.

Mushrooms on Toast

Choose small button mushrooms. Fry or grill with butter and put on to fingers of toast. Top with paprika and parsley.

Soft Roes on Toast

1 lb. soft herring roes; 2–3 oz. ($\frac{1}{4}$–$\frac{3}{8}$C) butter; seasoning; 3 tablespoons milk or thin cream (see Method 2); 3–4 large slices bread. *To garnish:* parsley; cayenne pepper or paprika.
Wash, dry and separate the roes.
Method 1 Heat 2 oz. ($\frac{1}{4}$C) of the butter and fry the roes in this until just tender, season well.
Method 2 (You need only 2 oz. ($\frac{1}{4}$C) butter in all for this method.) Put 1 oz. of the butter into a pan with the milk or cream. Add the roes and seasoning and simmer gently until nearly tender, then lift the lid so the liquid evaporates.

Toast the bread, spread with the remaining butter. Top with the roes and garnish with parsley and cayenne or paprika. *Serves 3–4 as a snack or 6–8 as an after dinner savoury.*

Storing and Freezing *These savouries must be eaten when fresh. Welsh Rarebit mixture stores well for 1–2 weeks in a covered container in the refrigerator. It could be frozen but dries out if kept for too long.*

Toasted cheese

Pastry Savouries

The savouries on this page are served in a pastry case. Short crust pastry can be used but the very crisp, faintly cheese-flavoured pastry seems particularly suitable for the ingredients used in the fillings.

Blue Print Recipe

Anchovy Boats

For the pastry: 6 oz. (1½C) plain flour · seasoning · pinch dry mustard · 3 oz. (⅜C) butter · 2 tablespoons grated Parmesan cheese · 1 egg yolk · little water to mix · For the filling: can anchovy fillets · 3 eggs · 2 tablespoons thick cream · pepper ·

To make Sieve the flour, seasoning and mustard. Rub in the butter, add the cheese, the egg yolk and water to mix. Roll out the pastry thinly and line 12 boat-shaped tins (or use round patty tins). See the sketches on the easiest way to line boat tins with pastry. Chop the anchovy fillets and put into the pastry cases. Beat the eggs and cream, add a good shake of pepper. Salt is unnecessary as the anchovies give this flavouring. Spoon the egg mixture over the anchovies.

To cook Bake towards the top of a moderately hot to hot oven, 400–425°F, Gas Mark 6–7, for 12–15 minutes.

To serve Hot. *All recipes based on this make 12 boats.*

AVOID *Too thick pastry, it should be thin and light in texture. The savouries must be elegant to look at too, so plan interesting garnishes to contrast in colour with the fillings.*

Storing and Freezing *Make the pastry cases, store in a tin and reheat before filling. They can be frozen if preferred. The fillings on this page are better if freshly made.*

To use any left over *The fillings are inclined to soften the pastry, so use up as soon as possible.*

Caviare Boats

Make the boats as the Blue Print. Prick well, bake 'blind' until crisp and golden brown. Allow to cool. Blend a small jar of caviare (the Danish variety is comparatively inexpensive) with the finely chopped whites 2 hard boiled eggs, 2 tablespoons thick cream and pepper. Flavour with a little lemon juice. Put into the pastry cases. Top with sieved or chopped hard boiled egg yolks.

Sardine and Cheese Boats

Make the boats as the Blue Print. Prick well, bake 'blind' until pale golden. Mash sardines with lemon juice and seasoning to taste. Put into the pastry cases. Top with grated Gruyère, Cheddar or Parmesan cheese. Return to the oven for a few minutes to melt the cheese. Garnish with tomato.

Devilled Tuna Boats

Make the boats as the Blue Print. Bake 'blind' until the pastry has just set, do not over-cook. Meanwhile open a medium-sized can of tuna, drain away the liquid. Flake then pound the fish until very smooth with 1 level tablespoon chutney, 1 teaspoon curry powder and 1 egg. Season well. Spoon the mixture into the pastry cases and return to the oven for about 6–8 minutes. Garnish with prawns and strips of red pepper or small celery leaves. Serve hot.

To vary

Devilled Ham Mince or chop about 4 oz lean ham, mix with 2 tablespoons thick cream, then add the chutney, curry powder, egg and seasoning as the recipe above and heat in the half cooked pastry cases. Garnish with sliced stuffed olives.

Crab and Tomato Tarts

Make the pastry as the Blue Print. Line 4–6 fairly large shallow patty tins or 12 small tins with the pastry. Prick and bake 'blind' until crisp and golden brown; keep warm. To make the filling, remove the meat from a medium-sized crab (or use canned crab-meat). Hard boil 1–2 eggs. Heat 2 oz. (¼C) butter in a pan, add 4 large skinned and chopped tomatoes, simmer until a fairly smooth purée. Add the crabmeat, the juice of ½ lemon, seasoning and 2–3 tablespoons mayonnaise or thick cream. Heat gently. Put into the pastry cases. Serve topped with rings of hard boiled egg. (Illustrated on page 201.)

To vary Use flaked lobster or prawns instead of crab.
Use diced cooked white fish instead of crab – this is less suitable for an after dinner savoury.

Anchovy boats, Caviare boats, Sardine and cheese boats and Devilled tuna boats

1. Put the boat-shaped tins close together on the baking tray or pastry board.
2. Support the pastry over the rolling pin.
3. Lay on top of the boat-shaped tins.

4. Press down with your fingers.
5. Move the rolling pin over the top of the tins, so cutting the pastry neatly.

Luxury Savouries

On this page are two soufflés and the recipe for small savoury choux, plus suggestions for filling these. They are admirable for after dinner savouries.

Cold Cheese Soufflé

3 eggs; aspic jelly to set ¾ pint (2C); ½ pint (1⅓C) water; ¼ pint (⅔C) thick cream; ¼ pint (⅔C) thin cream (or use all thick cream); 4 oz. (1C) very finely grated Cheddar or Gruyère cheese; seasoning. *To garnish:* gherkins; radishes; tomatoes.

Separate the eggs and put the yolks into a basin. Soften and then dissolve the aspic jelly in the very hot water. Whisk on to the egg yolks and continue whisking until blended. Allow to cool and begin to stiffen slightly. Meanwhile whisk the thick cream until it holds a shape, then gradually whisk in the thin cream, cheese and seasoning. Fold into the aspic jelly mixture. Lastly fold in the stiffly whisked egg whites. Spoon into a prepared soufflé dish and allow to set. Remove the band of paper and garnish with pieces of gherkin, radish, if liked and tomato. *Serves 6–8.*

Note The amount of aspic gives a very lightly set soufflé which is ideal, but it must be given adequate time to set. If worried about the time then use enough aspic to set 1 pint (2⅔C).

Smoked Haddock and Cheese Soufflé

6 oz. smoked haddock (weight without bones); ¼ pint (⅔C) water; 1 oz. butter; 1 oz. flour; ¼ pint (⅔C) thin cream; 4 eggs; 2 oz. (½C) grated cheese*; seasoning.

* Use Cheddar or Gruyère for a medium flavour; Parmesan for a strong taste.

Poach the haddock in the water, save this. Make a thick sauce of the butter, flour and thin cream, then add 3–4 tablespoons of the fish stock. If you like a soft soufflé use the larger quantity. Add the finely flaked fish,

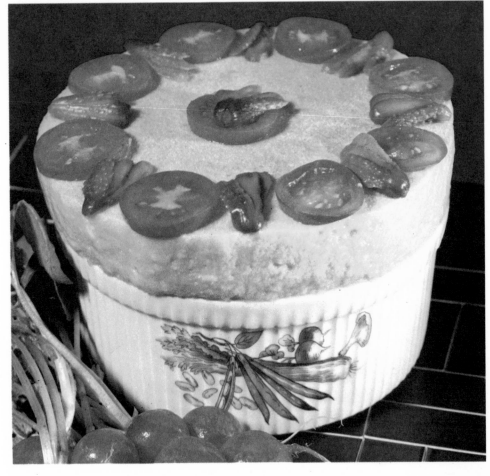

the egg yolks and the cheese. Taste and season as required. Lastly fold in the stiffly whisked egg whites. Turn into a soufflé dish and bake in the centre of a moderate to moderately hot oven, 375–400°F, Gas Mark 5–6, until lightly set and golden brown, approximately 25–30 minutes. Do not over-cook. *Serves 4–6.*

Savoury Choux

For the pastry: ¼ pint (⅔C) water; 1 oz. butter or margarine; seasoning; 3 oz. (¾C) flour, preferably plain; 2 eggs; 1 egg yolk. *For the fillings:* see below. *To garnish:* lettuce; tomato; parsley or unshelled prawns.

Put the water and butter or margarine into a pan, season well. Heat until the butter or margarine has melted. Remove the pan from the heat, then stir in the flour. Return to the

heat and cook until a thick ball. Remove once more from the heat and gradually beat in the eggs and the egg yolk, until a smooth mixture. For these savoury choux put teaspoons of the mixture on to well greased baking trays, allowing space for them to rise and spread. If preferred, put into a piping bag with a ¼-inch plain pipe and make the little rounds. Bake for a good 10 minutes, until well risen and firm, above the centre of a hot oven, 425–450°F, Gas Mark 6–7. I like savoury choux slightly browned on the outside, if you do not then lower the heat slightly. When quite firm remove from the oven, split and remove any slightly under-cooked centre. Return to the oven for 2–3 minutes to dry out. Cool and add the filling. Serve on a bed of lettuce garnished with tomato and parsley or prawns. *This makes about 30–allow 3–4 per person.*

Fillings for Savoury Choux

Mashed well seasoned sardines, or shell fish in a little seasoned cream.

Cooked or raw chopped mushrooms in thick well seasoned whipped cream.

Grated cheese blended with well seasoned whipped cream, and a few chopped nuts.

Glazed Choux

Fill the cooked choux buns, brush with a very little egg, sprinkle with grated cheese and return to the oven for a few minutes.

Storing and Freezing *The soufflés must be eaten fresh. The choux do not store but freeze perfectly with or without the fillings. Serve as soon as defrosted.*

Savoury choux

Making Sauces

Throughout the various parts of Perfect Cooking are recipes for sauces that are needed for a particular dish. In this, and the next pages, basic savoury sauces are described, with easy and interesting variations that can be served with various foods. An indication of the dishes with which they blend is given with each sauce.

Making Sauces

The following points are the most important when making any sauce.

1. Use the correct proportions for the consistency required, but if you have misjudged the amount of flour or liquid, this can be adjusted:
a) If too thick add more liquid.
b) If too thin let the sauce evaporate and thicken by cooking in an open pan.
2. Cook the flour adequately. If a sauce is cooked for too short a time there is a 'floury' taste which spoils the flavour. The times given in the Blue Print Recipe are minimum and a little longer cooking will be an advantage.
3. Stir the sauce as you add the liquid.
4. Stir as the sauce thickens to keep it smooth and prevent it sticking to the pan.
5. Taste to make sure the sauce is adequately seasoned.
6. Never let a sauce boil if adding egg or egg yolk, the sauce would curdle (become lumpy). Cook very gently. Other ingredients can cause curdling to a white or similar sauce, i.e. lemon juice, vinegar, wine.
7. Do not let a skin form on a sauce. There are two ways of preventing this:
a) Cover with very damp greaseproof paper. Remove the paper when ready to heat the sauce.
b) Use less liquid in making the sauce than stated in the recipe. Make the sauce, allow to thicken, then pour the cold liquid on top. This acts as a barrier between the sauce and the air. You will need a good layer of liquid so hold back about 25%. Stir the liquid slowly into the sauce before heating.

● **AVOID** *A lumpy sauce: An under-cooked sauce: A greasy sauce.*
● **TO RECTIFY** *Whisk a lumpy sauce hard and the lumps should come out. If not, sieve the sauce or emulsify in a liquidiser and reheat: Taste a sauce and if it has the roughness of uncooked flour or cornflour return to the heat for a little longer: A greasy sauce indicates too much butter (or other fat) to the amount of flour, so blend a little extra flour with cold liquid, stir into the sauce and continue stirring until thickened.*
● **SHORT CUTS** *Use the quick method of sauce making or sauce mixes.*
● **TO SLIMMERS** *Sauces should be avoided.*
Storing and Freezing *A sauce can be kept for 1–2 days then reheated. Cover with damp paper to keep it as moist as possible. Heat gently to serve. You will probably need to add a little extra liquid to give the desired consistency. It is a good idea to emulsify the sauce in the liquidiser after or before heating. Sauces can be frozen but they may separate as they are reheated. The possibilities of this happening are less if you make the sauce with cornflour (allow ½ oz. cornflour in place of each 1 oz. flour) or potato flour (allow the same weight as when using flour). Whisk or emulsify the defrosted sauce if it does separate or add a little extra flour or cornflour blended with cold liquid and cook slowly, stirring all the time, until the sauce thickens again.*

Caper sauce

Terms Used in Sauce Making

Roux This means the butter and flour mixture, which can be called a liaison. Stages 1–3 in the Blue Print Recipe for white sauce show how this is used.
Consistency The thickness of a sauce.
Coating consistency The sauce coats the back of a wooden spoon (shown in the picture).
Thin consistency The sauce pours easily. This is often used when adding a sauce to vegetables to make a soup. Follow the Blue Print Recipe but use 1 pint (2⅔C) milk instead of ½ pint (1⅓C) to the 1 oz. butter or margarine and 1 oz. flour.
Panada or binding consistency The sauce is very thick. This is used to bind ingredients together, e.g. in rissoles, and fish cakes (instead of an egg). Follow the Blue Print Recipe but use ¼ pint (⅔C) milk instead of ½ pint (1⅓C) to the 1 oz. butter or margarine and 1 oz. flour.

Blue Print Recipe

White Sauce

For a coating consistency
1 oz. butter or margarine · 1 oz. flour · ½ pint (1⅓C*) milk · seasoning ·
* This is fractionally less than ½ pint so be fairly generous with filling the cup.

1. Heat the butter or margarine in a fairly small saucepan. Do not over-heat, otherwise the butter or margarine darkens in colour.
2. Remove from the heat, stir in the flour.
3. Return to a low heat and stir for several minutes, until the 'roux' forms a dry looking ball.
4. Once again take the pan off the heat and gradually blend in the liquid.
5. Stir briskly with a wooden spoon as you do so.
6. Return once again to the heat and bring steadily to the boil, stirring or whisking all the time as the sauce thickens.
7. Add *a little* seasoning and continue stirring for 4–5 minutes. Taste and add more seasoning if required.
To serve A white sauce blends with most foods – eggs, fish, poultry, vegetables. *All recipes based on this serve 3–4.*

Adaptations

Blending method Use the same proportions as in the Blue Print Recipe for white sauce. Blend the flour carefully with the liquid. Put into a saucepan. Add the butter or margarine. Bring gradually to the boil, stirring all the time. Cook as Stage 7 of the Blue Print Recipe. This is found to be an easier method of making the sauce for some people.

Quick method Use the same proportions as in the Blue Print Recipe for white sauce. Proceed as Stages 1–3. Take the pan off the heat, add *all* the liquid. Return to the heat. Allow the liquid to come to the boil and whisk sharply. Continue as Stage 7.

Using cornflour If you wish to use cornflour instead of flour, remember cornflour thickens more than flour, so use ½ oz. cornflour in place of 1 oz. flour. Although a sauce made with cornflour thickens more quickly than one made with flour, it is important to cook it for some minutes.

When all milk should not be used in a white sauce

I prefer using half milk and half vegetable stock, or at least some vegetable stock, when making a sauce to coat vegetables. In this way you retain more of the flavour of the particular vegetables.

Use *some* fish, meat or poultry stock in the sauce when making a white sauce to serve with these foods, see velouté sauce below.

Recipes Based on White Sauce

In each case the proportions for the basic sauce are as the Blue Print Recipe. The flavourings are added at Stage 7, unless stated to the contrary.

Admiral sauce—for fish dishes.
Add 2 teaspoons capers, 2 teaspoons chopped parsley, few drops anchovy essence, ½ teaspoon grated lemon rind and 2 teaspoons lemon juice.

Anchovy sauce—for fish dishes.
Add enough anchovy essence to give a definite flavour and colour to the sauce. Be sparing with the salt.

Aurore sauce—for fish dishes.
Make white or béchamel sauce. Flavour with a little paprika and ½ teaspoon chopped tarragon. For luxury occasions, add 2 table-spoons pounded red lobster coral (roe).

Béchamel sauce A more sophisticated version of white sauce and used as a basis for other sauces in place of white sauce. Warm the milk with a piece of celery, carrot, onion and bay leaf for 2–3 minutes. Leave in the pan for about 30 minutes, strain, then add enough milk to give ½ pint (1⅓C) again. Proceed as white sauce. If desired you can flavour with a little grated nutmeg at Stage 7 of the Blue Print Recipe.

Bohemian sauce—for meat dishes (particularly beef).
Use half milk and half white stock. Add 1–2 teaspoons grated horseradish or horseradish cream. This sauce can be made by omitting the flour, heating the butter or margarine and milk and thickening with 1½ oz. (⅓C) soft white breadcrumbs, then adding seasoning, grated horseradish and a little cream.

Caper sauce—generally served with boiled lamb, but can be used with fish, ham or chicken.
Add 2–3 teaspoons capers (chopped or left whole) and a little vinegar from the bottle.

Cardinal sauce—for fish dishes.
Blend pounded lobster coral into a very creamy béchamel sauce.

Celery sauce—excellent with chicken or turkey.
Make white sauce with half milk and half celery stock (from boiling finely chopped celery). Add 4–5 tablespoons chopped cooked celery and a little thick cream.

Cheese sauce—to serve with fish, vegetables, meat, eggs.
Add a little made mustard to the thickened sauce or good pinch dry mustard to the flour. Stir in 3 oz. (¾C) grated cheese (Cheddar, Dutch Gouda or Gruyère—or use rather less Parmesan). Heat, do not boil.

Duchesse sauce—for boiled ham.

Blend 2–3 tablespoons chopped tongue and 2 oz. (½C) sliced mushrooms fried in 1 oz. butter into the sauce.

German sauce—for chicken or veal.
Make the sauce with half milk and half white stock. When thickened blend 2 egg yolks with 2–3 tablespoons thick cream. Stir into the sauce. Cook gently, *without* boiling, for several minutes.

Mornay sauce—as cheese sauce above or for a richer sauce use a béchamel sauce foundation.
Add 1–2 tablespoons cream blended with 1 egg yolk with the cheese.

Mustard sauce—to serve with herrings, very good with fried or grilled chicken.
Blend from 1 teaspoon to 1 tablespoon made mustard with the sauce or add from ½–2 teaspoons dry mustard to the flour.

Onion (soubise) sauce—excellent with many meat dishes, particularly roast mutton.
Boil 2 finely chopped onions until tender. Strain the liquid. Use ¼ pint (⅔C) of this and ¼ pint (⅔C) milk to make the sauce. Add the chopped onions to the thickened sauce. Add a little cream, cayenne pepper and/or grated nutmeg if desired.

Shrimp sauce—for fish or egg dishes.
Add 3–4 tablespoons whole or chopped shrimps (chopped prawns may be used instead) to the sauce.

Velouté sauce—for steamed or boiled chicken or other meat dishes.
Make béchamel sauce with half chicken stock and half milk or all chicken stock if preferred. When thickened blend in 3–4 tablespoons thick cream mixed with 1–2 tablespoons dry sherry. Heat gently *without* boiling.

White wine sauce—for fish, chicken or veal dishes.
Flavour a white or béchamel sauce with a little white wine:

A brown sauce is generally served with meat dishes and while most of the essential points in making the sauce are the same as for a white sauce the ingredients differ and are very important.

In order to give a very good flavour to a brown sauce, add 1–2 tablespoons of the meat jelly that forms under the dripping.

Blue Print Recipe

Brown Sauce

1 oz. (generous weight) fat (well clarified dripping, lard, cooking fat, margarine or butter) · 1 oz. flour · ½ pint (1⅓C) brown stock (see page 114) or water and 1 beef stock cube · seasoning.

To cook Put the selected fat into a pan. Stir in the flour and blend thoroughly. Allow the 'roux' to cook over a low heat, stirring occasionally, until it turns a golden brown. Do not over-cook at this stage, otherwise the sauce will be spoiled. If you are in a hurry, omit the browning of the flour and add a few drops of gravy browning instead. Add the brown stock or water and stock cube as described in the Blue Print Recipe for white

Brown, Vegetable and Fruit Sauces

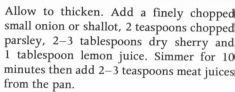

sauce on page 216 and cook until a smooth thickened sauce. Taste and season as required.

To serve Hot with grilled or fried meats or as a basis for casseroles (see below). *All recipes based on this serve 3–4.*

Consistency This may be varied in the same way as a white sauce (see page 216). The thin brown sauce is used as the liquid in some casseroles.

Flavouring Add a chopped onion, a little chopped celery and/or carrot and a *bouquet garni* to the sauce *with* the liquid or heat 2 oz. (¼C) fat and toss the vegetables in this, *then* add the flour. Either strain the sauce before serving or remove the *bouquet garni* and sieve or emulsify the vegetables and sauce then reheat. You may need a little extra stock or use sherry or red wine for additional flavour.

Recipes Based on Brown Sauce

Beefsteak sauce—serve with grilled or fried steak.
Make the brown sauce as the Blue Print.

Allow to thicken. Add a finely chopped small onion or shallot, 2 teaspoons chopped parsley, 2–3 tablespoons dry sherry and 1 tablespoon lemon juice. Simmer for 10 minutes then add 2–3 teaspoons meat juices from the pan.

Bordelaise sauce—serve with grilled or fried lamb or beef.
Make the brown sauce as the Blue Print. Allow to thicken. Add 2 teaspoons finely chopped onion or shallot, 1–2 teaspoons chopped parsley, ½–1 teaspoon chopped tarragon and 4 tablespoons red wine. Simmer for approximately 10 minutes.

Cavalier sauce—a pleasant alternative to tomato sauce to serve with pasta, meat, fish or poultry dishes.
Make the brown sauce as the Blue Print. Allow to thicken. Add 2 tablespoons sieved tomato purée, or use 1 tablespoon concentrated tomato purée, 2 teaspoons tarragon vinegar and 1 teaspoon French mustard. Heat, then add 1 tablespoon chutney, 2 teaspoons chopped gherkins and 2 teaspoons chopped capers.

Garibaldi sauce—to serve with fish or meat. Make the brown sauce as the Blue Print, but toss 1–2 crushed cloves garlic in the fat. When the sauce has thickened add 1–2 teaspoons capers (do not chop), ½ teaspoon curry paste, few drops anchovy essence and 1 teaspoon made mustard.

Espagnole (Spanish) Sauce

This is a more elaborate type of brown sauce, more difficult to make, but much more delicious than the Blue Print. The vegetables give a subtle flavour and pleasant colour to the sauce. This sauce can be served with meat, poultry and pasta dishes.

1–2 oz. (⅛–¼C) fat (see Blue Print); 1 rasher bacon; small piece chopped onion; 1 oz. (¼C) chopped mushrooms; 2 large chopped tomatoes; 1 oz. flour; ½ pint (1⅓C) brown stock; *bouquet garni*; seasoning; 1–2 tablespoons sherry.

Melt the fat (use the larger quantity if the bacon is lean). Add the chopped bacon and heat for a few minutes, then add the vegetables. Toss in the fat with the bacon. Stir in the flour and cook for 3–4 minutes. Add the stock, as the Blue Print Recipe for white sauce on page 216, together with the herbs. Bring to the boil, stirring all the time, and cook until thickened. Season to taste. Simmer for 10 minutes. Remove the herbs. This sauce is generally sieved (or it can be emulsified in the liquidiser). If preferred serve without sieving, in which case the tomatoes should be skinned. Heat with the sherry. *Serves 3–4.*

Recipes Based on Espagnole Sauce

Bressoise sauce—excellent with roast poultry, particularly duck, or with pork chops or cutlets.
Make the espagnole sauce (using an *extra*

Bressoise sauce

medium-sized onion for a stronger flavour). Sieve or emulsify, put into the pan and add 2–3 tablespoons orange juice and the finely chopped cooked duck or chicken liver (naturally this cannot be added with pork).
Burgundy sauce—serve with meat particularly tongue).
Make the espagnole sauce but use half brown stock and half red Burgundy wine. Sieve or emulsify. A quicker version is to make the brown sauce as the Blue Print with half brown stock and half red Burgundy wine.
Chateaubriand sauce—to serve with grilled steaks, but excellent with veal or venison.
Make the espagnole sauce. Sieve or emulsify, then reheat with 3 tablespoons white wine, 1–2 tablespoons meat jelly (from under the dripping), 1–2 teaspoons chopped parsley and 1 tablespoon red currant jelly.
Madeira sauce—serve with most meat (particularly tongue).
Make either the espagnole, or the brown sauce but use half brown stock and half Madeira wine. Sieve or emulsify the espagnole sauce. Heat the sauce with $\frac{1}{2}$ teaspoon made mustard; 1 tablespoon red currant jelly may be added as well.
Poivrade sauce—serve with meat, excellent with steaks.
Make the espagnole sauce, but simmer with about 12 peppercorns. Sieve or emulsify *with* the peppercorns—beware it is very hot. Reheat with a little brandy.

Blue Print Recipe

Tomato Sauce

Tomato sauce is one of the most versatile sauces, for it can be served with many foods.

1 small onion · $\frac{1}{2}$ small dessert apple · 1 rasher bacon or several bacon rinds · 1 clove garlic · 1$\frac{1}{2}$ lb. *ripe* tomatoes · 1 oz. butter · $\frac{1}{4}$ pint ($\frac{2}{3}$C) white stock or water · seasoning.

To make Peel the onion and apple and grate or chop finely. The rasher of bacon may be left whole if you wish to remove this. Crush the peeled garlic clove. Skin and chop the tomatoes.
To cook Heat the butter and bacon rasher or rinds then toss the onion, apple and garlic in the butter and bacon fat. Take care these do not discolour. Add the tomatoes and stock or water and heat until the tomatoes are tender. Remove the bacon rasher or rinds. Season well.
To serve This sauce can be served hot or cold. *All recipes based on this serve 5–6.*
To give a smooth textured sauce · Sieve or emulsify. Blend 1 oz. flour or $\frac{1}{2}$ oz. cornflour with $\frac{1}{4}$ pint ($\frac{2}{3}$C) extra white stock or water. Add to the tomato mixture, return to the pan and heat steadily, stirring all the time, until smooth and thick. Taste and add any extra seasoning. Serve hot.

To add extra flavour The Blue Print gives a very mild flavoured sauce, so to add extra flavour:
Blend 1–2 tablespoons concentrated tomato purée (from a can or tube) with the fresh tomato mixture.
Add a generous amount of cayenne pepper to the sauce.
Flavour with a *bouquet garni* of herbs and a little chopped celery. Omit the apple.
Add 1–2 teaspoons brown sugar.

Cumberland Sauce

This sauce is an ideal accompaniment to hot or cold ham or boiled bacon. There are many ways of making it but the sauce should contain orange and lemon juice, red currant jelly, mustard and port wine. Here is a recipe I find particularly good.
2 small oranges; 1 lemon; $\frac{1}{4}$ pint ($\frac{2}{3}$C) water; 2 teaspoons arrowroot or cornflour; $\frac{1}{4}$ pint ($\frac{2}{3}$C) ham or white stock; 2 teaspoons made mustard; 2 tablespoons port wine; 4–5 tablespoons red currant jelly; seasoning.
Cut the peel from the oranges. Remove the white pith then cut into thin matchsticks. A very little lemon rind may be treated in the same way if wished. Squeeze the juice from the fruits. Put the rind into a pan with the cold water. Soak for 1 hour then simmer very gently in a covered pan until nearly tender (about 15–20 minutes). Remove the lid towards the end of the cooking time so the liquid is reduced to 3 tablespoons. Blend the arrowroot or cornflour with the ham or white stock. Put into the pan with the fruit juice, mustard, wine and jelly. Stir over a low heat until thickened and clear. Season well. Serve hot or cold. *Serves 4–5.*

Storing and Freezing *See the comments on page 216. Espagnole and tomato sauce freeze well, particularly if not sieved.*
To use any left over *Store carefully in the refrigerator or cool place reheat gently.*

219

Cold Sauces

The most famous of all cold sauces is mayonnaise, and while excellent commercial mayonnaise is available the home-made variety has a flavour that it is difficult to surpass.

Blue Print Recipe

Mayonnaise

2 egg yolks · ½–1 teaspoon made English mustard or French mustard · ¼–½ teaspoon salt · good shake pepper · pinch sugar (optional) · ¼ pint (⅔C) olive oil · 1–2 tablespoons vinegar (white or brown malt or wine vinegar) or lemon juice · 1 tablespoon boiling water (optional).

To make Put the egg yolks, seasonings and sugar into a mixing bowl or basin. Beat well with a wooden spoon or with a whisk. Add the oil drop by drop, beating all the time. When the oil has been incorporated whisk in the vinegar or lemon juice. Taste once or twice to make sure you are not adding too much for *your* taste. Add the boiling water gradually at the end to give a very light creamy taste.
To serve Cold with salads.
To make a piping mayonnaise Add up to ½ pint (1⅓C) oil; the more oil added the thicker the mayonnaise.

Mayonnaise

● **AVOID** *Adding the oil too quickly, if you do the mayonnaise curdles.*
● **TO RECTIFY** *Put another egg yolk into a basin and whisk the curdled mayonnaise very gradually into this. Be sure the egg yolks and oil are at room temperature. If the eggs come from the refrigerator the mayonnaise is more likely to curdle.*
● **SHORT CUTS** *Use an electric whisk or a liquidiser (blender) is even quicker.*
● **TO SLIMMERS** *Avoid the oily mayonnaise and use the yoghourt dressing on this page.*

Mayonnaise in a Liquidiser

Ingredients as the Blue Print but the order of adding these is different. Put the egg yolks, seasonings and sugar into the liquidiser goblet, switch on for a few seconds. Add the vinegar or lemon juice. I would use the smaller amount the first time you make this. Switch on until blended. Switch to a low speed and pour the oil in *very steadily*. Taste and add any more vinegar or lemon juice required on low speed, then add the water.

Sauces Based on Mayonnaise

Andalouse sauce—especially good with shell fish.
Add 1–2 tablespoons fresh or concentrated tomato purée and 1 finely chopped red pepper (discard the core and seeds) to the thickened mayonnaise.
Ayoli (garlic) mayonnaise—for all salads.
Add 1–2 cloves finely chopped or crushed garlic to the thickened mayonnaise. Taste and add a little extra lemon juice if desired.

Green mayonnaise—especially good with fish salads.
Add freshly chopped herbs plus a little green colouring, or put a spinach leaf and the herbs into the liquidiser when the mayonnaise has thickened. Switch on until the herbs are chopped and the spinach blended.
Lemon mayonnaise—to serve in place of mayonnaise.
Add extra lemon juice and a little finely grated lemon rind to the thickened mayonnaise.
Tartare sauce—for all fish dishes.
Add up to 1 tablespoon chopped parsley, ½–1 tablespoon chopped gherkins and 1–2 teaspoons whole or chopped capers to the thickened mayonnaise. If making the mayonnaise in the liquidiser add the sprigs of parsley and whole gherkins to the thickened mayonnaise. Switch on until 'chopped' then add the capers.
Tomato mayonnaise—especially good with cheese or meat salads.
If making in a liquidiser, add 1–2 skinned tomatoes to the mayonnaise when thickened. Switch on until the tomatoes are blended. If mixing by hand sieve the tomatoes or use concentrated tomato purée.

Yoghourt Dressing

Blend seasoning, a little made mustard and 1 crushed sugar substitute tablet into ¼ pint (⅔C) natural yoghourt. Add ½–1 teaspoon finely grated lemon rind and 1 tablespoon lemon juice. 1 tablespoon olive oil may also be blended into the yoghourt to give a richer flavour. *Serves 4.*

French Dressing

Gradually blend 2 tablespoons olive or other good salad oil (corn oil if wished) into a little dry or made mustard (½–1 teaspoon). Add a good pinch of salt, shake of pepper, a pinch of sugar and 1 tablespoon vinegar or lemon juice.

Vinaigrette Dressing

This is often given as another name for French dressing, but this is not quite correct —it is French dressing plus 1–2 teaspoons freshly chopped herbs. A teaspoon finely chopped shallot or onion and 2 teaspoons chopped gherkin may also be added.

Storing and Freezing *Mayonnaise keeps well in the refrigerator for several weeks. Keep well covered so the mixture does not dry. French dressing keeps almost indefinitely which is why you can make a large quantity and store it in a screw topped bottle. Shake before using. I prefer to make vinaigrette dressing freshly. Mayonnaise will not freeze, it separates badly.*

COOKING WITH DAIRY PRODUCE

When you use the expression 'dairy produce' you are describing some of the most nutritious of all foods.

Milk has great nutritive value and is an essential food for all ages. It provides protein for building and maintaining healthy growth in the body and ensures a regular supply of many essential vitamins and mineral salts. Just think of the versatility of milk in the every day diet. We can drink it plain—hot or cold—we can turn it into delicious and unusual beverages and it is an essential ingredient in many soups, sauces, puddings and savoury dishes. You will find recipes using milk wisely and well in the first pages of this section. Most of us *enjoy* milk, but sometimes children or adults pass through a phase when they tire of the taste, so pages 222 and 223 give suggestions for incorporating milk into foods where its flavour will not be too obvious.

Cream gives a deliciously luxurious touch to many dishes. A tablespoon of cream added to sauces, soups or 'milky' dishes gives an improved flavour; a topping of cream can turn an every day cake or dessert into a party dish. One of the easiest meals of all is fresh bread, butter and cheese. We are fortunate in having such a range of cheeses from which to choose and many of the most important cheeses are described on pages 238 and 239.

During the past few years we have heard a great deal about yoghourt. Do not imagine that this is an entirely *new* food. It has been appreciated in most parts of the world for centuries, particularly in the Eastern European countries, where it is often associated with longevity. Yoghourt is produced from milk which is treated with a culture. This gives an interesting flavour and consistency to the milk, yet retains its valuable food properties. The reason yoghourt has become so popular is that it is now produced very widely and is easily available.

Soured cream is described on page 231. You will not find this as easy to obtain as yoghourt, but do try to buy it for the flavour it gives to dishes, particularly savoury foods, is most interesting. If you cannot obtain soured cream you can try the recipes if you substitute fresh cream and lemon juice.

Most of us would benefit from including a pint of milk a day in our diet, so plan ways to use milk wisely and well. Here is a brief summary of some of the ways in which it can be used:

In drinks—hot and cold.

In sauces—sweet and savoury.

To make milky puddings of all kinds.

As an ingredient in fish, meat and poultry dishes.

There is no need to use 'plain' milk all the time, yoghourt is another form of milk that opens up a wide field of new recipes and flavours. Cream, whether fresh or soured, has the value of milk, plus fat for energy.

The products made from milk and cream, i.e. cheese and butter, all add food value to our diets.

On this and the next page are some quick and easy recipes which introduce milk into savoury dishes.

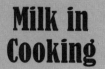

Milk in Cooking

Blue Print

Using Milk in Cooking

1. Milk will cause a sauce or stew to 'boil over' readily, so keep the heat low as the mixture cooks.

2. Stir well, to prevent any possibility of the sauce burning on the pan.

3. Milk absorbs a fair amount of seasoning, so taste and adjust the amount of salt and pepper accordingly.

4. If you like very moist fish, dip the fish in milk before putting under the grill, this is particularly valuable with rather fine, dry fleshed fish such as sole and whiting.

5. Liver, left to soak in milk for a while before cooking, becomes far less strong in flavour. This is particularly valuable when trying to encourage children to eat liver.

6. If you find a curry or other sauce a little too strong or salty in flavour add a little milk or cream, this absorbs the excess seasoning very well.

7. Use plenty of milk in creaming vegetables. Heat the milk first if possible, particularly when adding this to mashed potatoes, it makes the mixture whiter.

8. Have you ever tried cooking potatoes, carrots and turnips in milk—the flavour is delicious. Put into boiling milk instead of boiling water. Cook steadily and lift the lid of the pan towards the end of the cooking time, so the vegetables absorb the excess milk. Season well and mash.

9. Try mixing short crust pastry with milk instead of water, it gives a very crisp short texture. I find that short crust or sweet short crust pastry to be frozen keeps a better texture if made with milk rather than water.

10. If you cannot spare an egg, brush pastry and other foods with milk before baking to give a shine.

11. Dishes made with milk or cream are very satisfying so you can be a little more sparing with the amount of meat or fish.

12. In fact if your family are not great milk drinkers, add a little milk when you next make a stew, it will give a pleasant golden coloured sauce. If the stew contains acid ingredients such as vinegar, wine or tomatoes the liquid must simmer, rather than boil rapidly.

Chunky pork suprême

Sauces, using milk, need not take very long, for there are many dehydrated sauce mixes available that simply need blending with the milk and heating.

Chunky Pork Suprême

2 onions*; 1 lb. lean pork; 2 medium-sized carrots; 2–3 sticks celery; 1 small green pepper (optional); 3 oz. ($\frac{3}{8}$C) butter or margarine*; 2 oz. ($\frac{1}{2}$C) flour*; seasoning; 1 pint ($2\frac{2}{3}$C) milk; 1 bay leaf.

Method A *Omit the onions, 2 oz. ($\frac{1}{4}$C) butter or margarine and the flour and use a double packet of onion sauce mix. Prepare the sauce with the milk as the instructions on the packet, then toss the diced pork and vegetables in the 1 oz. butter or margarine and add to the sauce, proceed as Method B.

Method B Peel and chop the onions, dice the pork, peel and slice the carrots and chop the celery and the green pepper (discard the core and seeds). Heat all the butter or margarine in the saucepan, fry the prepared veget-

ables in this for a few minutes. Toss the pork in the flour, blended with seasoning and add to the vegetable mixture. Continue cooking gently until the pork is pale golden coloured. Gradually blend in the milk and stir over a low heat until a smooth thickened sauce. Add the bay leaf. Cover the pan, then simmer gently until the pork is tender, this takes approximately $1\frac{1}{4}$–$1\frac{1}{2}$ hours. Stir occasionally. Remove bay leaf before serving. *Serves 4–5.*

Gammon with Pineapple and Corn Sauce

4 small or 2 larger slices of lean gammon; about 2 oz. (about $\frac{1}{4}$C) butter; 3–4 rings of canned pineapple. *To garnish:* watercress. *For the sauce:* 1 onion; 1 oz. butter; 1 oz. flour; $\frac{1}{2}$ pint ($1\frac{1}{3}$C) milk, seasoning; 3–4 tablespoons cooked sweet corn; 2–3 teaspoons chopped parsley; 2 tablespoons syrup from the can of pineapple.

If you like very crisp fat on grilled gammon remove the rind. If you prefer the fat to be

fairly soft then leave the rind on. In either case snip the edges of the gammon, this prevents it curling. Never pre-heat the grill when cooking gammon, for if the grill is too hot it encourages the edges of the gammon to curl and burn. Brush with melted butter and cook for several minutes on the one side, turn, brush with more butter and continue cooking. When the gammon is nearly ready add the halved, well drained rings of pineapple to the grill pan. Brush these with butter and heat thoroughly. Place the gammon and pineapple on a plate and garnish with watercress. Serve the sauce separately. Make the sauce while the gammon is cooking. Chop the onion very finely. Heat the butter in a pan, stir in the flour and cook for several minutes. Gradually blend in the milk, add the onion. Bring to the boil and cook until thickened, stirring all the time. Season the sauce, add the sweet corn and parsley and keep warm until ready to serve. At the last minute whisk in the pineapple syrup. *Serves 4.*

The Curried Meat Balls, pictured on this page, are very popular in Scandinavia. They have a more delicate curry flavour than one generally meets.

Curried Meat Balls

These are a pleasant change from the usual brown curry. Both the meat balls and the sauce have a creamy taste.

1½ lb. beef (or choose a mixture of beef and veal); 2 medium-sized onions; 1 oz. butter; ½ teaspoon ground ginger; 1–2 teaspoons curry powder; 2 oz. (¾C) soft breadcrumbs; 2 egg yolks; 3–4 tablespoons thick cream. *For frying and the sauce:* 3 oz. (⅜C) fat or butter; 1 oz. flour; 1–2 teaspoons curry powder; ½ pint (1⅓C) white stock; ¼ pint (⅔C) thin cream or milk; seasoning. *To garnish:* 1–2 green peppers; 3–4 tomatoes; cooked rice.

Mince the meat very finely. Chop the onions very finely or grate coarsely. Heat the butter in a pan, stir in the onions and cook gently until nearly soft. Add the ginger and curry powder then the meat. Blend very thoroughly, then stir in the crumbs and egg yolks and mix well. Gradually add enough cream to give a soft creamy texture. Put into a cool place for about 30 minutes to stiffen slightly. Make into small balls the size of little walnuts. Heat the fat or butter in a large frying pan. Put in the balls and brown, turning round several times. Lift the balls out of the pan on to a large plate. Blend the flour with the fat remaining in the pan and cook for 1–2 minutes. Add the curry powder, then blend in the stock and bring to the boil. Cook gently until thickened, stir in the cream or milk and seasoning. Replace the meat balls and simmer gently for about 10 minutes. Spoon the balls and sauce on to a very hot dish, garnish with rings of pepper, slices of tomato and the hot rice. *Serves 5–6.*

To vary

Creamed Veal Curry Follow the recipe above, but fry small pieces of veal fillet in the butter instead of meat balls.

Macaroni and Egg Hot-Pot

6 oz. short cut macaroni; seasoning; 4 eggs; 1½ oz. butter or margarine; 1½ oz. flour; ¾ pint (2C) milk; 4 oz. cooked ham. *To garnish:* 2–3 tablespoons grated cheese; 1 tablespoon chopped parsley.

Put the macaroni into boiling salted water and cook until tender; with the quick cooking variety this takes about 8 minutes. Drain. Meanwhile hard boil and shell the eggs. Heat the butter or margarine in a pan, stir in the flour and cook for several minutes, stirring all the time. Remove the pan from the heat and gradually stir in the milk. Bring to the boil, cook until smooth and thickened, stir well during this time. Season the sauce. Mix the macaroni, three of the chopped eggs and the diced ham with the sauce. Heat gently for a few minutes only. Put into a hot casserole, top with the cheese and parsley, slice the remaining egg and arrange on top. *Serves 4–6.*

To vary This is an excellent way to use small 'untidy' pieces of cooked chicken.

Left over cooked vegetables may be added to the macaroni and eggs instead of cooked ham. Omit the eggs and stir about 4 oz. (1C) grated Cheddar cheese into the sauce.

If you wish to prepare this beforehand, to be reheated later, use 1 pint (2⅔C) milk to make the sauce, for the macaroni absorbs liquid in standing.

Savoury Cheese Pudding

4 oz. (1⅓C) soft white or brown breadcrumbs; ½ pint (1⅓C) milk; 3 eggs; 2 oz. (¼C) butter; 2 medium-sized onions; seasoning; 6 oz. (1½C) grated Cheddar cheese.

Put the crumbs into a basin. Add the warm milk and beaten eggs and allow the crumbs to stand for 20 minutes to soften. Meanwhile heat the butter and fry the finely chopped onions in this until transparent, do not brown. Blend with the crumb mixture. Add seasoning and finally the grated cheese. Put into a 2-pint (5–6C) pie, soufflé or oven-proof dish and bake in the centre of a moderate oven, 350–375°F, Gas Mark 4–5, until well risen and firm. This takes about 35 minutes in a pie dish, but a little longer in a deeper soufflé dish. *Serves 4–6.*

To vary Diced cooked ham or flaked cooked fish may be added to the above recipe or the onions may be omitted and the cheese pudding flavoured with a little made mustard. If omitting the onions omit the butter also.

Storing and Freezing *The dishes on these two pages vary so much that it is difficult to generalise about storage. All the cooked dishes store for 24 hours in a cool place, except the cheese pudding, which must be eaten when freshly cooked. The gammon is unlikely to be stored after cooking, but can be diced and added to salads. The sauce could be reheated. The Curried Meat Balls freeze very well indeed, but the sauces are not very successful in freezing, they tend to separate. If this happens then whisk sharply or emulsify in a liquidiser or blend a little extra thickening into the sauce and reheat carefully.*

If using cornflour instead of flour in these recipes the mixture keeps smoother when frozen, or potato flour is even better. Use ½ oz. cornflour to 1 oz. flour or 1 oz. potato flour to 1 oz. flour.

Gammon with pineapple

Curried meat balls

Family Milk Puddings

One of the best ways to make certain the family have milk in an enjoyable form is to serve a variety of milk puddings, hot or cold.

Blue Print Recipe

Rice Pudding

2 oz. (2 tablespoons) round grain rice · 1–2 oz. ($\frac{1}{8}$–$\frac{1}{4}$C) sugar · 1 pint (2$\frac{2}{3}$C) milk · small knob butter ($\frac{1}{2}$–1 oz.) · little grated nutmeg.

To make Put the ingredients into a pie dish.
To cook In the centre, or coolest part of a slow oven, 275–300°F, Gas Mark 1–2, for 1$\frac{1}{2}$ hours, or even longer at 250–275°F, Gas Mark $\frac{1}{2}$–1. Stir the pudding once or twice during cooking if possible.
To serve Hot by itself or with fruit. *All recipes based on this dish serve 4.*
To vary Long grain rice can also be used as in the picture.
Cook the pudding in a saucepan for about 25–30 minutes, stirring well, or about 45 minutes to 1 hour in the top of a double saucepan.
Use other cereals, i.e. tapioca, sago in the same way. It is better, when making these puddings, to simmer the milk, cereal, etc. for a few minutes in a saucepan and then transfer to the pie dish and cook in the oven.

● **AVOID** *Cooking milk puddings too quickly, otherwise they do not develop a creamy texture.*
● **SHORT CUT** *Heat canned milk puddings for a short time.*
● **TO SLIMMERS** *These recipes are not very suitable for slimming diets, but you can reduce the calories by using skimmed milk.*

Rice pudding

Caramelled Rice Pudding

Ingredients as Blue Print PLUS 4 oz. ($\frac{1}{2}$C) sugar (granulated or caster), 4 tablespoons water, 2 oz. ($\frac{1}{3}$C) sultanas, 1 oz. glacé cherries and 1 oz. chopped candied peel, but MINUS the nutmeg.
Put the 4 oz. ($\frac{1}{2}$C) sugar and the water into a saucepan. Stir until the sugar has dissolved. Boil steadily until a golden brown caramel. Pour half the caramel on to a small tin to set. Blend 1 tablespoon water with the remaining caramel to make a slightly thinner sauce. Pour into the bottom of the pie dish and leave until cold. Heat the rice, sugar, milk and butter in a saucepan for about 10 minutes, add the sultanas, chopped cherries and peel. Spoon over the caramel and bake as the Blue Print. Break the hard caramel (on the tin) into pieces. Sprinkle over the pudding just before serving.

Junket

This is a splendid milk pudding when you need something very light in texture. Heat 1 pint (2$\frac{2}{3}$C) milk with 1–2 tablespoons sugar to blood heat. Remove from the heat, add a little flavouring, i.e. about $\frac{1}{4}$ teaspoon vanilla or almond essence or 1–2 teaspoons instant coffee. Add 1 good teaspoon rennet. Pour into 3–4 individual dishes. Top with grated nutmeg if wished. Allow to clot at room temperature, do not move until quite firm, when the junkets may be chilled in the refrigerator. *Serves 3–4.*
Junket is delicious served with fruit.

Chocolate Walnut Meringue

1 packet chocolate blancmange powder; 1 pint (2$\frac{2}{3}$C) milk; 3 oz. ($\frac{3}{8}$C) caster sugar; 2 eggs; 2 tablespoons thin cream; 3 oz. ($\frac{3}{4}$C) chopped walnuts.

Blend the blancmange powder with a little cold milk to make a smooth paste. Heat the remainder of the milk with 1 oz. sugar, pour over the blancmange, stirring all the time. Return to the pan and stir over a low heat until the blancmange thickens. Remove from the heat, add the egg yolks blended with the cream and half the nuts. Cook, without boiling, for 2–3 minutes then put into an oven-proof serving dish. Whisk the egg whites until very stiff. Gradually whisk in the remaining sugar and nuts. Pile over the blancmange mixture. Bake for 20–25 minutes in the centre of a cool to very moderate oven, 300–325°F, Gas Mark 2–3, until golden. *Serves 4.*

Lemon Diplomat Pudding

1 lemon flavoured jelly; $\frac{1}{4}$ pint ($\frac{2}{3}$C) water; 3 oz. (1C) soft sponge cake crumbs or semi-sweet biscuit crumbs or macaroon biscuit crumbs; grated rind 1–2 lemons; 4 oz. ($\frac{2}{3}$C) sultanas; 1 oz. sugar; $\frac{3}{4}$ pint (2C) milk.
Dissolve the jelly in $\frac{1}{4}$ pint ($\frac{2}{3}$C) very hot water. Cool slightly then add the rest of the ingredients. Do not pour in the milk until the jelly is cold, this saves any problems of curdling. Rinse out a mould in cold water. Spoon in the mixture and allow to set. Turn out when ready to serve. *Serves 4–5.*
To vary Ingredients as above, but use sliced sponge cakes instead of crumbs. Put the sponge and sultanas into the mould. Dissolve the lemon jelly in the $\frac{1}{4}$ pint ($\frac{2}{3}$C) very hot water, add the lemon rind. Cool then add the $\frac{3}{4}$ pint (2C) cold milk. Pour over the sliced sponge cakes and fruit and allow to set.

Storing and Freezing *The milk puddings store quite well in a refrigerator for a limited time but do not freeze.*

Special Desserts

The desserts on this page are quite simple to make and yet they are ideal for a party.

Pineapple and Strawberry Ring

Scant 1 oz. powdered gelatine (or enough to set 1½ pints (4C)); 1 medium-sized can pineapple rings*; 1 lemon; 4 eggs; 2 oz. (¼C) caster sugar; ½ pint (1⅓C) milk. *To decorate:* ¼ pint (⅔C) thick cream; about 8 oz. strawberries.

*About 10–12 rings required.

Put the gelatine into a basin. Open the can of pineapple, strain off ¼ pint (⅔C) of the syrup. If inadequate add enough water to give ¼ pint (⅔C). Soften the gelatine in 3 tablespoons of the cold pineapple syrup. Heat the remainder of the pineapple syrup, pour over the gelatine and stir until completely dissolved. Grate the lemon rind very finely, put into a basin. Squeeze out the juice, add to the rind. Separate the eggs and put the yolks with the lemon rind and juice and the whites into a separate bowl. Add the sugar to the egg yolks, etc. and whisk over a pan of hot, but not boiling water until thick and creamy. Whisk in the pineapple and gelatine liquid. Allow the mixture to cool then add 6 *well drained* chopped pineapple rings and the cold milk. Leave the dessert to stiffen *slightly* (to hasten this process stand the mixing bowl in another bowl of ice cubes). Whisk the egg whites until very stiff. Fold into the pineapple mixture. Rinse a 9–10-inch ring mould with cold water. Spoon in the dessert and leave until firm. Turn out when ready to serve. Halve 3 pineapple rings and chop the remainder. Spoon most of the chopped pineapple into the centre of the ring and arrange the halved rings round the dish. Whip the cream and put into a piping bag with a small or ¼-inch rose pipe. Halve the strawberries and place on the top and round the sides of the dessert with the remaining chopped pineapple. Decorate with piped cream. *Serves 6–8.*

Note Do *not* use fresh pineapple, the dessert will not set.

Ice Cream Gâteau

The topping on this bought commercial ice cream gives a very imaginative dessert.

For the pastry cream topping: 1 oz. (2 level tablespoons) cornflour; ½ pint (1⅓C) milk; 3 oz. (⅜C) caster sugar; 3 egg yolks; ¼–½ teaspoon vanilla essence; 2 oz. mixed glacé fruits; 1 oz. glacé cherries. *For the base:* 1 block chocolate ice cream.

Blend the cornflour and milk, pour into a saucepan. Add the sugar. Cook over a low heat, stirring all the time until the mixture thickens. Remove from the heat, cool slightly, then add the well beaten egg yolks. Transfer to the top of a double saucepan or basin and cook over hot, but not boiling water for 5–8 minutes to give a thick creamy mixture. Stir in the vanilla essence, cover with damp greaseproof paper and allow to cool. Remove the paper. Add most of the chopped glacé fruits and glacé cherries. Put the ice cream on to the serving dish and top with the pastry cream and remaining glacé fruits and cherries. *Serves 4–6.*

Storing and Freezing *Both the pineapple ring and the pastry cream should be stored in the refrigerator—they do not freeze well. The ice cream keeps well in the freezing compartment of the refrigerator (the storage time depends upon the type of refrigerator) or in the home freezer.*

To use any left over *Store carefully and use as soon as possible.*

Pineapple and strawberry ring

Ice cream gâteau

Cream is one of the foods that can turn an ordinary dish into a special one, but if used to excess it makes food over-rich. Choose the dishes to which you add cream with great care.

The picture opposite and the one on page 221 illustrate the wise use of cream. A cold soufflé would lack substance if cream was not included among the ingredients.

Choux pastry, used to make cream buns, is light and delicate in texture, but is a pastry with little flavour, the cream filling provides this.

The Chicken in Lemon Sauce is a way of giving flavour and richness to the lemon flavoured stock.

Chicken in Lemon Sauce

1 young chicken (2½–3 lb. when trussed); seasoning; 1 bay leaf; *bouquet garni*; 2 lemons. *For the sauce:* 2 oz. (¼C) butter; 2 oz. (½C) flour; ½ pint (1⅓C) thick or thin cream. *To garnish:* lemons; tomatoes.

Put the chicken into a pan with water to cover. Bring the water to the boil, remove any scum that forms on the top, then add the seasoning, the bay leaf, *bouquet garni* and sliced lemons. Take the pips out of the lemons as they make the stock bitter. Simmer the liquid gently for about 1¼ hours or until the chicken is tender. Lift the chicken from the stock and strain a generous ½ pint (1⅓C) stock. Keep the chicken hot on a dish. Heat the butter in a pan, stir in the flour. Stir over a low heat for several minutes then gradually blend in the stock and bring to the boil, stirring all the time. Remove from the heat then add the cream slowly. Return to a gentle heat and stir until the cream is well blended. Taste and season as required. Cut the chicken into 4–6 joints and put on to a hot dish. Coat with the sauce and garnish with sliced lemons and sliced tomatoes. *Serves 4–6.*

Using Cream Wisely

Hazel-nut Soufflé

3 eggs; ¼ pint (⅔C) milk; 3 oz. (⅜C) caster sugar; 2 tablespoons brandy; ½ tablespoon powdered gelatine; ½ pint (1⅓C) thick cream; 1 oz. finely chopped hazel-nuts. *To decorate:* 2 oz. (½C) finely chopped hazel-nuts; nearly ¼ pint (nearly ⅔C) thick cream; about 16 whole hazel-nuts.

Separate the eggs. Put the yolks with the milk and sugar into a basin over hot water and whisk until thickened. Blend the brandy and gelatine, stir into the custard mixture and continue stirring until dissolved. Allow to cool. Whip the cream until it just holds a shape, add to the brandy mixture. Spoon out about one-third of the mixture into another basin, fold the hazel-nuts into this. Whisk the egg whites until very stiff. Add two egg whites to the plain mixture and one egg white to the nut mixture. Put the hazel-nut layer into a prepared soufflé dish, Sketches 1 and 2, then the plain layer on top. Allow to set. Remove the paper with the help of a knife. Press the nuts against the sides of the soufflé with

a palette knife, Sketch 3. Pipe a thick band of cream round the top of the soufflé and decorate with whole nuts. (Illustrated on page 221). *Serves 5–6.*

To vary The hazel-nuts for the top can be dipped in caramel, as in the picture.

Increase hazel-nuts to 3–4 oz. (¾–1C) and add all to the mixture.

Chocolate Cream Buns

Ingredients as the Blue Print PLUS nearly ½ pint (generous 1C) thick cream, 6 oz. plain or couverture chocolate, 1 tablespoon water, few drops olive oil or about ½ oz. butter.

Make the choux pastry as the Blue Print. Either put spoonfuls of the mixture on to lightly greased baking trays, see photograph 3, or pipe into rounds with a ½-inch plain pipe. Allow plenty of space for the choux pastry to rise. Bake for 15–20 minutes in the centre of a moderate to moderately hot oven, 375–400°F, Gas Mark 5–6, then lower the heat slightly and cook for a further 20 minutes until firm to the touch. Cool away from a draught. Slit the buns through the centre; if there is any uncooked dough, remove this and return the buns to the oven to dry out. Whip the cream until it holds its shape. Spoon into the *cool* buns. Melt the chocolate with the water, oil or butter in a basin over a pan of hot water. Spread over the top of the buns. Allow to set. *Makes up to 12 buns.*

Storing and Freezing *The soufflé should be eaten when freshly made, it is not improved by storing. Choux pastry and cream buns freeze very well; eat as soon as defrosted. They cannot be stored in any other way but freezing. The chicken dish is better eaten fresh.*

Buttermilk fruit cake, Yoghourt fruit salad, Chicken in lemon sauce and Chocolate cream buns

1.

Blue Print Recipe

Choux Pastry

¼ pint (⅔C) water · 1 oz. butter · pinch sugar · 3 oz. (¾C) flour, plain or self-raising · 2 eggs · 1 egg yolk.

To make Put the water, butter and sugar into a pan. Heat until the butter has melted. Remove the pan from the heat. Stir in the sieved flour. Return to the heat and stir over a low heat until a dry mixture, see photograph 1. Once again remove the pan from the heat and blend in the beaten eggs and yolk, until a smooth mixture, see photograph 2. Allow to cool and use the choux pastry in the cream bun recipe.

● **AVOID** *Adding the eggs too quickly to the flour mixture, if you do it is difficult to achieve a smooth mixture.*

2.

3.

Savoury Dishes Using Cream

Cream blends well with practically every type of fish or meat, giving richness and additional flavour to the sauce. It is particularly good with delicate flavoured foods such as veal and chicken, although the Creamed Kidneys on this page shows a dish where cream blends with a strong flavoured meat.

The Veal Fricassée is an excellent Blue Print for all 'creamy-type' stews. The sauce is thickened with egg yolks, blended with cream, as well as with flour. The egg yolks, cream and bacon garnish makes this a very satisfying dish, so a relatively small amount of meat is sufficient for up to 6 people.

Blue Print Recipe

Veal Fricassée

1–1¼ lb. veal (use stewing veal or fillet from the leg) · 2 medium-sized onions · 1 pint (2⅔C) white stock · *bouquet garni* · seasoning · 2 oz. (¼C) butter · 2 oz. (½C) flour · 2 egg yolks · 2 tablespoons lemon juice · ¼ pint (⅔C) thick cream · To garnish: 4 bacon rashers · 6–8 slices bread · 1–2 lemons · parsley.

To make Cut the veal into 1–2-inch pieces. Chop the onions finely. Put the meat and onions into a pan. Add nearly all the stock.

To cook Bring the stock to the boil, remove any scum that comes to the top of the liquid. Add the herbs and seasoning. Cover the pan and simmer very slowly for 1½ hours if using stewing veal or 1–1¼ hours with the more tender fillet. When the veal is cooked add the butter. Blend the flour with the remaining stock, add to the veal liquid. Stir as the sauce comes to the boil and boil steadily, stirring all the time as the sauce thickens. If the sauce is too thick adjust the consistency by adding a little extra stock or milk. Remove the *bouquet garni*. Mix the egg yolks with the lemon juice and cream. Take the pan of veal off the heat so the liquid no longer boils. Stir or whisk the egg and cream mixture into the sauce. Return to the heat and simmer for about 5 minutes, stirring all the time. Make the bacon into rolls, see the sketches, cook under the grill. Toast the bread, remove the crusts and cut into triangles (do this after thickening the veal liquid with the flour so you may give your undivided attention to the mixture when adding the cream).

To serve Spoon the veal and sauce on to a hot serving dish. Top with bacon rolls, triangles of lemon and parsley. Arrange the toast round the edge of the dish. Serve extra toast and lemon with the fricassée. *All recipes based on this dish serve 5–6.*

● **AVOID** *Cooking the meat too quickly: Boiling the liquid when adding the egg yolks, lemon juice and cream: The Sauce becoming lumpy.*

● **TO RECTIFY** *Keep the heat low under the stew: Whisk the sauce if it shows signs of becoming lumpy. You may prefer to lift the meat out of the stock before thickening this. Remove the meat from the pan with a perforated spoon or fish slice. Put on to a very hot dish, then thicken the liquid as the Blue Print.*

Fricassée of Chicken

Method as the Blue Print but use a jointed chicken or boiling fowl instead of veal. Simmer the chicken in the stock until tender then proceed as the Blue Print. You may need a little extra stock if cooking a boiling fowl. Never allow the sauce in a fricassée to be too thick, it should be a coating consistency. Jointed rabbit could be cooked in the same way.

A fricassée can be garnished with small cooked button mushrooms instead of, or in addition to, the bacon rolls.

Creamed Kidneys

1 green pepper; 1 red pepper; seasoning; 8 lambs' kidneys; 1 oz. flour; 2 oz. (¼C) butter; 3 tablespoons dry sherry; ¼ pint (⅔C) thin cream; 4–6 oz. (½–¾C) long grain rice.
Halve the peppers. Remove the cores and seeds then cut the flesh into neat strips. Blanch the strips of pepper by cooking them in boiling well seasoned water for 3–4 minutes only, then drain well. Skin the kidneys, halve and remove the white cores. Slice if wished. Season the flour, roll the kidneys in this. Heat the butter in a large pan. Fry the strips of pepper for a few minutes. Lift out of the pan on to a dish and keep hot. Cook the kidneys in the remaining butter until tender. This takes 8–10 minutes. Turn the meat several times so it does not harden in cooking. Blend the sherry and cream in a basin. Remove the pan from the heat, add the flavoured cream, stir well to mix the meat and sauce. Return to a low heat for 2–3 minutes only with some of the peppers. Boil the rice in salted water while cooking the peppers and kidneys. Arrange in a ring in a hot dish. Spoon the kidneys and sauce in the centre and top with the remaining pepper slices. *Serves 3–4.*

Paprika Beef

2 onions; 1 red pepper; 3 oz. (⅜C) butter; 1 lb. fillet steak; seasoning; 1 oz. flour; ¼ pint (⅔C) thin cream; 1 teaspoon paprika. *To garnish:* chopped parsley.
Cut the onions into rings, halve and slice the pepper (remove core and seeds). The strips of pepper may be blanched as in the recipe for Creamed Kidneys, but I like them rather firm in this dish. Heat half the butter and fry the onion and pepper for 5–8 minutes until *just* tender. Remove from the pan and keep hot. Cut the fillet steak into narrow strips. Toss in well seasoned flour and fry in the remainder of the butter. Blend the cream and paprika, pour over the meat and heat gently for several minutes. Lift the meat on to the serving dish and top with the onion and pepper. Garnish with parsley. This can be served with cooked rice or noodles or it is excellent with young green beans and a green salad. *Serves 3–4.*

Grilled Fish and Cream

4 portions white fish; little butter; seasoning; lemon juice; ¼ pint (⅔C) thick cream. *To garnish:* lemon; parsley; paprika.

Veal fricassée

Creamed kidneys

Stuffed plaice in cream

Pre-heat the grill so the fish cooks quickly. Put the fish on the buttered grid of the grill pan, season lightly and flavour with lemon juice. Top with melted butter. Grill until nearly tender, turn thick pieces of fish, thinner fillets do not need turning. Meanwhile whip the cream, season and flavour with a squeeze of lemon juice. Remove the grill pan from under the grill, lower the heat. Spread the cream over the fish and replace under the grill. Cook for a few minutes until the cream browns slightly. Serve at once garnished with slices of lemon, chopped parsley and paprika. *Serves 4.*

Stuffed Plaice in Cream

1 lb. cooked mashed potatoes; seasoning; 2 oz. ($\frac{1}{4}$C) butter; 4 large or 8 small plaice fillets; 3 oz. ($\frac{3}{4}$C) mushrooms; 3–4 rashers lean bacon; $\frac{1}{4}$ pint ($\frac{2}{3}$C) thick cream. *To garnish:* tomato; parsley.

Beat the potatoes with seasoning and 1 oz. butter. Put into a cloth bag with a $\frac{1}{4}$ or $\frac{1}{2}$-inch potato rose and pipe a border round the edge of a shallow oven-proof dish. Skin the fillets of plaice, or ask the fishmonger to do this. Roll the fillets from the tail to the head, secure with wooden cocktail sticks and put into the dish. Slice the mushrooms and chop the bacon. Heat the remaining butter and fry the mushrooms and bacon in this for a few minutes. Spoon into the centre of the fish rolls. Season the cream. Pour over the fish. Cover the dish lightly with foil, do not press this down and spoil the potato piping. Bake in the centre of a moderate oven, 350–375°F, Gas Mark 4–5 for 15 minutes until the fish is tender, do not over-cook. Meanwhile halve the tomato or cut in a Van-Dyke design, as in the picture, bake for a few minutes in the oven. Remove the foil and cocktail sticks, garnish with the tomato and parsley, serve at once. *Serves 4.*

Storing and Freezing *All these dishes must be stored in the refrigerator. If storing use within 24–36 hours. They are not very successful when frozen.*

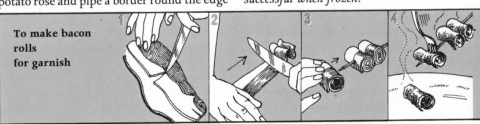

To make bacon rolls for garnish

1. Remove the bacon rinds. Half the rashers.
2. Stretch with a knife.
3. Form into rolls, put several on to a metal skewer, grill until crisp, turn several times.
4. Remove from the skewer with the prongs of a fork.

Put 1–2 tablespoons syrup and the hot or cold milk into the goblet. Put the lid on firmly and switch to the highest speed. Maintain for about 30 seconds to 1 minute. Pour into the tumbler.

Put a little crushed ice in the goblet with the syrup and milk. Switch on as described above. Put a spoonful of ice cream into the goblet, then add the syrup and milk. Switch on as described above.

Put fresh fruit, a few strawberries, piece of apple, orange or banana, into the goblet. Add the hot or cold milk. You can use crushed ice or ice cream with cold milk. Switch on as described above.

If you have no liquidiser—use the suggestions below. The mixture does not become quite as aerated, so use a little more milk to fill the tumbler.

Put into a cocktail shaker and shake hard.

Put into a jug or basin and whisk vigorously.

Chocolate and Coffee Milk Shakes

Use one of the methods of mixing above but flavour the milk with a little cocoa or chocolate powder or instant coffee, coffee essence, or strong coffee.

Iced Coffee

There are many ways of making iced coffee, but this is the method I use. Make very strong coffee, allow to cool then chill thoroughly. Put a little crushed ice into the glasses. Add enough coffee to come just over half way up the glass. Fill nearly to the top with ice cold milk then add a layer of thin cream. Sweeten as required. 1 pint ($2\frac{2}{3}$C) strong coffee, 1 pint ($2\frac{2}{3}$C) milk plus a little crushed ice and 4–5 tablespoons thin cream gives 4–5 glasses.

This can be varied by adding a spoonful of vanilla, coffee or chocolate ice cream just before serving or a spoonful of lightly whipped thick cream and a sprinkling of grated chocolate or ground cinnamon.

In order to produce iced coffee with no delay fill freezing trays with *strong* coffee. Put the dividers (to make ice cubes) into the trays. Freeze then pack the coffee ice cubes into containers and store in your freezer. All you need to do is to drop 1 or 2 of these cubes into cold milk and you have excellent iced coffee.

Yoghourt in Drinks

Yoghourt can be blended with many ingredients to give interesting drinks.

Yoghourt and tomato cocktail Whisk $\frac{1}{2}$ pint ($1\frac{1}{3}$C) chilled tomato juice, $\frac{1}{4}$ pint ($\frac{2}{3}$C) chilled natural yoghourt, 1 teaspoon Worcestershire sauce and seasoning together. Do this by hand or in the liquidiser. Pour into

Fruit milk shake

glasses and top with sprigs of mint. *Serves 4.*

Lemon fizz Blend $\frac{1}{4}$ pint ($\frac{2}{3}$C) natural or lemon flavoured yoghourt with a large bottle of bitter lemon. Pour into glasses, top with orange or lemon slices. *Serves 2.*

Hazel-nut and pineapple drink Blend 1 pint ($2\frac{2}{3}$C) sweetened canned pineapple juice with $\frac{1}{4}$ pint ($\frac{2}{3}$C) or $\frac{1}{2}$ pint ($1\frac{1}{3}$C) hazel-nut yoghourt. Pour into tall glasses over a little crushed ice. *Serves 3–4.*

Prune cream soda

Blend $\frac{1}{4}$ pint ($\frac{2}{3}$C) prune yoghourt and $\frac{1}{4}$ pint ($\frac{2}{3}$C) milk together. Chill and serve topped with a spoonful of ice cream. *Serves 1.*

Buttermilk Drinks

Buttermilk can be used in place of milk in any drinks. It is much lighter and the drinks are, therefore, less filling.

Coffee milk shake

Although milk is used more than any other dairy produce in drinks, yoghourt, buttermilk and cream contribute to interesting and health-giving beverages.

Milk Shakes

This is an excellent way of encouraging all the family to enjoy milk.

To give a fruit flavour Use fruit flavoured syrups, made especially to use in milk shakes; also blackcurrant and rose hip syrups or crushed fresh fruit.

If you have a liquidiser (blender) the methods of making the drinks are very simple; there are several ways to achieve these fluffy mixtures. Remember the liquidiser aerates the milk, so to produce a full tumbler of milk shake use barely $\frac{3}{4}$ tumbler of milk.

Many people have not yet had the opportunity to try soured cream in dishes. This is a pity, for dairy soured cream gives a particularly delicious flavour to both sweet and savoury dishes. It has a sharper, more piquant taste than fresh cream and seems less rich, so that dishes made with soured cream are never cloying. The distribution of this throughout the country is good, but not universal. If you have difficulty in obtaining it do not feel you cannot make the dishes given on this page and in other parts of Perfect Cooking; use fresh cream and to each ¼ pint (⅔C) allow 1 tablespoon lemon juice. In most dishes you are better to use thin, rather than thick cream, but this point is dealt with in the recipes below.

Blue Print

Using Soured Cream

1. It is excellent as a topping for soups, particularly if the soup has a rather bland flavour and needs a 'bite'. Add at the end of cooking and if reheating do this carefully and do not allow the soup to boil (see the recipe and picture on this page).
2. It is generally used to bind the ingredients in a 'dip' for it gives a certain piquancy to the mixture.
3. Often you will find soured cream among the ingredients in a cheese cake (see page 240).
4. One of the most famous dishes in the world using soured cream is Beef Stroganoff and a very simple version is given on this page.
5. Soured cream, blended with fresh fruit, makes a delicious filling for sponge cakes, tarts, etc.

● **AVOID** *Boiling sauces containing soured cream, otherwise they will curdle and spoil.*
● **TO RECTIFY** *The only remedy if the sauce does* curdle *is to sieve it or emulsify in a liquidiser.*

Crème Chambertin

2 medium-sized onions; 2 medium-sized potatoes; 2 oz. (¼C) butter; 1 pint (2⅔C) chicken stock; seasoning; 1 oz. flour; ½ pint (1⅓C) milk; 1 large carrot; 2 tablespoons chopped fresh herbs; ½ pint (1⅓C) soured cream.
Chop the onions and potatoes. Toss in the hot butter for a few minutes, take care the vegetables do not brown. Add the stock and simmer gently for 30 minutes. Season lightly. Sieve or emulsify the soup and return to the pan. Blend the flour with the milk and stir into the vegetable purée. Continue stirring over a low heat until the mixture thickens. Add the finely grated carrot, herbs, half the soured cream and a little extra seasoning. Simmer for 5–10 minutes. Do not boil. Top with the remainder of the soured cream. *Serves 6–8.*
To vary Add small sprigs cooked cauliflower after sieving.

Beef Stroganoff

1¼ lb. fillet steak; 4–6 oz. (1–1½C) button mushrooms; 1 small onion; 4 oz. (½C) butter; seasoning; nutmeg; ½ pint (1⅓C) soured cream; 2–3 tablespoons brandy (optional).
Cut the steak into 1-inch strips. Wash and dry the mushrooms, chop the onion finely. Heat 1 oz. of the butter in a pan, fry the mushrooms and season them. Heat the rest of the butter in a second pan, fry the onion until transparent, put in the steak and cook until tender; add a very little grated nutmeg, seasoning and the soured cream. Heat gently, put in the mushrooms and the brandy. Serve with rice or noodles. *Serves 4–5.*
Note The mushrooms may be fried in the same pan as the meat, but this tends to darken the sauce.
To vary Blend a little white wine and concentrated tomato purée with the soured cream.
You can also add a few drops of Worcestershire sauce to the soured cream.

Fried Chicken with Orange Cream

4 chicken breasts; 1 oz. flour; finely grated rind 1 orange; seasoning; 2–3 oz. (¼–⅜C) butter; ½ pint (1⅓C) soured cream; 1–2 tablespoons brandy or Curaçao. *To garnish:* 1 red pepper.

Wash and dry the chicken breasts well. If using frozen chicken allow to defrost thoroughly for this recipe. Mix the flour with the orange rind and seasoning. Coat the chicken in this. Heat the butter in a large pan and fry the chicken breasts steadily until tender, this takes about 12–15 minutes. Lift out of the pan on to a hot dish. Add the cream to the pan and stir well to incorporate the chicken juices. When ready to serve add the brandy or Curaçao, stir well. Pour over the chicken and top with slices of red pepper. The pepper should be halved and the core and seeds removed then the pulp cut into strips. If you wish to heat the pepper either fry in the pan with the chicken or cook in boiling well seasoned water until tender and strain. *Serves 4.*
To vary
Veal in soured cream
Use the recipe above, but substitute veal fillets for the chicken breasts and lemon rind for the orange rind.
If preferred omit the brandy or Curaçao from the above recipe and use orange juice in the sauce.

When Using Fresh Cream

On this page the recipes can be made with thin fresh cream and lemon juice but the soup is better with thick cream and lemon juice.

Storing and Freezing *The dishes on this page should be served when freshly cooked, although the soup can be reheated. They do not freeze well.*

Crème chambertin

Yoghourt and Buttermilk

Yoghourt, like most dairy produce, is a good mixer. It blends with sweet or savoury dishes. If you want to be truly lazy just eat yoghourt from the carton, which makes it ideal for packed meals.

The recipes on these pages mainly deal with natural yoghourt, but there are many flavours from which to choose. Natural yoghourt is low in calories, so it should be included in most slimming diets; it gives the food value of milk in an easy to digest form.

Blue Print

Using Yoghourt

1. Try it as an easy dessert, serve with fruit or simply mix with a little sugar or honey and ground nutmeg or cinnamon. The flavoured yoghourt is particularly good for desserts.
2. Blend yoghourt into a liquid jelly before it sets.
3. Stir yoghourt into white, cheese and other sauces, it gives a pleasant sharpness that blends with most foods but particularly with chicken, veal and white fish.
4. If you find mashed vegetables dull, add butter and yoghourt instead of butter and milk.
5. Yoghourt is an excellent basis for quick and easy salad dressings.
6. If a soup tastes a little dull, add some natural yoghourt. It is particularly good with vegetable soups.
7. In many countries yoghourt is an essential ingredient in savoury dishes as in the kebabs opposite.
Note Natural yoghourt is often sold in 5 oz. cartons which is $\frac{1}{4}$ pint ($\frac{2}{3}$C).

Storing and Freezing *Yoghourt and sauces made with yoghourt can be kept for a day or two in a refrigerator. They must not be frozen. The tea bread and cake are not particularly rich so should be eaten when fresh, or they can be frozen.*

Yoghourt Whip

Approximately $\frac{1}{2}$ pint ($1\frac{1}{3}$C) thick sweetened fruit purée; $\frac{1}{4}$ pint ($\frac{2}{3}$C) natural yoghourt; 1 egg white. *To decorate:* fruit.
The purée can be obtained in various ways. If using ripe strawberries or other soft fruit just mash, sieve or emulsify and add sugar to taste. Hard fruit should be cooked in the minimum of water (or omit water if possible) with sugar to taste, then mashed, sieved or emulsified. If using canned or defrosted frozen fruit, strain off the syrup (this can be used in a fruit salad or jelly), mash, sieve or emulsify. Add extra sugar if required.

Chill the yoghourt well then beat into the cold purée. Add the stiffly whisked egg white. Spoon into glasses, decorate with fruit and serve at once. The mixture tends to separate if left standing. *Serves 3–4.*

Jellied Whip

Recipe as above, but soften 1 teaspoon powdered gelatine in 2 tablespoons water or syrup from the fruit in a basin. Stand in a saucepan of very hot water and stir until dissolved. Add to the fruit purée, cool thoroughly then proceed as above. This small amount of gelatine prevents the mixture separating, so you can prepare the dessert and allow it to stand for some time in the refrigerator.

Savoury Yoghourt Whip

Add 1–2 tablespoons freshly chopped mint or other herbs, 2 tablespoons lemon, orange or grapefruit juice and seasoning to $\frac{1}{4}$ pint ($\frac{2}{3}$C) chilled natural yoghourt. This makes a pleasant beginning to a meal instead of fruit juice. *Serves 2.*

Yoghourt Jelly

Dissolve a 1 pint ($2\frac{2}{3}$C) fruit flavoured jelly in $\frac{3}{4}$ pint (2C) hot water. Allow to cool then whisk in $\frac{1}{4}$ pint ($\frac{2}{3}$C) yoghourt; this can be natural yoghourt or a flavour that blends with the jelly. Put into a rinsed mould or sundae glasses and allow to set. *Serves 3–4.*

Salad Dressings

Quantities give enough for 4 servings.
Cucumber dressing Blend 2 tablespoons finely diced cucumber, the grated rind and juice of $\frac{1}{2}$ lemon and 1 teaspoon sugar with $\frac{1}{4}$ pint ($\frac{2}{3}$C) natural yoghourt. Add 1 teaspoon chopped parsley and $\frac{1}{2}$–1 teaspoon chopped dill or fennel. Serve with fish.
Horseradish dressing Blend 2–3 tablespoons finely grated fresh horseradish with 2 teaspoons white vinegar or lemon juice, $\frac{1}{4}$ pint ($\frac{2}{3}$C) natural yoghourt, seasoning, a good pinch sugar and $\frac{1}{2}$ teaspoon made mustard. Serve with hot or cold beef. When fresh horseradish is not available blend 4 tablespoons bottled horseradish cream with the same amount of natural yoghourt. Season.
Mint and caper dressing Blend $\frac{1}{4}$ pint ($\frac{2}{3}$C) natural yoghourt with seasoning, 1 tablespoon freshly chopped mint and 2 teaspoons capers. This is excellent with cold lamb.

Yoghourt whip

Savoury Sauces

You can add a few spoonfuls of natural yoghourt to most savoury sauces if you feel the sauce *needs* a little extra flavour. Make sure the sauce is no longer boiling when you add the yoghourt and stir or whisk over a low heat. As yoghourt is a low fat food I find it better to heat sauces in a basin over hot water or the top of a double saucepan; this avoids any possibility of burning. Quantities give enough for 4 servings.
Golden cheese sauce Put 1 egg and $\frac{1}{2}$ pint ($1\frac{1}{3}$C) natural yoghourt into a basin over hot water or top of a double saucepan, add $\frac{1}{2}$–1 teaspoon made mustard, seasoning and heat well, stirring all the time. Add up to 4 oz. (1C) grated Cheddar cheese and heat until melted.
Piquant tomato sauce Put 2 tablespoons concentrated tomato purée, $\frac{1}{2}$ pint ($1\frac{1}{3}$C) natural yoghourt, 1 crushed clove garlic and seasoning into a basin over hot water or top of a double saucepan. Season well, add a little Worcestershire, soy or chilli sauce if desired. Stir until hot and smooth. Serve with grilled or fried fish or chicken or veal cutlets.
Mock hollandaise sauce Put 2 egg yolks, seasoning and 2 teaspoons lemon juice in a basin over hot water or top of a double saucepan. Whisk until fluffy then gradually whisk in $\frac{1}{4}$ pint ($\frac{2}{3}$C) natural yoghourt. Season well.

Yoghourt is equally as successful in sweet as in savoury sauces.
Yoghourt custard sauce Put 1 egg or 2 egg yolks and $\frac{1}{2}$ pint ($1\frac{1}{3}$C) natural yoghourt into a basin over hot water or the top of a double saucepan. Whisk until smooth, add sugar, honey or sugar substitute to sweeten. Serve with fruit or in a trifle. The custard may be flavoured with vanilla, chocolate or coffee or use flavoured yoghourt. *Serves 4–6.*
Russian fruit sauce Blend equal quantities of fruit purée and yoghourt (natural or flavoured) and heat these together. Serve

...ver sponge puddings, ice cream, etc. Instead of fruit you can use jam or jelly. Heat this then cool slightly and blend with the yoghourt.

Using Buttermilk

In the old days when so many people produced their own butter there was a plentiful supply of buttermilk available. Buttermilk is the skimmed milk left after removing the cream for butter. Because it is lighter than ordinary milk it is excellent for mixing the dough in scones, quick breads and family cakes. Two recipes on this page make use of buttermilk.

When you use buttermilk for drinks, remember it has not only a lighter texture than milk but it has a pleasantly soured flavour.

Buttermilk Fruit Cake

12 oz. (3C) self-raising flour or plain flour and 3 teaspoons baking powder; $\frac{1}{2}$–1 teaspoon allspice; 6 oz. ($\frac{3}{4}$C) butter or margarine; 6 oz. ($\frac{3}{4}$C) brown sugar; 1 level tablespoon black treacle or golden syrup; 2 eggs; $\frac{1}{4}$ pint ($\frac{2}{3}$C) buttermilk; 12 oz. (2C) mixed dried fruit.

Sieve the flour or flour and baking powder with the allspice. Rub in the butter or margarine, add the sugar, black treacle or syrup and the beaten eggs. Mix thoroughly then add the buttermilk and dried fruit. Stir well. Put into an 8-inch greased and floured cake tin and bake in the centre of a very moderate oven, 325–350°F, Gas Mark 3–4, for approximately $1\frac{1}{4}$–$1\frac{1}{2}$ hours. Check that the cake is not becoming over-brown at the end of about 50 minutes and reduce the oven temperature slightly if necessary. (Illustrated on page 227.)

Raisin and Walnut Bread

8 oz. (2C) self-raising flour or plain flour and 2 teaspoons baking powder; pinch salt; 2 oz. ($\frac{1}{4}$C) butter or margarine; 2 oz. ($\frac{1}{4}$C) sugar; 4 oz. ($\frac{2}{3}$C) raisins; 4 oz. (1C) chopped walnuts; 1 egg; 1 level tablespoon golden syrup; 7 tablespoons buttermilk. *For the topping:* 1 tablespoon sugar; 2 tablespoons chopped walnuts; little buttermilk.

Sieve the flour or flour and baking powder and salt. Rub in the butter or margarine, add the sugar, raisins, walnuts and beaten egg. Mix thoroughly. Stir the syrup into the buttermilk, add to the other ingredients and beat well. Grease and flour a $1\frac{1}{2}$–2-lb. loaf tin, spoon the mixture into this. Spread flat on top. Mix the sugar and nuts together. Brush the loaf with buttermilk, sprinkle the sugar and nuts over the top. Press gently with a palette knife. Bake for approximately 45–50 minutes in the centre of a moderate oven, 350–375°F, Gas Mark 4–5, until quite firm to the touch. Lower the heat after 30 minutes to very moderate if the loaf is browning too much. Turn out carefully. Slice and butter.

To vary The above gives a fairly shallow loaf. If preferred bake in a 1 lb. loaf tin for about 1 hour.

Use chopped dates in place of raisins.

Yoghourt and Fruit Salad Flan

Make an 8-inch sponge or pastry flan, bake and allow to cool.

Prepare 1–$1\frac{1}{4}$ lb. fresh fruit salad (enough for 6 people). Choose a good selection of fruit as shown in the picture on page 227. Blend with $\frac{1}{2}$ pint ($1\frac{1}{4}$C) natural yoghourt and a little sugar to taste. Spoon into the flan case and serve as soon as possible, so the flan case is not softened. *Serves 6.*

Yoghourt Fruit Salad

Blend freshly sliced and prepared fruit salad with yoghourt, using proportions as suggested in the recipe above. Allow to stand for about an hour for the flavours to blend. *Serves 6.*

Lamb Shish-Kebabs with Herbed Sauce

For the sauce: 1 bottle—about $\frac{1}{2}$ pint ($1\frac{1}{3}$C) tomato juice; 2 teaspoons made mustard; $\frac{1}{4}$ pint ($\frac{2}{3}$C) natural yoghourt; shake cayenne pepper; 2 teaspoons finely chopped mint; 2 teaspoons chopped chives or spring onions; seasoning; $\frac{1}{4}$ teaspoon ground cinnamon. *For the kebabs:* 1 lb. lean lamb (cut from the leg); 1 green pepper; 8–12 button mushrooms; 4 small tomatoes; 12 small cocktail onions; 1 oz. butter.

Mix all the ingredients for the sauce. Put into a shallow dish. Cut the lamb into 1-inch cubes. Put into the sauce and leave for 3–4 hours, turn several times. Lift the meat out of the sauce. Cut the flesh of the green pepper into 8–12 pieces, discard the core and seeds. Thread the meat and vegetables on to 4 long metal skewers. Brush the vegetables, but not the meat, with the melted butter, season lightly. Cook under the hot grill, turning several times, until tender. Brush the meat once or twice with the sauce. Serve with boiled rice or crusty bread. Heat the remaining sauce *gently* and serve with the kebabs. *Serves 4.*

Lamb shish-kebabs with herbed sauce

As you will see by the picture on this page, these colourful dishes would make a perfect warm weather dinner or luncheon menu. Each recipe though has the added advantage of being a good basic one that can be varied throughout the year and you will find suggestions for 'ringing the changes'.

Chilled Summer Soup

1 medium-sized lettuce; 1 bunch watercress or use a little parsley instead; 1 medium-sized bunch spring onions; 1½ oz. butter; 1½ pints (4C) chicken stock or water and 2 chicken stock cubes; 1½ oz. flour; seasoning; ½ pint (1⅓C) thin cream. *To garnish:* chopped parsley.

Wash and shred the lettuce, discard any tough outer leaves. Chop the watercress

Warm Weather Dishes

leaves or enough parsley to give 1 tablespoon. Chop the white part of the onions together with some of the green stems. Heat the butter in a saucepan and add the lettuce, watercress or parsley and onions. Lower the heat and cook for 10 minutes, stirring several times so the vegetables do not burn. Add most of the stock or water and stock cubes. Simmer gently for approximately 10 minutes, or until the vegetables are tender. Blend the flour with the remaining stock. Add to the soup and cook until thickened. Season well.

Sieve or emulsify the soup to give a very smooth purée. If you do this *after* thickening the soup a skin will not form. Allow to become really cold then whisk in most of the cream. Serve in a chilled tureen or soup cups. Top with the rest of the cream and chopped parsley. *Serves 4–6.*

To vary Use sprigged cauliflower with 1–2 chopped leeks instead of the lettuce, watercress and spring onions. Sieve or emulsify as above, garnish with paprika.

Use about 6 oz. shredded spinach and spring onions, omit the lettuce and watercress. Sieve or emulsify as above, garnish with cream and parsley.

Use a lettuce, ½ peeled chopped cucumber and 1 chopped onion together with the grated rind of 2 oranges. Omit the water-

Chilled summer soup, Salmon cream flan, Blackcurrant ice cream and Strawberry cream gâteau.

cress and spring onions. Sieve or emulsify as above. Garnish with diced cucumber, serve with sliced oranges, see the picture on the right.

Salmon Cream Flan

For the pastry: 6 oz. (1½C) flour, preferably plain; pinch salt; 3 oz. (⅜C) butter or margarine; water to bind. *For the filling:* 7½–8 oz. can red salmon; 2 eggs or 4 egg yolks (use the whites in the ice cream); ¼ medium-sized cucumber; ½ pint (1⅓C) thin cream; ¼ teaspoon anchovy essence; ½ small onion or 2–3 spring onions; seasoning. *To garnish:* sliced cucumber; parsley.

Sieve the flour and salt. Rub in the butter or margarine until the consistency of fine breadcrumbs. Gradually add enough cold water to make a rolling consistency. Roll out and line an 8-inch flan ring, on an upturned baking tray, or a sandwich tin. Put a piece of greased greaseproof paper into the pastry case (with the greased side touching the pastry). Cover with beans or crusts of bread and bake 'blind' in the centre of a moderately hot to hot oven, 400–425°F, Gas Mark 6–7, for 10–15 minutes, until golden coloured. Meanwhile flake the salmon in a basin, beat in the eggs or egg yolks. Peel and dice the cucumber, add to the fish mixture with the cream, anchovy essence, finely chopped or grated onion and seasoning. Remove the flan from the oven, take out the paper and beans or bread. Spoon the fish mixture into the pastry case. Lower the oven heat to very moderate, 325–350°F, Gas Mark 3–4, and bake for a further 30–35 minutes until the pastry is crisp and the filling firm. Garnish with the thinly sliced cucumber and parsley. Serve hot or cold with new potatoes and green peas. *Serves 4–6.*

To vary Use flaked white fish instead of salmon.
Use canned or cooked crab instead of salmon.
Use finely chopped chicken instead of salmon, omit the anchovy essence and substitute 1 teaspoon horseradish cream.
Add chopped parsley, chives or dill to the fish mixture.

Blackcurrant Ice Cream

1 lb. fresh blackcurrants; 2 tablespoons water; 2 oz. (¼C) sugar; ½ pint (1⅓C) thick cream; 4 level tablespoons sieved icing sugar; 4 egg whites.

Make sure the refrigerator is set to the coldest setting. Cut the ends from the blackcurrants (i.e. top and tail). Simmer with the water and sugar until just soft. Put some on one side for decoration and sieve or emulsify the remainder to give a purée. Cool thoroughly. Whip the cream *lightly*, do not over-whip. Blend with the icing sugar and the blackcurrant purée, put into the freezing trays. Freeze for about 30 minutes until just begin-

Apple cream sponge (left)
Chilled summer soup Version 3 (below)

ning to stiffen then remove from the refrigerator and put into a chilled bowl. Whisk the egg whites stiffly, fold into the half frozen fruit mixture. Return to the freezing trays and freeze until firm. When ready to serve spoon into dishes or goblets and top with the blackcurrants. *Serves 6–8.*

To vary Use any other fruit pulp—apricots, passion fruit, etc. instead of blackcurrants.

Strawberry Cream Gâteau

For the sponge: 4 large eggs; 4 oz. (½C) caster sugar; finely grated rind ½ lemon; 4 oz. (1C) flour, plain or self-raising; 2 teaspoons lemon juice. *For the filling:* ½ pint (1⅓C) thick cream; 1 oz. sieved icing or caster sugar; 1 lb. strawberries.

Put the eggs, sugar and lemon rind into a large mixing bowl or the electric mixer bowl and whisk until thick and creamy. You should see the trail of the whisk. Sieve the flour very thoroughly. In this sponge so much air should be incorporated into the eggs and sugar that self-raising flour is not

essential. Fold the flour gently and carefully into the eggs and sugar with a metal spoon or palette knife. Add the lemon juice. Grease and flour an 8-inch cake tin. Put in the mixture. Bake in the centre of a very moderate to moderate oven, 325–350°F, Gas Mark 3–4, for approximately 35–40 minutes, until just firm to the touch. Turn out of the tin and allow to cool. Cut into three slices. Whip the cream until it stands up in peaks. Fold in the sugar. Halve the strawberries. Sandwich the layers together with some of the cream and fruit. Top with the remainder of the fruit. Put the remaining cream into a piping bag with a small or ¼-inch rose pipe. Decorate the edges and top with piped cream. *Serves 8–10.*

To vary Use any fruit in season as a filling.

Apple Cream Sponge

Make and bake the sponge as above or cook in a 9-inch cake tin for about 30 minutes. Turn out and cool. Slice 1 or 2 dessert apples (do not peel), simmer in a very little water and sugar, with lemon juice to flavour, until tender but unbroken. Whip ¼ pint (⅔C) thick cream. Add 1 tablespoon sieved icing or caster sugar. Pipe or spread on top of the sponge. Drain the apple slices carefully and arrange on the cream with halved rings of canned or fresh pineapple

To vary Bake the sponge in a 10-inch ring tin and fill the centre of the ring with fruit and cream.

Storing and Freezing *All these dishes should be kept in a refrigerator for only about 24 hours. They can all be frozen, but the cucumber in the filling of the flan becomes limp. Serve the flan as soon as it is defrosted, otherwise the filling makes the pastry soft. You cannot freeze the cucumber garnish on the flan.*

Do not imagine that a dessert including cream is unduly extravagant. You need not use a great quantity of cream to give a good flavour. The desserts on this page serve 4–6 people and only one of them uses more than $\frac{1}{4}$ pint ($\frac{2}{3}$C) thick cream.

Cream Desserts

Cream Flan

For the flan case: 2 eggs; 3 oz. ($\frac{3}{8}$C) caster sugar; $2\frac{1}{2}$ oz. (just over $\frac{1}{2}$C) flour, plain or self-raising. *For the filling:* $\frac{1}{2}$ pint ($1\frac{1}{3}$C) thick cream or $\frac{1}{4}$ pint ($\frac{2}{3}$C) thick and $\frac{1}{4}$ pint ($\frac{2}{3}$C) thin cream; 8–12 oz. fruit (raspberries, strawberries, passion fruit pulp, peaches, etc.); little sugar.

Whisk the eggs and sugar until thick, see page 235 for a more detailed explanation. Fold in the sieved flour. Grease and flour an 8–9-inch sponge flan tin, spoon in the mixture and bake for about 12 minutes above the centre of a moderate to moderately hot oven, 375–400°F, Gas Mark 5–6, until firm to the touch. Turn out carefully and leave until quite cold. Whip the thick cream until it *just* holds a shape, or whip the thick cream then gradually whisk in the thin cream. Halve or mash most of the fruit and blend with the cream, add the sugar. Lift the sponge flan on to a serving plate. Fill with the cream mixture and decorate with fruit. Serve with extra cream or ice cream. *Serves 5–6.*

Strawberry Fruit Whip

1 strawberry flavoured jelly; generous $\frac{1}{2}$ pint ($1\frac{1}{2}$C) water; 2 eggs; 1 oz. sugar; $\frac{1}{4}$ pint ($\frac{2}{3}$C) thick cream.
Dissolve the jelly in the very hot water.

Strawberry fruit whip (above)
Cream flan (below)

Allow to cool. Separate the egg yolks from the whites. Beat the yolks and sugar until thick and creamy. Pour the warm jelly over the egg yolks. Allow to cool and begin to stiffen, then add the lightly whisked cream and the stiffly whisked egg whites. Spoon into 4 or 5 glasses and allow to set. *Serves 4–5.*
To vary This is delicious made with an orange or lemon jelly. Use the juice of 1 or 2 oranges or lemons made up to a generous $\frac{1}{2}$ pint ($1\frac{1}{2}$C) with water.
Use a little less water and add thick fruit

purée to the jelly and egg yolk mixture, allow to thicken slightly, continue as above.

Chocolate Cream Mousse

4 oz. cooking or plain chocolate; 4 eggs; 1 tablespoon caster sugar; $\frac{1}{4}$ pint ($\frac{2}{3}$C) thick cream.
Break the chocolate into pieces. Put into a large basin and stand this over a pan of hot, but *not* boiling water. Allow to soften slightly —do not leave too long. Separate the egg yolks from the whites. Add the yolks and the sugar to the chocolate. Beat the mixture until light and soft. Remove from the top of the pan. Continue beating as the mixture cools. When quite cool, but not set, fold in the lightly whipped cream and the stiffly whisked egg whites. Spoon into glasses and chill. *Serves 4–5.*

White Wine Syllabub

$\frac{1}{4}$ pint ($\frac{2}{3}$C) thick cream; $\frac{1}{4}$ pint ($\frac{2}{3}$C) thin cream; 1 lemon; 2 oz. ($\frac{1}{4}$C) caster sugar; up to $\frac{1}{4}$ pint ($\frac{2}{3}$C) sweet white wine. *To decorate:* crystallised rose petals.
Whip the thick cream until it holds a shape. Gradually whisk in the thin cream, the very finely grated lemon rind and sugar. Add the lemon juice and wine slowly to the fluffy cream until a soft mixture. Spoon into glasses and chill. Decorate with crystallised rose petals. *Serves 4–5.*

Storing and Freezing *All these desserts except the Syllabub, which is inclined to separate, store for 24 hours in the refrigerator. None freeze well.*

The recipes on this page need no cooking. They depend upon the good flavour given them by dairy produce, i.e. butter and cream.

Chocolate Cherry Slice

4 oz. (½C) butter, preferably unsalted; 3 *level* tablespoons golden syrup; 12 oz. digestive or semi-sweet biscuits; 2 oz. (⅓C) sultanas; 2 oz. (generous ¼C) glacé cherries; 4 oz. plain chocolate (this is better than cooking chocolate in this recipe); 2–4 oz. (⅓–⅔C) whole blanched almonds (optional). *For the icing:* 2 oz. plain chocolate; 1½ tablespoons water; 1 oz. butter; 6 oz. (1½C) sieved icing sugar. *To decorate:* 5–6 glacé cherries; angelica; 2 oz. (½C) chopped nuts, preferably almonds.

Melt the butter and syrup in a large pan, remove from the heat. Crush the biscuits with a rolling pin. Add the biscuit crumbs and sultanas to the melted mixture. Quarter the cherries, chop the chocolate and the nuts and tip into the pan. Stir over a gentle heat until the chocolate melts (this takes a very short time). Line the bottom of a Swiss roll tin, measuring about 11 × 7–8-inches, with greased greaseproof paper. Tip the chocolate mixture into this and flatten with a palette knife. Leave in a cool place for several hours to set. Cut into 3 slices across the tin, make sure these are of equal size. The mixture is easy to cut if you dip the knife in very hot water and shake reasonably dry.

To make the icing, break the chocolate into pieces. Put into a basin with the water and butter. Stand over a pan of hot, but not boiling water and leave until the chocolate has melted. Remove the basin from the pan, add the icing sugar and beat until smooth. Sandwich the 3 layers together with some of the icing. Spread the remainder on top, smooth flat, then mark on a design with a fork. Decorate with halved glacé cherries, leaves of angelica and a border of finely chopped nuts. Serve as a dessert or as a cake with coffee or tea.

Banana Fool

3 bananas; 1–2 oz. caster or sieved icing sugar (amount depends upon personal taste); 1 tablespoon lemon juice; 2 oz. (⅓C) raisins; ¼ pint (⅔C) thick cream; ¼ pint (⅔C) thin cream. *To decorate:* finely grated lemon rind; few raisins.

Peel the bananas and mash with half the sugar and the lemon juice, add the raisins. Pour the thick cream gradually over the bananas and beat until thick then gradually blend in half the thin cream. Beat hard until smooth. Spoon into individual glasses. Stir the remainder of the sugar into the thin cream. Pour over the banana mixture and decorate with the lemon rind and raisins. *Serves 4–6.*

To vary Add mashed berry fruit, passion

Uncooked Desserts

fruit pulp, finely chopped pineapple etc. The cream mixture may be flavoured with a little brandy or a liqueur.

Grape Meringue Flan

10–12 home-made or bought small meringues (see page 12); 2 oz. (¼C) butter; 3 oz. (nearly ½C) soft brown sugar; 3 oz. (nearly ½C) demarara sugar; 8 *level* tablespoons golden syrup; 8 oz. bran buds. *For the filling:* 8 oz. white grapes; 2–4 oz. black grapes; 4 level tablespoons sieved apricot jam; 3 tablespoons water.

If making meringues prepare these first. Melt the butter, the sugars and syrup in a large pan. Remove from the heat, add the bran buds. Mix well then press into an 8-inch flan ring on a serving plate. Leave in a cool place for 2–3 hours to harden. Halve the grapes, remove the pips. Heat the jam and water until a smooth glaze. Arrange the grapes in the flan and brush with the *warm* glaze. Leave to cool then put the meringues round the edge. Serve with cream. *Serves 5–6.*

To vary Use crushed biscuit crumbs or corn flakes instead of bran buds.

Top with other fresh fruit; as this is a very sweet base do not use sweetened canned fruit.

Storing and Freezing *The cherry slice and flan base keep well for several weeks in a tin or other covered container. There is no point in freezing them. The banana fool should be eaten fresh or it can be frozen as an ice cream.*

Know About Cheese

I wonder if you try as large a variety of cheese as you can? So often one is inclined to select the cheeses one knows and overlook the other kinds. Some of the cheeses available today are described on this page. Obviously not *every* cheese listed will be on show in *every* store, although in large stores there is generally an impressive selection. When a kind is described as 'dessert' cheese it simply means it is eaten at the end of a meal with bread or biscuits. Where the cheeses have other outstanding uses I have given them, for example Danish Blue is excellent as a filling for celery 'boats'.

Buying Cheese

Do not buy too much at one time, except when entertaining a large number, for most cheeses lose flavour or develop an unpleasantly strong taste if *too* mature. You may shop where the assistant is very helpful about the cheeses to buy and their condition, but there are simple ways of checking on this. If a soft cheese, such as Brie or Camembert, feels very firm and hard it is immature and must be allowed to mature before serving. Unfortunately these cheeses can be stored in such a cold temperature that sometimes they *never* mature properly, which is why it is important to buy cheese from a shop where they understand correct storage conditions. If the cheeses feel very soft they will be very ripe and strong. Ideally the cheese should 'give' to gentle pressure.

The veined cheeses, such as Gorgonzola and Stilton, should not smell unpleasantly strong or look very dry and hard.

The firm cheeses, such as Cheddar and Cheshire, should not look damp or be badly cracked and dry looking.

Storing Cheese

Many cheeses *can* be stored in a refrigerator. Wrap well in foil or put into a polythene container and keep as far away from the freezing compartment as possible, or put into the special cheese compartment. Bring the cheese out of the refrigerator for $\frac{1}{2}$–1 hour before a meal. Some cheeses are spoiled by being stored in the cool temperature of a refrigerator. I have indicated these by the words 'room temperature'.

The storage time given is just an indication of the period during which the cheese is at its best.

Freezing cheese is not normally recommended, but if I have a lot of cheese left over from a party I do freeze it, then take out one or two varieties as required. Allow to defrost at room temperature.

Bel Paese From Italy, the name means beautiful country. A firm, creamy white cheese with a nutty flavour.
Use: Delicious with fruit.
Store: Refrigerator—several days.

Bresse Bleu A soft French cheese with faint blue veining. Medium strong.
Use: Excellent in salads.
Store: Room temperature—about a week.

Brie This has a firm crust and creamy centre. From France, it has an over-strong flavour when ripe.
Use: Good after-dinner cheese.
Store: Room temperature—1–2 days.

Caboc An ancient Scottish Highlands double cream cheese rolled in toasted oatmeal.
Use: Goes well with full bodied wines.
Store: Refrigerator—1–2 weeks. Do not allow to dry.

Caerphilly A favourite with Welsh miners, this semi-smooth, creamy white cheese has a mild, slightly salty flavour.
Use: Good with apples in a salad.
Store: Refrigerator—several weeks.

Camembert Another soft textured creamy French cheese. Cut like a cake.
Use: A perfect dessert cheese. Although it cannot be stored in the refrigerator it is delicious if frosted lightly like an ice cream and served with fruit.
Store: Room temperature—1–2 days.

Cheddar A rich, mellow, nutty-flavoured cheese, close-textured and ranging from cream to deep yellow. Flavour strengthens as the cheese matures.
Use: All purposes in cooking and a dessert cheese.
Store: Refrigerator—2–3 weeks, but it does dry out during this time.

Cheshire The oldest known English cheese, with crumbly texture and mellow flavour that improves with age. Can be white or red.
Use: Dessert cheese, but excellent in salads and can be used in cooking.
Store: Refrigerator—2–3 weeks but it does dry out during this time.

Cottage Cheese A low calorie crumbly cheese.
Use: Can be served with fruit, excellent with salads and used in cooking.
Store: Refrigerator—in carton—several days.

Danish Blue Crumbly white cheese with blue veins, it becomes softer with maturity. A slightly sharp flavour.
Use: Particularly good as a filling in celery, blend with cream. Excellent diced as a cocktail snack.
Store: Room temperature—1 week.

Demi-Sel Soft French pasteurised cheese with a fairly good 'bite', slightly crumbly.
Use: Fill halved dessert pears, top with nuts.
Store: Refrigerator—1 week.

Derby A creamy white or honey-coloured, open-textured cheese. Mild flavour develops as it matures. There is also Sage Derby, which is flavoured with sage leaves giving green tinted layers.
Use: A very pleasant dessert cheese.
Store: Refrigerator—several weeks.

Dolcelatta An Italian soft delicately veined cheese; must be ripe to develop flavour.
Use: Excellent dessert cheese or with fruit.
Store: Room temperature—few days only.

Double Gloucester A smooth, deep cream to reddish cheese with a crumbly texture, it has a rich flavour similar to Cheshire. A slow maturing cheese.
Use: Excellent in Welsh Rarebit, but a good dessert cheese.
Store: Refrigerator—several weeks.

Dunlop Scottish cheese, rather like Cheddar.
Use: As Cheddar.
Store: Refrigerator—several weeks.

Edam Creamy, firm textured Dutch cheese with a red rind. Mild flavour.
Use: Very good in all forms of cooking, slices neatly for open sandwiches. Use in salads.
Store: Refrigerator—several weeks.

Emmenthal (or Emmenthaler) Famous Swiss cheese with mild, nutty flavour. Has fairly large holes.
Use: Used in Swiss Fondue. An excellent cooking cheese but can be eaten as a dessert cheese.
Store: Refrigerator—several weeks.

Esrom Mild flavoured Danish cheese, slightly aromatic, with butter-like texture and numerous irregular holes.
Use: A very good cheese in salads or with fruit.
Store: Refrigerator—1–2 weeks.

Fynbo Another mild Danish cheese, but firmer textured than Esrom with regular holes.
Use: As Esrom.
Store: Refrigerator—1–2 weeks.

Gjetöst A dark brown Norwegian goat's cheese—mild and rather sweet in flavour.
Use: Can be sliced neatly and thinly to use in open sandwiches.
Store: Refrigerator—some weeks.

Gouda Creamy, firm textured Dutch cheese, wheel-shaped with yellow rind. Mild flavour.
Use: Very good in cooking.
Store: Refrigerator—several weeks.

Gorgonzola From Italy, a soft textured cheese with grey-green veins and a sharp flavour.
Use: A splendid after-dinner cheese.
Store: Room temperature—several days.

uyère Firm textured French/Swiss cheese
th a few small holes, it has a unique, slightly
eet spiced flavour. Often confused with
mmenthal which is the cheese with the larger
les.
e: Excellent cooking cheese.
ore: Refrigerator—several weeks.

avarti A Danish cheese that used to be called
dsit.
re: After-dinner cheese, good with fruit.
ore: Refrigerator—1–2 weeks.

ncashire This crumbly white cheese matures
om mild to rather pungent.
e: A splendid accompaniment to apple pie or
umbled on top of soup.
ore: Refrigerator—1–2 weeks.

icester A crumbly, open textured cheese.
ch red-brown colour with mild flavour which
atures to piquant.
se: Good dessert cheese. Delicious in a salad.
ore: Refrigerator—1–2 weeks.

ozzarella A soft Italian cheese with very
efinite flavour. Sold in plastic covering so it
oes not dry.
se: One of the very good Italian cooking
eeses used in pizza and lasagna.
ore: Refrigerator—well wrapped—2–3 weeks.

. Paulin A soft French cheese covered with
ange coloured rind, fairly strong.
se: Ideal for the end of a meal where you have
rved food with a strong taste.
ore: Refrigerator—few days.

armesan Very hard Italian cheese usually sold
rated. A sharp strong flavour. You can buy
is in small containers already grated.
se: For cooking or sprinkling over other
ishes, i.e. soup.
ore: Cupboard—if in drums. Keeps almost
definitely.

Port Salut A French cheese, round in shape
with a fairly strong flavour.
Use: A good dessert cheese.
Store: Refrigerator—1–2 weeks.

Roquefort French cheese. Similar in appearance
to Danish Blue cheese; good mild flavour.
Use: In salads, as a dessert cheese, excellent
with fruit.
Store: Room temperature—few days.

Samsöe Staple cheese of Denmark, it is named
after the island where it was first made. Mild,
sweet nutty flavour with firm texture and round
shiny holes.
Use: Dessert cheese, excellent sliced for open
sandwiches.
Store: Refrigerator—several weeks.

Smoked Cheese Austrian sausage-shaped
cheeses, one variety is mixed with ham.
Use: Dessert cheese.
Store: Refrigerator—several weeks.

Stilton Connoisseur's cheese traditionally
associated with port. Open texture, creamy with
blue veins spreading from centre. Rich and
mellow with a tangy flavour from the veins.
White Stilton also available, which is milder.
Use: Perfect dessert cheese, often spooned from
centre rather than sliced.
Store: Room temperature—some weeks.

Tôme au Raisin (Tôme au Marc de Raisins)
French cheese, rather soft in texture and fairly
mild. Can be recognised by the covering of
grape pips which add a distinctive flavour.
Use: Dessert cheese.
Store: Refrigerator—up to 1 week.

Wensleydale A smooth, creamy white cheese
with a mild, slightly salty flavour.
Use: Another British cheese traditionally
associated with apple pie.
Store: Refrigerator—several weeks.

In addition there are the flavoured cheeses,
i.e. with herbs, nuts, garlic, etc.
Use: These are excellent dessert cheeses.
Store: Refrigerator—for a short time.

Cheese Dishes

Cheese and date bread

Throughout Perfect Cooking are many dishes
using cheese, but here are two particularly
easy and slightly less usual ways of using
cheese.

Cheese and Date Bread

8 oz. (2C) self-raising flour (or plain flour and
2 teaspoons baking powder); 1 level teaspoon
dry mustard; seasoning; 2 oz. (¼C) butter or
margarine; 4 oz. (1C) grated Cheddar,
Gruyère or Cheshire cheese; 2–3 oz. (nearly
½C) chopped dates; 2 eggs; ¼ pint (⅔C) milk
or buttermilk.
Sieve the flour or flour and baking powder
and the seasonings. Rub in the butter or
margarine, add the cheese and dates, 1 whole
beaten egg and nearly all the second egg
(save 1 good teaspoon to brush the top of the
loaf). Add the milk or buttermilk and beat
well. Grease and flour a 1½–2-lb. loaf tin.
Put in the mixture, brush with the beaten
egg. Bake for 45–50 minutes in the centre of
a moderate oven, 350–375°F, Gas Mark 4–5,
until quite firm to the touch. Lower the heat
after 30 minutes to very moderate if the loaf
is browning too much. Slice and butter. Serve
fresh.
To vary   The above gives a fairly shallow
loaf. If preferred bake in a 1 lb. loaf tin for
about 1 hour as in the picture.

Creamy Swiss Eggs

This is a delicious supper dish or first
course and much easier than making omelettes.
6 eggs; seasoning; 6 tablespoons cream,
preferably thick; 4 oz. (1C) grated Cheddar
or other firm cheese; 1 oz. butter.
Mix the eggs, seasoning, cream and cheese.
Butter a shallow oven-proof dish generously,
or use 4 small individual dishes, and pour
in the egg mixture. Set for 10–12 minutes
towards the top of a hot oven. Serve at once
with hot French bread or toast and butter.
Serves 3–4.

Cheese Cakes

Whatever recipe you choose for a cheese cake you have this very interesting combination of sweetness and the savoury flavour of cheese. In addition to the recipes on this page, see page 71.

Orange Cheese Cake

For the coating: 6 oz. digestive biscuits; 2 oz. ($\frac{1}{4}$C) butter; 1 tablespoon honey; grated rind 2 oranges; 2 oz. ($\frac{1}{4}$C) caster sugar. *For the filling:* 2 oz. ($\frac{1}{4}$C) butter; grated rind 1 orange; 3 oz. ($\frac{3}{8}$C) caster sugar; 2 eggs; 1 oz. cornflour; 12 oz. ($1\frac{1}{2}$C) cottage cheese; 2 tablespoons orange juice. *To decorate:* little sieved icing sugar; can mandarin oranges.

Crush the biscuit crumbs until most of them are very fine, but keep some crumbs a little coarser, see the picture. Cream the butter, honey, orange rind and sugar. Add the crumbs and use to line the sides and bottom of a 7–8-inch cake tin—*choose a tin with a loose base.* Cream the butter, orange rind and caster sugar together. Add the egg yolks, cornflour, cottage cheese (this can be sieved if wished, but it is not essential) and orange juice. Lastly fold in the stiffly whisked egg whites. Spoon into the biscuit case and bake for approximately 1$\frac{1}{4}$ hours in the centre of a slow to very moderate oven, 300–325°F, Gas Mark 2–3, until firm but pale golden. Allow to cool in the oven with the heat turned off (this stops the cake sinking). Remove from the cake tin. Sprinkle icing sugar over the top of the cheese cake and decorate with well drained mandarin orange segments. *Serves 7–8.*

Apricot Cheese Cake

1 medium-sized can apricot halves; 1 lemon; $\frac{1}{2}$ oz. powdered gelatine (enough to set 1 pint (2$\frac{2}{3}$C)); 8 oz. (1C—well pressed down) cream cheese; $\frac{1}{4}$ pint ($\frac{2}{3}$C) thick cream; 2 oz. ($\frac{1}{4}$C) sugar. *For the base:* 4 oz. digestive biscuits; 1 oz. sieved icing sugar; 2 oz. ($\frac{1}{4}$C) butter. *To decorate:* little thick cream.

Strain the juice from the apricots into a measure, add the grated rind and juice of the lemon and enough water to make up to $\frac{1}{2}$ pint (1$\frac{1}{3}$C). Soften the gelatine in a little of the cold apricot liquid, heat the rest. Add the gelatine and stir until dissolved. Cool then add to the cream cheese, put on one side to *stiffen slightly.* Keep 6 apricot halves for decoration, chop the remainder, mix with cream cheese. Whip the cream until it holds its shape, then whisk in the sugar. Fold into the cream cheese and jelly and spoon into a 7–8-inch cake tin (without a loose base) rinsed out in cold water. Set lightly. Crush the biscuit crumbs, blend with the icing sugar and creamed butter. Press on top of the lightly set mixture and leave for several hours. Turn out on to a serving dish. Decorate with whipped cream and apricot halves. *Serves 6.*

Storing and Freezing *Both these cheese cakes can be stored for 1–2 days in a refrigerator. Both can be frozen. The first freezes excellently, the second (jellied version) one should be used within 3–4 weeks, otherwise it loses its soft texture and becomes rather dry.*

Orange cheese cake

Many good foods are inexpensive to buy and you will find a selection of interesting dishes that form appetising, as well as cheap, meals in the next four pages. Dishes serve 4–6.

Be selective about shopping, choose foods that are in season, for those out-of-season are always more expensive and often not at their best.

Learn about the cheaper meats, stewing steak, minced beef (excellent for meat sauces, loaves, hamburgers), neck and breast of lamb.

Choose some of the inexpensive white fish and 'dress up' with flavoursome sauces.

Buy in larger quantities where practicable and save money that way.

Garbure (bean soup)

Chop 1 or 2 rashers inexpensive bacon, and fry lightly for a few minutes. Lift out of the pan, add 1 oz. fat to the bacon fat in the pan and heat. Chop 1 large or 2 medium-sized onions, crush a clove of garlic (if wished). Fry the onions and garlic in the fat until soft, but not brown. Add 2 coarsely grated or diced carrots, $1\frac{1}{4}$ pints (3C) beef or chicken stock or water and stock cubes. Simmer gently for about 15 minutes, then add a medium-sized can haricot beans, and the bacon. Heat thoroughly. Serve in hot soup cups, topped with chopped parsley and grated cheese.

Soaked and cooked haricot beans could be used instead of canned beans. This is sustaining enough for a light supper meal.

Devilled Cod

Wash and dry 4 or 6 portions of cod. Put into a well buttered dish. Melt 2 oz. ($\frac{1}{4}$C) margarine

MENU

1

Garbure (bean soup)

Devilled cod with Mixed Salad

Lemon Apple Meringue Pie

or butter, blend with 1–2 teaspoons curry powder, 1 teaspoon Worcestershire sauce, 1–2 tablespoons sultanas and 1 tablespoon sweet chutney. Add a good shake pepper and pinch salt, mix well, then stir 3 tablespoons soft breadcrumbs into the mixture. Spread over the top of the fish and bake for approxi-

mately 25 minutes towards the top of a moderately hot oven, 400°F, Gas Mark 6. Do not cover the dish if you want a slightly crisp topping. Garnish with lemon and watercress and serve with a mixed salad.

Lemon Apple Meringue Pie

Line a deep oven-proof dish or 7–8-inch flan with sweet short crust pastry, made with 5–6 oz. ($1\frac{1}{2}$C) flour etc. (as page 4.) Bake 'blind' (as page 5) until just pale golden brown, do not over-cook. Meanwhile peel, slice and cook 2 really large cooking apples, with the grated rind and juice of 1 lemon and 2–3 oz. ($\frac{1}{4}$–$\frac{1}{3}$C) sugar until a thick pulp. Beat or sieve until smooth, then add 2 beaten egg yolks. Spoon into the pastry case. Whisk the 2 egg whites until very stiff, then gradually beat in another 2–4 oz. ($\frac{1}{4}$–$\frac{1}{2}$C) sugar, see page 12 for details on meringues. Either bake for about 25–30 minutes in a very moderate oven 325°F, Gas Mark 3 and serve

hot, or bake for about 1 hour in a very slow oven 275°F, Gas Mark 1 and serve cold. Use the larger amount of sugar if serving cold. The meringue can be decorated with slices of eating apple (dipped in lemon juice to preserve the colour) a grated lemon rind, small pieces of angelica or glacé cherries if wished.

MENU 2

Steak Upside Down Pie

Lyonnaise Potatoes

Creamed Carrots

Grape and Orange Whip

Steak Upside Down Pie

Fry 2 medium-sized finely chopped onions, a few mushrooms (if cheap) or mushroom stalks and 2–3 skinned chopped tomatoes in 2 oz. ($\frac{1}{4}$C) dripping or fat until soft. Add $\frac{1}{2}$ pint ($1\frac{1}{3}$C) stock or water and a beef stock cube. Heat vegetables then add 12 oz. ($1\frac{1}{2}$C) raw minced beef. Stir until a smooth, thick mixture, season well and cook for about 15 minutes only in an uncovered pan. Stir from time to time. Meanwhile prepare the topping. Sieve 6 oz. ($1\frac{1}{2}$C) self-raising flour or plain flour and $1\frac{1}{2}$ teaspoons baking powder with a very good pinch salt, pepper and dry mustard. Rub in 2 oz. ($\frac{1}{4}$C) fat, add 2 oz. ($\frac{1}{2}$C) grated Cheddar cheese—this is an excellent way to use stale pieces. Bind with 1 egg yolk and enough milk to make a soft rolling consistency. Form into a 7–8-inch round. Put the meat mixture into a cake tin (without a loose base) or a round 7–8-inch oven-proof dish, top with the dough. Bake in the centre of a moderate oven, 350–375°F, Gas Mark 4–5 for about 50 minutes. Invert on to a hot serving dish and garnish with a border of creamed carrots.
Creamed Carrots: Cook and mash carrots with a knob of margarine or butter, 1–2 tablespoons top of the milk, a little grated nutmeg and plenty of seasoning. Top with chopped parsley.

Lyonnaise Potatoes

Slice about 1 lb. cooked potatoes fairly thickly. Slice about half this amount of raw onions very thinly. Heat 2 oz. ($\frac{1}{4}$ cup) fat or dripping in a pan and cook the onions until nearly tender. Add the potatoes and mix well, then heat gently until pale golden. Top with chopped parsley before serving.

Grape and Orange Whip

Halve 2–3 very large oranges carefully. Squeeze out the juice, but try and keep the orange cases intact. Measure the juice and add enough water to give just $\frac{3}{4}$ pint (2C). Dissolve an orange flavoured jelly in this and allow to cool, then begin to stiffen slightly. Whisk sharply then fold in 2–3 tablespoons thick cream and 1 stiffly beaten egg white (left from main dish). Put a layer of skinned de-seeded grapes at the bottom of each orange case, top with the jelly mixture and decorate with whole grapes.

MENU 3

Golden Cheese Soup

Milanaise Kidneys with Noodles

Cauliflower Polanaise

Honey Banana Creams

Golden Cheese Soup

Heat 2 oz. ($\frac{1}{4}$C) margarine or butter in a pan, stir in 2 oz. ($\frac{1}{2}$C) flour and cook gently for several minutes. Gradually stir in $\frac{1}{2}$ pint ($1\frac{1}{3}$C) milk and $\frac{3}{4}$ pint (2C) chicken stock or water and stock cubes. Bring to the boil, stir well until thickened. Add 2 grated carrots, cook for a few minutes only, as it is important to keep the slightly crisp texture of the carrots, then 4–6 oz. grated Cheddar cheese. Heat until melted. Pour into soup cups, top with chopped parsley, or watercress leaves and paprika.

Milanaise Kidneys

Fry 2–3 thinly sliced onions and about 4 large skinned tomatoes or canned tomatoes in a little fat until soft. Add about $\frac{1}{4}$ pint ($\frac{2}{3}$C) stock and about 7 halved lambs' kidneys. Season well and simmer steadily in a covered pan for about 10–15 minutes. If wishing to use the more economical sliced pigs' kidneys then use rather more liquid. Blend 1–2 teaspoons cornflour with a few tablespoons extra stock or cheap red wine. Stir into the mixture and continue stirring as the mixture thickens. Serve with noodles and garnish with grilled or fried snippets of bacon.

Cauliflower Polanaise

Break a cauliflower into neat sprigs. Cook until just tender, strain then arrange neatly in the serving dish. Fry 1–2 tablespoons soft breadcrumbs in a small knob of margarine, add 1–2 tablespoons chopped parsley and finally a chopped hard boiled egg. Spoon over the top of the cauliflower just before serving.

Honey Banana Creams

Mash 3 large ripe bananas with juice 1 large lemon. Heat 2–3 tablespoons honey in $\frac{1}{2}$ pint ($1\frac{1}{3}$C) milk, stir into the mashed bananas. Simmer the lemon rind in $\frac{1}{4}$ pint ($\frac{2}{3}$C) water for about 5–6 minutes to extract the maximum flavour, then blend the liquid with $\frac{1}{2}$ oz. softened powdered gelatine. When quite

clear add to the banana mixture. Allow to cool and stiffen very slightly then fold in 2–3 tablespoons lightly whipped cream. Spoon into 4–6 glasses, top with ice cream or cream just before serving.

Soufflé Eggs

Roast Chicken with Sweet Sour Stuffing

Roast Potatoes

Cooked Corn

Apple and Date Charlotte

Soufflé Eggs

Allow 1 egg per person. Separate the yolks from the whites and whisk the whites until very stiff. Butter individual oven-proof saucers or shallow dishes. Beat the egg yolks with a little thin cream, allow about $\frac{1}{2}$ tablespoon per egg yolk, season well and mix with tiny pieces of cooked ham or grated cheese. Spoon into the dishes, top with the well seasoned egg whites and a sprinkling of very finely grated cheese. Bake for about 10 minutes towards the top of a moderately hot to hot oven and serve at once. One eats these with a teaspoon.

Roast Chicken with Sweet Sour Stuffing

Stuffing is an excellent way to make the more expensive foods, poultry, meat and fish 'go further'. This is an easy and very delicious stuffing with chicken. Blend 1 lb. sausagemeat with 2–3 tablespoons seedless raisins, 2–3 tablespoons chopped walnuts 2–3 tablespoons chopped gherkins and 1 teaspoon liquid from the jar of gherkins. Add 1–2 teaspoons chopped herbs, 1 egg and mix well. To give a moist texture, add a little chicken stock (from simmering the giblets). Put into the chicken and weigh. Allow 15 minutes per lb. and 15 minutes over in a moderately hot to hot oven, 400–

425°F, Gas Mark 5–6. Always cover the breast of the chicken with fat to keep it moist during cooking. If preferred wrap in foil, but allow about 30 minutes longer cooking time and open the foil for the last 30 minutes to allow the bird to brown. Serve with thickened gravy, made from the giblet stock. If you wish to give this a slightly sweet sour flavour, add 2 teaspoons honey and a squeeze lemon juice after it has thickened.

For special occasions add 4–5 tablespoons chopped canned pineapple to the stuffing and a little syrup to the gravy. Serve with roast potatoes and cooked corn.

Apple and Date Charlotte

Cut about 6 slices bread and spread with margarine or butter, remove the crusts if wished. Cut the slices of bread into fingers. Simmer about 1 lb. peeled sliced apples in the minimum of water, adding 2–3 tablespoons sugar to sweeten. When soft add about 4 oz. ($\frac{1}{2}$C) chopped dates and a sprinkling powdered cinnamon to taste. Sprinkle the bottom of a pie dish with a little brown sugar. Put half the fingers of bread in the dish with the buttered side towards the sugar so it will brown and crisp. Cover with the apple mixture, then the rest of the slices of bread and butter, this time the buttered side uppermost. Sprinkle lightly with brown sugar. Bake for about 10–15 minutes in the centre of the oven, then leave in the oven when removing the chicken, but lower the heat to very moderate, 325°F, Gas Mark 3. Serve hot with custard, cream or ice cream.

Cook about 8–12 pancakes, as the recipe on page 13. Make $\frac{3}{4}$ pint (1$\frac{2}{3}$C) creamy white sauce using a little chicken stock for flavouring the sauce. Mix half of this with small pieces of cooked chicken, tiny pieces of stuffing, if available, and chopped green or red pepper and a little cooked corn. Fill the pancakes with this, then put into an oven-proof dish. Spoon over remaining sauce, soft breadcrumbs and a little grated cheese. Top with a little margarine or butter (melted or in small pieces) and heat for about 25 minutes just above the centre of a moderate to moderately hot oven, 375–400°F, Gas Mark 5–6. Serve at once.

Celery Coleslaw

Toss finely shredded cabbage and finely chopped raw celery in mayonnaise. Add tiny pieces of chopped gherkin and a few capers.

Caramel Crumb Custard

Make the custard sauce as page 12. Dice small pieces of plain sponge cake and put into individual glasses. Moisten with a very little fruit juice, sherry or white wine, then top with sliced cooked apples, or other fresh or cooked fruit. Spoon the warm custard over the top and allow it to cool. Meanwhile make the caramel as the Blue Print on page 13. When the sugar mixture is brown pour it on to a tin and let it set. Crush with a rolling pin and sprinkle over the top of each dessert.

Ham and Mushroom Flan

Make short crust pastry with 8 oz. (2C) flour, pinch salt, 4 oz. ($\frac{1}{2}$C) butter or fat and water to mix. Roll out and make a 9–10-inch flan case as shown on page 5. Bake 'blind' until crisp and golden brown. Meanwhile heat 1$\frac{1}{2}$ oz. butter or margarine in a pan, stir in 1$\frac{1}{2}$ oz. flour and cook for several minutes. Gradually blend $\frac{3}{4}$ pint (2C) milk into the roux, bring to the boil and cook until thickened. Add 6–8 oz. (approximately 1C) neatly diced cooked ham, 4–6 tablespoons grated cheese and seasoning. Heat for a few minutes only. Fry 12 button mushrooms in 1 oz. butter or fat. Fill the *hot* pastry case with the *hot* ham mixture. Top with the well drained cooked mushrooms and serve as soon as possible.

Cucumber and Tomato Salad

Put a layer of watercress into a shallow dish. Arrange thin slices of cucumber and tomato over this. Flavour with salt, pepper, a little vinegar or lemon juice and chopped chives or spring onions.

Peach and Cherry Trifle

Make 1 pint (2$\frac{2}{3}$C) egg custard sauce as page 10. Put thin strips of lemon or orange rind into the milk and remove when the custard has thickened. Arrange 6 fingers of Swiss Roll or sponge cake, split and spread with jam, in a serving dish. Top with 1–2 sliced fresh peaches (when cheap) or $\frac{1}{2}$ can drained canned peaches. Spoon the hot custard sauce over the sponge and fruit and allow to cool. Decorate with 1 or 2 thinly sliced fresh peaches (dipped in lemon juice) or the remainder of the canned fruit, $\frac{1}{4}$ pint ($\frac{2}{3}$C) whipped cream and canned, glacé or fresh cherries. At the bottom of the Blue Print on page 18 are two suggestions for a lighter and more economical cream topping. You can of course, omit some of the peaches.

Peach and cherry trifle

MENU

5

Grapefruit and Melon Cocktails

Chicken Stuffed Pancakes au Gratin

Celery Coleslaw

Caramel Crumb Custard

MENU

6

Avocado Cocktail

Ham and Mushroom Flan

Cucumber and Tomato Salad

Peach and Cherry Trifle

Grapefruit and Melon Cocktails

This is an excellent way of using part of a melon. Make a ginger flavoured syrup by boiling together 2 oz. ($\frac{1}{4}$C) sugar and $\frac{1}{4}$ pint ($\frac{2}{3}$C) water. Flavour with a tablespoon sherry and a little ginger. Take the segments from 2 large halved grapefruit and mix with the diced fruit from about $\frac{1}{2}$ small melon. Put into glasses. Spoon over the syrup and chill.

Chicken Stuffed Pancakes au Gratin

This is a good way to use left over pieces of chicken.

This menu provides a buffet or formal meal for 6 people at a reasonable cost.

Avocado Cocktail

Cut away the peel and pith from 1 grapefruit and remove the fruit segments. Put 6 segments on one side for garnish. Cut the remainder into small pieces, put into a basin. Halve 1 ripe avocado pear, remove the stone, skin and slice the fruit neatly. Mix with the grapefruit pieces, 2 oz. shelled prawns and a little mayonnaise. Arrange a little finely shredded lettuce in individual glasses or on small dishes, top with the avocado and prawn mixture and garnish with the reserved grapefruit segments.

Let us take a new look at cold weather meals.

Once it was felt that the ideal fare for a winter's day was to start with a large filling breakfast, to have a really 'warming' main mid-day meal, perhaps soup, followed by a plate piled high with meat in some form, plenty of potatoes and other vegetables and to end the meal with a good 'old fashioned' pudding and cheese. This would probably be repeated with a similar type of menu in the evening. All this may sound sensible and wise for 'keeping out the cold', but it is *not* the perfect choice for wintry months. Firstly, most people would put on unwanted weight with such a diet, and this, plus the surfeit of food, would create a feeling of lethargy. The more energetic one can be in cold weather the easier it is to exercise and keep warm. Fresh air, plus a *sensible* diet, is the best way to 'fight' colds and 'flu. Start the day with fresh citrus fruit or fruit juice; if you like a cooked breakfast that is splendid, but do not follow it with too much bread, toast or

Menu Maker two
COLD WEATHER MENUS

MENU
7

Spiced Orange Juice

Beef Goulash with Red Cabbage

Cheese and Biscuits with Celery and/or Chicory

crispbread and preserves. Certainly it is wise to enjoy warming soups, but if they are thick and filling, plan a lighter main course. All menus serve 4 people unless stated otherwise.

Spiced Orange Juice

This is not only refreshing, but as warming as hot soup. Heat fresh or canned orange juice, and as it heats infuse a stick of cinnamon in this. Pour into hot glasses, top with grated nutmeg and put a cinnamon stick into each glass if liked.

Beef Goulash with Red Cabbage

Make the goulash as page 30, either with or without the potatoes. Shred the red cabbage and cook in the minimum of salted water, strain then tip back into the pan with a small knob of butter or margarine. Flavour with a few caraway seeds if wished.

Cheese Board

Select a good variety of cheeses, i.e. a hard cheese such as Cheddar or Cheshire, a soft cheese with 'bite' like Camembert or Brie and a delicate cheese, Bel Paese, for example.

This very satisfying menu can be prepared and cooked within a very short period.

Speedy Borsch

Peel and grate or chop 1 medium-sized onion and toss it in a small knob fat, until softened, but not brown. Add about 1½ pints (4C) canned or home made consommé, or beef stock and heat thoroughly. Season well; include a good pinch garlic salt. Cut a large cooked beetroot into thin strips or grate this, add to the soup and warm through. Spoon into individual soup cups, top with a little yoghourt or soured or fresh cream and chopped parsley.

Sweet and Sour Ham

Buy 4 good slices cooked ham (about ½–¾-inch thick). Put 1½ oz. butter or margarine, 1 oz. brown sugar, 3 tablespoons brown or white vinegar and 3 tablespoons red currant or apple jelly into a frying pan, stir over a gentle heat until the mixture forms a smooth sauce. Add 1–2 teaspoons made mustard and a good shake of pepper. A little salt can be added if the ham is mild in flavour. Put in the slices of ham and heat gently.

Crisp Topped Noodles

Cook enough noodles for 4 people, strain, toss in a small knob of butter or margarine then put in a heat-proof dish. Top with breadcrumbs and a little grated cheese and brown for a few minutes only in the oven or under the grill. Serve the slices of ham on this and spoon the sauce over the top.

Green Beans and Tomatoes

Cook frozen or fresh green beans or heat canned beans. Strain, then mix in the pan with several skinned, thickly sliced, fresh tomatoes and seasoning. Heat for a few minutes only, so the tomato slices remain a good shape, and serve.

Cherry Grapefruit Alaska

Halve 2 good-sized grapefruit, remove the segments of fruit. Discard pith, skin and pips. Put the grapefruit pieces back into the

cases, together with some canned black cherries. Sweeten to taste. Put a spoonful of ice cream over the fruit. Whisk 3 egg whites until very stiff, then gradually whisk in 4 oz. (½C) caster sugar. Pile over the ice cream and fruit and decorate with a few well drained cherries. Heat for 4–5 minutes in a very hot oven.

In this menu, the main dishes may be left in the oven to cook without attention.

Cheese Stuffed Mushrooms

Select about 16 large mushrooms, remove the stalks, wash and chop these. Skin the mushroom caps, wash and dry. Blend 2 egg yolks with 3 tablespoons soft breadcrumbs, 3 tablespoons grated Gruyère or Cheddar cheese and seasoning. Add the mushroom stalks to this mixture, and small strips of cooked ham can also be included. Spread over 8 mushrooms, then cover with the rest of the mushrooms. Dip in beaten egg yolk, blended with a little water, and coat in crumbs, then fry in hot shallow fat until brown on one side, turn and brown on the second side. If lightly cooked these may be warmed gently in the oven or kept hot for a short time. Serve with quarters of lemon and garnish with lettuce or watercress.

Chicken Hot-Pot

Put a layer of peeled thinly sliced potatoes into a casserole, cover with a layer of very thinly sliced onions and thickly sliced skinned tomatoes. Season each layer well. Put 4 joints of well seasoned uncooked chicken over the vegetables, add about ¼ pint (⅔C) well seasoned stock and a light sprinkling of chopped fresh or dried rosemary or lemon thyme, then a layer of tomatoes, onions, and a topping of potato slices. Season well, and put small pieces of margarine over the potatoes. Cover the casserole with a lid and cook in or near the centre of a very moderate oven, 325–350°F, Gas Mark 3–4, for approximately 1¼–1½ hours. Remove the lid for the last 20–30 minutes if wished, to brown the potatoes. Garnish with chopped parsley.

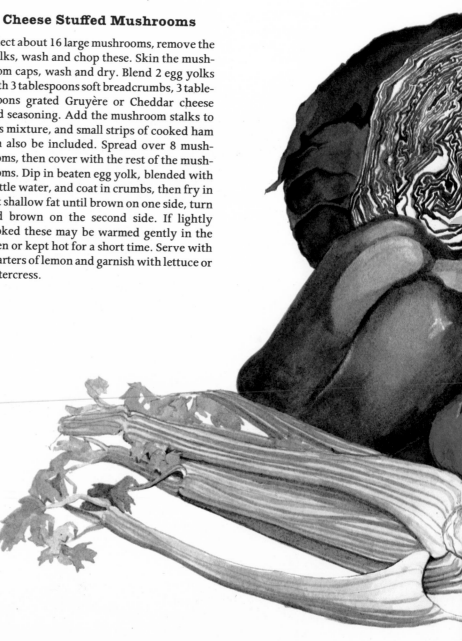

Caramel Topped Rice Pudding

Put 2 tablespoons round grain rice into a pie or oven-proof dish. Add 1–2 tablespoons sugar and 1 pint (2⅔C) milk. Bake in the coolest part of the oven for about 1 hour. Remove the dish from the oven, top with a layer of brown sugar and return to the oven for about 20–25 minutes, lowering the heat to slow, to allow the topping to caramelise.

Ginger Pears

Peel and halve firm pears. Put into a casserole and cover with ginger ale or ginger beer. Put a lid on the casserole and bake for about 1 hour in the coolest part of the moderate oven.

MENU
10

Aubergines Niçoise

Fish Kebabs with Rice and Fried Courgettes

Chocolate Pudding and Rum Sauce

This menu serves 4–5.

Aubergines Niçoise

Wash and dry 2 medium-sized aubergines (egg plants), slice thinly, but do not peel. Sprinkle lightly with salt and leave for about 15–20 minutes. This minimises the slightly bitter taste of the vegetable. Crush 1–2 cloves garlic, chop 1 large onion. Heat 1 tablespoon oil and 1 oz. butter in a saucepan. Fry the garlic and onion gently for a few minutes, then add 4–5 large skinned and chopped tomatoes. Simmer gently until the tomatoes become a purée, then add the aubergine slices. Season well. Mix well with the tomato purée, put a lid on the pan and simmer steadily for 45–50 minutes. Serve hot topped with chopped parsley.

Fish Kebabs

Choose a firm fleshed white fish, such as cod, fresh haddock or hake. Cut 1¼–1½ lb. into 1½-inch cubes, removing any skin or bones. Wash and dry about 24 small mushrooms and cut the flesh of a red and a green pepper into squares. Put the fish, mushrooms and squares of pepper on to 4 or 5 metal skewers. Heat 4 oz. (½C) butter or margarine, the juice of a large lemon, salt, pepper and a few drops of chilli sauce. Brush the fish and vegetables with a little of the mixture. Cook under a hot grill, turning several times, until the fish is cooked. Serve the kebabs on boiled rice. Heat the remaining butter mixture, add about 1 tablespoon chopped parsley and spoon over the kebabs.

Fried Courgettes

Wash, dry and cut courgettes into ¼–½-inch slices. Coat in well seasoned flour and fry until crisp and golden brown. Drain on absorbent paper before serving.

Chocolate Pudding with Rum Sauce

Put 2 oz. plain chocolate, a few drops vanilla and 2 oz. (¼C) butter or margarine into a basin and melt over a pan of hot water. Remove the basin from the pan, cool the chocolate mixture slightly. Add 3–4 oz. (⅜–½C) caster sugar and blend thoroughly. Beat in 2 eggs then 6 oz. (1½C) self-raising flour and 6 tablespoons (½C) milk. Grease and flour a 2-pint basin, put in the mixture, cover well and steam for 1 hour. Turn out and serve with a rum flavoured sauce.

Rum Sauce

Blend 2 tablespoons cornflour with ½ pint (1⅓C) milk. Put into a saucepan with 2 tablespoons sugar and heat, stirring well, until thickened. Add 1–2 tablespoons rum to taste.

Banana and lemon cream

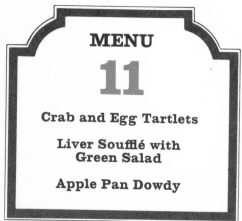

MENU
11

Crab and Egg Tartlets

Liver Soufflé with Green Salad

Apple Pan Dowdy

Crab and Egg Tartlets

Make short crust pastry with 4 oz. (1C) plain flour, pinch salt, 2 oz. (¼C) fat and water to mix. Roll out very thinly and line 8 small patty tins and bake 'blind' in a hot oven until crisp and golden brown (see page 5). Arrange on a dish and keep warm. Scramble 3 well-seasoned eggs, blended with a tiny can flaked crab meat, in a knob of butter. When lightly set pile into the pastry cases and serve as soon as possible.

Liver Soufflé

Make a thick sauce with 1 oz. butter or margarine, 1 oz. flour and ¼ pint (⅔C) milk. Add 12 oz. minced raw lamb's or calf's liver. Season well and add pinch sugar. Beat in 3 egg yolks then fold in 4 stiffly whisked egg whites. Put into a lightly greased 7-inch soufflé dish. Bake in the centre of a moderate oven, 350–375°F, Gas Mark 4–5, for 35 minutes or until lightly set. Remember, cooked soufflés cannot be kept waiting.

Apple Pan Dowdy

Peel and slice 3 good-sized cooking apples. Put into a greased 1½-pint pie dish with 1–2 tablespoons brown sugar, 1–2 tablespoons golden syrup and a sprinkling of grated nutmeg and ground cinnamon. Do not add any water. Cover the dish with foil and bake in the centre of a moderate oven for about 15–20 minutes until the apples are nearly soft. · Meanwhile make a thick batter mixture by blending 4 oz. (1C) self-raising flour, pinch salt, 2 oz. (¼C) sugar, 1 egg, 4 tablespoons milk and 2 oz. (¼C) melted butter or margarine. Spoon the mixture over the apples, sprinkle lightly with sugar and bake in the centre of a moderate oven for 30–35 minutes. Turn the pudding upside down on to a dish, serve with cream, hard sauce or vanilla-flavoured sauce (made as the rum sauce in the previous menu but using ½–1 teaspoon vanilla essence instead of rum).

MENU
12

Tournedos Béarnaise with Creamed Potatoes and Cauliflower

Banana and Lemon Cream

Cheese Board and Salad

Do not imagine a cold weather menu must be 'stodgy'; this menu, for a special occasion, is satisfying, and uses the foods needed in cold weather. This menu serves 4–6.

Tournedos Béarnaise

Make the sauce before cooking the meat and keep it hot over a very low heat. Tie (or ask the butcher to do this) 4–6 fillet steaks into rounds (tournedos). Brush with butter and follow the instructions for grilling as the Blue Print on page 25. Serve with Béarnaise Sauce, creamed potatoes and cauliflower.

To make the Béarnaise Sauce: Put 3 tablespoons white or white wine vinegar and 3 tablespoons tarragon vinegar into a pan with a peeled shallot or small onion. Simmer the vinegars until reduced to 2–2½ tablespoons, then allow to cool. Put 3 egg yolks and the strained vinegars into the top of a double saucepan or a basin over a pan of hot, but not boiling water. Whisk until thick. While this is thickening allow 4 oz. (½C) butter to soften slightly. Gradually whisk in the butter—*do this very gradually*. Lastly add ½–1 teaspoon each of chopped fresh tarragon and chervil or use a good pinch dried herbs. Season well. Remove from the heat and stand in a warm place until ready to serve.

Banana and Lemon Cream

Dissolve a lemon flavoured jelly in ¾ pint (2C) boiling water. Add 2 teaspoons lemon juice and 1 tablespoon sugar. Chill until beginning to set. To hurry this process stand over a bowl of ice cubes or use ¼ pint (⅔C) boiling water in which to dissolve the jelly and add ½ pint (1⅓C) crushed ice. When the jelly is firm whip until frothy, then add nearly ½ pint (1⅓C) thick cream, whipped until it stands in peaks. Add 2 stiffly whipped egg whites and 3 small sliced bananas. Spoon into a 2-pint (5–6C) tin or mould (rinsed in cold water). When set turn out. Press cream-coated sponge fingers round the edge, top with remaining whipped cream, sliced bananas (dipped in lemon) and cherries.

One cannot plan a sensible beauty routine without considering the value of various foods and their effect upon good health and beauty.

The menus that follow are designed to give interesting and appetising meals that are planned round the many foods that contribute to a nutritious diet.

The footnote after each menu indicates why I have chosen these. All menus serve 4 unless stated otherwise.

Menu Maker three
BALANCED MENUS FOR BEAUTY

Add 3 egg yolks and beat well. Fold in the 3 stiffly whisked egg whites. Put into a buttered or oiled 6-inch soufflé dish and bake for 20–25 minutes in the centre of a moderate oven, 350–375°F, Gas Mark 4–5. Do not over-cook as this soufflé is nicer when not too set.

A delicious variation is to put a layer of shrimps, prawns or crab meat at the bottom of the dish.

Analysis

Avocado pears are an unusual fruit for they are rich in protein, so the first course of this meal is equally suitable for a light lunch. Try to have potatoes cooked in their jackets as often as possible, as you have extra flavour, roughage and Vitamin C. Dried apricots are an excellent source of iron.

MENU
14

Tomato and Celery Soup

Beef Spirals with Peas, Carrots and Watercress

Apple Raisin Mould

MENU
13

Avocado Soufflé

Cold Beef with Jacket Potatoes and Mixed Salads

Apricot Fool

Avocado Soufflé

Halve 2 small (or 1 large) ripe avocados, remove the stones and scoop the pulp from the skins. Mash with the juice of 1 small lemon, 2 teaspoons olive oil and seasoning.

Apricot Fool

Soak 8 oz. (about 1C) dried apricots in $\frac{1}{2}$ pint ($1\frac{1}{3}$C) water and the juice of 1 lemon for 12–24 hours. Simmer until tender. Sieve or emulsify and sweeten with sugar or sugar substitute. Blend with about $\frac{1}{4}$ pint ($\frac{2}{3}$C) whipped cream, thick custard or natural yoghourt. Spoon into 4 glasses and top with flaked browned almonds.

Tomato and Celery Soup

Chop 2 medium-sized onions and 3–4 sticks celery. Toss in 1 oz. margarine for a few minutes. Stir well so the vegetables do not burn. Add 1 lb. chopped tomatoes, $\frac{1}{2}$ pint ($1\frac{1}{3}$C) white stock and simmer for 15 minutes. Sieve or emulsify. Return to the pan, heat for a few minutes, add seasoning and 1 tablespoon concentrated tomato purée. Pour into

soup cups. Garnish with little curls of celery and chopped celery leaves.

This soup is also excellent cold.

Beef Spirals

Buy a generous 1 lb. rump steak (cut in one piece) and beat until rather thin. Spread with 2 oz. ($\frac{1}{4}$C) butter or margarine then with 2–3 tablespoons chopped parsley and/or 1 finely chopped green or red pepper (discard the core and seeds). Roll like a Swiss roll, cut into 8 slices and secure the spirals with wooden cocktail sticks. Grill or fry until tender. Serve in a border of peas and sliced carrots. Garnish with watercress.

Apple Raisin Mould

Simmer 2 good-sized peeled and cored cooking apples with $\frac{1}{2}$ pint (1$\frac{1}{3}$C) water, the finely grated rind of 1 orange and sugar or sugar substitute to taste. Beat, sieve or emulsify until smooth. Soften $\frac{1}{2}$ oz. powdered gelatine (or enough to set 1 pint (2$\frac{2}{3}$C)) in the cold orange juice. Measure the apple pulp and you should have *nearly* 1 pint (2$\frac{2}{3}$C); if insufficient add a little hot water to make the correct amount. Blend the gelatine with the hot apple purée and stir until dissolved. Put 2–3 tablespoons seedless raisins into the bottom of a mould rinsed out in cold water. Spoon the apple mixture over these. Leave to set. Turn out, decorate with fresh orange slices and serve with natural yoghourt.

Analysis

The soup is warming and satisfying without being fattening. The meat portions are relatively small so I have added extra protein in the form of the peas. Be generous with the watercress garnish to provide iron. The dessert is refreshing, easy to digest, low in calories and the oranges give Vitamin C, the vitamin that helps towards a clear skin. Raisins also contain iron and this is important for healthy blood.

MENU
15

Herring Hors d'œuvre

**Cheese and Onion Hot-Pot
with Chicory Coleslaw**

Fresh Fruit

This menu serves 4–6.

Herring Hors d'œuvre

Fillet 4 medium-sized herrings. Season, brush with a little oil and grill carefully so the flesh does not break—*do not over-cook*. Cool, then cut into neat pieces. Blend 1 herring with a finely chopped small onion, a finely chopped dessert apple and a little sherry. Blend the second herring with mayonnaise flavoured with curry powder. Mix $\frac{1}{2}$–1 tablespoon concentrated tomato purée with 2–3 tablespoons natural yoghourt, toss the third herring in this mixture.

Mix the last herring with 1 grated raw carrot, 1 teaspoon grated raw onion and 1 chopped hard boiled egg.

Arrange the four mixtures on a bed of lettuce and watercress. Garnish with lemon twists. For a more savoury hors d'oeuvre use well drained Rollmops or Bismarck herrings instead of grilled fresh herrings.

Cheese and Onion Hot-Pot

Peel and slice 1 lb. potatoes and 1 lb. onions very thinly. Slice or grate about 8 oz. Cheddar cheese. Put layers of the potatoes, cheese and onions into a casserole, seasoning each layer and brushing with a little melted margarine. Begin and end with potatoes. Pour $\frac{1}{4}$ pint ($\frac{2}{3}$C) milk over the mixture. Bake in the centre of a very moderate oven, 325–350°F, Gas Mark 3–4, for about 1$\frac{1}{4}$ hours.

Chicory Coleslaw

Shred the heart of a small cabbage finely, mix with a grated raw carrot and the chopped base of 3–4 heads of chicory (the white vegetable often called endive). Blend 4 tablespoons natural yoghourt with 1–2 teaspoons made mustard and a squeeze lemon juice. Toss the vegetables in this. Put into a shallow dish, top with chopped parsley and arrange the tips of chicory round the dish.

Analysis

Herrings are an excellent source of protein, fat (for creating a feeling of warmth), and Vitamin A which also helps to give a good skin and healthy eyes. Although potatoes are a 'starchy' vegetable, which must be omitted in a very stringent slimming diet they *do* contain Vitamin C and like all starches (eaten in sensible amounts) provide energy. Cheese gives calcium for strong teeth, bones and nails as well as protein. This meal has plenty of raw vegetables for roughage.

MENU
16
**Prawn and
Grapefruit Cocktails**

**Alpine Eggs with
Creamed Spinach**

Hot Melon and Ginger

Prawn and Grapefruit Cocktails

Halve 2 grapefruit, remove the segments carefully. Blend with 3–4 tablespoons defrosted frozen, or well drained canned or shelled fresh prawns. Toss in mayonnaise or well seasoned natural yoghourt. Put a layer of finely shredded lettuce into each grapefruit 'shell' or into glasses. Top with the prawn and grapefruit mixture. Garnish with slices of tomato.

Alpine Eggs

Cut 4 thin slices of wholemeal or brown bread. Put into a long shallow oven-proof dish. Spread with butter or margarine then cover with a generous layer of cottage or cream cheese and a sprinkling of finely chopped onion or chives. Heat for 10 minutes above the centre of a moderately hot oven, 375–400°F, Gas Mark 5–6. Separate the whites of 4 eggs and put into a basin. Pour the egg yolks carefully into the centre of each slice of bread. Whisk the egg whites until very stiff, season with salt, celery salt, cayenne and ordinary pepper. Pile the meringue mixture round the egg yolks, so all the bread and cheese is covered. Return to the oven for 15 minutes, lowering the heat to very moderate (this gives time to eat the first course).

Hot Melon and Ginger

This is an excellent way to serve the less luxurious melons which often have relatively little flavour.

Either slice or halve the melon and remove the seeds, then dice the flesh or cut into balls (with a vegetable scoop). Heat the juice of 1 lemon, $\frac{1}{4}$ pint ($\frac{2}{3}$C) water, 2 oz. ($\frac{1}{4}$C) sugar, or use sugar substitute and 2–3 tablespoons diced preserved or crystallised ginger. Add the melon and heat for a few minutes only. Spoon into glasses.

Analysis

Shell fish is a low caloried protein and combines with fresh grapefruit (which gives Vitamin C) for an interesting hors d'oeuvre. Eggs and cheese are as nutritious as meat or fish for a main dish and remember that bread also provides protein. Spinach is a vegetable that is rich in iron. Melon has no real vitamin value but is low in calories and very refreshing.

Chicken Liver Scramble

Chop 4 chickens' livers finely. Heat in 2 oz. ($\frac{1}{4}$C) butter, add 4 well-seasoned eggs and scramble lightly. Serve on or with crisp wholemeal toast.

Cottage Cheese and Nut Salad

Blend a little freshly chopped parsley and/or mint with about 12 oz. ($1\frac{1}{2}$C) cottage cheese. Pile on to a bed of green salad, top with salted or plain peanuts or cashew nuts. Arrange rings of apple, dipped in mayonnaise and topped with more nuts, around the cottage cheese. Serve a dish of sliced well-seasoned tomatoes and cucumber separately. ·

Yoghourt California

Cover 8 oz. (nearly $1\frac{1}{2}$C) prunes with cold water, add a little grated orange rind and fresh orange juice.

Leave soaking overnight, then simmer until tender, unless using tenderised prunes which will become quite soft with soaking alone. Chill and serve with natural yoghourt. Add a little honey to the prunes for a sweeter flavour.

Analysis

Wholemeal bread gives valuable Vitamin B and mineral salts. Liver, eggs and prunes are all excellent sources of iron, a mineral that is often neglected in modern diets. The cheese,

with nuts, liver and eggs ensures plenty o protein in this meal and cottage cheese, lik all cheese, is an excellent source of calcium while being low in calories. Fresh tomatoe give Vitamin C and yoghourt is one of the easiest and most nutritious desserts. En courage all the family to eat yoghourt.

MENU
18

Citrus Fruit Cocktails

Grilled Sole and
Cauliflower Niçoise

Gingerbread
with Apple Sauce

Citrus Fruit Cocktails

Squeeze the juice from 1 large grapefruit, mix with the juice of $\frac{1}{2}$ or 1 small lemon and 3–4 large oranges. Add a little sugar, sugar substitute or honey to sweeten and a few bruised mint leaves. Serve in small glasses.

Grilled Sole

Soak 4 medium-sized soles in a little milk for 30 minutes. Drain, then brush with butter and grill. Garnish with parsley.

Cauliflower Niçoise

Cook a medium-sized cauliflower (for 4) in boiling salted water. Meanwhile chop 2 small onions and fry in 2 oz. margarine. Add 4 large, skinned chopped tomatoes and cook until a thick purée. Blend $\frac{1}{4}$ pint ($\frac{2}{3}$C) cauliflower water with 1 teaspoon cornflour, add to the tomato mixture with 1 tablespoon chopped gherkins and seasoning. Cook until thickened, spoon over the cauliflower.

Gingerbread with Apple Sauce

Make the gingerbread as page 49. Cut enough portions for 4, warm in the oven, top with apple sauce.

Analysis

Fresh citrus fruits are an excellent start to any meal. They ensure an adequate amount of Vitamin C, which is needed daily and cannot be stored in the body. Fish is a low calorie source of protein, and grilling the most digestible method of cooking. All too often vegetable liquid is not used and this retains valuable mineral salts, so the sauce gives interest and flavour, as well as added nutrients to the meal. Black treacle is used rarely, except in gingerbreads, but it is one of the best sources of iron.

MENU
17

Chicken Liver Scramble

Cottage Cheese and
Nut Salad

Yoghourt California

There are a number of occasions when a light menu is required. Many people dislike a heavy luncheon, particularly when working hard. A light meal is ideal for a high tea, a late supper or when one is over-tired or has some digestive disorder.

four

MENUS FOR LIGHT MEALS

If light meals are chosen for medical reasons, avoid highly spiced or exotic dishes containing rich sauces. There are many interesting dishes based on milk, eggs and fish which are easily digested. All menus serve 4 unless stated otherwise.

Haddock Charlotte

Cut the crusts from 4–5 large slices of bread and butter. Flake 1–1¼ lb. uncooked fresh haddock finely or put this through a mincer. Blend with 1 egg, ¼ pint (⅔C) milk, seasoning, 1 teaspoon finely grated lemon rind and 1–2 teaspoons finely chopped parsley. Cut the bread into fingers and put half at the bottom of a 2-pint pie dish with the buttered side touching the bottom of the dish. Spoon the fish mixture over this. Top with fingers of bread and butter with the buttered side uppermost. Bake for 45–55 minutes in the centre of a very moderate to moderate oven, 325–350°F, Gas Mark 3–4, until the bread topping is crisp. Garnish with segments of tomato and lemon.

Creamed Carrots

Cook and mash carrots, then blend with a knob of butter or margarine and 2–3 table-

MENU

19

Haddock Charlotte with Creamed Carrots and Duchesse Potatoes

Peach Madrilenes

spoons thin cream or top of the milk. Pile into the serving dish.

Duchesse Potatoes

Cook and mash potatoes, sieve to ensure all

the lumps are removed. Beat a generous amount of butter or margarine (about 2 oz. (¼C) to each lb. cooked potatoes) and 1 or 2 egg yolks into the mashed potato. Do not add milk as this makes the potato shapes spread badly. Pipe or pile into large rose or pyramid shapes on a greased oven-proof dish or baking tray. Heat through and brown in the oven.

Peach Madrilenes

Halve and de-seed about 12 grapes, skin if wished. Remove the skin, pith and pips from 1 orange and cut the fruit into neat pieces. Whip ¼ pint (⅔C) cream until it just holds its shape. Sweeten to taste. Add the grapes and orange segments and pile into 4 large or 8 smaller peach halves.
To vary Thick smooth custard, soured cream or natural yoghourt may be used in place of cream.

This menu is illustrated on the previous page.

MENU

20

Tomato Soufflés

**Salad Sandwich Loaf
with Green Salad**

Fresh Fruit

Tomato Soufflés

Choose 4 very large firm tomatoes. Halve these and scoop out the pulp carefully so the tomato cases are intact. Season the cases. Chop the pulp very finely, add the yolks of 3 eggs and about 2 tablespoons fine bread-crumbs or smooth potato to make a creamy consistency. Blend with a generous amount of seasoning and 1–2 teaspoons finely chopped chives or onion and fold in 2 stiffly beaten egg whites. Spoon the mixture into the tomato cases. Stand on an oven-proof flat dish and bake for about 12 minutes in a moderately hot oven, 375–400°F, Gas Mark 5–6. Serve at once.

To vary Use grated cheese in place of breadcrumbs or potato.

Salad Sandwich Loaf

Remove the crusts from a small loaf and cut the loaf into 4 slices lengthways. Spread each slice with butter or margarine.

Layer 1 Put the first slice on a board and spread with cream cheese and sliced tomato.

Layer 2 Top with the second slice and flaked canned or cooked salmon, and well seasoned sliced cucumber.

Layer 3 Put the third slice of bread on this and cover with chopped hard boiled eggs, blended with mayonnaise and finely shredded lettuce.

Cover with the last slice of bread and butter (buttered side downwards). Coat the top and sides of the sandwich with soft cream cheese and press salted peanuts against the sides. Lift on to a bed of green salad and garnish the top with twists of cucumber, radish roses and/or a lattice of well drained anchovy fillets. The salad can be served separately if preferred.

MENU
21

Waldorf Salad

Curried Sea-food Scallops

Cheese and Biscuits

Waldorf Salad

This rather sweet salad is a pleasant start to a meal.

Put a layer of crisp lettuce into the salad bowl. Blend equal quantities of diced dessert apple and crisp celery, then mix with mayonnaise. Pile on to the lettuce and top with chopped walnuts. Garnish with fresh or well drained canned grapefruit segments and grapes or melon balls. This salad is also an excellent accompaniment to cooked ham.

Curried Sea-food Scallops

Make a creamy curry sauce with $1\frac{1}{2}$ oz. butter or margarine, $1\frac{1}{2}$ oz. flour, 1–2 teaspoons curry powder and $\frac{1}{2}$ pint ($1\frac{1}{3}$C) milk. When thickened add seasoning and 2–3 tablespoons thin cream. Blend with about 1 lb. mixed fish, i.e. flaked cooked white fish, shell fish and a little canned tuna. Put into scallop shells. Top with fine breadcrumbs and heat under the grill or in the oven.

To vary To make a more substantial dish, arrange a layer of cooked long grain rice in a shallow heat-proof dish. Top with the curry mixture and heat as above. The sauce may be flavoured with cheese, anchovy essence or parsley instead of curry.

Strain off the juice. Put a layer of apricots at the bottom of a 1½-pint (4C) greased basin. Crumble 2–3 sponge cakes, spread over the apricots. Beat 3 eggs and 2 oz. (¼C) sugar, add ¾ pint (2C) warm milk and 3–4 tablespoons of the apricot syrup. Pour over the sponge cakes. Cover the basin with greased foil or greaseproof paper and steam for about 1¼ hours over hot, but not boiling, water. By this time the pudding should be nearly set. Lift off the cover and arrange the rest of the apricots over the custard mixture. Cover again and continue steaming for 15–30 minutes. Serve hot or cold but allow the pudding to stand for about 5 minutes before turning out of the basin.

To vary   Crushed pineapple, either fresh or canned could be used in place of apricots. An unusual and delicious variation is to substitute fresh or canned passion fruit for the apricots.

Cauliflower surprise

MENU 22

Omelette Espagnole with Broccoli

Cottage Cheese and Apple Rings with Biscuits and Butter

MENU 23

Cauliflower Surprise with Crispbread and Butter

Apricot Diplomat

MENU 24

Boiled Ham with Sweet and Sour Onions

Mushroom Salad

Cucumber Yoghourt Salad

Fresh Fruit

Omelette Espagnole

This has almost exactly the same kind of ingredients as the usual Tortilla (Spanish Omelette) but the omelette is a soufflé type. Chop 1 onion, 2–3 skinned tomatoes, 1 green pepper and a few mushrooms and fry in a little oil for a few minutes. Add 2–3 tablespoons stock so the mixture is kept hot and moist. Season well and put in strips of cooked ham or sausage if wished, together with diced cooked potato and any other cooked vegetables. Put about 2 oz. (¼C) butter into a large shallow oven-proof dish. Put this into the oven to heat. Beat 5–6 egg yolks with seasoning and 2 tablespoons milk, then fold in the stiffly whisked egg whites. Remove the dish from the oven, pour in the omelette mixture. Bake for about 15 minutes above the centre of a hot oven until lightly set. Slip out of the dish if wished, top with the hot vegetable mixture and serve at once. **To vary**   If preferred cook as ordinary omelettes and fill with the mixture.

Cottage Cheese and Apple Rings

Core dessert apples and cut into rings, spread with cottage cheese and top with raisins and/or nuts. Serve with cheese biscuits and butter.

This menu serves 4–6.

Cauliflower Surprise

This *looks* like Cauliflower Mornay (cauliflower cheese) but underneath you have a layer of savoury vegetables that turn this into a 'meal in a dish'. Slice 2–3 medium-sized onions, 2 skinned tomatoes and about 6 mushrooms and toss in 2 oz. (¼C) margarine until tender. Add a small well drained can of corn, a few cooked or canned peas and a few tablespoons diced cooked ham. Heat gently but do not over-cook. Meanwhile cook a medium-sized cauliflower in boiling salted water until just tender and make a white sauce with 2 oz. (¼C) margarine, 2 oz. (½C) flour, ¾ pint (2C) milk, ¼ pint (⅔C) cauliflower stock and seasoning. When the sauce has thickened blend about one-quarter with the vegetable mixture and put into a hot deep serving dish or casserole. Put the cauliflower on top. Add about 4–6 oz. (1–1½C) grated cheese to the remaining sauce, spoon over the cauliflower. Brown under the grill and serve at once.

Apricot Diplomat

Open a medium-sized can halved apricots.

Boiled Ham

Either serve the cooked ham cold, or heat in a little stock or water with a stock cube. To give extra flavour, add a small amount of red wine. Slice neatly.

Sweet and Sour Onions

Blend 2 teaspoons cornflour with ¼ pint (⅔C) white wine vinegar, 2 tablespoons honey, 2–3 tablespoons tomato chutney, ¼ pint (⅔C) white stock and seasonings. Put the sauce into a pan and cook until thickened. Add 1 large finely diced or grated cooked beetroot and leave until cold. Pour over about 12 well drained pickled onions and leave for several hours, if possible.

Mushroom Salad

Slice well washed new button mushrooms, toss in well seasoned oil and vinegar and top with chopped fresh herbs if liked.

Cucumber Yoghourt Salad

Slice cucumber and mix with, or top with, yoghourt mixed with seasoning, lemon juice and paprika. Serve very cold.

The menus that follow are for dishes to be cooked in covered containers in the oven.

If you have insufficient casseroles use cake tins, with fixed, not loose, bases or oven-proof dishes. Cover the tins or dishes with foil. If the recipe contains an appreciable amount of liquid it can spoil the cake tin slightly, causing the cake mixture to stick. To avoid this,

Set the oven at very moderate to moderate, 325–350°F, Gas Mark 3–4. The soup takes about 1 hour, the Lamb Lyonnaise 1¼ hours, the pudding about 1½ hours, but if this is over-cooking reduce the heat when removing the lamb from the oven.

Vegetable Rice Soup

Choose a really deep casserole so the soup does not boil over. Peel and chop about 12 oz.–1 lb. mixed vegetables—onions, carrots, tomatoes, turnips, etc., fairly finely. Put into the casserole with 1½ pints (4C) hot chicken stock or water and 2 stock cubes, *bouquet garni*, seasoning and 1 tablespoon rice. Cover and place in a fairly cool part of the oven. Chop parsley and/or chives and sprinkle over the soup before serving. Serve with crispy rolls or French bread.

Menu Maker
five
CASSEROLE MEALS

MENU
25

Vegetable Rice Soup

Lamb Lyonnaise with Green Salad

Apple Crumb Pudding

Lamb Lyonnaise

Peel and slice 1 lb. potatoes and 1 lb. onions *very thinly*. Put half the potatoes and onions into a shallow, preferably long oven-proof dish. Season very well and top with a very

grease cake tins very well after use as a casserole.

Never cook green vegetables in casseroles in the oven, for they lose colour, flavour and vitamins.

Other vegetables should be put into a dish, covered with cold water, salted, then covered with foil or a very tightly fitting lid. All menus serve 4 unless stated otherwise.

little chopped sage or rosemary. Put 4 large or 8 smaller thick, *lean* lamb chops over the potato mixture. Add the rest of the onions then the potatoes and season well. If you like a moist mixture add about ¼ pint (⅔C) stock or water and ½ stock cube. Cover the dish tightly and put the dish in the hottest part of the oven. Before serving, garnish with slices of raw tomato and/or watercress. Serve with green salad.

To vary Put a little fat over the sliced potatoes and lift the lid 40 minutes before serving to allow the potatoes to brown.

Use veal chops instead of lamb.

Add thickly sliced tomatoes to the potatoes and onions.

Apple Crumb Pudding

Cream 2 oz. (¼C) butter or margarine, 2–3 oz. (⅓C) brown sugar and 1 tablespoon golden

syrup. Add 1 teaspoon mixed spice, 8 oz. (2⅔C) breadcrumbs and the grated rind of 1 lemon. Put half this mixture into a greased casserole. Peel and slice 2–3 good-sized cooking apples, mix with 2 oz. (¼C) sugar, the juice of 1 lemon and 2–3 oz. seedless raisins. Put over the crumb mixture, then top with the rest of the crumbs and a foil covering or a lid. Bake in a cool part of the oven. Lift the lid when 'dishing-up' the meat course so the crumbs can crisp. Serve with a syrup sauce which can be heated in the oven in a small covered casserole.

Syrup Sauce

Mix 3 tablespoons golden syrup with the grated rind and juice of 1 lemon and ¼ pint (⅔C) water.

---

does not press down over the crumbs or leave the dish uncovered for a very crisp topping. Bake in the coolest part of the oven.

Rhubarb and Date Pudding

Rub 3 oz. (⅜C) margarine into 6 oz. (1½C) self-raising flour or plain flour sieved with 1½ teaspoons baking powder. Add 4 oz. (½C) caster sugar, 1 egg and enough milk to make a sticky consistency. Add about 8 oz. (1¼C) chopped raw rhubarb and 4 oz. (nearly ¾C) stoned, chopped dates. Put into a greased 8-inch cake tin or a 2-pint (5–6C) pie dish. Stand this in another container of water*. Put a sheet of foil over both the pudding and container. Cook in the hottest part of the oven.
*Have the water as high as possible in the container, but not so high that it boils over.

---

frozen peas (separate these if frozen in block), in a casserole. Cover with cold water, add salt and mint to taste. Cover with foil and cook in a fairly hot part of the oven.

Hawaiian Nut Pudding

Cut away the peel from 6 oranges. Stand each orange on a ring of canned pineapple and put into a casserole. Heat 2 oz. (¼C) butter in a pan, add 2 oz. (¼C) caster sugar and stir until the sugar has dissolved. Add about ⅜ pint (⅔C) syrup from the pineapple can and the juice of a fresh orange or 2 tablespoons Curaçao. Pour into the casserole and cover this. Bake in the coolest part of the oven for about 45 minutes. Lift out and cover the oranges with chopped nuts. Serve cold or warm with cream.

Baked Cheese Fingers

Cut 12 fingers of bread and butter and make sandwiches with sliced Cheddar or Gruyère cheese. Beat 1 egg with seasoning and 4 tablespoons milk. Dip the sandwiches in this and arrange in a shallow buttered casserole. Bake for about 15 minutes in the coolest part of the oven. An electric oven can be turned out if wished and the sandwiches baked in a warmer part of the oven while the heat drops. Garnish with watercress and celery curls just before serving.

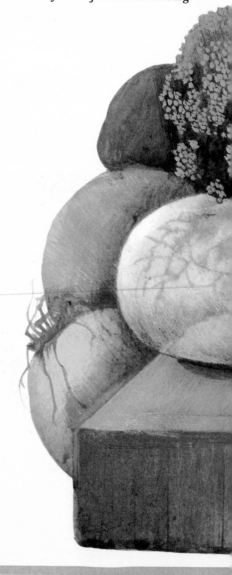

MENU 26

Oven-baked Risotto with Aubergines and Tomatoes au Gratin

Rhubarb and Date Pudding

Set the oven at moderate, 350–375°F, Gas Mark 4–5, for 1 hour for the risotto and aubergine dishes and about 1¼ hours for the pudding. This menu serves 4–6.

Oven-baked Risotto

Heat 2 tablespoons oil in a pan, toss 1 crushed clove garlic, 2 peeled sliced onions, 1 diced green pepper and 4 oz. sliced mushrooms in this. Next add 7–8 oz. (about 1C) long grain rice, 1¼ pints (3⅓C) chicken stock or water and 1–2 chicken stock cubes, seasoning, 2–3 oz. sultanas and 4–6 oz. diced chickens' livers or diced calf's liver. Bring the stock to the boil then spoon the mixture into a deep casserole. Wrap foil round the outside of the casserole to be certain the rice does not dry. Cover tightly. Put into the coolest part of the oven. Spoon out of the casserole on to a hot serving dish. Top with chopped parsley and lots of grated cheese.

Aubergines and Tomatoes au Gratin

Slice very thinly, but do not peel, 2 large aubergines and 1 lb. tomatoes. Put one third of the tomatoes in the casserole, season well. Add half the aubergines, seasoning, 1 tablespoon melted butter, half the remaining tomatoes, the rest of the aubergines, seasoning, butter and the last of the tomatoes. Top with a thick layer of crumbs, preferably brown, and a little butter. Put on a lid that

---

MENU 27

Chicken and Avocado Casserole with Jacket Potatoes, Peas and Carrots

Hawaiian Nut Pudding

Baked Cheese Fingers

Set the oven at moderate to moderately hot, 375–400°F, Gas Mark 5–6. Allow about 1 hour for the chicken dish with vegetables, 45 minutes for the pudding and about 15 minutes for the cheese fingers. This menu serves 6.

Chicken and Avocado Casserole

Coat 6 joints of young chicken in 1 oz. seasoned flour, mixed with ¼ teaspoon dried, or 1 teaspoon fresh chopped, thyme and the very finely grated rind of 1 lemon. Brown in 2 oz. (¼C) butter then put into a casserole. Add another 1 oz. butter to the saucepan, toss 2 sliced onions in this for a few minutes, add ½ pint (1⅓C) dry white wine and ¼ pint (⅔C) chicken stock or water and ½ stock cube, blended with 1 tablespoon flour. Bring to the boil and cook until thickened. Pour over the chicken. Cover the casserole and cook for nearly 1 hour in a fairly hot part of the oven. Remove from the oven, cool slightly so the liquid is no longer boiling, stir about ¼ pint (⅔C) thick cream into the mixture. Halve, peel and remove the stones from 2 ripe avocado pears. Slice and sprinkle with lemon juice. Put on top of the chicken mixture, brush with a little oil. Return to the coolest part of the oven for 10 minutes.

The jacket potatoes should be medium-sized only and put round the chicken casserole when placed in the oven.

Dice young carrots, mix with fresh or

Braised beef whirls

the coolest part of the oven. Strain, then top with a little margarine and chopped parsley.

Rice Pudding de Luxe

Put 2 oz. ($\frac{1}{4}$C) rice with 1–2 tablespoons sugar, 1 pint (2$\frac{2}{3}$C) milk, $\frac{1}{4}$ pint ($\frac{2}{3}$C) thin cream, 2–3 tablespoons sultanas and 1–2 tablespoons halved glacé cherries into a pie dish. Cook in the coolest part of the oven.

MENU
30

Piquant Fish Casserole

Paprika Scalloped Potatoes

Broccoli Spears

Banana and Coconut Bake

Set the oven at moderate, 375°F, Gas Mark 4–5. Allow 1$\frac{1}{4}$ hours for the scalloped potatoes, 40 minutes for the fish casserole and 25–30 minutes for the Banana and Coconut Bake.

Piquant Fish Casserole

Slice 4–6 oz. mushrooms, toss in 1 oz. hot margarine or butter. Add 1 tablespoon chopped spring onion or chives and/or 1 tablespoon chopped parsley, $\frac{1}{4}$ pint ($\frac{2}{3}$C) thin cream and 2 teaspoons Angostura bitters. Put 4 portions of white fish into a buttered casserole, season lightly, spoon the mushroom and cream mixture over the fish. Cover the dish and bake in the coolest part of the oven.

Paprika Scalloped Potatoes

Heat about $\frac{3}{4}$ pint (2C) milk with 2 oz. ($\frac{1}{4}$C) margarine or butter, good pinch salt, shake pepper and 1–2 teaspoons paprika. Put about 1 lb. peeled and very thinly sliced potatoes into a 2–3-pint pie dish. Add the milk mixture, do not cover. Cook in a fairly hot part of the oven.

The broccoli spears should be cooked in the top of the oven.

Banana and Coconut Bake

Heat 1 oz. butter, 2 oz. ($\frac{1}{4}$C) brown sugar and the juice of 2 oranges or $\frac{1}{4}$ pint ($\frac{2}{3}$C) canned orange juice until the sugar melts. Put 4 large or 8 small peeled bananas in a casserole. Add the orange liquid. Press a layer of desiccated coconut over the bananas. Bake in a fairly hot part of the oven.

This is delicious with Zabaione or Orange Zabaione (see page 100) or serve with fresh cream.

MENU
28

Stuffed Onion Casserole with Duchesse Potatoes and Green Beans

Compôte of Fruit

Set the oven at moderate to moderately hot, 375–400°F, Gas Mark 5–6. Allow about 45 minutes for all the menu, except the potatoes which need 25 minutes.

Stuffed Onion Casserole

Peel and boil 4 large onions in salted water until *nearly* soft. Remove from the water, cool enough to handle. Remove the centre of each onion, chop finely and mix with 3 oz. ($\frac{3}{4}$C) soft breadcrumbs, 8 oz. (about 1C) minced, cooked meat (pork and ham are particularly good in this dish) 1 oz. margarine, $\frac{1}{4}$ teaspoon dried, or 1 teaspoon chopped fresh, sage and seasoning. Press firmly into the middle of each onion, put into a casserole. Make a little thick brown sauce from some of the onion liquid in the pan. Pour round the onions, add a small packet of frozen green beans (broken up so they can be spread round the onions) and a little extra seasoning. Cover the casserole and cook in the fairly hot part of the oven.
To vary Finely chopped raw lambs' kidneys can be used in place of minced meat.

Duchesse Potatoes

Beat 1–2 oz. margarine and 1–2 egg yolks into 1 lb. mashed potato. Pile in shapes on a greased dish, heat and brown in the hottest part of the oven.

Compôte of Fruit

Put 1–1$\frac{1}{2}$ lb. prepared firm fruit, i.e. apples, plums, etc., into a casserole. Make a syrup of

---

sugar and water. Pour the syrup over the fruit. Put a lid on the casserole and cook in the coolest part of the oven. Turn or switch off the heat when removing the onions and potatoes from the oven.

MENU
29

Braised Beef Whirls

Macedoine of Vegetables

Rice Pudding de Luxe

Set the oven at slow to very moderate, 300–325°F, Gas Mark 2–3. Allow about 2 hours for the whole menu.

Braised Beef Whirls

Cut 4 slices topside beef in half and chop 1 onion and about 6 oz. ox-kidney fairly finely. Mix the onion and kidney with 1 tablespoon chopped parsley, 1 oz. margarine or shredded suet and seasoning. Divide this between the 8 pieces of meat and roll firmly. Secure with wooden cocktail sticks or fine string. Peel and slice 2–3 large onions and about 6 large carrots. Put at the bottom of the casserole. Heat 2 oz. ($\frac{1}{4}$C) fat in a pan. Coat the meat whirls in 1 oz. seasoned flour and then toss in the hot fat until golden coloured. Lift out on top of the vegetables. Blend $\frac{1}{2}$ pint (1$\frac{1}{3}$C) brown stock or water and 1 beef stock cube with the fat remaining in the pan. Pour round the beef whirls. Cover the casserole and cook in the fairly cool part of the oven.

Macedoine of Vegetables

Cut potatoes, swedes and turnips into dice. Put into a casserole. Cover with water, add salt and cover the casserole tightly. Cook in

---

These menus are planned for families with small children. No busy mother wants to cook two separate meals, one for the adults and another for young children, but the needs and tastes of grown-ups and children are not necessarily exactly the same. It is, however, often possible to adapt the dishes, so they are ideal for all the family. Children vary, of course, some young children will enjoy adult flavourings so some adaptations may not be necessary.

Quantities given are for 2 adults and 2 young children (who would have smaller portions).

MENU
31

Cheese and Bacon Kebabs with Mixed Vegetables

Blackcurrant Flummery

Cheese and Bacon Kebabs

Cut the rind from rashers of bacon and cut each rasher in half. Cut firm Cheddar cheese into cubes, then roll the bacon round the cheese. Put the bacon rolls on to a metal skewer.

For children Add segments of ripe eating apple, between the bacon rolls.

For adults Either add apple as above or add rings of green pepper, small mushrooms and partially cooked tiny onions (brushed with melted fat).

Cook under the grill, turning round until the bacon is evenly cooked. Do not over-cook the cheese as it then becomes less easily digested. Serve on a bed of diced cooked vegetables.

Blackcurrant Flummery

Dissolve a lemon jelly in ½ pint (1⅓C) very hot water. Cool slightly then add 2–3 table-spoons blackcurrant syrup. Allow to cool and begin to stiffen *very slightly* then spoon into a large basin. Gradually whisk nearly ½ pint (1⅓C) evaporated milk into the mixture. Pile into 4 glasses and leave to set. Decorate with slices of crystallised lemon.

For adults If the flavour of this dessert is too 'bland', put half the blackcurrant mixture into one basin and the rest into a second basin. Whisk ¼ pint (⅔C) evaporated milk into half the jelly and ¼ pint (⅔C) yoghourt into the remainder.

To vary Use an orange jelly and the juice of a fresh orange.

MENU

32

Grape and Melon Coûpe

Fried Liver, Bacon, and Brown Gravy Carrots and Creamed Potatoes

Butterscotch Raisin Pudding

Grape and Melon Coûpe

Halve about 4 oz. (1C) grapes and halve a small, or part of a larger, melon. Remove the seeds from both fruits. Dice the melon neatly. Arrange the fruit in 4 glasses. Make a syrup by boiling ¼ pint (⅔C) water with 1–2 tablespoons sugar or honey.

For children Cool the syrup slightly, spoon a little over the children's portions (unless they like ginger flavouring).

For adults Add ½ teaspoon ground ginger to the remaining syrup and spoon over the adult portions.

Fried Liver and Bacon

Fry rashers of bacon for *all* the family *lightly*, so they do not over-cook while being kept waiting. Coat sliced lambs' or calf's liver (about 10–12 oz.) with a *very little* seasoned flour and fry in the pan until tender. If the bacon fat is inadequate, add a little extra fat before putting the liver into the pan so it does not dry. Lift out when cooked and make a brown gravy in the pan.

For children Liver is such an important food, that it is worthwhile taking a little trouble to ensure children enjoy it. Liver has a slightly bitter taste, which children may not like, so add a little sugar to the flour coating. When the gravy is made, you can also add a pinch of sugar to part of this. Presentation is important to children, so form part of the creamed potatoes into 2 'nests'. Chop the bacon and liver, pile into the 'nests' and top with a little gravy.

For adults The gravy can be made more piquant for adults by adding a little made mustard.

Butterscotch Raisin Pudding

Put 3 oz. (⅓C) brown sugar and 1 oz. butter into a pan, stir over a low heat until the sugar has dissolved. Cool slightly, then add ¾ pint (2C) milk. Heat gently until the milk absorbs

the butterscotch. Pour over 3 oz. ($\frac{1}{2}$C) raisins and 3 oz. (1C) breadcrumbs. Leave for about 20 minutes to soften the crumbs. Add 2 well beaten eggs. Pour into a pie dish, stand in a container of water and bake for about 1 hour in the centre of a slow to very moderate oven, 300–325°F, Gas Mark 2–3.

For children   This dessert should be popular with children as well as being nutritious.

For adults   The dessert may be too insipid, so serve with lemon flavoured yoghourt, i.e. add grated lemon rind and juice to natural yoghourt.

MENU

33

Chicken Charlotte with Stuffed Tomatoes

Fresh Fruit Salad

Chicken Charlotte

Cut 5–6 slices bread into fingers. Do not cut away the crusts. Fry the bread fingers in hot margarine, butter or well clarified dripping until crisp and golden. Drain on absorbent paper. Make a white sauce with 1 oz. margarine or butter, 1 oz. flour and just *over* $\frac{1}{2}$ pint (1$\frac{1}{2}$C) milk, or milk and chicken stock. Add about 12 oz. (1$\frac{1}{2}$C) diced cooked chicken and 4 oz. ($\frac{1}{2}$C) diced cooked lean ham, or use all chicken. Put half the bread fingers into an oven-proof dish, top with the sauce mixture, then the rest of the fried bread fingers. Heat in the oven for a few minutes only.

For adults   Put part of the chicken and ham mixture at one end of the dish for the children. Add chopped chives and/or chopped lemon thyme to the remaining sauce to make the mixture more piquant.

To vary   Use 1 lb. smoked or cooked white fish in place of the chicken.

Use veal in place of chicken.

Stuffed Tomatoes

Halve tomatoes, scoop out the pulp, season and mix with cooked peas and/or cooked sweet corn. Pile into the tomato cases. When tomatoes are at their best serve cold, or heat for a short time only.

For children   If the children are very small, sieve the tomato pulp to avoid the pips.

Fresh Fruit Salad

Encourage children to enjoy raw fruit. Adapt the fruits in the salad to the children's taste. Do not over-sweeten.

For children Moisten with a little fresh orange juice.

For adults Moisten with a little white wine, or Kirsch for special occasions.

MENU
34

**Sausage Boats
with Jacket Potatoes
and Cauliflower**

Crisp-topped Banana Rice

Sausage Boats

Cook 6–8 large sausages. Cut 6–8 very thin slices of fresh bread. Spread one side of the bread with margarine. Put a sausage in the centre of each slice, gather up the sides to form a 'boat' shape and secure with a wooden cocktail stick. Brush the outside of the bread with melted margarine and crisp in a hot oven.

For children Bake really small jacket potatoes, otherwise the meal is too 'solid'. Make the cauliflower look attractive by topping with a little red paprika (not hot but sweet pepper) and a chopped hard boiled egg. If the children like a moist texture, top the cauliflower with a cheese or white sauce or make a gravy to serve with the sausages.

For adults Spread the bread with mustard and/or cottage or cream cheese before putting the sausage on the bread.

Crisp-topped Banana Rice

Make a creamy rice pudding or use canned creamed rice. Put into a dish and heat gently. Top with sliced bananas and brown sugar and heat under a low grill until the sugar bubbles.

MENU
35

**Salmon Fish Cakes
with Cheese Sauce
and Creamed Spinach**

Date and Nut Pie

Salmon Fish Cakes

Flake about 12 oz. (1½C) canned salmon. Mix with an equal quantity of mashed potato. If using dehydrated potato, make this a little more stiff than usual. Blend with 2 egg yolks and seasoning. Form into flat cakes, dust with seasoned flour. Brush with the 2 egg whites and coat with crisp breadcrumbs. Fry in a little hot fat, or bake for about 15 minutes on a well greased and heated baking tray in a moderately hot oven, or 25 minutes in a moderate oven. Serve with a cheese sauce and chopped or sieved cooked spinach, blended with a little top of the milk.

For children or adults Frying is a less easily digestible form of cooking, so bake.

For adults Blend 1–2 teaspoons capers and a little anchovy essence with some of the fish.

To vary Use flaked tuna or white fish instead of salmon.

Date and Nut Pie

Blend 3 oz. (⅜C) semolina and 3 oz. (¾C) plain or self-raising flour. Add 4 oz. (½C) caster sugar and 3 oz. (⅜C) melted margarine or butter. Chop 8 oz. (1¼C) dates. Put into a basin. Add 3 tablespoons (¼C) boiling water, 2 tablespoons honey, 1 tablespoon orange or lemon juice and 2 peeled, grated, medium-sized apples. Stir together until smooth. Sprinkle half the semolina mixture in the bottom of a 7-inch shallow oven-proof dish. Add the date mixture.

For adults Spread a generous quantity of coarsely chopped walnuts over part of the date mixture. These are not very suitable for small children.

Top the date or date and nut mixture with the rest of the semolina mixture. Bake for about 35–40 minutes in the centre of a moderate oven, 375°F, Gas Mark 4–5. Reduce the heat after 20 minutes if the topping is becoming too brown.

MENU
36

**Beef Darioles
with Hot Coleslaw,
Savoury Rice and
Tomato Sauce**

Orange Coffee Cream

Beef Darioles

Heat 2 oz. (¼C) fat and fry 1–2 finely chopped or grated onions for a few minutes. Stir in 1 oz. flour and cook for several minutes. Gradually add ¼ pint (⅔C) canned tomato juice or home-made tomato pulp. Bring the tomato mixture to the boil and cook until thickened. Stir in 12 oz.–1 lb. (1½–2C) freshly minced beef, 1 oz. (⅓C) soft breadcrumbs and seasoning. Put into 8 greased dariole tins (castle pudding tins). If these are not available, use old cups or small moulds. Cover with greased greaseproof paper or foil and steam for 30 minutes. Meanwhile make the tomato sauce. Blend 1 oz. flour with ¾ pint (2C) tomato juice or pulp. Put into a pan with 1 oz. margarine and seasoning. Bring to the boil and cook until thickened.

For adults Add 1–2 teaspoons capers to the sauce and a few drops Tabasco sauce.

Hot Coleslaw

Cook finely shredded cabbage in the minimum of salted water for a very short time so it retains its crisp texture. Children often enjoy very crisp cabbage and it retains more mineral salts and vitamins.

For adults Try the Continental 'trick' of adding a teaspoon of caraway seeds and a knob of butter to the hot cabbage.

Savoury Rice

Serve well seasoned boiled rice.

For children A sprinkling of grated cheese and/or a few sultanas will make the rice more interesting.

Orange Coffee Cream

Beat 2 eggs with 1 oz. sugar. Add ½ pint (1⅓C) warm milk. Cook in a basin over *hot* water or the top of a double saucepan until the custard thickens enough to coat the back of a wooden spoon. Meanwhile open a can of mandarin oranges. Pour out ¼ pint (⅔C) syrup from the can, blend with ½ tablespoon sweetened coffee essence. Soften ½ oz. gelatine (or enough to set 1 pint (2⅔C)) in 2 tablespoons cold coffee-orange liquid. Heat the rest of the liquid, add the gelatine and stir until dissolved. Allow both the gelatine mixture and the custard to cool, then whisk together. Put into a mould, rinsed in cold water. Allow to set. Turn out and top with mandarin oranges, cream, and a little angelica if liked.

For children The blending of flavours is delicious and should be popular with all the family. Do not give the children any, or too much, cream topping.

Try to keep busy, so you have little time to think about the food you cannot eat. Do not eat between meals. It is the odd biscuit or sweet that can make the difference between a successful or unsuccessful diet.

Do not miss meals, otherwise you will feel unwell and lack energy.

Never start a strict slimming diet without medical advice.

Do not talk about your diet and become a bore.

If you do 'eat out' with friends and have to accept a dish that is not particularly low calorie, eat and enjoy it then have one or two smaller meals the next day.

Do not imagine that slimming menus are necessarily monotonous and dull. Obviously if you wish to lose weight, there are many high-calorie or fattening foods you must avoid but if you make slimming meals interesting and imaginative (within the limits of the diet) there is a much greater chance of the diet being followed.

It is not easy for one member of a family to eat entirely different meals from the rest. I have therefore planned

menus that are relatively low in calories and added hints for the 'non-slimmers' as well. All menus serve 4.

seven
MENUS FOR SLIMMING

MENU
37

Clear Tomato Soup

Citrus Lamb Cutlets with Green Salad

Frosted Apple

Clear Tomato Soup

Heat canned tomato juice, add finely chopped celery, spring onions, parsley and seasoning. The soup can be topped with a spoonful of yoghourt if wished.

For non-slimmers Top each portion with a little soured cream or spoonful of thick fresh cream.

To vary This is delicious as an ice-cold soup for hot weather.

Citrus Lamb Cutlets

Bake or grill lamb cutlets—do not fry these. Add slices of orange to the grill or roasting tin a few minutes before the meat is cooked.

For non-slimmers Serve with jacket, creamed or new potatoes.

Green Salad

Eat plenty of green salads when on a slimming diet—they are low in calories and give you valuable vitamins and mineral salts. Choose the low-calorie salad ingredients, i.e. lettuce, endive, chicory, cucumber and green or red pepper. Shred or chop and arrange a generous portion of salad in bowls or on plates. To make a low-calorie dressing, blend natural yoghourt with plenty of seasoning and a squeeze of lemon juice.

Frosted Apple

Cook peeled and cored apples until a smooth thick purée. Add a little sugar substitute to sweeten. Allow to cool. To each ½ pint (1⅓C) apple purée allow 1 egg. Blend the yolk with the apple, then fold in the stiffly beaten egg white. Freeze lightly.

For non-slimmers   Top each portion with cream or vanilla ice cream, and chopped nuts or grated or desiccated coconut.

MENU

38

Watercress Eggs

Devilled White Fish with Grilled Tomatoes and Spinach

Yoghourt and Orange Sundae

Watercress Eggs

Hard boil 4 eggs and halve lengthways. Remove the yolks, mash with seasoning. Add squeeze lemon juice, 2 tablespoons skimmed milk (to give a soft consistency) and 3–4 tablespoons chopped watercress leaves. Press into the white cases and serve on a bed of lettuce.

Note   If you are being extra careful with calories, have half an egg only as an hors d'oeuvre.

For non-slimmers   Top each portion with mayonnaise.

To vary   Use chopped canned asparagus tips in place of watercress.

Devilled White Fish

Blend 1–2 teaspoons Worcestershire sauce, ½ teaspoon curry powder, pinch cayenne pepper and ¼–½ teaspoon celery salt with 1 oz. melted butter. Brush over 4 portions of white fish and cook under a hot grill. Serve with grilled tomatoes and spinach.

For non-slimmers   Top the grilled fish with a generous portion of extra flavoured butter.

To vary   Use lemon butter, parsley butter, tomato butter or anchovy butter.

Yoghourt and Orange Sundae

Cut the peel from 6 oranges and then cut the fruit into rings or segments. Divide between 4 glasses and top with natural yoghourt.

For non-slimmers   Add a generous portion of sweetened whipped cream or sweeten the orange slices (honey or brown sugar is delicious).

MENU

39

Harlequin Soufflé Omelette with Broccoli

Hot Melon with Ginger

Harlequin Soufflé Omelette

Separate the whites from the yolks of 6–8 eggs. Beat the yolks with 8 oz. (1C) cottage cheese and seasoning until a smooth well-blended mixture. Add 1 tablespoon chopped parsley and 1–2 tablespoons chopped chives or spring onions. Next fold in the stiffly beaten egg whites. Heat 2 oz. (¼C) butter in a very large frying pan or a little less in a 'non-stick' pan. Pour in the egg mixture. Cook

steadily for about 5–6 minutes, then put the pan under a medium grill and cook for a further 3–4 minutes until set. Slip out of the pan (do not try and fold) on to a hot dish. Top with slices of red pepper, or tomato and green pepper. Serve at once.

For non-slimmers Add toast, bread or rolls to the meal.

Hot Melon with Ginger

Slice ripe melon, remove the seeds. Moisten with fresh orange juice, sprinkle with a little ground ginger and warm in the oven.

For non-slimmers Blend a little preserved ginger with the orange juice and top with pieces of preserved ginger. Omit the ground ginger if wished.

MENU

40

Prawns in Aspic

Stuffed Steaks with Spinach

Junkets and Fresh Fruit

Prawns in Aspic

Put 4–6 oz. shelled prawns into 4 small moulds or dishes. Make up ¾ pint (2C) aspic jelly according to the instructions on the packet. Add 1 tablespoon concentrated tomato purée and a few drops Worcestershire sauce and pour over the prawns. Leave to set. Turn out of the moulds or leave in the dishes.

For non-slimmers Top with a spoonful of mayonnaise.

Stuffed Steaks

Buy 4 fairly thick fillets or pieces of rump steak. Cut horizontally across three-quarters of each steak to make a 'pocket'. Chop 2 lambs' kidneys finely, season well, add a little chopped parsley and 2 skinned chopped tomatoes. Insert the stuffing into the steaks and grill until as cooked as you like. Use the minimum amount of melted fat to baste the meat. If preferred, wrap each steak in a square of foil and bake for 20–35 minutes (depending upon how you like the meat cooked) in a hot oven; 20 minutes will give a very 'rare' steak. Serve with freshly cooked or frozen spinach.

For non-slimmers Blend a little chopped bacon or good knob of butter with the kidney filling. The spinach can be sieved or chopped and blended with a little thick cream. Season well.

To vary Use 6 oz. lamb's or calf's liver in place of kidney in the stuffing.

Use fillet of veal in place of steak. Lay the veal on a board and divide the filling between the four pieces of meat. Roll up and secure with wooden skewers or fine string. Bake in foil in a hot oven, for about 35–45 minutes.

Junkets

Take the cream off the milk. Heat 1 pint (2⅔C) skimmed milk to blood heat. Add a little sugar substitute. Add 2 teaspoons rennet (this amount is necessary with pasteurised milk). Pour into 4 dishes, top with grated nutmeg and allow to clot at room tem-

liquid sugar substitute. Put back into the grapefruit cases. Top with foil and heat for about 10 minutes in a moderate oven.
For non-slimmers Mix with a little brown sugar instead of sugar substitute. Put the fruit back into the grapefruit cases, top with a very little butter and omit the foil. Heat in the oven. If preferred, the grapefruit can be grilled when topped with butter.

Country Bake

Cook enough fresh or frozen spinach to give a good portion for 4 people. Chop or sieve the vegetable. Season well and put into a

MENU
42
**Fish in Wine Sauce
with Baked
Stuffed Mushrooms**

**Cheese and
Starch-reduced Roll**

Fish in wine sauce

perature. Top with a few slices of fresh unsweetened fruit (avoid banana) just before serving.
For non-slimmers Spoon lightly whipped cream (sweetened to taste) on the junkets then add the fruit. Do not break the junket otherwise it becomes 'watery'.

MENU
41

Spiced Hot Grapefruit

Country Bake

Coffee Jelly

Spiced Hot Grapefruit

Halve grapefruit. Remove the segments of fruit from the skin, discard the pips. Mix with a very little allspice and few drops

shallow oven-proof dish. Cover with about 8 oz. (1C) cottage cheese. Break 4 eggs over the cheese, then pour ½ pint (1⅓C) well seasoned yoghourt over the eggs. Top with 2–3 teaspoons freshly chopped herbs (parsley, chives, mint, very little thyme). Bake for approximately 20 minutes just above the centre of a moderate oven, 375°F, Gas Mark 4–5.
For non-slimmers Although all the foods chosen in this dish are low in calories, it is very sustaining as well as being quite delicious. Serve with new potatoes, toast or hot crispy rolls.

Coffee Jelly

Make 1 pint (2⅔C) moderately strong coffee. Sweeten with sugar substitute. Soften 1 tablespoon gelatine or an envelope (enough to set 1 pint (2⅔C)) in a little cold coffee from the pint. Heat the rest. Add the softened gelatine and stir until dissolved. Pour into a rinsed mould or 4 sundae glasses. If using a mould, turn out when set.
For non-slimmers Serve with chocolate flavoured ice cream or top with sweetened whipped cream.
Note Home-made fresh fruit jellies (see page 9) are ideal desserts for slimmers which will be enjoyed by all the family.

Fish in Wine Sauce

Fish is a low-calorie, high protein food, so is ideal for slimmers.
Choose fillets of whiting, plaice, sole or other white fish. Season and fold the fillets. Put into a shallow oven-proof dish. Cover with dry inexpensive white wine, add a few halved de-seeded grapes, a little diced green and red pepper and cover the dish. Bake for 20–30 minutes (according to the size of the fillets) in the centre of a moderate oven, 375°F, Gas Mark 4–5.

Baked Stuffed Mushrooms

Buy 8–12 oz. fairly large mushrooms. Wash and remove the stalks. Chop these and blend with 2–3 large skinned chopped tomatoes, 1 small grated onion, 1 oz. butter or margarine, 1 tablespoon chopped parsley and seasoning. Put the mushrooms on a large greased oven-proof dish. Top with the stuffing. Cover with foil and cook in the oven for the same length of time as the fish. Serve hot.
For non-slimmers Top the mushrooms with a little butter or margarine and serve another cooked vegetable with the meal.

The very large range of convenience foods available means that good meals, interesting meals and nutritious meals can be prepared within minutes.

Canned Foods

Meat, fish, fruit, vegetables all add variety to a menu and the food needs little, if any, heating. Canning does not affect the protein value of meat, but canned vegetables do not contain the vitamins present in freshly grown, and carefully cooked, or raw vegetables. This is why you will find fresh fruit juices or tomatoes added to some of the menus.

Canned soups are an excellent stand-by. Use them for sauces, when you are short of time. It takes but a few minutes to add extra flavouring or garnish to canned soups and make them completely individual.

eight
MEALS IN MINUTES

MENU
43

Queensland Cocktail

Curried Hard Boiled Eggs with Mixed Vegetables

Mock Savarin

Frozen Foods

These have caused a mild 'revolution' in our kitchens. The vegetables, which retain an appreciable amount of vitamins, also keep much of the flavour and appearance of fresh vegetables. Frozen fish and meat are also excellent.

Dehydrated Foods

Many modern dried foods no longer require prolonged soaking and cooking, and they are packaged in such a compact manner that they need relatively little room in the store-cupboard.

Fresh 'Convenience Foods'

Cooked meats, cheese, milk, bread and many fruits and vegetables can be termed 'convenience foods', for they can provide the basis of speedy and interesting meals.

All menus serve 4 people.

Queensland Cocktail

Halve 1 large or 2 small avocado pears, remove skin and dice the flesh. Blend with mayonnaise immediately so the pear does not discolour. Mix with the contents of a small can of crabmeat and a diced green pepper. Shred part of a lettuce finely, put at the bottom of 4 glasses. Top with the avocado mixture. Quarter 1 lemon and put a section on top of each glass. Serve with a teaspoon.

To vary Use fresh crab or other cooked shell fish.

Use canned or fresh grapefruit segments in place of avocado pear.

Add a little tomato purée or ketchup to the sauce.

Curried Hard Boiled Eggs

Put 4–8 eggs on to cook (depending upon your appetite). Meanwhile heat a fairly large can of mulligatawny soup, add a little curry powder if wished (the soup already has a curry taste), 1–2 teaspoons chutney, 1 tablespoon raisins, 1 tablespoon desiccated coconut and 1 large well drained can of mixed vegetables. Crack the hard boiled eggs, re-

move the shells. Put the eggs into a heated dish, add the curried mixture. Serve with bread and butter, creamed dehydrated potatoes or long grain rice.

To make the curry more interesting, serve chutney, nuts, sliced bananas and/or orange in individual dishes.

To vary   It is possible to buy canned curry sauce. Use this instead of the soup.

Use chicken soup instead of mulligatawny.

Use flaked canned tuna instead of eggs.

Use frozen mixed vegetables and simmer in the soup until tender.

Use dehydrated vegetables and cook as the directions on the packet, then add to the soup.

Mock Savarin

Open a medium-sized can of fruit (preferably mangoes, apricots, peaches or pineapple). Pour $\frac{1}{4}$ pint ($\frac{2}{3}$C) of the syrup into a saucepan. Add 2 tablespoons rum and heat. Put a small plain Madeira cake or sponge on a dish, spoon the sauce over this. Top with the canned fruit.

To vary   Use fresh instead of canned fruit and make the syrup with $\frac{1}{4}$ pint ($\frac{2}{3}$C) water and 2 oz. ($\frac{1}{4}$C) sugar. Honey or golden syrup could be used instead of sugar. Add the rum as above.

Add a few drops rum essence in place of rum.

This menu is illustrated on the previous page.

Chicken Borshch

Open a medium-sized can of chicken soup, tip into a pan. Heat. Add a little top of the milk and the liquid from a small can of beetroot. Garnish with chopped parsley.

To vary   Add diced or grated carrot or cooked beetroot to the soup, top with yoghourt or soured cream.

Sardines Niçoise

Open a small can of tomatoes. Tip into a pan, add seasoning and simmer until a *thick* pulp. Mash the sardines from a medium-sized can, season lightly. Toast 4 crumpets or slices of bread. Butter, then spread with the sardines. Heat under the grill for a few minutes. Top with the tomato pulp, anchovy fillets and black olives.

MENU
45

**Danish Kebabs
with Mustard Sauce
and Green Salad**

Orange Condé

Cheese Wafers

Danish Kebabs with Mustard Sauce

Open three cans for interesting kebabs—a small can of luncheon meat or ham and pork, a small can of Frankfurters and a small can (or use a tube) of pâté. Cut the luncheon meat into neat 1½-inch cubes. If the Frankfurters are large halve these. Split the Frankfurters carefully and spread with a little pâté then sandwich together again. Quarter firm tomatoes. Put the food on to 4 long or 8 smaller metal skewers. Brush with a little melted margarine or butter and heat under the grill.

Heat a small can of chicken soup or make up a small quantity of dehydrated chicken soup. Flavour with a generous amount of French or English mustard. Serve as a sauce with the kebabs and green salad.

To vary Diced canned tongue, ham, bacon rolls, canned or fresh mushrooms, small pickled onions and small, firm, canned new potatoes may be used for the kebabs.

Orange Condé

Cut the peel from 3 or 4 oranges and slice the fruit neatly. Open a can of creamed rice, blend some of the fruit with the rice. Spoon into 4 individual dishes or 1 larger dish. Heat 2–3 tablespoons marmalade, apricot jam or red currant jelly. Arrange the rest of the oranges on the rice, top with the hot marmalade, jam or jelly.

To vary Use other fresh or canned fruit in place of oranges.

Blend a little fresh or canned cream with the rice.

Cheese Wafers

Sandwich ice cream wafer biscuits with thin slices of processed or Cheddar cheese, or spread cream cheese over half the wafers and top with the remainder. Put on to a baking tray, brush with a little melted butter or margarine and heat for about 3 minutes only in a hot oven.

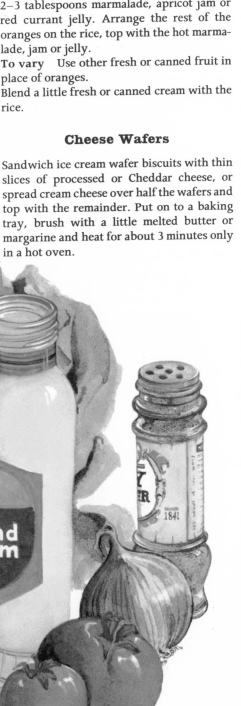

MENU
46

Paprika Mushrooms

**Chicken Fricassée
with Crumbed Potatoes
and Garlic Beans**

Coffee Pear Alaska

Paprika Mushrooms

Blend a can of cream with 1–2 teaspoons paprika and a few drops of vinegar. Season well. Heat canned button mushrooms, drain well, put on rounds of toast or fried bread. Heat the cream mixture for 1–2 minutes only. Spoon over the mushrooms and top with chopped parsley.

To vary Serve as a savoury at the end of the meal instead of a 'starter'.

Use fresh button mushrooms in place of canned mushrooms. Simmer in seasoned stock until just tender.

Use ¼ pint (⅔C) soured cream in place of canned cream. Omit the vinegar.

Chicken Fricassée

Cut a cooked chicken into neat pieces. Remove the skin if wished. Open a large can of asparagus soup, tip into a large saucepan or a deep frying pan. Blend ½–1 chicken stock cube with nearly ¼ pint (⅔C) boiling water. Add to the soup, stir over a gentle heat until a smooth fairly thin mixture. Put in the chicken pieces. Heat gently, without covering the pan, for about 10 minutes. The sauce should then be the right consistency. Garnish with triangles of toast.

To vary Use chicken instead of asparagus soup, add diced canned red pepper for colour and flavour.

Crumbed Potatoes

Heat a can of new potatoes in a pan. Drain very thoroughly. Melt 1½–2 oz. (nearly ¼C) butter or margarine in the saucepan, add 2–3 tablespoons crisp breadcrumbs (raspings). Put in the potatoes and turn until coated.

To vary Add a little curry powder to the crumbs.

Garlic Beans

Heat canned green beans or cook dehydrated beans. Drain well. Heat 1 oz. butter or margarine in the pan. Add a clove of garlic (crushed or finely chopped). Put in the beans and blend well.

Coffee Pear Alaska

Put a block of very firm coffee ice cream into an oven-proof serving dish, or on an oven-proof serving plate. Peel, core and quarter 2 or 3 pears, arrange round the ice cream. Whip 4 or 5 egg whites until *very stiff*. Gradually whisk in 2–3 oz. ($\frac{1}{4}$–$\frac{3}{8}$C) caster sugar, then fold in another 2–3 oz. ($\frac{1}{4}$–$\frac{3}{8}$C) sugar. Pile or pipe over the ice cream and fruit. Brown for 3–5 minutes in a very hot oven. This dessert can be 'kept waiting' after cooking for about 15–20 minutes without spoiling.

To vary   Put the ice cream and fruit on to a shallow sponge cake. This can be moistened with strong sweetened coffee, flavoured with a little Tia Maria (the coffee flavoured liqueur).

Choose vanilla ice cream and other fruit, fresh or canned.

MENU
47

Fresh Grapefruit

Speedy Moussaka with Green Vegetable

Coconut Gâteau

Speedy Moussaka

Peel and grate 2–3 potatoes and 2–3 onions. Heat 2–3 oz. ($\frac{1}{4}$–$\frac{3}{8}$C) margarine or dripping in a frying pan. Cook the potatoes and onions *steadily* until just tender. This takes about 8 minutes. Tip a large can of stewed steak into the frying pan and blend with the vegetables. Heat thoroughly. Meanwhile make a white sauce by the speedy method, i.e. blend 1 oz. flour or $\frac{1}{2}$ oz. cornflour with $\frac{1}{2}$ pint (1$\frac{1}{3}$C) milk. Tip into the saucepan with 1 oz. margarine or butter, stir until thickened. Season well, add 2–3 oz. ($\frac{2}{3}$–1C) grated Cheddar cheese, heat gently until melted. Put the meat and vegetables into a heated shallow casserole. Top with the sauce and a little grated nutmeg and serve at once. Serve with a green vegetable.

Note   Use less grated Parmesan cheese. This is an excellent·'stand-by' in the cupboard as it keeps well in drums.

To vary   Add a finely sliced or diced aubergine (egg plant) to the potatoes and onions in the frying pan. You will need a little more margarine or dripping (or use oil if wished). Add a beaten egg to the cheese sauce, cook for 1–2 minutes.

Add several sliced tomatoes to the potatoes and onions *after* about 5 minutes cooking. This makes certain the tomatoes do not become too soft.

Coconut Gâteau

Blend 2 oz. ($\frac{1}{4}$C) butter, 2 oz. (generous $\frac{1}{4}$C) brown sugar with the finely grated rind and juice of 1 lemon. Add 2–3 tablespoons desiccated coconut. Split a 7-inch sponge cake across the centre. If not spread with jam, cover the bottom half with a little jam then half the coconut mixture. Put the two halves together again. Spread the top of the sponge with the rest of the coconut mixture and brown under a low grill. Serve warm or cold with a jam sauce, made by heating a little jam.

To vary   Flavour the coconut mixture with orange instead of lemon or with diced preserved ginger and syrup from the ginger. Decorate with glacé cherries or canned cherries.

MENU
48

Corn Scramble with Rolls

Speedy Grill

Cornflake Flan

Corn Scramble

Heat 1 oz. margarine or butter in a pan with 2 tablespoons top of the milk. Add a small can of sweet corn and heat. Beat 4 eggs with seasoning. Scramble lightly and serve with rolls.

Speedy Grill

Open a can of Frankfurters and a can of corned beef or chopped pork or ham. Brush the sausages and sliced meat with melted margarine and cook under the grill for a few minutes. Serve with canned heated mushrooms or tomatoes.

To vary   Buy fresh sausages or bacon and combine these ingredients with sliced canned ham, or buy frozen Hamburgers which cook very quickly.

Cornflake Flan

Cream 2 oz. ($\frac{1}{4}$C) butter or margarine, 2 oz. ($\frac{1}{4}$C) caster sugar and 2 teaspoons golden syrup. Add 4 oz. (good 3C) slightly crushed cornflakes. Form into a flan shape. Either set in a cool place for a short time or brown for 10 minutes in a very moderate oven. Fill with canned fruit and decorate with cream if liked.

Cornflake flan

Most of us enjoy hot weather, but it can have a disastrous effect upon one's appetite. If people are very hot and/or very tired, they often lose their taste for food. It is a sensible idea to have a cool, refreshing drink and relax for a while before eating.

Do not make the mistake of having all cold dishes in hot weather, this is boring and monotonous; many hot dishes are light and 'easy to eat'. Avoid food that is very solid and take special care that food *looks* interesting and inviting. Try to cook meals in the oven, rather than on top of the cooker; this keeps the kitchen *and* the cook cool.

This menu serves 4–6.

Mushroom Vichysoisse

Peel 2 large old potatoes and clean 3 large leeks. Chop the vegetables and simmer in 1 pint (2⅔C) chicken stock for about 35–40 minutes. Add 2 oz. (½C) sliced button mushrooms towards the end of the cooking time. Sieve or emulsify, cool. Blend with ¼ pint (⅔C) thin cream and season well. Top with a little cream and chopped chives. The soup should be the consistency of a thick pouring cream.
To vary Omit the mushrooms.
Use a little less stock and add white wine with the cream.

nine
HOT WEATHER MENUS

MENU
49

Mushroom Vichysoisse

Terrine en Croute with New Potatoes and Green Beans

Raspberry Princess with Almond Snaps

Terrine en Croute

This is made as the recipe on page 175, using chicken in the filling.

Raspberry Princess

Make up a raspberry flavoured jelly with ½ pint (1⅓C) very hot water, pour over ¼ pint (⅔C) crushed raspberries. Allow to cool and stiffen *very slightly*. Whisk 3 egg whites very stiffly. Gradually whisk 1–2 tablespoons sugar into the egg whites. Fold into the raspberry mixture. Spoon into 4–6 glasses, piling the fluffy mixture fairly high. Decorate with raspberries and leave to set.
To vary The above is a fairly firm mixture, for a softer mixture crush about ½ pint (1⅓C) raspberries. Put a little pulp in each glass, then add the rest to the jelly, as the recipe above.

Almond Snaps

Grease 2–3 baking trays with oil before making the biscuits. Whisk 2 large egg whites stiffly, add 2–3 drops almond essence. Fold in 4 oz. (½C) caster sugar and 4 oz. (1C) ground almonds or crushed almonds (i.e. chop or emulsify until nearly as fine as ground almonds). Divide the mixture into about 18 balls. Put these on the trays, allowing space for them to spread out to about 3 inches in diameter. Flatten with your fingers. Bake for approximately 12 minutes just above the centre of a moderate oven, 350–375°F, Gas Mark 4–5. Watch carefully as they cook, and bake one batch at a time. Remove from the oven, allow to cool for about 1 minute, so the biscuits set sufficiently to handle. Lift the first biscuit from the tin and roll round the greased handle of a wooden spoon. Remove and cool on a wire tray. Repeat this process with other biscuits. Store in an airtight tin when cold. *Makes about 18.*

Golden Tomatoes

Parcelled Veal with Yoghourt and Sherry Sauce and Mixed Salad or Summer Vegetables

Peach and Strawberry Baskets

This menu serves 4.

Golden Tomatoes

Choose 4 medium-sized tomatoes. Dip into boiling water for about 30 seconds, remove and cool. Take off the skins. Meanwhile hard boil 2 eggs. Shell, halve and put the yolks on one side. Chop the whites, put into a basin. Add about 4 oz. ($\frac{1}{2}$C) cream cheese and 2–3 tablespoons finely diced cucumber. Cut a slice from each tomato, scoop out the pulp, chop and add to the egg white mixture. Beat until fairly smooth. Season well. Spoon into the tomatoes, smooth flat on top, coat with thick mayonnaise and the chopped egg yolks. Serve on a bed of sliced cucumber.

Parcelled Veal with Yoghourt and Sherry Sauce

Chop 3–4 rashers fairly fat bacon into narrow strips, slice 4 oz. (1C) mushrooms and mix with the bacon. Add 1 tablespoon chopped parsley, 1 small grated onion, 2 oz. ($\frac{1}{4}$C) butter or margarine, 3 oz. ($\frac{3}{4}$C) soft breadcrumbs, 1 egg and seasoning. Stir well until the mixture binds. Cut 4 squares of foil, brush with melted butter or oil. Put a veal chop or fillet of veal in the centre of each piece of foil. Spoon the stuffing on top and wrap the foil round the meat and stuffing to make a neat parcel. Lift into a meat tin and bake for approximately 30–35 minutes for thin fillets or 40–45 minutes for chops, towards the top of a hot oven, 425–450°F, Gas Mark 6–7. To make the sauce, put approximately $\frac{1}{2}$ pint ($1\frac{1}{3}$C) yoghourt into a basin over hot water, add a little chopped parsley, seasoning and 2 tablespoons sherry. Heat gently, then add 2 teaspoons capers and 1 teaspoon made mustard. Unwrap the 'parcels' carefully. Lift on to a dish, garnish with lemon and parsley and serve with the sauce.

Peach and Strawberry Baskets

Halve 4 peaches or use 8 canned peach halves. If using fresh peaches make sure the cream mixture covers the cut surface to prevent discolouration. Slice about 4 oz. strawberries do *not* mash. Blend with $\frac{1}{4}$ pint ($\frac{2}{3}$C) whipped cream and 1 tablespoon sieved icing sugar. Spread over the peach halves (cut side uppermost). Top with whole strawberries. Decorate with strawberry leaves where possible.

Gazpacho

Ham and Tongue Loaf with Corn Salad

Chocolate Macaroon Trifle

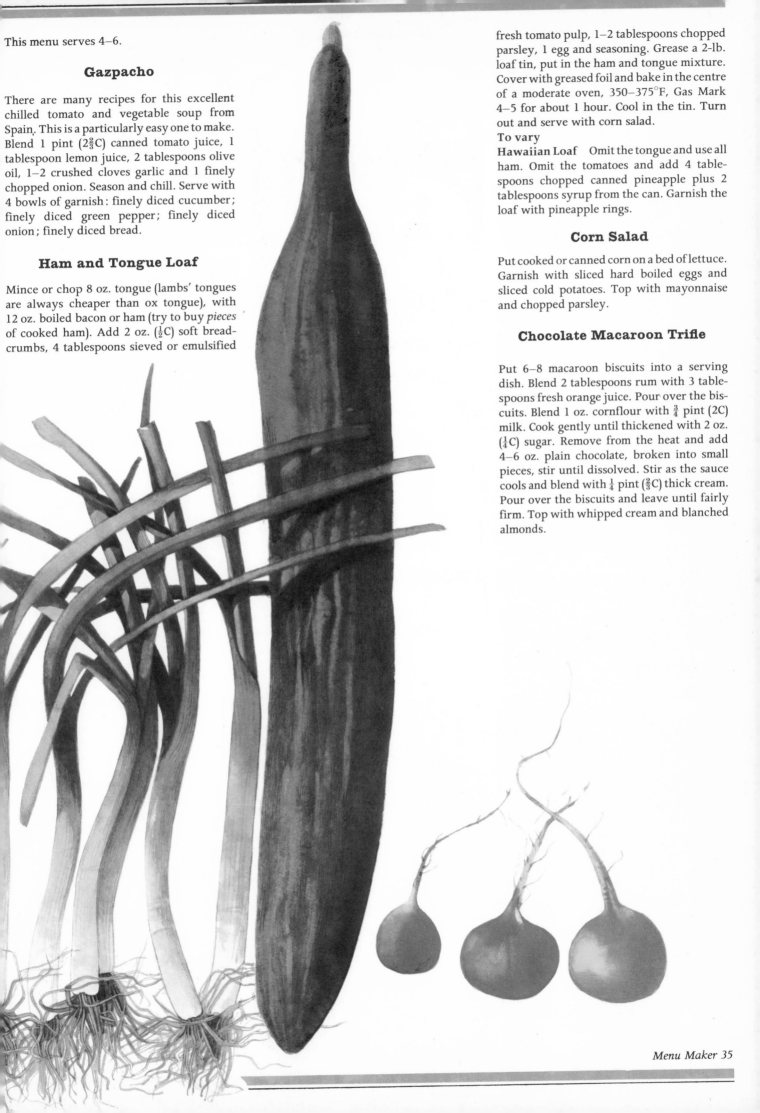

This menu serves 4–6.

Gazpacho

There are many recipes for this excellent chilled tomato and vegetable soup from Spain. This is a particularly easy one to make. Blend 1 pint (2⅔C) canned tomato juice, 1 tablespoon lemon juice, 2 tablespoons olive oil, 1–2 crushed cloves garlic and 1 finely chopped onion. Season and chill. Serve with 4 bowls of garnish: finely diced cucumber; finely diced green pepper; finely diced onion; finely diced bread.

Ham and Tongue Loaf

Mince or chop 8 oz. tongue (lambs' tongues are always cheaper than ox tongue), with 12 oz. boiled bacon or ham (try to buy *pieces* of cooked ham). Add 2 oz. (½C) soft bread-crumbs, 4 tablespoons sieved or emulsified

fresh tomato pulp, 1–2 tablespoons chopped parsley, 1 egg and seasoning. Grease a 2-lb. loaf tin, put in the ham and tongue mixture. Cover with greased foil and bake in the centre of a moderate oven, 350–375°F, Gas Mark 4–5 for about 1 hour. Cool in the tin. Turn out and serve with corn salad.

To vary

Hawaiian Loaf Omit the tongue and use all ham. Omit the tomatoes and add 4 table-spoons chopped canned pineapple plus 2 tablespoons syrup from the can. Garnish the loaf with pineapple rings.

Corn Salad

Put cooked or canned corn on a bed of lettuce. Garnish with sliced hard boiled eggs and sliced cold potatoes. Top with mayonnaise and chopped parsley.

Chocolate Macaroon Trifle

Put 6–8 macaroon biscuits into a serving dish. Blend 2 tablespoons rum with 3 table-spoons fresh orange juice. Pour over the bis-cuits. Blend 1 oz. cornflour with ¾ pint (2C) milk. Cook gently until thickened with 2 oz. (¼C) sugar. Remove from the heat and add 4–6 oz. plain chocolate, broken into small pieces, stir until dissolved. Stir as the sauce cools and blend with ¼ pint (⅔C) thick cream. Pour over the biscuits and leave until fairly firm. Top with whipped cream and blanched almonds.

MENU 52

Tomato Juice Cocktail

Savoury Cheese Log with Garlic Bread

Pineapple Soufflé Pudding

This menu serves 4–6.

Tomato Juice Cocktail

Blend 1 pint ($2\frac{2}{3}$C) tomato juice with celery salt, pinch cayenne pepper, a little Worcestershire sauce and a few bruised mint leaves. Chill and serve in glasses frosted with chopped mint or parsley. To frost the glasses, brush the rims with egg white, turn upside down and dip in very finely chopped mint or parsley.

Savoury Cheese Log

Grate 1–$1\frac{1}{4}$ lb. Cheddar cheese finely. Mix with 2–3 tablespoons of each of the following: diced cucumber; sliced stuffed olives; sliced radishes and chopped walnuts.

Moisten with enough mayonnaise to make the consistency of very thick whipped cream. Form into a long roll. Garnish with olives, halved walnuts and radishes, chill well. Serve on a bed of green salad with halved tomatoes, cooked peas (topped with chopped spring onions) and sliced cucumber. Serve extra mayonnaise or oil and vinegar dressing separately.

Garlic Bread

Make $\frac{1}{2}$–$\frac{3}{4}$-inch cuts in a French loaf, almost to the base, then pull gently apart with your hands. Blend 2 oz. ($\frac{1}{4}$C) butter with garlic salt or crushed garlic. Spread a little of the garlic butter in each cut. Wrap in foil and leave for about 10–15 minutes in a moderately hot oven or about 25–30 minutes in a very moderate to moderate oven.

Pineapple Soufflé Pudding

Cream 2 oz. ($\frac{1}{4}$C) margarine or butter with 2 oz. ($\frac{1}{4}$C) caster sugar and the grated rind of 1 lemon. Gradually beat in 2 egg yolks and 2 oz. ($\frac{1}{2}$C) self-raising flour or plain flour sieved with $\frac{1}{2}$ level teaspoon baking powder. Add 12 tablespoons (1C) canned pineapple juice and the juice of 1 lemon. Fold in the 2 stiffly beaten egg whites. The mixture may look curdled at this stage, but it does not matter. Pour into a pie dish, stand this in a container with a little cold water. Bake in the centre of a very moderate to moderate oven, 325–350°F, Gas Mark 3–4, for about 40 minutes. Serve hot. The pudding separates during cooking, you have a sauce layer at the bottom of the dish with a light soufflé mixture on top.

To vary Serve with rings of hot pineapple or with ice cream.

Fruit meringue trifle

MENU 53

Sour and Sweet Eggs

Salami and Potato Salad

Orange Cherry Creams

This menu serves 4–6.

Sour and Sweet Eggs

Hard boil 4–6 eggs. Crack and shell. *Do not over-cook* as they must be simmered for a short time in the sauce. Grate or chop 1 large onion. Toss in 2 oz. ($\frac{1}{4}$C) butter for a few minutes. Stir in 1 oz. flour and cook over a low heat, then gradually add $\frac{1}{2}$ pint ($1\frac{1}{3}$C) chicken stock or water and 1 chicken stock cube. Bring to the boil and cook until thickened. Add 2 tablespoons brown malt vinegar, 1 tablespoon honey, and seasoning. Put in the eggs and 2 tablespoons diced gherkins. Cover the pan and simmer for 2–3 minutes.

Salami and Potato Salad

Dice about 1 lb. cooked new potatoes, mix with a few cooked green beans, few sliced radishes, sliced cucumber, chopped celery, chopped spring onions and mayonnaise to bind. Pile in the centre of a bed of lettuce. Arrange 12 oz.–1 lb. sliced salami or other sausage round the edge of the dish.

Orange Cherry Creams

Cut a slice from 4 very large or 6 medium-sized oranges. Remove the pulp very carefully with a spoon. Drain the pulp and put the juice into a measure and the pieces of pulp on one side. Remove any pips and skin from the pulp. Add enough water to the orange juice to give $\frac{3}{4}$ pint (2C) liquid. Heat and dissolve an orange jelly in this. Allow to cool and begin to stiffen then whisk with $\frac{1}{4}$ pint ($\frac{2}{3}$C) whipped cream. Taste and add a little sugar if wished. Put the orange pulp and a few stoned ripe or canned cherries at the bottom of each orange case. Spoon the orange cream over the fruit. Decorate with cherries.

MENU 54

Salami Hors d'Oeuvre

Summer Omelettes with Peas and New Potatoes

Fruit Meringue Trifle

This menu serves 6–8.

Salami Hors d'Oeuvre

Arrange slices of salami on a bed of lettuce or other green salad. Garnish with sliced tomatoes and cucumber. Serve with mustard or a mustard pickle.

Summer Omelettes

Make omelettes in the usual way and fill with lightly cooked summer vegetables, i.e. chopped spring onions, sliced baby carrots, diced young turnip. The cooked vegetables can be tossed in hot butter or margarine or heated in a white or cheese sauce.

Fruit Meringue Trifle

Prepare $1\frac{1}{4}$–$1\frac{1}{2}$ lb. dessert fruit. The picture shows raspberries, but sliced fresh peaches, apricots, pears, or a mixture of fruit may be used. Put the fruit into a bowl and sprinkle with sugar. Add a little white wine or lemon juice to peaches, apricots or pears to prevent their discolouring. White wine can also be added to the berry fruit.

Whip $\frac{3}{4}$ pint (2C) thick cream until it holds its shape. Put a little on one side for decoration. Gradually blend up to $\frac{1}{4}$ pint ($\frac{2}{3}$C) white wine with the remaining cream. Sweeten to taste. Break about 8 medium-sized home-made or bought meringue shells into fairly large pieces. Put a layer at the bottom of a dish. Add half the fruit, then the cream and wine layer then nearly all the rest of the fruit (save a little for decoration). Top with meringue pieces, piped cream and fruit. This must be served within an hour of preparation so the meringue pieces keep crisp.

There are many occasions when one needs to take a packed meal. Perhaps you are travelling, and do not wish to break your journey; it may be your husband has no facilities for obtaining a meal at work and has to take packed meals; or may be it is a family picnic for a day on the beach or in the country. I have added suggestions for Barbecue Meals also where applicable. There is a range of equipment available today for carrying food, apart from picnic baskets.

INSULATED CARRYING CASES These keep food and drinks hot for several hours. They are equally efficient for keeping iced drinks, salads and desserts pleasantly cold. Naturally these cases are more expensive than some other utensils.

VACUUM FLASKS To keep food and drinks hot *or* cold. *Always* warm the flask with a little hot water before adding boiling or very hot liquid. *Never* put large pieces of ice into a vacuum flask, they can break the lining. Crush the ice then add this to the drink. Wide-necked flasks enable you to carry stews, cooked fruits or chilled fruit salad and ice cream.

ten
PACKED MEALS AND PICNICS

MENU
55

Mixed Cold Meats

Green Mayonnaise Salad

Stuffed French Loaves

Fruit and Cheese

POLYTHENE BAGS OR BOXES These keep food fresh and moist for a long period.

FOIL WRAPPING This also keeps food fresh and moist. Remember you can buy foil dishes of various sizes and shapes. Bake *and* carry pies etc. in their foil dishes.

WAXED CARTONS FOR JELLIES All menus serve 4 unless stated otherwise.

This is one of the easiest picnic meals.

Green Mayonnaise

Blend freshly chopped parsley, mint, tarragon and thyme with mayonnaise. Carry in a screw topped bottle.

Stuffed French Loaf

For each loaf allow a little butter for spreading the loaf and the filling as below.
Cream 2 oz. ($\frac{1}{4}$C) butter with 1–2 teaspoons made mustard and 2 tablespoons tomato ketchup or other savoury sauce. Add 1 tablespoon chopped gherkins, 1–2 tablespoons chopped spring onions or chives. Gradually mix with about 12 oz. liver sausage or cooked

minced or chopped cooked beef. Split the loaf lengthways, spread with butter and the filling. It is easier to carry the loaves, butter and filling separately and put them together at the last minute.

Also included in the picture are thick slices of galantine, from Menu 56.

Barbecue tip   If you wish to plan this meal as part of a barbecue, wrap the filled loaves in foil and heat over the barbecue fire. Cook jacket potatoes to serve with the meal.

MENU

56

Tomato Cream Soup

Chicken and Nut Galantine with Rolls and Butter

Fruit Coleslaw

Cheese

This menu serves 6.

Tomato Cream Soup

Heat 1½ oz. (nearly ¼C) butter or margarine. Chop and fry a small bunch of spring onions in the hot butter or margarine, then add 1½ lb. ripe skinned chopped tomatoes, seasoning, 1–2 teaspoons brown sugar, ½ pint (1⅓C) chicken stock (see next recipe) and a little chopped parsley. Simmer for 10 minutes. Sieve or emulsify. Reheat and put into the warmed vacuum flask or chill and put into the cool flask. Take cream separately and use a spoonful to top each portion of soup.

Chicken and Nut Galantine

Cut all the meat from an uncooked medium-sized roasting chicken. Put the bones and giblets into a saucepan with 1 pint (2⅔C) water and seasoning. Cover the pan and simmer for 1 hour. Meanwhile mince the chicken meat plus the meat from the giblets, when these are cooked. Add 4 oz. (about 1C) chopped nuts, 2 oz. (⅔C) soft breadcrumbs, preferably brown, 2 eggs and ¼ pint (⅔C) chicken stock. Season well. Put into a well greased 2-lb. loaf tin, cover with greased foil or paper. Stand in a container with a little cold water. Bake for 1¼–1½ hours in the centre of a very moderate to moderate oven, 325–350°F, Gas Mark 3–4. Cool in the tin and put moderate-sized weights on top as the galantine cools, this makes it easier to slice.

Fruit Coleslaw

Shred the heart of a small cabbage, put into a bowl and add 2–3 oz. (nearly ½C) raisins, 2 peeled, diced dessert apples, 1–2 peeled, diced oranges and enough mayonnaise to moisten. Put into a polythene box, cover, and keep in a cool place until the last minute.

Cheddar Scotch Eggs

Lettuce and Tomatoes

**Shortbread Flapjacks
with Dessert Apples**

Cheddar Scotch Eggs

Hard boil 4 eggs, shell and halve. Remove the yolks very carefully, mash, then add 3 oz. (1C) grated Cheddar cheese, 1 oz. butter and seasoning. Mix well and press back again into the white cases. Put the halves together, then coat each egg in about 3 oz. sausage-meat (you need 12 oz. for the 4 eggs). Make sure the sausagemeat covers the eggs neatly. Roll in seasoned flour, then beaten egg and crisp breadcrumbs. Fry in hot fat until crisp and brown, and the sausagemeat is cooked. Drain on absorbent paper then wrap carefully.

Shortbread Flapjacks

Cream 2 oz. ($\frac{1}{4}$C) butter and 1 oz. caster sugar, add 4 oz. (1C) plain flour and enough milk to bind. Add as little milk as possible. Press out to an 8-inch round. Put into a greased cake tin with a loose base or on a flat baking tray.

To make the flapjack topping, melt 1$\frac{1}{2}$ oz. (nearly $\frac{1}{4}$C) butter or margarine with 1 oz. brown sugar and 1 tablespoon golden syrup in a fairly large pan. Add 4 oz. (2C) rolled oats and blend well. Spoon the flapjack mixture on top of the shortbread. Spread flat with the back of a damp metal spoon or palette knife. Bake in the centre of a very moderate to moderate oven, 325–350°F, Gas Mark 3–4 for about 30 minutes. Mark into sections while warm. Cool in or on the tin. Carry in a polythene box or tin. *Makes about 6 portions.*
Barbecue tip Warm the Cheddar Scotch eggs over the barbecue fire and serve with a **Spicy sauce.** To make this, blend 3 table-spoons tomato ketchup, 1 tablespoon Worcestershire sauce, 1 tablespoon vinegar, 2 teaspoons brown sugar and 1 teaspoon made mustard. Spoon over each egg just before serving. Bake apples over the barbecue fire and serve with hot golden syrup flavoured with ginger or lemon juice.

**Country Burgers
with Lettuce**

Date and Nut Fingers

This menu is a very simple one. It can be made more ambitious by serving well chilled melon balls and grapefruit segments as the first course. The sweet date fingers are excellent with apples and Cheddar cheese.

Country Burgers

Remove the rind and chop 2–3 rashers of bacon very finely, fry in a pan with 1 oz. fat until nearly crisp. Add 1 grated onion and 4 oz. (1C) chopped mushrooms. Mix with 12 oz. (average-sized can) flaked corned beef, 3 oz. (1C) soft breadcrumbs, seasoning and a good pinch dried mixed herbs or teaspoon chopped fresh herbs. Form the mixture into 8 flat cakes. Roll in crushed potato crisps then allow to cool. Put in halved soft buttered rolls or if you are 'counting calories', put between lettuce leaves.

Date and Nut Fingers

Crush 8 oz. sweet biscuits and put into a mixing bowl. Add the finely grated rind of 1 lemon, about 1 tablespoon lemon juice, 4 oz. (1C) chopped nuts and 4 oz. ($\frac{1}{2}$C) stoned chopped dates. Mix well, then add up to $\frac{1}{4}$ pint ($\frac{2}{3}$C) sweetened condensed milk to bind. Coat a sandwich tin, about 8-inches in diameter, with a generous amount of sieved icing sugar. Put in the mixture, smooth flat and top with icing sugar. Leave for several hours in the refrigerator to set. Carry in the tin, cut into fingers.

MENU
59

Seafood Salad
Fried Chicken Drumsticks
with Tomatoes and
French Bread
Ice Cream
Fresh Fruit

Seafood Salad

Boil long grain rice in salted water until just tender. Drain, toss in mayonnaise while the rice is still hot. Cool. Blend with cooked peas and sweet corn, flaked canned tuna or salmon, chopped prawns or flaked canned or cooked crabmeat and diced cucumber. As the fish is highly perishable this salad should be carried in a container in an insulated bag or in a wide-necked vacuum flask. Serve with lettuce.

Fried Chicken Drumsticks

Skin and coat chicken drumsticks with seasoned flour then beaten egg and crumbs. Fry until the chicken is cooked, crisp and golden brown. Drain on absorbent paper. Any joints of chicken may be fried and taken on a picnic meal, but drumsticks are easier to eat with your fingers. Pack in greaseproof paper and foil.

Barbecue tip Do not cook the chicken at home, but over the barbecue fire. It is not necessary to coat the joints. Simply brush with oil or melted butter, flavoured with a little made mustard and a few drops Worcestershire or chilli sauce. Cook sausages, tomatoes and jacket potatoes, wrap the French bread in foil and heat over the barbecue fire.

This menu serves 6.

Farmhouse Pie

Make a savoury short crust pastry. Sieve 12 oz. (3C) plain flour with a good pinch of salt, celery and garlic salts, mixed dried herbs and mustard. Add a shake of pepper. Rub 6 oz. (¾C) margarine or cooking fat into the flour. Bind with water. Roll out and use about three-quarters to line a 2-lb. loaf tin. Fry 2 peeled and chopped onions and 3 large skinned chopped tomatoes in 2 oz. (¼C) margarine. Blend with 1 lb. diced cooked or canned lambs' tongue (lambs' tongues are an excellent buy) or tongue mixed with diced cooked chicken. Season and add 1–2 tablespoons sweet pickle or chutney. Put into the pastry lined tin. Damp the pastry edges with a little water. Roll out the remainder of the pastry, make a 'lid' to fit on the pie and a few pastry 'leaves'. Place the lid in position, flute the edges together. Brush the top of the pie with beaten egg, put the 'leaves' in position and brush these with egg. Make 1 or 2 slits on top for the steam to escape. Bake the pie in the centre of a hot oven, 425–450°F, Gas Mark 6–7 for about 20 minutes, then lower the heat to very moderate for a further 20 minutes.

Ham and Potato Salad

Dice 1 or 2 thick slices of cooked ham or boiled bacon, mix with 12 oz.–1 lb. diced cooked potatoes, chopped parsley, little grated onion and mayonnaise. Put into a polythene box and top with chopped chives.

To carry salads

Use polythene boxes or bags, foil or a wide-necked vacuum flask. Wash green salad vegetables, shake dry. Pack at once and keep cool for as long as possible.

To carry fruit salads

Blend fresh fruits with canned fruit and the syrup from the can. If using all fresh fruit make a syrup by boiling a little sugar and water. Put the fruit and syrup into polythene containers, with a well-fitting seal or into screw topped jars or wide-necked vacuum flasks. Keep as cool as possible.

The essence of most family meal planning is to create interesting meals, without being unduly extravagant, or taking too long in preparation.

It is important to give the family meals that are nutritionally well balanced. All the family need adequate amounts of protein. Fortunately there are many ways in which we can obtain protein—from meat and poultry, fish, eggs, cheese, from the pulses (beans, peas, lentils), milk and bread.

These menus concentrate on nutritious meals that provide pleasant tasting and attractive looking dishes which do not require a great deal of time spent on them.

When you are busy, and when one has a family time for cooking can be restricted, it is a wise plan to 'think ahead', for often you can prepare a large quantity of a sauce or a particular vegetable and use some of the food in one meal, and the remainder (in an entirely different recipe) in another meal. At the end of most of the recipes you will also find tips entitled Planning Wisely to help you plan ahead and save time.

All menus serve 4 unless stated otherwise.

eleven
FAMILY MEALS

MENU
61

Fresh Orange Juice

Salad Nicoise

Liver and Steak Casserole with Jacket Potatoes and Cauliflower

Cheese Tray with French Bread

This menu is designed to turn a very simple one-course family meal into a special one. The Salad Niçoise is sustaining, as well as interesting, so will help you if you are trying to make meat 'go further'.

Salad Nicoise

Open a can of tuna fish and a can of anchovy fillets. Dice the fish and separate the fillets. Make a salad of lettuce, tomatoes and hard boiled eggs. Add sliced cooked new potatoes and cooked beans when available. Add the tuna fish and the anchovy fillets. Toss in either mayonnaise or well seasoned oil and vinegar. The salad may be garnished with black or green olives.

Liver and Steak Casserole

This is an excellent way of adding liver to a menu. Many people dislike liver, which is a pity, as it is such a nutritious meat, but in this casserole the flavour is not too strong. If you add a little brown sugar and orange juice to the brown stock this 'takes away' any bitter taste.

Cut about 8 oz. lambs' liver and about 1 lb. stewing steak into small pieces. Coat in approximately 1 oz. seasoned flour and fry in 2 oz. ($\frac{1}{4}$C) margarine or dripping. Gradually add 1 pint ($2\frac{2}{3}$C) brown stock plus 1 table-

spoon concentrated tomato purée and 2 teaspoons Worcestershire sauce. Cover the pan and simmer for about 1½ hours. Add 8 small peeled onions and about 4 oz. (1C) button mushrooms, then continue cooking for a further ¾–1 hour until the steak is tender. Top with chopped parsley. *The casserole serves 4–6 normally, but with the salad could serve 8 people.*

Planning wisely Warm the oranges, if using, before you halve and squeeze out the juice—you will have a bigger yield of juice. If you have no small onions for the Liver and Steak Casserole use pickled onions instead, they give a very good flavour to the dish.

MENU
62

**Cold Pork or other
Cold Meat
Sauté Potatoes and Salad
Chutney**

**Apple Lemon Mould
with Ice Cream or Cream**

Sauté Potatoes

Slice cooked potatoes neatly. Fry in a little hot fat until golden on both sides. Drain on absorbent paper, serve topped with chopped parsley.

Apple Lemon Mould

Stir the grated rind of 2 lemons into 1 pint (2⅔C) hot *thick* apple purée. Blend ½ oz. powdered gelatine with the juice from the lemons. Stir into the hot apple purée with 2 tablespoons golden syrup. Put into a rinsed mould and allow to set. Turn out and serve with ice cream or cream.

MENU
63

**Cheese Pudding
with Mixed Root
Vegetables**

Treacle Tart

This menu serves 4–6.

Cheese Pudding

Put 4 oz. (1⅓C) soft breadcrumbs into a basin. Heat ¾ pint (2C) milk with 1 oz. butter or margarine, pour over the crumbs and leave for 10 minutes. Add 6 oz. (about 2C) grated Cheddar cheese, 3 well beaten eggs and seasoning. Pour into a 2-pint (5–6C) pie dish and bake in the centre of a moderately hot oven, 400°F, Gas Mark 6 for about 30–35 minutes until well risen and golden brown. If baking the mixture in a deeper dish, i.e. a soufflé dish, allow about 40–45 minutes at a slightly lower temperature. Cook diced mixed vegetables until tender, strain and serve with a parsley sauce or topped with well seasoned tomato purée.

Treacle Tart

Make short crust pastry with 6 oz. (1½C) flour, etc. Roll out and line an 8–9-inch pie plate. Prick the pastry and bake 'blind' towards the top of a moderately hot oven, 400°F, Gas Mark 6 until set. Meanwhile grate the rind of ½ lemon, mix with 1 tablespoon lemon juice and 4 good tablespoons golden syrup. Cover the pastry with this and top with a sprinkling of breadcrumbs or crushed cornflakes. Move to a cooler part of the oven,

or lower the heat slightly, and continue cooking for a further 15–20 minutes until the pastry is crisp.

Planning wisely The 'tired', rather dry, pieces of cheese may be grated, stored in bags or jars in a cool place and used-up in dishes, such as the cheese pudding.

MENU 64

**Pineapple Meat Cakes
Tomatoes
Green Salad or Green
Vegetable**

Cheese and Biscuits

Fresh Fruit

Pineapple Meat Cakes

Peel and chop 1 large onion and 1 clove garlic (optional) finely. Heat 2 oz. ($\frac{1}{4}$C) margarine or fat in a pan. Fry the onion and garlic until soft. Blend with 1 lb. sausagemeat, 1 egg and a little extra seasoning if desired. Form into 8 flat cakes. Fry or grill until the sausagemeat is cooked (about 10–12 minutes). Sandwich the 8 cakes together with 4 rings of pineapple. Top with rings of uncooked tomato. Serve with grilled or fried tomatoes.

Planning wisely Keep a container of dehydrated (dried) onion in the house and use this as per instructions on the packet when you are short of time—it saves chopping a fresh onion. Use garlic salt instead of crushed garlic.

MENU 65

**Tipsy Chops
with Savoury Potato Cake
Green Vegetables**

Saucer Pancakes and Fruit

Tipsy Chops

Season 4 large or 8 smaller lamb chops. Put into an oven-proof dish. Spoon 4 tablespoons red wine over these or if preferred use orange juice or stock; each gives an entirely different flavour of course. Cover with foil and cook for about 25–30 minutes in the centre of a hot oven, 425°F, Gas Mark 7.

Savoury Potato Cake

Peel or scrape about 1 lb. potatoes and slice very thinly. Peel and slice 2 large onions equally thinly. Pack a greased tin with layers of potato and onion, season each layer well and begin and end with potatoes. Brush the top layer with melted margarine or oil. Cover tightly. Bake in the coolest part of a hot oven, 425°F, Gas Mark 7 for about 1–1$\frac{1}{4}$ hours. Turn out like a cake. This can also be cooked for about 1$\frac{3}{4}$–2 hours in a very moderate oven.

Saucer Pancakes

Cream 2 oz. ($\frac{1}{4}$C) margarine or butter with 2 oz. ($\frac{1}{4}$C) caster sugar until soft. Beat in 2 large eggs. Fold in 4 oz. (1C) plain flour, sieved with a pinch salt, then add $\frac{1}{4}$ pint ($\frac{2}{3}$C) milk. Grease 8 shallow oven-proof dishes or tins well. Warm thoroughly in the oven, then spoon the batter into these. Bake for 10–15 minutes (according to the depth of the cooking utensils) towards the top of a hot oven, 425°F, Gas Mark 7. Serve with hot fruit purée, apple, cherry, raspberry, apricot and gooseberry are ideal.

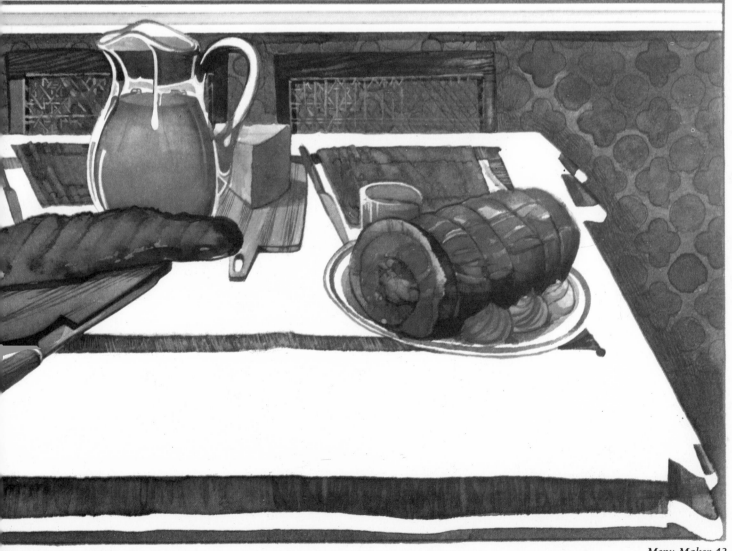

This menu serves 6

A simple mixed hors d'oeuvre turns an ordinary family meal into a special one. It need not be too expensive, and can often incorporate left over ingredients, such as cooked rice and potatoes, small quantities of salad ingredients and left over fish and meat.

Mixed Hors d'Oeuvre

Rice and pepper salad Mix cooked rice with chopped green pepper and a little onion. Toss in oil and vinegar dressing and top with chopped parsley.

Prawn eggs Hard boil 3 eggs, halve, remove the yolks and mash with mayonnaise. Add a few chopped prawns, pile into the white cases and top with whole prawns.

Tomato slices Toss sliced tomatoes in a little oil, vinegar, seasoning and finely chopped onion. Top with chopped parsley.

Sardines Lightly season sardines and sprinkle with lemon juice and chopped parsley.

Onions and cream Slice onion into rings. Toss in a little thin cream, soured cream or yoghourt and season. Top with paprika.

Diced cucumber Toss peeled and diced cucumber in a little oil, vinegar, seasoning and chopped chives.

MENU
66
Mixed Hors d'Oeuvre
Roast Pork with Apricot Stuffing   Apple Sauce
Roast Potatoes
Green Vegetable
Fruit Pie

Apricot Stuffed Pork

Buy about $4\frac{1}{2}$ lb. loin of pork, have this boned so it can be rolled round the stuffing. Blend 4 oz. ($1\frac{1}{3}$C) soft crumbs, preferably wholemeal, with 2 oz. ($\frac{1}{4}$C) melted margarine, a generous $\frac{1}{4}$ pint (1C) chopped canned or cooked apricots, 3 oz. (nearly $\frac{1}{2}$C) raisins, 1–2 tablespoons flaked almonds (optional), seasoning, 1 tablespoon chopped parsley and a little apricot syrup. Cooking time includes the weight of the stuffing so allow about 2 hours. Brush the fat with a little oil. Start in a hot oven, 425–450°F, Gas Mark 7–8 and reduce heat to moderately hot, 400°F, Gas Mark 6 after about 45 minutes. Roast potatoes in hot fat in a separate tin.

Fruit Pie

Choose about $1\frac{1}{2}$–2 lb. fairly 'sharp' fruit to follow the rather rich flavoured pork, e.g. plums, greengages, mangoes or sharp gooseberries. Add the minimum of water and a little sugar. Put into the pie dish, top with short crust or flaky pastry made with 6–8 oz. ($1\frac{1}{2}$–2C) flour, etc. Bake for about 40–45 minutes until the pastry is crisp and brown and the fruit soft. Reduce the heat or lay a piece of paper over the pastry if it is becoming too brown. Sprinkle with caster or icing sugar before serving.

Planning wisely Make the hors d'oeuvre earlier and put this, on its platter, in the refrigerator or a cool place. Cover very lightly with damped kitchen paper and it will stay fresh looking for 2–3 hours.

If you make a quantity of soft crumbs, when you have a little time, store them in jars or polythene boxes in a cool place or in the refrigerator or freezer then you can remove the quantity required for the apricot stuffing or any other stuffings.

Something to celebrate often means a special meal. It may be the start of a new job or a new school, a celebration dinner party for an anniversary, or a birthday party. The menus on the next pages give ideas for several different types of celebration meals.

High tea or Supper meal. Ideal for older children or for an anniversary or birthday where all ages will be present.

Allow 2–3 oz. tongue, 2 tablespoons Russian salad, ½ egg and 2 tablespoons salad, 1 open sandwich (have a few extra), 1 sausage roll, a slice of tart and a cream horn per person.

Advance preparations   Cook and press the tongue, page 28 gives details of this process. Alternatively buy a canned tongue or portion of tongue. The meat keeps better if you buy it in one thick piece, rather than having it ready sliced. Cook the vegetables and make the Russian salad. Make or buy the puff pastry. The recipe for sausage rolls is on page 98 and the cream horns on page 60.

Russian Salad

Dice and cook as many mixed root vegetables as possible or use frozen or canned vegetables.

twelve
CELEBRATION MENUS

MENU
67

Cold Pressed Tongue with Russian Salad
Cheddar Eggs
Open Sandwiches
Sausage Rolls
Apple and Apricot Tart
Strawberry Cream Horns

Drain well after cooking, or opening the can and blend with mayonnaise. Avoid too strong flavours if small children are present, but you can add a little curry powder, crushed garlic, or 1–2 teaspoons horseradish

cream to the mayonnaise. The original Russian salad always had chopped hard boiled egg mixed with the vegetables.

Cheddar Eggs

Allow 4 oz. (1C) finely grated Cheddar cheese to every 4 hard boiled eggs. Remove the egg yolks, sieve or mash, add the cheese and a little mayonnaise or softened butter and seasoning. Pile or pipe the mixture back into the white cases. Serve with shredded lettuce, sliced tomatoes or any other salad ingredients.

Open Sandwiches

The success of open sandwiches is to have as great a variety as possible and to choose as colourful toppings as you can. Butter thin slices of bread. Put on the toppings. The picture shows:

1 Cottage cheese with canned pineapple and canned mandarin oranges on a bed of lettuce, with a garnish of watercress.
2 Sliced lean ham, spread with pâté or chutney, rolled neatly, put on a bed of lettuce and garnished with tomato and cucumber twists and a cooked prune, if liked.
3 Potato salad on a bed of lettuce, garnished with segments of tomato and cucumber, and sprigs of watercress.
4 Well drained sardines on a bed of lettuce, garnished with slices of tomato and lemon.

The open sandwiches in the picture are fairly large, so you may see them easily, but for an occasion like this I would make smaller ones. If rather small allow 2–3 sandwiches per person instead of 1 large sandwich.

Apple and Apricot Tart

Make a sweet short crust pastry. Sieve 8 oz. (2C) plain flour and a pinch salt, rub in 4 oz. ($\frac{1}{2}$C) butter or margarine. Add 1 oz. sugar and bind with 1 egg and water or egg yolk and water. Roll out. Use most of the pastry to line an 8-inch flan ring on an upturned baking tray or a sandwich tin. Put the rest of the pastry on one side for the lattice topping. Prepare the filling, peel, slice and cook 3 large apples with the very minimum of water and a very little sugar until a thick purée. Blend with 2 oz. ($\frac{1}{2}$C) chopped nuts and 2 tablespoons apricot jam. Stir well to mix. Meanwhile bake the pastry case 'blind' for 10–15 minutes in a moderately hot oven 400°F, Gas Mark 6 until the pastry is set. Remove from the oven, spread with a thin layer of apricot jam, then add the apple and apricot filling and top with a little melted apricot jam. Roll out the remaining pastry and make a lattice work over the top of the tart. Return to the oven, reducing the heat to moderate, and bake for approximately 15–20 minutes until the pastry is crisp and brown. Top with desiccated coconut or shredded nuts, if liked. Serve hot or cold. *Serves about 8.*

Strawberry Cream Horns

The recipe for making cream horns is on page 60. These horns are filled with crushed sweetened strawberries (fresh, frozen or well drained canned fruit) then topped with whipped cream and whole strawberries. Do not put the filling into the horns until just before the meal. Use jam if you have no strawberries and decorate with chopped nuts or a little red currant jelly in place of strawberries.

A special dinner or luncheon menu which would be easy to prepare and serve. Quantities are for 6 people.

Advance preparations Prepare the fresh lobster stock. Make the thick sauce in the pan for the soufflé and the thin sauce for the accompaniment, cover both with damp paper. You can emulsify the pouring sauce in a liquidiser before transferring to the double saucepan (see the recipe) to make sure it is very smooth. Prepare the cutlets and chestnut purée. Cut the potatoes, shell the peas; keep both potatoes and peas in cold water. Peel and slice the onions. Make the gâteau, fill and store in a cool place.

Lobster Soufflé

Buy a small lobster or a medium-sized can of lobster. If using fresh lobster, remove the meat from the shell. Put the shell into a saucepan, add about $\frac{1}{2}$ pint (1$\frac{1}{3}$C) water and seasoning. Cover the pan and simmer for 15 minutes. Measure the stock and put $\frac{1}{4}$ pint ($\frac{2}{3}$C) on one side for the soufflé, simmer the rest until it is reduced to about 2 tablespoons only (this is for the sauce). If using canned lobster remove the meat, save the small amount of liquid from the can to use in the sauce to serve with the soufflé. Heat 1$\frac{1}{2}$ oz. butter in a large pan, stir in 1 oz. flour and cook for several minutes. Gradually blend in the $\frac{1}{4}$ pint ($\frac{2}{3}$C) lobster stock, or use milk with canned fish. Bring to the boil, stirring well, and cook until a thick sauce, draw to one side, then add 3 tablespoons thick cream and most of the flaked lobster meat. Save the neatest pieces to go into the sauce. Next add 5 egg yolks and seasoning, lastly fold in the stiffly whisked egg whites. Put into a buttered 7–8-inch soufflé dish and bake for approximately 35 minutes in the centre of a moderate oven, 350–375°F, Gas Mark 4–5. Serve when risen and firm with the sauce. To make the sauce, heat 1 oz. butter in a pan. Stir in 1 oz. flour, cook for several minutes. Gradually blend in $\frac{1}{2}$ pint (1$\frac{1}{3}$C) milk and the small amount of lobster stock. Bring to the boil, stirring well, and cook until thickened. Add a few drops of anchovy essence. Transfer to the top of a double saucepan or basin over hot water, cover with very damp greaseproof paper. Add about 4 tablespoons thick cream, any extra seasoning required and the tiny pieces of chopped lobster just before serving. This is not a large quantity of sauce, but the soufflé is fairly moist.

Cutlets of Veal or Venison with Chestnut Purée

Buy 12 medium-sized cutlets veal or venison. Put the cutlets into a marinade made of 2 tablespoons olive oil and 2 tablespoons white wine vinegar or white wine (you can use red wine vinegar or red wine for venison if wished). Add a crushed clove of garlic, seasoning and a little chopped parsley. Turn the cutlets and leave for several hours. This tenderises the meat and counteracts the very dry texture of these particular meats. Lift the cutlets from the marinade, but do not drain. Put into an oven-proof dish, top with

a very little butter and cover with foil. Bake for about 40 minutes towards the top of the oven, garnish with sliced tomatoes, lemon and parsley. If the cutlets are put in the oven 10 minutes after the soufflé goes in they will be ready to serve after eating the soufflé. To make the chestnut purée, simply heat canned chestnut purée with enough brown stock to make a soft consistency. Season very well and keep hot in an attractive serving dish. This saves making gravy or sauce for the cutlets.

Savoury Scalloped Potatoes

Scrape or peel about $1\frac{1}{2}$ lb. new or old potatoes, cut into wafer thin slices. Cut 2 onions into wafer thin slices as well. Heat $\frac{1}{2}$ pint ($1\frac{1}{3}$C) milk with plenty of seasoning and 2 oz ($\frac{1}{4}$C) butter. Put a layer of potatoes into an attractive oven-proof serving dish, then a layer of onions, continue like this, ending with potatoes. Pour the milk over the potatoes. Bake for about $1\frac{1}{4}$ hours in the coolest part of the oven, until crisp and golden brown and the milk is absorbed.

Peas French Style

Line an attractive casserole with very damp lettuce leaves. Add about $1\frac{1}{4}$ lb. shelled peas or the equivalent in frozen peas, 1 oz. butter, seasoning and a few chopped spring onions. Cover with about 2 tablespoons water and very damp lettuce leaves. Wrap the *outside* of the dish with foil, so the lettuce does not scorch and cook on the same shelf as the potatoes for about 1 hour. To serve, just remove the top layer of lettuce. Do not strain the peas, the little liquid in the dish is delicious.

Pear and Chocolate Gâteau

Cream 8 oz. (1C) margarine or butter with 8 oz. (1C) caster sugar until soft and light. Gradually beat in 4 large eggs. Sieve together 6 oz. (1½C) self-raising flour (or plain flour and 1½ teaspoons baking powder) and 1 oz. cocoa. Add 2 oz. (½C) ground almonds. Fold into the creamed mixture, add 1 tablespoon warm water to give a soft consistency or nearly 2 tablespoons if the eggs are only medium-sized. Line the bottom of two 9-inch sandwich tins with greased greaseproof paper. Grease and flour the sides of the tins. Divide the mixture between these and bake just above the centre of a moderate oven, 350–375°F, Gas Mark 4–5, for approximately 25–30 minutes, until just firm to the touch. Turn out very carefully. Allow to cool. Open a large can of pears, drain well. Whip about ½–¾ pint (1⅓–2C) thick cream. Flavour with a little brandy. Spread some of the cream over one of the cakes, top with sliced pears and the second cake. Spread some of the remaining cream over the cake. Decorate with pear slices, browned flaked almonds and piped cream.

MENU
69

Open Sandwiches

American Celebration Cake

Champagne

This menu would be suitable for an older couple giving a party to celebrate a wedding anniversary. It may sound very plain, but if the open sandwiches were imaginative it could look splendid.

Advance preparations Make the cake and prepare the toppings for the sandwiches. Pages 104 and 105 give a number of ideas and there are several others under Menu 67.

Celebration Cake

The three tiers shown are 11 inch, 9 inch and 7 inch. The amount of mixture given below is sufficient for all three tiers. Choose cake, rather than sandwich tins.
Cream 1½ lb. (3C) margarine or butter and 1½ lb. (3C) caster sugar until soft and light. Add the finely grated rind of 3 oranges and 2 lemons (be careful that you do not use any of the bitter white pith). Gradually beat in 12 eggs. If the mixture shows signs of curdling add a little of the sieved flour. Fold in 1¼ lb. (6C) sieved self-raising flour (or plain flour and 6 level teaspoons baking powder). Next add 4 tablespoons orange juice. Grease

and flour the cake tins or line with greased greaseproof paper. Put the mixture into the tins, as you will see the cakes are not much deeper than a Victoria sandwich. Bake just above the centre of a very moderate oven, 325–350°F, Gas Mark 3–4. The 7-inch layer takes about 30 minutes. The 9-inch layer about 35–40 minutes and the 11-inch layer about 40–45 minutes. Lower the heat for the large cake if it is becoming too brown. Turn the cakes out of the tins carefully and allow to cool.

Make up butter icing for filling and decoration. Cream 1½ lb. (3C) butter and 2 lb. (generous 7C) sieved icing sugar, add a little grated lemon and orange rind and about 2 tablespoons fruit juice. Tint golden with a few drops of yellow food colouring. Split each cake and sandwich together with some of the butter icing. Spread the base of the 9-inch cake with some butter icing and put on to the 11-inch cake. Spread the base of the 7-inch cake with some of the butter icing and put on to the 9-inch cake. Make up lemon flavoured glacé icing to coat the whole cake. This must be very soft so it flows over the cakes easily. Blend 1½ lb. (5½C) sieved icing sugar with 3 tablespoons lemon juice and enough water to give a flowing consistency. Pour over the cakes and allow to set. Lift carefully on to the serving tray and decorate with a piping of butter icing, and bows or ribbon, as shown in the picture.
This gives about 40 portions.

Celebration cake

MENU
70

Asparagus Eggs

Braised Ham and Tongue with Savoury Creamed Potatoes

Peaches with Cherry Sauce

Cheese Canapés

This is an entirely store-cupboard meal, to celebrate the arrival of a welcome, but unexpected guest. Quantities are for 4 people with footnotes to make it stretch to 6.

There are no advance preparations here, but in order that the meal can be prepared in the minimum of time and have everything cooked, this is the order I would follow. Make up the dehydrated potatoes and put them into the dish, then prepare the ham and tongue, the cherry sauce and the cheese canapés. Finally cook the first course.

Asparagus Eggs

Open a can of cream of asparagus soup. If the concentrated (condensed) variety, then dilute to the consistency of thick cream. If the thinner variety, allow it to simmer for a short

time to become a little thicker. Pour into a shallow oven-proof casserole, top with 4 eggs and a little butter. Bake in a moderately hot oven for about 10 minutes, until eggs are set. *Note* The can of soup will provide enough sauce for 6 eggs.

Braised Ham and Tongue

Open a small can of tomatoes or use 3–4 fresh tomatoes. Skin and chop fresh tomatoes, simmer with a little water and seasoning or simmer canned tomatoes for a few minutes. Emulsify or beat until fairly smooth, then blend 1 teaspoon cornflour with ¼ pint (⅔C) water, add to the tomatoes, with ½ beef stock cube and cook, stirring well, until thickened. Add a can of mixed vegetables. Put at the bottom of an oven-proof serving dish and top with slices of canned ham and tongue. Cover with greased foil and heat for a short time in the oven.
Note If garnished with crisp triangles of toast the dish is more substantial.

Savoury Creamed Potatoes

Make up a packet of dehydrated potatoes, following the instructions on the packet. Add chopped parsley, a little celery salt, seasoning and top of the milk. Pile into an oven-proof serving dish, top with a little margarine or butter and brown in the oven.

Peaches with Cherry Sauce

Open a can of peaches, strain and arrange in a serving dish. Open a can of cherries, strain off the juice, add the juice of the peaches, the juice of a lemon and blend with 1 teaspoon arrowroot or cornflour. Put into a saucepan with 2 tablespoons red currant or apple jelly. Stir well over a gentle heat until slightly thickened and clear. If too thin allow to simmer for a short time. Add the cherries. Pour over the peaches.
Note If you have very few peaches add rings of dessert apple, dipped in lemon juice.

Cheese Canapés

Grate or crumble some cheese, blend with a little butter. Spread over cheese biscuits, top with a gherkin or stuffed olive slices.

Complete Index

Entries in blue indicate Blue Print Recipes. MM refers to recipes in the Menu Maker section.

290

PUT IT RIGHT

Cake sunk in the centre

Cut out the centre carefully, turn the outside into a ring cake. Ice or decorate if wished.

Either crumble the cake from the centre, blend with an egg and steam for 35–40 minutes then serve as a hot pudding. Or slice the centre neatly, dip in beaten egg, fry in hot butter, sprinkle with sugar and serve as fritters.

Cake in which the fruit sinks

Slice across the original cake to give two shallow cakes, one plain and one fruit. Turn the cut surface to the bottom.

Sauce, soup or stew that is too salty

Put 2 or 3 peeled sliced potatoes into the liquid. Simmer for 10 minutes, remove. If still rather too salty, blend in a little milk or cream (this absorbs the flavour).

Biscuits or small cakes spread out too much as they bake

Take a pastry cutter or a knife and pull the edges towards the centre again to give a neat shape.

Cake or pastry that is burned

Rub a fine grater gently over the cake or pastry to remove the burned part. Dust a cake with sieved icing sugar, a sweet pie with sieved icing or caster sugar, and a savoury pie with finely grated cheese, mixed with a little chopped parsley.

Sauces or stews with a lumpy sauce

Whisk the sauce sharply, rub through a sieve, or put into a liquidiser and emulsify until smooth. Lift the meat and any vegetables from the liquid in the stew and keep warm while you deal with the sauce as above. Reheat, then add the meat etc.

Sauce, soup or stew that is burned

Do not stir—pour gently and carefully into a clean pan. Flavour with curry, chutney or mustard to camouflage the burnt taste. If a sweet sauce, try vanilla or almond essence.

Cake in which the fruit sinks